THE MEDIA
of Mass Communication
CANADIAN EDITION

JOHN VIVIAN

Winona State University

PETER MAURIN

Brock University

Allyn and Bacon Canada

Scarborough, Ontario

Canadian Cataloguing in Publication Data

Vivian, John
    The media of mass communication
1st Canadian ed.
ISBN 0-205-26897-8

1. Mass media.   I. Maurin, Peter.   II. Title.

P90.V58 1997   302.23   C96-932068-X

© 1997 Prentice-Hall Canada Inc., Scarborough, Ontario
A Division of Simon & Schuster/A Viacom Company

Allyn & Bacon, Inc., Needham Heights, Massachusetts
Prentice-Hall International (UK) Limited, London
Prentice-Hall of Australia, Pty. Limited, Sydney
Prentice-Hall Hispanoamericana, S.A., Mexico City
Prentice-Hall of India Private Limited, New Delhi
Prentice-Hall of Japan, Inc., Tokyo
Simon & Schuster Southeast Asia Private Limited, Singapore
Editora Prentice-Hall do Brasil, Ltda., Rio de Janeiro

ISBN 0-205-26897-8

Vice-President, Editorial Director: Laura Pearson
Acquisitions Editor: Cliff Newman
Development Editor: Imogen Brian
Production Editor: Susan James
Copy Editor: Deborah Viets
Editorial Assistant: Carol Whynot
Production Coordinator: Sharon Houston
Permissions/Photo Research: Marijke Leupen
Art Director: Mary Opper
Cover Design: Monica Kompter
Cover Image: Paul Watson
Page Layout: Bill Renaud

Original edition published by Allyn & Bacon Inc.
A Simon & Schuster Company
Needham Heights, MA 02194-2315
Copyright © 1997 by Allyn & Bacon Inc.

2 3 4 5   BB   01 00 99 98
Printed and bound in Canada.

Visit the Prentice Hall Canada Web site! Send us your comments, browse our catalogues, and more. **www.phcanada.com** Or reach us through e-mail at **phabinfo_pubcanada@prenhall.com**

Photo credits are listed on page 432, which constitutes a continuation of this copyright page.

To Harold Vivian, my father,
who sparked my curiosity about the mass
media at age five by asking what was black and
white and read all over.

And to Elaine Vivian, my mother,
who nurtured this curiosity by keeping the
house stocked with books, magazines and
reading material of every sort.

J. V.

To Kim, Sonja and Joshua; you guys mean the world to me.
To Bohdan, Jeannette, Jim, Walter and students in
Communications 1F90 and 3F60; thanks for letting me
call Brock "home" for the last ten years.

P. M.

CONTENTS-AT-A-GLANCE

CONTENTS

PREFACE

As Canadians, we consume both Canadian and American media. For example: How did you keep up to date on the Paul Bernardo drama? On the U.S. military intervention in Haiti? Why did you choose one brand of athletic shoes over another? Do you trust Bill Clinton? Jean Chrétien? Saddam Hussein? David Letterman? If you saw the movie *The Lion King* but not *Exotica*, why? How did you learn about the existence of the latest CD or tape you purchased? Would you agree if your local library removed *Playboy* magazine from the shelves? Should *In the Night Kitchen* be banned? *Grapes of Wrath? Huckleberry Finn?* Who decides what music gets played on the radio? Who chooses the news stories? Can you trust *The Globe and Mail? The National Enquirer?* CBC Newsworld? *Frank?* Should you worry about little children imitating Rambo? Barbie? Butt-head? Is there too much sex on television?

Everybody faces these kinds of questions in this age of mass communication. The media are everywhere, and they affect almost every aspect of our lives, including our knowledge of the world around us, the decisions we make as consumers and the values we embrace. The Canadian edition of *The Media of Mass Communication* is designed to help you become more informed and discerning as a user of the mass media. It is also designed to provide a comprehensive foundation for students in the analysis of media using various theories and models.

New in this edition is a chapter on the emerging new media. You will learn what is at stake on the information superhighway everyone is talking about. You also will get a peek at the forms the media will take in the future. For example, the next generation of college students probably won't be learning from a textbook like this one. What will replace it? Read on.

HOW THIS BOOK IS ORGANIZED

OVERVIEW. Chapter 1 orients you to the mass media and the process of mass communication. You will learn some of the themes that come up in later chapters. Included is a section on semiotics.

THE MEDIA. Separate chapters deal with each major mass medium in the sequence they developed: newspapers, sound recordings, movies, radio and television.

NEW MEDIA. "Mass Media Tomorrow" is new in this edition. You will learn about the emerging technology that is transforming the mass media.

MEDIA ISSUES.   The remaining nine chapters focus on media research, theories, effects and ethics.

LEARNING GOALS.   Chapters begin with learning goals to help guide your thoughts as you read.

STUDY PREVIEWS.   Chapters include frequent summaries of the material in subsequent paragraphs. These study previews can help prepare you for the material ahead.

BOXES.   Throughout the book, you will find four kinds of boxes that illustrate significant points. *Media People* boxes introduce personalities who have had a major impact on the media or whose stories illustrate major points of media history. *Media Abroad* boxes tell about practices in other countries to help you assess our own media's performance. The *Media Databank* boxes contain tables to help you see certain facts about the mass media at a glance. In the *Media and You* boxes, you will be challenged to bring your experience as a media consumer to major issues and come to your own conclusions.

QUESTIONS FOR REVIEW.   These questions are keyed to the major topics and themes in the chapter. Use them for a quick assessment of whether you caught the major points.

QUESTIONS FOR CRITICAL THINKING.   These questions ask you both to recall specific information and to use your imagination and critical thinking abilities to restructure the material. They will also give you an opportunity for outside research.

FOR FURTHER LEARNING.   If you have a special interest in the material introduced in a chapter, you can use the end-of-chapter bibliographies to identify more detailed examinations in other sources. The notes can help orient you to the perspective of the authors of these sources, as well as to the level at which they are written. The sources range from easily digested articles in popular magazines to scholarly works that press the boundaries of human knowledge and understanding.

FOR KEEPING UP TO DATE.   These sections list professional and trade journals, magazines, newspapers and other periodical references to help you keep current on media developments and issues. Most of these periodicals are available in college and university libraries.

INTERNET RESOURCES.   This listing of sites on the Internet will help you keep up to date. Sites for both Canada and the U.S. are included.

An Instructor's Resource Manual and supplementary videotape are available.

We wish to sincerely thank the following people for reviewing the manuscript for the Canadian Edition: Dr. Harris Breslow, York University (Calumet College); Dr. Lyle Cruickshank, Dawson College; Dr. Richard Lewis, University of Windsor.

CHAPTER 1

THE MEDIA of Mass Communication

The mass media are pervasive in our everyday lives

The primary mass media are built on print, electronic and photographic technologies

Scholars have devised models that help explain the mass media

Most mass media organizations must be profitable to stay in business

The mass media are undergoing change, including global consolidation

Mass communicators create mass messages that are sent through mass communication via mass media to mass audiences

Scholars have devised models to explain the mysterious process of mass communication

MEDIA IN THEORY

Mass Communication Models: The Semiotic School

The semiotic school of thought looks at the creation of meaning in communication. Later in this chapter we discuss a second model of mass communication called the process school of communication, which focuses on the sending and receiving of media messages.

What are some of the differences between the semiotic and process schools? Let's take the example

of a particular program, say, "Hockey Night in Canada." The semiotic school would be interested in how viewers find and create meaning while watching the program. For example, during a game between the Calgary Flames and Edmonton Oilers, how would fans of each team decode the messages being communicated? How would each find pleasure in watching the hockey game? What meaning does each fan find in the broadcast? On the other hand, the process school would be interested in how this program gets transmitted from point A to point B, how the show is produced, who produces it and who it is aimed at.

This approach to communication theory draws on the work of French cultural theorist Roland Barthes and the idea of signs, what they refer to, and the influence of culture on those references.

To understand what semiotics is and what signs are, it is important to see how Barthes expanded on the work of Swiss linguist Ferdinand de Saussure. For de Saussure idea of the sign is composed of a signifier and a signified, as shown in Figure 1.1.

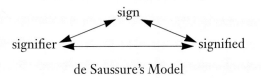

de Saussure's Model

For example, the words "maple leaf" constitute a sign. This sign is composed of a signifier, the letters in the words "m-a-p l e-l-e-a-f," and its signified, the mental concept of leaves from a maple tree that accompanies the words. Together, the signifier and signified form the sign of the "maple leaf." The relation between the signifier and its signified is entirely arbitrary. The words "maple leaf" denote what they do solely because of the linguistic conventions of the English language.

DENOTATION AND CONNOTATION

Barthes took this idea of signification one step further. For Barthes, there is not only one level of signification (the mental concept of "maple leaf"), but two: first- and second-order signified. He called these levels of meaning denotation and connotation respectively. Barthes' conceptualization of signs is shown in Figure 1.2.

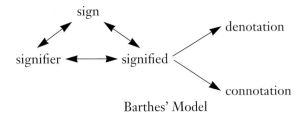

Barthes' Model

Denotation is the same as de Saussure's idea of the signified. It is what Barthes calls the simple, every

day meaning in the sign. For example, "maple leaf" signifies, or denotes, a type of leaf from a particular tree. But, it can also mean many other things. There is a difference in its connotation, which deals with an additional level of meaning. For example, a maple leaf can signify Canada, or an NHL team, as well as signifying a leaf from a maple tree. For Barthes, this second-level meaning is a vehicle for cultural ideology. For example, a picture of a soldier holding a flag isn't just what it denotes; it may carry with it a connotation of patriotism. The word "dog" may denote a furry four-legged creature. However, because of cultural ideology (or myth) it can also mean an unattractive person or a sexually promiscuous person. It's only because we are Canadians that the maple leaf signifies Canada to us. Hockey fans will interpret a maple leaf as signifying the team from Toronto. The multitude of meanings that can be associated with a sign is also arbitrary and depends largely on cultural conventions. That's what semiotics looks at—the many different types of meanings that are created by cultural influences.

By analyzing the relationship between denotation and connotation in popular culture, Barthes believed that hidden ideologies (or what he called "mythologies") could be uncovered. A myth can also be defined as a culture's belief system. In Barthes' view, these myths "naturalized" (or established) the interests and values of the dominant class in society. By exposing these bourgeois mythologies as arbitrary, Barthes believed they could be eliminated.

Not all signs are created equal. Communication theorist C. S. Pierce designed a way to classify signs according to their level of connotation or denotation. Pierce divided signs into three categories: icons, indexes and symbols.

Icons are signs that resemble what they represent because the signifier looks like what is signified. For example, a map of Canada is an icon of Canada because it looks like the geographic layout of the country. A picture of Preston Manning is an icon of the leader of the Reform Party. A statue of John A. Macdonald is an icon of the first prime minister. If the sign is denotative and not connotative, it is an icon.

An index is directly related to what it represents. A popular example of an index is smoke, which usually indicates there is a fire. Smoke is an index of fire because smoke has a connection with fire. An index is a mixture of connotation and denotation. Smoke by itself is largely denotative, but it connotes something else: fire. A Mountie's hat is also an index; it is not only a hat but has come to represent an RCMP officer. Former prime minister Pierre Trudeau wore a rose on his lapel. The rose became an index of Trudeau. Another former prime minister was often depicted in political cartoons as possessing a large, protruding chin. That physical characteristic became an index of Brian Mulroney.

A symbol is a sign that is entirely connotative because there is no clear connection between the signifier and the signified. Words are symbolic of what they represent. The Canadian flag, the fleur-de-lis, and the beaver are all Canadian symbols. They don't look like Canada but they have all become symbolic of various aspects of our culture. Symbols develop their meaning over time through convention. The meaning given to symbols is arbitrary and can change.

These categories are not carved in stone and are not mutually exclusive. It is possible to have an icon that is also symbolic. Take a statue of John A. Macdonald, for instance. On a denotative level, it's a representation of the former prime minister. On a connotative level, standing beside the statue may evoke feelings of patriotism, which would also make the statue symbolic of Canada. It's also possible to have an index that is symbolic. Some political cartoonists may view the protruding chin not only as an index of Brian Mulroney but also as a symbol of several Canadian political issues: the GST, NAFTA and the Meech Lake Accord.

EXPOSING DENOTATION AND CONNOTATION

Take any pop song and analyze its lyrics in terms of both denotation and connotation. Look for first- and second-order signifieds. Here are some songs to get you started:

- "American Pie" by Don McLean
- "At the 100th Meridian" by The Tragically Hip
- "Harvest Moon" by Neil Young
- "The Last Song" by Elton John
- "I'm an Adult Now" by The Pursuit of Happiness

Another interesting way to expose connotation is to hear the same song done different ways. For example, have a listen to the following songs and discuss the differences in connotations:

- "Layla" by Eric Clapton versus "Layla" by Derek and the Dominoes
- "Killing Me Softly" by Roberta Flack and the remake by the Fugees
- "Take a Chance on Me" by Abba and by Erasure

Remember: you're trying to expose meaning on a deeper level. Look for hidden meanings in your reading of the lyrics. What various readings of these lyrics are possible?

The Royal Canadian Air Farce. Is this comedy team's portrayal of life in a doughnut shop an example of what Barthes might call "Canadian-ness?" What Canadian signifiers would you argue are present in this photo?

IMPORTANCE OF MASS MEDIA

STUDY PREVIEW   Mass media usually are thought of as sources of news and entertainment. They also carry messages of persuasion. Important, though often overlooked, is how mass messages bind people into communities, even into nations.

PERVASIVENESS

Mass media are pervasive in modern life. Every morning we wake up to clock radios. Political candidates spend most of their campaign dollars on television to woo voters. The economy is dependent on advertising to create mass markets. Children see 30 000 to 40 000 commercial messages a year. With mass media so influential, we need to know as much as we can about how they work. Consider:

- Through the mass media, we learn almost everything we know about the world beyond our immediate environs. What would you know about Karla Homolka's deal or the Stanley Cup if it were not for newspapers, television and other mass media?
- An informed and involved citizenry is possible in modern democracy only when the mass media work well.
- People need the mass media to express their ideas widely. Without mass media, your expression would be limited to people within earshot and to whom you write letters.
- Powerful forces use the mass media to influence us with their ideologies and for their commercial purposes. The mass media are the main tools of propagandists, advertisers and other persuaders.
- How is Canadian culture shaped by American media? Consider that the average Canadian watches more American television than Canadian television.

The Canadian mass communication context is unique in the world. Besides living next door to the largest exporter of mass media products, Canada is officially multicultural and bilingual. People who live outside Quebec rarely heard

EDIA AND YOU

Looking for Canadian Signs and Myths

In a book called *Mythologies*, Barthes looked at various forms of popular culture and subjected them to semiotic analysis. In one of the essays, entitled "Wine and Milk," the two drinks carry the following connotations:

"Wine: high class, French, good for the soul."

"Milk: pure, innocent."

The "Newfie" is a well-known Canadian signifier. The Newfoundland government took aim at the negative

mythology surrounding the province with an ad campaign to sell its Economic Diversification and Growth Enterprises program in 1996. The ads, showing pictures of fish, stated "If you think this is all Newfoundland and Labrador exports ... think again."

Using Barthes' ideas, think of some mythical Canadian signifiers; try to get beyond Mounties and beavers. What Canadian icons, indexes and symbols can you think of?

Robert Charlebois, Beau Dommage, Diane Tell or Nanette Workman. While these singers have collectively sold millions of records in Quebec, they are largely unknown in the rest of Canada. Denys Arcand is one of Quebec's finest filmmakers, yet many in the rest of Canada have never seen *Decline of the American Empire* or *Jesus of Montreal*.

More often than not, Canadians choose American popular culture over home-grown popular culture. Statistics Canada viewing data indicates that the majority of Canadians watch American programming in prime time. Even if they are tuned into a Canadian station, chances are that the programming will be American, unless the channel is CBC. This has serious implications for Canadian culture.

INFORMATION SOURCE

The most listened-for item in morning newscasts is the weather forecast. People want to know how to prepare for the day. The quality of their lives is at stake. Not carrying an umbrella to work if rain is expected can mean getting wet on the way home, perhaps catching pneumonia, at worst dying. There used to be a joke that the most important thing the mass media did was to tell us whether a tornado was coming or whether the Russians were coming.

Media in Revolution. Control of the mass media is a high priority for both the government and insurgents during a revolution. In 1989, in a revolution that ousted Romanian strongman Nicolae Ceausescu, the fiercest fighting was at the government-controlled Bucharest television headquarters.

The heart of the media's informing function lies in messages called *news*. Journalists themselves are hard pressed to agree on a definition of news. One useful definition is that news is reports on things that people want or need to know. Reporters try to tell the news without taking sides.

Advertising also is part of the mass media's information function. The media, especially newspapers, are bulletin boards for trade and commerce. People look to grocery advertisements for specials. Classified advertisements provide useful information.

ENTERTAINMENT SOURCE

The mass media can be wonderful entertainers, bringing together huge audiences not otherwise possible. No matter how many people saw Charlie Chaplin on the vaudeville stage, more people saw him in movie houses. Even more have been entertained by his impersonator in the IBM personal computer advertisements on television and in magazines and newspapers.

Almost all mass media have an entertainment component. The thrust of the American movie industry is almost wholly entertainment, although there can be a strong informational and persuasive element. Even the most serious newspaper has an occasional humour column. Most mass media are a mix of information and entertainment—and also persuasion.

PERSUASION FORUM

People form opinions from the information and interpretations to which they are exposed, which means that even news coverage has an element of persuasion. The media's attempts to persuade, however, are usually in editorials and commentaries whose purposes are obvious. Most news media separate material designed to persuade from news. Newspapers package their opinion articles in an editorial section. Commentary on television is introduced as opinion.

MEDIA ABROAD

Mass Media and National Development

The British Broadcasting Corporation and the United Nations periodically gather data on the number of television and radio sets around the globe. The data underscore the importance of an advanced mass media system with national development.

	Radios per 1000 People	Televisions per 1000 People		Radios per 1000 People	Televisions per 1000 People
Western Democracies			*Developing Countries*		
United States	2043	612	Yemen	20	3
Canada	n/a	458	Ethiopia	89	40
Australia	1301	395	India	55	4
United Kingdom	993	359	Bangladesh	8	1
Japan	713	250	Burkina Faso	19	5

The most obvious of the media messages designed to persuade is *advertising*. Ads exhort the audience to action—to go out and buy toothpaste, cornflakes and automobiles. *Public relations* is subtler, seeking to persuade but usually not to induce immediate action. Public relations tries to shape attitudes, usually by persuading mass media audiences to see an institution or activity in a particular light.

BINDING INFLUENCE

The mass media bind communities together by giving messages that become a shared experience. A rural newspaper editor scrambling to get out an issue may not be thinking about how her work creates a common identity among readers, but it does. The town newspaper is something everyone in town has in common. In the same way, what Metro riders in Montreal read on their way to work in the morning gives them something in common. A shared knowledge and a shared experience are created by mass media, and thus they create a base for community.

The same phenomenon occurs on a national level. Stories on the 1986 *Challenger* space shuttle disaster bound Americans together in a nationwide grieving process. Coverage of the Iran-Contra scandal prompted a nationwide dialogue on what U.S. foreign policy should be. The importance of mass media in binding people into nationhood is clear in every revolution and coup d'état: the leaders try to take over the national media system right away.

PRIMARY MASS MEDIA

STUDY PREVIEW The mass media fall into three categories based on the technology by which they are produced—print, electronic and photographic. The primary print media are books, magazines and newspapers. The primary electronic media are television, radio and sound recordings. The one primarily photographic medium is movies.

PRINT MEDIA

Books, magazines and newspapers can generally be distinguished in the following four categories: binding, regularity, content and timeliness:

	Books	*Magazines*	*Newspapers*
Binding	Stitched or glued	Staples	Unbound
Regularity	Single issue	At least quarterly	At least weekly
Content	Single topic	Diverse topics	Diverse topics
Timeliness	Generally not timely	Timeliness not an issue	Timeliness important

Although these distinctions are helpful, they cannot be applied rigidly. For example, timeliness is critical to *Time* and *Maclean's*. Over the past 20 years, book publishers have found ways to produce "instant books" on major news events within a couple of weeks so that their topics can be timely.

The definition problem was illustrated when comedian Carol Burnett sued the *National Enquirer* for reporting falsely that she had been tipsy at a restaurant. The case was tried in California, where state law was more tolerant of slanderous stories in newspapers than those in magazines. Defending itself, the *National Enquirer* tried to convince the judge that it was a newspaper. The judge did not buy the argument, and the *National Enquirer* was tried under the magazine rules and lost. But it was not an easy call. The *National Enquirer* has characteristics of both a newspaper and a magazine.

The technological basis of books, magazines and newspapers, as well as that of lesser print media such as brochures, pamphlets and billboards, is the printing press, which for practical purposes dates back to the 1440s. Print media messages are in tangible form. They can be picked up physically and laid down, stacked, and filed and stored for later reference. Even though newspapers may be used to wrap up the leftovers from dinner for tomorrow's garbage, there also is a permanency about the print media.

ELECTRONIC MEDIA

Television, radio and sound recordings flash their messages electronically. Pioneer work on electronic media began in the late 1800s, but they are mostly a 20th-century development. Unlike print messages, television and radio messages disappear as soon as they are transmitted. Messages can be stored on tape and other means, but usually they reach listeners and viewers in a nonconcrete form. Television is especially distinctive because it engages several senses at once with sound, sight and movement.

PHOTOGRAPHIC MEDIA

The technology of movies is based on the chemistry of photography. Movies, however, may not be with us much longer as a chemical medium. While Hollywood still makes movies on film that is pulled "through the soup," a lot of video production, including some prime-time television, is shot on tape and stored digitally. Photography itself is moving from chemistry to digital technology, which means

Digital Photography. Today, images can be captured, stored, manipulated and reproduced digitally, without using chemicals. Kodak has a system that stores images on CD-ROM, which allows them to be viewed on a computer and television screens. And with a computer, images can be easily enhanced and changed in ways a photographer in a darkroom could never have done. Because this digital technology is easy to use and study too, it is rapidly displacing the chemistry that had been the sole basis of photography.

production and editing occur on computer screens rather than in darkrooms. The end may be coming soon for darkrooms, hypo and fixer.

MASS MEDIA MODELS

STUDY PREVIEW   Scholars have devised numerous ways to dissect and categorize the mass media. These include the hot-cool, entertain-inform and elitist-populist models. Each offers insights, but all of them have shortcomings in explaining the mass media.

HOT AND COOL

Born in Edmonton in 1911, Canadian communication theorist *Marshall McLuhan* taught at Assumption College in Windsor (now the University of Windsor) and at St. Michael's College at the University of Toronto. In 1954 he founded *Explorations*, a journal devoted to the analysis of popular media and culture. While the phrase has become something of a cliché, McLuhan developed the theory that the "medium is the message." McLuhan examined how we perceive media messages: not only looking at the content of the message, but how the message is delivered, that is its form. He used the metaphor of a lightbulb to explain his idea. He argued that while everyone notices the content of the lightbulb (the light it provides), no one notices the form, that is the bulb itself. The same holds true for

Marshall
McLuhan

Hot and Cool. Canadian scholar Marshall McLuhan, whose work is often associated with the "Toronto School," developed the idea of *hot* and *cool* media. The more the audience is immersed in the message, the warmer McLuhan considered the medium. He saw movies as very warm because they can engage so many human senses simultaneously with a darkened environment and huge screen keeping out competing stimuli.

content in the context of the media. People notice the content of the media (a speech on radio, a comedy on television) but not the medium that transmits the message. McLuhan came to believe that the medium influences how we perceive the message.

McLuhan developed an innovative model to help explain the mass media. To McLuhan's thinking, books, magazines and newspapers were *hot media* because they require a high degree of thinking to use. To read a book, for example, you must immerse yourself to derive anything from it. The relationship between medium and user is intimate. The same is true with magazines and newspapers. McLuhan also considered movies a hot medium because they involve viewers so completely. Huge screens command the viewers' full attention, and sealed, darkened viewing rooms shut out distractions.

In contrast, McLuhan classified electronic media, especially television, as cool because they can be used with less intellectual involvement and hardly any effort. Although television has many of the sensory appeals of movies, including sight, motion and sound, it does not overwhelm viewers to the point that all else is pushed out of their immediate consciousness. When radio is heard merely as background noise, it does not require any listener involvement at all, and McLuhan would call it a *cool medium*. Radio is warmer, however, when it engages listeners' imaginations, as with radio drama. The same classification can be applied to children's programing. Some programming, due to rapid editing and violent content, can be seen as cool, while other more engaging fare is hot. For example, the "Power Rangers" can be classified as cool, while "Mr. Dressup" is hot.

McLuhan's basic argument here deals with how active or passive we are when we consume media messages. Generally speaking, for McLuhan, watching television is a passive process, not requiring much energy on the part of the viewer. Since television uses both audio and video channels to communicate its message, there is little for the viewer to do but be passive. The expression "couch potato" is an example of how watching television is generally seen as passive (and therefore cool). In contrast, since reading a newspaper requires more input from the reader, it is clearly an active process, and newspapers are considered a hot medium.

McLuhan's point is underscored by research that has found people remember much more from reading a newspaper or magazine than from watching television or listening to the radio. The harder you work to receive a message from the media, the more you remember.

There is still much debate about hot and cool media. How would you categorize the following, hot or cool?

- Dancing the "Macarena"
- Watching a hockey game at an arena
- Watching a hockey game on television
- Reading a novel by Margaret Atwood
- Channel surfing
- Surfing the Internet

ENTERTAINMENT AND INFORMATION

Many people find it helpful to define media by whether the thrust of their content is entertainment or information. By this definition, newspapers almost always are considered an information medium, and audio recording and movies are considered entertainment. As a medium, books both inform and entertain. So do television and radio, although some networks, stations and programs do more of one than the other. The same is true with magazines, with some titles geared more for informing, some for entertaining.

Although widely used, the entertainment-information dichotomy has limitations. Nothing inherent in newspapers, for example, precludes them from being entertaining. Consider the *National Enquirer* and other supermarket tabloids, which are newspapers but which hardly anybody takes seriously as an information source. The neatness of the entertainment-information dichotomy doesn't work well with mainstream newspapers either. Most daily newspapers have dozens of items intended to entertain. Open a paper and start counting with Calvin and Hobbs, Garfield and the astrology column.

The entertainment-information dichotomy has other weaknesses. It misses the potential of all mass media to do more than entertain and inform. The dichotomy misses the persuasion function, which you read about earlier in this chapter. People may consider most movies as entertainment, but there is no question that Steven Spielberg has broad social messages even in his most rollicking adventure sagas. In the same sense, just about every television sitcom is a morality tale wrapped up in an entertaining package. The persuasion may be soft-pedaled, but it's everywhere.

Dividing mass media into entertainment and information categories is becoming increasingly difficult as newspapers, usually considered the leading information medium, back off from hard-hitting content to woo readers with softer, entertaining stuff. For better or worse, this same shift is taking place also at *Time* and *Maclean's.* This melding even has a name that's come into fashion: *infotainment.*

While the entertainment-information model will continue to be widely used, generally it is better to think in terms of four media functions—to entertain, to inform, to persuade, and to bind communities—and to recognize that all media do all of these things to a greater or lesser degree.

ELITIST VERSUS POPULIST

An ongoing tension in the mass media exists between advancing social and cultural interests and giving broad segments of the population what they want. This tension, between extremes on a continuum, takes many forms:

- Hana Gartner's "National Magazine" versus Camilla Scott.
- Classical music versus pop music.
- Nudes in art books versus nudes in *Playboy* magazine.
- *Saturday Night* versus the *National Enquirer.*
- A Salman Rushdie novel versus pulp romances.
- A Public Broadcasting Service documentary on crime versus Fox Television's "Ten Most Wanted" re-creations.

At one end of the continuum is serious media content that appeals to people who can be called *elitists* because they feel the mass media have a responsibility to contribute to a better society and a refinement of the culture, regardless of whether the media attract large audiences. At the other end of the continuum are *populists,* who are entirely oriented to the marketplace. Populists feel the mass media are at their best when they give people what they want.

The mass media have been significant historically in shaping social and cultural values. Media committed to promoting these values generally forsake the largest possible audiences. In New York City, the serious-minded *Times*, which carries no comics, has generally lagged in circulation behind the *Daily News*, a screaming tabloid that emphasizes crime and disaster coverage, loves scandals and sex, and carries popular comics. The *Times* can be accused of *elitism*, gearing its coverage to a high level for an audience that appreciates thorough news coverage and serious commentary. The *Daily News*, on the other hand, can be charged with catering to a low level of audience and providing hardly any social or cultural leadership. The *Daily News* is in the populist tradition.

A lot of media criticism can be understood in the context of this *elitist-populist* continuum. People who see a responsibility for the mass media to provide cultural and intellectual leadership fall at one extreme. At the other extreme are people who trust the general population to determine media content through marketplace dynamics. Certainly there are economic incentives for the media to cater to mass tastes.

Most mass media in the United States are somewhere in the middle of the elitist-populist continuum. Fox Television offers some serious fare, not only hyped crime re-creations, and the *New York Times* has a sense of humour that shows itself in the wit of its columnists and in other ways.

ECONOMICS OF MASS MEDIA

STUDY PREVIEW   Most mass media are privately owned and must turn a profit to stay in business.   Except for books, sound recordings and movies, most media income is from advertising, with lesser amounts directly from media consumers. These economic realities are potent shapers of media content.

ECONOMIC FOUNDATION

The mass media are expensive to set up and operate. The equipment and facilities require major investment. Meeting the payroll requires a bankroll. Print media must buy paper by the ton. Broadcasters have gigantic electricity bills to pump their messages through the ether.

To meet their expenses, the mass media sell their product in two ways. Either they derive their income from selling a product directly to mass audiences, as do the movie, record and book industries, or they derive their income from advertisers who pay for the access to mass audiences that the media provide, as do newspapers, magazines, radio and television. In short, the mass media operate in a capitalistic environment, and, with few exceptions, they are in business to make money.

ADVERTISING REVENUE.   Advertisers pay the mass media for access to potential customers. From print media, advertisers buy space. From broadcasters, they buy time.

The more potential customers a media company can deliver to advertisers, the more advertisers are charged for time or space. NBC had 40 million viewers for the 1994 Super Bowl, and it charged $900 000 for a 30-second commercial. A spot on a daytime program, with a fraction of the Super Bowl audience, typically goes for $85 000. *Time* magazine, claiming a 4.6 million circulation, charges $138 200 for a full-page advertisement. If *Time*'s circulation were to plummet, so would its advertising rates. With some exceptions, newspapers, magazines, television and radio support themselves with advertising revenues.

Book publishers once relied solely on readers for revenue, but that has changed. Today, book publishers charge for film rights whenever Hollywood turns a book into a movie or a television program. The result is that publishing houses now profit indirectly from the advertising revenue that television networks pull in from broadcasting movies.

Movies too have come to benefit from advertising. Until the 1950s, movies relied entirely on box-office receipts for profits, but moviemakers now calculate what profits they can realize not only from movie house traffic but also from recycling their movies through advertising-supported television and home videos. The home video aftermarket, in fact, now accounts for the lion's share of movie studio income. Today, moviemakers even pick up advertising directly by charging commercial companies to include their products in the scenes they shoot.

CIRCULATION REVENUE.   While some advertising-supported mass media, such as network television, do not charge their audiences, others do. *Globe and Mail* readers pay 75 cents a copy at the newsrack. *The Hockey News* costs $3.25. Little if any of the newsrack charge or even subscription revenue ends up with the *Globe* or *The Hockey News*. Distribution is costly, and distributors all along the way take their cut. For some publications, however, subscription income makes the difference between profit and loss.

Direct audience payments have emerged in recent years in broadcasting. Cable subscribers pay a monthly fee. Audience support is the basis of subscription television like commercial-free TMN and Moviepix. Noncommercial broadcasting, including TVOntario, relies heavily on viewer and listener contributions. Record makers, moviemakers and book publishers depend on direct sales to the consumer.

GOVERNMENT SUBSIDIES.   While the idea of government support for the mass media might seem to some a waste of public money, both the U.S. and Canadian governments support some form of public broadcasting. The U.S. Congress gives about $90 million a year to the Corporation for Public Broadcasting. Here in Canada, the Canadian Broadcasting Corporation (the CBC) current-

---

MEDIA DATABANK

Buying Space and Time

Here is a sampler of rates for time and space in major media for one-time placements. Major advertisers pay less because they are given discounts as repeat customers.

Los Angeles Times	Sunday full page	$ 52 900
Wall Street Journal	Full page	99 400
Globe and Mail	Saturday full page	41 000
NBC, "Cheers"	30-second spot	400 000
NBC, Super Bowl	30-second spot	900 000
CBC, "Hockey Night in Canada"	30-second spot	15 500

ly receives about $950 million a year from Ottawa, augmented by about $350 million a year in advertising revenue.

The CBC was formed in 1936 by an Act of Parliament. It provides broadcasting services in both official languages. This programming takes the following forms:

- English and French Television
- English and French Radio—both AM and FM
- CBC North—broadcasts not only in French and English but in eight native languages
- RDI (Le Réseau de l'information) and Newsworld, 24-hour-a-day all-news channels in French and English (These services don't receive any government support; they are solely funded by cable subscribers and advertising revenue.)

Government support for public broadcasting seems to be dropping off, as both Canadian and U.S. government funds for public broadcasting have been cut drastically in the last few years.

ECONOMIC IMPERATIVE

Economics figures into which messages make it to print or the airwaves. To realize their profit potential, the media that seek large audiences choose to deal with subjects of wide appeal and to present them in ways that attract great numbers of people. A subject interesting only to small numbers of people does not make it into *Canadian Living*. CTV drops programs that do not do well in the television ratings. This is a function of economics for those media that depend on advertising revenue to stay in business. The larger the audience, the more advertisers are willing to pay for time and space to pitch their goods and services.

Even media that seek narrow segments of the population need to reach as many people within their segments as possible to attract advertisers. A jazz radio station that attracts 90 percent of the jazz fans in a city will be more successful with advertisers than a competing jazz station that attracts only 10 percent.

Media that do not depend on advertising also are geared to finding large audiences. For example, a novel that flops does not go into a second printing. Only successful movies generate sequels.

UPSIDE AND DOWNSIDE

The drive to attract advertising can affect media messages in sinister ways. For example, the television station that overplays the ribbon-cutting ceremony at a new store usually is motivated more by pleasing an advertiser than by telling news. The economic dependence of the mass media on advertising income gives considerable clout to advertisers who threaten to yank advertising out of a publication if a certain negative story appears. Such threats occur, although not frequently.

At a subtler level, lack of advertiser support can work against certain messages. During the 1950s, as racial injustice was emerging as an issue that would rip apart the nation a decade later, American television avoided documentaries on the subject. No advertisers were interested.

The quest for audience also affects how messages are put together. The effect is relatively benign, although real, when a television preacher like Oral Roberts avoids mentioning that he is a Methodist so as not to lose listeners of other faiths. Leaving things unsaid can be serious. For years, many high school science textbooks have danced gingerly around the subject of evolution rather than become embroiled with creationists and lose sales.

MASS MEDIA TRENDS

STUDY PREVIEW   Giant corporations with diverse interests have purchased most North American mass media, and this trend toward conglomeration is accelerating on a global scale. Two other trends, contradictory in some ways, are the moves to seek both ever larger and narrower audiences. Meanwhile, technological advances, mostly electronic, are blurring old distinctions among media.

CONGLOMERATION

The trend toward *conglomeration* involves a process of mergers, acquisitions and buy-outs that consolidates the ownership of the media into fewer and fewer companies. The deep pockets of a wealthy corporate parent can see a financially troubled media unit, such as a radio station, through a rough period, but there is a price. In time, the corporate parent wants a financial return on its investment, and pressure builds on the station to generate more and more profit. This would not be so bad if the people running the radio station loved radio and had a sense of public service, but the process of conglomeration often doesn't work out that way. Parent corporations tend to replace media people with career-climbing, bottom-line managers whose motivation is looking good to their superiors in faraway cities who are under serious pressure to increase profits. Management experts, not radio people, end up running the station, and the quality of media content suffers.

A myopic profit orientation is not surprising, considering that the executives of parent corporations are responsible to their shareholders to return the most profit possible from their diverse holdings. When a conglomerate's interests include

Conrad Black. The actions of both Conrad Black and Ted Rogers have recently raised concerns in Canadian media circles about who owns how much of the media.

enterprises as diverse as soccer teams, airlines, newspapers and timberland, as did the business empire of the late Robert Maxwell, it is easy to understand how the focus is more on the bottom line than on the product. The essence of this phenomenon was captured by *Esquire* magazine when it put this title on an article about the hotel magnate and financier who took over CBS in 1986 and, some say, hastened its decline: "Larry Tisch, Who Mistook His Network for a Spreadsheet."

How extensive is conglomeration? In 1989, media critic *Ben Bagdikian* offered these statistics, which remain true today:

- Six publishing houses have most of North America's book sales.
- Six companies have most of the magazine revenues.
- Three companies have most of the television audience and revenues.
- Three major studios have most of the movie business.

Critics like Bagdikian say conglomeration affects the diversity of messages offered by the mass media. Bagdikian portrays conglomeration in bleak terms: "They are trying to buy control or market domination not just in one medium but in all the media. The aim is to control the entire process from an original manuscript or new series to its use in as many forms as possible. A magazine article owned by *the company* becomes a book owned by *the company*. That becomes a television program owned by *the company*, which then becomes a movie owned by *the company*. It is shown in theaters owned by *the company*, and the movie sound track is issued on a record label owned by *the company*, featuring the vocalist on the cover of one of *the company* magazines. It does not take an angel from heaven to tell us that *the company* will be less enthusiastic about outside ideas and production that it does not own, and more and more we will be dealing with closed circuits to control access to most of the public."

Concentration of ownership is an issue in Canada. For example, after taking over Maclean Hunter, Ted Rogers (and Rogers Communications) owned, or par-

Alternative Media. Advertisers are putting more dollars into new media that reach consumers in the marketplace as they shop. The VideoCart Company, for example, makes a video screen that mounts on shopping carts and plays messages as shoppers wheel through aisles where certain products are shelved. Such place-based alternative media are a threat to traditional media, such as magazines, newspapers, radio and television, which are losing the near-monopoly they once held for reaching consumers with retail advertising.

tially owned, the majority of cable systems in Canada, the Rogers video store chain, *Maclean's* magazine, all the *Sun* newspapers, the *Financial Post*, Cantel and Unitel. The CRTC forced Rogers to sell off the Sun publishing chain, including the *Financial Post*, in 1996. The chain sold for over $400 million. Meanwhile, two newspaper chains, Southam and Hollinger, own the majority of dailies in Canada. Hollinger is now the majority owner of Southam.

DEMASSIFICATION

Another contemporary economic phenomenon is *demassification*. The mass media are capable of reaching tremendous numbers of people, but most media today no longer try to reach the largest possible audience. They are demassifying, going after narrower and narrower segments of the mass audience.

This demassification process, the result of technological breakthroughs and economic pressures, is changing the mass media dramatically. Radio demassified early in the 1950s, replacing formats designed to reach the largest possible audiences with formats aimed at sectors of the audience. Magazines followed in the 1960s and the 1970s, and today most consumer magazines cater only to the special interests of carefully targeted groups of readers. Today, with dozens of television program services available via cable in most households, television also is going through demassification.

The effects of demassification are only beginning to emerge. At first, advertisers welcomed demassification because they could target their pitches to groups of their likeliest customers. Although demassification dramatically changed the mass media—network radio went into a decline, for example—the economic base of the mass media remained advertising. Local radio stations found new profitability from advertisers anxious to support demassified formats. Today, however, technology has found ways for advertisers to bypass the mass media to reach mass audiences. The latest trend in demassification has advertisers producing their own media to carry their messages by mail to potential customers who, through computer sorting and other mechanisms, are more precisely targeted than magazines, newspapers, television and radio could ever do. The new *alternative media*, as they are called, include:

- Direct mail catalogues and flyers to selected addresses.
- Television commercials at the point of purchase, such as screens in grocery store shopping carts.
- Place-based media, such as magazines designed for distribution only in physicians' waiting rooms.
- Telemarketing, in which salespeople make their pitches by telephone to households determined by statistical profiles to be good potential customers.
- Cable advertising, on information channels like Prevue Guide, which offers advertisers an alternative to traditional media.
- Sport Scope, a Canadian information service, offers 2 million cable subscribers up-to-the-minute sports information, 24 hours a day. It also offers advertisers a way to reach a large, mostly male, audience. It is an example of two media, in this case print and television, "melding" to form a new medium.

If advertisers continue their shift to these and other alternative media, the revenue base of magazines, newspapers, radio and television will decline. Wholly new ways to structure the finances of these media will be necessary, probably with readers, listeners and viewers picking up the bill directly rather than indirectly by buying advertised products, which is the case today.

Sport Scope. New media alternatives for advertisers are emerging, including Sport Scope, a Canadian 24-hour sports information channel. A channel like Sport Scope can reach a narrowly defined audience for advertisers.

MELDING

The seven primary mass media as we know them today are in a technological transition that is blurring the old distinctions that once clearly separated them. For example, newspapers are experimenting with electronic delivery via cable and telephone lines—"no paper" newspapers. Through personal computers, thousands of people have access to data banks to choose the news coverage they want. In the 1980s the Massachusetts Institute of Technology media lab developed *configurable video* systems that integrated printed articles and video segments that a person could read and view in any sequence desired. The MIT system was an integration of traditional print and electronic media with a new twist: An individual, sitting at a screen, could control the editing by passing unwanted portions and focusing on what was most valuable.

Some media melding has come about because competitors have recognized how partnerships could be mutually beneficial. When television became a media force in the 1950s, Hollywood lost millions of moviegoers and declared war on its new rival. For several years, the movie industry even forbade television from playing movies, and Hollywood developed distinctive technical and content approaches that television could not duplicate. The rivalry eased in time, and today Hollywood and the television industry are major partners. Hollywood produces a significant amount of programming for the television networks, and there are all kinds of joint ventures.

MASS COMMUNICATION PROCESS

STUDY PREVIEW   Mass communication is the process mass communicators use to send their mass messages to mass audiences. It is a process that is related to other kinds of communication but that also is distinctive. It is a process that is not well understood.

FOUR BASIC COMPONENTS

The mass media are a relatively recent arrival in human experience. The oldest mass medium, the printed book, has been around more than 500 years, and the newest medium, television, only 50 years. These media affect us in many ways, but we know much less than we should about how they work. One way to understand how the mass media work is to define these different but related terms:

MASS MESSAGES.   A news item is a message, as are a movie, a novel, a recorded song and a billboard advertisement. The *message* is the most apparent part of our relationship to the mass media. The people who create messages include journalists, lyricists, scriptwriters, television anchors, radio disc jockeys, public relations practitioners, and advertising copywriters.

MASS MEDIA.   The *mass media* are the vehicles that carry messages. The primary mass media, as we have discussed, are books, magazines, newspapers, television, radio, sound recordings, and movies. Most theorists view media as neutral carriers of messages. The people who are experts at media include technicians who keep the presses running and who keep the television transmitters on the air. Media experts also are tinkerers and inventors who come up with technical improvements, such as compact discs, AM stereo radio and newspaper presses that can produce high-quality colour.

MASS COMMUNICATION.   The process through which messages reach the audience via the mass media is called *mass communication*. This is a mysterious process about which we know far less than we should. Researchers and scholars have unraveled some of the mystery, but most of how it works remains a matter of wonderment. For example: Why do people pay more attention to some messages than to others? How does one advertisement generate more sales than another? Is behaviour, including violent behaviour, triggered through the mass communication process? There is reason to believe that mass communication affects voting behaviour, but how does this work? Which is most correct—to say that people can be controlled, manipulated, or influenced by mass communication? Nobody has the answer.

MASS AUDIENCES.   The size and diversity of mass audiences add complexity to mass communication. Only indirectly do mass communicators learn whether their messages have been received. Mass communicators are never sure exactly of the size of audiences, let alone of the effect of their messages. Mass audiences are fickle. What attracts great attention one day may not the next. The challenge of trying to communicate to a mass audience is even more complex because people are tuning in and tuning out all the time, and when they are tuned in, it is with varying degrees of attentiveness.

MYSTERY OF MASS COMMUNICATION

The mass communication process is full of mystery. Major corporations commit millions of dollars to advertising a new product and then anxiously hope the promotional campaign works. Sometimes it does. Sometimes it doesn't. Even experts at mass communication, such as the people at advertising agencies, haven't unlocked the mysteries of the process, nor have scholars who try to understand the influence of mass communication on society and individuals. One of the enduring questions of our time is whether the media trigger violent behaviour.

Despite the mystery and the uncertainties, there is no alternative to mass communication in modern society. Therefore, it is important for people who create mass media messages to learn all that can be known about the process. It is no less important that people who receive the messages have a sense of the process that is being used to inform, entertain and persuade them.

COMMUNICATION TYPES

The communication in which the mass media engage is only one form of communication. One way to begin understanding the process of mass communication is to differentiate it from other forms of communication:

INTRAPERSONAL COMMUNICATION.   We engage in *intrapersonal communication* when we talk to ourselves to develop our thoughts and ideas. This intrapersonal communication precedes our speaking or acting.

INTERPERSONAL COMMUNICATION.   When people talk to each other, they are engaging in *interpersonal communication*. In its simplest form, interpersonal communication is between two persons physically located in the same place. It can occur, however, if they are physically separated but emotionally connected, like lovers over the telephone.

The difference between the prefixes *intra-* and *inter-* is the key difference between intrapersonal and interpersonal communication. Just as *intrasquad* athletic games are within a team, *intrapersonal* communication is within one's self. Just as *intercollegiate* games are between schools, *interpersonal* communication is between individuals.

GROUP COMMUNICATION.   There comes a point when the number of people involved reduces the intimacy of the communication process. That's when the situation becomes *group communication*. A club meeting is an example. So is a speech to an audience in an auditorium.

MASS COMMUNICATION.   Capable of reaching thousands, even millions, of people is *mass communication*, which is accomplished through a mass medium like television or newspapers. Mass communication can be defined as the process of using a mass medium to send messages to large audiences for the purpose of informing, entertaining or persuading.

In many respects the process of mass communication and other communication forms is the same: Someone conceives a message, essentially an intrapersonal act. The message then is encoded into a common code, such as language. Then it's transmitted. Another person receives the message, decodes it and internalizes it. Internalizing a message is also an intrapersonal act.

In other respects, mass communication is distinctive. Crafting an effective message for thousands of people of diverse backgrounds and interests requires different skills than chatting with a friend across the table. Encoding the message is more complex because a device is always used—for example, a printing press, a camera or a recorder.

One aspect of mass communication that should not be a mystery is spelling the often-misused word "communication." The word takes no "s" if you are using it to refer to a *process*. If you are referring to a communication as *a thing*, such as a letter, a movie, a telegram or a television program, rather than a *process*, the word is "communication" in singular form and "communications" in plural. The term "mass communication" refers to a process, so it is spelled without the "s."

- -

MASS COMMUNICATION MODELS: THE PROCESS SCHOOL

STUDY PREVIEW   Scholars have devised numerous models that illustrate the communication process. The models discussed previously fell within the semiotic school of communication. We will now examine the process school, which focuses on the sending and receiving of messages.

BASIC MODEL

Many ways have been devised to display the communication process to help explain how it works. One model was laid out in 1948 by two Bell telephone engineers, *Claude Shannon* and *Warren Weaver*, who were working on advanced computer applications in telephone systems. Shannon and Weaver needed a reference point for their research, so they devised a model that has become a standard baseline for describing the communication process.

STIMULATION.   In the Shannon-Weaver model, communication begins with a source who is stimulated internally to want to communicate a message. The stimulation can result from many things. Emotions can be stimuli, as can something that is sensed—seeing a beautiful panorama, feeling a cold draft or hearing a child cry.

ENCODING.   The second step is encoding. The source puts thoughts into symbols that can be understood by whomever is destined to receive the message. The symbols take many forms—for example, the written word, smoke signals or pictographs.

TRANSMISSION.   The message is the representation of the thought. In interpersonal communication, the message is almost always delivered face to face. In mass communication, however, the message is encoded so that it is suitable for the equipment being used for transmission. Shannon and Weaver, being telephone engineers, offered the example of the sound pressure of a voice being changed into proportional electrical current for transmission over telephone lines. In technical terms, telephone lines were channels for Shannon and Weaver's messages. On a more conceptual basis, the telephone lines were the *media*, in the same way that the printed page or a broadcast signal is.

DECODING.   The receiver picks up signals sent by the transmitter. In interpersonal communication, the receiver is a person who hears the message or sees it, or both. An angry message encoded as a fist banging a table is heard and perhaps felt. An insulting message encoded as a puff of cigar smoke in the face is smelled. In mass communication, the first receiver of the message is not a person but the equipment that picks up and then reconstructs the message from the signal. This mechanical decoding is necessary so that the human receiver of the message can

Failures to Communicate

When was the last time you misunderstood something you learned about from the mass media? Try to reconstruct the situation and identify what went wrong. Perhaps you had trouble following the plot of a television movie or could not determine the premier's position on some issue from a newspaper article. Ask yourself:

■ Was encoding at fault? Decoding?
■ Did channel, environmental or semantic noise interfere?

■ Did filters interfere?
■ Were gatekeepers at fault, giving you insufficient background or perhaps cluttering a message with irrelevancies that obscured the message?
■ Was homophyly lacking?
■ Would the misunderstanding have occurred if you had had an opportunity for immediate feedback with the source of the message that you misunderstood?

Classic Communication Model. This is the classic communication model to which people like Claude Shannon and Warren Weaver began adding the mechanical and electronic components of mass communication in the 1940s. In mass communication, the transmitter is not the human voice or a writing utensil but, in the case of a radio, a transmitter. The receiver is not a human ear but a radio receiver. The conception of a message by a sender and the internalization by the receiver remain human functions in mass communication. The terms *encoder* and *decoder* were added by scholar Wilbur Schramm.

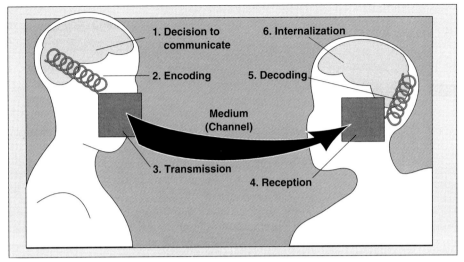

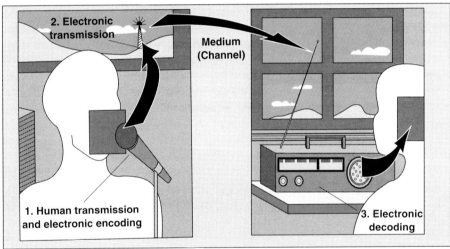

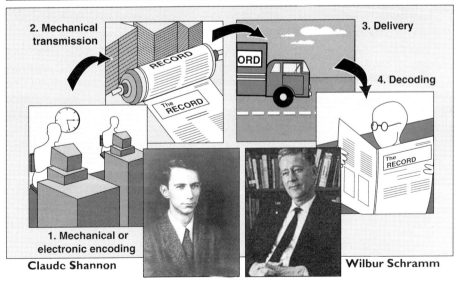

understand it. As Shannon and Weaver put it, "the receiver ordinarily performs the inverse operation that was done by the transmitter."

INTERNALIZATION.   In mass communication, a second kind of decoding occurs with the person who receives the message from the receiving equipment. This is an intrapersonal act, internalizing the message. For this second kind of decoding to work, the receiver must understand the communication form chosen by the source in encoding. Someone who reads only English will not be able to decode a message in Greek. Someone whose sensibility is limited to punk rock will not understand Handel's water music. In other words, the source and the receiver must have enough in common for communication to occur. This common experience, which can be as simple as speaking the same tongue, is called *homophyly*. In mass communication, the encoder must know the audience well enough to shape messages that can be decoded accurately and with the intended effect.

NOISE.   If speakers slur their words, the effectiveness of their messages is jeopardized. Slurring and other impediments in the communication process are called *noise*. In mass communication, which is based on complex mechanical and electronic equipment, the opportunities for noise interference are countless because so many things can go wrong. Noise occurs in three forms. *Channel noise*, such as transmission static, faulty microphones and smudged pages, occurs in the transmission of messages. *Environmental noise*—a doorbell that interrupts someone's reading an article or shouting kids who distract a viewer from the six o'clock news—interferes with the decoding process. *Semantic noise*, such as sloppy wording, involves problems in crafting messages.

Mass communicators go to special lengths to guard against noise interfering with their messages. For example, in encoding, broadcast scriptwriters avoid "s" sounds as much as possible because they can hiss gratingly if listeners are not tuned precisely on the frequency. Because words can be unintentionally dropped in typesetting, newspaper reporters write that a verdict was "innocent" rather than "not guilty." It would be a serious matter if noise resulted in the deletion of "not."

To keep noise at a minimum, technicians strive to keep their equipment in top-notch condition. Even so, things can go wrong. Also, mass communicators cannot control noise that affects individual members of their audience—such as the siren of a passing fire truck, a migraine headache or the distraction of a pot boiling over on the stove. Clear enunciation, whether sharp writing in a magazine or clear pronunciation on the radio, can minimize such interference, but noise is mostly beyond the communicator's control.

Repetition is the mass communicator's best antidote against noise. If the message does not get through the first time, it is repeated. Rare is an advertisement that plays only once. Radio newscasters repeat the same major news stories every hour, although they rehash the scripts so they will not bore people who heard the stories earlier.

FEEDBACK.   Because mass communication is not the one-way street that the Shannon-Weaver model indicated, later theorists embellished the model by looping the process back on itself. The recipient of a message, after decoding, responds. The original recipient then becomes the sender, encoding a response and sending it via a medium back to the original sender, who becomes the new destination and decodes the response. This reverse process is called *feedback*.

Semantic Noise. In every issue, the *Columbia Journalism Review* delights in reproducing bad headlines and other newspaper gaffes as a reminder to journalists to be more careful. These gaffes are examples of semantic noise, in which ambiguous wording and other poor word choices interfere with clear communication.

In interpersonal communication, you know if your listener does not understand. If you hear "Uhh?" or see a puzzled look, you restate your point. In mass communication, feedback is delayed. It might be a week after an article is published before a reader's letter arrives in the newsroom. Because feedback is delayed and because there usually is not very much of it, precise expression in mass communication is especially important. There is little chance to restate the point immediately if the television viewer does not understand. A mass communicator cannot hear the "Uhh?"

OTHER IMPORTANT COMMUNICATION TERMS

INFORMATION.   The content of the message that is being sent is important to communication researchers. Content can include photographs, words and song lyrics. In the process of mass communication, information is usually coded and transmitted through at least one channel.

CHANNEL.   This refers to the way the message (information) is sent; radio uses sound waves, television can use co-axial cables to carry a combination of audio and video signals, telephones and the Internet use telephone wires.

MEDIUM.   A medium is the way the message is transformed in order to be sent through a channel. As McLuhan observed, which medium is used to communicate a message has important implications. John Fiske divides media into three categories:

Presentational   The body is a presentational medium. In interpersonal communication, we can send messages nonverbally, through gestures and facial expressions. Both the sender and receiver must be present for the act to be defined as presentational. Therefore, watching a play at the Charlottetown Festival is a way of witnessing a presentational medium. The actors are the medium through which much of the play's content is communicated.

Representational   This kind of medium includes most artifacts that we would usually define as mass media: movies, books, magazines, newspapers, music videos and television programming are all representational media. They are "texts" that can be consumed by a mass public. They are works of communication. Neither the receiver nor the sender need be present at the same time.

Mechanical   The mechanical media help communicate presentational and representational media. Radio, television, the Internet and telephones are forms of mechanical media.

As with many definitions in communication studies, these categories are not mutually exclusive. For example, a politician's speech, viewed in person, is presentational in nature. A radio station broadcasting that speech live makes the speech representational through the use of a mechanical medium. The speech has not changed, but the form used to convey it has. Think of viewing a baseball game in person or at home on TSN. The event has not changed, but your perception of it has. Placing all mechanical media in the same category is also problematic, as a news story written in the newspaper or read on the radio will not be the same. In each instance a different channel is used to communicate information.

REDUNDANCY.   In the context of communication redundancy is beneficial; it helps the process of communication. A redundant message is easily decoded by the receiver; there is little room for error. The term is used by communication theorists to explain how predictable a message is. A catchy slogan or jingle needs to be redundant to be effective. Can any hockey fan hear the theme music from "Hockey Night in Canada" and not know what it is? A redundant message only needs a passive receiver in order to be understood. A redundant message may also be called a conventional message.

The success of the TV show "Friends," on Global, is a good example of redundancy and convention. Due to the show's success, many "clones" were produced. These clones followed the same conventions as "Friends" and so convey redundant messages. When someone watches "Friends" or one of its imitators, he or she knows what to expect.

ENTROPY.   This is the opposite of redundancy. An entropic message is not easy to decode and is clearly not conventional. An entropic message may need a more active receiver in order to be understood. This is usually seen as a problem in the process of communication, particularly in mass communication, where the aim is to appeal to a large audience.

Artists often break convention in the construction of their media messages. Directors like Fellini, Bergman and Canada's Atom Egoyan often break with convention in their (entropic) films in order to attract a more active audience. The television programs "Twin Peaks" and "Murder One" also broke with the conventional structure of television and paid the price in lost viewers. While both shows initially received critical and public acclaim, viewers found them difficult to watch and decode. As a result, both programs ultimately fell in the ratings.

CONCENTRIC CIRCLE MODEL

The Shannon-Weaver model can be applied to all communication, but it misses some things unique to mass communication. In 1974 scholars *Ray Hiebert, Donald Ungurait* and *Thomas Bohn* presented an important new model—a series of concentric circles with the encoding source at the centre. One of the outer rings was the receiving audience. In between were several elements that are important in the mass communication process but less so in other communication processes.

GATEKEEPERS. Mass communication is not a solo endeavour. Dozens, sometimes hundreds, of individuals are involved. A Stephen King thriller passes through several editors before being published. When it's adapted as a screenplay, substantial modifications are made by many other individuals, all expert in the medium of the movie. Later, when it is adapted for television, experts in television

Concentric Circle Model.
The scholars who designed the concentric circle model suggest thinking of it as a pebble being dropped in still water. The ripples emanating outward from the communicator go through many barriers before reaching the audience or having any effect. The model takes note of feedback, media amplification, noise and distortion introduced by the media.

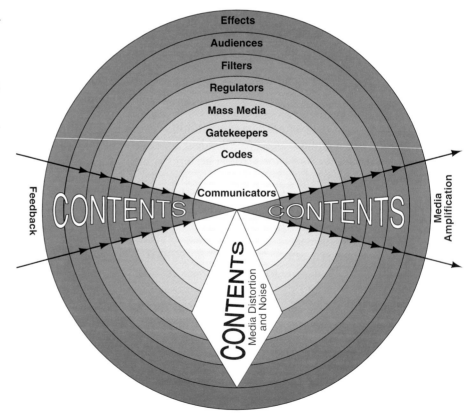

as a mass medium make further changes, and so might the network program standards office. Anyone who can stop or alter a message en route to the audience is a *gatekeeper*. Newscast producers are gatekeepers because they decide what is aired and what is not. They make decisions about what to emphasize and what to deemphasize. Magazine and newspaper editors do the same, sorting through hundreds of stories to choose the relatively few that will fit in their publications. When gatekeepers make a mistake, however, the communication process and also the message suffer.

REGULATORS.   The concentric circle model also recognizes *regulators* as a force that shapes and reshapes mass-communicated messages before they reach the mass audience. Regulators are nonmedia institutions that influence media content. The Canadian Radio-television and Telecommunications Commission is a government agency that serves as a regulator. Pressure groups like MediaWatch also have an effect. Peer pressure is institutionalized in trade and professional organizations. Other regulators include theatre licensing procedures, libel laws and fair trade requirements in advertising.

FILTERS.   Hiebert, Ungurait and Bohn note that receivers are affected by a variety of filters in decoding a message. They call the language or symbols used for a message *informational filters*. If the sender and receiver are not in tune with the same symbols, the communication process is flawed. If you did not know how to read, an informational filter would be interfering right now with your understanding this sentence.

Physical filters exist when a receiver's mind is dimmed by fatigue.

If a receiver is a zealous animal rights activist, *psychological filters* likely will affect the reception of news on medical research involving animals. Being on a different wavelength can be a filter. Imagine two women friends going to the movie *Fatal Attraction* together. One woman is married and monogamous, the other is involved with a married man. Having different ideas on and experiences with marital fidelity, which is at the heart of the movie, the women hear the same words and see the same images, but they see two "different" movies.

EFFECTS.   A decoded message can do more than prompt verbal feedback. It can also affect how someone votes or even provoke a riot. The outermost ring of the concentric circle model, the effects of a message, goes beyond the Shannon-Weaver model to include this important point.

AMPLIFICATION.   An outgoing arrow in the concentric circle model points out that mass media have the ability to amplify, which is related to gatekeepers. Amplification is a process by which mass communication confers status to issues and personalities merely by covering them.

Status conferral can work positively and negatively. For example, some scholars claim that the U.S. government overreacted in 1980 to the 444-day Iran hostage situation because media coverage kept fueling public reaction. Oliver North's name would not have become a household word had it not been for saturation media coverage of the Iran-Contra issue.

Status conferral is not limited to the news media. Ballads and music, amplified through the mass media, can capture the public's imagination and keep an issue alive and even enlarge it. In World War I, catchy songs such as "Over There" helped rally support for the cause. Fifty years later, "An Okie From Muskogee" lent legitimacy to the hawkish position on Vietnam. Bob Dylan's 1975 song "Hurricane" reopened the investigation into the murder conviction of Reuben "Hurricane" Carter. Movies also have the power to move people and sustain issues. Sidney Poitier movies of the 1960s, including "Guess Who's Coming to Dinner," helped keep racial integration on the American agenda.

NARRATIVE MODEL

Yale professor *Harold Lasswell*, an early mass communication theorist, developed a useful yet simple mass communication model. The Lasswell model is not diagrammed. Instead, it is in narrative form and poses four questions: Who says what? In which channel? To whom? With what effect?

You can easily apply the model. Pick any bylined story from the front page of a newspaper.

- Who says what? The newspaper reporter tells a story, often quoting someone who is especially knowledgeable on the subject.
- In which channel? In this case, the story is told through the newspaper, a mass medium.
- To whom? The story is told to a newspaper reader.
- With what effect? The reader decides to vote for Candidate A or B, or perhaps readers just add the information to their reservoir of knowledge.

CHAPTER WRAP-UP

The mass media are the vehicles that carry messages to large audiences. These media—books, magazines, newspapers, records, movies, radio, television and sound and video recordings—are so pervasive in modern life that many people do not even notice their influence. Because of that influence, however, we should take time to understand the mass media so that we can better assess whether they are affecting us for better or worse.

The mass media are essential. By keeping people on top of current issues, the media enable people to participate intelligently in public policy discussion and decision making. The media also are the vehicles by which people debate the issues and try to persuade each other of different points of view. Even when they provide us with entertainment, the mass media are capable of portraying and shaping values that enrich our dialogue on social issues and public policy. Sometimes the media perform these functions well, sometimes not. Studying the media gives people the tools to know whether the media are living up to their potential as facilitators of democracy.

The mass media work through a process called mass communication. This is an important distinction: Mass media are *things*, mass communication is a *process*.

The study of mass communication teaches a great deal about the influence of the mass media.

Technology is central to mass communication. Magazines and newspapers are possible only because the printing process was invented. Television, likewise, is dependent on electronic equipment. Because media technology is complex, mass communication is possible only through organizations that bring together many people with a range of specialized skills. These organizations include television networks, book publishers and newspaper chains, almost all of which exist only because they generate profits for their owners. A related approach to studying the mass media, therefore, involves examining the competitive economic context within which they operate.

QUESTIONS FOR REVIEW

1. How are the mass media pervasive in our everyday lives?

2. What are the three technologies on which the primary mass media are built?

3. Explain three models that scholars have devised to explain the mass media.

4. How do mass media organizations make money to stay in business?

5. What are the major changes that the mass media are undergoing? And what are the effects?

6. How do these items relate to each other? Mass communicators, mass messages, mass communication, mass media, mass audiences.

7. What is the difference between the process school and the semiotic school?

8. Who were de Saussure, Barthes and Pierce? What are signs?

9. Explain the differences between an icon, an index and a symbol.

QUESTIONS FOR CRITICAL THINKING

1. How is each of these types of communication—intrapersonal, interpersonal, group and mass—difficult to master?

2. All communication involves conceiving, encoding, transmitting, receiving and decoding, but some of these steps are more complicated for mass communication. In what way?

3. Some people were confused when Marshall McLuhan called electronic media cool and print media hot because, in their experience, radios and television sets heat up and newspapers are always at room temperature. What did McLuhan mean?

4. The effectiveness of messages communicated through the mass media is shaped by the technical limitations of each medium. One limitation of radio is that it cannot accommodate pictures; another that most radio news formats limit stories to 40 seconds. Can you provide examples of content limitations of certain media? What are the audience limitations inherent in all mass media?

5. For many years CBS television programs drew a

generally older and more rural audience than the other networks. Did that make CBS a niche-seeking mass media unit? Did it make the CBS audience any less heterogeneous?

6. Describe some of the limitations of both the process and semiotic schools of communication.

7. Which mass media perform the informing purpose best? The entertaining purpose? The persuading purpose? Which of these purposes does the advertising industry serve? Public relations?

8. Why do revolutionaries try to take over the mass media right away?

9. Which is more important to the mass media—profits or doing social good? What about the goals of supermarket tabloids like the *National Enquirer*?

10. Which mass media rely directly on consumer purchases for their economic survival? Advertising provides almost all the revenue for commercial radio and television stations, but indirectly consumer purchases are an important factor. In what way?

11. Are any types of mass media not dependent on

advertising or consumer purchases?

12. Analyze some Canadian signs using the semiotic approach. What Canadian connotations emerge?

What do these connotations say about Canadians and our culture? How do you think these connotations developed?

FOR FURTHER LEARNING

Ken Auletta. *Three Blind Mice: How the TV Networks Lost Their Way* (Random House, 1991). Auletta takes a dim view of media conglomeration in this examination of the corporate takeovers of ABC, CBS and NBC in the 1980s.

Ben H. Bagdikian. "Special Issue: The Lords of the Global Village." *The Nation* 248 (June 12, 1989):23, 805–20. Bagdikian, a media critic, argues that the concentration of media ownership into a few global conglomerates is diluting the vigour of news and other content.

Roland Barthes. *Mythologies* (Paladin, 1973).

Arthur Asa Berger. *Media USA: Process and Effect* (Longman, 1988). This is a collection of articles on media issues, including economic aspects of the mass media.

John Fiske. *Introduction to Communication Studies.* (Routledge, 1990). Fiske offers an excellent introduction to the study of communication from both the process and semiotic perspectives.

Stephen W. Littlejohn. *Theories of Human Communication*, 3rd ed. (Wadsworth, 1989). Professor Littlejohn traces developments in communication theory and synthesizes current research. One chapter focuses on mass communication.

Eric McLuhan and Frank Zingrone. *Essential McLuhan.* (Anansi, 1995). A collection of McLuhan's works including the famous *The Medium Is the Message*.

Marshall McLuhan. *Understanding Media*. (Signet, 1964)

Denis McQuail. *Mass Communication Theory* (Sage, 1987)

Denis McQuail and Sven Windahl. *Communication Models for the Study of Mass Communication* (Longman, 1981). McQuail and Windahl show dozens of models from the first 30 years of mass communication research with explanatory comments. Included is discussion on the narrative, Shannon-Weaver and helix models.

Anthony Smith. *The Age of the Behemoths: The Globalization of Mass Media Firms* (Priority Press, 1991). In this brief volume, media scholar Smith details the recent growth of giant global media companies, including Bertelsmann, Sony and Time Warner, and discusses implications of this development.

Alexis S. Tan. *Mass Communication Theories and Research* (Macmillan, 1986). Drawing on the growing body of behavioural communication research, Professor Tan explains mass communication functions, processes and effects. Although it is written for serious students, the book requires no background in communication theory, methodology or statistics.

FOR KEEPING UP TO DATE

Scholarly discussion on the communication process can be found in *Communication Yearbook*, published since 1977, and *Mass Communication Review Yearbook*, published since 1986.

The Canadian Communication Association is a group of scholars and students who share an interest in issues of mass communication in Canada. *The Canadian Journal of Communication* is published quarterly by Wilfred Laurier Press.

The Journal of Communication is a quarterly scholarly publication from Oxford University Press.

Many mass media developments abroad are tracked in the monthly London-based *Censorship Index*.

Newsmagazines including *Time* and *Maclean's* cover major mass media issues more or less regularly, as do the *Globe and Mail* and other major newspapers.

CHAPTER 2

THE PRINTED WORD
Newspapers and Magazines

The mass production of the written word in the 1400s fundamentally changed human history

Newspapers are the major source of news for most North Americans

Most newspapers are owned by chains

Canada and the United States are largely nations of local and regional newspapers

Most of the leading North American newspapers are metropolitan dailies

Television and retailing changes have cut into newspaper display advertising

Thriving newspapers include counter-culture, gay and ethnic papers aimed at narrow readerships

Magazines have been innovators as a journalistic and as a visual medium

Sponsored magazines and trade journals far outnumber consumer magazines that are available at newsracks

The magazine industry continues to demassify with products aimed at audiences with more narrowly focused interests

MEDIA IN THEORY

Newspaper Content

Communication theorists view newspapers as works of communication that are representational in nature. They are texts that primarily use words to communicate ideas. Words are probably the most common sign in communication. As symbols, they signify something other than themselves. They operate on a denotative level in the sense that they name objects in our world,

and they also work on a connotative level in the sense that they convey cultural beliefs and values.

The Sapir-Whorf hypothesis claims that language, while not wholly determining our perceptions, does have an effect on how we see the outside world. Benjamin Lee Whorf and Edward Sapir were both linguistic anthropologists who studied language use and patterns among several cultures. The Sapir-Whorf hypothesis has a strong and a weak version. The strong one implies that language determines how we see the world; the other suggests that language and thought are linked. Most theorists discard the strong theory, deeming it too reminiscent of George Orwell's *1984*, in which citizens were told that being a slave was really being free.

The weak version of the hypothesis, which says that language can subtly affect our perception, the way we "see" the world, can be illustrated by asking a skier how many different words (signs) there are for snow. An experienced skier will see and label a wide variety: corn snow, champagne snow, packed powder and loose granular, to name just a few. Most subcultures have their own way of talking, which affects how they interpret the world around them. The Sapir-Whorf hypothesis claims that language also works on a societal level to guide interpretations and understandings.

An excellent example of this theory in action occurred during the 1990 Persian Gulf War: Iraqi people weren't killed during bombings; they became "collateral damage," while Americans soldiers who were killed by American weapons were killed by "friendly fire." The Sapir-Whorf (weak) hypothesis would suggest that the Pentagon, by choosing its words carefully, was able to control public opinion.

Because of this idea, many communication scholars are worried that, with ownership concentrated in fewer and fewer hands, only a narrow selection of connotations and interpretations will be reported. Applying the ideas of Barthes, they fear that ultimately only the connotations of the dominant ideology will be communicated by newspapers. However, many would argue that the recent explosion in counter-culture, ethnic and gay newspapers offers the various subcultures within Canada a chance for their voices to be heard.

GUTENBERG AND MOVABLE TYPE

Johannes Gutenberg was eccentric—a secretive tinkerer with a passion for beauty, detail and craftmanship. By trade, he was a metallurgist, but he never made much money at it. Like most of his fellow 15th-century Rhinelanders, he pressed his own grapes for wine. As a businessman, he was not very successful, and he died penniless. Despite his unpromising combination of traits, quirks and habits—perhaps because of them—Johannes Gutenberg wrought the most significant change in history: the mass-produced written word. He invented movable metal type.

Despite the significance of his invention, there is much we do not know about Gutenberg. Even to friends, he seldom mentioned his experiments, and when he did he referred to them mysteriously as his "secret art." When he ran out of money, Gutenberg quietly sought investors, luring them partly by the mystique he attached to his work. What we know about Gutenberg's "secret art" was recorded only because Gutenberg's main backer didn't realize the quick financial return he expected on his investment and sued. The litigation left a record from which historians have pieced together the origins of modern printing.

The date that Johannes Gutenberg printed his first page with movable type is unknown, but historians usually settle on 1446. Gutenberg's printing process was widely copied—and quickly. By 1500, presses all over western Europe had published almost 40 000 books.

Today, Gutenberg is remembered for the Bibles he printed with movable type. Two hundred Gutenberg Bibles, each a printing masterpiece, were produced over several years. Gutenberg used the best paper. He concocted an especially black ink. The quality amazed everybody, and the Bibles sold quickly. Gutenberg could have printed hundreds more, perhaps thousands. With a couple of husky helpers, he and his modified wine press could have produced 50 to 60 imprints an hour. However, Johannes Gutenberg, who never had much business savvy, concentrated instead on

First Mass-Produced Written Word. Johannes Gutenberg and his assistants could produce 50 to 60 imprints an hour with their modified wind press, but Gutenberg's real contribution was movable metal type. His movable type expedited the putting together of pages and opened the age of mass communication.

Gutenberg Masterpiece. The craftsmanship that Johannes Gutenberg put into his Bibles made them sought after in the 1450s and still today. Of the 47 remaining, one sold at an auction for $2.4 million in 1978.

Scribist Monk. Until the invention of movable type by Johannes Gutenberg in the 1440s, books were produced one at a time by scribes. It was tedious work, production was slow and scribes were not always faithful to the original.

quality. Forty-seven Gutenberg Bibles remain today, all collector's items. One sold in 1978 for $2.4 million.

BOOKS IN HUMAN HISTORY

The introduction of mass-produced books in the 15th century marked a turning point in human history. Before then, books were handwritten, usually by scribist monks who copied existing books onto blank sheets of paper letter by letter, one page at a time. These scribists could turn out only a few hand-lettered books in a lifetime of tedium.

In the mid-1400s, *Johannes Gutenberg*, a tinkerer in what is now Germany, devised an innovation that made it possible to print pages using metal letters. Printing itself was nothing new. Artisans in ancient China had been printing with a process that is still an art form:

- Impressions are carved in page-size wooden blocks.
- The blocks are laid on a flat surface and inked.
- A sheet of paper is carefully laid on the blocks.
- Pressure is brought down on the inked blocks.
- The carved-out niches in the block remain uninked, and the surface of the block becomes inked figures impressed on the paper.

Gutenberg's revolutionary contribution was in applying metallurgy to the process. The idea occurred to Gutenberg in the mid-1430s. Instead of wood, which often cracked in the pressing process, he experimented with casting individual letters in a lead-based alloy. He built a frame the size of a book's page and then arranged the metal letters into words. Once a page was filled—with letters and words and sentences—he put the frame into a modified wine press, applied ink, laid paper, and pressed. The process made it possible to produce dozens, even hundreds and thousands, of copies.

Gutenberg's impact cannot be overstated. The duplicative power of movable type put the written word into wide circulation and fueled quantum increases in literacy. One hundred years after Gutenberg, the state of communication in Europe had undergone a revolution. Elaborate postal systems were in place. Standardized maps produced by printing presses replaced hand-copied maps, with all their inaccuracies and idiosyncracies. People began writing open letters to be distributed far and wide. Newspapers followed.

IMPORTANCE OF NEWSPAPERS

STUDY PREVIEW   Newspapers are the primary mass medium from which people receive news. In most cities, no other news source comes close to the local newspaper's range and depth of coverage. This contributes to the popularity and influence of newspapers.

NEWSPAPER INDUSTRY DIMENSIONS

The newspaper industry dwarfs other news media by almost every measure. The data are staggering:

- In Canada, 106 dailies publish about 5 million copies each day.

- In the U.S. about 1 570 daily newspapers put out 60 million copies a day.
- Community weeklies in Canada publish over 10 million copies and are read by 1.6 people per household.
- The Canadian newspaper industry is multicultural: 39 Canadian ethnic groups publish almost 300 newspapers.

(Source: Canadian Advertising Rates and Data (CARD), June 1996)

What makes a newspaper Canadian? Changes to the 1988 Income Tax Act state that a newspaper is Canadian if:

- the type is set in Canada (excluding ads or feature stories)
- it is wholly printed in Canada (exluding comics)
- it is edited and published by people living in Canada.

(Source: Canadian Income Tax Act with income tax regulations consolidated to 22 September 1988.)

Perhaps because television has stolen the glitz and romance that newspapers once had, the significance of newspapers is easy to miss. But the newspaper industry is large by every measure. In an article marveling at an issue of a newspaper as "the daily creation," the *Washington Post* said: "Roughly 11,000 people are involved in the production and distribution each day, enough bodies to fill all the billets of an Army light infantry division." Although the *Post* stretched to include even the delivery boys and girls in its startling number, the point is valid: In Washington and everywhere else, including Canada, newspapers far outdistance other news media in the number of people who gather, edit and disseminate news.

Except for brief downturns in the overall economy and an occasional exceptional situation, daily newspapers have been generally profitable enterprises through the 20th century. As a mass medium, the newspaper is not to be underrated.

CONTENT DIVERSITY AND DEPTH

In most communities, newspapers cover more news at greater depth than competing media. A metropolitan daily like the *Hamilton Spectator* typically may carry hundreds of items—more than any television or radio station and at greater length. Magazines, for example, offer more depth on selected stories, but the magazines are published relatively infrequently and run relatively few articles.

Newspapers have a rich mix of content—news, advice, comics, opinion, puzzles and data. It's all there to tap into at will. Some people go right for the stock market tables, others to sports or a favourite columnist. Unlike radio and television, you don't have to wait for what you want.

People like newspapers. Some talk affectionately of cuddling up in bed on a leisurely Sunday morning with their paper. The news and features give people something in common to talk about. Newspapers are important in people's lives, and as a medium they adapt to changing lifestyles. Ads in Sunday papers are often their guide for shopping excursions.

All this does not mean that the newspaper industry is not facing problems from competing media, new technology and ongoing lifestyle shifts. But to date, newspapers have reacted to change with surprising effectiveness. To offset television's inroads, newspapers put new emphasis on being a visual medium and shed their

MEDIA AND YOU

News Habits

Confirming what was widely suspected, a 1990 study found that young people by and large don't read newspapers. According to the study, only 30 percent of people under 35 read a newspaper the day before. Twenty-five years earlier, the Gallup polling people found the rate was 67 percent.

Newspaper executives have cause to worry. Unless they entice young readers, their medium will decline as older people, the bulk of their audience, die. But the problem may be even more serious. The study found that it isn't just newspapers that young people are avoiding but news itself. Of respondents between ages 18 and 29, 40 percent are less likely than their elders to be able to identify significant figures in the news, and 20 percent said they were less likely to follow even major events.

The study overturned the notion that young people prefer television to newspapers for news. Only four of every 10 respondents under age 35 had watched television news the day before. Twenty-five years earlier it was five of 10. Except for sports and issues that affect them directly, like abortion, young people are less and less interested in news.

Conduct your own informal survey to test whether the younger generation in your community also has less interest in newspapers and in news. Ask these questions to a dozen people under 35 and another dozen people over 35:

- Did you read a newspaper yesterday?
- Did you watch a television newscast yesterday?
- Did you follow the NAFTA debate closely?
- Are you following the latest constitutional debate?

If you were a newspaper editor or a television news executive, what would you do to attract more people to your product?

drab graphics for colour and aesthetics. To accommodate the work schedule transition over recent years from factory jobs starting at 7 a.m. to service jobs starting at 9 a.m., newspapers have emphasized morning editions and phased out afternoon editions. Knowing that the days of ink-on-paper technology are limited, the newspaper industry is examining electronic delivery methods for the 21st century.

Some problems are truly daunting, like the aversion of many young people to newspapers. Also, chain ownership has raised fundamental questions about how well newspapers can do their work and still meet the profit expectations of distant shareholders.

THE HISTORY OF THE PRESS IN CANADA

STUDY PREVIEW Canadian communication scholar Wilfred Kesterton has pointed out that the growth of the Canadian newspaper industry follows trends that are integral to any capitalist venture. First, technology must be available to produce the commodity so that it can be sold. The second factor is social; there have to be enough people in order to market the newspaper. While Gutenberg provided the printing technology in the mid-1400s, it wasn't until 300 years later that Canada had its first newspaper.

THE EARLY DAYS OF CANADIAN NEWSPAPERS

Because of its important role in transportation and communication in Canada's early days, the East Coast became the centre for immigration. *Bartholomew Green* set up the first printing press in Canada in 1751 in Halifax. One year later, Green published Canada's first newspaper, the *Halifax Gazette*. By today's standards, it wasn't what we would consider a newspaper. Other than a few advertisments for area merchants, there wasn't much local content; most of the articles focused on government or international news. The *Gazette* appeared every two weeks and had about 70 subscribers. This small subscriber base was typical of early newspapers. Even Charlottetown's *Royal American Gazette* started with only 50 subscribers in 1787, while the *Quebec Gazette* had about 150 subscribers when it first began publishing in 1764. As conditions improved and immigrants began moving down the St. Lawrence and into Upper Canada, the *Upper Canada Gazette* began publishing in Niagara-on-the-Lake in 1793.

Following the War of 1812, immigration in Canada flourished, particularly in Upper Canada, where the population doubled by the mid-1820s. Combine this population surge with the effects of the Industrial Revolution and you will begin to understand the changing social climate in Canada. People stopped working at home or in the fields and began to work in factories. These factors contributed to the growth of newspapers. At the end of the War of 1812, Canada had only a handful of newspapers; by the mid-1820s, that number had risen to almost 300.

During the latter half of the 1800s immigration and migration became two important factors in the growth of Canadian newspapers. As the Canadian population moved west and north, newspapers followed. The Gold Rush made Victoria, British Columbia, a centre for commerce and transportation. In 1858, the Victoria *Gazette* and *Anglo American* began publishing. Other early newspapers in western Canada included the *Nor'Wester* in 1859, the Saskatchewan *Herald* in 1878, the *Edmonton Bulletin* in 1880 and the *Yukon Sun* and *Klondike Nuggett*, both in 1898. New papers also began publishing in central and eastern Canada: The *Montreal Star* in 1869, the Toronto *Telegram* in 1876, and the *Ottawa Journal* in 1885. By the turn of the century, over 1200 newspapers were serving Canada's population, which at that time stood at close to 5.5 million people.

CANADIAN NEWSPAPERS IN THE 20TH CENTURY

In the 1900s, the newspaper came of age in Canada. Although immigration levels and migration patterns were inconsistent due to the world wars and the Depression during the first half of the century, improvements in technology helped the newspaper grow to new heights. This technology included better printing presses, and better quality newsprint, which helped improve the form of the newspaper, while the introduction of the news wire helped broaden the content of the daily. Improvements in communication and transportation improved distribution. Due to these changes and the continuing growth of cities, the large metropolitan daily as a business enterprise became the norm for many newspapers. The number of dailies in Canada was about 120; by 1951, there were only 94. However, while the number of dailies decreased, circulation increased. The average circulation for a daily in Canada by 1951 was around 40 000; an 800 percent increase since the turn of the century.

Since the 1950s several factors have contributed to the current state of Canadian newspapers. Television arrived in 1952. People began turning to television, not only as an entertainment medium but as their source for news. Remember what

Marshall McLuhan had to say about the differences between media? Television was a cool medium while newspapers were hot. Watching television simply takes less energy and is less taxing than reading a newspaper. Fewer readers meant that advertising revenue began to drop, making it more difficult for newspapers to turn a profit. These factors, combined with higher production costs, made newspaper publishing less lucrative than it had been in the past. Some newspapers folded; others began to buy out troubled competitors. As a result, fewer newspapers were owned by fewer people.

NEWSPAPER CHAIN OWNERSHIP

STUDY PREVIEW   Through the 20th century, newspapers have been incredibly profitable, which, for better or worse, encouraged chain ownership. Today, chains own most newspapers.

TREND TOWARD CHAINS

Reasoning that he could multiply profits by owning multiple newspapers, *William Randolph Hearst* put together a chain of big-city newspapers in the late 1880s. Although Hearst's chain was not the first, his empire became the model in the public's mind for much that was both good and bad about newspaper chains. Like other chains, Hearst also expanded into magazines, radio and television. The trend toward chain ownership continues, and today chains own the majority of dailies in the United States and Canada. Chain ownership is also coming to dominate weeklies, which had long been a bastion of independent ownership.

Newspaper profitability skyrocketed in the 1970s and 1980s, which prompted chains to buy up locally owned newspapers. Single-newspaper cities were especially attractive because no competing media could match a local newspaper's large audience. It was possible for new owners to push ad rates up rapidly, and local retailers had to go along. The profit potential was enhanced because production costs were falling dramatically with less labour-intensive back-shop procedures, computerized typesetting and other automation. Profits were dramatic. Only soft drink companies did better.

The Gannett media conglomerate's growth typifies how newspapers became chains and then grew into cross-media conglomerates. In 1906 the chain was six upstate New York newspapers. By 1982 Gannett had grown to almost 90 dailies, all profitable medium-size newspapers. Swimming in money, Gannett launched *USA Today*. Gannett not only absorbed *USA Today's* tremendous start-up costs for several years but also had enough spare cash to outbid other companies for expensive metropolitan newspapers. In 1985 and 1986 Gannett paid $1.4 billion for the *Detroit News, Des Moines Register* and *Louisville Courier-Journal*. Along the way, Gannett acquired Combined Communications, which owned 20 broadcasting stations. Today Gannett owns 82 daily newspapers, 39 weeklies, 16 radio and 8 television stations, the largest billboard company in the U.S., and the Louis Harris polling organization. It renamed and beefed up a national Sunday newspaper magazine supplement. No longer just a newspaper chain, Gannett has become a mass media conglomerate.

ASSESSING CHAIN OWNERSHIP

Is chain ownership good for newspapers? The question raised in Hearst's time was whether diverse points of view were as likely to get into print if ownership were concentrated in fewer and fewer hands. That concern has dissipated as chains have become oriented more to profits than to participating in public dialogue. Executives at the headquarters of most chains focus on management and leave editorials to local editors. While local autonomy is consistent with journalistic values, a corporate focus on profits raises a dark new question: Are chains so concerned about profits that they forget good journalism? These are the types of questions that were the basis of two Royal Commissions in Canada.

GOVERNMENT COMMISSIONS INTO THE CANADIAN NEWSPAPER INDUSTRY

In 1970 a special Senate Committee on the status of the mass media in Canada, headed by Senator Keith Davey, released its report about the state of Canadian newspapers. Part of the rationale for this committee was the growing concern regarding concentration of newspaper ownership in Canada. In its report, the committee noted that "the media is passing into fewer and fewer hands, and that the experts agree that this trend is likely to continue." In terms of newspaper ownership, at the time of its publication, the Davey Commission noted that genuine competition existed in only five Canadian cities; that at the turn of the century, 35 Canadian cities and towns were multi-newspaper towns (meaning they had two or more newspapers), but by 1970, there were only 15. In five of those 15 cities, both papers were published by the same owner. In 1930 116 daily newspapers were owned by 99 publishers, but by 1970 three newspaper chains: Southam, Thomson and F.P. had a controlling interest in three-quarters of newspaper circulation in Canada.

The Davey Report made many recommendations. Among them was the creation of a press ownership review board. The role of the board would be to monitor ownership changes and proposed mergers between newspapers in order to control the trend toward concentration of ownership. The board would have the power to veto any sale of a newspaper if it meant an increase in concentration of ownership. The governement's response to the recommendations was lukewarm at best and such a board was never created.

A little more than 10 years later the situation had not improved. Ownership of Canada's newspapers, particularly in Quebec, had fallen into fewer and fewer hands. The 1981 Kent Commission into newspaper ownership in Canada, headed by Tom Kent, came about following an incident that was too convenient to be coincidental. On the same day in August of 1980, the *Ottawa Journal*, which had been publishing for 94 years and was owned by Thomson, and the 90-year-old *Winnipeg Tribune*, owned by Southam, closed their doors and ceased publication, leaving Winnipeg and Ottawa as one-newspaper towns. Each city still had a daily newspaper—the *Winnipeg Free Press*, owned by Thomson and the *Ottawa Citizen*, owned by Southam. Within a week, the Kent Commission was born. Its mandate was to look into the state of newspapers in Canada and to propose a course of action for the government. Its mandate was considerably broader than its predecessor's. A multivolume report, the Kent Commission made recommendations not only on concentration of ownership but on editorial expression and the quality of journalism in Canada. The goal of the commission was to establish legislation governing the newspaper industry in Canada. Among those recommendations it was stated that

- no owner could control more than 5 percent of Canada's total newspaper circulation
- no owner could own more than five newspapers
- no owner could own more than one newspaper within a radius of 500 kilometres
- newspaper editors would have to report each year to a governement body (a press rights panel) about the editorial content of the newspaper. Such a report would be mandatory if the newspaper was owned by a chain; it would be voluntary if the paper was an independent. In this way, an editor would be accountable to the government and not to the owner of the newspaper for the content of the paper in the hopes that editorial selection would lie with the editor, not with a board of directors in a city far away.
- to sustain and improve the quality of newspaper journalism in Canada, newspapers would be taxed if it was found the quality of content had suffered, while excellence would be rewarded through subsidies and tax incentives. Part of the tax would go to help develop and expand the Canadian Press wire service.
- to stop the trend towards chains, several papers, including Thomson, would be ordered to "divest" themselves of some of their newspaper holdings.

As was the case with the Davey Commission, the Kent Commission's suggestions died before becoming law. In 1984 while the Newspaper Act was being debated in Parliament, an election was held. When Parliament reconvened, the bill died.

CURRENT STATE OF THE NEWSPAPER INDUSTRY IN CANADA

The landscape has changed dramatically since the Kent Commission in 1981. It has changed in terms of who the players are but not in terms of the fears of either Kent or Davey.

In 1981 Thomson owned twice as many newspapers as Southam. Although it stills owns the *Globe and Mail,* Thomson has sold off many of its newspapers, focusing its resources on electronic information services. Southam is now the largest newspaper player in Canada, with an average daily circulation of 1.4 million newspapers, or 27 percent of total daily newspaper circulation in Canada. Some of the papers owned by Southam include the Montreal *Gazette,* the *Ottawa Citizen,* the *Calgary Herald,* both Vancouver dailies: the *Sun* and the *Province,* the *Edmonton Journal* and the *Hamilton Spectator,* which the company has owned since 1877. In total the Southam Empire includes 17 dailies and 33 weeklies in Ontario, British Columbia and Alberta. Southam owns five of the top 10 dailies in Canada. In addition to newspapers, they also publish business magazines, product information and, like Thomson, are involved in electronic databases and information. They provide content for America On-Line (AOL) Canada.

Conrad Black's Hollinger, an international publisher whose Canadian holdings include many small-town dailies and weeklies, is Canada's second-largest publisher. While it owns such international papers as the *Chicago Sun-Times* and the *Jerusalem Post,* it has recently set its sites on Southam. In 1996 Hollinger acquired 41 percent of Southam. This situation has communication scholars worried. This gives one corporation control over the majority of daily newspapers in Canada. It would

MEDIA DATABANK

Top 10 Canadian Newspapers

Here are the top 10 Canadian newspapers ranked by average circulation, Monday-Friday:

Toronto Star	491 000	Torstar	*Edmonton Journal*	162 500	Southam
Globe and Mail	315 100	Thomson	Vancouver *Province*	153 750	Southam
Le Journal de Montréal	270 600	Québecor	Montreal *Gazette*	148 800	Southam
Toronto Sun	240 800	Toronto Sun Publishing	*Ottawa Citizen*	146 000	Southam
Vancouver *Sun*	214 750	Southam			
Montréal *La Presse*	179 600	Probec			

Source: Canadian Advertising Rates and Data (CARD), June 1996

appear that the fears of the Davey and Kent commissions were well-founded: If Hollinger continues to buy Southam shares, one publisher may well control the majority of newspapers in Canada. Peter Desbarats, who was a senior consultant to the 1981 Kent Commission, is concerned about the future of newspaper publishing and journalism in Canada:

The Globe and Mail, Tuesday, May 28, 1996

Conrad Black and the Newspaper Universe

by Peter Desbarats

MEDIA / In the light of the 1981 report of the Royal Commission on Newspapers, Mr. Black's new control of Southam should be considered a national disaster; but this isn't 1981, or even 1984. The picture is much more complex than it was 15 years ago.

When the Royal Commission on Newspapers reported on concentration of ownership in 1981, two groups dominated the English-language newspaper scene in Canada: Thomson and Southam. Thomson owned more than twice as many dailies, but Southam's 14 newspapers generated 8.6 million aggregate weekly circulation, about 20 per cent more than Thomson's total.

On the staff of the commission, we sometimes talked about the nightmare scenario: One of the giant chains would take over the other, leaving the vast majority of English-language newspaper readers at the mercy of a single proprietor. At the time, Thomson was usually envisaged as the aggressor.

Conrad Black, 15 years ago, was a mere dot in the media firmament. His Sterling group owned 11 dailies, but most were in British Columbia and together they had a weekly circulation of only 292,000, little more than 8 per cent of the weekly circulation of the Toronto Star.

Since then Mr. Black has become a media supernova, overtaking and absorbing newspapers at an explosive rate. (His Hollinger Inc. last week raised its stake in Southam to 41 per cent of the shares from 20.5, and says it plans to buy more.) The nightmare scenario of 1981 is unfolding, except that the players are different and the concentration is even more massive. Apart from the Toronto Sun group of newspapers, the dwindling remains of Thomson's Canadian newspaper empire, a few regional clusters and an insignificant number of independents, Conrad Black owns the nation's daily newspapers. He has made history by becoming the first publisher to establish a significant presence in both English and French Canada.

A measure of his power is the influence he now wields over the future of The Canadian Press, the co-operative news exchange organized by newspapers in the early years of the century and seen ever since as one of the hidden pillars of national unity.

In the light of the 1981 royal commission report, Mr. Black's new control of Southam should be seen as a national disaster with ominous consequences for freedom of the press, political discourse and the very cohesiveness of the country. But this isn't 1981, or even 1984, and many things have changed in the intervening years.

In 1981 the newspaper industry was already looking back on the glory days when it had been the second most profitable in the country, next to brewing. Since then, circulations have stagnated or declined, costs have increased and profits have deteriorated, though there remain a few money-making anomalies at either end of the scale, such as The Globe and Mail and some of the popular tabloids.

Nothing illustrates this decline more dramatically than the Thomson group's decision to shift its emphasis from newspapers to electronic data bases, and nothing illustrates the difficulty of forecasting media futures more effectively than the contrasting investment strategy of Hollinger. Thomson's strategy is obviously aimed at the longer term, while Mr. Black has decided that a great deal of money can be made from newspapers in the immediate future, particularly if costs are controlled.

These differing philosophies would simply be grist for the financial pages if it weren't for the nagging question of public interest. Newspapers are not a business like any other; they create and disseminate ideas, propagate trends, shape political attitudes and help to make or break political careers.

No one understands this better than Conrad Black, one of the few modern newspaper proprietors who enjoy dealing in ideas as well as newspaper shares. He has always been a writer as well as an entrepreneur, and he approaches the newspaper business with zest.

Unfortunately, not many newspaper journalists still do. Typical was an editor from a Vancouver daily who called me in Ottawa several weeks ago. We had never met, and at first I was puzzled. Was this an interview? Was he looking for advice? It turned out he just wanted to have a good cry about the downsizing and demoralization of his newsroom and the generally dismal state of the industry.

Newspaper journalists have been badly shaken by years of staff reductions, cutbacks in editorial budgets and predictions that important dailies may start to close over the next decade. Now television and radio journalists working for the CBC are going through the same process.

Understanding that change is inevitable doesn't make it any easier for many of these journalists. If you were starting a daily newspaper from scratch in 1996, it wouldn't make sense to construct it on the old model. A nucleus of senior editors and designers would be the only permanent staff required. Almost everything else could be done on freelance contract, often at the end of a modem. Conrad Black may be working his way toward this type of structure. In the same way, a television news operation could be staffed almost entirely by freelancers, guided by a small editorial core.

For older journalists like me, this is a difficult media world to imagine. Newspapers have always been part of our lives. Intellectually, we realize that daily newspapers were themselves the result of the development of certain technologies, just as the Internet is today, and that they can be made obsolete by technology. Emotionally, many of us can't really accept this.

We want to know what will replace the newspaper as the mirror and mentor of its community. We have trouble imagining electronic journalism without a strong public broadcasting presence. We are worried about the amount of power now in the hands of Conrad Black, but our concern about the public interest is confused by our obvious concerns for our own jobs, and those of our friends and colleagues.

The picture is much more complex than it was 15 years ago, and the answers are more elusive. In the trade-off between freedom and accountability, Canada and most other developed nations have opted traditionally for freedom of the press barons as an acceptable substitute for some purer form of editorial independence. So far it has worked reasonably well, and certainly better than state-controlled media in most countries.

Whether it will continue to provide an acceptable pattern for the development of computer-based journalism, and whether this will be even recognizable to us as "journalism" in future, is an intriguing and important question that is only beginning to emerge.

Why all the concern about concentration of ownership in Canada? After all, in a capitalist society, one should be able to venture into any enterprise he/she wants to. One might also argue that since Montreal and Toronto each have several daily newspapers there is competition for readers. Both the Davey and Kent Commissions leave us with these points to think about when discussing the effects of concentration of ownership:

News is a product, it needs a variety of voices to be produced. Without this variety, newspapers "become more alike, less individual, less distinctive." In short, concentration of ownership limits choice on the part of the reader.

As newspapers become part of a large corporation, the people who run them won't likely have a background in journalism, but a background in business or management. Given this scenario, profits become more important than editorial content and the whole news gathering and writing process.

Too much power in too few hands contradicts the role of the press in a democracy. Concentration of press ownership in Canada may mean power without accountability.

While it's true that newspapers have competition from radio and television, it's newspapers that have traditionally been used to record history. Radio and television newscasts are not archived in the same manner as newspapers. This has serious implications for future historical research.

NATIONAL DAILIES

STUDY PREVIEW Although most newspapers in Canada and the U.S. are local papers, several dailies have national circulation. In the U.S. the *Wall Street Journal* and *USA Today* are distributed nationally. In Canada the *Globe and Mail* calls itself "Canada's National Newspaper."

THE *GLOBE AND MAIL*

The *Globe* was founded in 1844 in Toronto by Scottish immigrant *George Brown*. His love of publishing was evident in the paper's first edition, published on March

5, 1844. In the opening column on the front page was a poem entitled "The Newspaper." An excerpt from it follows:

> In gown and slippers loosely dressed,
> and breakfast brought—a welcome guest—
> What is it gives the meal a zest?
>
> The paper.
>
> Abroad, at home infirm or stout,
> In health, or raving from the gout,
> Who possibly can do without
>
> The paper?

(Source: *The Globe and Mail: 150 Years in Canada*)

Although labeled as politically conservative, Brown was also somewhat of a publishing innovator. He expanded the format of the paper and the *Globe* began publishing daily in 1853. He also published a weekly edition for readers living outside of Toronto. He was rewarded for his efforts; by 1872, circulation had almost tripled to 45 000. By the turn of the century, it had increased to 80 000. The *Globe* merged with the *Mail and Empire* in November of 1936.

True to George Brown's innovations, the *Globe* was the first Canadian newspaper to offer electronic services. In 1980 it created *InfoGlobe*, an electronic information and research tool. An online version of the paper became available in 1984. Due to the competition in the Canadian newspaper industry in the mid-1980's, it became clear that the paper needed to look beyond its traditional southern Ontario market. Thanks to satellite distribution, it was possible for readers in Vancouver and Halifax to get the *Globe* in the morning. The *Globe* had previously been distributed using airplanes. *Globe* readers in Edmonton, Whitehorse and Montreal had been able to get the paper delivered the same day, but it didn't hit the newsstands until the afternoon. In the mid-1980s the *Globe* also began to publish *Report on Business Magazine* and other glossy magazines on a regular basis in the hope of broadening national circulation and increasing advertising revenue.

The *Wall Street Journal*

The *Wall Street Journal*, America's largest newspaper, began humbly. *Charles Dow* and *Edward Jones* went into business in 1882, roaming the New York financial district for news and then scribbling notes by hand, which they sent by courier to their clients. As more information-hungry investors signed up, the service was expanded into a newsletter, and in 1889 the *Wall Street Journal* was founded.

The *Wall Street Journal* might have remained a relatively small albeit successful business paper had it not been for the legendary *Barney Kilgore*, who joined the newspaper's San Francisco bureau in 1929. Within two years, Kilgore was the *Journal*'s news editor and in a position to shift the newspaper's journalistic direction. Kilgore's formula was threefold:

- Simplify the *Journal*'s business coverage into plain English without sacrificing thoroughness.
- Provide detailed coverage of government but without the jargon that plagued much of Washington reporting.

Barney Kilgore

- Expand the definition of the *Journal*'s field of coverage from "business" to "everything that somehow relates to earning a living."

USA TODAY

A strict format, snappy visuals and crisp writing give *USA Today* an air of confidence and the trappings of success, and the newspaper has its strengths. In less than a decade, circulation has reached 1.6 million, behind only the *Wall Street Journal*, and Gannett executives exude sureness about long-term prospects. The optimism is underscored by the confident if not brash Page 1 motto: "The Nation's Newspaper."

The fact, however, is that except for an occasional profitable month, *USA Today* lost money over its first 11 years of publication, and Gannett has come nowhere near recouping the startup costs, reported as high as $40 million. In 1993, analysts thought the newspaper might have its first profitable year, even though the company declined to break out financial details of *USA Today* operations for either the public or its shareholders.

Whatever the financial situation at *USA Today*, the newspaper has had a significant impact. Like the *Wall Street Journal*, *USA Today* seeks well-heeled readers, although in different ways. *USA Today* has relatively few subscribers, going instead after single-copy sales mostly to business people who are on the run and want a quick fix on what the news is. Many of *USA Today's* sales are at airport newsracks, by which corporate executives and middle-management travelers pass. Gannett offers deep discounts to upscale hotels to buy the papers in bulk and slip free under guests' doors as a morning courtesy. Stories strain to be lively and upbeat to make the experience of reading the paper a positive one. In contrast to the *Wall Street Journal*, almost all *USA Today* stories are short, which diverts little of a reader's time from pressing business. The brevity and crispness of *USA Today*, combined with the enticing graphics, has led some critics to liken the newspaper to fast food and dub it "McNewspaper"—not bad for you but not as nourishing as, say, the *Wall Street Journal*.

USA Today Graphics. When the *Challenger* exploded after takeoff, *USA Today* demonstrated how graphics can tell some stories better than words alone. Most of Page 1 was turned over to a team of artists and reporters who explained through pictures and very few words what had happened. One of the influences of *USA Today* has been to revive interest in newspapers as a visual medium.

Innovations include:

HIGH STORY COUNTS.   Most stories run no more than 10 sentences, which creates room for many more stories per issue than in other newspapers. Even lengthier pieces, limited to only four per issue, are capped at 35 sentences. Among journalists, this is known as a "high story count."

SPLASHY DESIGN.   *USA Today* emphasizes colour photographs and illustrations, moving away from words alone to tell the news and explain issues.

GRAPHS, TABLES, CHARTS.   The newspaper offers data graphically, not just accompanying stories but standing alone in separate displays.

The introduction of *USA Today* came at a time when most newspapers were trying to distinguish themselves from television news with longer, exploratory and interpretive stories. While some major newspapers like the *New York Times* and the *Los Angeles Times* were unswayed by *USA Today*'s snappy, quick-to-read format, many other newspapers moved to shorter, easily digested stories, infographics and more data lists. Colour became standard. *USA Today* has influenced today's newspaper style and format.

HOMETOWN NEWSPAPERS

STUDY PREVIEW   Big-city dailies are the most visible hometown newspapers, but medium-size and small dailies have made significant strides in quality in recent decades and eroded the metros' outlying circulation.

METROPOLITAN DAILIES

In every region of the United States and Canada, there is a newspaper whose name is a household word. These are metropolitan dailies with extensive regional circulation. In New England, for example, the Boston *Globe* covers Boston but also prides itself on extensive coverage of Massachusetts state government, as well as coverage of neighbouring states.

Here are snapshots of two leading metro dailies:

THE *TORONTO STAR*.   The *Toronto Star* is not only a metropolitan daily, it also has the largest daily circulation of any newspaper in Canada: almost half a million copies. The *Star* was founded in 1892 as the Toronto Star and Publishing Company. Its founding fathers were 21 printers who were on strike (or were locked out, depending on who you listen to). They had worked for the *Toronto News* until a new typesetting process threatened their jobs. Within days of losing their jobs, they borrowed old printing presses and, with each printer assuming the roles of writer, reporter, ad salesperson and proofreader, the first *Evening Star* was printed on November 3, 1892. The masthead proclaimed "A paper for the people." It's this incident that gave rise to the *Star* being identified as a "liberal" paper for many years.

Today the *Star* employs more than 4500 people, including almost 400 people

Hometown Coverage. The *Toronto Star* has the highest circulation of any Canadian daily. It began publishing in 1892.

MEDIA DATABANK

Daily U.S. Newspaper Circulation

	Daily	Sunday		Daily	Sunday
Wall Street Journal	1.8 million		New York *Daily News*	764 000	927 000
USA Today	1.5 million		Long Island *Newsday*	747 000	825 000
New York Times	1.1 million	1.8 million	*Chicago Tribune*	690 000	1.1 million
Los Angeles Times	1.0 million	1.5 million	Detroit *Free Press*	556 000	1.2 million
Washington Post	814 000	1.2 million	San Francisco *Chronicle*	544 000	705 000

in its newsroom. The *Star*'s press centre produces almost 4 million newspapers each week. Unlike the *Los Angeles Times*, it is the Saturday edition of the *Toronto Star* that is likely to make quite a thump on the front step. The *Saturday Star* has a circulation of almost three quarters of a million.

The *Star* is owned by Torstar Corporation, which publishes community newspapers, distributes mail-order catalogues and also publishes the successful Harlequin romance series.

LOS ANGELES TIMES.   The *Los Angeles Times* edged out the declining New York *Daily News* in 1990 as the nation's largest metropolitan daily when circulation reached 1.3 million. By many measures, the *Times* is huge. A typical Sunday edition makes quite a thump on the doorstep at two kilograms and 444 pages.

The *Times* has 1300 editors and reporters, some in 27 foreign bureaus and 13 U.S. bureaus. Fifty-seven reporters cover the federal government in Washington alone. To cover the 1991 war against Iraq, the *Times* dispatched 20 reporters and photographers to the Gulf region, compared to 12 for the *New York Times* and 10 for the *Washington Post*, the traditional leading U.S. metro dailies for foreign coverage. Critics say the *Los Angeles Times* is sometimes disappointing in local coverage, but it is applauded for the coverage to which it channels resources.

HOMETOWN DAILIES

With their aggressive reporting on national and regional issues, the metro dailies receive more attention than smaller dailies, but most people read hometown dailies. By and large, these locally oriented newspapers, most of them chain-owned, have been incredibly profitable while making significant journalistic progress since World War II.

Fifty years ago, people in small towns generally bought both a metropolitan daily and a local newspaper. Hometown dailies were thin and coverage was hardly comprehensive. Editorial pages tended to offer only a single perspective. Readers had few alternative sources of information. Since then, these smaller dailies have hired better-prepared journalists, acquired new technology and strengthened their local advertising base.

Hometown dailies have grown larger and more comprehensive. The years between 1970 and 1980 were especially important for quantum increases in news coverage. The space available for news, called the *news hole*, increased. Many hometown dailies also gave much of their large news holes to bigger and more diverse opinion sections. Most editorial sections today are smorgasbords of perspectives.

Australia's Transcontinental Newspaper

Canada has Conrad Black, Australia has Rupert Murdoch. When his father died in 1955, Murdoch, who was 21 years old, inherited a second-rate newspaper in Adelaide, Australia. Through mergers and acquisitions, young Murdoch parlayed his inheritance into a company that included papers in five of Australia's six state capital cities. Ever growth-minded, Murdoch set his sights on a new kind of newspaper in 1964: a national daily to be circulated coast to coast. It would be a radical departure. At the time, Australia was a nation with provincial newspapers that had only local circulation. The expanse of the nation, almost 3000 miles coast to coast, had precluded the kinds of national papers that existed in relatively small countries.

Murdoch established the *Australian* in Canberra, the national capital, where editors could be on top of federal news that would be of nationwide interest. For the newspaper's second staple, foreign news, he arranged for news agencies and set up a modest foreign staff. Murdoch hoped that local circulation and advertising income in Canberra would keep the paper going until it attracted a national readership and advertising.

To deliver the paper nationally, whole pages were photographed and converted into lightweight printing plates. These plates were flown overnight to the major cities of Sydney and Melbourne, each 200 miles away,

Rupert Murdoch

where Murdoch-owned presses printed copies for local distribution the next morning. Meanwhile, editions were printed in Canberra for air delivery to cities coast to coast.

It was an exciting time in Murdoch's life, not just because of the unprecedented scope and risk of the endeavour but because of Canberra's notorious fog. Stories abound about Murdoch on the fog-shrouded tarmac at Canberra in his pajamas, egging pilots on by telling them that it really wasn't fog, just a light mist.

Today, the paper is printed in Sydney, Melbourne and Brisbane, the nation's largest cities, none of which have Canberra's fog problem. Besides local distribution, copies are dispatched throughout the continent by airplane.

Although the *Australian* became the crown jewel of Rupert Murdoch's Australian newspaper media empire, it did not keep his attention. Next he expanded into Australian television, and then British newspapers, and today his interests include the Fox Television network, *TV Guide* and HarperCollins books in the United States. At various times, Murdoch has owned the *Boston Herald, Chicago Sun-Times, New York Post,* and the *San Antonio News* and *Express.* His attempt at a national newspaper in the United States was the racy scandal sheet *Star.*

CHALLENGES FOR DAILY NEWSPAPERS

STUDY PREVIEW   Daily newspaper circulation is stagnant, and other media are eroding the dominance of the newspaper as an advertising medium. Even so, the newspaper industry is financially strong, and newspapers have inherent advantages over competing media.

CIRCULATION PATTERNS

The circulation decline has been heaviest among evening newspapers. Television is largely responsible. The decline in evening newspapers, called *PMs,* has been especially severe in blue-collar towns, where most families once built their lifestyle around 7 a.m. to 3 p.m. factory shifts. Today, as we shift from an industrial to a service economy, more people work 9-to-5 jobs and have less discretionary time in the afternoon and evening to read a newspaper. Predictably, advertisers have followed readers from evenings to mornings, and one by one afternoon newspapers in two-newspaper cities folded. In many places, afternoon newspapers have followed their readers' life-style changes and converted to the morning publication cycle.

ADVERTISING PATTERNS

Even morning papers are having advertising problems. The heady days when newspapers could count on more advertising every year seem over. Projections for the rest of the 1990s indicate that newspaper advertising will be lucky to hold its own. Television's growth is a factor, but other media, including ads distributed by mail, are eating into the historic dominance of the newspaper as an advertising medium.

Besides television, daily newspaper advertising revenue has taken a hit from the consolidation of retailing into fewer albeit bigger companies. Grocery, discount and department store mergers cut down on advertising revenue. Fewer competing retail chains meant fewer ads. This was a major loss because the grocery, discount and department stores were newspapers' largest source of income.

A growing advertising practice, bypassing the traditional mass media and sending circulars and catalogues directly to potential customers, also is cutting into newspaper advertising income. This *direct mail* trend took off in the 1970s and accelerated into the 1990s. To win back advertisers who switched to direct mail, newspapers are willing to tuck preprinted advertising circulars, mostly from large retailers, inside the regular paper. In one sense, *preprints*, as they are called, represent lost revenue because in the days before direct mail those ads would have been placed in the regular pages of the newspaper at full ad rates. Newspaper preprint rates are discounted deeply to compete with postal rates.

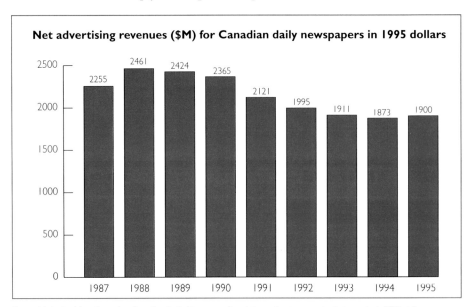

Net advertising revenues ($M) for Canadian daily newspapers in 1995 dollars

Source: Marketing Magazine, using Canadian Daily Newspaper Association estimates converted into constant 1995 dollars.

PROSPECTS FOR THE DAILY PRESS

While daily newspapers, both metros and smaller dailies, face problems, hardly are they on the verge of extinction. While competing media have taken away some newspaper retail advertising, the want ads, formally called *classified advertising*, may not be glamorous to anybody except newspaper owners. At some newspapers, classifieds generate more than half of the revenue. Television and radio have not found a way to offer a competing service, and not even free-distribution papers devoted to classified advertising have reversed the growth in daily newspaper classified revenue.

Also, the newspaper remains the dominant advertising medium for most major local advertisers: grocery stores, department stores, automobile dealerships and discount stores.

On the downside, daily newspapers have suffered major losses over the years in national advertising, mostly to magazines and network television. Despite the losses, newspapers have not given up on national advertising. Every newspaper has a broker, called a *national representative*, whose business is to line up national advertising for its client newspapers.

Daily newspapers have inherent advantages that competing media cannot match, at least not now.

PORTABILITY.   Newspapers are a portable medium. People can pick up a newspaper any time and take it with them, which is hardly possible with newspaper's biggest rival for advertisers, television. In the long term, as television sets are installed in more places and with the arrival of miniaturized, battery-operated television receivers, this newspaper advantage may erode.

VARIETY.   A newspaper has more room to cover a greater variety of events and provide a greater variety of features than competing media units. The entire script for a 30-minute television newscast can fit on a fraction of a single newspaper page. This advantage may dissipate as people have greater access to new specialized television services and zip and zap among them: the Weather Channel on cable, TSN, information channels, ticker-tape streamers on cable. Also, 900-number telephone services offer scores, game details and sports news on demand, although they are more expensive than buying a newspaper.

INDEXED CONTENT.   Newspapers remain quick sources of information, ideas and entertainment. Readers can quickly find items that interest them by using headlines as an indexing device. With television, people have to wait for the items they want.

DEPTH COVERAGE.   Newspapers have room for lengthy, in-depth treatments, which most contemporary broadcast formats preclude. Rare are radio newscasts with stories longer than 120 words, and most television focuses only on highlights.

These traditional advantages that accrue to the newspaper as a medium are being eroded, but the newspaper remains the only package that has them all. In general, newspaper companies are in a good position to survive because of an asset that competing media lack: the largest, most skilled newsroom staffs in their communities. Television stations have relatively minuscule news-gathering staffs, and they lack the tradition and experience to match the ongoing, thorough coverage of newspapers. The strength of newspaper companies is their news-gathering capability, not their means of delivery. Since the 1970s newspapers have experimented with facsimile and television text delivery, gaining familiarity with alternate technology for disseminating their main product, which is news, not newsprint.

WEEKLY NEWSPAPERS

STUDY PREVIEW Many community weekly newspapers, especially in fast-growing suburbs, are thriving, while others, especially rural weeklies, have fallen on hard times. In all areas, free-distribution advertising sheets called *shoppers* have attracted strong followings.

COMMUNITY WEEKLIES

Weekly newspapers are making strong circulation gains, especially in suburban communities, and some have moved into publishing twice a week. To the detriment of metro dailies, many advertisers are following their customers to the suburban weeklies. Advertisers have found that they can buy space in weeklies for less and reach their likeliest customers. Ralph Ingersoll, whose weeklies give fits to the daily Long Island *Newsday* in New York, explained it this way in an interview with *Forbes*: "If you're an automobile dealer on Long Island, you can pay, say, $14,000 for a tabloid page in *Newsday*, most of which is wasted because the people that get it will never buy a car in your neck of the woods, or you can go into one of the weekender publications and pay a few hundred dollars and reach just the people likely to drive over to your shop."

Some weeklies, particularly those in upscale suburbs, offer sophisticated coverage of community issues. Others feature a homey mix of reports on social events such as who visited whom for Sunday dinner. The success of these weeklies some-

Community News. Suburban weeklies are thriving: readers like the detailed local coverage and advertisers like the target market and the relatively low cost of ads.

times is called "telephone book journalism" because of the emphasis on names, the somewhat overdrawn theory being that people buy papers to see their names in print. Weeklies have in common that they cover their communities with a detail that metro dailies have neither staff nor space to match. There is no alternative to keeping up with local news.

Rural weeklies generally have fallen on rough times. Part of their problem is the diminishing significance of agriculture in the U.S. and Canadian economies and the continuing depopulation of rural North America. In communities that remain retail centres, rural weeklies can maintain a strong advertising base. However, the Main Street of many small towns has declined as improved roads and the construction of major retail stores draw customers from 60 to 90 kilometres away. In earlier days, those customers patronized hometown retailers, who placed significant advertising in hometown weeklies. Today, many of these Main Street retailers, unable to compete with giant discount stores, are out of business.

SHOPPERS

Free-distribution papers that carry only advertisements have become increasingly important as vehicles for classified advertising. In recent years, *shoppers* have attracted display advertising that earlier would have gone to regular newspapers. Almost all shoppers undercut daily newspapers on advertising rates. The number of shoppers has grown, and they no longer are merely an ignorable competitor for daily newspapers for advertising.

By definition, shoppers are strictly advertising sheets, but beginning in the 1970s some shoppers added editorial content, usually material that came free over the transom, such as publicity and occasional self-serving columns from legislators. Some shoppers have added staff members to compile calendars and provide a modicum of news coverage. Most of these papers, however, remain ad sheets with little that is journalistic. Still, their news-gathering efforts and expenses are minuscule compared to those of a daily newspaper.

ALTERNATIVE AND MINORITY NEWSPAPERS

STUDY PREVIEW Most newspapers attempt broad coverage for a broad audience, but more specialized newspapers are important in the lives of many people.

COUNTER-CULTURE NEWSPAPERS

A group of friends in the Greenwich Village neighbourhood of New York, including novelist Norman Mailer and Don Wolf, decided to start a newspaper. Thus in 1955 was born the *Village Voice*, a free-wheeling weekly that became a prototype for a 1960s phenomenon called the *alternative press* and that has continued to thrive.

In its early days, the *Village Voice* was a haven for bohemian writers of diverse competence who volunteered occasional pieces, some lengthy, many rambling. Many articles purported to be investigative examinations of hypocritical people and institutions, but, as *Voice* veteran Nat Hentoff has noted, nobody ever bothered to check "noisome facts," let alone the "self-righteous author." The *Voice* seemed to scorn traditional, detached, neutral reporting. Despite its flaws, the amateurism gave the *Voice* a charm, and it picked up readership.

The *Voice* today is more polished and journalistically serious. The characteris-

Ethnic Newspapers. As the percentage of Chinese-speaking people in Canada has increased, so has the circulation of Chinese-language newspapers. Whether this growth will be sustained depends on the assimilation process. Earlier foreign-language newspapers went through explosive growth that accompanied immigration patterns and then withered as immigrants eased into the mainstream language and lifestyles..

tics that made it distinctive in its early history, and which were picked up by other counter-culture newspapers, include:

- Antiestablishment political coverage with a strong antimilitary slant.
- Cultural coverage that emphasizes contrarian music and art and exalts sex and drugs.
- Interpretive coverage focusing more on issues of special concern to alienated young people.
- Extensive entertainment coverage and listings of events.
- Conversational, sometimes crude style that includes four-letter words and gratuitous expletives for their shock value.
- Extensive personals for dating and sex liaisons.

By delivering a loyal readership that was hard to reach through mainstream media, many counter-culture newspapers became fat with advertising. Today, about 100 alternative newspapers are published in the United States, and many are prospering. With a circulation of 172 000, the *Village Voice* is widely available in big-city newsracks and by mail throughout the country.

Canada has its share of alternative newspapers, mostly distributed free at bus stops, bars, restaurants and malls. These publications are typically regional in nature, with each metropolitan centre boasting at least one such newspaper.

GAY NEWSPAPERS

Jim Michaels began publishing the first gay newspaper, the Los Angeles *Advocate*, out of his living room in 1967. Today, gay newspapers in North America have a total circulation of more than 1 million. Most are free papers distributed at gay bars, nightclubs and businesses. However, mainstream advertisers are beginning to take notice of the loyalty of gay readers to their newspapers. In 1990 the Columbia CD Club tested a membership ad offering eight discs for $1 in 12 gay newspapers. The response rate was so high that the club began placing the ad in 70 gay papers within a year. Other advertisers followed Columbia into the gay press.

ETHNIC NEWSPAPERS

The ethnic press has always been an important tool in maintaining ethnic boundaries. One of the earliest studies on the role of the ethnic press was done by Robert Park in the early 1920s. Park examined the ethnic press in the U.S. and its role in the process of assimilation. He found that most immigrants said they only planned to live in America temporarily and would return to their native country once they had earned enough money. Some researchers feel that ethnic social institutions, such as churches and the press, slowed down the process of assimilation into the dominant culture. However, Park felt that the ethnic press might help the process of assimilation by making immigrants, many of whom couldn't read English, feel part of the wider community.

On the other hand, in their study of the Portuguese community in Quebec, Alpalhao and Da Rosa (1990) found that in some areas of Quebec the existence of an ethnic means of mass communication, as well as other ethnic institutions (social services, churches, etc.), "... permit a large percentage of the community to live as if they were still in the milieu of origin. ..." Therefore, the ethnic media may hinder assimilation into the broader, dominant culture.

Given Canada's official status as a multicultural country, it's not surprising that numerous foreign language newspapers exist. According to recent data, many different voices are heard in Canadian ethnic newspapers. For example, Canada's Italian community publishes almost 30 newspapers, while the Jewish and First Nations communities each publish 20 newspapers. According to recent data, other ethnic groups that publish their own papers include the Spanish, Ukrainian, Greek, German, Urdu and Middle Eastern communities.

THE INFLUENCE OF MAGAZINES

STUDY PREVIEW   Today, as through their whole history, magazines are a mass medium through which culture is brought to a national audience. The periodicals pack great literature and ideas into formats that, unlike books, almost anybody can afford.

A NATIONAL ADVERTISING MEDIUM

Advertisers used magazines through the 1800s to build national markets for their products, which was an important factor in transforming North America from an agricultural economy into a modern economy. This too contributed to a sense of nationhood. The other mass media could not do that as effectively. Few books carried advertisements, and newspapers, with few exceptions, delivered only local readership to advertisers.

MASSIVE MAGAZINE AUDIENCE

People have a tremendous appetite for magazines. According to magazine industry studies, almost 90 percent of adults read an average of 10 magazine issues a month. While magazines are affordable for most people, the household income of the typical reader is 5 percent more than average. In general, the more education and higher income a person has, the greater the person's magazine consumption. A 1989 study by the Magazine Research Institute found:

- Of people who have postsecondary education, 94 percent read at least one magazine issue a month, and, as a group, they average 11.1 issues a month.
- Of people whose annual household income exceeds $40 000, 93 percent read at least one issue a month and average 11.1 issues.
- Of people in professional and managerial jobs, 95 percent read at least one issue a month and average 13.3.

In short, magazines are a pervasive mass medium. Magazines, however, are not only for the upper crust. Many magazines are edited for "downscale" audiences, which means the medium's role in society is spread across almost the whole range of people with literacy skills. Even illiterates can derive some pleasure and value from magazines, which by and large are visual and colourful.

The massiveness of the audience makes the magazine an exceptionally competitive medium. About 12 000 publications vie for readers, ranging from general-interest publications like *Reader's Digest* to such specialized publications as *Winetidings*, for people interested in wine, and *Canadian Thoroughbred*, for racehorse aficionados. In recent years, new titles have been launched annually, although only one in five survives into the third year. Even among major magazines, a huge following at the moment is no guarantee of survival. Magazine publishing is a risky business.

WHAT MAKES A MAGAZINE CANADIAN?

To determine whether or not a magazine is "Canadian," we must look at the Income Tax Act of 1988. A magazine is considered "Canadian" if

- the type is set in Canada (excluding advertisements)
- it is printed in Canada
- it is published and edited in Canada by people living in Canada.

It is not a Canadian magazine if more than 20 percent of the issue (not including advertising) is the same as a magazine printed, edited or published outside of Canada. It's also not Canadian if it's printed or published under a licence granted by someone who publishes outside of Canada.

These guidelines exist to ensure that Canadian voices are heard in Canadian magazines. The government's concern about this issue stemmed from early Canadian issues of *Time* and *Reader's Digest*, which didn't contain much Canadian content. Acting on a recommendation of the 1970 Davey Commission, Parliament changed the Income Tax Act. Advertising had always been a legitimate business expense. However, as of 1970 for magazine advertising to qualify, the magazine had to meet the guidelines outlined above. The legislation worked; advertisers began to run ads in Canadian magazines, such as *Saturday Night* and *Maclean's*, instead of publications that were only nominally Canadian.

MAGAZINES AS MEDIA INNOVATORS

STUDY PREVIEW Magazines have led other media with significant innovations in journalism, advertising and circulation. These include investigative reporting, in-depth personality profiles and photojournalism.

INVESTIGATIVE REPORTING

Muckraking, usually called "investigative reporting" today, was honed by magazines as a journalistic approach in the first years of the 20th century. Magazines ran lengthy explorations of abusive institutions in the society. It was *Theodore Roosevelt*, the reform president, who coined the term "muckraking." Roosevelt generally enjoyed investigative journalism, but one day in 1906, when the digging got too close to home, he likened it to the work of a character in a 17th-century novel who focused so much on raking muck that he missed the good news. The president meant the term derisively, but it came to be a badge of honour among journalists.

PERSONALITY PROFILES

The in-depth *personality profile* was a magazine invention. In the 1920s *Harold Ross* of the *New Yorker* began pushing writers to a thoroughness that was new in journalism. They used multiple interviews with a range of sources—talking not only with the subject of the profile but with just about everyone and anyone who could comment on the subject, including the subject's friends and enemies. Such depth required weeks, sometimes months of journalistic digging. It's not uncommon now in newspapers, broadcasting or magazines, but before Harold Ross, it didn't exist.

Under *Hugh Hefner, Playboy* took the interview in new directions in 1962 with in-depth profiles developed from a highly structured question-and-answer format. The *Playboy* Q-A format became widely imitated.

PHOTOJOURNALISM

Magazines brought *visuals* to the mass media in a way books never had. *Harper's Weekly* sent artists to Civil War battles, leading the way to journalism that went beyond words.

The young editor of the *National Geographic, Gilbert Grosvenor,* drew a map proposing a route to the South Pole for an 1899 issue, putting the *Geographic* on the road to being a visually oriented magazine. For subsequent issues, Grosvenor borrowed government plates to reproduce photos, and he encouraged travelers to submit their photographs to the magazine. This was at a time when most magazines scorned photographs. However, Grosvenor was undeterred as an advocate for documentary photography, and membership in the National Geographic Society, a prerequisite for receiving the magazine, swelled. Eventually the magazine assembled its own staff of photographers and gradually became a model for other publications that discovered they needed to play catch-up.

Aided by technological advances involving smaller, more portable cameras and faster film capable of recording images under extreme conditions, photographers working for the *Geographic* opened a whole new world of documentary coverage to their readers. Among *Geographic* accomplishments were:

- A photo of a bare-breasted Filipino woman field-worker shocked some *Geographic* readers in 1903, but Grosvenor persisted against Victorian sensitivities to show the peoples of the world as they lived.

Photojournalism Innovator. The *National Geographic*, a sponsored membership magazine, has been a leader in photographic coverage. A 1903 photo of a bare-breasted Filipino woman irked some people, but the *Geographic* defended itself as showing the peoples of the world as the maga-

Life **Defined America.** The giant general-interest magazines like *Life* gave meaning to the word "photojournalism." The grisliness of war was indelible in George Strock's shot of G.I.s felled in their steps in New Guinea in World War II. After the war, *Life* chronicled the suburbanization of America with photo and text coverage of Leavittown.

zine found them. In 1911 the *Geographic* demonstrated with a dramatic 17-page foldout of the Canadian Rockies that format need not limit photojournalism's portrayal of the world. The magazine has also led in underwater colour and dramatic aviation and space photography.

Photojournalism Arrives. The oversize pages of *Life*, which opened to 34 x 52.5 cm, did justice to great photography. Margaret Bourke-White's medieval tones captured the immensity of Fort Peck Dam under construction in Montana for the cover of the inaugural issue. Bourke-White became a star photographer for *Life*. She was among a handful of women journalists who covered World War II for American readers.

- The first photographs from Tibet, by Russian explorers, appeared in 1905 in an 11-page spread, extraordinary visual coverage for the time that confirmed photography's role in journalism.
- A 17-page, 2.5 m foldout panorama of the Canadian Rockies in 1911 showed that photojournalism need not be limited by format.
- The magazine's 100th anniversary cover in 1988 was the first hologram, a three-dimensional photograph, ever published in a mass-audience magazine. It was a significant production accomplishment.

Life magazine brought photojournalism to new importance in the 1930s. The oversize pages of the magazine gave new intensity to photographs, and the magazine, a weekly, demonstrated that newsworthy events could be covered consistently by camera. *Life* captured the spirit of the times photographically and demonstrated that the whole range of human experience could be recorded visually. Both real life and *Life* could be shocking. A 1938 *Life* spread on human birth was so shocking for the time that censors succeeded in banning the issue in 33 cities.

ANALYZING PHOTOGRAPHS

How do we "read" photographs and derive meaning from them? Photographs are signs; they are iconic representations of reality, and as such, they are of interest to communication theorists. The meaning of photographs is ambiguous; the old saying "a picture is worth a thousand words" certainly fits. The photograph is a message without a code; it needs something to help anchor meaning. Look at the photographs from *Life* in this chapter; did you know what each photograph signified before you read the words beside it? Let's consider what Roland Barthes says about press photos in his essay "The Photographic Message." According to Barthes, there are three texts to consider when examining press photographs and how we decode them. The first is the photograph itself, the second the written words that accompany the photo, while the third is the text that is constructed when the photograph and the written text meet. It is Barthes' view that in order to analyze the photograph, we need to look at the following six codes and how they work to create "connotation" or meaning:

1. *Trick effects.* Usually reserved for supermarket tabloids, trick effects involve doctoring photographs in order to create meaning. Take for example a photo of our prime minister and a photo of a space alien. Separately, these subjects signify one thing; place both subjects in the same photograph and they signify something else.

2. *Pose.* The pose of the subject can communicate meaning nonverbally. Facial expression, eye contact, posture and body type are cultural codes that help create meaning. In the last federal election the Progressive Conservative ad campaign used press photographs that accentuated Jean Chrétien's facial expression. The conservatives hoped to establish the connotation that he did not "look" like a prime minister.

3. *Objects.* Objects within the photograph also help to lay the foundation for meaning. Take the example of a doctor who has been photographed wearing a white lab coat with a stethoscope around her neck and her medical degrees on the wall. The lab coat, stethoscope and office, as objects, help lay the foundation for the meaning that is created: this woman is a doctor. Photograph her in ripped jeans and a Tragically Hip T-shirt and the image of "doctor" does not come to mind. She

Photo Comparison. Consider these photographs of O.J. Simpson. What would Barthes say about the connotations created by the pose, photogenia, trick effects and other factors?

may well be a doctor, but the objects in the photograph would contradict the message.

4.   *Photogenia.* Barthes uses this fancy word to describe the methods photographers employ to be creative: lighting, exposure and printing.

5.   *Aestheticism.* By this, Barthes means the overall look of the photograph—is it artistic?

6.   *Syntax.* When several photographs are used in sequence, meaning can be created. Consider the Calvin and Hobbs comic strip in this chapter when thinking of syntax; each section within the panel builds on the previous one. The meaning of the comic strip is only created when we have read all the panels. A series of photographs works in much the same way.

In regard to the written text that accompanies a given photograph, Barthes focuses on the following three factors:

- How does the text help speed up the process of connotation? How quickly does it take away the ambiguity of the photograph?
- How is the text presented? Different fonts and colours carry with them various

---

MEDIA DATABANK

Magazine Circulation Leaders: United States

These are the circulation leaders among United States magazines.

Reader's Digest	16.3 million	Family Circle	5.3 million
TV Guide	14.5 million	Good Housekeeping	5.1 million
National Geographic	9.7 million	Consumer Reports	5.0 million
Better Homes & Gardens	8.0 million	Ladies' Home Journal	5.0 million
Cable Guide	5.9 million	Woman's Day	4.8 million

---

connotations. A big, bold, red headline in a newspaper connotes urgency or perhaps disaster, while a small, black headline would be interpreted as somewhat insignificant.

■ How often does the written text create an entirely unexpected meaning in the photograph? Viewing a photograph of a crying man might make you think he is sad; perhaps he has lost a loved one or his home has been destroyed by fire. However, after reading the written text, you might discover the tears were tears of joy. He might have just won the 6/49 Lottery.

CONSUMER MAGAZINES

STUDY PREVIEW   The most visible category of magazines is general-interest magazines, which are available on newsracks and by subscription. Called *consumer magazines*, these include publications like *Reader's Digest* that try to offer something for everybody, as well as magazines edited for narrower audiences.

NEWSMAGAZINES

Although it is often compared to *Time*, *Maclean's*, "Canada's Weekly Newsmagazine," was founded in 1905, almost 20 years before *Time* first appeared. However, the magazine we now know as *Maclean's* was called *Busy Man's Magazine* until 1911. Originally, it was a large-format magazine, about the size of *Life*, but in 1969 it was reduced to a standard size. In content, *Maclean's* is similar to *Time*, with an emphasis on in-depth coverage of national and international stories. Columnists like Peter C. Newman (a former editor of *Maclean's*), Barbara Amiel and Allan Fotheringham have offered their various perspectives to Canadians in the pages of this magazine.

Fresh out of Yale in 1923, classmates *Henry Luce* and *Briton Hadden* begged and borrowed $86,000 from friends and relatives and launched a new kind of magazine: *Time*. The magazine provided summaries of news by categories such as national affairs, sports and business. It took four years for *Time* to turn a profit, and some people doubted that the magazine would ever make money, noting that it merely rehashed what daily newspapers had already reported. Readers, however, came to like the handy compilation and the sprightly, often irreverent writing style that set *Time* apart. The Canadian edition of *Time*, published in Toronto, has a circulation of 300 000.

While *Time* and *Maclean's* cover a broad range of subjects, specialized news-

Newsmagazines. Canada's counterpart to *Time* magazine is *Maclean's* magazine. It brings the Canadian journalism tradition of analysis to the newsstands.

magazines focus on narrower subjects. The largest category is those featuring celebrity news, including the gossipy sort. The supermarket tabloid *National Enquirer* focuses on the rich and famous, hyped-up medical research and sensational oddball news and is an incredible commercial success.

While the *National Enquirer* treads the line between being a magazine and being a newspaper, its numerous imitators include publications that are distinctly magazines. In 1974 Time-Life created the consumer magazine *People*, aimed at the same supermarket checkout-line customers as the *National Enquirer*. *People*, however, concentrates on celebrities and avoids much of the *National Enquirer*'s blatant rumour mongering and sensationalism.

People proved a quick success and also spawned a slew of imitators. Even the New York Times Company joined the bandwagon with *Us*. Together the celebrity-focused magazines robbed circulation from the sensationalistic tabloids.

WOMEN'S MAGAZINES

The first magazine edited to interest only a portion of the mass audience, but otherwise to be of general interest, was *Godey's Lady's Book*. It was started by *Sarah Josepha Hale* in 1830 to uplift and glorify womanhood. Its advice on fashions, morals, taste, sewing and cooking developed a following, which peaked with a circulation of 150 000. The *Godey's* tradition is maintained today in competing magazines: *Better Homes & Gardens, Family Circle, Good Housekeeping, Ladies' Home Journal, McCall's, Redbook* and *Woman's Day*. While each can be distinguished from her siblings, there is a thematic connection: concern for home, family and quality living from a traditional woman's perspective. Canadian offerings like *Homemakers, Chatelaine* and *Canadian Living* also fit the mold.

MEDIA DATABANK

Magazine Circulation Leaders: Canada

Top 10 Canadian Magazines: Average circulation

Homemakers Magazine	1 600 000	*Canadian Living*	595 000
Reader's Digest	1 200 000	*Maclean's*	507 000
Chatelaine	809 000	*Health Watch Canada*	490 000
TV Guide	790 000	*Westworld BC*	455 000
Leisure Ways	631 000	*Legion*	446 000

Average circulation includes copies distributed free and by subscription.

Source: Canadian Advertising Rates and Data, June 1996

Another woman's magazine is *Cosmopolitan*. Under Helen Gurley Brown, *Cosmopolitan* has geared itself to a subcategory of women readers—young, unmarried and working. It's the most successful in a large group of women's magazines seeking narrow groups. Among them are *Elle*, focusing on fashion; *Playgirl*, with its soft pornography; *Mirabella*, which mixes fashion and social issues; *Essence*, for black women; *Seventeen*, for teenage girls; and *Self*, for women of the "me generation." In Canada, *Flare*, *Images* and *Focus on Women* are also geared toward narrow audiences.

MEN'S MAGAZINES

Founded in 1933, *Esquire* was the first classy men's magazine. It was as famous for its pin-ups as its literary content, which over the years has included articles from Ernest Hemingway, John Dos Passos and Gay Talese. Fashion has also been a cornerstone in the *Esquire* content mix.

Hugh Hefner learned about magazines as an *Esquire* staff member, and he applied those lessons when he created *Playboy* in 1953. With its lustier tone, *Playboy* quickly overtook *Esquire* in circulation. At its peak, *Playboy* sold 7 million copies a month. The magazine emphasized female nudity but also carried journalistic and literary pieces whose merit attracted many readers. Readers embarrassed by their carnal curiosity could claim they bought the magazine for its articles. Critics sniped, however, that *Playboy* published the worst stuff of the best writers.

Playboy imitators added raunch—some a little, some a lot. The most successful, Bob Guccione's *Penthouse*, has never attracted as many readers or advertisers as *Playboy*, but it has been a success.

Social observers credit Hefner with capitalizing on the post–World War II sexual revolution in the United States and fanning it. A moral backlash developed in the mid-1980s, and *Playboy* and other sex-oriented men's magazines suffered. The major blow was the 1986 decision by 7-Eleven convenience stores to discontinue selling *skin magazines*. Seven-Eleven was the largest among retail outlets that responded to pressure from moralists. The 7-Eleven decision especially hurt *Penthouse*, which relied on newsrack sales more than *Playboy*, but *Playboy* was hurt too. *Playboy*'s circulation dipped to 3.5 million and *Penthouse*'s to 1.8 million. Both have recovered some circulation but still are far short of their peaks. With less circula-

Magazine Survival

Hundreds of new magazines come into existence every year. Most are doomed to fail in the intense competition for readers and advertisers. While magazines fail for many reasons, media scholar Theodore Peterson has identified three principles for a magazine's success:

- Find a readership that no other magazine is serving or that is being inadequately served.
- Adapt as conditions and readers' tastes change.

- Reflect the personality of the editor or publisher.

As you read this chapter, reflect on the success of magazines *you* read. What voids or niches do these magazines find and fill? How do they reflect the vision and personality of the person in charge? From your own point of view, how have these magazines, as well as others you know about, adapted to changing conditions?

---

tion, they have had to adjust advertising rates downward. Also, they have lost some advertisers who had been attracted by the earlier large circulations.

Not all men's magazines dwell on sex. The outdoor life is exalted in *Field & Stream*, whose circulation tops 2 million. Fix-it magazines, led by *Popular Science* and *Popular Mechanics*, have a steady following.

MAGAZINES FOR THE INTELLIGENTSIA

Magazines such as *Saturday Night, Harper's* and *Atlantic* that approach issues cerebrally are *high-brow slicks*. Articles are exploratory and essayish. Fiction is included. The nonfiction focuses in depth on literary, cultural and political issues. All three have grand traditions going back to the 1800s.

NON-NEWSRACK MAGAZINES

STUDY PREVIEW   Many organizations publish magazines for their members. While these sponsored magazines, including *National Geographic, Modern Maturity* and *Smithsonian,* resemble consumer magazines, they generally are not available at newsracks. In fact, consumer magazines are far outnumbered by sponsored magazines and by trade journals.

SPONSORED MAGAZINES

The founders of the National Geographic Society decided in 1888 to put out a magazine to promote the society and build membership. The idea was to entice people to join by bundling a subscription with membership and then to use the dues to finance the society's research and expeditions. Within a few years, the *National Geographic* had become a phenomenal success both in generating membership and as a profit centre for the National Geographic Society. Today, more than 100 years old and with circulation near 10 million, the *Geographic* is the most widely recognized sponsored magazine in the U.S. Other sponsored magazines include *Modern Maturity*, published by the American Association of Retired People for its members. Its circulation exceeds 22 million. In Canada, *Legion*, with a circulation of 446 000 and *CARP News*, published by the Canadian Association of Retired Persons, are sponsored magazines.

Many sponsored magazines carry advertising and are financially self-sufficient. In fact, the most successful sponsored magazines compete aggressively with consumer magazines for advertising. In 1991 *National Geographic*'s advertising staff put together an elaborate pitch to the Ford Motor Company for more of its ads. Impressed with the *Geographic*'s readership data, Ford increased its *Geographic* advertising for 1992 models by 250 percent—at a time when Ford was cutting back overall in magazine advertising.

Many sponsored magazines do not seek advertising. These include many university magazines, which are considered something that a university should publish as an institutional expense to disseminate information about research and scholarly activities and, not incidentally, to promote itself. Other sponsored magazines that typically do not carry advertising include publications for union members, in-house publications for employees, and company publications for customers. These publications do not have the public recognition of consumer magazines, but many are as slick and professional as consumer magazines. All together, they employ more editors, photographers and writers than consumer magazines.

TRADE JOURNALS

Everyone in a profession or trade has at least one magazine for keeping abreast of what is happening in the field. In entertainment, *Billboard* provides a solid journalistic coverage on a broad range of subjects in music: new recording releases, new acts, new technology, new merger deals and so forth. *Billboard*, a trade journal, is essential reading for people in the industry. About 4000 trade journals cover a mind-boggling range of businesses and trades. Consider the diversity in these titles: *Rock and Dirt*, *Progressive Grocer*, *Canadian Plastics*, *Hogs Today* and *Hardware Age*.

Like consumer magazines, the "trades" rely mostly on advertising for their income and profits. Some charge for subscriptions, but many are sent free to a carefully culled list of readers whom advertisers want to reach. As an example, listed below are advertisers in *Broadcaster*, a Canadian trade journal for people with radio, television and cable jobs:

- Panasonic, which sells all forms of audio/video production equipment.
- Maxell, promoting industrial-quality video and audio tape.
- Shure, a company that produces audio equipment.

CRITICISM OF TRADE MAGAZINES

Many trade magazine companies have reputations for honest, hard-hitting reporting of the industries they cover, but the trades have a mixed reputation. Some U.S. trade magazines are loaded with puffery exalting their advertisers and industries. For years, *Body Fashions*, formerly *Corset and Underwear Review*, unabashedly presented ads as news stories. As many trade journals do, it charged companies to run stories about them and covered only companies that were also advertisers. At some trades, the employees who solicit ads write news stories that echo the ads. These trades tend to be no more than boosters of the industries they pretend to cover. Kent MacDougall, writing in the *Wall Street Journal*, offered this especially egregious example: *America's Textile Reporter*, which promoted the textile industry from a management perspective, once dismissed the hazard of textile workers' contracting brown lung disease by inhaling cotton dust as "a thing brought up by venal doctors" at an international labour meeting in Africa, "where inferior races are bound to be afflicted by new diseases more superior people defeated years ago." At the time, in 1972, 100 000 U.S. textile workers were afflicted with brown lung. Many trade magazines persist today in pandering to their trades, professions and industries, rather than approaching their subjects with journalistic truth-seeking and truth telling.

Responsible trade journals are embarrassed by some of their brethren, many of which are upstarts put out by people with no journalistic experience or instincts. Because of this, and also because it takes relatively little capital to start a trade magazine, many bad trade magazines thrive. Several trade magazine professional organizations, including the American Business Press and the Society of Business Press Editors, work to improve both their industry and its image. Even so, as former ABP President Charles Mill said, trades continue to be plagued "by fleabag outfits published in somebody's garage."

Trade magazines covering the Canadian and American mass media include *RPM*, *The Record* and *Billboard* for the music industry; *Marketing* Magazine for advertising and marketing; *The Publisher*, for the newspaper industry and *Broadcaster* and *Cablecaster* for the Canadian radio and television industries.

MAGAZINE GLOBALIZATION

STUDY PREVIEW Many magazines are seeking readers and revenue beyond their national borders. Some have created foreign editions, each with distinctive editorial content and advertising. More magazines are establishing foreign editions, and the growing number of multinational media companies is accelerating the trend.

EXPORTED MAGAZINES

With their *Reader's Digest* a phenomenal success in the United States and with a growing list of subscribers abroad, the magazine's founders, DeWitt and Lila Wallace decided in 1938 to set up a London office and launch a foreign edition. By the end of World War II, *Digest* circulation reached 9 million in the United States and 4 million overseas. Meanwhile, *National Geographic* also found an international following.

The potential of foreign editions was not lost on other major U.S. magazines, and today *Cosmopolitan*, *Newsweek* and *Time* derive substantial revenue from international editions. With the development of the global economy, *Business Week*, *Fortune* and *Forbes* have gone with a variety of editions to build an international audience, and the *Playboy* and *Penthouse* men's magazines have increased their readership with international editions. In 1991 Hearst brought out United Kingdom editions of *Esquire* and *Vanity Fair*. The leader, however, remains *Reader's Digest*, which is published in 18 languages and sells more than 12.2 million copies abroad, including 1.2 million copies in Canada.

Foreign editions of U.S. magazines are not always mere rehashes or translations of the U.S. editions. *Reader's Digest* discovered early that some articles of interest to American readers were offensive abroad. In the 1960s, many U.S. articles on the civil rights movement, including "Why Negroes Riot," did not go into

Reader's Digest in Russian

One hundred thousand people in the Ukrainian city of Kharkov opened their mail in August 1991 to find a four-page flier announcing that "the world's most popular journal" soon would be available. The flier marked the entry of *Reader's Digest,* that homey embodiment of conservative, middle-class American values, into areas that were once part of the closed Soviet empire. A few days later, 50 000 copies of the 160-page debut issue were delivered to newsracks in Kharkov, Kiev, St. Petersburg and Moscow, and they sold out. The people liked the mix of brief articles on international life, health and psychology. The press run soon was increased to 100 000.

Although the Russian-language *Reader's Digest* sells for the ruble equivalent of $1.50, twice as much as most Russian magazines, the Reader's Digest Association of Pleasantville, New York, was not seeking early profits. Start-up and distribution costs were high, and the inaugural issue carried a mere five pages of advertising—from Coca-Cola, Colgate toothpaste, Pepsi-Cola, Smirnoff vodka and Toshiba televisions.

The marketing-savvy *Reader's Digest* organization viewed the Russian-language edition as an investment. The company wanted to learn how to reach mass audiences in the former Soviet Union with the goal eventually of selling not only magazines but also books, music and other products.

Mass mailing, a key to the success of *Reader's Digest* elsewhere, is a special challenge in the former Soviet republics. Not only are the mails slow and unreliable, but the remnants of the notorious Soviet black market system include the postal structure, which swallows attractive products, including slick, colourful magazines, before they reach addressees. Instead of being mailed to subscribers, Russian *Reader's Digests* are sent to newsracks individually, where clerks hold copies for subscribers.

Thievery in the postal system even cuts into mailings of subscription offers, which prompted the decision to stick to black-and-white fliers for advertising *Reader's Digest.* To distribute books, tapes and other products at some future date, the company assumes it may need to go with unadorned plain brown wrappers.

A key to the Reader's Digest Association's marketing success with mass mailing elsewhere has been computerized, cross-indexed mailing lists that match people with the products they are likeliest to order. In the former Soviet Union, where consumer mailing lists are virtually nonexistent, that aspect of marketing is starting from scratch.

While early issues produced hardly any advertising revenue—only $6000 a page—the Reader's Digest Association was not unmindful that the introduction of capitalism in the old Soviet Union meant advertising could become a profit centre some day.

the edition for racially segregated South Africa. In deference to Roman Catholicism, *Digest* editions in heavily Catholic areas, including France, Germany, Ireland, Italy, Latin America and Quebec, did not carry articles on birth control. The *Digest*'s fervent anti-Communism, a mainstay in U.S. editions, was skipped in the Finland edition, whose readers, not to mention their government, feared their Soviet neighbour.

Newsweek and *Time* also offer distinctive content in their foreign editions. Editors boil down domestic U.S. news and carry more coverage from their foreign staffs. The rules on advertising acceptability are geared to local mores. As mentioned previously, Canadian editions of foreign publications must meet certain criteria.

COOPERATIVE INTERNATIONAL ARRANGEMENTS

To gain experience in new markets and to reduce risk, magazine companies go into joint ventures. Time Warner and Hachette have teamed for a French edition of *Fortune*. Time Warner joined with a Milan company for an Italian edition of *Time*. Hachette is in a joint agreement with a Shanghai publishing house for the Chinese edition of *Elle* in Chinese and with a Moscow publishing house for a Russian-language edition of *Paris Match* (without the prefix *Paris*). The Hungarian edition of *Penthouse* is published under license to a Swiss company. With a Hong Kong company, *Forbes* is producing an edition aimed at the 40 million Chinese who do not live on the still-closed mainland. *Newsweek* has an arrangement with the Australian newsmagazine *Bulletin*.

The first U.S. and Western European magazines into the former Soviet Union during the perestroika reforms had to forge special arrangements because dealings had to be in rubles, which could not be taken out of the country. The Russian-language edition of *Scientific American* was published through a royalty arrangement with a government agency. The Russian-language *Business Week* is a joint venture with a Moscow publisher.

Major magazine publishers worldwide are anxious to position themselves as the choice of advertisers for internationally marketed goods. The potential is obvious with the democratization and capitalistic reforms in the former Soviet bloc, the economic unification of Europe and the growing international commerce in consumer goods.

MAGAZINE DEMASSIFICATION

STUDY PREVIEW   Giant mass-audience magazines were major influences in their heyday, but television killed them off by offering larger audiences to advertisers. Today, the magazine industry thrives through demassification, the process of seeking audiences with narrow interests. Critics feel demassification has changed the role of magazines in society for the worse.

A NARROWER FOCUS

With the demise of many general-interest magazines doomsayers predicted that magazines were a dying breed of media. The fact, however, was that advertisers withdrew only from magazines with broad readerships. What advertisers discov-

Magazine Demassification. Advertisers favour magazines that are edited to specific audience interests that coincide with the advertisers' products. Fewer and fewer magazines geared to a general audience remain in business today. Communication theorists refer to the process of demassification as narrowcasting.

ered was that although it was less expensive to use television to peddle universally used products like detergents, grooming aids and packaged foods, television, geared at the time for mass audiences, was too expensive for products appealing to narrow groups. Today, relatively few magazines seek a truly mass audience.

Special-interest magazines, whose content focused on limited subjects and whose advertising rates were lower, fit the bill better than either television or the giant mass-audience magazines for reaching customers with special interests. For manufacturers of $3000 video systems, for example, it made sense to advertise in a narrowly focused videophile magazine like *Video News and Reviews.* In the same way, neither mass-audience magazines nor television was a medium of choice for top-of-the-line racing skis, but ski magazines were ideal. For hockey cards, *Canadian Sportscard Collector* made sense.

Among new magazines that emerged with the demassification in the 1960s were regional and city magazines, offering a geographically defined audience to advertisers. Some of these magazines, which usually bore the name of their city or region, including *Voilà Québec, Vancouver Magazine, Cityscope* (Calgary) and *Hamilton Magazine*, offered hard-hitting journalistic coverage of local issues. Many, though, focused on soft life-style subjects rather than antagonize powerful local interests and risk losing advertisers. Indeed, hypersensitivity to advertisers is a criticism of today's demassified magazines.

CRITICS OF DEMASSIFICATION

Norman Cousins, once editor of the high-brow *Saturday Review of Literature,* criticized demassified magazines for betraying their traditional role of enriching the culture. Cousins said specialization had diluted the intellectual role of magazines in the society. Advertisers, he said, were shaping magazines' journalistic content for their commercial purposes—in contrast to magazine editors independently deciding content with loftier purposes in mind.

Scholar Dennis Holder put this "unholy alliance" of advertisers and readers this way: "The readers see themselves as members of small, and in some sense, elite groups—joggers, for example, or cat lovers—and they want to be told that they are terribly neat people for being in those groups. Advertisers, of course, want to reinforce the so-called positive self-image too, because joggers who feel good about themselves tend to buy those ridiculous suits and cat lovers who believe lavishing affection on their felines is a sign of warmth and sincerity are the ones who purchase cute little cat sweaters, or are they cat's pajamas." Magazine editors and writers, Holder said, are caught in the symbiotic advertiser-reader alliance and have no choice but to go along.

Norman Cousins and Dennis Holder were right that most consumer magazines today tend to a frothy mix of light, upbeat features, with little that is thoughtful or hard-hitting. However, most readers want to know about other people, particularly celebrities, and a great many trendy topics, and advertisers want to reach those readers, avoiding controversies that might hurt sales. So profitability for most magazines and their advertisers is locked into providing information their target audiences are interested in rather than serving an undefinable "public interest." The emphasis on profits and demassification saddens a number of people who believe that magazines have a higher calling than a cash register. These critics would agree with Cousins, who warned that emphasizing the superficial just because it sells magazines is a betrayal of the social trust that magazine publishers once held. "The purpose of a magazine," he said, "is not to tell you how to fix a leaky faucet, but to tell you what the world is about."

There is no question that demassification works against giving readers any kind of global view. In demassified magazines for auto enthusiasts, as an example, road test articles typically wax as enthusiastically as the advertisements about new cars. These demassified magazines, edited to target selected audiences and thereby attract advertisers, make no pretence of broadening their readers' understanding of substantive issues by exploring diverse perspectives. The narrowing of magazine editorial content appears destined to continue, not only because it is profitable but also because new technologies, like Time Warner's geodemographic TargetSelect program, make it possible for magazine publishers to identify narrower and narrower segments of the mass audience and then to gear their publications to those narrower and narrower interests.

MAGAZINE CHALLENGES

STUDY PREVIEW   Magazines face new challenges as cable television becomes a demassified advertising medium. Other problems include fickle audiences for narrowly focused magazines, finding a balance between newsrack and subscription sales and ever-rising costs.

HAZARDS OF DEMASSIFICATION

While many magazines have prospered through demassification by catering to special interests, serving a niche of readers has its hazards. One problem is that a narrow audience may turn out to be transitory. Citizen's band radios were the rage in the 1970s, and CB magazines suddenly cropped up, only to die as public interest in CBs waned.

A second problem stems from the fact that, in coming years, specialized magazines may feel competition from other media, which are going through their own belated demassification. Radio is already demographically divided, with stations using formats designed for narrow audiences, and the narrowing is continuing. At the start of the 1990s, major cities had stations that aired only comedy, only financial news and only motivational talk. Specialized magazines were losing their monopoly on narrow audience segments.

NEW COMPETITION

Another ominous sign for magazines is the cable television industry, which is eating into magazine advertising with an array of demassified channels, such as TSN, Bravo! and the Life Network. The demassified cable channels are picking up advertisers that once used magazines almost exclusively to reach narrow slices of the mass audience with a presumed interest in their products and services.

Another drain on magazine revenue is the growth of direct-mail advertising. Using sophisticated analysis of potential customer groups, advertisers can mail brochures, catalogues, fliers and other material, including video pitches, directly to potential customers at their homes or places of business. Every dollar that goes into direct-mail campaigns is a dollar that in an earlier period went into magazines and other traditional advertising media.

CUTTING COSTS

Besides the soft advertising situation, magazines are facing rising costs. Hikes in paper costs prompted the once-oversize *Ladies' Home Journal* and *Esquire* to trim their page size. In 1991 even the fashion magazines *Elle* and *Mirabella*, whose fashion ads erupted off huge, oversize pages, abandoned the large European formats that had been standard for fashion magazines. The change allowed the magazines to fit better into newsrack slots, and, conceded publisher Grace Mirabella, "to save precious dollars on expensive paper." Trimming down also saves mailing costs, one of a magazine's largest expenses. When *Premiere* reduced the page dimensions, its weight dropped 2 percent, which was hardly insignificant at the postal meter.

NEWSRACKS OR SUBSCRIPTIONS

A magazine's financial health can hinge on finding the right balance between single-copy sales at newsracks and subscriptions. Subscriptions represent long-term reader commitment, but they are sold at deep discounts. Newsrack sales generate more revenue. Finding the right balance is complicated because advertisers have different points of view on which delivery system is better for reaching potential customers. Some advertisers reason that readers who pay cash for individual issues are more attentive to the content than people who routinely receive every issue via mail. Other advertisers are impressed by the loyalty implicit in subscriptions. Also, there are advertisers who flip-flop on the question.

To find the right balance, magazines manipulate their subscription rates and newsrack prices. When its advertisers shifted to a newsstand preference, *Cosmopolitan* lowered its single-copy price and hiked subscription rates until 95 percent of its circulation was through newsracks. The shift helped make the magazine attractive to advertisers.

Single sales benefit magazines in another way. They are more profitable than subscriptions, which means that magazines can keep their advertising rates down because readers pick up more of the bills. In general, the shift through the 1970s and 1980s was toward single-copy sales. The shift helped magazines improve their competitive stance against television.

CHAPTER WRAP-UP

Can newspapers survive? Even if people were to stop buying newspapers tomorrow, newspaper organizations would survive because they have an asset that competing media lack: the largest, most skilled newsroom staffs in a given community. The presses and ink-on-newsprint medium that carry the message may not have a long future, but newspapers' news-gathering capability will endure. Some Canadian newspapers are experimenting with facsimile delivery, while others are available over the Internet. Perhaps the future of newspaper organizations will lie in selling information. Thomson is already headed this way.

In addition to the daily national, metropolitan and hometown newspapers that are available, thousands of weekly community newspapers and special interest papers are published in Canada and the U.S. By focusing on audiences with special interests, many of these newspapers are attracting more advertisers and either solidifying their existing financial base or building strong foundations for the future.

Recent developments at Southam and Hollinger have rekindled interest in concentration of newspaper ownership in Canada. The concerns of the Davey Committee and the Kent Commission are still relevant in the 1990s.

Magazines have been an adaptable medium, adjusting to the times and to changing audience interests. This is clear in the medium's long history of innovations, which other media have subsequently copied. These innovations include in-depth personality profiles, photojournalism and muckraking. A troubling question about contemporary magazines is whether they are still enriching culture. Through most of their history, magazines have made important literature and ideas available at reasonable cost to the general public. Critics worry that many of today's specialty magazines have lost a sense of society's significant issues. Troubling too, say critics, is that these magazines have forsaken a detached, neutral journalistic approach in an enthusiasm for their specialized subjects, in effect selling out to the commercial interests of their advertisers rather than pursuing the truth.

QUESTIONS FOR REVIEW

1. How did the mass production of the written word fundamentally change human history?

2. Describe the rise of newspaper chains.

3. Why are Canada and the U.S. nations of mostly morning, regional newspapers?

4. What challenges to their dominance as a news and advertising medium do newspapers and magazines face?

5. Community newspapers are booming. Why?

6. Describe the growth of alternative and minority newspapers.

7. Explain the Sapir-Whorf hypothesis and its relevance to newspaper content.

8. Outline the growth of newspapers in Canada.

9. Why are the O'Leary, Kent and Davey commissions important to publishing in Canada?

10. How have magazines been innovative as a journalistic and a visual medium?

11. What is demassification?

12. Explain how Barthes says we read a photograph.

QUESTIONS FOR CRITICAL THINKING

1. Take any newspaper or magazine editorial and analyze it from the standpoint of the Sapir-Whorf hypothesis. How does the author carefully select words to make you agree with the editor's main point? Remember to look beyond the denotative nature of the words; what connotations are created?

2. Take any press photograph from a newspaper or magazine and analyze the signs and the codes. Without looking at the written text, what do you think the photograph communicates? Then look at as many of the six codes outlined by Barthes as is appropriate: trick effects, pose, objects, photogenia, aestheticism and, if appropriate, syntax. What meaning is created by the photograph? Then look at the written text; what role does it play in your interpretation of the message that is being communicated?

3. How useful have the Royal Commissions into newspaper ownership been?

4. How has a newspaper like *USA Today* changed the way we read news?

5. To some, the word "muckraking" has a negative connotation. How can muckraking be seen in a positive light? Why do you think that muckraking is more of an American journalistic style than a Canadian one?

6. Is demassification good or bad for the magazine industry? For readers?

7. How can you explain the declining number of newspapers and their losses in market penetration in view of the newspaper industry's profitability?

8. How have newspapers met challenges to their advertising revenue from radio, television, direct mail and shoppers?

9. Can you explain why there are more morning newspapers than afternoon papers?

10. Identify advantages and disadvantages in the consolidation of newspapers, daily and weekly, into chains and cross-media conglomerates.

11. How have improvements in newspapers led to fewer households taking more than a single newspaper?

FOR FURTHER LEARNING

J. Antonio Alpalhao and Victor Da Rosa. *A Minority in a Changing Society: The Portuguese Communities of Quebec* (University of Ottawa Press, 1980). A case study of the Portuguese community includes an examination of the role of the Portuguese ethnic media in the daily life of the community.

Roland Barthes. "The Photographic Message." In *Image-Music-Text* (Fontana, 1973).

James L. Baughman. *Henry R. Luce and the Rise of the American News Media* (Tawyne, 1987). Baughman, a historian, traces the influence of Luce on the presentation of news in other media through his innovations at *Time* and other magazines.

Bill Bishop. "A Warning from Smithville: Owning Your Own Weekly," *Washington Journalism Review* 10 (May 1988):4, 25–32. Bishop offers a first-person case study on how chains are consolidating the weekly newspaper industry. He deals with the pleasure and pain of publishing an independent rural weekly.

Leo Bogart. *Preserving the Press: How Daily Newspapers Mobilized to Keep Their Readers* (Columbia University Press, 1991). Bogart, a newspaper industry analyst, describes the strengths and weaknesses of newspapers in times of changing technology, reader life-style changes and preferences, and new options for advertisers through other media.

Reginald Bragonier, Jr., and David J. Fisher. *The Mechanics of a Magazine* (Hearst, 1984). This lavishly illustrated book details every facet of the creation of an issue of *Popular Mechanics*.

Walter M. Brasch. *Forerunners of Revolution: Muckrakers and the American Social Conscience* (University of America Press, 1990). Professor Brasch distinguishes muckraking from investigative reporting. Muckrakers, he says, seek to expose misdeeds that undermine the social fabric of society, while investigative reporters focus on abuses of the public trust and schemes that bilk people.

Canada. Royal Commission on Newspapers, 1981. Known as the Kent Commission, this eight-volume report includes an in-depth look at newspapers and journalism in Canada in the early 1980s.

Canada. Senate Special Committee on the Mass Media, *Report*. 3 vols. (Ottawa, 1970). Known as the Davey Committee, this report includes an analysis of newspapers and magazines in Canada in 1970.

J. William Click and Russell N. Baird. *Magazine Editing and Production*, 5th ed. (Wm. C. Brown, 1990). This textbook focuses on the mechanics of producing a magazine.

Ellis Cose. *The Press* (Morrow, 1989). Cose profiles

the *Washington Post;* Times Mirror, owner of the *Los Angeles Times;* the *New York Times;* and the Gannett and Knight-Ridder chains.

Jonathan Curiel. "Gay Newspapers," *Editor & Publisher* 224 (August 3, 1991):32, 14–19. Curiel, a San Francisco *Chronicle* reporter, gives a history of gay newspapers and their growing attractiveness as an advertising medium.

Francis X. Dealy. *The Power and the Money: Inside the Wall Street Journal* (Birch Lane Press, 1993). Dealy, a former Dow Jones employee, claims the *Journal* has gone soft, citing a lack of investigative fervour in the 1980s excesses in American business. Dealy argues that the newspaper missed scandals that would not have escaped its attention in an earlier era.

Peter Desbarats. *Guide to the Canadian News Media* (Harcourt, Brace, Jovanovich, 1990). A thorough examination of newspapers in Canada, from early to contemporary days.

Edwin Diamond. *Behind the Times: Inside the New York Times* (Villard Books, 1994). Diamond, media columnist for *New York* magazine, updates Gay Talese's classic 1969 study of the most prestigious newspaper in the United States.

Robert Draper. *Rolling Stone Magazine: The Uncensored History* (Doubleday, 1990). In this lively and colourful account, Draper is enthusiastic about the early days of the music magazine *Rolling Stone* but less so about its founder, Jann Wenner, and what the magazine has become.

Elizabeth L. Eisenstein. *The Printing Press as an Agent of Change: Communications and Cultural Transformation in Early-Modern Europe,* 2 vols. (Cambridge University Press, 1980). Eisenstein offers a thorough examination of the advent of printing and how it changed even how we see ourselves.

Douglas Fetherling. *The Rise of the Canadian Newspaper* (Oxford University Press, 1990). A good historical look at the press in Canada; includes an analysis of the "party press" in Canada.

Otto Friedrich. *Decline and Fall* (Harper & Row, 1969). Friedrich, a *Saturday Evening Post* editor, details the power struggle that made drama of the magazine's demise.

Douglas H. George. *The Smart Magazines: 50 Years of Literary Revelry and High Jinks at Vanity Fair, the New Yorker, Life, Esquire and the Smart Set.* (Archon Books, 1991). George, an English professor, offers lively, anecdote-laden accounts of magazines whose appeal was giving readers a sense of participation in society's upper crust. The magazines are profiled separately.

The Globe and Mail: 150 Years in Canada. 1994.

Dennis Holder, Robert Love, Bill Meyers and Roger Piantadosi, contributors. "Magazines in the 1980s." *Washington Journalism Review* 3 (November 1981):3, 28–41. Holder's article, "The Decade of Specialization,"

looks at social implications of magazines seeking market niches.

Ernest C. Hynds. *American Newspapers in the 1980s* (Hastings House, 1980). Hynds, a journalism professor, offers a snapshot of all aspects of the newspaper industry.

M. Thomas Inge, ed. *Handbook of American Popular Culture,* 2nd ed. (Greenwood, 1989). Inge includes a thoroughly annotated article on magazines.

Amy Janello and Brennon Jones. *The American Magazine* (Harry N. Abrams, 1991). Janello and Jones focus on magazines as a creative medium, editorially and visually. The book includes essays by magazine people and more than 500 illustrations, including many magazine covers and spreads.

Lauren Kessler. *Against the Grain: The Dissident Press in America* (Sage, 1984). Kessler surveys the newspapers of minority and persecuted groups through U.S. history.

Wilfred Kesterton, "The Growth of the Newspaper in Canada", 1981. In *Communications in Canadian Society,* edited by Benjamin Singer (Addison-Wesley, 1983). Kesterton traces the history of the press in Canada up to the Kent Commission in 1981.

Michael Leapman. *Arrogant Aussie: The Rupert Murdoch Story* (Lyle Stuart, 1985). Leapman, who worked at two newspapers at the time of Murdoch's takeovers, offers an unfriendly portrait of how Murdoch's media empire was built.

A. Kent MacDougall. *The Press: A Critical Look From the Inside* (Dow Jones Books, 1972). In this collection of reprints from the *Wall Street Journal,* MacDougall has included his article on the dark side of trade magazines. The article details trade magazine boosterism of their subjects and pandering to advertisers, rather than journalistic coverage.

Barbara Matusow. "Allen H. Neuharth Today," *Washington Journalism Review* 8 (August 1986):8, 18–24. Media commentator Matusow traces Neuharth's career, quirks and all, to the eve of his retirement as chief executive officer of the Gannett media chain.

Richmond M. McClure. *To the End of Time: The Seduction and Conquest of a Media Empire* (Simon & Schuster, 1992). McClure, a former Time Inc. executive with many inside sources, chronicles the deal-making that merged Henry Luce's Time-Life empire into the Time Warner media conglomerate. Luce's vision was lost in the process, and McClure is not sympathetic.

Al Neuharth. *Confessions of an S.O.B.* (Doubleday, 1989). Neuharth, who created *USA Today,* explains his controversial newspaper management style in this sprightly autobiography.

Alan and Barbara Nourie. *American Mass-Market Magazines* (Greenwood, 1990). The Nouries offer histories of 106 current and defunct consumer magazines.

Andrew M. Osler, "From Vincent Massey to Thomas Kent: The Evolution of National Press Policy in Canada,"

1981. In *Communications in Canadian Society*, edited by Benjamin Singer (Addison-Wesley, 1983). Osler offers an analysis of press policy, or, in hindsight, the lack thereof in Canada.

Theodore Peterson. *Magazines in the Twentieth Century* (University of Illinois Press, 1964).

Sam G. Riley, ed. *Corporate Magazines in the United States* (Greenwood Press, 1992). This is a pioneering attempt at an overview of the publications that corporations produce for free circulation among employees, customers and other groups. The diversity of these publications makes a profile difficult. Sometimes called "public relations magazines," these publications employ many more people than the more visible consumer magazines.

Sam G. Riley and Gary W. Selnow, eds. *Regional Interest Magazines of the United States* (Greenwood Press, 1991). Riley and Selnow profile city and regional magazines, including *Arizona Highways*, *Southern Living*, *Texas Monthly*, *Chicago* and *Philadelphia*.

Edward E. Scharfe. *Worldly Power: The Making of the Wall Street Journal* (Beaufort, 1986). Traces the history of the *Journal* with emphasis on its editorial leadership since World War II.

William Shawcross. *Murdoch* (Simon & Schuster, 1993). Shawcross chronicles the rise of Rupert Murdoch as a global media baron and attempts to explain what motivates the man. Shawcross, a British journalist, relies extensively on interviews with people around Murdoch and Murdoch himself.

Ted Curtis Smythe. "Special Interest Magazines: Wave of the Future or Undertow." In Michael Emery and Smythe. *Readings in Mass Communication*, 6th ed. (Wm. C. Brown, 1986). Smythe examines trends in the magazine industry.

James D. Squires. *Read All About It! The Corporate Takeover of America's Newspapers* (Times Books, 1993). Squires, a former *Chicago Tribune* executive, makes a case that newspaper managers are preoccupied with advertising and profits. As a result, the traditional separation of advertising and news staffs has been eroded, which in turn has led to news coverage that is compromised by newspapers' financial interests.

Jim Strader. "Black on Black," *Washington Journalism Review* 14 (March 1992):2, 33–36. Strader, a Pittsburgh reporter, discusses the decline of national black newspapers and their hopes to beef up local coverage to restore their influence.

W. A. Swanberg. *Luce and His Empire* (Scribners, 1972). Swanberg, a biographer of major journalists, is at his best with Henry Luce of Time-Life.

William H. Taft. *American Magazines for the 1980s* (Hastings House, 1982). In this overview, Professor Taft describes the American magazine industry and trends at the start of the 1980s.

John Tebbel. *A History of Book Publishing in the United States*, Vols. 1–3 (R. R. Bowker, 1972–1977).

John Tebbel and Mary Ellen Zuckerman. *The Magazine in America, 1741–1990* (Oxford University Press, 1991). Tebbel and Zuckerman provide a great amount of information, much of it colourful, on the evolution of magazines in the United States. They make the case that magazines have been a major shaper of American life.

Times Mirror Center for The People and The Press. *The Age of Indifference* (Times Mirror Company, 1990). This major study found that young people have significantly less interest in news than the generations before them. They read fewer newspapers and watch less news on television.

David S. Thomson, "Worlds Shaped by Words." In *Human Behavior: Language*. (Winthrop, 1974). A good, readable explanation of the Sapir-Whorf hypothesis and its implications for modern society.

Eric Utne. "Tina's *New Yorker*." *Columbia Journalism Review* 31 (March/April 1993):6, 31–37. Utne, a self-described magazine junkie, is far from convinced that the commercial-driven changes that Tina Brown is bringing to the *New Yorker* are making a better magazine.

Benjamin Lee Whorf, "The Relation of Habitual Thought and Behaviour to Language." In *Language, Culture and Society*, edited by Ben Blount (Winthrop, 1974). The Sapir-Whorf hypothesis from one of its originators.

FOR KEEPING UP TO DATE

CARD (Canadian Advertising Rates and Data) is a listing of newspapers and magazines published in Canada. It includes circulation data and current ad rates.

Editor & Publisher is a weekly trade journal for the newspaper industry.

Folio is a trade journal on magazine management. Among major newspapers that track magazine issues in a fairly consistent way are the *New York Times*, the *Wall Street Journal* and *USA Today*.

NewsInc. is a monthly trade journal on newspaper management.

Newspaper Research Journal is a quarterly dealing mostly with applied research.

Presstime is published monthly by the American Newspaper Publisher's Association.

Publisher's Weekly is the trade journal of the book industry.

Many general interest magazines, like *Maclean's*, cover print media issues on a regular basis.

CHAPTER 3

SOUND RECORDINGS
Spinning the Music

Recorded music is important because it evokes human emotions

Sound reproduction has shifted from mechanical to electromagnetic to digital forms

Music videos have revitalized the sagging recording industry

Several new formats and megadeals with performers are risky for the recording industry

The glitz and glamour of the recording industry mask serious business enterprise

The recording industry depends on radio to promote new music

Six companies dominate the record business, which critics say works against innovation

Payola, censorship and home dubbing are continuing critical issues for the recording industry

MEDIA IN THEORY

Analysis of Canadian Content

Since 1970 the CRTC has required that Canadian radio stations play 30 percent Canadian content between the hours of 6 a.m. and midnight. However, the system is not without its problems. At first, there was not much Canadian content to play. Canadian production houses and distribution networks simply did not exist. The Canadian musical talent might have been there, but it was hard to fight the machinery of large U.S. record distributors. While some good Canadian singers and groups emerged in the early 1970s, Canadian music was difficult to find at the time. As a result, some Canadian recordings were compared unfavourably with American ones. The resulting myth that Canadian music wasn't as good as

American music plagued this country's artists for several years. Canadian music has only recently been able to escape this negative mythology.

Adding to this negative myth about Canadian music, certain broadcasters played little Canadian content during the day, instead choosing to "bury" it after 10 p.m. on weeknights and early in the morning on weekends when fewer people listened to the radio. The 30 percent CanCon requirement was not consistently measured at all times of the day; CanCon was calculated as a portion of the station's weekly playlist. As a result fewer Canadian songs were played during rush-hour periods when people were driving to or from work. This practice was also reported in 1994, following a two-year study of FM radio stations sponsored by SOCAN and CIRPA (the Canadian Independent Record Production Association). In its report, the task force found that during morning drive times only 18 percent of music was Canadian, while Canadian music accounted for 26 percent of the music played during the corresponding afternoon period.

While the system seems to favour Canadian artists, it can also discriminate against Canadian singers. Songs by America, Jennifer Warnes, Joe Cocker and Rod Stewart are considered CanCon because these singers recorded songs written by Canadians. The recent Bryan Adams controversy is a good example of discrimination against Canadian singers. His song from *Robin Hood: Prince of Thieves* "Everything I Do, I Do It For You," and other songs on his album *Waking Up the Neighbours* were not considered Canadian content because he co-wrote them with a British songwriter. Due to the controversy that ensued from this classification, the CRTC amended the MAPL formula to allow for Canadian songwriters to collaborate with foreigners. This amendment only applied to songs recorded after September 1991. The song from *Robin Hood: Prince of Thieves* was released in early 1991 and thus still does not qualify as CanCon.

Have the Canadian content regulations worked? The regulations had two general objectives: to promote Canadian culture and to help stregthen the Canadian music industry. Given the rise in popularity of Canadian artists and songs in the 1990s, one could easily argue that the music industry is stronger today than it was in 1970. As for promoting Canadian culture, since music and lyrics (as signs) signify something other than themselves, one might ask, What does the lyrical content of "CanCon" say about Canadian culture?

An examination of songs that reached number one on the CHUM chart for a 13-year period before and a 13-year period after the implementation of the CanCon regulations might help answer these questions. The survey reveals that 13 Canadian songs reached number one between 1957 and 1969, while between 1970 and 1982, there were 19 number-one Canadian songs. On the surface, this seems to show that the regulations were successful in promoting Canadian talent and the music industry as six more Canadian songs reached number one. But a closer analysis of the songs shows that these songs had few Canadian signifiers in the lyrics.

During the period before the regulations, 1957 to 1969, at least four of the Canadian songs that reached number one were recorded by Americans. They included: "It Doesn't Matter Anymore," written by Paul Anka and recorded by Buddy Holly; "Love Child," written by Canadian R. Dean Taylor and recorded by Diana Ross and the Supremes; "Aquarius" and "Let the Sun Shine In" written by a trio of songwriters from Montreal and recorded by the Fifth Dimension; and "Sugar, Sugar," written by Andy Kim and sung by the Archies. These songs undoubtedly helped Canadian songwriters to make money, but their lyrics say little, if anything, about Canada. In essence they are American songs, written for the U.S. market.

In addition, two of the number-one Canadian songs were included on American movie soundtracks. For example, "Born to Be Wild" by Steppenwolf was featured in the film *Easy Rider*, while "One Tin Soldier" by The Original Caste was used in the movie *Billy Jack*. These songs did little to promote Canadian culture. If anything, they promoted the American myths of the biker and the cowboy all the while disguised as Canadian content by CRTC regulations.

Several other songs written by Canadians reflected American or British values instead of mirroring Canadian culture. Examples include "Diana" by Paul Anka, "My True Love" by Jack Scott, "Which Way You Goin' Billy?" by the Poppy Family and "Charlena" by Richie Knight and the Mid-Knights. Two singles were hits in Toronto: "Gaslight" by the Ugly Ducklings and "Cornflakes and Ice Cream" by the Lords of London. These groups were popular in Yorkville and their success was reflected in the musical charts. Still, these songs, like the others above, said nothing about Canada or Canadian culture.

The only Canadian song to reach number one that was explicitly about Canada was the novelty song

"Clear the Track, Here Comes Shack" by Douglas Rankine and the Secrets. The song was a tribute to Eddie Shack, a hockey player for the Toronto Maple Leafs.

After the Canadian content regulations came into effect in 1970, the number of Canadian number-one singles on the CHUM charts increased from 13 to 19. However, the same patterns that had existed before the CanCon regulations came into effect were still evident: American artists continued to record songs written by Canadians. For example, "Puppy Love," recorded by Donny Osmond, and "She's a Lady," sung by Tom Jones, were written by Paul Anka. "Woodstock," which was about the mythic American music festival, was written by Joni Mitchell and recorded by Crosby, Stills, Nash and Young. Meanwhile, the "Theme from S.W.A.T.," by the T.H.P. Orchestra was the theme music to the American television program of the same name. Perhaps only two number-one Canadian singles in Canada during this period were openly nationalistic. The first was "American Woman" (which also reached number one in the United States) by the Guess Who. Appropriately, the band had dubbed itself the Guess Who in 1965 to avoid facing prejudice against Canadian artists by Canadian radio stations. The song's lyrics made clear distinctions between Canadian and American culture. The other uniquely Canadian number-one single was "Take Off" by Bob and Doug Mackenzie (SCTV comics Rick Moranis and Dave Thomas).

However, like "Clear the Track, Here Comes Shack," this brand of nationalism was humorous in nature and perhaps reached number-one status due to its novelty.

Other songs that reached number one during this period were mainly nondescript American-style songs. They included: "As Years Go By" by Mashmakan, Ocean's "Put Your Hand in the Hand," R. Dean Taylor's "Gotta See Jane," "Sweet City Woman" by The Stampeders, The Bells' "Stay Awhile," Neil Young's "Heart of Gold," "Heartbeat, It's a Lovebeat" by the DeFranco Family, "Last Song" by Edward Bear, "Seasons in the Sun" by Terry Jacks, Rush's "New World Man," and three number-one songs by Bachman Turner Overdrive—"Taking Care of Business," "You Ain't Seen Nothing Yet" and "Hey You." Still, none of these songs were distinctly Canadian. As before 1970, they were clearly variations on American pop music.

The lyrics of several Canadian songs have contained Canadian signifiers. See if you can decode the Canadian references in songs like:

- "Down by the Henry Moore" by Murray McLauchlan
- "Wheat Kings" by The Tragically Hip
- "Running Back to Saskatoon" by the Guess Who
- "Locked in the Trunk of a Car" by The Pursuit of Happiness
- "The Wreck of the Edmund Fitzgerald" by Gordon Lightfoot.

RECORDED MUSIC AS A SOCIAL FORCE

STUDY PREVIEW Culturally, the words and music of a song signify something outside of themselves. In other words, symbolically, a song can become greater than the sum of its parts. Music is a potent form of human expression that can mobilize hearts and minds. Think about the effects of hymns and anthems, martial music and love songs. For better or worse, these powerful effects are magnified by the technology of sound recording.

RALLYING POWER

Released in 1984, "We Are the World" right away was the fastest-climbing record of the decade. Four million copies were sold within six weeks. Profits from the record, produced by big-name entertainers who volunteered, went to the USA for Africa project. The marketplace success paled, however, next to the social impact. The record's message of the oneness of humankind inspired one of the most massive outpouring of donations in history. Americans pumped $20 million into USA for Africa in the first six weeks the record was out. Within six months, $50 million in medical and financial support was en route to drought-stricken parts of Africa. "We Are the World," a single song, had directly saved lives. Canadian artists formed Northern Lights and recorded "Tears Are Not Enough" in the spring of 1985.

The power of recorded music is not a recent phenomenon. In World War I, "Over There" and other records reflected an enthusiasm for American involvement in the war. Composers who felt strongly about the Vietnam war wrote songs that put their views on vinyl. "The Green Berets" cast American soldiers in a heroic vein, "An Okie From Muskogee" glorified blind patriotism, and there were antiwar songs, dozens of them. "American Woman" by The Guess Who symbolized Canada's stormy relationship with the U.S., while Joni Mitchell's "Big Yellow Taxi" was environmentally conscious long before that became the norm.

Political speech writers know the political value of tapping into popular music. It was no accident in the 1992 primaries when George Bush paraphrased a Nitty Gritty Dirt Band song to a New Hampshire crowd: "If you want to see a rainbow, you've got to stand a little rain." In his state-of-the-union message, the president borrowed from Paul Simon's "Boy in the Bubble" to make a point on the economy: "If this age of miracles and wonders has taught us anything, it's that if we can change the world, we can change America." At his inauguration, Bill Clinton used Fleetwood Mac's "Don't Stop" to symbolize hope for the future.

In short, music has tremendous effects on human beings, and the technology of sound recording amplifies these effects. The bugle boy was essential to Company B in earlier times, but today reveille is on tape to wake the troops. Mothers still sing Brahms's lullaby, but more babies probably are lulled to sleep by Brahms on tape. For romance, lovers today lean more on recorded music than their own vocal cords. The technology of sound recording gives composers, lyricists and performers far larger audiences than would ever be possible through live performances.

BRINGING ABOUT CHANGE

Besides explicit advocacy and its immediate, obvious effects, recorded music can have a subtle impact on the course of human events. *Elvis Presley*, "the white boy who sang coloured," hardly realized in the mid-1950s that his music was helping pave the way for American racial integration. It was the black roots of much of Presley's music, as well as his suggestive gyrations, that made him such a controversial performer. Whatever the fuss, white teenagers liked the music, and it blazed a trail for many black singers who became popular beyond the black community. A major black influence entered mainstream culture. There also was a hillbilly element in early rock, bringing the concerns and issues of poor, rural whites— another oppressed, neglected minority—into the mainstream consciousness. Nashville ceased to be an American cultural ghetto.

REFLECTION OF CHANGING VALUES

While recorded music has the power to move people to war and peace, to love and to sleep, it also reflects changing human values. In 1991, as troops were massing at the Persian Gulf to reclaim Kuwait, American record-makers issued music that reflected public enthusiasm for the war. Arista records put Whitney Houston's Super Bowl version of "The Star-Spangled Banner" on a single, which sold 750 000 audio copies in only eight days. It was the fastest selling single in Arista's history. In addition, Arista sold more than 100 000 videos. Boston Dawn's remake of the Shirelles' oldie "Soldier Boy," expressing a woman's love for her soldier overseas, included some rap lines from the soldier. It was very much a song of the times, and the record company, American Sound, had 25 000 back orders for the record almost as soon as it was released.

The Persian Gulf war also had protest music, of a sort. The Rolling Stones's "Highwire," a single issued two weeks ahead of the U.S.-led ground war in Iraq, blamed the war on the industrialized world's greed for oil. Even the protest music was largely in sync with mainstream American opinion. In "Highwire," for example, the chorus was in the background singing support for the troops as Mick Jagger attacked the war. When "Highwire" was included in an album released a month after the coalition victory, it went mostly unnoticed in the public's war euphoria.

SOUND RECORDING TECHNOLOGY

STUDY PREVIEW   The recording industry, as with all mass media, has been built on technological advances and break-throughs, beginning with Thomas Edison's mechanical phonograph. Today, the technology is all electrical and digital.

VIBRATION-SENSITIVE RECORDING

For years scientific journals had speculated on ways to reproduce sound, but not until 1877 did anyone build a machine that could do it. That was when inventor *Thomas Edison* applied for a patent for a talking machine. He used the trade name *Phonograph*, which was taken from Greek words meaning "to write sound."

The heart of Edison's invention was a cylinder wrapped in tin foil. The cylinder was rotated as a singer shouted into a large metal funnel. The funnel channeled the voice against a diaphragm, which fluttered to the vibrations. A *stylus*, which most people called a "needle," was connected to the diaphragm and cut a groove in the foil, the depth of the groove reflecting the vibrations. To listen to a recording,

Thomas Edison. Prolific inventor Thomas Edison devised a machine that took sound waves and etched them into grooves on a foil drum. When the drum was put on a replacing mechanism and rotated, you could hear the recorded sound. Edison's *Phonograph,* as he called it, was never a commercial success because his recordings could not be duplicated. It was a later inventor, Emile Berliner, who found a way to mass produce recorded music in Montreal.

you put the cylinder on a player and set a needle in the groove that had been created in the recording process. Then you placed your ear to a megaphone-like horn and rotated the cylinder. The needle tracked the groove, and the vibrations created by the varying depths of the groove were fed through the horn.

Edison's system contained a major impediment to commercial success: a recording could not be duplicated. In 1887 *Emile Berliner* introduced a breakthrough in Montreal. Rather than recording on a cylinder covered with flimsy foil, as Edison did, Berliner used a sturdy metal disc. From the metal disc, Berliner made a mold and then poured a thermoplastic material into the mold. When the material hardened, Berliner had a near-perfect copy of the original disc—and he could make hundreds of them. Berliner's system, called the *gramophone*, led to mass production. His company, the Berliner Gramophone Company, began to produce and market sound recordings in Canada.

ELECTROMAGNETIC RECORDING

In the 1920s, the Columbia and Victor record companies introduced records based on an electrical system perfected by *Joseph Maxwell* of Bell Laboratories. Metal funnels were replaced by microphones, which had superior sensitivity. For listening, it was no longer a matter of putting an ear to a mechanical amplifying horn that had only a narrow frequency response. Instead, loudspeakers amplified the sound electromagnetically.

Magnetic tape was developed in Germany and used to broadcast propaganda in World War II. In 1945 American troops brought the German technology home with them. Ampex began building recording and playback machines. The 3M Company perfected tape. Recording companies shifted from discs to magnetic tape to record master discs. An advantage of tape was that bobbles could be edited out. Creative editing became possible.

Early Mechanical Recording. Band music was popular in the early days of sound recording. Brass sounds picked up well on the primitive mechanical recording equipment. In recording's early days, John Philip Sousa recorded hundreds of cylinders because the technology did not permit duplicating copies from masters. Each cylinder sold to a customer was an original. Some recording studios had up to 10 recording horns—which allowed 10 cylinders to be made at once. Still, recording was time-consuming.

While magnetic tape suggested the possibility of long-playing records, the industry continued to use brittle shellac discs that revolved 78 times a minute. One problem with the 10-inch 78-rpm disc was that it could accommodate only three to four minutes of sound on a side.

VINYL RECORDS AND MICROGROOVES

One day *Peter Goldmark*, chief engineer at Columbia Records, was listening to a 78-rpm recording of Brahms's Second Piano Concerto, Arturo Toscanini conducting. The concerto was divided onto six discs, 12 sides. Fed up with flipping discs, Goldmark got out his pencil and calculated whether a slower spin and narrower grooves could get the whole concerto on one disc. It was possible, although it would take both sides. At least the break could come between movements.

In 1948 Goldmark's long-playing record was introduced. Each side had 240 *microgrooves* per inch and contained up to 25 minutes of music. Offering several advantages, LPs soon replaced the 78-rpm record. Not only did each record have more music, but also the sound was better. The records were of vinyl plastic, which meant less hissing and scratching than shellac records. Also, vinyl discs were harder to break than the brittle 78s.

Refusing to be upstaged, RCA, which earlier had dabbled unsuccessfully with 33⅓-rpm records, introduced extended-play records called EPs. They were small 45-rpm discs with a large spindle. Thus was launched the *battle of the speeds*, which pitted RCA and Columbia against each other. RCA, which manufactured phonographs, included only 78-rpm and 45-rpm speeds on its machines—no 33⅓-rpm. The battle was costly. Unsure which would prevail, the public hesitated to buy phonographs and records. Record sales slumped.

A truce came, finally, when conductor Arturo Toscanini took RCA boss *David Sarnoff* aside and pointed out the obvious—that Brahms's Second Piano Concerto could not fit even on two sides of an RCA 45-rpm disc. Toscanini convinced Sarnoff to add a 33⅓ speed to RCA phonographs for classical music. The 45-rpm disc, meanwhile, became the standard for pop music, with one song on each side. Discs sold for a dollar, within the means of the teenagers who ushered in the rock 'n' roll era in the 1950s.

THE STEREO AND DIGITAL REVOLUTIONS

Technical progress until the late 1970s produced nothing as revolutionary as the microgroove, but the improvements, taken all together, made for dramatically better sound. Anyone who has grown up with Tom Cochrane would hardly believe that record-buyers accepted the sound quality of Bill Haley records only 30 years earlier. Better fidelity, called high fidelity, or *hi-fi*, was introduced in the early 1950s. The full audio range of the human ear could be delivered to listeners exactly as it was recorded. *Stereo* came in 1961. Multiple microphones recorded on separate tracks. Records played the sound back through two speakers, simulating the way people hear—through their left and their right ears. Consumers went for the new quality. FM stereo radio was introduced about the same time.

Except for tapes, Edison's 1877 technology, refined by Maxwell half a century later, was at the heart of sound recording for 101 years. The technology was called *analog recording* because it converted the waves that were physically engraved in the grooves of the record into electrical pulses that coincided analogously with the waves in the grooves. It worked this way:

- As the record rotated, a stylus suspended from an arm over the record tracked waves embedded in the grooves.
- A gizmo called a *transducer*, located in the arm, converted the physical energy created by the stylus moving through the grooves into electrical energy.
- The resulting electrical pulses moved through an *amplifier* and then to a loud-speaker.
- The *loudspeaker* converted the pulses back into physical energy, which took the form of sound waves moving through the air.

Record-makers developed a technological revolution in 1978: the *digital recording.* No longer were continuous sound waves inscribed physically on a disc. Instead, sound waves were captured at millisecond intervals, and each wave was logged in computer language as an isolated on-off binary number. When discs were played back, the digits were translated back to the sound at the same millisecond intervals they were recorded. The intervals would be replayed so fast that the sound would seem continuous, just as the individual frames in a motion picture become a moving blur that is perceived by the eye as continuous motion.

By 1983 digital recordings were available to consumers in the form of *compact discs*, silvery 4.7-inch platters. The binary numbers were pits on the disc that were read by a laser light in the latest version of the phonograph: the *CD player.* The player itself converted the numbers to sound.

Each disc could carry 70 minutes of uninterrupted sound, more than Peter Goldmark dared dream. Consumers raved about the purity. Some critics argued, however, that there was a sterility in digital recording. The sound was too perfect, they said. Instead of reproducing performances, said the critics, compact discs produced a quality more perfect than a performance. Traditional audiophiles had sought to reproduce live music perfectly, not to create a perfection that could never be heard in a live performance.

BUMPY ECONOMIC PROGRESS

STUDY PREVIEW If a single word could describe the economic history of the record industry, it would be "volatile." In the beginning, there was a struggle to determine whether recorded sound could even turn a profit. Booms were spectacular, but not even the industry giants like RCA and Columbia escaped the bad times.

FINDING A MARKET

At first, nobody realized the economic potential of sound recordings. When Thomas Edison's hand-cranked phonograph was taken on tour, it attracted attention on the vaudeville circuit and in lecture halls, but not even the inventive and entrepreneurial Edison foresaw its home entertainment possibilities.

Seeking commercial applications, entrepreneur *Jesse Lippincott* bought the Edison and a passel of other phonograph patents in 1888 and formed the *Columbia Phonograph Co.* Times were tough, and Lippincott almost went under. At a crucial moment an aide suggested installing phonographs at arcades and charging people who wanted to listen. At a nickel a song, Lippincott was rescued. The nickelodeons whetted consumer interest. Eventually sales picked up.

Emile Berliner went into business with his superior disc technology. The sound was better than cylinders, and discs were far easier to store. In 1896 the Berliner gramophone and some other patents were combined in a commercial venture, the *Victor Talking Machine Co.*, which aimed at a home entertainment market and eventually became RCA. In time, Columbia abandoned cylinders and introduced its own disc machine.

BOOM AND BUST

The recording business received a big boost in 1913 when a dance craze hit North America. Then World War I songs became popular, further fueling demand. Record production, 27 million discs in 1914, quadrupled to 107 million in 1919. The boom continued into the early 1920s, but in 1924 sales of records and record players dropped 50 percent as a mushrooming number of radio stations drew customers away from records.

Then came the 1929 stock market crash. The *jukebox* helped keep the recording industry going through the difficult 1930s. The machines were installed in restaurants, saloons and soda fountains. By 1940 jukeboxes were taking nickels throughout the land. Jukeboxes kept the public interested in recorded music.

THE ROCK 'N' ROLL JOLT

When shellac was scarce during World War II, the major record-makers gave up the small black rhythm 'n' blues market. After the war, these major companies expected big profits from contracts with proven performers like Bing Crosby and Frank Sinatra. When rock 'n' roll came along in the 1950s, the major record-makers ignored it as a momentary flash. How wrong they were. Almost overnight, the small companies were swamped with orders. The Sun label, now almost forgotten, put out such enduring stars as Elvis Presley, Roy Orbison, Johnny Cash and Carl Perkins. From 1955 to 1957 the number of records on the trade journal *Billboard*'s Top 10 charts from independent companies quintupled from 8 to 40.

Even though they were losing market share, the major record-makers were slow to respond. In one cautious reaction, they issued toned-down remakes of rock 'n' roll songs that were catching on, a practice they called *covering*. As profits plummeted, they tightened their business practices. They streamlined their systems for getting records to customers. Some formed music publishing companies. Some even bought retail outlets. The result was that their music passed through fewer hands to get to market. Fewer intermediaries meant more profits.

Despite their success, the scrappy independents had relatively small repertoires and lacked the resources to put together competitive distribution systems. One at a time, as the major recordmakers realized that rock 'n' roll was here to stay, the independents sold out to them. Giant Warner, for example, first bought independents Atlantic and Reprise, and then Elektra, another independent, was merged into the company. These acquisitions and mergers shaped today's recording industry, which is dominated by a handful of giant companies.

The emergence of rock 'n' roll, from Bill Haley and the Comets to Elvis Presley and then the Beatles, pushed the record industry to unprecedented profitability. Record sales outpaced even movies by the mid-1970s.

The King. Exuberant fans welcome Elvis Presley at a 1956 outdoor concert in his hometown of Tupelo, Mississippi. Elvis was among early rockabillies who blended black rhythm 'n' blues with rural, white grassroots music to form what became a social force. The new rock 'n' roll fueled a period of fantastic growth in the record industry.

ROCK 'N' ROLL IN CANADA

While Rock 'n' Roll is an American musical genre, many Canadians have been successful rock 'n' rollers. *Paul Anka* is the most obvious Canadian success story. His good looks, combined with his singing and songwriting abilities, brought him success not only at home, but in the United States. "Diana," "Lonely Boy," "Put Your Head on my Shoulder" and "Puppy Love" all reached the Top 10 in both countries. Other artists also recorded Anka's material, including Buddy Holly, who recorded "It Doesn't Matter Anymore," and Elvis, whose "My Way" was co-written by Anka.

Anka wasn't alone in having success south of the border. The Guess Who, led by Burton Cummings and Randy Bachman, reached the top of the charts in both countries with "These Eyes," "Undun," and, of course, "American Woman." Bachman's success in the United States continued when he left The Guess Who and formed Bachman Turner Overdrive, which reached number one with "You Ain't Seen Nothin' Yet." Throughout the 60s, 70s and 80s, Canadians like Anne Murray, Gordon Lightfoot, Rush, Neil Young, Blood, Sweat and Tears (led by Canadian David Clayton Thomas), The Four Lads, Joni Mitchell, The Diamonds, The Crew Cuts and others became pop music stars in the U.S. In the 90s, Bryan Adams, Shania Twain and Alanis Morrisette continue the Canadian assault across the border. Morrisette's album "Jagged Little Pill" has sold more copies than that of any other female artist in history.

Within Canada, there have been other success stories. While not achieving much fame in the U.S., several singers and groups were popular in Canada. For example, Thunder Bay, Ontario's Bobby Curtola, who never reached Billboard's Top 40, had nine Top 10 records and 16 Top 40 records in Canada. Pretty amazing when you realize that Curtola wasn't with a major record label. While on tour, he used to sell records and memorabilia out of the trunk of his car. He was also the first Canadian artist to record a commercial jingle (it was for Coca-Cola). Other artists who succeeded at home during this period include The Beau-Marks, The Five-Man Electrical Band, Trooper, Kim Mitchell, Lighthouse, The Bells, Chilliwack, Ian Thomas and Murray McLauchlan. During the 1990s, Jann Arden, Sloan, Sarah McLachlan, Colin James, Bare Naked Ladies and The Tragically Hip developed loyal followings in Canada, but had limited success in the U.S.

THE JUNO AWARDS

The year 1996 marked the 25th Anniversary of the *Juno Awards*. The awards were named after *Pierre Juneau*, who was head of the CRTC when the Canadian content regulations were implemented. The idea of honouring the Canadian music industry came from *Walt Grealis* and *Stan Klees*, who publish *RPM* Magazine, a music industry trade journal. The Junos have been televised by the CBC since 1975.

Every year in October, nomination forms are sent to members of the Canadian Association of Recording Arts and Sciences (CARAS) asking for nominations in a number of categories. The winners are chosen in different ways:

- The Entertainer of the Year nominees are selected by CARAS; the winner is chosen by the public.
- The Best-Selling Albums (Francophone, foreign and domestic) are determined by sales.
- Nominees for Single of the Year are based on chart success, but CARAS members vote in order to select the winner.
- The nominations for the categories Album of the Year, Female Vocalist of the Year, Male Vocalist of the Year and Group of the Year are determined by sales.

The winner is selected after a vote by CARAS members.

In January of each year, the nominees are announced and ballots are sent to CARAS members. The firm KPMG Peat Marwick Thorne tabulates the results and keeps them confidential until the Junos are presented in the spring.

Each year at the Junos, a Canadian is inducted into the Canadian Music Hall of Fame. The list is a Who's Who of Canadian music:

1978: Oscar Peterson and Guy Lombardo
1979: Hank Snow
1980: Paul Anka
1981: Joni Mitchell
1982: Neil Young
1983: Glenn Gould
1984: The Crew Cuts, The Diamonds and The Four Lads
1985: Wilf Carter
1986: Gordon Lightfoot
1987: The Guess Who
1988: The Band
1989: Maureen Forrester
1990: Leonard Cohen

The Juno Awards. The Junos have signified excellence in the Canadian music industry since 1971.

1991: Ian and Sylvia
1992: Anne Murray
1993: Rush
1994: Buffy St. Marie
1995: David Clayton Thomas, Denny Doherty, John Kay,
            Domenic Troiano and Zal Yanovsky

HORRIFIC 1979

Record companies released extraordinary hits in the late 1970s. The "Rumours" album by Fleetwood Mac sold 13 million copies. The "Saturday Night Fever" and "Grease" soundtracks did spectacularly. While things looked good on the surface, there was a big problem. Except for the megahits, sales were flat—a fact masked by the big sellers and a $1-per-album price hike.

The year 1979 produced no megahits. Worse, sales were off because teenagers were plugging quarters into video games, not saving them to buy records. At the same time, an oil shortage sparked huge increases in the price of petroleum, a raw material used in record manufacturing. The industry's problems went even deeper. Wrongly assuming that their earlier spectacular growth would continue, the companies had overexpanded. With sales down and manufacturing costs rising, the industry had no choice but to scale back. Here is how the industry retrenched:

- **Layoffs.** Record companies laid off an estimated 5000 people.
- **Contracts.** Lavish long-term contracts like Stevie Wonder's $13 million and Elton John's $8 million deals became rarer.
- **Focused marketing.** Fewer records were released. In lusher times, the companies put out a lot of new recordings, knowing that most would flop. The idea, called the *buckshot philosophy*, was to throw dozens of releases "up against the wall to see which stuck." Not anymore. By 1984 record-makers had halved the number of releases.
- **Fewer artists.** The number of artists under contract was reduced, which allowed companies to focus reduced resources on their remaining artists.
- **Inventories.** Companies reduced their inventory in the distribution chain. Retailers could no longer return any unsold records they had ordered.

Leaner, the industry survived to rise again.

RESURGENCE IN THE 1980s

Promotional and technical innovations led a record industry revival that cannonballed through the 1980s. By 1990 record-buyers were shelling out billions of dollars a year for recorded music. The key factors were music videos and digital technology.

MUSIC VIDEOS.   Because strictly regulated European radio does not play much pop music, record-makers there needed to be especially innovative in promoting new music. In the 1970s, seeking new ways to interest young people in their products, European record companies created videos that featured recording artists acting out their music. Dance clubs played the videos, and record sales picked up. American record-makers, desperate to reverse slumping sales, borrowed the idea and made videos available to cable television channels to play between movies. The videos developed a following.

In 1981 the Warner media conglomerate, whose divisions included Warner records, gambled that a full-time music video cable channel would attract enough viewers to interest advertisers and make money, while simultaneously promoting records. At first there were doubters, but by 1984 the *Music Television Channel, MTV* for short, claimed 24 million viewers, more than any other cable channel. Warner was right too about a correlation between music videos on television and record sales. The MTV audience was mostly teenagers and young adults, the same people who buy most records. It was no surprise when surveys found that almost three out of four record-buyers reported that MTV influenced their choices at the record shop.

In Canada, *MuchMusic* was launched in August of 1984. Like MTV, it is also a success story. Surveys indicate that 42 percent of teens and 41 percent of young adults (18 to 25) tune into MuchMusic at least once a week. Since its inception, MuchMusic and Quebec's MusiquePlus, have expanded to include MuchUSA, Argentina's MuchaMusica and Jyrki, a 90-minute after school show in Finland, patterned after the conventions of MuchMusic.

DIGITAL TECHNOLOGY.   The record industry gave itself another shot in the arm in the 1980s by switching to compact disc digital playback equipment and software. The quality of CD sound attracted attention, and many people began replacing their tape and record collections with CDs. By the mid-1980s, the record industry was clearly out of its slump.

UNCERTAINTIES AHEAD

STUDY PREVIEW New digital disc and tape formats, introduced in the 1990s, are intended to spur hardware and software sales, but doubters fear that consumers might hold off buying music until one or two formats emerge as dominant. There is concern too that the industry might again be overextending itself with megabuck deals with performers.

NEW DISC AND TAPE FORMATS

By 1992 only a few tiny, obscure record companies were still pressing vinyl discs, and most record shops had given up stocking 33⅓ LPs. The transition to digital technology, however, had just begun. The Japanese manufacturers next introduced digital audio tape (DAT) playback machines. DAT had the clarity of the CD with the additional feature of a dubbing capacity. Compact discs had been designed for listening only. With DAT, people could record as well as listen. It seemed at first that the process of people replacing their music collections with a new format would repeat itself, again bolstering sales not only of recordings but also the equipment to play them. In their first year on the market, however, DAT machines were bought by only 30 000 people, less than one-third of the manufacturers' expectation. The expanded variety of formats had given too many choices to consumers, reminiscent of the RCA-CBS battle of the speeds in the late 1940s when people put off purchasing phonographs and records rather than be stuck with an orphaned format. Again, people were sitting out the "war" to see who would win.

The format confusion worsened in 1995 when playback manufacturers expanded the options. Besides CDs and DATs, there suddenly was Philips's DCC, short for *digital compact cassette*, which lacked DAT's audio range but which could play both digital and ordinary tapes. Sony simultaneously introduced *Mini Disc* (MD), a small 2½-inch CD onto which 70 minutes of music could be crammed, albeit with some quality loss. The MD was the logical successor to Sony's portable Walkman, which played only traditional tapes. Just as in the LP versus the EP war between CBS and RCA, the new 1990s competition was taking form as a war to the finish. On its side, Philips lined up fellow hardware manufacturer Matsushita and the Radio Shack retail chain, and it sent the rock group Dire Straits on a 300-city global tour to promote DCCs. As both a music software and hardware company, Philips had plenty of muscle to push DCCs in both audio equipment stores and record stores. On behalf of MDs, Sony had the muscle not only in its traditional strength and hardware, but also in its 1988 acquisition of CBS Records, itself a major force in music software.

PERFORMER MEGADEALS

Big star megadeals became the fashion again in the 1990s, despite the experience of 1979 when the bottom fell out of the music business and record companies found themselves locked into extravagant commitments. Michael Jackson signed a long-term deal with Sony in 1991 for $65 million, five times more than Stevie Wonder's deal that typified the record industry's earlier overextension. Sony guaranteed Jackson not only $65 million but also a 50-50 split on profits. Next, Time Warner inked a similar 50-50 deal with Madonna, with her guarantee reported to be $75 million, a new benchmark. Among groups, the heavyweight hard-rock Aerosmith's $50 million deal with Sony eclipsed a $28 million Rolling Stones contract.

The scale of the new megadeals reflected the corporate mergers that were consolidating the mass media into the hands of fewer but bigger companies. Sony had

The Fab Four. The Beatles from Liverpool, England, as they appeared on Ed Sullivan's television show in New York in the 1960s.

just bought CBS Records and Columbia Pictures and was eager to lock up proven talent like Michael Jackson for its new software enterprises. With Sony flashing so much cash, the newly created Time Warner media conglomerate felt it had little choice but to sweeten its deal with Madonna to keep her from straying. The contract kept Madonna on Sire records and in Warner films. Her percentage of the retail price of recordings went from 18 to 30 percent.

With the biggest names under long-term agreements, the record companies eased away from megadeals in the mid-1990s. There was also the experience of Michael Jackson's problems, with both Sony and Jackson backing off from several of their anticipated projects.

MAKING AND SELLING RECORDS

STUDY PREVIEW   Record companies spend a lot of energy on the glitzy aspects of their business, including celebrity artists, but much more is involved in bringing recorded music to market.

ARTISTS AND REPERTOIRES

Record companies have *A&R*, short for *artist and repertoire departments*, to work with stars. Before rock 'n' roll, A&R people signed new artists and even arranged their music and supervised recording sessions. They nurtured performing styles, worked on grooming and wardrobe to make a performer saleable, arranged interviews and worried about things like overexposing their stars. In his book *Solid Gold*,

Serge Denisoff quotes a former Capitol executive about how the A&R system once worked: "The company would pick out 12 songs for Peggy Lee and tell her to be at the studio Wednesday at 8, and she'd show up and sing what you told her. And she'd leave three hours later and Capitol'd take her songs and do anything it wanted with them. Her art was totally out of her—the artist's—hands. . . . That was a time when the artist was supposed to shut up and put up with anything the almighty recording company wanted."

Today, performers do not lean nearly so much on A&R people. Many insist on producing their own work, some in their own studios with their own producers. A&R people still scout the country for talent, checking small clubs and colleges, but most A&R activity today is office work: listening to *demo tapes* sent in by aspiring musicians and tending to contract details.

RECORDING STUDIOS

Making records is a complex process that occurs in a recording studio. Based on preliminary discussions with A&R people, record producers and the recording artists, engineers set up the studio. Dozens of microphones can be used, sometimes one for every performer or instrument. Baffles separate different sound sources to keep spillover to a minimum. Days can go into *miking* a studio. No matter how experienced the engineers, there is an element of trial and error in choosing the right microphones, placing them for best effect and adjusting settings.

Once a recording session begins, the producer is in charge. In an ideal session, everything goes perfectly the first time. That happens rarely. The producer might insist that a song be done over and over. Tapes may be played back so that performers can hear deficiencies that concern the producer. Not infrequently, arrangements are modified during a recording session.

A recording may include three or four dozen tracks, each from a separate microphone. The tracks are consolidated onto two tracks in a complicated process called *mix-down*. In mixing-down, some tracks can be emphasized and others deemphasized or even deleted. Special effects can be dubbed in. Decisions are made concerning which sounds go on the right and the left tracks.

AIRPLAY AND MARKETING

Record companies ship new releases to radio stations in hope of airplay. Few make it. Stations are inundated with more records than they can possibly audition. Also, most stations stick to a playlist of already popular music rather than risk losing listeners by playing untried records. To minimize the risk and yet offer some fresh sounds, most radio station music directors rely heavily on *charts* of what music is selling and being played elsewhere. The most-followed charts appear in the trade journal *Billboard*. Canadian radio music directors also read *RPM*, which began publishing in 1964. Another record industry journal is *The Record*, which first appeared in 1981. There also are *tip sheets*, which leading disc jockeys and music directors put out as a sideline and sell by subscription.

Airplay is valuable because it is the way in which most people are first exposed to new releases that they might go out and buy. Also, airplay is efficient for record-makers because it is free.

This may soon change. In 1996, Parliament considered changing the Copy-

In-Store Promotion. An HMV megastore includes a performance area for recording artists to give customers a live sample of albums for sale. Whether this new marketing approach works in the long term could determine whether the record industry continues to rely so much on radio airplay to promote new music. Here the jazz group Special FX hopes its HMV performance will generate the kind of success that folk singer Suzanne Vega achieved for her album *Days of Open Hand.* Without much airplay at all, it sold almost 1 million copies.

right Act which would force Canadian radio stations to begin paying royalities to artists and record companies. At the time of publication, radio stations are only required to pay a licence fee to the Society of Composers, Authors and Music Publishers of Canada (SOCAN). SOCAN periodically samples the playlists of Canadian radio stations to ensure that the writer(s) of any piece of music broadcasted during the survey period is compensated. After the survey period, songwriters are paid royalties by SOCAN. Canadian television stations are also surveyed by SOCAN.

Promotion also includes advertising campaigns. Record companies place ads on television and radio and in magazines to promote their records and performers. Because an estimated 13 percent of record purchases are on impulse, promotional point-of-purchase displays also are important.

Tours can generate enthusiasm for an album, but interest in tours has declined among performers unless a record company is willing to pick up the expenses. Costs have skyrocketed, not only for special effects and backups but also for security. When Larry Gatlin gave up recording in 1991, he blamed the exhaustion of touring and the expenses. Overexuberant fans take their toll too, especially when a concert goes sour. Guns 'n' Roses won few friends or fans after a mêlée at a St. Louis concert that ended with 60 people injured, $200 000 in damages, and numerous lawsuit threats.

A variation on concert tours was pioneered by CBS Records in 1990. With nothing to lose, CBS sent little-known Mariah Carey on a low-budget nationwide tour singing in record stores. Within weeks and with virtually no airplay, her debut album reached Number 1. Next, Musicland, the 1000-store U.S. record retailer, stocked its stores with the meandering, synthesized New Age album of Yanni and asked him to perform in stores. The album sold 900 000 copies, not bad for a hitherto obscure Greek-born musician whose music received hardly any airplay.

MEASURES OF COMMERCIAL SUCCESS

About half the records sold today are pop, a broad category that ranges from Barry Manilow's mellow sentimentalism to Mötley Crüe's hard-edged rock. The rest are country, classical, jazz and the other musical genres, as well as children's records and the minor although growing category of recorded literature and self-help cassettes.

The measure of success in the record-making business is the *gold record*. Once a single sells 1 million or an album sells 500 000 copies, the Recording Industry Association of America confers a gold-record award. A *platinum record* is awarded for 2 million singles sold or 1 million albums. In Canada, The Canadian Recording Industry Association awards a Gold Seal for sales of 50 000, a Platinum Seal for sales of 100 000 and a Diamond Seal for recordings that sell 1 000 000 copies in Canada.

INTERDEPENDENCE WITH RADIO

STUDY PREVIEW The radio and record industries need each other. Record companies rely on the publicity that comes when radio stations play their records, and radio stations rely on the record industry as a source of low-cost programming.

RECORD—RADIO PARTNERSHIP

The radio and record industries are intimately connected. In the 1940s, when records by performers like Bing Crosby and Frank Sinatra were promoted over the radio, sales soared. One by one, radio stations also discovered that they could both build audiences and cut costs by building more and more programming around records. Spinning records was far less expensive than the big-name productions that had been radio's main programming.

The relationship between the radio and record industries was a two-way street. Not only did radio stations need records, but record-makers needed jockeys to air their products. Records that won airplay were almost assured success. Record companies scrambled to curry favour with leading disc jockeys. This interdependence expanded to television in the 1980s when cable television services, like MTV and MuchMusic, built their programming on video versions of popular music.

As mentioned previously, since 1970 the CRTC has required radio stations in Canada to play at least 30 percent Canadian content, or CanCon, for short. One of the reasons for this policy was to help strengthen the Canadian music industry by encouraging radio to support Canadian songwriters, performers and those involved in the production of Canadian music. Prior to these regulations, some estimate that only about 4 percent of all music heard on Canadian radio was Canadian.

What makes a song "Canadian?" In 1970 Stan Klees of *RPM* Magazine developed the "CanCon MAPL" to help the industry define Canadian content. To be categorized as CanCon, a song must generally fulfil two of the following four conditions:

- M: The *music* must be written by a Canadian (citizen or landed immigrant).
- A: The music or lyrics must be principally performed by a Canadian *artist*.

- P: The recording must have been either *produced* in Canada or *performed* and broadcast live in Canada.
- L: The *lyrics* must be written by a Canadian.

There are some exceptions to these rules:

- If the song was recorded before January 1972, it need only meet one of the four criteria.
- Due to the lack of Canadian material from the first half of this century, if a radio station only plays songs recorded prior to 1956, the CanCon level need only be 2 percent. If 90 percent of the material broadcast is pre-1956, the level of Canadian content should be 10 percent.
- An instrumental piece written by a Canadian.
- If the song was recorded after September 1991, a Canadian who co-writes a song with a non-Canadian will receive half the credit for lyrics and music.

PAYOLA

Alan Freed had always liked music. At Ohio State University, Freed played trombone in a jazz band called the Sultans of Swing. After an army stint during World War II, he landed an announcing job at a classical radio station in Pennsylvania. Later Freed went to Cleveland and became host for a late-night radio show. He played records by Frank Sinatra, Jo Stafford, Frankie Laine and other popular performers of the day.

That was before rock 'n' roll. In 1951 Cleveland record store owner *Leo Mintz*, who sponsored Freed's "Record Rendezvous" on WJW, decided one day to show Freed his shop. Neither the radio nor the record industry was ever the same again. Freed saw Mintz's shop full of white teenagers. They weren't listening to Perry Como or Rosemary Clooney. They were dancing in the aisles to rhythm 'n' blues—"Negro music," as it was called then. And they were buying it.

Alan Freed. On his "Moon Dog House" radio show in Cleveland, Alan Freed laid the groundwork for rock 'n' roll in the early 1950s. By the time he reached New York, Freed was a major influence in the success of young, new performers.

Freed went back to WJW and talked management into a new show, "Moon Dog House." With the new show and a variety of promotions, Freed built a white audience for black music in Cleveland. Word spread. Soon Freed was syndicated on faraway stations with music he called "rock 'n' roll." Within three years he was the top disc jockey in New York City. Rock 'n' roll was here to stay, and the U.S. record industry would be shaken to its roots.

Alan Freed embodied the best and the worst of the intertwined businesses of music, records and radio. He was an innovator at a pivotal point in music history. The rock 'n' roll he played transformed musical tastes almost overnight. Critics charged that his rock 'n' roll was corrupting a generation of teenagers, the same kind of controversy that still plagues the record business today. For Freed, as with many people in the music industry, life was in the fast lane. He became involved in shady deals with record-makers eager for him to play their music on the air, and he was prosecuted—some say persecuted—in the first of many payola scandals. Like many in the faddish record and music industry, Freed rose fast and died young, in 1965 at age 43.

The relationship between the radio and record industries has had problems. Alan Freed was at the heart of one: the first *payola* crisis. In 1958 the grapevine was full of stories about record companies' bribes to disc jockeys to play certain records. One audit found that $263 000 in "consulting fees" had been paid to radio announcers in 23 cities. The Federal Trade Commission filed unfair competition complaints against record companies. Radio station managers, ever conscious that their licences from the Federal Communications Commission could be yanked for improprieties, began demanding signed statements from disc jockeys that they had not accepted payola. Dozens of disc jockeys in major markets quietly left town. Alan Freed did not go quietly. He refused to sign an affidavit requested by ABC, which owned a New York station running one of Freed's programs. He called the request a slur on his reputation. ABC fired him. Freed maintained he had done nothing unethical, and some observers contend that the news media overplayed the payola question.

Whether legitimate or hyped, payola scandals did not end with the 1950s. Competition for airplay has continued to tempt record promoters to "buy" airtime under the table. There were indictments again in the 1970s. And in 1988 two independent promoters were charged with paying $270 000 to program directors at nine widely imitated radio stations to place records on their playlists. One station executive was charged with receiving $100 000 over two years. Some payola bribery involved drugs.

Payola scandals illustrate the relationship that has taken shape between the record and radio industries. It is an interdependent relationship, but radio holds the upper hand. It is the record industry's need for airplay that precipitates the scandals.

HOME-DUBBING REVENUE DRAIN

The lopsidedness of the relationship between the radio and record industries became obvious in another way in the 1970s. Instead of buying records and tapes at $9 each, people began sharing records and dubbing them onto relatively inexpensive blank tapes. Phonograph manufacturers offered machines that not only could dub tapes from records but also could record from the air at the flick of a toggle.

Many FM stereo radio stations catered to home dubbers by announcing when they would play uninterrupted albums. The economic effect of home dubbing on the record industry is hard to measure precisely, but the CRIA (Canadian Recording Industry Association) estimates the industry lost $324 million in 1995 because of home taping.

Record companies tried to dissuade stations from playing albums uninterrupted, but it did not work. Stations were not about to give up the audience they had cultivated for their made-for-dubbing programs. The record companies had no recourse. Cutting off pre-releases to radio stations would mean throwing away free airplay, and airplay was too important. Again, the record industry's dependence on radio was clear. Record-makers were powerless to close a major drain on their revenues.

The dependence of the record industry on radio again was demonstrated in the 1980s when many radio stations shifted to oldies. Traditionally, the record industry derived most of its profits from new music, whose marketing was boosted by radio airplay. In the 1980s, however, stations played more old songs to reach the huge audience of baby boomers who grew up in the 1950s and 1960s and who, like generations before them, preferred the music that was popular when they were young. The change in radio programming worked against the record industry, which, although it was in an economic partnership with radio, was not in control of the relationship.

While record-makers were unable to strike a deal with the radio industry to plug the home-dubbing revenue drain, progress was made on another front in 1991. The record-makers and their long-time foe on the home-dubbing issue, the manufacturers of home electronic equipment, agreed on a "taping tax." Anyone purchasing a blank tape would pay a fee to be passed on to songwriters, music publishers and others who lose royalty income from home dubbing.

AUDIO AND VIDEO PIRACY

Criminal *piracy* involves dubbing records and videos and selling the dubs. An estimated 18 percent of the records and tapes sold are from shadowy pirate sources, mostly in Asia but also in other countries, including Saudi Arabia. These pirate operations have no A&R, royalty or promotion expenses. They dub tapes produced by legitimate companies and sell them through black-market channels. Their costs are low, and their profits are high.

These pirate operations are well financed and organized. It is not uncommon for a Bangkok pirate operation to have 100 "slave" tape-copying machines going simultaneously 24 hours a day and even to ship illegal copies before the official release by the distributor. Local authorities have other priorities and antipiracy laws are weak. In an interview with *Fortune* magazine, Frank Knight, a Bangkok investigator who specializes in these cases, said: "Anybody who's been involved in past mischief, such as drug exports, finds this to be a highly lucrative crime that's easier and less punishable." Knight has tracked exports of illegal tapes to South Africa, to the Indian subcontinent, throughout the Asian Rim, and to the United States.

Bootleg recordings are also a concern of the Canadian recording industry. A *bootleg* is an illegal recording of a performer in concert. As of January 1, 1996, the Antibootleg amendment to the Canadian Copyright Act became law. It is now illegal to record a performance and sell it. Anyone caught can be sued by the performer under the Criminal Code of Canada. The maximum penalty for this form

Recording Piracy. Pirating operations in Bangkok are so well organized that illegal copies of music and videotapes find their way into local shops ahead of their release through legal channels. A tape of the movie *Pretty Woman* went for $5 in a blank cassette box weeks before the distributor put it on the market.

of copyright infringement is a $1 000 000 fine or imprisonment for up to five years, or both penalties.

A CONSOLIDATED INDUSTRY

STUDY PREVIEW The record industry is concentrated in six major companies. This consolidation worries cultural sociologists, who say that the industry's size and bent for profits discourage musical innovation.

MAJORS AND INDIES

Records, like the other mass media, are big business. Six companies dominate the recording industry. Each of these *majors* is, in turn, part of a larger media conglomerate:

- CBS Records is owned by Sony, the Japanese electronic hardware company, which purchased it in 1988 from CBS Inc. Labels include Columbia, Epic and WTG.
- Capitol is owned by Electrical and Musical Instruments of England and Paramount Communications of the United States. Labels include Chrysalis.
- MCA, formerly Music Corporation of America, is owned by Matsushita Electrical Industrial Corp. of Japan. It has numerous media interests, including Universal Pictures. Labels include MCA, Decca, Kapp, Geffen and UNI.
- PolyGram is part of a London-based company owned by Philips of the Netherlands. Labels include A&M, Deutsche Grammophon, Island, Mercury and Motown.
- RCA Records is a subsidiary of the German media giant Bertelsmann, which purchased it in 1988 from General Electric. RCA labels include Arista.

■ Warner Music is owned by Time Warner, the conglomerate that resulted from the 1989 merger of Warner Communications, whose interests included Warner movies and Time-Life, the magazine giant. Labels include Atco, Atlantic, East West, Elektra, Giant, Nonesuch, Reprise, Sire and Warner Brothers.

As *Paul Audley* points out in his book *Canada's Cultural Industries*, the recording business in Canada is largely controlled by American interests. All of the major U.S. labels have offices in Canada. Political economists refer to this as a branch plant economy. This means that while a company may have a corporate presence in Canada, the majority of the power and profit lies outside Canada, usually in America.

The remaining portion of the record market is held by independent companies. Although many *indies* are financially marginal, they are not to be written off. Some indies prosper in market niches. Windham Hill succeeded with high-tech jazz recordings in the 1980s, as did 415 Records with its own brand of rock. A single hit can propel an independent label from a relatively obscure market niche into a *major independent*. For Rounder Records, it was releases by George Thorogood and the Destroyers in the late 1970s. For Windham Hill, it was a hit by pianist George Winston. IRS scored with the group R.E.M.

CULTURAL HOMOGENIZATION

Many media critics bemoan the concentration of the music industry in a few big companies. One result, they say, is *cultural homogenization*. In their book *Rock 'n'*

MEDIA DATABANK

Conglomeration and Globalization

The major record companies are all part of larger corporations with diverse interests. Japan-based Sony, which acquired CBS Records in 1988 and Columbia Pictures in 1989, represents the extent to which media conglomeration and globalization are occurring. Here is a thumbnail list of Sony's U.S. units, excluding its subsidiaries elsewhere, and a sampler of their products:

CBS Records	Michael Jackson
Digital Audio Disc Corp.	Compact discs
Sony Magnetic Products Group	Video- and audio-tape
Sony Engineering and Manufacturing	Television, video, audio hardware
Columbia Pictures	First-run movies
Tri-Star Pictures	"Wheel of Fortune"
Columbia Pictures Television	Recycled movies for home video
Columbia Tri-Star Home Video	Movie houses
Loews theaters	Electronic games
Sony Electronic Publishing	Video distribution
SVS	Semiconductors
Material Research Corp.	In-flight entertainment
Sony Trans Com Corp.	

Roll is Here to Pay, Steve Chapple and Reebee Garofalo argue that the greatest creativity in pop music comes from lean and hungry independent companies, not the fat majors. They note, for example, that the rockabilly innovators of the mid-1950s, like Elvis Presley, Bill Haley and Carl Perkins, recorded for scrappy little risk-taking companies. These companies contributed new richness and diversity to the culture. Chapple and Garofalo contrast the rockabilly innovations with "the Philadelphia schlock" of slick packager *Dick Clark*, who watered down the work of the innovators into commercially safe pap that would sell to a mass audience. An example, from the 1950s, was a song by the Midnighters, an obscure black group, with the suggestive title, "Work With Me, Henry." Major label pop singer Georgia Gibbs changed the title to "Dance With Me, Henry" and toned down the lyrics, and it became a big hit. This process of modifying a song to pander to vanilla mass market tastes, called *covering*, has been repeated hundreds of times. Each time, say cultural historians, artistic authenticity is compromised. The financial rewards and lures go to homogenization, not originality. Art that springs from the grassroots, they say, doesn't have much of a chance with mass marketers, and the result is that authentic culture is co-opted.

Cultural homogenization became a high-visibility issue in the 1990s when many music reviewers panned the record industry's Grammy Awards for favouring *derivative artists* who may be popular, as was Georgia Gibbs, but whose artistic merits are second rate. The issue erupted in 1990 when Rob Pilatus and Fab Morvan, who performed as Milli Vanilli, were embarrassed into surrendering a Grammy when it was learned that somebody else recorded their popular records and they lip-synced the videos.

The cultural homogenization issue became more focused when Sinéad O'Connor, considered an especially talented rock artist, announced that she would boycott the 1991 Grammy ceremony. The awards, she said, were merely the record industry's hype to promote sales and had little to do with authentic artistry. Her point was underscored by reviewers who noted that previous Grammy winners had included such dubious talents as Debby Boone and the group Toto.

The biggest factor in cultural homogenization is the major record companies, whose quest for marketplace success often supersedes any sense of responsibility to foster artistic contributions. Music commentator David Hadelman, writing in *Rolling Stone*, made the point this way: "It's no revelation that teenybopper acts like Abdul, the New Kids, Milli Vanilli, Rick Astley and Kylie Minogue are primarily poster-ready hunks and babes and barely singers at all. In this age of the producer-auteur, their vocals are the last element added to a record." About the Grammys, *Time* music critic Jay Cocks said: "The Grammys have the most unfortunate reputation for often making saccharine choices that toady shamelessly to the marketplace." Joe Smith, president of Capitol records, was unwittingly revealing about the profit-over-art orientation of the major record companies when he defended the televised Grammy awards by saying: "They get good ratings. This is not the International Red Cross."

Record industry critics say that cultural homogenization has accelerated since the 1950s, coinciding with the disappearance of many independent record companies. The major labels have acquired most of the independents, which prided themselves on distinctive music. These include the black label *Motown*, known once for a distinctive "Detroit sound" but which moved to Los Angeles and went for the mass market before being swallowed up by a major label in 1988. *Arista*, the last so-called *major independent*, was bought by a major, Time Warner, in 1989.

RECORD CENSORSHIP

STUDY PREVIEW A perennial problem for record-makers is pressure to sanitize lyrics to protect young listeners. Some would-be censors are at the reactionary and radical fringes of society, but others have received serious attention from congressional committees. By and large, the record industry has headed off government sanctions with voluntary labels on records.

OBJECTIONABLE MUSIC

Campaigns to ban records are nothing new. In the Roaring 20s, some people saw jazz as morally loose. White racists of the 1950s called Bill Haley's rock "nigger music." War protest songs of the Vietnam period angered many Americans.

Government attempts to censor records have been rare, yet they indirectly keep some records off the market. The CRTC and FCC can take a dim view of stations that air objectionable music, which guides broadcasters toward caution. Stations do not want to risk their licenses. Because the record industry is so dependent on airplay, hardly any music that might seriously offend makes it to market.

The politically active radical right affects what record-makers do. The radical right has campaigned against specific artists and records in protests, boycotts against stations and record-burning rallies. The flavour of these campaigns is reflected in the titles of books by David Noebel, who is part of evangelist Billy James Hargis's Christian Crusade: *Communism, Hypnotism and the Beatles: An Analysis of the Communist Use of Music; The Beatles: A Study in Drugs, Sex and Revolution;* and *Rhythm, Riots, and Revolution,* which Noebel announced he would retitle

Kurt Cobain. The Seattle rocker and his band Nirvana created music in which a new generation of alienated teenagers found identity. The defining moment, according to Anthony DeCurtis when writing Cobain's obituary for *Rolling Stone* was the 1991 release "Smells Like a Teen Spirit." The message was an anticommercial, antipolitical and resentful reaction to the self-indulgence and greed of the 1980s. Cobain shot himself to death in 1994.

The Marxist Minstrels. Televangelist Jimmy Swaggart and coauthor Robert Lamb followed the same theme in their 1987 book *Religious Rock 'n' Roll: A Wolf in Sheep's Clothing.*

What effect have the radical right had on the recording industry? In his book *Solid Gold,* Serge Denisoff says, "Depending upon geography and political climate, both the Right and the FCC have influenced musical fare in America. Fear of these entities forced CBS to remove Bob Dylan's 'Talking John Birch Society Blues' from his second album and from the Ed Sullivan Show. Pete Seeger was blacklisted from commercial radio and television for nearly 17 years. Ed Sullivan changed the title of the Rolling Stones' 'Let's Spend the Night Together' to 'Let's Spend Some Time Together.' Barry McGuire's 'Eve of Destruction' and Crosby, Stills, Nash and Young's 'Ohio' were blacklisted in many parts of the country."

RECORD LABELING

In the 1980s complaints about lyrics narrowed to drugs, sexual promiscuity and violence. In the U.S. a group led by Tipper Gore and wives of several other influential members of Congress, *Parents' Music Resource Center,* claimed links between explicit rock music and teen suicide, teen pregnancy, abusive parents, broken homes, and other social ills. The group objected to lyrics like Prince's "Sister," which extolls incest; Mötley Crüe's "Live Wire," with its psychopathic enthusiasm for strangulation; Guns n' Roses' white racism; and Ice T and other rap artists' hate music.

The Parents' Music Resource Center argued that consumer protection laws should be invoked to require that records with offensive lyrics be labeled as dangerous, like cigarette warning labels or the movie industry's rating system. Record companies began labeling potentially offensive records: "Explicit Lyrics—Parental Advisory." In some cases, the companies printed lyrics on album covers as a warning.

Gangsta Rap. For Charles Broadus, escaping his past seemed too big a task. As gangsta rapper Snoop Doggy Dogg, Broadus rapped about his gang roots in Long Beach, California, but just as his career was about to take off, he was arrested. The night of the 1993 MTV Awards, where he made a presentation, Broadus was arrested and charged with first-degree murder. Police said his bodyguards fired two bullets into the back of a man Broadus claimed had threatened him. As *Newsweek* commented: "Authenticity was his asset and his downfall."

LYRICS AND YOUNG PEOPLE

Despite countless studies, it is unclear whether mores are affected by lyrics. Two scholars from California State University at Fullerton found that most high school students are hazy on the meaning of their favourite songs. Asked to explain Bruce Springsteen's "Born in the U.S.A.," about the hopelessness of being born in a blue-collar environment, many teenagers were simplistically literal. "It's about the town Bruce Springsteen lives in," said one. Led Zeppelin's "Stairway to Heaven" has been criticized for glorifying drug or sexual rushes, but many teenagers in the study were incredibly literal, saying the song was about climbing steps into the sky. What does this mean? Professor Lorraine Prinsky of the Fullerton study concluded that teenagers use rock music as background noise. At most 3 percent, she said, are fully attentive to the lyrics.

Critics, however, see an insidious subliminal effect. Some songs repeat their simple and explicitly sexual messages over and over, as many as 15 to 30 times in one song. Said a spokesperson from the Parents' Music Resource Center: "I can't believe it's not getting through. It's getting into the subconscious, even if they can't recite the lyrics."

CHAPTER WRAP-UP

Prospects for the record industry are upbeat, as long as record-makers stay in tune with the changing tastes of the young people comprising their major market. Citing huge profits, analyst Allan Dodds Frank says, "Gold hasn't flowed from black vinyl disks in such quantities in many years." Compact discs have caught on, and profits are high. The discs cost $3 each to make, not including $1 or so in royalties, and sell for $8 and up wholesale and $13 to $25 retail. Record-makers clear $4 or so a disc, which makes for happy shareholders.

Technological advances continue to create new profit opportunities by rendering old formats obsolete. Just as record-makers reissued old 78-rpm music on EP and LP when the microgroove was introduced, they later added stereo versions. Then they went to eight-track tapes, which eventually lost favour to cassette tapes, which later were replaced by CDs. As consumers buy improved playback equipment, they need to update their music collections with recordings in the new formats. While this can churn profits for record companies, promoters of new formats run a risk with the introduction of so many competing formats: Customers may shy away from buying any of them until they know which will survive. It is doubtful, for example, that over the long haul CD, DAT, DCC and MD equipment will all find a sufficient marketplace following to justify record companies' manufacturing in all the formats or record stores' stocking them all.

The future has other challenges. Home-dubbing equipment could be an unstoppable leak on profits. There also are antitrust questions about whether the public or our culture would be better served by a less concentrated recording industry.

The long-term future of the recording industry, however, rests more on each new generation of young people than anything else. Since the turn of the century, when a separate youth culture began taking form, teenagers have looked to new music to set their generation apart. They have bought records that irritated their parents, that represented the social causes of the day and that were fun to listen to. Today almost 50 percent of recording industry sales are to people under the age of 25.

But young people can be fickle. When record sales plummeted in 1924, young people were turning on the radio. In 1979 they played video games and sent the record industry into depression. For the most part, though, young people have been a loyal, growing market, and they will continue to be as long as recordings are an affordable vehicle to identify their generation, to celebrate their values, to demonstrate youthful rebellion and to dance to.

QUESTIONS FOR REVIEW

1. Why is recorded music important?
2. How did mechanical sound reproduction work? How about electromagnetic reproduction? How about digital reproduction?
3. What effect did music videos have on the recording industry when they were introduced?
4. What is the effect of new formats and megadeals with performers on the recording industry?
5. Is making money easy in the recording industry?
6. What is the relationship of the recording and radio industries?
7. Does conglomeration in the recording business affect innovation?
8. What is the effect of payola, censorship and home dubbing on the recording business?
9. Define MAPL. Should radio stations be required to play a certain amount of Canadian material, or should the marketplace decide what gets played on the radio?
10. What are the Junos?

QUESTIONS FOR CRITICAL THINKING

1. Three principal methods for storing sound for replaying have been developed. Distinguish each type, explain the advantages of each and place them in a historical perspective. The methods are mechanical media, like the phonograph disc; magnetic media, like cassette tapes; and digital media, like compact discs.
2. Two types of piracy are plaguing the recording industry. Describe illegal copying of both records and tapes for resale and home dubbing, and discuss what can be done.
3. Of the major technological developments in sound recording, which was the most significant? Support your case. Consider but do not limit yourself to these developments: the Phonograph of Thomas Edison in 1877, electromagnetic applications by Joseph Maxwell in 1924, the 33⅓ LP by Peter Goldmark and the compact disc.
4. The year 1979 was disastrous for the recording industry. Of the industry's problems that year, which have been addressed successfully? Which have not? What lies ahead? Is it realistic to expect continued growth? Consider home dubbing and piracy, a loose distribution system for getting products to consumers and megabuck contracts with star performers.
5. What are the common and the distinguishing characteristics of the six major U.S. recording companies? They are Capitol, CBS, MCA, PolyGram, RCA and Warner.
6. Discuss the relationship of the independent recording companies and the majors, with particular attention to Windham Hill, Rounder and Motown. Consider that Motown was acquired by a major label in 1988.
7. Historically, the direction of radio has had major effects on the U.S. recording industry. Discuss the effects brought about by Alan Freed's record programs in the 1950s and demographics-based programming shifts from a teenage to an older, larger audience.
8. Some historians divide the recording industry into periods. Using information in this chapter, cite specifics on what characterizes each of these periods: the age of discovery (1877–1924), the age of electrical recording (1925–1945), the age of the LP and rock 'n' roll (1948–1960), the age of maturing rock and high profits (1960–1978), the age of retrenchment (1979–1984) and the age of video and digital resurgence (1985 on).
9. What criteria would make sense to protect teenagers from the records to which Parents' Music Resource Center objects? Do teenagers need to be protected? Are cover labels enough? Does printing lyrics on album covers make a difference?

10. Explain how the record-making industry and the manufacturers of playback equipment came to be divided on the home-dubbing issue. How did conglomeration, including Sony's purchase of CBS Records, ease this antagonism?

11. What kind of solution is the taping tax to the revenue drain that home dubbing represents for the recording industry? How can the taping tax encourage more creative activity among lyricists and musical performers?

12. Using the approach outlined in this chapter, can you think of any songs by Canadian groups or artists that say something about Canadian culture? How do they communicate this?

13. Music has many "sounds:" the Motown sound, the Nashville sound to name just two. Has a Canadian sound emerged in the legacy of the Canadian content regulations?

◼️**F**OR FURTHER LEARNING

Paul Audley. *Canada's Cultural Industries* (Lorimer and Company, 1983). A look at the economic side of Canada's so-called cultural industries, including record production.

Iain Chambers. *Urban Rhythms: Pop Music and Popular Culture* (St. Martin's, 1985). Chambers, a British scholar, sees post–World War II pop music as a liberator for the masses of people against traditional cultural forces.

Steve Chapple and Reebee Garofalo. *Rock 'n' Roll Is Here to Pay: The History and Politics of the Music Industry* (Nelson-Hall, 1977). This interpretive look at the music industry is built on the premise that authentic cultural contributions are co-opted by profit motives.

R. Serge Denisoff with William Schurk. *Tarnished Gold: The Record Industry Revisited* (Transaction Books, 1986). Denisoff, a sociologist, examines the recording industry by accepting popular music as a cultural phenomenon within a commercial framework. This is an update of his 1975 book, *Solid Gold.*

Peter Fornatale and Joshua E. Mills. *Radio in the Television Age* (Overlook Press, 1980). This interestingly written account of radio from the 1950s through the 1970s suggests that the payola scandals were overplayed in the media because of other events of the time.

Roland Gelatt. *The Fabulous Phonograph: From Tin Foil to High Fidelity* (J.B. Lippincott, 1955). This is a comprehensive history through the battle of the speeds and the demise of the 78-rpm record.

Peter Goddard and Phillip Kamin, editors. *Shakin' All Over: The Rock and Roll Years in Canada* (McGraw Hill Ryerson, 1989). A series of essays on the Canadian pop music experience that focus on such stars as Dan Hill, Carole Pope, Terry David Mulligan and Bernie Finkel-

stein. The book also provides short biographies of several (English and French) Canadian artists.

Ron Hall. *The CHUM Chart Book* (Stardust Publications, 1984). Hall provides a thorough listing of all the songs charted by CHUM radio in Toronto between 1957 and 1983.

Ted Kennedy. *Oh! Canada Cuts* (Canadian Chart Research, 1989). A listing of all Canadian singles that made the national charts in both *RPM* (during the period 1964 to 1989) and *The Record* (from 1983 to 1989). Wherever possible, chart data from *Billboard* magazine is also included.

Martin Melhuish. *Heart of Gold: 30 Years of Canadian Pop Music* (CBC Enterprises, 1983). The companion book to the CBC-TV series of the same name is an exellent chronicle of Canadian popular music.

Mike Roberts. *Finger on the Pulse: MuchMusic Still Strong after 10 Years*, Montreal *Gazette*, January 22, 1995.

Barry L. Sherman and Joseph R. Dominick. "Violence and Sex in Music Videos: TV and Rock 'n' Roll." *Journal of Communication* 36 (Winter 1986):1, 79–93. Scholars Sherman and Dominick tackle the influence of music videos from numerous perspectives. Their report is part of a 68-page special music video section in this issue of the *Journal of Communication.*

Justin Smallbridge. "Think Global: Act Local," in *Canadian Business*, June 1996.

Dick Weissman. *The Music Business: Career Opportunities and Self-Defense* (Crown Publishers, 1979). After 20 years of learning the ropes of the music business as a performer, Weissman wrote this excellent primer for anyone aspiring to a career in music.

FOR KEEPING UP TO DATE

Consumer magazines that track popular music and report on the record industry include *Rolling Stone* and *Spin*.

Entertainment Weekly has a regular section on music, as does *Maclean's*.

RPM Magazine and *The Record* are good sources for the current state of the music business in Canada.

CHAPTER 4

RADIO A Medium of Instant Communication

Radio reaches people everywhere with opinion, news, entertainment and advertising

Radio signals move through the air by piggybacking on already existing electromagnetic waves

Canadian radio operates in both the private and public sectors

Radio has an entertainment rather than an educational thrust

News is becoming less important in the programming mix of radio, while Talk Radio is becoming a dominant format

MEDIA IN THEORY

What Makes Radio Different?

What makes radio different from other media? Andrew Crissell, a cultural theorist, refers to radio as a blind medium: you can't see it with your eyes, like you can television, a movie or a newspaper. You can only see the pictures in your mind. Radio broadcasters use time, not space as their canvas to communicate their messages. Building on the ideas of Barthes, radio uses four signs to create its imagery: words, sounds, music and silence.

As discussed earlier, words can be symbolic in that they represent something other than themselves: The phrase "maple leaf" isn't a real maple leaf, it is only a label that our culture attaches to the physical object of a leaf. This naming process is entirely arbitrary. However, words in radio differ from words in print. Why? Because they are spoken. It's not so much what you say, but how you say it. The way in which an announcer or radio performer speaks also communicates meaning. Words end up working on two levels; not only do the words themselves stand for something else, but the way in which they are spoken signifies something as well. For example the announcer can say "great!" and mean it in two different ways, one positive, one negative.

Sounds or sound effects are indexical signs. The sound of a creaking door is an index of the sound of a creaking door. To someone listening to Tom Cheek and Jerry Howarth broadcast a Blue Jays game, the loud crack of a bat and the cheering of a crowd signify that Joe Carter has just hit a home run. Like the words that help us decode the meanings of a press photograph, sounds anchor the meaning or image created by radio; this is important due to the invisible nature of radio. Sounds let us know where we are and what's going on.

The third sign of radio, music, works on several levels. The music you hear on a radio station helps you to identify the station. When you hear Charlie Major or Michelle Wright on the radio, you know you're listening to a country station; if you're listening to Slik Toxik or Kim Mitchell, you know the station is not country. Music can also act as a bridge between segments of a radio show, newsmagazine or play or it can be used to create a mood in a radio play.

An absence of any of the three signs signifies something in itself. As a sign, silence works to communicate meaning two ways. First, it can be symbolic. A minute of silence on Remembrance Day symbolizes respect and honour for soldiers who died in war. But silence can also be an index that something's wrong with the broadcast—a power outage, or a faulty microphone or radio transmitter problems can all cause what is known as "dead air."

It is through these conventional signs that radio broadcasters are able to create various connotations. Unfortunately, many radio stations are rigidly formatted, leaving little room for the announcers to use signs creatively. One exception to this rule is the "Royal Canadian Air Farce," whose cast members have won a dozen ACTRA awards for radio comedy; *Maclean's* magazine included these actors on their honour roll of Canadians who make a difference and they have honorary degrees from Athabasca University in Alberta and Brock University in Ontario. Luba Goy, Don Ferguson, Roger Abbott, John Morgan and Dave Broadfoot have been entertaining Canadian radio audiences on CBC Radio since 1973. Each week, their skits poke fun at Canada's newsmakers. Pierre Trudeau, Brian Mulroney, Preston Manning, Lucien Bouchard, Sheila Copps and Jean Chrétien have all been lampooned by the "Royal Canadian Air Farce." The show's humour is always topical and has a distinctly Canadian flavour.

What makes the "Air Farce" so different is not only its content, but its form. In these days of formatted radio the "Air Farce" borrows from the old school to create comedy. Sound effects and a live studio audience are part of the program. The show is taped primarily at the Glenn Gould Studio in Toronto on Friday nights or Saturday mornings and broadcast that weekend, on CBC Radio and CBC Stereo. The members of the "Air Farce" stand on stage, in front of microphones, scripts in hand, and perform before the audience. It's really a page out of the old days of radio. The "Air Farce" is proof that radio can be more than time, temperatures and tunes. It can be a very creative medium.

SIGNIFICANCE OF RADIO

STUDY PREVIEW   Radio is an important medium for opinion, news, entertainment and advertising. The portability of radio means it is everywhere in our daily lives.

RADIO AS A MOTIVATOR

Radio can motivate people to action. When members of Congress were mulling a 51 percent pay hike for themselves in 1988, radio talk-show host Jerry Williams decided it was time for another Boston tea party. He stirred his Boston listeners to send thousands of tea bags to Congress as a not-so-subtle reminder of the 1765

A Canadian Comedy Institution. The "Royal Canadian Air Farce" comedy troupe specializes in fast-paced topical humour with a distinctly Canadian flavour, taped before a live audience.

colonial frustration over taxes that led to the Revolutionary War. Talk-show hosts elsewhere joined the campaign, and Congress, swamped with tea bags, scuttled the pay raise proposal.

Record companies know the power of radio. Without radio stations playing new music, a new record release is almost certainly doomed. Airplay spurs people to go out and buy a record. Advertisers value radio to reach buyers. Only newspapers, television and direct mail have a larger share of the advertising dollars spent, and radio's share is growing.

UBIQUITY OF RADIO

Radio is everywhere. The signals piggyback on naturally occurring waves in the electromagnetic spectrum and reach every nook and cranny. Hardly a place in the world is beyond the reach of radio. In spite of this, radio is often a forgotten medium.

Imagine this scenario: scores of media academics driving to school or to a conference to discuss the evils and perils of the modern mass media. Topics like sexism in advertising, the impact of viewing television violence on children, and how Canadian culture is being smothered by U.S. media conglomerates are at the top of their research lists. The scholars ponder these important questions en route while listening to CBC Radio in their Volvos. Many of them overlook what may be the most pervasive medium of all, radio.

The general public, not just academics, overlook radio for numerous reasons. The main reason is this. While radio is a medium of mass communication, it is also a medium of interpersonal communication. It acts as a friend. We usually listen to a radio station that reflects our taste in music, our political orientation and our overall ideology. We listen to what we are in the mood for. Radio is so personal that we often do not see it as a mass medium.

But it is a mass medium. Here are some interesting facts on where and how we use radio:

- Three out of every four bedrooms have a radio.
- Two out of every three kitchens have a radio.
- Ninety-five percent of all cars have radios.
- Two out of every three offices have a radio station on.
- Radio reaches 96 percent of all Canadians; the typical Canadian listens to about 22 hours of radio each week.
- According to the Spring 1996 *Broadcaster Directory*, Canada has 548 privately owned radio stations.

Despite this proliferation of radio signals, the Canadian Association of Broadcasters reports that Canadian radio stations have collectively lost $180 million since the early 1990s.

TECHNICAL DEVELOPMENT

STUDY PREVIEW Human mastery of the electromagnetic spectrum, through which radio is possible, is only a century old. In 1895 an Italian physicist and inventor, Guglielmo Marconi, was the first to transmit a message through the air. Later came voice transmissions and better sound.

ELECTROMAGNETIC SPECTRUM

Radio waves are part of the physical universe. They have existed forever, moving through the air and the ether. Like light waves, they are silent—a part of a continuing spectrum of energies, the *electromagnetic spectrum*. As early as 1873, physicists speculated that the electromagnetic spectrum existed, but it was a young Italian nobleman, *Guglielmo Marconi*, who made practical application of the physicists' theories while in Canada.

Young Marconi became obsessed with the possibilities of the electromagnetic spectrum and built equipment that could ring a bell by remote control—no strings, no wires. The Marconi device shaped a radio wave in such a way that another device could intercept it and decipher a message from the wave's shape. In 1895, when he was 21, Marconi used his wireless method to transmit codes for more than a mile on his father's Bologna estate.

On December 12, 1901, Marconi stood on Signal Hill in Newfoundland and received the Morse code signal for the letter "S" from Cornwall, England. This day has been well documented as a significant date in the study of broadcasting. However, Canadian *Reginald Fessenden* played an equally important role in the early days of radio. He constantly vied with Marconi for both funding and fame. On Christmas Eve, 1906, he broadcast music and voices to ships at sea. The broadcast took place from Brant Rock, Massachusetts. Fessenden played the violin for his listeners as a Christmas present. He also played an Ediphone recording of

Reginald Fessenden. Canadian Reginald Fessenden competed with Marconi in the early days of radio technology.

Handel's *Largo*. It is significant that the first radio musical broadcast also featured one of the world's first musical recordings. But history has not been kind to Fessenden. In spite of his contributions, Marconi is the one who is remembered as the father of radio.

Marconi patented his invention in England, and his mother, a well-connected Irish woman, arranged British financing to set up the Marconi Wireless Telegraph Co. Soon ocean-going ships were equipped with Marconi radiotelegraphy equipment to communicate at sea, even when they were beyond the horizon, something never possible before.

TRANSMITTING VOICES

Breakthroughs came quickly. In 1906 *Lee De Forest* created the *audion tube*, which made voice transmissions possible. Technical development stalled during World War I. Military and civilian research concentrated on other things, and work on the newfangled wireless was put off. After the war, Americans were wary as never before about the dangers of dependence on foreign goods. They worried about being cut off if another war disrupted transoceanic commerce. The worry extended to patents, even those in friendly countries, like Marconi's British wireless patent. At the urging of the federal government, three American companies, General Electric, Westinghouse and American Telephone & Telegraph, pooled their resources in 1919 and bought Marconi's American subsidiary and patents. Although the consortium broke up within a few years, it helped to refine the technology further. In this same period, physics department experiments at many universities added to the technology, which gave further impetus to radio's development.

Static-free transmission was developed by *Edwin Armstrong*, a Columbia University researcher. In 1939 Armstrong built an experimental station in New Jersey

Before Tape Recorders. It was no small task when radio stations arranged remote broadcasts in the early days. Staff members packed a lot into this sedan for a field production.

using a new system called *frequency modulation,* FM for short. FM's system, piggy-backing sound on airwaves, was different from the older *amplitude modulation,* or AM method. In time, Armstrong developed FM stereo with two soundtracks, one for each ear, duplicating the sensation of hearing a performance live.

CHARACTERISTICS OF RADIO

STUDY PREVIEW   The radio industry established itself early in the private, free enterprise sector of the economy. It also chose entertainment, rather than news, information and education, as its main programming thrust. However, fearful of too much U.S. programming on Canadian radio, the government soon stepped in and changed the face of radio in Canada.

CHARACTERISTICS OF CANADIAN RADIO

In 1919, the Montreal-based radio station *XWA* (now CIQC) was the first station to get a broadcasting licence from the federal government. Its first broadcast took place in May 1920, under the supervision of Marconi. XWA was the first station to have regularly scheduled programs, the first of which was a musical program broadcast locally to the Royal Society of Canada in Montreal. This was not only the first radio broadcast in Canada but also in North America, contrary to what KDKA in Pittsburgh claims. In 1922 *CKAC* in Montreal, which still broadcasts today, was licensed as the first French-language station in Canada.

During the 1920s, radios became an integral part of Canadians' living rooms. These were big radios, some as large as today's home entertainment units. People listened to the radio then in much the same way we watch television: after supper, with or without the family. A radio was considered a status symbol and much of the programming reflected this: broadcasts included concerts, political commentary, dramas and comedies.

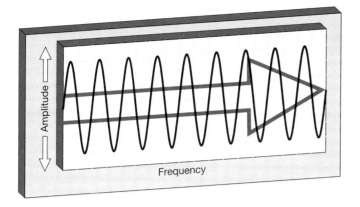

Guglielmo Marconi

Unmodulated Wave. If you could see electromagnetic waves, they would look like the cross-section of a ripple moving across a pond, except they would be steady and unending. Guglielmo Marconi figured out how to hitch a ride on these waves to send messages from Signal Hill, Newfoundland, in 1901.

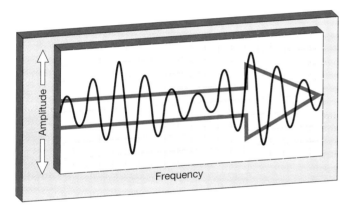

Lee De Forest

Amplitude-Modulated Wave. Lee De Forest discovered how to adjust the height of electromagnetic waves to coincide with the human voice and other sounds. De Forest's audion tube made voice transmission possible, including an Enrico Caruso concert in 1910.

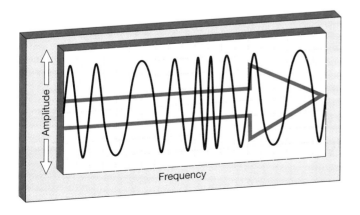

Edwin Armstrong

Frequency-Modulated Wave. FM radio transmissions squeeze and expand electromagnetic waves without changing their height. Edwin Armstrong introduced this form of broadcasting, which had superior clarity and fidelity, in the 1930s. Not even lightning interferes with transmission.

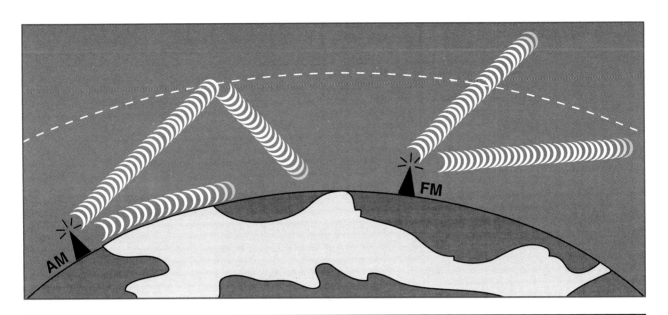

Bounce-Back Effect. When AM electromagnetic waves are transmitted, many of them follow the contour of the earth, which extends their range beyond the line-of-sight from the transmitter. Some AM waves go upward, and many of these are bounced back to earth by reflective layers in the ionosphere, which further extends a station's range. The bounce-back effect is weaker during the day when the sun warms the ionosphere and reduces its reflective properties. FM transmissions have a shorter range than AM because the signals move in straight lines and tend not to adhere to the earth's contours. Also, upward-moving FM waves pass through the ionosphere rather than being reflected back.

Another place where Canadians listened to radio in the 1920s was on the *Canadian National Railway* (the *CNR*). Like many entrepreneurs at the time, the president of the CNR thought that radio was the ideal medium for promoting Canada and train travel. You could travel from Ottawa to Toronto and be entertained by radio music and other radio programs. Most of this programming was highbrow: it featured singers, orchestras and dramas. By the end of the decade the CNR had established a sizable private network, with radio stations in Ottawa, Montreal and Moncton; it was also leasing stations from coast to coast. By 1932, 20 radio stations made up the CNR's regional and national network.

An interesting phenomenon occurred in the 1920s, one that is still with us: Canadians were listening to more American programming than domestic programming. This was partly due to geography and the availability of many U.S. radio signals. Canadians also claimed American radio offered them more choice. And why not? A number of U.S. radio stars were also Broadway or vaudeville celebrities. There was, however, one notable exception to the rule—hockey. Broadcasts of hockey games were the most popular radio programs of the period. They began in 1923 with *Foster Hewitt*. Within a decade, Saturday night hockey broadcasts became a tradition in Canada.

In the early days, most stations were on the air at night with hotel tea-time music. It was pleasant programming, offensive to no one. Sandwiched among the *potted-palm* music, as it was called, were occasional soloists, poets and public speakers. As broadcasting expanded into the daytime, stations used more recordings, which introduced a bit more variety. In the 1930s, evening programming became more varied. Potted-palm music gave way to symphonies and big bands. Guy Lombardo, the Dorsey Brothers and Benny Goodman all found that radio helped promote their record sales in both Canada and the U.S.

With more varied programs, radio attracted a true mass audience in the 1930s. Fred Waring and his Pennsylvanians demonstrated that variety shows could attract large audiences. Jack Benny, Milton Berle and Bob Hope did the same with comedy. George Burns and Gracie Allen put together the first continuing situation comedy. Drama series were introduced—murders, soap operas, Westerns, thrillers. Quiz shows became part of the mix.

RADIO'S EARLY ROLE IN UNIFYING CANADA

Unlike American radio, Canadian politicians saw radio not only as a way to promote entertainment but also as a tool to unite the country. In its early days, Canadian radio succeeded in uniting the country in a way that had never been done before. On July 1, 1927, on Canada's 50th birthday, CNR's network of telephone and telegraph lines joined orchestras in several Canadian cities from Halifax to Vancouver through its 23 private radio stations across the nation. About 5 million people in Canada and the U.S. tuned into the *Diamond Jubilee Broadcast,* which originated in Ottawa. The program was also broadcast on shortwave radio. It must have been an interesting sight; people gathered in the streets to listen to it on speakers and on telephone party lines. In Montreal, an estimated 20 000 people congregated at Fletcher's Field to listen to the performance of the "Maple Leaf Forever." For the first time in history, Canadians were linked from coast to coast via a mass medium. *Wilson MacDonald*, a farmer from Saskatchewan, was so stirred by the performance, he wrote the following poem:

> A silence there, expectant, meaning,
> And then a voice clear pitched and tense,
> A million hearers, forward leaning,
> Were in the thrall of eloquence
>
> A pause, a hush, a wonder growing,
> A prophet's vision understood,
> In that strange spell of his bestowing,
> They dreamed, with him, of Brotherhood.

(Source: *50 Years of CBC Radio*)

In August of 1927, Canada's prime minister, *Mackenzie King*, also sang the praises of radio, citing the Diamond Jubilee event the previous month. His speech was delivered at the Canadian National Exhibition and was also broadcast on radio. He claimed that Canadians from coast to coast were moved by the message of Canadian unity and that the regions of Canada had become one during that Diamond Jubilee broadcast on July 1, 1927.

YOU'RE "ON THE AIRD": CANADA'S FIRST ROYAL COMMISSION ON BROADCASTING

The idea that radio could help build a country was one of the factors behind the first Royal Commission on Broadcasting. The fact that Canadians were listening to more American than Canadian programming worried Ottawa. For the first time (and certainly not the last time) in Canadian media history, politicians began to worry about the domination of Canada by American mass media. To solve this problem they set up the first of many Royal Commissions on broadcasting in

BBC: "This Is London"

All over the world, people listen to their radios for the premier British Broadcasting Company program, "This Is London." It goes out in 39 languages to an estimated 75 million people, some listening to shortwave signals direct from BBC transmitters, others to their local stations, which relay the program. The popularity of "This Is London," which offers news, culture and entertainment, rests in part with the respect the BBC gained in World War II for consistent and reliable foreign coverage. Later, BBC's international reputation was strengthened by quality television documentaries and dramas, which were exported widely.

BBC's quality sometimes is attributed to the fact that it need not be overly concerned with ratings. Overseas services are funded by Parliament and domestic services through a Parliament-approved tax on the sale of radio and television sets. Like CBC Radio, BBC takes no advertising. Although its financial base is dependent on Parliament, the BBC functions through a governance structure that buffers it from political pressure.

The BBC went on the air in 1922, and five years later received a royal charter as a nonprofit public corporation. By 1939 the BBC was operating a number of shortwave services to other Commonwealth nations in addition to foreign language services to other countries.

BBC held a home monopoly until 1954, when Parliament authorized a second domestic broadcast system. Even though the new ITV television and ILR radio networks use advertising as their revenue base, the British never embraced commercial broadcasting of the North American sort. All advertisements are placed before or after programs—never in the middle—so they will not interrupt.

Canada. The *Aird Commission* (named after *Sir John Aird*) was created to examine the danger that American programming posed to Canadian culture. The verdict it reached in 1929 wasn't surprising: American networks were a threat to our airwaves and our culture.

The commission recommended that Canada set up and fund a public broadcasting network, like the BBC in England. This network would produce and broadcast Canadian programs for and by Canadians. This recommendation caused quite a conflict between the owners of private radio stations, who were making a tidy profit, and those who preferred the public system. By 1932 Prime Minister Bennett laid out the government's official position on radio broadcasting in Canada. Canada would have both public and private radio stations. The government's proposal regarding public broadcasting revolved around three issues, issues that were very different from those relating to the American system:

- National sovereignty was to be preserved.
- Broadcasting services were to be made available to anyone in Canada, no matter where they lived.
- Broadcasting was not to be exploited by private interests.

In 1932 the Canadian Radio Broadcasting Act was passed, resulting in the creation of the *Canadian Radio Broadcasting Commission*, which began broadcasting in 1933. The CRBC was a direct product of the Aird Commission. Initially it broadcast for only one hour a day. By the time it was replaced by the *CBC* in 1936, it was reaching just under half the Canadian population. By 1936 the *Canadian Broadcasting Corporation* (CBC) was formed. In addition to being a national radio network, it was responsible for granting licences to private radio broadcasters, even though the government did not officially recognize private broadcasting—an ideal position for the government to be in. In 1957 the *Fowler Commission* changed the name of the CBC's board of governors to the board of broadcast governors (BBG) to emphasize their power, and by 1958 the BBG was given the power to regulate broadcasting in Canada. The CBC was now simply a broadcasting network with no control over private broadcasting. In 1968, the BBG became the *Canada Radio-Television Commission* (CRTC). It had the power to license radio and television stations in Canada and was the forerunner of today's CRTC.

CBC RADIO PROGRAMMING

As Canada's public broadcaster, *CBC Radio* brought Canadian programming home to Canadians. Some of the programming highlights from the CBC English-language archives include:

- The abdication of the throne by Edward VIII due to his love for a "common" woman.
- Lorne Greene's news broadcasts which made everyone sit up and listen.
- *The Investigator*, a play written by Rueben Ship and directed by Andrew Allan in 1954. It poked fun at the Communist hunt in America spearheaded by Joseph McCarthy. It was so controversial that it was banned in the U.S.
- Paul Henderson scoring the winning goal at the 1972 Canada Cup.
- The 1976 Olympics.
- Comedy programs, which have always been a staple of CBC programming. Besides the "Royal Canadian Air Farce," the CBC has also featured "Radio-Free Friday," "Funny You Should Say That" and "Dr. Bundolo's Pandemonium Medicine Show."
- Some strange shows. During the 1940s, fashion shows and tap-dancing lessons were also offered on the air. Given how the four signs of radio work and the limitations of the medium, it is difficult to imagine how these shows communicated their content effectively.

Today, CBC Radio broadcasts in both official languages on both AM and FM. Some of its most popular English-language programs include "Morningside" with Peter Gzowski, "Disc Drive" with Jurgen Gothe, "Ideas" with Lister Sinclair, "Cross Country Checkup", and the newsmagazines, "As It Happens" and "Sunday Morning." Its French-language counterpart, Société Radio-Canada (SRC) broadcasts French programming nationally.

CBC Stereo, CBC Radio and SRC do not carry commercials. True to the CBC's original mandate, its programming is funded by Parliament.

U.S. RADIO IN THE PRIVATE SECTOR

A Pittsburgh engineer, *Frank Conrad*, fiddled with radiotelegraphy in his home garage, playing music as he experimented. People with homemade receivers liked what they heard from Conrad's transmitter, and soon he had a following. When Conrad's Westinghouse bosses learned that he had become a local celebrity, they saw profit in building receivers that consumers could buy at $10 a set and take home to listen to. To encourage sales of the receivers, Westinghouse built a station to provide regular programming of news, sports and music—mostly music. That station, KDKA, became America's first licensed commercial station in 1920.

The licensing of KDKA was important because it demonstrated the United States' commitment to placing radio in the private sector. In Europe, broadcasting was a government monopoly. KDKA's entertainment programming also sent American broadcasting in a certain direction. In many other countries, radio was used mostly for education and high culture, not mass entertainment.

ROLE OF ADVERTISING

Like the CNR, Westinghouse never expected radio itself to make money, only to spur sales of their $10 home receivers. The economic base of KDKA and the rest of American broadcasting changed in 1922 when WEAF in New York accepted $50 from a real estate developer and allowed him 10 minutes to pitch his new Long Island apartments. Then the Gimbel's department store tried radio advertising. Within months, companies were clamouring for air time. The Lucky Strike Orchestra produced programs, as did the Taystee Loafers from the Taystee bread company, and the A&P Gypsies, the Goodrich Silvertown Orchestra, and the Interwoven Pair from the sock company.

Unlike Canadian radio in those first years of the 1920s and 1930s, American radio took on these distinctive traits:

- Private rather than state ownership of the broadcasting systems.
- An entertainment thrust to programming that emphasized popular culture.
- An economic foundation based on selling time to advertisers who needed to reach a mass audience of consumers.

RADIO AS ENTERTAINMENT

STUDY PREVIEW   Radio stations today are known by a wide range of formats, each geared to attracting narrow segments of the population. In earlier times, radio stations sought broader mass audiences with programs that had wide appeal. Today's more segmented programming came about when radio began losing the mass audience to television in the 1950s.

FORMATS FOR SPECIFIC AUDIENCES

Comedies, dramas and quiz shows moved to television beginning in the late 1940s, and so did the huge audience that radio had cultivated. The radio networks, losing advertisers to television, scaled back what they offered stations. As the number of listeners dropped, local stations played more recorded music, which was far cheaper than producing programs.

Although most stations in the pre-television period offered diversity, a few stations emphasized certain kinds of programming. Some stations carried only religious programs. In the 1950s, Alan Freed introduced rock 'n' roll, which became the fare at hundreds of stations and began wide-scale fragmentation in radio programming. Today, hardly any station tries to offer something for everyone, but everyone can find something on the radio to like. There is a format for everyone.

After Freed came the *Top 40* format, in which the day's top songs were repeated in rotation. The wizard of radio formatting, *Gordon McLendon*, developed the format by mixing fast-paced newscasts, disc jockey chatter, lively commercials and promotional jingles, and hype with the music. It was catchy, almost hypnotizing—and widely imitated. McLendon designed *beautiful music* as a format in

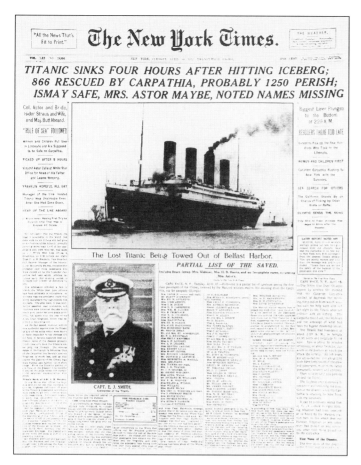

"Radio" Becomes a Household Word. When the *Titanic* sank in 1912, newspapers relied on young radio operator David Sarnoff for information on what was happening in the mid-Atlantic. For 72 hours Sarnoff sat at his primitive receiver, which happened to be on exhibit in a department store, to pick up details from rescue ships. The newspaper coverage of the disaster made "radio" a household word, which paved the way for consumer acceptance over the next few years.

1959; *all-news* in 1961; *all-classified ads*, in 1967. In all of his innovations, McLendon was firm about a strict structure. In Top 40, for example, there were no deviations from music in rotation, news every 20 minutes, naming the station by call letters twice between songs, upbeat jingles and no dead-pan commercials. McLendon's classified-ad format bombed, but the others have survived in both Canada and the U.S.

Radio's fragmented programming has reduced its role as a culturally unifying factor. Almost everyone listens to radio, but listening to a hard-rock station gives a person hardly anything in common with people who listen to public affairs–oriented stations, or soul stations, or beautiful-music stations. Today, the shared experience of radio does not extend beyond narrow segments of the population. Some see this local nature of radio as one of its strengths and not a weakness.

Here are terms used to distinguish radio's major music formats for private radio in Canada:

ADULT CONTEMPORARY. Many advertisers like adult contemporary stations because so many people in the big-spending 25 to 40 age group listen. The format is sometimes called "light rock" or "adult rock."

TOP 40. Top 40, also called "CHR," short for "contemporary hits radio," emphasizes current rock but not as strictly as McLendon insisted. These stations target teenagers.

MEDIA AND YOU

Assessing Hometown Radio

The demassification of radio has led to a great many formats, each designed to appeal to a segment of the mass audience. The shape of demassification varies from region to region, reflecting different interests. You can assess the flavour of radio programming in your area by listening to all the daytime signals you can pick up and categorizing them by these criteria:

■ **Formats.** What percentage of stations falls into major format categories? Almost everywhere, the adult contemporary format is dominant, but in some regions other formats are unusually strong—like country in the West, ethnic in Toronto, and polka in Wisconsin. You may find some stations dabble in so many programming genres that they are difficult to categorize. Generally, though, one type of content best characterizes a station.

■ **Audience.** What age group is each station most appealing to? Top 40 tends to be a teenage audience, classical much older. Are some formats more appealing to women? All-sports stations have strong male followings.

■ **Market.** Listen to local advertisements to determine what socioeconomic level each station is geared to. Ads on all-news stations will show that advertisers believe they have listeners with higher incomes than most other formats. Stations that carry advertisements for luxury products, like Cadillacs, have wealthier audiences than stations that carry ads from muffler shops.

It is important to do this exercise during the daytime because many AM signals at night are from distant cities that won't reflect your area's distinctiveness.

NEWS AND TALK.   As FM stations drew listeners away from AM with their superior sound for music, many AM stations switched to news and talk programming. Talk radio is becoming a dominant format. There is at least one talk radio station in every major market in Canada, including Vancouver, where talk radio has been popular since the 1960s. Most of these stations are on AM. Given that most people tune into FM for music, AM radio had to offer something else to remain profitable, so they opted for talk and information.

Casey's Hits. For almost a quarter century, honey-voiced Casey Kasem has been counting down the Top 40 hits on a nationally syndicated weekly radio show. About 8 million people tune in. Analysts say it's more than the music that draws listeners. An editor at the trade journal *Billboard,* Paul Grein, told a *Newsweek* interviewer: "Countdown shows are very orderly, very ritualistic, and people love a ritual." Today, more than a dozen syndicated countdown shows, built on Kasem's concept, are available to local stations.

COUNTRY.   Once called "country and western," or "CW" for short, this format goes back to the WSM "Grand Old Opry" program from Nashville, Tennessee, in 1925. The music varies significantly from twangy western ballads to what's called "urban country." In Canada, "Young Country" and "New Country" have become two popular music formats. By abandoning Tammy Wynette and George Jones for Shania Twain and Patricia Conroy, new country radio stations have been able to attract younger listeners. Traditional country fans are older males; fans of the new formats are a mix of younger males and females, making it easier to attract listeners and advertisers.

ALBUM-ORIENTED ROCK.   AOR formats offer songs from the 100 best-selling albums. A casual listener might confuse AOR with Top 40, but album stations go back a couple of years for wider variety. Audiences tend to be aged 18 to 24.

OLDIES.   Oldies stations play music that the 30-something generation grew up with, mostly music of the 1960s and 1970s. Sometimes it's called "classic hits."

MIDDLE OF THE ROAD.   Some radio people still use the term "MOR," but this traditional format has been largely subsumed by newer categorizations. MOR avoids the extremes of potted-palm music and hard rock, not concerned about being on top of the latest hits and not hesitant about older music as long as it's not too hard, not too soft.

BEAUTIFUL MUSIC.   Modern variations on this McLendon format provide lavishly orchestrated standards that many people like as background music. This format, sometimes called "musical wallpaper" and "elevator music," was popular in the 1970s and 1980s, especially among women 18 to 45, but much of that audience has switched to "lite" or easy-listening stations that meld MOR and AOR.

ETHNIC.   More than 9 million Canadians belong to ethnic groups other than First Nations, French or British. These people represent over 70 different cultures. Given this fact and Canada's official status as a multicultural country, it's not surprising that full-time, ethnic radio stations have taken root in many of Canada's

Gordon McLendon. The views of radio programming guru Gordon McLendon were widely sought in the 1950s. It was McLendon who created the Top 40 and all-news formats that enabled radio to survive massive audience losses to television.

urban centres. Vancouver has CJVB and CHMB, Edmonton, CKER and Toronto has CHIN. Many other radio stations feature ethnic programming on a part-time basis, during the evenings and on weekends.

CLASSICAL.   This format offers the basic repertoire of enduring music since the Baroque era, although some classical stations also play experimental symphonies, operas and contemporary composers. Because high-brow music has a limited following, most classical stations are supported not by advertising but by listener donations, by universities and by government funding. CBC Stereo broadcasts classical music on a national basis.

RELIGIOUS.   Inspirational music is the programming core of religious stations. The music is interspersed with sermons from evangelists who buy time for their programs, seeking both to proselytize and to raise funds to support ministries.

TALK RADIO

STUDY PREVIEW   Listener call-in programs have become a popular format that has potential as a forum on public issues. These talk formats that feature live listener telephone calls emerged as a major genre in radio in the 1980s.

TALK FORMATS

Call-in formats were greeted enthusiastically at first because of their potential as forums for discussion of the great public issues, but there was a dark side. Many stations with music-based formats used the advent of news and talk stations to reduce their news programming. In effect, many music stations were saying, "Let those guys do news and talk, and we'll do music." The rationale really was a profit-motivated guise to get out of news and public affairs, which is expensive. Playing records is cheap. The result was fewer stations offering serious news and public affairs programming.

Disturbing too was that talk formats failed to live up to expectations that they would be serious forums on public policy. While talk shows provided opportunities for immediate listener feedback, many of the most popular ones degenerated into advice programs on hemorrhoids, psoriasis, face-lifts and psychoses. Sports trivia went over big. Talk shows gave an illusion of being news, but in fact they were low-brow entertainment. The call-in shows that focused on public issues, mostly late at night, attracted many screwballs and hate-mongers who diminished the quality of public dialogue on the great issues. The shows were vulnerable to people who tried to divide communities. A Denver talk show host, Alan Berg, who was Jewish, was shot to death by an anti-Semite who became fired up over what he heard on the radio. In Houston, talk shows encouraged the airing of a rash of antigay sentiments. Talk shows, by their nature, lend themselves to misinformation, even disinformation, from crackpots, fanatics and ignoramuses.

Talk radio may offer access to the "commoners," or so it would seem. *Paul Rutherford*, a Communication professor at the University of Toronto, says that talk radio is "providing a voice for people who otherwise wouldn't have one."

This was especially true during the late 1980s and early 1990s, a time when the government was dealing with issues such as the GST, Meech Lake and Free Trade. At the time, many Canadians felt a sense of alienation; they believed that their politicians simply weren't listening to them. To vent their frustrations, many turned to talk radio. This gave listeners a sense that they were finally being heard.

Shock Jock. Blunt and uninhibited on the air, radio personality Howard Stern is the epitome of the "shock jock." He has expanded into television on the E! channel, and in 1993 he wrote a best-selling autobiographical book. Although his New York-based program has strong listenership, Stern's crude humour is not universally popular. Fox television boss Rupert Murdoch got cold feet about creating a program for Stern in 1994, and the FCC has fined stations that carry his radio program $1.2 million.

MEDIA: PEOPLE

Howard Stern

Would he have become so popular if he had been a Canadian talk show host?

No wonder they call Howard Stern a "shock jock." The New York disc jockey is outrageous, cynical and vulgar. But people listen to his bathroom-wall jokes and his topless female studio guests. Not surprisingly, the Federal Communications Commission, which regulates U.S. broadcast stations, doesn't cotton well to Stern's brand of humour. That hasn't bothered Stern much. In fact, he told listeners he was praying that the prostate cancer of FCC Chairman Alfred Sikes would spread.

No matter how obnoxious he is, Stern has a following. In fact, he is the crown jewel air personality of Infinity Broadcasting, the nation's fourth largest radio company, which syndicates Stern's show coast to coast. The company had $150 million in revenue in 1992, up 11 percent from the year before.

Stern has been expensive for Infinity Broadcasting, not just because he commands top dollar in salary but because the FCC has fined stations carrying Stern $1.2 million for his "references to sexual and excretory activities and functions." Infinity can afford to pay the fine, but it is fighting it on First Amendment grounds. Infinity's president, Mel Karmazin, calls it a harassing attempt at censorship of something that thousands of people want to hear. Those who don't like it can listen elsewhere, Karmazin says: "That's why they make on-off buttons."

Howard Stern has known controversy a long time. At Boston College, he worked at the campus radio station— until they fired him for a show on Godzilla going to Harlem. Later at WNBC in New York, a bit called "Bestiality Dial-a-Porn" got him fired again.

At WXRK in New York, Stern proved he could draw listeners. The station shot from number 21 to number 1 in morning ratings after he signed on in 1985. At his current Infinity home, the blue humour, as well as his racism, sexism, homophobia, misogyny and bad taste, continue to attract a large, profitable audience.

Depending on who you talk to, Howard Stern represents the best in American radio, meeting the interests and needs of a mass audience, or the worst, pandering to the lowest instincts in the society and getting rich in the process.

His autobiographical 1993 book, *Private Parts*, was further evidence of his commercial success. Publisher Simon and Schuster was into a sixth printing within weeks of the release. At that point, sales were 750 000 and climbing.

How is Canadian talk radio different from American talk radio? Many differences exist, according to those who claim that Canadians are "kindler, gentler" talk show participants. Rutherford claims that there are two types of talk show hosts: *warriors* and *father figures*. The warrior is clearly American: confrontational and in your face. Male Canadian talk show hosts tend to be father figures, with a few exceptions—namely, Rafe Mair in British Columbia, Gilles Proulx in Quebec and John Michael in Ontario. Bill Rowe in Newfoundland and Jane Hawtin in Toronto offer more thought-provoking and well-researched fare and belong to neither category.

Perhaps one of the reasons talk radio is different in Canada is the regional or local nature of talk shows. Compared to America, which boasts numerous national talk show hosts, Canadian talk show hosts are local in character. Gary Slaight of Standard Broadcasting says there's only one real issue in America, "and that's whether you're left-wing or right-wing. Whether you're in New York or Seattle, it's the same question. Not in Canada, where we're defined so many ways: English/French, East/West."

CHAPTER WRAP-UP

The proliferation in radio programming can be expected to continue with stations narrowcasting into more and more specialized niches. Broadcast industry commentator Erik Zorn predicts hundreds of formats, some as narrow as all-blues music stations, business news stations, Czech-language stations and full-time stations for the blind. In this new world of *demand programming*, any listener will be able to choose among hundreds of programs at any time—a far cry from pre-television days when mainstream radio was truly a mass medium and sought the whole audience with every program.

Technology has created problems. The advent of FM stereo drew listeners away from AM in the 1980s. With its superior quality of sound, FM held more than 70 percent of the radio audience by the 1990s. Many AM stations shifted to news and talk formats, which did not require stereo transmissions to attract an audience, but these audiences were smaller and AM ended up with fewer listeners. The resale value of AM stations sank, even for old-line big-name stations. Some AM stations entered bankruptcy.

There is no question that radio will continue as a strong medium of mass communication, but the shape of the radio industry is less certain. As in the past, government regulation, technological innovation and competition from other mass media will be major players in determining radio's future.

QUESTIONS FOR REVIEW

1. Why is radio called a ubiquitous and influential medium?
2. How does radio move invisibly through on electromagnetic waves?
3. What are characteristics of the radio industry in Canada? In the U.S.?
4. Why has U.S. radio historically had an entertainment thrust? Why is Canadian radio different?
5. Outline what CBC Radio does.
6. Explain how the four signs of radio help create meaning.

QUESTIONS FOR CRITICAL THINKING

1. The telegraph was invented by Samuel Morse in 1844. Roughly 50 years later Guglielmo Marconi introduced radio wireless telegraphy. What was the difference?
2. Lee De Forest was a technical and programming innovator. Explain the significance of his audion tube and his 1916 broadcast of election returns.
3. A new way of transmitting radio was developed by Edwin Armstrong in the 1930s, and by the 1980s it had left the original AM broadcast system in economic peril. Discuss Armstrong's invention and how it has reshaped radio.
4. American radio was shaped by the networks in the 1920s and 1930s and reshaped by the advent of television in the 1950s. Explain these influences, and be sure to cite radio's transition from literal *broadcasting* toward *narrowcasting*. What about the influence of Gordon McLendon? What of the future?
5. Explain the significance of KDKA of Pittsburgh, and XWA in Montreal.
6. Was enthusiasm about radio's role in the early development of Canadian culture because of the message or the medium? Remember radio was still in its infancy. Could people have been swayed not so much by *what* was said, but by *how* it was said? Remember Marshall McLuhan; was the medium the real message in 1927 at the Dominion Day ceremonies?
7. What makes watching a baseball game on TV dif-

ferent from listening to it on the radio? Analyze the signs used by both media in the broadcast of the same game.

8. Analyze the signs and codes used by the radio stations in your area. How are signs used differently to create meaning in different formats?

9. What do you think the role of CBC radio should be? Should its funding be cut and should it start to accept advertising on air?

10. Which model best describes talk radio in your area: the "warrior" or the "father figure" model?

FOR FURTHER LEARNING

Erik Barnouw. *A Tower in Babel, A History of Broadcasting in the United States to 1933* (Oxford, 1966); *The Golden Web, A History of Broadcasting in the United States, 1933–1953* (Oxford, 1968); *The Image Empire, A History of Broadcasting in the United States, 1953–On* (Oxford, 1970). Barnouw's trilogy is thorough and readable.

John R. Bittner. *Broadcast Law and Regulation* (Prentice Hall, 1982).

"CAB Fires Back at Music Industry Radio Content Claims." *Broadcaster* Industry News (April 1996).

Canadian Association of Broadcasters. *A Broadcaster's Guide to Canada's Cultural Mosaic*, 1988.

Gerald Carson. *The Roguish World of Dr. Brinkley* (Holt, Rinehart & Winston, 1960). Carson's lightly written account tells how the Goat Gland Surgeon took the issue of broadcast regulation to court and lost.

CBC Enterprises. *Fifty Years of Radio: A Celebration of CBC Radio 1936–1986.*

Andrew Crissell. *Understanding Radio* (Methuen, 1990). In the Fiske tradition of cultural studies books, Crissell offers analysis of talk radio, sports and other radio programming.

"The Fowler Years: A Chairman Who Marches to His Own Drummer," *Broadcasting* 112(March 23, 1987): 12, 51–54. An analytical summary of the FCC's deregulation policy under commission chair Mark Fowler.

Peter Goddard. "It's Talk, Talk, Talk All Over the Radio," *Toronto Star* (October 29, 1995).

Lynne Schafer Gross. *Telecommunications: An Introduction to Radio, Television and Other Electronic Media*, 2nd ed. (Wm. C. Brown, 1986). Professor Gross's survey of broadcasting includes an excellent explanation of how the electromagnetic spectrum works.

Laurel Hyatt. "Radio's Recipe for Success," *Broadcaster* (April 1996), 12–15.

Donald Jack. *Sinc, Betty and the Morning Man* (Macmillan, 1977). Although Jack is clearly a fan of CFRB radio, this book does offer some good insights into the growth of the private radio station, from its beginnings to its heyday as one of the most listened to stations in Canada.

Murray B. Levin. *Talk Radio and the American Dream* (D.C. Heath, 1987). Levin, a political scientist, argues that talk radio programs are unique in the American mass media as a voice of common people.

Kirk Makin. "Brrrrring....brrrrring: You're on the Air," *Globe and Mail* (July 16, 1994).

Sandy Stewart. *A Pictorial History of Radio in Canada* (Gage, 1975) An excellent historical look at radio in Canada, especially its early days. Stewart's analysis of Fessenden's role in developing radio in this country is especially good.

Erik Zorn. "Radio Lives!" *Esquire* 101(March 1984):3, 45–54; "The Specialized Signals of Radio News," *Washington Journalism Review* 8(June 1986):6, 31–33. Zorn, a news reporter whose beat is radio and television, tracks changes in broadcasting.

FOR KEEPING UP TO DATE

The weekly trade journals *The Record* and *RPM* keep abreast of news and issues.

Other news coverage can be found in the *Wall Street Journal*, the *New York Times*, the *Los Angeles Times* and the *Globe and Mail.*

Scholarly articles can be found in the *Journal of Broadcasting*, the *Canadian Journal of Communication* and *Journalism Quarterly.*

CHAPTER 5

MOVIES Not Always a Glamour Medium

Movies have a powerful impact

The technological basis of movies is photographic chemistry

Movies had their heyday as a mass medium in the 1940s

Television was a serious threat to Hollywood beginning in the late 1940s

Hollywood today is a major producer of television programming

The movie exhibition business faces challenges from home video

Moviemakers are in an expensive, high-risk business

Hollywood has opted for self-policing to quell censorship threats

The movie business is becoming more concentrated

MEDIA IN THEORY

American vs. Canadian Movies

Why are Canadian movies different from American movies? Notice that the question doesn't imply that Canadian movies are "worse" than American movies, although that seems to be the mythology. For students of communication and decoders of texts, the questions really should be: what makes Canadian movies different from American films and what do our films say about our culture?

While certainly funding, marketplace economics and distribution have all played a role in the development of the Canadian film industry and the "look" of Canadian films, there may be other differences as well. Peter Harcourt, in his essay *Introduction* (1976), argues that Canadian movie scripts symbolically reflect "our own social uncertainties—both our uncertainty of action as a nation and our own present lack of security in dealing with ethnic and cultural problems which, throughout our vast nation, we are trying to define ourselves."

Uncertainty is part of the Canadian way of life; the uncertainties of the French—English debate and the uneasiness of living next door to the United States have all helped shape Canadian culture. Do you see this theme as part of the content of Canadian films? Do an analysis of any Canadian film you have seen. Is this theme present? How is it signified? Here's a list of

Canadian films (French and English) that will help get you started:

Nobody Waved Goodbye (1964)
Mon Oncle Antoine (1971)
Paperback Hero (1973)
The Apprenticeship of Duddy Kravitz (1974)
Decline of the American Empire (1987)
Exotica (1994)
Whale Music (1994)

IMPORTANCE OF MOVIES

STUDY PREVIEW The experience of watching a movie, uninterrupted in a darkened auditorium, has entranced people since the medium's earliest days. It is an all-encompassing experience, which has given movies a special power in shaping cultural values.

OVERWHELMING EXPERIENCE

Movies have a hold on people, at least while they are watching one, that is more intense than any other medium. It is not unusual for a movie reviewer to recommend taking a handkerchief, but never will you hear such advice from a record reviewer and seldom from a book reviewer. Why do movies have such powerful effects? It is not movies themselves. With rare exception, these evocative efforts occur only when movies are shown in a theatre. The viewer sits in a darkened auditorium in front of a giant screen, with nothing to interrupt the experience. The rest of the world is excluded. Movies, of course, can be shown outdoors at drive-in theatres and on television, but the experience is strongest in the darkened cocoon of a movie house.

People have been fascinated with movies almost from the invention of the technology that made them possible, even when the pictures were nothing more than wobbly, fuzzy images on a whitewashed wall. The medium seemed to possess magical powers. With the introduction of sound in the late 1920s, and then colour and a host of later technical enhancements, movies have kept people in awe. Going to the movies remains a thrill—an experience unmatched by other media.

HOLLYWOOD'S CULTURAL INFLUENCE

When Clark Gable took off his shirt in the 1934 movie *It Happened One Night* and revealed that he was not wearing anything underneath, American men in great numbers decided that they too would go without undershirts. Nationwide, undershirt sales plummeted. Whether men prefer wearing underwear is trivial compared to some concerns about how Hollywood portrays life and its influence:

■ Sociologist Norman Denzin says the treatment of drinking in American movies has contributed to a misleading bittersweet romanticism about alcoholism in the public consciousness.

Steven Spielberg

Steven Spielberg. Perhaps no other moviemaker can project stories so compellingly across such a diverse range of subjects as Steven Spielberg. His *Jurassic Park*, which raised questions about DNA preservation of extinct life forms, became the most profitable movie in history, surpassing *E.T.* by over $165 million. *Schindler's List*, which depicts one aspect of the World War II Holocaust, etched powerful, not-to-be-forgotten images into viewers' consciousness.

- Scholars using content analysis have found exponential increases in movie violence that far outpace violence in real life but that nonetheless correspond with perceptions that violence is a growing problem in modern life.
- Utility company executives were none too pleased with the widespread public concern about nuclear power created by James Bridges's 1979 movie, *The China Syndrome*.
- Political leaders express concern from time to time that movies corrupt the morals of young people and glamorize deviant behaviour. Congressman Parnell Thomas once raised questions that Hollywood was advocating the violent overthrow of the government.

Movies are part of our everyday lives in more ways than we realize. Even the way we talk is loaded with movie metaphors. The *New Yorker* magazine noted this introducing an issue on Hollywood: "Our personal scenarios unspool in a sequence of flashbacks, voice-overs and cameos. We zoom in, cut to the chase, fade to black."

Because of the perceived influence of movies, some real, some not, it is important to know about the industry that creates them. This is especially true now that television entertainment programming has been largely subsumed by Hollywood and that the book, magazine and sound recording industries are closely tied into it.

MEDIA: PEOPLE

Robert Flaherty

Explorer *Robert Flaherty* took a camera to the Arctic in 1921 to record the life of an Eskimo family. The result was a new kind of movie: the *documentary*. While other movies of the time were theatrical productions with scripts, set and actors, Flaherty tried something different —recording reality.

His 57-minute *Nanook of the North* was compelling on its own merits when it started on the movie house circuit in 1922, but the film received an unexpected macabre boost a few days later when Nanook, the father of the Eskimo family, died of hunger on the ice. News stories of Nanook's death stirred public interest and attendance at the movie, which helped establish the documentary as an important new film genre.

Flaherty's innovative approach took a new twist in the 1930s, when propagandists saw reality-based movies as a tool to promote their causes. In Germany the Nazi government produced propaganda films, and other countries followed. Frank Capra directed the vigorous five-film series *Why We Fight* for the U.S. War Office in 1942. During this time, Flaherty served as a consultant to the National Film Board (NFB) of Canada.

After World War II, there was a revival of documentaries in Flaherty's style—a neutral recording of natural history. The NFB's documentary style owes much to the Flaherty style.

Today, documentaries are unusual in American movie houses, with occasional exceptions like *Mother Teresa* in 1986 and movies built on rock concerts.

The CBS television network gained a reputation in the 1950s and 1960s for picking up on the documentary tradition with "Harvest of Shame," on migrant workers, and "Hunger in America." In the same period, the National Geographic Society established a documentary unit, and French explorer Jacques Cousteau went into the television documentary business.

Such full-length documentaries mostly are relegated to the Public Broadcasting Service and cable networks today. The major networks, meanwhile, shifted most documentaries away from full-length treatments. Typical was CBS's "60 Minutes," a weekly one-hour program of three minidocumentaries. These new network projects, which included ABC's "20/20," combined reality programming and entertainment in slick packages that attracted larger audiences than traditional documentaries.

Robert Flaherty

Nanook of the North. The documentary became a film genre with explorer Robert Flaherty's *Nanook of the North* in 1921. This film was an attempt to record reality—no actors, no props. The film was especially potent not only because it was a new approach and on a fascinating subject but also because, coincidentally, Nanook died of starvation on the ice at about the time that it was released.

TECHNICAL HERITAGE OF MOVIES

STUDY PREVIEW   Motion picture technology is based on the same chemical process as photography. The medium developed in the 1880s and 1890s. By the 1930s movie houses everywhere were showing "talkies."

AN ADAPTATION FROM PHOTOGRAPHY

The technical heritage of motion pictures is photography. The 1727 discovery that light causes silver nitrate to darken was basic to the development of motion picture technology. So was a human phenomenon called *persistence of vision*. The human eye retains an image for a fraction of a second. If a series of photographs captures something in motion and if those photographs are flipped quickly, the human eye will perceive continuous motion.

The persistence of vision phenomenon was demonstrated photographically in 1877 by *Eadweard Muybridge* in California. Former Governor Leland Stanford had found himself in a wager on whether horses ever had all their legs off the ground when galloping. It was something the human eye could not perceive. All anyone could make out of the legs of a galloping horse was a blur. Stanford asked Muybridge if photography could settle the question. Muybridge stationed 24 cameras along a track with trip strings to open the shutters. The galloping horse hit the strings, and Muybridge had 24 sequential photographs that showed that galloping horses take all four legs off the ground at the same time. Stanford won his $25,000 bet.

More significant to us was that the illusion of a horse in motion was possible by flipping Muybridge's photographs quickly. The sequential photographic images, when run rapidly by the human eye, made it appear that the horse was moving. All that was needed was the right kind of camera and film to capture about 16 images per second. Those appeared in 1888. *William Dickson* of Thomas Edison's laboratory developed a workable motion picture camera. Dickson and Edison used celluloid film perfected by *George Eastman*, who had just introduced his Kodak camera. By 1891 Edison began producing movies.

Edison movies were viewed by looking into a box. In France, brothers *Auguste* and *Louis Lumière* brought projection to motion pictures. By running the film in

Reality Bites. Young adults in their 20s, dubbed "Generation X" by novelist Douglas Coupland, have been the subject of several recent films, including 1993's *Reality Bites*. X-ers (a.k.a. "Slackers," from the Richard Linklater film of the same name) complain that their cultural image is entirely media-created, and in fact is meaningless, except as a convenient demographic category for advertisers.

front of a specially aimed powerful lightbulb, the Lumières projected movie images on a wall. In 1895 they opened an exhibition hall in Paris—the first movie house. Edison recognized the commercial advantage of projection, and himself patented the *Vitascope* projector, which he put on the market in 1896.

Movies came to Canada in June of 1896 when a private demonstration of the Vitascope was held in Montreal. Those in attendance included the mayor of Montreal and other members of the elite. They witnessed another example of what McLuhan would refer to as the medium becoming the message. The report in Montreal's *La Presse* explains what they saw and how they reacted to the imagery of a cavalry charge: "You see each and every man in all his glory. There are a thousand of them. They are coming right onto the stage. You are going to be crushed—but no, at the crucial moment everything vanishes and you remain gaping. All that was needed to complete the illusion was colour and a phonograph to reproduce sounds. That is soon to come."

ADDING SOUND TO PICTURES

Dickson at Edison's lab came up with a sound system for movies in 1889. In the first successful commercial application, Fox used sound in its 1922 Movietone

High-Brow Movies

European movie directors, especially the Swede *Ingmar Bergman,* have been favourites of a high-brow American moviegoing crowd since the 1950s. These directors looked to film as a sophisticated literary form, not escapist entertainment. Among Bergman's 50 films, several explored the turbulent relationship he witnessed as a child between his depression-prone father and his emotionally cool mother. The Italian director *Federico Fellini*'s *La Dolce Vita* in 1960 commented with poetic abstraction on human rituals.

High-brow foreign movies never attracted huge American audiences, but they developed a loyal, influential following. They also reminded entertainment-oriented Hollywood of the artistic and literary possibilities of film as a medium. Bergman's 1982 *Fanny and Alexander* won four of Hollywood's Academy Awards.

Occasionally, foreign art films find their way into major movie houses, but usually they are exhibited at small specialized theatres in major cities and near universities. These movies also are popular at film society meetings.

The Remains of the Day. The Ismail Merchant and James Ivory producer-director team created a series of high-brow films, most with a small but intense following. *The Remains of the Day* in 1993, starring Anthony Hopkins and Emma Thompson, dealt with class, politics, and repressed desire in England between the wars. Earlier Merchant-Ivory films, adapted from English novels, included *A Room with a View* and *Howards End.*

newsreels. But it was four upstart moviemakers, the brothers *Albert, Harry, Jack* and *Sam Warner,* who revolutionized movies with sound. In 1927 the Warners released *The Jazz Singer* starring Al Jolson. There was sound for only two segments, but it caught the public's fancy. By 1930, 9000 movie houses around the country were equipped for sound.

THREE CRISES THAT RESHAPED HOLLYWOOD

STUDY PREVIEW   In quick succession, Hollywood took three body blows in the late 1940s. Right-wing political leaders sent some directors and screenwriters to jail in 1947 and intimidated moviemakers into creative cowardice. In 1948 the U.S. Supreme Court broke up the economic structure of the movie industry. Then television stole people from the box office.

THE HOLLYWOOD 10

Hollywood had a creative crisis in 1947 when Congressman *Parnell Thomas,* chair of the House Un-American Activities Subcommittee, began hearings on communists in Hollywood. Thomas summoned 47 screenwriters, directors and actors and demanded answers to accusations about leftist influences in Hollywood and the Screen Writers Guild. Ten witnesses who refused to answer insulting accusations went to jail for contempt of Congress. It was one of the most highly visible manifestations of *McCarthyism,* a post–World War II American overreaction to Soviet communism as a national threat.

The Thomas hearings had longer deleterious effects. Movie producers, afraid the smear would extend to them, declined to hire the *Hollywood 10.* Other careers were also ruined. One expert identified 11 directors, 36 actors, 106 writers and 61 others who suddenly were unwelcome in their old circles and could not find work.

Among the Hollywood 10 was screenwriter *Dalton Trumbo.* His powerful pacifist novel *Johnny Got His Gun* made Trumbo an obvious target for the jingoist Thomas committee. After Trumbo refused to answer committee questions, he was jailed. On his release, Trumbo could not find anybody who would accept his screenplays, so he resorted to writing under the pseudonym Robert Rich. The best he could earn was $15 000 per script, one-fifth his former rate. When his screenplay for *The Brave One* won an Academy Award in 1957, Robert Rich did not dare show up to accept it.

In a courageous act, *Kirk Douglas* hired Trumbo in 1959 to write *Spartacus.* Then *Otto Preminger* did the same with *Exodus.* Besides Trumbo, only screenwriter *Ring Lardner Jr.* rose from the 1947 ashes. In 1970, after two decades on the blacklist, Lardner won an Academy Award for *M*A*S*H.*

The personal tragedies resulting from the Thomas excesses were bad enough, but the broader ramification was a paucity of substantial treatments of major social and political issues. Eventually, moviemakers rallied with sophisticated treatments of controversial subjects that, it can be argued, were more intense than they might otherwise have been. It was an anti-McCarthy backlash, which did not occur until the mid-1950s, when Hollywood began to reestablish movies as a serious medium. By the 1970s, there were even cinematic exposés of this vicious period in American political history, including *The Way We Were,* a 1973 film starring Robert Redford and Barbra Streisand, and *The Front,* a 1976 satire starring Woody Allen and Zero Mostel.

Divided Hollywood. When some members of Congress set out in 1947 to unearth a communist infiltration in Hollywood, they heard what they wanted to hear from actor Robert Taylor. He testified that he had seen plenty of things "on the pink side" in Hollywood. Other Hollywood people saw through the congressional probe as a witch hunt, and refused even to testify. Ten of them went to jail.

COURT BANS ON VERTICAL INTEGRATION

The U.S. government has acted twice to break up the movie industry when it became so consolidated that there was no alternative way to prevent abuses. *Adolph Zukor*'s Paramount became a major success as a producer and distributor of feature films in the 1920s, but Zukor wanted more. He began buying movie houses, and eventually owned 1400 of them. It was a classic case of *vertical integration*, a business practice in which a company controls its product all the way from inception to consumption. Paramount not only was producing and distributing movies but also, through its own movie houses, was exhibiting them. It was profitable, and soon other major Hollywood studios also expanded vertically.

Still not satisfied with his power and profits, Zukor introduced the practice of *block booking*, which required non-Paramount movie houses to book Paramount films in batches. Good movies could be rented only along with the clunkers. The practice was good for Zukor because it guaranteed him a market for the failures. Exhibitors, however, felt coerced, which fueled resentment against the big studios.

The U.S. Justice Department began litigation against vertical integration in 1938, using Paramount as a test case. Ten years later, in 1948, the U.S. Supreme Court told Paramount and four other major studios to divest. They had a choice of selling off either their production or distribution or exhibition interests. Most sold their theatre chains.

The effect shook the whole economic structure on which Hollywood was based. No longer could the major studios guarantee an audience for their movies by booking them into their own theatres, and what had come to be known as the *studio system* began to collapse. There was now risk in producing movies because movie houses decided what to show, and there was also a hitherto missing competition among studios.

Movie scholars say the court-ordered divestiture, coming when it did, had a more damaging effect than the Justice Department and the courts foresaw. It was about this time that Parnell Thomas and his congressional committee were bashing producers, which undermined Hollywood's creative output. Now the whole way in which the industry operated was required to change overnight. Hollywood was coming apart.

THE CHALLENGE FROM TELEVISION

Movie attendance peaked in 1946 at over 90 million tickets a week. Every neighbourhood had a movie house, and people went as families to see the latest shows, even those that were not very good. Movies, rivaled only by radio, had become the nation's dominant entertainment medium.

Then came television. The early television sets were expensive, and it was a major decision in many families whether to buy one. In many households there were family conferences to decide whether to divert the weekly movie budget to buying a television. By 1950 movie attendance plummeted to 60 million a week and then 46 million by 1955.

Not only had Hollywood been pummeled by Congress into creative timidity, and then been broken up by the courts, but also it had lost the bulk of its audience. Doomsayers predicted an end to Hollywood.

HOLLYWOOD'S RESPONSE TO TELEVISION

STUDY PREVIEW   Ironic as it seems, television has been the greatest force shaping the modern movie industry. When television began eroding movie attendance in the 1950s, moviemakers responded with technical innovations such as wraparound screens. There also were major shifts in movie content, including treatments of social issues that early television would not touch.

TECHNICAL INNOVATION

When television began squeezing movies in the late 1940s, moviemakers scrambled for special effects to hold their audience. Colour movies had been introduced in the 1930s. In the 1950s they came to be the standard—something that early television could not offer. Other technical responses included wraparound Cinerama screens, which put images not only in front of audiences but also in their peripheral vision. Television's small screen could not match it. Cinerama also permitted moviemakers to outdo television with sweeping panoramas that were lost on small television screens. Offsetting its advantages, Cinerama was a costly attempt to increase audience involvement. It required multicamera production, and theatres had to be equipped with special projectors and remodeled for the curved screens. Cinema-Scope gave much the same effect as Cinerama but less expensively with an image 2½ times wider than it was high, on a flat screen. CinemaScope did not fill peripheral vision, but it seemed more realistic than the earlier squarish screen images. Gimmicky innovations included *three-dimensional pictures*, which gave viewers not only width and height but also depth. Smellovision was a dubious, short-lived technique. Odours wafted through movie houses to enhance the audience's sensual involvement.

CONTENT INNOVATION

Besides technical innovations, moviemakers attempted to regain their audiences with high-budget movies, with innovative themes and, finally, by abandoning their traditional mass audiences and appealing to subgroups within the mass audiences.

Media Abroad

Movies of India

At 13 cents a seat, people jam Indian movie houses in such numbers that some exhibitors schedule five showings a day starting at 9 a.m. Better seats sell out days in advance in some cities. There is no question that movies are the country's strongest mass medium. Even though per capita income is only $206 a year, Indians find enough rupees to support an industry that cranks out 800 movies a year, four times more than American moviemakers. Most are B-grade formula melodramas and action stories. Screen credits often include a *director of fights*. Despite their flaws, Indian movies are so popular that it is not unusual for a movie house in a Hindi-speaking area to be packed for a film in another Indian language that nobody understands. Movies are produced in 15 Indian languages.

The movie mania centres on stars. Incredible as it may seem, M. G. Ramachandran, who played folk warriors, and M. R. Radha, who played villains, got into a real-life gun duel one day. Both survived their wounds, but Ramachandran exploited the incident to bid for public office. He campaigned with posters that showed him bound in head bandages and was elected chief minister of his state. While in office, Ramachandran continued to make B-grade movies, always as the hero.

Billboards, fan clubs and scurrilous magazines fuel the obsession with stars. Scholars Erik Barnouw and Subrahmanyam Krishna, in their book *Indian Film*, characterize the portrayals of stars as "mythological demigods who live on a highly physical and erotic plane, indulging in amours." With some magazines, compromising photos are a specialty.

A few Indian moviemakers have been recognized abroad for innovation and excellence, but they generally have an uphill battle against B-movies in attracting Indian audiences. Many internationally recognized Indian films, such as those by *Satyajit Ray*, flop commercially at home.

India Fan Mags. Prolific moviemakers in India crank out movies (most of them not very good) in 15 languages to meet a seemingly insatiable public demand. Fans track the off-screen antics of their favourite stars in celebrity magazines like these in English, Gujarati and Hindi.

High-budget movies called *spectaculars* became popular in the 1950s. How could anybody, no matter how entranced by television, ignore the epic *Quo Vadis*, with one scene using 5500 extras? There were limits, however, to luring Americans from their television sets with publicity-generating big-budget epics. The lavish *Cleopatra* of 1963 cost $44 million, much of which Twentieth Century-Fox lost. It just cost too much to make. Even so, moviemakers continued to risk occasional big-budget spectaculars. No television network in the 1960s would have put up $20 million to produce the profitable *The Sound of Music*. Later, the *Star*

Wars movies by George Lucas were huge successes of the sort television could not contemplate.

Television's capture of the broad mass audience was a mixed blessing. Television was in a content trap that had confined movies earlier. To avoid offending big sections of the mass audience, television stuck with safe subjects. Moviemakers, seeking to distinguish their products from television, began producing films on serious, disturbing *social issues*. In 1955 *Blackboard Jungle* tackled disruptive classroom behaviour, hardly a sufficiently nonthreatening subject for television. Also in 1955 there was *Rebel Without a Cause*, with James Dean as a teenager seeking identity. Marital intimacy and implied homosexuality were elements in the movie adaptation of Tennessee Williams's *Cat on a Hot Tin Roof*, starring Paul Newman and Elizabeth Taylor.

Television continued to be squeamish about many social issues into the 1960s, but movies continued testing new waters, notably with violence and sex. The slow-motion machine-gun deaths of bank robbers Bonnie and Clyde in Arthur Penn's 1967 classic left audiences awed in sickening silence. Nevertheless, people kept coming back to movies with graphic violence. Sex was taboo on television but not at the movies. It was the theme in *Bob and Carol and Ted and Alice*, *Carnal Knowledge* and *I Am Curious Yellow*. Sex went about as far as it could with the hard-core *Deep Throat* of 1973, which was produced for porno houses but achieved crossover commercial success in regular movie houses.

Movies came to be made for a younger crowd. By 1985, regular moviegoers fell into a relatively narrow age group—from teenagers through college age. Fifty-nine percent of the tickets were purchased by people between the ages of 12 and 24. Even so, the industry did not produce exclusively for a young audience. Moviemakers recognized that the highest profits came from movies with a *crossover audience*. These were movies that attracted not only the regular box-office crowd but also infrequent moviegoers. Essential, however, was the youth audience. Without it, a movie could not achieve extraordinary success. The immensely profitable *E.T.* was an example. It appealed to the youth audience, to parents who took their small children, and to film aficionados who were fascinated with the special effects.

MELDING OF MOVIES AND TELEVISION

STUDY PREVIEW   Hollywood's initial response to television was to fight the new medium, an effort that had mixed results. Next Hollywood adopted the idea that if you can't beat them, join them. Today, most of the entertainment fare on television comes from Hollywood.

RECONCILIATION OF COMPETING INDUSTRIES

Despite Hollywood's best attempts to stem the erosion in attendance caused by television, the box-office sales continued to dwindle. Today, an average of only 16 million tickets are sold a week, one-fifth of attendance at the 1946 box-office peak. Considering that the U.S. population has grown steadily during the period, the decline has been an even more severe indication of television's impact on movie attendance.

Despite a near 50-year slide in box-office traffic, Hollywood has hardly lost its war with television. The movie industry today, a $4 billion a year component of the U.S. economy, is so intertwined with television that it is hard to distinguish them. Three-quarters of the movie industry's production today is for television.

There remains, however, an uneasy tension between the exhibitors who own movie houses and television. Theatre traffic has not recovered, and while moviemakers and distributors are profiting from new distribution channels, especially home videos, these new outlets are hurting theatre traffic.

FIRST RUNS AND AFTER-MARKETS

When moviemakers plan films today, they build budgets around anticipated revenues that go beyond first runs in movie houses. Unlike the old days, when movies either made it or didn't at the box office, today moviemakers earn more than 17 percent of their revenue from pay television services like HBO after the movie has played itself out in movie houses. Another 8 percent comes from selling videotapes.

For most movies, foreign release is important. Movies are usually released in the United States and abroad simultaneously. Foreign distribution revenues can be significant. The box-office revenue from U.S. movies abroad, in fact, is significant in balance-of-trade figures with other nations.

After-market revenue comes from pay-per-view television channels and the home video market.

MOVIE EXHIBITORS

STUDY PREVIEW Most moviegoers today go to multiscreen theatres that show a wide range of movies. These multiplexes are a far cry from the first commercially successful exhibition vehicles, peep show machines that only one viewer at a time could watch. Intermediate exhibition vehicles ranged from humble neighbourhood movie houses to downtown palaces.

EARLY EXHIBITION FACILITIES

In the early days, movie patrons peered into a box as they cranked a 50-foot loop over sprockets. These were called *peep shows.* When Thomas Edison's powerful incandescent lamp was introduced, peep show parlours added a room for projecting movies on a wall. Business thrived. Typical admission was a nickel. By 1908 just about every town had a *nickelodeon,* as these early exhibition places were called.

Exhibition parlours multiplied and became grander. In 1913 the elegant *Strand Theatre,* the first of the movie palaces, opened in New York. By the early 1940s there were more than 20 000 movie houses in operation. Every neighbourhood had one.

As television gained prominence in the 1950s, many movie houses fell into disrepair. One by one they were boarded up. *Drive-in movies* eased the loss. At their peak, there were 4000 drive-ins in Canada and the U.S., but that did not offset the movie houses that had closed. Furthermore, drive-ins were hardly 365-day operations, especially in northern climates, like Canada.

MULTISCREEN THEATRES

Since a nadir in 1971, when annual attendance dropped to 875 million, the exhibition business has evolved into new patterns. Exhibitors have copied the European practice of *multiscreen theatres*—and they built them mostly in suburbs. The new multiscreen theatres allow moviegoers to choose among several first-run movies, all nearby in a multiplex theatre with as many as 12 screens. A family can split up in the lobby—mom and dad to one screen, teenagers to another, and the little kids to a G-rated flick.

Showing rooms are smaller today, averaging 340 seats compared with 750 in 1950. Most multiplexes have large and small showing rooms. An advantage for exhibitors is that they can shift popular films to their bigger rooms to accommodate large crowds and move other films to smaller rooms.

Multiplex theatres have lower overhead. There might be 12 projectors, but only one projectionist, one ticket taker and one concession stand. The system has been profitable. Multiplexes account for approximately 2500 movie screens in Canada.

BOX-OFFICE INCOME

Movie houses usually split box-office receipts with a movie's distributors. The movie house percentage is called the *nut*. Deals vary, but a 50-50 split is common the first week. *Exhibitors*, as the movie houses are called, take a higher percentage the longer the run. A frequent formula is 60 percent the second week and 70 percent the third, and sometimes more after that. Besides the nut, the concession stand is an important revenue source for exhibitors. Concessions are so profitable that exhibitors sometimes agree to give up their nut entirely for a blockbuster and rely on popcorn and Twizzlers to make money. Movie-house markups on confections are typically 60 percent, even more on popcorn.

The *distributors* that market and promote movies claim a share of movie revenue, taking part of the nut from exhibitors and charging booking fees plus expenses to the moviemakers. Distribution expenses can be significant. Advertising and marketing average $6 million per movie. Making multiple prints, 1200 copies at $1200 apiece, and shipping them around the country is expensive too. Distributors also

Edison's Kinetoscope. Among the earliest mechanisms for watching movies was inventor Thomas Edison's kinetoscope. A person would look through a peephole as a strip of film was wound over a light bulb. The effect was shaky. Later, Edison borrowed a technique from the Lumière brothers of Paris for the Vitascope system of projecting images on a wall.

Movies from the Front Seat. Drive-in theatres, with speakers that attach to the car window, were especially popular with teenagers, who often refer to them as "passion pits." Today, the number of drive-ins has diminished to about 100 in Canada.

take care of after-markets, including foreign exhibition, videocassette distributors and television—for a fee plus expenses.

With some movies not enough box-office income is generated for the producers to recoup their production expenses. These expenses can be staggering, about $24 million on average. However, when production budgets are kept low and the movie succeeds at the box office, the return to the producers can be phenomenal.

FINANCING FOR MOVIES

STUDY PREVIEW   The financing of movies is based more on hardball assessments of their prospects for commercial success than on artistic merit. The money to produce movies comes from major movie studios, banks and investment groups. Studios sometimes draw on the resources of their corporate parents.

THE LESSON OF *INTOLERANCE*

The great cinematic innovator *D. W. Griffith* was riding high after the success of his 1915 Civil War epic, *The Birth of a Nation*. Griffith poured the profits into a new venture, *Intolerance*. It was a complex movie that examined social injustice in ancient Babylon, Renaissance France, early 20th-century America and the Holy Land at the time of Christ. It was a critical success, a masterpiece, but film audiences had not developed the sophistication to follow a theme through disparate historical periods. At the box office it failed.

Intolerance cost $2 million to make, unbelievable by 1916 standards. Griffith had used huge sets and hundreds of extras. He ended up broke. To make more movies, Griffith had to seek outside financing. The result, say movie historians, was a dilution in creativity. Financiers were unwilling to bankroll projects with dubious prospects at the box office. Whether creativity is sacrificed by the realities of capitalism remains a debated issue, but there is no doubt that moviemaking is big business.

ARTISTIC VERSUS BUDGET ISSUES

Today, finding financial backing is easier for some moviemakers than others. Producer-actor Clint Eastwood has no problem because of his record for producing not only popular but also low-cost films, always within budget. Steven Spielberg, who produces big-budget movies like *Jurassic Park*, has an almost Eastwoodlike reputation for careful planning, good organization and delivering projects close to budget.

Raising money is harder for producers known for overspending. Michael Cimino reached an extreme with *Heaven's Gate*, a western budgeted originally at $10 million for production. Cimino spent $45 million in pursuing his compulsion for historical detail. The film ended up as a masterpiece by many standards, every scene a cinematographic postcard. It also almost put United Artists out of business.

Francis Ford Coppola has a similar reputation for refusing to compromise on detail, whatever the budget implications. For his war movie *Apocalypse Now*, Coppola asked the Pentagon to provide troops and equipment. The Pentagon declined, concerned about Coppola's focus on bizarre sideshows of the Vietnam War. So Coppola built his own army—an expensive artistic decision. In contrast, when the Army objected to a scene of trainee brutality in Clint Eastwood's *Heartbreak Ridge*,

MEDIA DATABANK

Top-Earning Movies

These are the top-earning movies of all time.

Movie	Director	Gross	Year
Jurassic Park	Steven Spielberg	$870 million	1993
E.T.: The Extra-Terrestrial	Steven Spielberg	$702 million	1982
Ghost	Jerry Zucker	$520 million	1990
Star Wars	George Lucas	$510 million	1977
Indiana Jones: Last Crusade	Steven Spielberg	$500 million	1989
Terminator 2	James Cameron	$490 million	1991
Home Alone	Chris Columbus	$480 million	1990
Jaws	Steven Spielberg	$460 million	1975
Pretty Woman	Garry Marshall	$450 million	1990
Batman	Leslie Martinson	$420 million	1989

Eastwood dropped the scene and received the military support he wanted—a budget-conscious decision.

FINANCING SOURCES

Just as in D. W. Griffith's time, movies are expensive to make—about $24 million on average. Then there are the big-budget movies. Depending on how the expenses are tallied, the 1991 movie *Terminator 2* cost $90 million to $110 million to make. The 1987 box-office flop *Ishtar* ran up bills of $40 million. *Who Framed Roger Rabbit?* exceeded $60 million. Where does the money come from?

MAJOR STUDIOS.   Major studios finance many movies with profits from their earlier movies. Most movies, however, do not originate with major studios but with *independent producers*. While these producers are autonomous in many respects, most of them rely on major studios for their financing. The studios hedge their risks by requiring that they distribute the movies, a profitable enterprise involving rentals to movie houses and television, home video sales and merchandise licensing.

The studios, as well as other financial backers, do more than write checks. To protect their investments, some involve themselves directly in film projects. They examine budgets and production schedules in considering a loan request. It's common for them to send representatives to shooting sites to guard against budget overruns.

Major studios that are part of conglomerates can draw on the resources of their corporate parents. In 1952 giant MCA acquired the ailing Universal studio and plowed its record business profits into the studio. Universal turned profitable, and MCA became even stronger by having another profitable subsidiary. The Gulf and Western conglomerate later did the same with Paramount. Coca-Cola acquired Columbia in 1982 with a promise to help Columbia through the rough times that had beset the movie company.

The Oscars. Canadian Anna Paquin won an Academy Award for best supporting actress for the 1993 movie *The Piano*. The Oscar is recognized as a mark of accomplishment because it is the film industry itself, the Academy of Motion Picture Arts and Sciences, who selects the winners.

In the 1980s several studios acquired new corporate parents, which made it easier to finance movies. The Japanese electronics giant Sony bought Columbia in 1989. At $3.4 billion, it was the biggest Japanese takeover of an American corporation in history. The size of the deal was a sign of the new resources Columbia could tap to make movies. By the early 1990s three of the largest U.S. studios were owned by giant foreign companies with the ability to generate cash from other enterprises to strengthen their new U.S. movie subsidiaries.

INVESTOR GROUPS.   Special investment groups sometimes are put together to fund movies for major studios. Among them is Silver Screen Partners, which provided millions of dollars in financing for Disney projects at a critical

MEDIA: PEOPLE

Spike Lee

Spike Lee, a bright, clever young film director, was in deep trouble in 1992. He had persuaded Warner Brothers, the big Hollywood studio, to put up $20 million for a film biography of controversial black leader Malcolm X, one of his heroes. Lee insisted on expensive foreign shooting in Cairo and Soweto, and now, not only was the $20 million from Warner gone but so was $8 million from other investors. To finish the movie, Lee put up his own $3 million up-front salary to pay, he hoped, all the production bills.

The crisis was not the first for Lee, whose experience as a moviemaker illustrates several realities about the American movie industry, not all of them flattering:

- Hollywood is the heart of the American movie industry, and it is difficult if not impossible for feature filmmakers to succeed outside of the Hollywood establishment.
- Hollywood, with rare exceptions, favours movies that follow themes that already have proven successful rather than taking risks on innovative, controversial themes.
- Fortunes come and go in Hollywood, even studio fortunes. Although Warner is a major studio and often flush with money, it was on an austerity binge when Spike Lee came back for more money in 1992.
- The American movie industry has been taken over by conglomerates, which, as in the case of Warner Brothers, a subsidiary of Time Warner, was being pressured in 1992 to maximize profits to see the parent company through a difficult economic period.

To hear Spike Lee tell it, his problem also was symptomatic of racism in the movie industry. Addressing the Los Angeles Advertising Club during the *Malcolm X* crisis, Lee, who is black, was blunt: "I think there's a ceiling on how much money Hollywood's going to spend on black films or films with a black theme."

Although studio executives would deny Lee's charge, his perceptions were born of experience in making five movies, all critically acclaimed and all profitable but all filmed on shoestring budgets and with little or no studio promotion.

As a student at Morehouse College, Spike Lee had dabbled in film, and when he graduated he decided to commit himself fully to making movies. He enrolled in the film program at New York University. As his master's thesis he put together *Joe's Bed-Stuy Barbershop: We Cut Heads*. It won a 1982 student Academy Award and became the first student film ever shown in the Lincoln Center's new films series in New York.

That would seem to make a young filmmaker a sought-after talent in Hollywood, but such would not be Lee's experience. Despite the acclaim for *Joe's Bed-Stuy Barbershop*, which called for an awakening of American black consciousness, Lee could not interest Hollywood in financing any of his ideas for more black-oriented films. On his own, Lee raised $175,000 in 1986 to produce *She's Gotta Have It*, a sharp, witty movie that upset Hollywood's conventional wisdom by making $8 million.

Bristling with ideas for more films, Lee again went hat in hand to Hollywood, but the response was lukewarm. For lack of financing, he put his movie ideas on a back burner and kept busy as a filmmaker with an Anita point in Disney's revival in the 1980s. Canadian tax laws allow tax breaks for investors who back Canadian filmmakers. The capital cost allowance (CCA) lets investors write off the cost of investing in a Canadian film.

Less proven producers, or those whose track records are marred by budget overruns and loose production schedules, often seek financing from *risk investors*, who include venture capitalists, tax-shelter organizers and foreign distributors. Risk investors often take a bigger share of revenue in exchange for their bigger risk. It sometimes is a surprise who puts up the money. For *Willie Wonka and the Chocolate Factory*, it was Quaker Oats.

BANKS. To meet front-end production expenses, studios go to banks for loans against their assets, which include their production facilities and warehouses of vin-

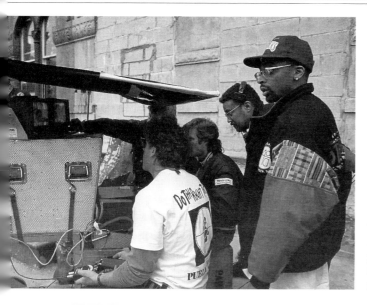

"Public Enemy." Between movie projects, Spike Lee produces television commercials and videos, including the popular "Public Enemy." There have been many slow periods between movies for Lee, who finds Hollywood money hard to come by for his work, even though he is acclaimed as one of his generation's great moviemakers. Lee blames racism among those who control Hollywood purse strings.

Baker music video, the "Horn of Plenty" short for "Saturday Night Live," and the "Hangtime" and "Cover" ads for Nike, with basketball star Michael Jordan and himself playing his Mars Blackmon streetwise hustler character from *She's Gotta Have It.*

The videos won awards, and the Nike ads sold a lot

of shoes, which finally enabled Lee to persuade Columbia Pictures to put up some money for a new movie, *School Daze,* although only one-third of the studio's usual commitment for a movie. Columbia's hesitancy was understandable from a commercial perspective. The movie seemed risky. Not only did it delve into sensitive racial issues, including social stratification between light-skinned and dark-skinned blacks, but also, being a musical, it had complex production numbers that might confound a young director, even one as promising as Spike Lee.

Columbia's hesitancy, it turned out, was misplaced. Despite weak studio publicity, *School Daze* turned out to be Columbia's top-grossing movie of 1988. Especially significant about *School Daze* was that Columbia had given Lee complete creative control, unusual even for many veteran filmmakers. That, of course, made the movie's success even a greater credit to Lee, and in 1989 *Newsweek* magazine proclaimed Lee one of the nation's 25 leading innovators.

Lee followed *School Daze* with *Do the Right Thing, Mo' Better Blues* and *Jungle Fever.* None had strong studio financial backing. He remained an outsider. Not only was he a black person in a white-dominated business, but he also insisted on living in the New York neighbourhood where he grew up.

When he proposed *Malcolm X,* Warner put up $20 million, unprecedented for a black film, but still short of the whole budget. Lee was sent out to raise the remainder of the $28-million budget from other sources, and then, when the cost overruns came in, he found himself putting his own salary into the project to pay the bills and keep the project alive.

tage films awaiting rerelease. By bankrolling movies, the California-based Bank of America grew into one of the nation's biggest banks.

GOVERNMENT FUNDING

Financing for Canadian movies can also come from the public sector. *Telefilm*, a federal government agency, provides loans and grants to Canadian filmakers to help them develop, produce and distribute movies (and television programs) in Canada. The idea behind Telefilm, and its predecessor, the Canadian Film Development Corporation, was to help foster and support a Canadian film industry. Legislation tabled in 1966 by Judy LaMarsh was passed by Parliament in 1967. Telefilm's 1995 budget was $152 million. One hundred and twenty-two million dollars came from taxpayers; the rest of the money came from revenues and other sources. Telefilm's budget will be reduced in the future as will other government-funded agencies in these days of cutbacks. Heritage Canada has decreased its contribution to Telefilm to $110 million in 1996, and further cuts are expected in 1997.

MOVIE CENSORSHIP

STUDY PREVIEW   The movie industry has devised a five-step rating system that alerts people to movies they might find objectionable. Despite problems inherent in any rating scheme, the NC-17, R, PG-13, P, and G system has been more successful than earlier self-regulation attempts to quiet critics.

MORALITY AS AN ISSUE

It was no wonder in Victorian 1896 that a movie called *Dolorita in the Passion Dance* caused an uproar. There were demands that it be banned—the first but hardly last such call against a movie. In 1907 Chicago passed a law restricting objectionable motion pictures. State legislators across the land were insisting that something be done. Worried moviemakers created the *Motion Picture Producers and Distributors of America* in 1922 to clean up movies. *Will Hays*, a prominent Republican who was an elder in his Presbyterian church, was put in charge. Despite his efforts, movies with titillating titles continued to be produced. A lot of people shuddered at titles such as *Sinners in Silk* and *Red Hot Romance*, and Hollywood scandals were no help. Actor Wallace Reid died from drugs. Fatty Arbuckle was tried for (and acquitted of) the slaying of a young actress. When the Depression struck, many people linked the nation's economic failure with "moral bankruptcy." Movies were a target.

Under pressure, the movie industry adopted the *Motion Picture Production Code* in 1930, which codified the kind of thing that Will Hays had been doing. There was to be no naughty language, nothing sexually suggestive and no bad guys going unpunished.

Church people led intensified efforts to clean up movies. The 1930 code was largely the product of *Father Daniel Lord*, a Roman Catholic priest, and *Martin Quigley*, a Catholic layperson. In 1934, after an apostolic delegate from the Vatican berated movies in an address to a New York church convention, United States bishops organized the *Legion of Decency*, which worked closely with the movie industry's code administrators.

The legion, which was endorsed by religious leaders of many faiths, moved on several fronts. Chapters sprouted in major cities. Some chapters boycotted theatres for six weeks if they showed condemned films. Members slapped stickers marked "We Demand Clean Movies" on car bumpers. Many theatre owners responded, vowing to show only approved movies. Meanwhile, the industry itself added teeth to its own code. Any members of the Motion Picture Producers and Distributors of America who released movies without approval were fined $25 000.

MOVIES AND CHANGING MORES

In the late 1940s the influence of the policing agencies began to wane. The 1948 Paramount court decision was one factor. It took major studios out of the exhibition business. As a result, many movie houses could rent films from independent producers, many of whom never subscribed to the code. A second factor was the movie *The Miracle*, which became a First Amendment issue in 1952. The movie was about a simple woman who was sure St. Joseph had seduced her. Her baby, she felt, was Christ. Critics wanted the movie banned as sacrilege, but the Supreme Court sided with exhibitors on grounds of free expression. Filmmakers became a bit more venturesome.

At the same time, with mores changing in the wake of World War II, the influence of the Legion of Decency was slipping. In 1953 the legion condemned *The Moon Is Blue*, which had failed to receive code approval for being a bit racy. Despite the legion's condemnation, the movie was a box-office smash. The legion contributed to its own undoing with a series of incomprehensible recommendations. It condemned significant movies like Ingmar Bergman's *The Silence* and Michelangelo Antonioni's *Blow-Up* in the early 1960s while endorsing the likes of *Godzilla vs. the Thing*.

CURRENT MOVIE CODE

Moviemakers sensed the change in public attitudes in the 1950s but realized that audiences still wanted guidance they could trust in regard to movies. Also, there remained some moralist critics. In 1968 several industry organizations established a new rating system. No movies were banned. Fines were out. Instead, a board representing movie producers, distributors, importers and exhibitors, the *Classification and Rating Administration Board*, placed movies in categories to help parents determine what movies their children should see. The categories, as modified through the years, in various jurisdictions, include:

- **F:** Suitable for *family viewing*, including young children.
- **G:** Suitable for *general audiences* and all ages.
- **PG:** *Parental guidance* suggested because some content may be considered unsuitable for preteens.
- **PG-13:** *Parental guidance* especially suggested *for children younger than 13* because of partial nudity, swearing or violence.
- **AA:** Anyone under 18 must be *accompanied by an adult* (over 18)
- **R:** *Restricted*—not open to anyone younger than 18.
- **NC-17:** *No children under age 17* should be admitted.

Whether the rating system is widely used by parents is questionable. One survey found two out of three parents couldn't name a movie their teenagers had seen in recent weeks.

ONGOING ISSUES

STUDY PREVIEW Movie companies in the U.S. have taken advantage of the federal government's hands-off attitude toward business, which began in the Reagan administration, and integrated themselves vertically. Critics fret that this integration has the same potential for abuse as earlier consolidations that were broken up by the government. In Canada, NAFTA and government cutbacks to Telefilm have also raised new issues.

VERTICAL INTEGRATION

Despite the U.S. Supreme Court's 1948 Paramount decision, movie studios clearly are back in the exhibition business, resurrecting vertical integration. Tri-Star Pictures, 23 percent of which was owned by Columbia Pictures, bought the Loew's movie-house chain in 1986. Within months the Cannon Group, Paramount, MCA and Warner also bought exhibition chains either directly or through their corporate parents.

These acquisitions raised questions about whether the 1948 Paramount decision against vertical integration was being violated. Entering the 1990s, the government was not in a trust-busting mood. The Reagan and Bush administrations, in office from 1981 to 1993, eased government regulation of business activities.

At the same time, some people, concerned that Hollywood was again too powerful, were advancing the same kinds of arguments that led to the 1948 divestiture. These trust-busting arguments noted not only that vertical integration had returned but also that the coerciveness of Zukor's block booking had never disappeared. Distribution companies, some owned by studios, had taken to selling movies to television in batches, winners being available only with clunkers.

The new vertical integration could go even further. The technology is available for movie distribution companies to move directly into exhibition by beaming movies via satellites to local movie houses. It sounds like Zukor's outlawed Paramount vertical integration, albeit with electronic impulses, not celluloid, as the vehicle to streamline the intermediary distribution step.

In Canada, the Famous Players chain of movie theatres is controlled by Paramount Pictures. Investment Canada is looking into how the recent merger between Paramount and Viacom will affect the Paramount Famous Players chain.

THE FUTURE OF FUNDING

American lobby groups are putting pressure on the Canadian goverment to stop subsidizing Canadian film projects, as they feel any assistance given to cultural industries is a violation of the North American Free Trade Agreement. Several production companies have already secured private funding for feature films through agreements with American film companies. The movie and subsequent television series *Due South* was a coproduction between Alliance, a Canadian production company, CTV and CBS. In 1995 Alliance signed a three-picture contract with Universal Studios, the first multipicture deal between the two countries.

COMMERCIAL VERSUS ARTISTIC PRIORITIES

Moviemakers are expanding their supplemental incomes by charging other companies to use movie characters, themes and music for other purposes. This has raised questions about whether commercial imperatives have more priority than artistic considerations.

MERCHANDISE TIE-INS.   Fortunes can be made by licensing other companies to use characters and signature items from a movie. In one of the most successful *merchandise tie-ins*, Twentieth Century-Fox and George Lucas licensed Ewok dolls, R2D2 posters and even *Star Wars* bed sheets and pillowcases. By 1985, seven years after the movie's release, tie-ins had racked up sales of $2 billion. The licensing fee typically is 10 percent of the retail price of the merchandise. *Batman* tie-ins rang up $500 million in sales in 1989, within six months of the movie's release, and Warner Bros. was earning 20 percent of the retail revenue on some products. The totals aren't in yet from the dinosaur mania that followed the 1993 release of *Jurassic Park* or the cave life mugs, T-shirts and trinkets that followed the 1994 release of *The Flintstones*.

Tie-ins are not new. Music, for example, was a revenue source for moviemakers even before talkies. Just about every early movie house had a piano player who kept one eye on the screen and hammered out supportive mood music, and sheet-music publishers bought the rights to print and sell the music to musicians who wanted to perform it on their own. This was no small enterprise. D. W. Griffith's *The Birth of a Nation* of 1915 had an accompanying score for a 70-piece symphony.

Today, music has assumed importance besides supporting the screen drama. It has become a movie-making profit centre. *Saturday Night Fever* was the vehicle for a host of hit songs. *Urban Cowboy* was as much a recording industry enterprise as a film endeavour.

PRODUCT PLACEMENT.   Moviemakers also have begun building commercial products into story lines in a subtle form of advertising. It was no coincidence that Tom Cruise downed Pepsi in *Top Gun*. Some movie producers work brand names into their movies for a fee. When the alien E.T. was coaxed out of hiding with a handful of candy, it was with Reese's Pieces. The Hershey company, which makes Reese's, paid to have its candy used. Sales soared in the next few months. Producers first offered the Mars company a chance for the candy to be M&Ms, but Mars executives were squeamish about their candy being associated with anything as ugly as E.T. They did not realize that moviegoers would fall in love with the little alien.

After *E.T.*, the product placement business boomed. Miller beer paid to have 21 references in *Bull Durham*. The same movie also included seven references for Budweiser, four for Pepsi, three for Jim Beam, and two for Oscar Meyer. A simple shot of a product in the foreground typically goes for $25 000 to $50 000. Some advertisers have paid $350 000 for multiple on-screen plugs.

Critics claim that *product placements* are sneaky. Some want them banned. Others say the word "advertisement" should be flashed on the screen when the products appear. Movie people, on the other hand, argue that using real products adds credibility. In the old days, directors assiduously avoided implicit endorsements. In a bar scene, the players would drink from cans marked "beer"—no brand name. Today, says Marvin Cohen, whose agency matches advertisers and movies, "A can that says

'Beer' isn't going to make it anymore." The unanswered question is how much product-placement deals affect artistic decisions.

CANADIAN FILM INDUSTRY

While Hollywood made glamorous blockbusters, the Canadian film industry pursued another direction. The National Film Board of Canada has won innumerable awards for documentaries and animation. Feature films in Canada have also followed the documentary tradition.

THE EARLY DAYS

In his article "American Domination of the Motion Picture Industry," Garth Jowett points out that Canada has always been dependent on Hollywood for movies. Jowett writes "from the outset, Canada because of its geographic situation was considered to be merely one of the many marketing areas designated by the American film industry." Jowett also claims that most Canadians have always preferred Hollywood movies to British or Canadian films. However, this does not mean filmmaking traditions do not exist in this country.

From the earliest days of the medium, movies were shot and produced in Canada. Douglas Fetherling says that the first film shot in Canada was in Manitoba in 1897. Many other short films followed; however, the first Canadian feature film wasn't made until 1913. *Evangeline* was a five-reel film produced by the Canadian Biograph Company of Halifax. Based on a poem by Longfellow about the flight of the Acadians, it was shot on location in the Annapolis Valley. It featured

---

MEDIA DATABANK

Top-Earning Canadian Movies

One of the problems for Canadian productions is screen time. Some estimate that screen time for Canadian films in Canadian theatres is about 2 percent. Famous Players and Cineplex Odeon, the two major theatre chains in Canada, have arrangements with Hollywood companies to screen their films. There simply isn't much time left for Canadian movies.

Movie	Gross
Porky's	$10 million
Decline of the American Empire	$2.5 million
Black Robe	$2.4 million
Jesus of Montreal	$2.3 million
Ding et dong: le film	$2.0 million
Heavy Metal	$1.9 million
The Gate	$1.7 million
The Care Bears Movie	$1.7 million
Grenouille et baleine	$1.6 million
La Florida	$1.5 million
Exotica	$1.0 million

(Source: Holmes and Taras, *Seeing Ourselves*, 1996)

an American cast and turned a profit. The Canadian Biograph Company was never able to match the success of *Evangeline*. The same was true of other early Canadian filmmakers; it's estimated that only about 70 Canadian feature films were produced before 1939, the year the National Film Board of Canada was established.

NATIONAL FILM BOARD

One of the most high-profile Canadian film organizations is the *National Film Board* (NFB). Formed by an Act of Parliament in 1939 to "interpret Canada to Canadians," the board's first commissioner was *John Grierson*, a British documentary filmmaker. Grierson advocated a strong national film industry. He wanted to make movies that celebrated Canada's geographic and social diversity. In a statement about government film policy, Grierson said that while Canada could never compete with the glamour of Hollywood, it should not abandon the idea of a national film industry. Grierson felt that making short, inexpensive films about Canadians and their experiences could complement more expensive Hollywood fare, while still giving Canadians a cinematic voice. Grierson also believed that films should tackle social issues and that filmmakers should try to produce films that make a difference.

During the Second World War, the NFB produced several propaganda films in support of the war effort. *The World in Action* and *Canada Carries On*, both narrated by Lorne Greene, were two popular NFB war films. A 1941 feature, *Churchill's Island*, won the first of nine Oscars for Canada's National Film Board. During the war period, the NFB didn't just make propaganda films. *Alexis Tremblay: Habitant* (1943) examined the mythical lifestyle of rural French Canadians, while *Eskimos of the Eastern Arctic* (1944) portrayed Inuit life. Robert Flaherty acted as a consultant to the NFB on this film.

After the war, Grierson returned to England, but the NFB continued to make successful documentary films. During this time, it became known for a style called *cinéma vérité*, which roughly translated means "truth in cinema." For the NFB, cinéma vérité has meant documentaries by Canadians about Canadians.

The NFB is also known for its animation. The board's animation roots can be traced back to the arrival of *Norman McLaren* in 1941. Although he made 59 films for the NFB, inlcuding the propaganda movies *V for Victory* (1941) and *Keep Your Mouth Shut* (1944), animation was McLaren's first love. While his films have won more than 200 international awards, his best-known work is the 1953 Oscar-winning short *Neighbours*. The eight-minute antiwar film is about two neighbours fighting over a flower. The dispute escalates into tribal warfare. The film used live actors, but they were animated with the same techniques used to animate puppets and drawings.

In 1950 Parliament passed the National Film Act, which changed the NFB's mandate to include producing, promoting and distributing films in the national interest. In the NFB's early days, it would send projectionists from city to city and town to town to show its latest offerings in arenas, community centres and even fields. These films were also shown in movie houses and eventually on television. NFB films were (and still are) distributed by public libraries, schools, universities and colleges. Today, the NFB enjoys regular showings on television on several channels, including Bravo!

Like other government agencies, the NFB has faced its share of budget cuts in the 1990s. Its budget for 1994 was $75 million, down from $81 million in 1993.

FEATURE FILMS IN CANADA

Despite its success in the documentary and animated areas, Canada, with the exception of Quebec, has left the bulk of dramas and literary adaptations to the Americans. The feature film industry in Canada remained largely dormant until the 1960s. In 1964 two films marked the unofficial start of the feature film industry in Canada. They were Don Owen's *Nobody Waved Goodbye* and Gilles Groulx's *Le Chat dans le sac*. Both these films were NFB productions, but they were feature films shot in the documentary tradition and featured regional themes without the glamour of Hollywood movies. The better-known Canadian films from this era include *Goin' Down the Road* (1970), *Mon Oncle Antoine* (1971), *Paperback Hero* (1973), *Between Friends* (1973) and the classic *The Apprenticeship of Duddy Kravitz* (1974).

By the late 1970s government incentives and tax breaks for producers investing in Canadian feature films created a glut of product—some good, some bad. Films like *Why Shoot the Teacher?* (1978), *Outrageous* (1979), *Atlantic City* (1980), *Scanners* (1981) and the largest-grossing Canadian movie of all time, *Porky's* (1982) were all produced during this time.

How successful Telefilm and other government tax initiatives were in stimulating the Canadian film industry is difficult to measure, as some years were better than others for Canadian movies. However, the recent success of *Whale Music*, *Exotica*, *Louis 19: King of the Airwaves* and *Thirty-two Short Films about Glenn Gould* can be attributed to the CFDC and Telefilm. Canadian movie-making has come a long way since *Porky's*. Pay-television services like TMN and Moviepix offer Canadians a chance to see Canadian movies that they might not otherwise see.

CHAPTER WRAP-UP

Movies passed their 100th birthday in the 1980s as an entertainment medium with an especially strong following among young adults and teenagers. From the beginning, movies were a glamorous medium, but beneath the glitz were dramatic struggles between competing businesspeople whose success depended on catching the public's fancy.

The most dramatic period for the movie industry came at midcentury. Fanatic anti-communists in Congress intimidated moviemakers into backing away from cutting-edge explorations of social and political issues, and then a government antitrust action forced the major studios to break up their operations. Meanwhile, television was siphoning people away from the box office. Movie attendance fell from 90 million to 16 million per week.

It took a few years, but the movie industry regrouped. More than ever, political activism and social inquiry have become themes in American movies. Moviemakers met the threat from television by becoming a primary supplier of TV programming. In response to the antitrust orders, the big studios sold their movie houses and concentrated on financing independent productions and then distributing them. In short, the movie industry has proved itself remarkably resilient and adaptive.

The movie industry has three primary components: production, marketing and exhibition. Most movie fans follow production, which involves stars, screenplays and big money. Major studios control most production, either by producing movies themselves or by putting up the money for independent producers to create movies, which the studios then market. Marketing, called "distribution" in the trade, involves promotion and profitable after-markets like television and home video sales. Since the 1948 antitrust action, exhibition has been largely independent of Hollywood, although the corporations that own the major studios have again begun moving into the movie-house business.

Throughout their history, movies have been scrutinized by moralists who fear their influence. Today, the critics seem fairly satisfied with the NC-17, R, PG-13, PG, and G rating system that alerts parents to movies that they might find unsuitable for their children.

The Canadian film industry, like other media in Canada, is a mixture of public and private interests. The National Film Board, founded in 1939, has made films that help explain Canada to Canadians. Feature films in Canada have often been supported through government funding, although recent co-production agreements with American companies have opened new doors for Canadian filmmakers and companies.

QUESTIONS FOR REVIEW

1. Why do movies as a mass medium have such a strong impact on people?
2. How does the technological basis of movies differ from the other primary mass media?
3. Why did movies begin fading in popularity in the 1940s?
4. What was Hollywood's initial response to television?
5. What is the relationship between Hollywood and the television industry today?
6. How has the movie exhibition business changed over the years?
7. How do moviemakers raise cash for their expensive, high-risk projects?
8. How has Hollywood responded to criticism of movie content?
9. What was the effect of the Reagan administration's relaxed posture toward business?
10. What is meant by the NFB's mandate to "explain Canada to Canadians?"
11. Who were Norman McLaren and John Grierson?

QUESTIONS FOR CRITICAL THINKING

1. How would you describe the success of these innovations—Cinerama, CinemaScope, 3-D and Smellovision—in the movie industry's competition against television?
2. Epic spectaculars marked one period of moviemaking, social causes another, sex and violence another. Have these genres had lasting effect?
3. Can you explain why films geared to baby boomers, sometimes called teen films, dominated Hollywood in the 1970s and well into the 1980s? Why are they less important now?
4. How did Eadweard Muybridge demonstrate persistence of vision, and how did that lead to early moviemaking? Cite the contributions of William Dickson, George Eastman and the Lumière brothers.
5. Explain how these three developments forced a major change in Hollywood in the 1950s: the 1947 Thomas hearings, the 1948 Paramount court decision and the advent of television.
6. Once the number of movie exhibitors in North America was measured in terms of movie houses. Today it is measured by the number of screens. Why?
7. Explain how moviemakers finance their movies. What are the advantages and disadvantages of each method?
8. What has been the role of these institutions in

shaping movie content: Motion Picture Producers and Distributors of America, Legion of Decency, and Classification and Rating Administration Board?

9.   What do you think makes Canadian movies different from American movies?

FOR FURTHER LEARNING

Thomas W. Bohn and Richard L. Stromgren. *Light and Shadows: A History of Motion Pictures* (Alfred Publishing, 1975). This is a lively, comprehensive examination.

Larry Ceplair and Steven Englund. *The Inquisition in Hollywood: Politics in the Film Community, 1930-1960* (Doubleday, 1980). Ceplair and Englund examine the 1947 congressional smear that depopulated Hollywood of some of its most talented screenwriters and directors.

David Clandfield. *Canadian Film* (Oxford University Press, 1987). A series of critical articles dealing with film-making in Canada.

Norman K. Denzin. *Hollywood Shot by Shot: Alcoholism in American Cinema* (de Gruyter, 1991). Denzin, a sociologist, tracks Hollywood portrayals of alcoholism from 1932 to 1989 for trends to interpret how they came to be and their effects.

Joan Didion. "In Hollywood." *The White Album* (Pocket, 1979). Didion discredits the notion that the major studios are dying with the emergence of independent producers. The studios both bankroll and distribute independent films and, she says, make lots of money in the process.

Douglas Fetherling. *Documents in Canadian Film* (Broadview Press, 1988). A series of articles that looks at the Canadian film industry from several perspectives.

Seth Feldman and Joyce Nelson. *Canadian Film Reader* (Peter Martin and Associates, 1977). A staple in university film courses. Feldman and Nelson present an anthology of articles about cinema in Canada.

Douglas Gomery. *The Hollywood Studio System* (St. Martin's, 1986). Gomery examines the movie industry of the 1930s and 1940s, a period when Hollywood moved into mass production, global marketing and a centralized distribution system.

Thomas Guback. "The Evolution of the Motion Picture Theatre Business in the 1980s." *Journal of Communication* 37 (Spring 1987):3, 70–77. Why are so many new movie screens being built in the United States even though a smaller percentage of the population goes to movies? Guback lays out an array of economic factors from popcorn prices to new vertical integration schemes.

Garth Jowett and James M. Linton. *Movies as Mass Communication* (Sage, 1980). Jowett and Linton examine the social impact of movies and the economic determinants of the movie industry in this brief, scholarly book.

Lary May. *Screening Out the Past: The Birth of Mass Culture and the Motion Picture Industry* (Oxford University Press, 1980). A thoroughly documented early history.

Victor Navasky. *Naming Names* (Viking, 1980). This is another treatment of the congressional investigation into the film industry.

Murray Schumach. *The Face on the Cutting Room Floor: The Story of Movie and Television Censorship* (Da Capo, 1974).

Variety, International Film Guide 1995.

FOR KEEPING UP TO DATE

People who are serious about movies as art will find *American Film* and *Film Comment* valuable sources of information.

Trade journals include *Variety* and *Hollywood Reporter.*

Among consumer magazines with significant movie coverage are *Premiere, Entertainment Weekly,* and *Rolling Stone.*

The *Wall Street Journal, Maclean's* and the *Globe and Mail* track the movie industry.

TELEVISION Electronic Moving Pictures

Television can influence people in the short term and the culture in the long term

Television relies on electronic technology, in contrast to movies, a chemical-based medium

The structure for television was built around local over-air stations

Radio was a role model for early television programming

Television has evolved into an efficient purveyor of information

Local stations affiliated with networks can play a major role in network programming

The four primary sources of television programming are networks, motion picture companies, independent production companies, and local stations

New technologies and programming services are cracking the big networks' monopoly

MEDIA IN THEORY

Analyzing Television Content: The World of Wrestling

In his essay "The World of Wrestling" Roland Barthes investigates televised professional wrestling. Barthes claims that the wrestlers and their bodies are the basic sign of professional wrestling. Barthes believes two character types, the "Bastard" and the "Hero," fit into three second-order signifieds in wrestling: Suffering, Defeat and Justice. The dominant cultural values and ideology define those positions for the spectator through the basic conventions of professional wrestling. The function of the wrestler is "not to win, but to go exactly through the motions that are expected of him."

Studies like this tend to close off any possible interpretation except the one that is culturally defined, or what Stuart Hall calls the "preferred reading" of the text. Barthes assumes that fans of professional wrestling will simply align themselves along the ideological (Good vs. Bad) lines that are drawn in the wrestling ring. This approach is unfortunate because the related research has neglected a variety of connotations associated with wrestling. Professional wrestling, like other forms of sport on television, is an area where meanings can be and often are created by the viewer.

Barthes states in "The World of Wrestling" that the function of the wrestler "is not to win, but to go exactly through the motions that are expected of him." However, some fans expect something different than the "average" fan does. These fans still find some enjoyment in reading wrestling the conventional way, but they find more pleasure in reinterpreting the performance. For example, these "smart" fans (as they refer to themselves) are not interested in who wins or loses or in the signified of Good versus Evil, but rewrite the conventional signs of professional wrestling. For example, while watching wrestling on television, smart fans rewrite the traditional meanings of the signifiers in a match:

- The "Hero" is called the babyface, while the "Bastard" is known as a heel.
- TV matches are called "squash matches" when the heel or babyface easily defeats an inferior wrestler, who in turn is called a "jobber," because it's his/her job to lose.
- The matches aren't labeled "fake," rather they are "worked." Wrestlers are categorized not as Heroes or Bastards, but according to how well they work. A wrestler's workrate is how well a wrestler works and

how well he/she makes a match look real. This is done by taking "bumps," that is, making punches and dropkicks look like they actually hurt.
- Successful wrestlers create "heat," meaning the fans accept them in their roles of Hero or Bastard and respond appropriately with cheers or boos.

Therefore, for the smart fan, the signifieds of Suffering, Defeat and Justice do not depend on cultural ideology. The wrestlers do not signify moral or political opposites. Instead, the signifier (wrestler) is simply a worker whose job it is to wrestle. These fans view the match in terms of the signified of "workrate," or how well the two wrestlers work together to make the action appear "real." A wrestler's workrate is signified by the "bumps" he takes during the course of the match. The Suffering, Defeat and Justice signified by each match are the successful creation of "heat."

If Barthes can look at professional wrestling on television, then Canadian students of communication can look at their own cultural artifacts for meanings. Using Barthes, examine the following signs on Canadian television for cultural ideology. Remember, you're trying to examine each of these programs for different connotations and how those connotations are created:

- Don Cherry on Coach's Corner; is he the mythical "Canadian"?
- How does hockey on Fox differ from Molson's "Hockey Night in Canada"?
- How has Fox changed "Canada's" game?
- How does MuchMusic differ from MTV? TSN from ESPN? Newsworld from CNN? "Liberty Street" from "Beverly Hills 90210"?

IMPACT OF TELEVISION

STUDY PREVIEW In a remarkably short period, television became the most popular medium for entertainment and later for news. Older media were muscled out of their former prominence and had to adapt with whatever audience and advertising segments were left. Today, television has become so central in modern culture that it is almost impossible for anyone looking at society to ignore it.

MASS MEDIA SHAKE-UP

In a brash moment in 1981, television tycoon *Ted Turner* predicted the end of newspapers within 10 years. The year 1991 came and went, and, as Turner had predicted, television was even more entrenched as a mass medium—but newspapers too were still in business. Turner had overstated the impact of television, but he was right that television would continue taking readers and advertisers from newspapers, just as it had from the other mass media.

Research by the TV Bureau of Canada indicates just how popular a medium television has become for Canadians. TV ranked as the number one choice for entertainment, excitement, information, education and believability. It was a close second behind radio for relaxation.

Since its introduction in the early 1950s, the presence of television has reshaped the other media. Consider the following areas of impact:

BOOKS.   The discretionary time people spend on television today is time that once went to other activities, including reading, for diversion and information. To stem the decline in reading, book publishers have responded with more extravagant promotions to draw attention to their products. A major consideration with fiction manuscripts at publishing houses is their potential as screenplays, many of which end up on television. Also, in deciding which manuscripts to accept, some publishers even consider how well an author will come across in television interviews when the book is published.

NEWSPAPERS.   Evening television newscasts have been a major factor in the steady decline of afternoon newspapers, many of which have ceased publication or switched to mornings. Also, newspapers have lost almost all of their national advertisers, primarily to television. Most newspaper redesigns attempt to be visual in ways that newspapers never were before television.

MAGAZINES.   Television took advertisers from the big mass circulation magazines, forcing magazine companies to shift to magazines that catered to smaller segments of the mass audience that television could not serve.

RECORDINGS.   The success of recorded music today hinges in many cases on the airplay that music videos receive on television on MuchMusic or YTV's Hit List.

MOVIES.   Just as magazines demassified after television took away many of their advertisers, Hollywood demassified after television stole its audience. Today, savvy moviemakers plan their projects for both the big screen and for reissuing to be shown on television, via the networks and for home video rental. These after-markets, in fact, have come to account for far more revenue to major Hollywood studios than their moviemaking.

RADIO.   Radio too demassified with the arrival of television. The television networks first took radio's most successful programs and moved them to television. After losing its traditional programming strengths, radio then lost both the mass audience and advertisers it had built up since the 1920s. For survival, individual radio stations shifted almost entirely to recorded music and geared the music to narrower and narrower audience segments.

PERVASIVE MEDIUM, PERSUASIVE MESSAGES

The data from the Bureau of Broadcast Measurement offer this picture of Canadians and television viewing:

- There are 111 television stations in Canada; 23 are publicly owned, 88 are privately owned.
- Ninety-eight percent of Canadians households have at least one television set; almost 60 percent have two or more.
- The average Canadian views about 23 hours of television per week. Teens watch the least amount of television (17.1 hours per week), while women over 60 watch the most (36.4 hours per week).
- Albertans watch the least amount of TV (20.6 hours per week), while Francophones in Quebec watch the most (26.2 hours per week).

There is no question that television has changed lifestyles, drawing people away from other diversions that once occupied their time. Churches, lodges and neighbourhood taverns once were central in the lives of many people, and today they are less so. For 26 million people, "60 Minutes" is a Sunday night ritual that was not available three generations ago.

Television can move people. Revlon was an obscure cosmetic brand before it took on sponsorship of the "$64,000 Question" quiz show in the 1950s. Overnight, Revlon became a household word and an exceptionally successful product. In 1992 Procter & Gamble spent $995 million advertising its wares on television; Philip Morris, $795 million (for its noncigarette products); and General Motors, $664 million.

The influence of television on serious matters was demonstrated in 1962, when President John Kennedy spoke into the camera and told the American people that the nation was in a nuclear showdown with the Soviet Union. People rallied to the president's decision to blockade Cuba until the Soviet Union removed the ballistic missiles it was secretly installing. Today, it is rare for a candidate seeking public office not to use television to solicit support:

- During the 1984 and 1988 election campaigns, Brian Mulroney swayed voters by using his powerful rhetorical skills to squash his opponents in televised debates. Television images can also backfire; during the 1993 election campaign, the Progressive Conservatives used "negative" images of Jean Chrétien in a series of ads leading up to election day. The public was outraged and Kim Campbell apologized for the error, but it was too late. The Tories lost the election and won only two seats in Parliament.
- Ross Perot chose CNN's "Larry King Live" talk show to test the waters for his long-shot presidential bid, and he returned to the show again and again to take viewer calls live.
- George Bush knew the television cameras were rolling when he made his no-new-taxes, "read my lips" pledge in 1988. It was a memorable campaign moment, which analysts saw as a key to Bush's election, and, later, as part of his 1992 undoing when, in fact, he found no recourse but to raise taxes.

Fictional television characters can capture the imagination of the public. Perry Mason did wonders for the reputation of the law profession. Mary Tyler Moore showed that women could succeed in male-dominated industries. Alan Alda was the counter-macho model for the bright, gentle man of the 1970s. In this same sense, Bart Simpson's bratty irreverence toward authority figures sent quivers through parents and teachers in the 1990s. Then came the alarm that Beavis and Butt-head's fun with matches might lead kids from all over the country to set everything in sight on fire.

CULTURAL IMPACT

While television can be effective in creating short-term impressions, there also are long-term effects. Today, a whole generation of children is growing up with "The Power Rangers" as part of their generational identity. These long-term effects exist at both a superficial level, as with "The Power Rangers," and at a serious level. Social critic *Michael Novak* puts the effect of television in broad terms: "Television is a molder of the soul's geography. It builds up incrementally a psychic structure of expectations. It does so in much the same way that school lessons slowly, over the years, tutor the unformed mind and teach it how to think."

What are the "lessons" to which Novak refers? Scholars *Linda and Robert Lichter* and *Stanley Rothman*, who have surveyed the television creative community, make a case that the creators of television programs are social reformers who build their political ideas into their scripts. The Lichters and Rothman identify the television creative community as largely secular and politically liberal. Among program creators whom they quote is Garry Marshall, the creative force behind "Happy Days" and later "Mork and Mindy": "The tag on 'Mork' is almost like the sermon of the week. But it doesn't look like that. It is very cleverly disguised to look like something else, but that's what it is." In many ways, Norman Lear, the creator of Archie Bunker, is the archetype program creator for the Lichter-Rothman profile. And Lear's liberal political and social agenda doesn't go away. He was back with a summer series in 1994, "704 Houser Street," set in the Bunker house—new characters, same issues.

Scholars have different views on the potency of television's effect on society, but they all agree that there is some degree of influence. Media scholar George Comstock, in his book *Television in America*, wrote: "Television has become an unavoidable and unremitting factor in shaping what we are and what we will become.

TECHNOLOGICAL DEVELOPMENT

STUDY PREVIEW   Television is based on electronic technology. Light-sensitive cameras scan a scene with incredibly fast sweeps across several hundred horizontally stacked lines. The resulting electronic blips are transmitted to receivers, which recreate the original image by sending electrons across horizontally stacked lines on a screen.

ELECTRONIC SCANNING

In the 1920s *Vladimir Zworykin*, a Westinghouse physicist, devised a vacuum tube that could pick up moving images and then display them electronically on a screen. Zworykin's main inventions, the *iconoscope* and the *kinescope*, sent electrons repeatedly across stacked horizontal lines on a tiny screen, each pass following the previous one so fast that the screen showed the movement as picked up by a camera. As with the motion picture, the system froze movement at fraction-of-a-second intervals and then replayed it to create an illusion of movement, but there was a significant difference. Motion pictures used chemical-based photographic processes. Zworykin used electronics, not chemicals, and the image recorded by a camera was transmitted instantly to a receiving tube. Zworykin's picture quality was not sharp, with electrons being shot across only 30 horizontal lines on the screen compared to 525 today, but the system worked.

Westinghouse, RCA and General Electric pooled their television research in 1930, and Zworykin was put in charge of a team of engineers to develop a national

MEDIA: PEOPLE

Ted Turner

When his father died, Ted Turner inherited a floundering Atlanta television station that hardly anybody watched. Back then, in 1963, many televisions sets could not pick up channels higher than 13, which meant that Turners' WTGC, like other UHF stations, was nonexistent in many households. Advertising revenue was thin, and it was not easy to pay the rent for the decrepit building that housed the studios. Only 60 people were on the payroll. Fumigators sprayed for fleas weekly.

Young Turner threw himself energetically into making something of the inheritance. He did everything himself, even stocking the soda machine. More important, he recognized that WTGC was condemned to a shoe string future unless he could offer viewers more than old B movies and sitcom reruns. Desperate to diversify programming, Turner borrowed enough money to buy the cellar-dwelling Atlanta Braves and Atlanta Hawks teams in the mid-1970s. The purchases spread Turner's finances even thinner, but they gave WTGC something distinctive to offer.

Turner then turned to his other major problem—WTGC's obscure UHF channel. Learning that HBO was planning to beam programs to an orbiting satellite for retransmission to local systems nationwide, he decided to do the same. Turner redubbed his station WTBS in 1976, bought satellite time and persuaded cable systems to add his "superstation" to their package of services. Overnight, Turner multiplied the audience for his old movies, sitcom reruns, and Atlanta pro sports. WTBS began attracting national advertising, something WTGC never could.

Ted Turner stopped refilling the soda machine himself, but he still worked hard. He kept an old bathrobe at his office and slept on the couch when he worked late. His mind never stopped. He considered a second cable network—a 24-hour television news service. In 1980, again stretching his finances to the limit, Turner bought an old mansion, outfitted it with the latest electronic news-gathering and editing equipment, hired two dozen anchors and launched *Cable News Network*. A few months later, with CNN still deep in red ink, Turner learned that ABC and Westinghouse were setting up the Satellite News Channel, which would compete with CNN. To discourage cable systems from picking up the competitor, Turner decided over a weekend to establish a second news network himself, and *Headline News* was born. The gamble worked, and ABC and Westinghouse sold their news network to Turner, who promptly shut it down.

There were setbacks. Turner started a rock 'n' roll cable network, but it could not compete with MTV, so he sold it. Detractors found the stogie-puffing Turner easy to criticize. He was called "the Mouth of the South" for his brash outspokenness. Operating at the edge financially, making major decisions alone and sometimes impulsively, he seemed to be an entrepreneurial loose cannon. Or was it genius? Or luck? The mystique was fueled by Turner's high profile, including his defence of the the America's Cup sailing championship. His strongest detractors, local television station executives, called him unscrupulous, charging that he was leasing old movies and sitcoms for WTBS at the going rate for a local station while making a killing by charging national ad rates. They called on the FCC to reinstate the syndex rule, which had guaranteed local exclusivity to stations buying syndicated programs. Because WTBS was running the same syndicated programs as over-air stations, the move was clearly aimed at drying up Turner's program supply. The syndicating companies also felt angry that Turner was exploiting his rental agreements.

Turner's previous successes had been masterstrokes—buying pro sports teams to create programming, using satellites to make himself a national television presence and establishing an around-the-clock television news channel. Now, facing a programming crisis if the syndex rule were restored, Turner looked for another masterstroke. He decided in 1985 to buy CBS, which not only could generate lots of programming but also would put him firmly in both the new cable and the traditional broadcasting industries. The buyout plan backfired, and Turner lost $21 million. Worse, he still did not have the new programming supply he needed.

A few days later, a Hollywood financier who knew Turner's programming predicament called him and offered to sell MGM/United Artists including the MGM movie library. Turner agreed on the spot, not even challenging the exorbitant $1.4 billion asking price. He mortgaged TBS to the hilt, but even then he could not raise enough. Facing foreclosure, Turner managed, barely, to keep the MGM films by selling off the rest of MGM/UA bit by bit. With MGM's 3700 movies, including *Gone With the Wind, Casablanca* and *Citizen Kane*, Turner had significant programming that could be run and rerun forever. It was a buffer against program vendors, which turned out to be important when the syndex rule was reinstated in 1989.

On the downside, the CBS and MGM ventures left Turner so debt-ridden that he had no choice but to sell

Chapter 6 Television: Electronic Moving Pictures **159**

Ted Turner. Atlanta television station owner Ted Turner saw orbiting satellites as an inexpensive way to beam his Atlanta stations to local cable systems that were hungry for programming in the early 1980s. Almost overnight Turner's WTBS became a superstation available to viewers nationwide. CNN, Headline News and TNT followed, making Turner Broadcasting a major player in the U.S. television industry. Turner was named *Time* magazine's Man of the Year in 1992.

chunks of TBS. Sensation-mongering media mogul Rupert Murdoch expressed interest. General Electric, which recently had bought NBC, also inquired. Cable companies, however, did not want control of WTBS, CNN and Headline News to go to outside interests. The Turner networks had become essential parts of the cable companies' packages for subscribers. John Malone, chief of the giant TeleCommunications cable company, pulled together 31 cable chains to bail out Turner. They put up $562 million. Said Malone: "If we hadn't rescued Ted Turner, TBS would have been bought by Rupert Murdoch, and CNN now would be running 'Murder of the Week.'"

In exchange for the cash infusion, Turner agreed to share control and operate less impulsively, but his mind kept going. To capitalize on the MGM film library, he proposed a fourth cable service. In 1988 *Turner Network Television*, TNT for short, began transmitting to 17 million cable households—five times more than any previous cable network. TNT began mostly with old MGM movies, but TBS's new directors budgeted $280 million to produce miniseries, made-for-TV movies, and high-profile events to go up against the traditional over-air networks. Turner hoped to bid against the major networks for events like the World Series, Rose Bowl, Indianapolis 500 and Academy Awards.

Almost overnight in 1991, a lynch pin in Turner's vision came to fruition. CNN leaped to industry dominance with its 24-hour coverage of the Persian Gulf War. Government and industry leaders worldwide watched it for quicker and better information than they could obtain through their own sources. Not infrequently, other news organizations ended up quoting CNN because they couldn't match the network's no-holds-barred commitment to thoroughness and timeliness. Turner's audience swelled, as each day CNN earned greater and wider respect. Back when it went on the air, CNN had been laughed at as "Chicken Noodle News." No more.

Ted Turner's odyssey from WTGC in 1963 embodies ongoing dynamics in the television industry:

■ The expansion of satellite-delivered and cable-delivered programming, like Turner networks.
■ The fragile state of even the oldest, proudest television organizations, demonstrated by upstart Turner's takeover run on CBS.
■ The important role of program vendors in network and local programming.
■ The constant need for programmers to find and air programs, demonstrated by Turner's acquisition of the MGM library.

television system. In 1939 RCA flamboyantly displayed the Zworykin invention at the New York World's Fair. Although the British had introduced a system three years earlier, RCA had superior picture quality. Soon, 10 commercial stations were licensed and several companies were manufacturing home receivers. Then came World War II. The companies that were developing commercial television diverted their research and other energies to the war effort.

INTEGRATED STANDARDIZATION

Even after the war, there were delays. The Federal Communications Commission, wanting to head off topsy-turvy expansion that might create problems later, halted further station licensing in 1948. Not until 1952 did the FCC settle on a comprehensive licensing and frequency allocation system and lift the freeze. The freeze gave the FCC time to settle on a uniform system for the next step in television's evolution: colour. RCA wanted a system that could transmit to both existing black-and-white and new colour sets. CBS favoured a system that had superior clarity, but people would have to buy new sets to pick it up, and even then they would not be able to receive black-and-white programs. Finally, in 1953, the FCC settled on the RCA system.

STRUCTURE OF TELEVISION

STUDY PREVIEW   The television system was built on both a local and a national foundation. As they did with radio, the FCC and CRTC licensed local stations with the goal of a diversified system. At the same time, networks gave the system a national character. In Canada, regulation of this national character has been the topic of much debate.

TELEVISION IN CANADA

While there were several experimental television broadcasts in Canada through the 1930s and 1940s, Canadians were first exposed to American television signals. If you lived close enough to the border and had access to a television, you probably watched Milton Berle or wrestler Gorgeous George on the Dumont network. Television officially arrived in Canada in 1952. As had been the case with the first radio station 30 years earlier, the first television station was in Montreal. CBFT, a public station, began broadcasting on September 6, 1952, with CBLT Toronto, broadcasting two days later. At first programming was a mix of Canadian and American fare. A microwave link between Buffalo and Toronto made it possible to carry American programs live. The first privately owned television station was CKSO in Sudbury, Ontario. It started broadcasting in 1953.

The evolution of television in Canada paralleled the growth of radio; a system with both public and private broadcasting. Initially, private television broadcasters had to apply to the CBC for broadcast licences. Private broadcasters were not happy; they felt a conflict of interest existed. How could the CBC, a broadcaster itself, also be responsible for overseeing private broadcasting?

THE FOWLER COMMISSION

In 1955 a royal commission into broadcasting was formed. *The Fowler Commission*, headed by *Robert Fowler*, analyzed Canadian broadcasting from the points of view of culture and regulations. Its report, tabled in 1957, formed the basis of the Broadcasting Act of 1958. Diefenbaker's Conservatives passed the act in July 1958. Among the changes to Canadian broadcasting policy were:

- The forming of the Board of Broadcast Governors (BBG), which would oversee the granting of broadcasting licences.
- Official government recognition of private broadcasters in Canada. This allowed stations to affiliate themselves with a body other than the CBC. This would lead to the formation of Canada's first private television network, CTV.
- Programming that was as Canadian in "content and character" as possible. In 1959 government policy decreed that 45 percent of programming had to be Canadian in nature and that the percentage was to rise to 55 percent by 1962.

Needless to say, private broadcasters did not appreciate the last change to the Broadcasting Act. They were making tidy profits broadcasting American programming to Canadians just as private radio broadcasters had 30 years earlier. They felt that Canadian shows were inferior to American ones and that it would cost more to produce Canadian programming than to import American series and specials. Lobby groups such as the Canadian Association of Broadcasters fought this ruling and won. The content legislation was loosened so much that even the World Series came to be defined as "Canadian."

THE 1968 BROADCASTING ACT

In March of 1968 another Broadcasting Act further defined the broadcast system and the function it should serve in Canada. This act resulted in the formation of the *Canadian Radio-Television Commission* (CRTC). The changes to television were as follows:

- The CRTC replaced the BBG and had the power to regulate brodcasting in Canada.
- The CBC was given its mandate to provide a national broadcasting service in both official languages and to provide Canadian programming that helped develop national unity and allowed for Canadian cultural expression.
- Television broadcasters should provide 60 percent Canadian content.
- Canadian broadcasting should be owned and operated by Canadians.

THE 1991 BROADCASTING ACT

In 1975 the CRTC became the *Canadian Radio-television and Telecommunications Commission* when it assumed responsiblity for regulating the telephone industry. In 1991 a new Broadcasting Act was issued to help further define broadcasting and cultural issues in Canada. The new Act:

- Stressed the importance of programming that was Canadian in content and character. The act also admitted that it was easier to fill Canadian content quotas than to produce progams that audiences would watch.
- Redefined the CBC's role as the national broadcaster which was to help create a "Canadian consciousness." However, no attempt to define the term "Canadian consciousness" was made; nor was the issue of funding addressed.
- Explained that cable companies should efficiently deliver Canadian services and stations at a reasonable cost.

In *Canada's Cultural Industries*, Paul Audley sums up the history of television in Canada well. He writes "the general pattern from the beginning of television in 1952 until the present has been one of a rapidly expanding private television broadcasting system and an underfinanced public system." Writing in *Maclean's*, Peter C. Newman argues that Canadians need the CBC to become important again. Says Newman, "with our kids watching 900 hours or more of TV a year—and at least 80 percent of it spreading the gospel of the American way of life—we must maintain a vibrant indigenous alternative." Private broadcasters would disagree with Newman, claiming that the Canadian identity can be preserved by the private sector.

DUAL NATIONAL SYSTEM—THE UNITED STATES

Congress and the Federal Communications Commission were generally satisfied with the American radio system that had taken form by the 1930s, and they set up a similar structure for television. The FCC invited people who wanted to build stations in local communities to apply for a federal licence. As a condition of their FCC licence, station owners raised the money to build the technical facilities, to develop an economic base and to provide programming. These stations, which broadcast over the airwaves, the same as radio, became the core of a locally based national television system. It was the same regulated yet free-enterprise approach that had developed for radio. By contrast, governments in most other countries financed and built centralized national television systems.

Even though the FCC regulated a locally based television system, the American system soon had a national flavour. NBC and CBS modeled television networks on their radio networks and provided programs to the new local television stations. Today, American television still has a backbone in the networks. Of 900 local com-

MEDIA DATABANK

Top-rated Shows on Canadian TV

Canadians love to watch television; here are the top-rated Canadian and American shows on Canadian television from 1995, according to the A.C. Nielsen Company:

The Top 5 Canadian TV Shows: 1995 Season

Show	Audience	Network
Due South	1 750 000	CTV
CTV Sunday Movie	1 689 000	CTV
Hockey Night in Canada	1 349 000	CBC
CTV Monday Movie	1 339 000	CTV
CTV News	1 307 000	CTV

The Top 5 American TV Shows: 1995 Season

Show	Audience	Network
ER	2 385 000	CTV
America's Funniest Home Videos	2 119 000	CTV
Larroquette	1 877 000	CTV
Roseanne	1 794 000	CTV
Murphy Brown	1 497 000	CTV

mercial stations, two-thirds are affiliates of one of the three major networks, ABC, CBS or NBC. In almost every city, it is the network-affiliated stations that have the most viewers.

The national television system in both countries began to undergo major changes in the 1980s. Dozens of new networks, led by TSN, First Choice, and SuperChannel and other cable program services, bypassed local stations, delivering programs via satellite and local cable systems into individual homes.

NETWORK–AFFILIATE RELATIONS

A network affiliation is an asset to local stations. Programs offered by the networks are of a quality that an individual station cannot afford to produce. With quality network programs, stations attract larger audiences than they could on their own. Larger audiences mean that stations can charge higher rates for local advertisements in the six to eight minutes per hour the networks leave open for affiliates to fill. Stations also profit directly from affiliations. The networks share their advertising revenue with affiliates.

Network–affiliate relations are not entirely money-making bliss. The networks, whose advertising rates are based on the number of viewers they have, would prefer that all affiliates carry all their programs. Affiliates, however, sometimes have sufficient financial incentives to preempt network programming. Broadcasting a state basketball tournament can generate lots of local advertising. The networks would also prefer that affiliates confine their quest for advertising to their home areas, leaving national ads to the networks. Local stations, however, accept national advertising on their own, which they schedule inside and between programs, just as they do local advertising.

The networks have learned to pay more heed to affiliate relations in recent years.

Talk Shows. When CBS put David Letterman opposite the venerable "Tonight" show, the network had a lot at stake. The success of the show depended on how many of the network's affiliates would air it on a scheduled basis. Many CBS affiliates had earlier found it more profitable to play old movies and sitcom reruns than CBS's previous attempts to compete with "Tonight." Affiliates decide which network programs to carry. For CBS, the Letterman gamble paid off—his offbeat humour attracted a large following.

Unhappy affiliates have been known to leave one network for another. Television chains like Group W or Gannett have a major bargaining chip with networks because, with a single stroke of a pen, they can change the affiliations of several stations. This happened in 1994 when Fox lured 12 stations away from the big three networks, eight of them from CBS alone.

Also, affiliates are organized to deal en masse with their networks. In 1982 the affiliates forced CBS and NBC to abandon plans to expand the evening network newscasts to 60 minutes. An hour-long newscast would have lost lucrative station slots for local advertising. One estimate is that the stations would have lost $260 million a year in advertising revenue, far more than network payments would have brought in.

Networks once required affiliates to carry most network programs, which guaranteed network advertisers a large audience. Most stations were not bothered by the requirement, which dated to network radio's early days, because they received a slice of the network advertising revenue.

ENTERTAINMENT PROGRAMMING

STUDY PREVIEW Early national television networks patterned their programs on their successful radio experience, even adapting specific radio programs to the screen. Until "I Love Lucy" in 1951, programs were aired live. Today, most entertainment programming is taped and then polished by editing.

RADIO HERITAGE

In the early days of television, the networks provided their affiliate stations with video versions of popular radio programs, mostly comedy and variety shows. Like radio, the programs originated in New York. With videotape still to be invented, almost everything was broadcast live. Early television drama had a live theatrical on-stage quality that is lost with today's multiple taping of scenes and slick editing. Comedy shows like Milton Berle's and variety shows like Ed Sullivan's, also live, had a spontaneity that typified early television.

Early Canadian programming also reflected its roots in radio. "Wayne and Shuster" was a staple of Canadian television during the 1960s and 1970s, while "Hockey Night in Canada", which began on radio in the 1920s, continues to draw a huge audience for the CBC on Saturday nights.

Desi Arnaz and *Lucille Ball*'s "I Love Lucy" situation comedy, introduced in 1951, was significant not just because it was such a hit, but because it was not transmitted live. Rather, multiple cameras filmed several takes. Film editors then chose the best shots, the best lines, and the best facial expressions for the final production. Just as in movie production, sequences could be rearranged in the cutting room. Even comedic pacing and timing could be improved. Final responsibility for what went on the air shifted from actors to editors. Taping also made possible the libraries of programs that are reissued by syndicates for rerunning.

"I Love Lucy" also marked the start of television's shift to Hollywood. Because Desi and Lucy wanted to continue to live in California, they refused to commute to New York to produce the show. Thus, "Lucy" became television's first Los Angeles show. Gradually, most of television's entertainment production went west.

Entertainment programming has grown through phrases. Cowboy programs became popular in the 1950s, later supplemented by quiz shows. The cowboy genre was replaced by cop shows in the late 1960s. Through the changes, sitcoms have remained popular, although they have changed with the times, from "Father Knows Best" in the 1950s through "All in the Family" in the 1970s to "Home Improvement" and "Full House" in the 1990s.

Canadian genres that were popular during the heyday of radio continue to be popular on television. These include news, information, comedy, sports and variety shows.

CHANGING PROGRAM STANDARDS

Vulgar lines and risqué scenes once were verboten on the television networks. Critics complained that the networks' prudery was stifling creative licence, but the networks had two overriding concerns. One was that they wanted to avoid putting their affiliates at risk. Offended viewers might object to the government, which could revoke licences. Also, network people also talked of decency for decency's sake. Each network maintained a *Standards and Practices Department* to review all entertainment programs and commercials. The "censors," as they were called, insisted that Rob and Laura Petrie of "The Dick Van Dyke Show" sleep in separate beds, sent suggestive commercials back to agencies for revising, and even banned Smothers Brothers' antiwar jibes at President Lyndon Johnson.

In the 1980s, with deregulation lessening licence worries and with society generally more tolerant of vulgarity and licentiousness, local stations began offering non-network programs that ventured into areas the network never had. These independent programs included lurid recreations of crimes, as on "America's Most

The Innovative "I Love Lucy." The long-running television series "I Love Lucy," starting in 1951, was taped and then edited for polish. This practice was a departure from other television programs, which, being broadcast live, lacked "Lucy's" slickness. The program also was significant because Desi Arnaz and Lucille Ball, who created the series, refused to live in New York where most television programs were being produced. The show thus became a Hollywood production and marked the beginning of the shift of television entertainment program production to California.

Wanted"; frank examinations of once-taboo subjects on Phil Donahue and other syndicated talk shows; and unbridled blue humour on comedy club programs. Local stations found audiences for what detractors called "tabloid journalism" and "trash TV."

Suddenly concerned about their programs being bypassed by affiliates for racier programs available from independent sources, networks reassessed their standards. Also figuring into the reassessment was that cable was siphoning viewers to programs that Standards and Practices reviewers would never approve. Also, viewers were being lost to home videos that even included smutty movies. Amid encroachments on their traditional viewership, the networks acquired new corporate parents, all profit-conscious in ways that network bosses had never been. The issue of network tastes peaked in 1988 when NBC aired a two-hour Geraldo Rivera special on satanism. The network drew the line at ritualistic draining and drinking of human blood, but the program included dismembered corpses, bloody orgies and programmed child abuse. Ratings were high.

Now, network sitcom couples no longer sleep in separate beds, and hardly ever in pajamas.

Melrose Place. In 1987, the Fox television network began with a handful of programs two evenings a week and gradually expanded. With hits like "Beverly Hills 90210" and "Melrose Place," Fox became the most profitable network, primarily with low-cost entertainment shows and by not going against the Traditional Big Three networks with a full schedule of programming. Also, Fox didn't rush into expensive news programming. Behind Fox are the financial resources of international media mogul Rupert Murdoch.

"NYPD Blue." Even before Steven Bochco's "NYPD Blue" was on the air, moralists rallied against it because of reports that the script was heavy with vulgarities and skin. Despite pressure on advertisers to back away from sponsorship, ABC stuck to its position that the program was high-calibre drama. The protest withered. Audiences loved the show, and it won numerous awards. It has also earned high ratings for CanWest-Global in Canada.

TELEVISION NEWS

STUDY PREVIEW The television networks began newscasts in 1947 with anchors reading stories into cameras, embellished only with occasional newsreel clips. Networks expanded their staffs and programming over the years. Documentaries, introduced in the 1950s, demonstrated that television could cover serious issues in depth.

TALKING HEADS AND NEWSREELS

The networks began news programs in 1947, CBS with "Douglas Edwards and the News" and NBC with John Cameron Swayze's "Camel News Caravan." The 15-minute evening programs rehashed AP and UPI dispatches and ran film clips from movie newsreel companies. Television news began in Canada in 1953. "The News at Seven" was a 15-minute nightly newscast on the CBC. The networks eventually built up their own reporting staffs and abandoned the photogenic but predictable newsreel coverage of events like beauty contests and ship launchings. With on-scene reporters, network news focused more on public issues. In 1963 the evening newscasts expanded to 30 minutes with NBC's Chet Huntley–David Brinkley team and CBS's Walter Cronkite in nightly competition for serious yet interesting accounts of what was happening. When Walter Cronkite retired in 1981, surveys found him the most trusted man in the country—testimony to how important television news had become. Although news originally was an unprofitable network activity, sometimes referred to as a "glorious burden," it had become a profit centre by the 1980s as news programs attracted larger audiences, which in turn attracted more advertisers.

Television's potential as a serious news medium was demonstrated in 1951 when producer *Fred W. Friendly* and reporter *Edward R. Murrow* created "See It Now," a weekly investigative program. Television gained new respect when Friendly and Murrow exposed the false, hysterical charges of Senator Joseph McCarthy about Communist infiltration of federal agencies.

Fifth Estate. Shows like CBC Television's "fifth estate" exemplify the fact that investigative journalism has long been a part of the Canadian news tradition.

In *A Guide to Canadian News Media*, Peter Desbarats reports that by the late 1950s, Canadian news programs were becoming analytical. René Lévesque's "Point de mire" and Pierre Berton's "Close-Up" were popular newsmagazine-style shows. CTV aired its first nightly newscast in 1961 with Harvey Kirck as the anchor.

Probably the best-known newsmagazine in the 1960s was "This Hour Has Seven Days," hosted by Laurier LaPierre and Patrick Watson. It become known for its controversial style and was taken off the air in 1966. "W5" began broadcasting in 1966 on CTV and has become the longest-running newsmagazine in both Canada and the United States. Today, people tune in to the trustworthy images of Lloyd Robertson and the "CTV National News" or Peter Mansbridge on CBC's "The National."

Canada has two all-news cable channels: the English-language Newsworld and the French RDI. Neither receive any government support; all of their funding comes from advertising and cable subscribers. Perhaps taking its cue from the NFB tradition of filmmaking, Canadian television news has tended to be documentary in style.

LOCAL NEWS

Local television news imitated network formats in the early days, but by the 1970s many innovations were occurring at the local level. Local reporting staffs grew, and some stations went beyond a headline service to enterprising and investigative reports. Many stations were quick to latch onto possibilities of satellite technology in the 1980s to do their own locally oriented coverage of far-away events. This reduced the dependence of stations on networks for national stories. Today, large stations send their own reporters and crews with uplink vans to transmit live reports back home via satellite.

TELEVISION NETWORKS TODAY

STUDY PREVIEW   The dominance of ABC, CBS and NBC in American television and CBC and CTV in Canada is being challenged. Public television and independent stations have nibbled away at network audiences. So have new programming sources and delivery systems. Today, cable can deliver more channels than are available over the air.

THE TRADITIONAL NETWORKS: CANADA

There are two national networks in Canada: the CBC and CTV. The CBC, as Canada's public broadcaster, owns and operates 23 television stations—18 English ones and five French ones. The CBC was Canada's only national network during television's infancy. As mentioned previously, CBC television began broadcasting in September 1952, with stations in Toronto and Montreal. The CBC's entire prime-time lineup is now Canadian. Some of the network's most popular Canadian programs, other than "Hockey Night in Canada," include "Rita and Friends," "The Royal Canadian Air Farce," "Marketplace" and "The Fifth Estate."

While CBC is Canada's public network, CTV is Canada's only private network. It began broadcasting in 1961 with only eight affiliates: CJCH (in Halifax), CFCF (in Montreal), CJOH (in Ottawa) CFTO (in Toronto), CKY (in Winnipeg), CFCN (in Calgary), CFRN (in Edmonton) and BCTV (in Vancouver). Today, CTV has 18 affiliates and seven supplementary affiliates.

CTV's mandate, as specified by the CRTC in CTV's licence, is to provide:

- Sixty percent Canadian programming, 50 percent of that in prime time, calculated on an annual basis.
- Three hours of Canadian drama per week in prime time.
- Forty-eight hours of Canadian features in prime time per year.
- Between 18 and 26 hours of Canadian specials per year.

Some of CTV's Canadian programming consists of U.S.-style genre programs, shot in Canada. "Lonesome Dove: The Series," "TekWar," "Robocop" and "F/X" all qualify as Canadian programs, although none of them have anything to do with Canada. The lone exception is "Due South," which attracts a large following in Canada. The bulk of CTV's ratings success comes when it carries American shows, as the chart of the top-rated shows in Canada in this chapter indicates. CTV's news and public affairs programs include "Canada AM" and "The CTV National News."

In addition to these two national networks, Canada also supports several regional networks, among them, the Baton Broadcasting System (BBS) and Can-West Global. BBS is a communications company whose holdings include stations in Ontario and Saskatchewan. It produces several shows aired on CTV, including Blue Jays baseball. It hopes to add stations from Alberta to its roster soon. Meanwhile, CanWest Global, with stations in seven provinces, is a strong player in Canadian television. CanWest boasts several of the top-rated shows in Canada: "Seinfeld," "The X-Files," "Friends," "The Simpsons," "Mad About You" and "Frasier." It has also produced several made-for-Canadian television series, including "Traders" and "Destiny Ridge." Numerous failed attempts to build a national network haven't dimmed the spirits of CEO Izzy Asper, who seems intent on giving Canadians a third national network.

THE TRADITIONAL NETWORKS: UNITED STATES

Television had four networks to begin with, but few cities had more than two stations. Because NBC and CBS both had been household words since the early days of radio, they were the first choices of local stations in lining up an affiliation. Upstart ABC, in the radio business only since 1943, survived in television through a cash infusion that accompanied a 1953 merger with United-Paramount Theaters. The DuMont Network, namesake of picture-tube developer *Allen DuMont*, folded in 1955. Meanwhile, as more cities acquired a third station, ABC grew and eventually rivaled the other networks for viewers. In the late 1970s, ABC unseated CBS as the ratings leader with youth-oriented comedies and Monday night football. In 1985, with the Bill Cosby sitcom and "Miami Vice," NBC displaced ABC. Today, the three networks are well matched in their affiliate bases and resources.

With federal funding provided in 1967, the *Public Broadcasting Service* began providing programs to noncommercial stations. While PBS has offered some popular programs, such as "Sesame Street," commercial stations did not see it as much of a threat. In fact, with its emphasis on informational programming such as the "Mac-Neil-Lehrer News Hour," "Nova" and quality drama and arts, PBS relieved public pressure on commercial stations for less profitable high-brow programming. Even so, relations between commercial and noncommercial stations were never warm, and they cooled in the 1980s when the FCC allowed public stations to acknowledge their supporters with on-air messages that come close to all-out advertising. In effect, public stations were free to join the competition for local advertising dollars.

Media baron *Rupert Murdoch* launched a fourth network in 1987 after buying seven nonnetwork stations in major cities and the Twentieth Century-Fox Film Corporation, which gave him production facilities and a huge movie library. Murdoch's new Fox network recruited affiliates among other independent stations nationwide with a late-night talk show, then Sunday night programming, and then Saturday night shows. By 1994, with a full prime-time lineup and having outbid CBS for NFL football, Fox raided eight stations from CBS.

Today, the older networks—ABC, CBS and NBC—each have about 200 affiliates. Fox, with about 180, is catching up, but many Fox stations don't have evening newscasts to draw viewers into a whole evening of programming, which means Fox has far fewer viewers than the other networks. Also, most Fox affiliates are UHF stations which, in general, have fewer viewers than stations in the VHF lower-end of the television spectrum.

THE CABLE CHALLENGE

Today the major commercial networks, which deliver programming via over-the-air local affiliates, face a significant challenge from cable television. It was not always so. In the late 1940s, the networks were pleased that communities beyond the range of television stations built master antennas that would catch distant signals and then distribute the signals house to house by wire.

In 1972 the networks watched helplessly as a new company, Home Box Office, began providing movies and special sports events by microwave relay to local cable companies, which set up a separate channel and charged subscribers an extra fee to tune in to the programs. HBO made hardly a dent in network viewership, but in 1975 the company switched to an orbiting satellite to relay its programs, which made the service available to every cable system in the country and 265 000 homes. HBO itself still was hardly a threat to the Big Three networks, but within months

MEDIA: PEOPLE

Christine Craft

Kansas City television anchor Christine Craft was stunned. Her boss, the news director, had sat her down in his office and announced he was taking her off the anchor desk. He flashed a consultant's report at her. "We've just gotten our research back," he said. "You are too old, too unattractive, and not sufficiently deferential to men." He went on, "When the people of Kansas City see your face, they turn the dial."

Christine Craft was incredulous. During her few months at KMBC, in 1981, the station had climbed to number one for the first time in three years. She was an experienced television journalist who had anchored in her hometown, at KEYT in Santa Barbara; reported in San Francisco, at KPIX; and anchored a sports show on the CBS network. At 36, she was hardly over the hill. What did her news director mean that she was "not sufficiently deferential to men"? He explained that she had not played second fiddle to male co-anchors. "You don't hide your intelligence to make the guys look smarter. People

don't like that you know the difference between the American and the National league."

Angry, Chris Craft sued. She charged that KMBC was demoting her on sexist grounds, claiming that male anchors were not held to the same standards in age, appearance or deference. Further, she said, the station had paid her unfairly, $38,500 compared to $75,000 for her male co-anchor. It was an important moment in television, triggering an overdue sensitivity to equal opportunity and treatment for women and men. Craft won her jury trial and even an appeal trial before a second jury. In further appeals, the Metromedia conglomerate, which owned KMBC, prevailed, but Craft had made her point on behalf of women broadcasters.

Within two years, Craft was back as an anchor and happy at KRBK in Sacramento. Then she was named news director and managing editor, the first woman to hold the positions at a Sacramento television station.

the owner of an independent station in Atlanta, Ted Turner, began beaming his signal to an orbiting satellite that retransmitted the signal to subscribing cable systems—the start of Superstation WTBS. This increasing variety of cable-delivered programming, plus the wiring of more and more communities for cable in the 1970s, began draining viewers from the traditional networks.

Today, cable is available in more than 20 000 communities in the United States. Six out of 10 U.S. households, representing 180 million people, subscribe, and the number is growing. This has hurt the traditional networks, whose local affiliates are losing viewers to cable.

The Big Three were also losing viewers to nonnetwork stations. In the early days, most television sets were designed to pick up only the *VHF* channels, 2 to 13, which meant most people could not receive independent stations, which tended to be on higher frequencies. In 1962 the FCC ruled that all new sets had to be able to receive the *UHF* channels, 2 to 83. Gradually, as people replaced their old sets, the audience potential for independent stations grew.

In some markets, independent stations established their own news departments and became serious competitors for viewers. Some major-market nonnetwork stations pooled their resources to create the Independent News Network, offering an alternative to network stations. Others tapped into CNN and other sources for national and international newscasts. Also many independents boosted ratings by signing with Rupert Murdoch's new Fox network, which built viewership with several popular programs, including "Married . . . With Children," "America's Most Wanted" and "Melrose Place."

Ken Burns

Ken Burns and the Civil War. The Public Broadcasting System again demonstrated its unique place in American television with Ken Burns's "Civil War" series in 1991. It was the kind of serious, high-quality television to which commercial networks give little attention, yet it drew massive numbers of viewers, skunking the traditional fare on the other networks night after night.

MEDIA AND YOU

Media Use

The Nielsen audience research company tracks how much time people spend watching television. Using this partial breakdown of Nielsen data (from the U.S.), which are divided by age groups into hours and minutes of viewing, how do your viewing patterns coincide with these averages? What patterns do you see in these data, and how do you explain these patterns?

	Women			Men		
	18–24	25–54	55 up	18–24	25–54	55 up
Monday–Friday 10 a.m.–4:30 p.m.	5:41	5:43	8:04	3:11	2:58	5:35
Monday–Friday 4:30 p.m.–7:30 p.m.	3:50	4:20	7:08	2:51	3:19	6:09
Monday–Friday 8 p.m.–11 p.m.	1:08	1:28	1:34	1:21	1:24	1:26
Monday–Sunday 11:30 p.m.–1:30 a.m.	7:05	9:26	12:19	6:06	8:58	11:32
Saturday 7 a.m.–1 p.m.	:40	:44	:38	:35	:41	:39

CABLE IN CANADA

Ironically, cable TV arrived in Canada before the first Canadian television station, perhaps reflecting our desire for American programming. An experiment with redistributing U.S. antenna signals in 1951 in London, Ontario, marked the start of cable TV in Canada. Research by BBM indicates that Canadians love cable television:

- Seventy-six percent of Canadians are wired for cable TV, from a high of 87 percent in British Columbia to a low of 61 percent in Saskatchewan.
- Forty percent of Canadian cable services, like TMN, TSN, MuchMusic, Super Écran and Viewers Choice reach the Canadian population, while 27 percent of U.S. speciality services, like A&E, CNN and ESPN also reach Canadian cable subscribers.

INTERACTIVE TELEVISION

Television is being put to new uses. Amid talk and speculation about a future of *interactive television*, in which people can send and receive messages through their television sets, home-shopping networks are doing it now. It is true that viewers don't order merchandise by using their television set, which would be truly interactive, but viewers do react immediately to television pitches for products on home-shopping networks by placing their orders by telephone. Home shopping has tremendous potential. Today it is a mainstay in the $2 billion a year electronic retailing industry.

PROGRAM SOURCES

 The networks and local stations produce almost all of their own news, sports and public-affairs programming, but most entertainment programming originates with outside sources.

PRODUCING NEWS PROGRAMS

Because of the prestige associated with quality news programs, the networks and local stations produce their own programs, each with its own stamp: "*ABC* World News Tonight," "The National," "The CTV News." For spot news when their own reporters are not at the scene, the networks buy videotape and stills from free-lancers and even amateurs. However, the networks hardly ever risk the reputations of their news operations by farming out newscast and news documentary production to outsiders. For the same reason, most stations produce all their own news programs, although some stations occasionally air a documentary by an independent producer.

The role of freelance television producers is limited mostly to contracted projects. For example, the PBS documentary program "Nova" is built on freelance projects. For its specials, the National Geographic issues contracts to producers to cover specific subjects.

At local stations, little programming besides news, sports and public affairs is produced. Local variety and quiz shows, even dramas, were attempted in the 1950s, but they were amateurish compared to network shows. Only in big markets where stations have major resources available are local entertainment programs produced anymore.

PRODUCING ENTERTAINMENT PROGRAMS

The networks produce some entertainment programs themselves, but in the U.S. because of FCC regulations that limited network profits for their own programs over many years, the networks rely mostly on independent companies for their shows. The independent companies create prototype episodes called "pilots" to entice the networks to buy the whole series, usually a session in advance. When a network buys a series, the show's producers work closely with network programming people on details. Because networks are responsible for the programs they feed their affiliates, the networks have standards and practices people who review every program for content acceptability. They order changes to be made. Although it is gatekeeping, not true censorship, these people who control the standards and practices are sometimes called "censors."

At all three major U.S. networks, the "censorship" units have been downsized in recent years—in part because of greater audience and government acceptance of risqué language and forthright dramatizations. This does not mean there are no limits. In 1993 ABC pushed some people's tolerance with the new "NYPD Blue" program. Many advertisers were cautious at first about signing up for the program. The criticism, mostly from the religious right, led by the Reverend David Wildmon, was offset by the critical acclaim the program received. The program also drew large audiences. Many advertisers, despite the criticism, couldn't pass up "NYPD Blue" as an effective vehicle to air their messages. Undeterred, in 1994 Wildmon and his followers launched a $3 million campaign against the program, the network and the sponsors, but decision makers, including regulators, weren't

Japanese Television

Anyone who owns a television set in Japan can expect a knock on the door every couple of months. It is the collector from NHK, the Japan Broadcast Corporation, to pick up the $16 (U.S.) reception fee. This ritual occurs six times a year in 31 million doorways. The reception fee, required by law since 1950, produces $2.6 (U.S.) billion annually to support the NHK network.

NHK is a Japanese tradition. It went on the air in 1926, a single radio station whose first broadcast was the enthronement of Emperor Hirohito. Today, NHK operates three radio and two domestic television networks. It also runs Radio Japan, the national overseas shortwave, which transmits 40 hours of programs a day in 21 languages.

The primary NHK television network, Channel One, offers mostly high-brow programming, which gives NHK its reputation as the good gray network. Medieval samurai epics have been a long-term staple.

NHK also is known for programs like the 1980 "Silk Road," 30 hours total, which traced early Europe-Japan trade across Asia. NHK airs about 600 hours a year of British and American documentaries and dramas from the BBC and PBS. The network prides itself on its news.

Some NHK programs, such as the 15-minute Sunday morning "Serial Novel," have huge followings. Ratings regularly are 50 percent. Most Japanese viewers, however, spend most of their television time with stations served by four networks, all with headquarters in Tokyo: Fuji, NHK, NTV and Tokyo Broadcasting System. A few independent stations complete Japan's television system.

The commercial stations all offer similar fare: comedies, pop concerts and videos, quiz shows, sports and talk shows. In recent years news has gained importance in attracting viewers and advertisers, encroaching on one of NHK's traditional strengths.

listening. This kind of opposition is seen less often in Canada, but may be on the rise.

Besides buying programs from independent producers, networks buy motion pictures, some that have already been on the movie-house circuit and on pay television, and others made expressly for the networks. Hollywood studios are among the largest producers of network entertainment programs.

Like the networks, single stations also buy independently produced entertainment programs. To do this, the stations go to distributors, called *syndicators*, who package programs specifically for sale to individual stations, usually for one-time use. Syndicators also sell programs that previously appeared on the networks. These *off-network programs*, as they are called, sometimes include old episodes of programs still playing on the networks. "Murder, She Wrote," a successful CBS program, went off-net in 1987 to the USA cable network while new episodes were still being produced for CBS. Local stations, like the networks, also buy old movies from motion picture companies for one-time showing.

PRODUCING ADVERTISEMENTS

Many television stations have elaborate facilities that produce commercials for local advertisers. In some cities, stations provide production services free, but the general practice is to charge production fees. These fees, usually based on studio time, vary widely but can run hundreds of dollars an hour. They can be a significant revenue source for stations. Except in the smallest markets, stations do not have a monopoly on producing commercials. Independent video production houses are also available to advertisers to put together commercials, which then are provided ready-to-play to stations.

FRAGMENTING AUDIENCE

STUDY PREVIEW Innovations in delivering television programs are dividing the audience into more and more segments. New and coming services have changed the vocabulary of television with terms and acronyms like PPV (pay-per-view), superstations, LPTV (low-power television), DBS (direct broadcast satellite) and STV (subscriber television).

CABLE INNOVATIONS

Gerald Levin. Television was revolutionized in the mid-1970s when Gerald Levin put HBO on satellite, giving local cable systems relatively inexpensive access to the service. Previously, television signals were transmitted via microwave towers spaced a few miles apart. With hundreds of relays across the countryside, the microwave system was expensive and prone to failure. With a satellite, however, it was one beam up and one beam down. Levin eventually moved up the ranks of HBO's parent corporation, Time-Life, and in 1992, was put in charge of the successor corporation, Time Warner.

Television entered a new era in 1975 when *Gerald Levin* took over *Home Box Office*, a Time Inc. subsidiary. HBO had been offering movies and special events, such as championship fights, to local cable systems, which sold the programs to subscribers willing to pay an extra fee. It was a *pay-per-program* service. Levin converted HBO to a *pay-per-month* service offering 24 hours a day of programming, mostly movies. To make the expanded system work, Levin needed somehow to cut the tremendous expense of relaying HBO programs across the country from microwave tower to microwave tower. It occurred to Levin that he could bypass microwaving if the HBO signal could be sent instead to an orbiting satellite, which then could send it back in one relay to every local cable company in the country. Levin put up $7.5 million to use the Satcom 1 satellite, which allowed him to cut microwave costs while expanding programming and making HBO available to more of the country.

It was a significant development. Until then, most television viewers had a choice only of network-affiliated stations; one, possibly two independent stations. Suddenly, HBO was a widely available alternative. Although HBO made hardly a dent in ABC, CBS and NBC ratings, the Levin innovation opened the way for other satellite-delivered cable networks. The potential of HBO's satellite delivery was not lost on Ted Turner, who put his nonnetwork Atlanta station on a satellite and called it a superstation. Others followed—WGN of Chicago, WWOR of New York, KPIX of San Francisco, KTLA of Los Angeles, and KTVT of Fort Worth, Texas. By 1990 cable subscribers had access to more than 60 cable networks, most of them specializing in program niches that the Big Three American networks, in the quest for general audiences, could not match.

NETWORK BELT-TIGHTENING

The effect was profound on the three traditional U.S. commercial networks. The networks had claimed 93 percent of American viewers in 1978, before cable networks began offering alternatives. Within six years, ABC, CBS and NBC together drew only 77 percent. With fewer viewers, the traditional commercial networks inevitably faced declining advertising revenue. The networks responded by cutting back on expenses. At CBS the news division was cut from 1400 to 1000 employees in one swoop. Similar cuts followed at ABC and NBC. CTV and CBC also downsized.

The networks also tried to establish footholds in the growing cable industry with their own networks. Some early efforts failed, including CBS Cable, which

---

MEDIA DATABANK

Specialty Channels

Canadian speciality channels like WTN, Showcase, Bravo! and Life offer Canadians niche programming. A.C. Nielsen Canada reports the top specialty channels in Canada are:

Channel	% Share of the Market
YTV	3.5
TSN	3.0
Newsworld	1.5
Discovery	1.5
MuchMusic	1.0
Bravo!	.8
Showcase	.6
Weather Network	.5
Vision	.5
Life	.5
WTN	.4
Canadian Home Shopping	.1

(Source: Holmes and Taras, *Seeing Ourselves*)

New Canadian specialty channels, announced in the fall of 1996, include CTV N-1, a 24-hour headline news service and ROBTV, an all-business news channel from the *Globe and Mail*. In all, 23 new specialty services were granted licences by the CRTC.

---

featured serious concerts, opera and drama; and Satellite News Network, an all-news venture of ABC and Westinghouse, which never overcame CNN's head start. ABC did better with its stake in the ESPN cable sports network and the low-budget USA entertainment network. NBC has found success with its CNBC consumer-oriented business network, which went up against the Financial News Network in a niche it had created. (NBC eventually bought out FNN.) CBC's Newsworld is one of the most watched Canadian specialty channels.

EVEN MORE CHANNELS

DBS, short for *direct broadcast satellite* service, could be cable's own comeuppance. DBS allows companies to transmit an array of channels directly to subscribers who have special antenna dishes—bypassing local cable companies. Early DBS experiments had mixed results, but DBS companies, without the expense of wiring communities, seem to have the potential to undercut cable company rates and further fragment the television market.

Telephone companies, meanwhile, are upgrading their lines with *fibre-optic* cables. These cables can carry a great number of high-quality signals, including video, which means that telephone companies have the potential to compete with cable companies in delivering television services. Because far more homes are wired for telephone than for cable, especially in rural areas, today's cable companies may face stiff new competition from the telephone companies.

Satellite Repair Job. Although satellites are highly reliable for relaying television and radio signals, when something does go wrong it is a major project to repair it. In 1992, astronauts Richard Hieb, Tom Akers and Pierre Thuot from the spacecraft *Endeavor* went space walking to capture the Intelsat VI satellite for repairs. While the Intelsat was out of commission, broadcast transmissions were channeled to alternate satellites.

PAY SERVICES

Meanwhile, other pay services joined HBO. These included Showtime, Cinemax, Disney and Playboy, which further divided the television audience. In Canada pay services included TMN, Moviepix and the Family Channel. In addition, pay-per-view services, offered by cable companies to subscribers who are charged for each program they watch, were coming into their own. The largest PPV, Viewer's Cable, is available in more than 2.5 million homes in the U.S., while Viewer's Choice Canada is available in 90 percent of Canadian homes with cable.

A PPV variation that does not deliver programming through cable companies is subscriber television—called *STV*. STV companies send scrambled signals through the air directly to subscribers who rent a decoder from the STV company. STV has worked in populous areas not yet wired for cable, but because STV offers only one channel, it is disadvantaged once cable reaches a neighbourhood. It is also susceptible to piracy. Decoding boxes are easily copied and sold on the black market.

CHAPTER WRAP-UP

Television patterned itself after radio. From the beginning, television was a system of locally owned commercial stations and national networks. Companies that were heavily involved in radio were also the television heavyweights. Even television's programming mimicked radio's. Networks like CTV, CBC, NBC, CBS and ABC were the most powerful shapers of television, leading in entertainment programming and news. They also pioneered many of the technological advances. Today, program packaging and further technical innovations are challenging network dominance, and the television industry is undergoing a major restructuring.

Gerald Levin and then Ted Turner led the restructuring when they realized that they could deliver programs to local cable companies via orbiting satellite. Levin's HBO and Turner's WTBS, both movie services, became unique features of cable companies in the 1970s. The threat to local over-air stations and the Big Three American networks was minor at first, but cable companies began wiring more neighbourhoods, and additional cable networks came to be, among them Turner's 24-hour news service. With cable into more than 70 percent of Canada's homes today, the cable networks are siphoning major advertising from the traditional networks, and many local cable companies are going after local advertisers. In some cities, independent local stations have become major players for advertising, which further contributes to the restructuring.

Satellite technology is contributing to major changes in a second way. Network affiliates discovered in the 1980s that they could use their new downlink equipment, which received network transmissions from satellites, to pick up programming from other sources. Suddenly, these stations could pick and choose programs, even news video, as never before. Many stations expanded their newscasts and assembled their own far-away coverage with video from a variety of network and nonnetwork sources. Larger stations acquired mobile uplink equipment and sent crews great distances to cover news. It was not unusual for some stations to send crews abroad several times a year. No longer were local over-air stations so dependent on their networks to succeed.

QUESTIONS FOR REVIEW

1. How does television influence people and society in the short term and the long term?
2. How is television technology different from movie technology?
3. How was radio the role model for early television programming?
4. How has television news evolved into its present format?
5. Why does the United States have a two-tier structure for the television industry?
6. What role do affiliates have in network programming?
7. What are the main sources of television programming?
8. How are the traditional television networks being affected by new technology that is available to their affiliates?
9. What developments in television are threatening the traditional over-air stations and the networks that supply much of their programming?
10. Describe how CBC and CTV complement each other as national networks.

QUESTIONS FOR CRITICAL THINKING

1. How did Vladimir Zworykin's iconoscope and kinescope employ electronics to pick up moving images and relay them to far-away screens? Explain the difference between television and film technology.

2. What was the relationship of radio and early television programming? You might want to review Chapter 5 to explain the effect of television on radio.

3. Trace the development of television news from the newsreel days. Include the heyday of documentaries and explain what happened to them. What was the contribution of Fred Friendly and Edward R. Murrow? Explain expanded network newscasts and the importance of Walter Cronkite. What contribution has PBS made? Include magazine and talk-show programs in your answer.

4. Outline the development of television networks. Besides the major networks, include Allen DuMont's, Ted Turner's and Rupert Murdoch's networks. Explain challenges faced today by the major networks, including how independent stations have become stronger, the innovation pioneered by Gerald Levin, the effect of deregulation, expanded program production by syndicators, and new technologies. How do you regard the observation of some critics that the networks will not exist in their present form by the year 2000?

5. Historically, why have American television stations sought affiliations with ABC, CBS and NBC? Discuss changes in network–affiliate relations. Is a network affiliation as attractive today as it was 20 years ago? Why or why not?

6. What happened to network Standards and Practices Departments in the late 1980s? Why?

7. How is the television industry funded? Remember that the financial base is different for the commercial networks, network–affiliated stations, independent stations, noncommercial networks and stations, superstations, cable networks, cable systems, and subscriber services.

8. How does the career of Ted Turner epitomize the emergence of new program and delivery systems as a challenge to the traditional structure of television?

9. The data indicate that the majority of programs watched by Canadians are American, so do we need a national public network that produces shows by and about Canadians? Should the task of producing television programs become totally privatized?

FOR FURTHER LEARNING

Erik Barnouw. *Tube of Plenty: The Evolution of American Television* (Oxford, 1975). Barnouw, the preeminent biographer of television, deals with evolutions in network programming and the powerful personalities that shaped the industry.

Warren Bennis and Ian Mitroff. *The Unreality Industry* (Carol Publishing 1989). Professors Bennis and Mitroff claim that television has turned America into a "24-hour entertainment society." It is for the worse, they say. By treating complex issues in slick 15-, 30-, and 60-second segments of information, television has lulled viewers into believing that the modern world can be understood with hardly any effort.

Roger Bird. *Documents in Canadian Broadcasting* (Carleton University Press, 1988). A chronological listing of government broadcasting documents from 1900 up to 1986.

Bureau of Broadcast Measurement. *1995-1996 Television Databook*.

Mary Lu Carnevale. "Untangling the Debate over Cable Television." *Wall Street Journal* 71 (March 19, 1990):107, B1, B5, B6. The *Journal* offers a package on the status of the cable industry, including competition from fibre-optic networks owned by telephone companies and from direct-to-home satellite services.

Mark Christensen and Cameron Stauth. *The Sweeps* (Morrow, 1984). An examination of special network programs, including miniseries and scandal reports, to attract viewers during ratings periods when advertising rates are set.

Christine Craft. *Too Old, Too Ugly, and Not Deferential to Men* (Dell, 1988). An anchorwoman recounts the sad emphasis on image over journalistic substance at a profitable, tight-fisted metropolitan station. It is a personal story that details her removal as an anchor because her bosses did not think she was young or pretty enough.

Don Dawson, Peter J. Maurin and Ken Phillips. *It's Only Wrestling: Everyone's Guide to Professional Grunt and Groan.* (Shooting Star Press, 1996). A look at the economic, historical and social elements of wrestling.

Peter Desbarats. *A Guide to the Canadian News Media* (Harcourt Brace, 1996).

Helen Holmes and David Tara. *Seeing Ourselves: Media Power and Policy in Canada.* A series of critical articles on Canadian television are included in this Canadian media reader.

Ed Joyce. *Prime Times, Bad Times* (Doubleday, 1988). A former president of CBS News explains network television journalism from the inside, up to the economic crunch of the late 1980s.

Joshua Meyrowitz. *No Sense of Place: The Impact of the Electronic Media on Social Behavior* (Oxford, 1985). Meyrowitz summarizes research on television's effects on human behaviour, concluding that the effect has been powerful.

Peter C. Newman. "Save the Country by Salvaging the CBC," *Maclean's* (February 19, 1996).

Lucas A. Powe, Jr. *American Broadcasting and the First Amendment* (University of California Press, 1987). Powe challenges the premise that broadcasting must be regulated to serve the public interest.

John P. Robinson and Mark R. Levy. *The Main Source* (Sage, 1986). Robinson and Levy argue that television news programs leave viewers with a false sense that they have been informed. The core problem, they say, is deficiencies inherent in the medium, rather than programs.

Mary Vipond. *The Mass Media in Canada* (James Lorimer and Company, 1992).

Jennifer Wells. "Izzy's Dream," *Maclean's.* (February 19, 1996).

Hank Whittemore. *CNN: The Inside Story* (Little, Brown, 1990). This is an enthusiastic account about Ted Turner and a small group of visionaries who proved that television had more potential as a news medium than the three major American networks had shown.

FOR KEEPING UP TO DATE

Broadcaster is a monthly trade journal for the radio, television and cable industries.

Channels is a monthly trade journal.

Journal of Broadcasting and Electronic Media is a quarterly scholarly journal published by the Broadcast Education Association.

Television/Radio Age is a trade journal.

Consumer magazines that deal extensively with television programming include *Entertainment* and *TV Guide.*

Newsmagazines that report television issues more or less regularly include *Newsweek* and *Time.*

Maclean's and *Canadian Business* track television as a business.

Major newspapers with strong television coverage include the *Los Angeles Times,* the *New York Times* and the *Wall Street Journal.*

CHAPTER 7

JOURNALISM Gathering and Telling News

Many mass media practices originated during major periods in American history

Journalists rely largely on individual judgment in deciding what to report

Many variables beyond a journalist's control affect what ends up being reported

Journalists bring many personal, social and political values to their work

Studies have found that journalists identify themselves as middle of the road politically

News is concerned with change, which gives currency to the charge that news has a liberal slant

Factors outside the newsroom influence how news is reported

Gatekeeping is both essential and hazardous in the news process

News organizations rely heavily on common sources, like news services and syndicates

MEDIA IN THEORY

Personal Values in News: The Role of the Journalist

After years of wrestling to come up with a definition for news, NBC newscaster Chet Huntley threw up his hands and declared: "News is what I decide is news." Huntley was not being arrogant. Rather, he was pointing out that events that go unreported aren't news. Regardless of an event's intrinsic qualities, such as the prominence of the people involved and the event's consequence and drama, it becomes news only when it's reported. Huntley's point was that the journalist's judgment is indispensable in deciding what's news.

Huntley's conclusion underscores the high degree of autonomy that individual journalists have in shaping what is reported. Even a reporter hired fresh out of college by a small daily newspaper and assigned to city hall has a great deal of independence in deciding what to report and how to report it. Such trust is unheard of in most other fields, which dole out responsibility to newcomers in small bits over a lengthy period. Of course, rookie journalists are monitored by their newsroom superiors, and editors give them assignments and review their stories, but it is that city hall reporter, no matter how green, who is the news organization's expert on city government.

This contributes to the independence and autonomy that characterize news work. Journalists know they have a high level of responsibility in deciding what to report as news. While most reporters will agree on the newsworthiness of some events and issues, such as a catastrophic storm or a tax proposal, their judgments will result in stories that take different slants and angles. On events and issues whose newsworthiness is less obvious, reporters will differ even on whether to do a story.

JOURNALISTS' PERSONAL VALUES

The journalistic ideal, an unbiased seeking of truth and an unvarnished telling of it, dictates that the work be done without partisanship. Yet as human beings, journalists have personal values that influence all that they do, including their work. Because the news judgment decisions that journalists make are so important to an informed citizenry, we need to know what makes these people tick. Are they left-wingers? Are they ideological zealots? Are they quirky and unpredictable? Are they conscientious?

A sociologist who studied stories in the American news media for 20 years, Herbert Gans, concluded that journalists have a typical American value system. Gans identified primary values, all in the American mainstream, that journalists use in making their news judgments:

ETHNOCENTRISM.   Journalists see things through their culture's eyes, which colours news coverage. In the 1960s and 1970s, Gans notes, North Vietnam was consistently characterized as "the enemy." American reporters took the view of the American government and military, which was hardly detached or neutral. This ethnocentricity was clear at the end of

the war, which American media headlined as "the *fall* of South Vietnam." By other values, Gans said, the Communist takeover of Saigon could be considered a *liberation*. In neutral terms, it was a *change in government*. Words can carry strong connotations, as the Sapir-Whorf hypothesis suggests.

This ethnocentrism creates problems as the news media become global. During the Persian Gulf war in 1991, CNN discovered that the commonly used word "foreign," which to American audiences meant anything non-American, was confusing to CNN audiences in other countries. Eager to build a global audience, CNN boss Ted Turner banned the word "foreign" and told anchors and scriptwriters that they would be fired for uttering the word. "International" became the substitute word, as awkward as it sometimes sounded to American ears. The semantic change was cosmetic, however, for the CNN war coverage continued, inevitably, to be largely from the American perspective, just as Gans found in his earlier studies. It is hard for all people, including journalists, to transcend their own roots.

COMMITMENT TO DEMOCRACY AND CAPITALISM.   Gans found that American journalists favour democracy of the American style. Coverage of other governmental forms dwells on corruption, conflict, protest and bureaucratic malfunction. The unstated idea of most U.S. journalists, said Gans, is that other societies do best when they follow the American ideal of serving the public interest.

Gans also found that American journalists are committed to the capitalist economic system. When they report corruption and misbehaviour in American business, journalists treat them as aberrations. The underlying posture of the news coverage of the U.S. economy, Gans said, is "an optimistic faith" that businesspeople refrain from unreasonable profits and gross exploitation of workers or customers while competing to create increased prosperity for all. In covering controlled foreign economies, American journalists emphasize the downside.

It may seem only natural to most Americans that democracy and capitalism should be core values of any reasonable human being. This sense itself is an ethnocentric value, which many people do not even think about but which nonetheless shapes how they conduct their lives. Knowing that American journalists by and large share this value explains a lot about the news coverage they create.

SMALL-TOWN PASTORALISM. Like most of their fellow citizens, journalists romanticize rural life. Given similar stories from metropolitan Vancouver and tiny Estevan, Saskatchewan, editors usually opt for the small town.

Cities are covered as places with problems; rural life is celebrated. Suburbs are largely ignored. This small-town pastoralism, said Gans, helps explain the success of Charles Kuralt's long-running "On the Road" series on CBS television and the soft news program "On The Road Again" on CBC.

INDIVIDUALISM TEMPERED BY MODERATION. Gans found that journalists love stories about rugged individuals who overcome adversity and defeat powerful forces. This is a value that contributes to a negative coverage of technology as something to be feared because it can stifle individuality. Gans again cited "On the Road," noting how Charles Kuralt found a following for his pastoral features on rugged individuals.

Journalists like to turn ordinary individuals into heroes, but there are limits. Rebels and deviates are panned as extremists who go beyond another value—moderation. To illustrate this propensity toward moderation, Gans noted that "the news treats atheists as extremists and uses the same approach, if more gingerly, with religious fanatics. People who consume conspicuously are criticized, but so are people such as hippies who turn their backs on consumer goods. The news is scornful both of the overly academic scholar and the over simplifying popularizer; it is kind neither to high-brows nor to low-brows, to users of jargon or users of slang. College students who play when they should study receive disapproval, but so do 'grinds.' Lack of moderation is wrong, whether it involves excesses or abstention."

In politics, Gans says, both ideologues and politicians who lack ideology are treated with suspicion: "Political candidates who talk openly about issues may be described as dull; those who avoid issues entirely evoke doubts about their fitness for office."

SOCIAL ORDER. Journalists cover disorder—earthquakes, industrial catastrophes, protest marches, the disintegrating nuclear family, and transgressions of laws and mores. This coverage, noted Gans, is concerned not with glamorizing disorder but with finding ways to restore order. To critics who claim that the news media concentrate on disruption and the nega-tive, Gans noted a study of television coverage of the 1967 race riots: Only 3 percent of the sequences covered the riots, and only 2 percent dealt with injuries and deaths. A full 34 percent of the coverage focused on restoring order. *Newsweek*'s coverage, according to the same study, devoted four times as many words to police and Army attempts to restore order as to describing the disturbances.

The journalistic commitment to social order also is evident in how heavily reporters rely on persons in leadership roles as primary sources of information. These leaders, largely representing the Establishment and the status quo, are the people in the best position to maintain social order and to restore it if there's a disruption. This means government representatives often shape news media reports and thus their audiences' understanding of what is important, "true" or meaningful. No one receives more media attention than the president of the United States, who is seen, said Gans, "as the ultimate protector of order."

JOURNALISTIC BIAS

Critics of the news media come in many colours. Conservatives are the most vocal, charging that the media slant news to favour liberal causes. Liberal critics see it in the opposite light. The most recurrent charge, however, is that the media are leftist, favouring liberal over conservative views, and change over the status quo.

The fact is that journalists generally fall near the political centre. A landmark 1971 survey by John Johnstone found 84.6 percent of journalists considered themselves middle-of-the-road or a little to the left or right. In 1983 David Weaver and Cleveland Wilhoit found 91.1 percent in those categories.

Despite such evidence, charges persist that journalists are biased. The charges are all the stranger considering that most news organizations pride themselves on a neutral presentation and go to extraordinary lengths to prove it. To avoid confusion between straight reporting and commentary, opinion pieces are set apart in clearly labeled editorial sections. Most journalists, even those with left or right leanings, have a zealous regard for detached, neutral reporting. Although they see their truth-seeking as unfettered by partisanship, they recognize that their news judgments often are made in confusing situations against deadline pressure, and they are the first, in self-flagellating postmortems, to criticize themselves when they fall short of the journalistic goals of accuracy, balance and fairness.

Considering the media's obsession with avoiding partisanship, how do the charges of bias retain any currency? First, critics who paint the media as leftist usually are forgetting that news, by its nature, is concerned with change. Everybody, journalists and media consumers alike, is more interested in a volcano that is blowing its top than in one that remains dormant. This interest in what is happening, as opposed to what is not happening, does not mean that anyone favours volcanic eruptions. However, the fact is that change almost always is more interesting than the status quo,

although it is often more threatening and less comfortable. When journalists spend time on a candidate's ideas to eliminate farm subsidies, it is not that the journalists favour the change, just that the topic is more interesting than stories about government programs that are unchallenged. Because conservatives favour the status quo, it is natural that they would feel threatened by news coverage of change and proposals for change, no matter how disinterested and dispassionate the coverage, but this is hardly liberal bias.

In short, journalists' concern with change is not born of political bias. It is inherent in the nature of their work.

Mainstream Values. Although the most powerful news media in North America are located in Toronto, Ottawa, New York, Washington, D.C., and other urban, cosmopolitan areas, studies by sociologist Herbert Gans have found that journalists for these organizations bring mainstream values to their work. Among these values is a fascination with rural life and small-town pastoralism. CBS correspondent Charles Kuralt built a following by criss-crossing the U.S. for stories about common people doing interesting things, mostly in small-town and rural settings.

MEDIA: PEOPLE

The Composite Journalist

Here is a look at journalists, drawn from numerous studies in recent years:

- **Age.** Journalism is more a young person's line of work than most career areas, probably because of stresses from deadlines, uncooperative news sources and difficult reporting assignments. Forty-five percent are 25 to 34 years old.
- **Gender.** Women comprise 53 percent of the new reporters hired by the media. Many women leave the field, however. Among long-term reporters, 65 percent are men. The number of women in manage-

ment is increasing but remains small. Of managing editors, 26 percent are women; of editors, 16 percent; of general managers, 8 percent; of publishers, 6 percent.
- **Education.** Most young journalists hold degrees in journalism or mass communication, and gradually such degrees are increasing. Among television journalists, the percentage of journalism and mass communication degrees is 63 percent; daily newspapers, 56 percent; news services, 53 percent; radio, 53 percent; weekly newspapers, 50 percent; and newsmagazines, 26 percent.

Peter Arnett in Baghdad.
CNN's Peter Arnett provided exclusive coverage from Baghdad during the 1991 Persian Gulf war. The coverage troubled many Americans and some journalists who, in their ethnocentrism, saw Arnett as being used by the enemy. While the Iraqis controlled much of Arnett's access to information, he wrote his own dispatches. He consistently reminded viewers of the conditions under which he was gathering information, including that Iraqi officials were his primary source.

NEWS MEDIA TRADITIONS

STUDY PREVIEW Journalism has evolved through four distinctive eras—the colonial, partisan, penny and yellow press periods. Each of these periods made distinctive contributions to contemporary news media practices in both Canada and the U.S.

COLONIAL PERIOD

Benjamin Harris published the first colonial newspaper, *Publick Occurrences*, in Boston in 1690. He was in hot water right away. Harris scandalized Puritan sensitivities, alleging that the king of France had dallied with his son's wife. In the colonies just as in England, a newspaper needed royal consent. The governor had not consented, and Harris was put out of business after one issue.

Even so, Harris's daring was a precursor for emerging press defiance against authority. In 1733 *John Peter Zenger* started a paper in New York in competition with the existing Crown-supported newspaper. Zenger's New York *Journal* was backed by merchants and lawyers who disliked the royal governor. From the beginning the newspaper antagonized the governor with items challenging his competence, and finally the governor arrested Zenger. The trial made history. Zenger's attorney, *Andrew Hamilton*, argued that there should be no punishment for printing articles that are true. The argument was a dramatic departure from the legal practice of the day, which allowed royal governors to prosecute for articles that might undermine their authority, regardless of whether the articles were true. Hamilton's argument prevailed, and Zenger, who had become a hero for standing up to the Crown, was freed. To the governor's chagrin, there was great public celebration in the streets of New York that night.

Zenger's success against the Crown foreshadowed the explosive colonial reaction after Parliament passed a stamp tax in 1765. The colonies did not have elected representatives in Parliament, so the cry was a defiant "No taxation without representation." The campaign, however, was less ideological than economic. Colonial printers, who stood to lose from the new tax, which was levied on printed materials, led the campaign. Historian *Arthur Schlesinger* has called it the *newspaper war on Britain*. The newspapers won: the tax was withdrawn. Having seen their potential to force the government's hand, newspapers then led the way in stirring other ill feelings against England and precipitating the American Revolution.

These traditions from the colonial period remain today:

- The news media, both print and broadcast, relish their independence from government censorship and control.
- The news media, especially newspapers and magazines, actively try to mold government policy and mobilize public sentiment. Today this is done primarily on the editorial page.
- Journalists are committed to seeking truth, which was articulated as a social value in Zenger's "truth defence."
- The public comes down in favour of independent news media when government becomes too heavy-handed, as demonstrated by Zenger's popularity.
- In a capitalistic system, the news media are economic entities that sometimes react in their own self-interest when their profit-making ability is threatened.

PARTISAN PERIOD

After the Revolution, newspapers divided along partisan lines. What is called the Federalist period in American history is also referred to as the *partisan period* among newspaper historians. Intense partisanship characterized newspapers of the period, which spanned roughly 50 years to the 1830s.

Initially the issue was over a constitution. Should the nation have a strong central government or remain a loose coalition of states? James Madison, Alexander Hamilton, Thomas Jefferson, John Jay and other leading thinkers exchanged ideas with articles and essays in newspapers. The *Federalist Papers*, a series of essays printed and reprinted in newspapers throughout the nation, were part of the debate. Typical of the extreme partisanship of the era were journalists who reveled in nasty barbs and rhetorical excesses. It was not unusual for an ideological opponent to be called "a spaniel" or "a traitor."

After the Constitution was drafted, partisanship intensified, finally culminating lopsidedly when the Federalist party both controlled the Congress and had their leader, John Adams, in the presidency. In firm control and bent on silencing their detractors, the Federalists ramrodded a series of laws through Congress in 1798. One of the things these laws, the *Alien and Sedition Acts*, prohibited was "false, scandalous, malicious" statements about government. Using these laws, the Federalists made 25 indictments, which culminated in 10 convictions. Among those indicated was *David Bowen*, a Revolutionary War veteran who felt strongly about free expression. He put up a sign in Dedham, Massachusetts, that said: "No stamp tax. No sedition. No alien bills. No land tax. Downfall to tyrants of America. Peace and retirement to the president [the Federalist John Adams]. Long live the vice president [the Anti-Federalist Thomas Jefferson] and the minority [the Anti-Federalists]. May moral virtues be the basis of civil government." If only critics of recent presidents were so mild! But the Federalists were not of a tolerant mind. Bowen was fined $400 and sentenced to 18 months in prison.

Federalist excesses were at their most extreme when *Matthew Lyon*, a member

When Words Failed, 1798-Style. The partisanship during the crude partisan period peaked in 1798 when Roger Griswold impugned the war record of fellow congressman Matthew Lyon. Lyon spat in Griswold's eye. The next day, on the floor of the U.S. House of Representatives, Griswold went after Lyon with his cane, and Lyon beat him back with a handy set of fire tongs. This political cartoon, one of the first, captured the hand-to-hand combat. Later, after Lyon mildly insulted President Adams in print, the Federalists put him in jail.

of Congress, was jailed for a letter to a newspaper editor that accused President Adams of "ridiculous pomp, foolish adulation, selfish avarice." Lyon, an anti-Federalist, was sentenced to four months in jail and fined $1000. Although he was tried in Rutland, Vermont, he was sent to a filthy jail 40 miles away. When editor Anthony Haswell printed an advertisement to raise money for Lyon's fine, he was jailed for abetting a criminal. The public was outraged at Federalist heavy-handedness. The $1000 was quickly raised, and Lyon, while still in prison, was re-elected by a two-to-one margin. After his release from prison, Lyon's supporters followed his carriage for 12 miles as he began his way back to Philadelphia, the national capital. Public outrage showed itself in the election of 1800. Jefferson was elected president, and the Federalists were thumped out of office, never to rise again. The people had spoken.

Here are traditions from the partisan period that continue today:

- Government should keep its hands off the press.
- The news media are a forum for discussion and debate.
- The news media should comment vigorously on public issues.
- Government transgressions against the news media will ultimately be met by public rejection of those committing the excesses, which has happened periodically throughout American history.

PENNY PRESS PERIOD

In 1833, when he was 22, the enterprising *Benjamin Day* started a newspaper that changed American journalism: the New York *Sun*. At a penny a copy, the *Sun* was within reach of just about everybody. Other papers were expensive, an annual subscription costing as much as a full week's wages. Unlike other papers, distributed mostly by mail, the *Sun* was hawked every day on the streets. The *Sun*'s content was different too. It avoided the political and economic thrust of the traditional papers, concentrating instead on items of interest to common folk. The writing was simple, straightforward and easy to follow. For a motto for the *Sun*, Day came up with "It Shines for All," his pun fully intended.

Day's *Sun* was an immediate success. Naturally, it was quickly imitated, and the *penny press period* began. Partisan papers that characterized the partisan period continued, but the mainstream of American newspapers came to be in the mold of the *Sun*.

Merchants saw the unprecedented circulation of the penny papers as a way to reach great numbers of potential customers. Advertising revenue meant bigger papers, which attracted more readers, which attracted more advertisers. A snowballing momentum began that continues today with more and more advertising being carried by the mass media. A significant result was a shift in newspaper revenues from subscriptions to advertisers. Day, as a matter of fact, did not meet expenses by selling the *Sun* for a penny a copy. He counted on advertisers to pick up a good part of his production cost. In effect, advertisers subsidized readers, just as they do today.

Several social and economic factors, all resulting from the Industrial Revolution, made the penny press possible:

- **Industrialization.** With new steam-powered presses, hundreds of copies an hour could be printed. Earlier presses were hand operated.
- **Urbanization.** Workers flocked to the cities to work in new factories, creating a great pool of potential newspaper readers within delivery range. Until the urbanization of the 1820s and 1830s, the population had been almost wholly agricultural and scattered across the countryside. Even the most populous cities had been relatively small.

Penny Press Period. When Benjamin Day launched the New York *Sun* in 1833 and sold it for one cent a copy, he ushered in an era of cheap newspapers that common people could afford. The penny press period also was marked by newspapers with stories of broad appeal, as opposed to the political and financial papers of the preceding party period.

- **Immigration.** Waves of immigrants arrived from impoverished parts of Europe. Most were eager to learn English and found that penny papers, with their simple style, were good tutors.
- **Literacy.** As immigrants learned English, they hungered for reading material within their economic means. Also, literacy in general was increasing, which contributed to the rise of mass circulation newspapers and magazines.

In 1844, late in the penny press period, *Samuel Morse* invented the telegraph. Soon the world was being wired. When the U.S. Civil War started in 1861, correspondents used the telegraph to get battle news to eager readers. It was called *lightning news*, delivered electrically and instantly. The Civil War also gave rise to a new convention in writing news, the *inverted pyramid*. Editors instructed their war correspondents to tell the most important information first in case telegraph lines failed—or were snipped by the enemy—as a story was being transmitted. That way, when a story was interrupted, editors would have at least a few usable sentences. The inverted pyramid, it turned out, was popular with readers because it allowed them to learn what was most important at a glance. They did not have to wade through a whole story if they were in a hurry. Also, the inverted pyramid helped editors fit stories into the limited confines of a page—a story could be cut off at any paragraph and the most important parts remained intact. The inverted pyramid remains a standard expository form for telling event-based stories in newspapers, radio and television.

Several New York newspaper publishers, concerned about the escalating expense of sending reporters to gather far-away news, got together in 1848 to share stories. By together sending one reporter, the newspapers cut costs dramatically. They called their cooperative venture the *Associated Press*, a predecessor of today's giant global news service. The AP introduced a new tone in news reporting. So that AP stories could be used by member newspapers of different political persuasions, reporters were told to write from a nonpartisan point of view. The result was a fact-oriented kind of news writing often called *objective reporting*. It was widely imitated and still is the dominant reporting style for event-based news stories in all the news media.

There are traditions of today's news media, both print and electronic, that can be traced to the penny press period:

- Inverted pyramid story structures.
- Coverage and writing that appeals to a general audience, sometimes by trying to be entertaining or even sensationalistic. It's worth noting that the egalitarian thinking of Andrew Jackson's 1829–1837 presidency, which placed special value on the "common man," coincided with the start of the penny press and its appeal to a large audience of "everyday people."
- A strong orientation to covering events, including the aggressive ferreting out of news.
- A commitment to social improvement, which included a willingness to crusade against corruption.
- Being on top of unfolding events and providing information to readers quickly, something made possible by the telegraph but that also came to be valued in local reporting.
- A detached, neutral perspective in reporting events, a tradition fostered by the Associated Press.

Yellow Journalism's Namesake. The Yellow Kid, a popular cartoon character in New York newspapers that by today's standards is a grotesque caricature, became the namesake for the sensationalist "yellow journalism" of the 1880s and 1890s. Many newspapers of the period, especially in New York, hyperbolized and fabricated the news to attract readers. The tradition remains in isolated areas of modern journalism, such as the supermarket tabloids and trash documentary programs on television.

YELLOW PERIOD

The quest to sell more copies led to excesses that are illustrated by the Pulitzer-Hearst circulation war in New York in the 1890s.

Joseph Pulitzer, a poor immigrant, made the St. Louis *Post-Dispatch* into a financial success. In 1883, Pulitzer decided to try a bigger city. He bought the New York *World* and applied his St. Louis formula. He emphasized human interest, crusaded for worthy causes, and ran lots of promotional hoopla. Pulitzer's *World* also featured solid journalism. His star reporter, *Nellie Bly,* epitomized the two faces of the Pulitzer formula for journalistic success. For one story, Bly feigned mental illness, entered an insane asylum and emerged with scandalous tales about how patients were treated. It was enterprising journalism of great significance. Reforms resulted. Later, showing the less serious, show biz side of Pulitzer's formula, Nellie Bly was sent out to circle the globe in 80 days, like the fictitious Phileas Fogg. Her journalism stunt took 72 days.

In San Francisco, Pulitzer had a young admirer, *William Randolph Hearst.* With his father's Nevada mining fortune and mimicking Pulitzer's New York formula, Hearst made the San Francisco *Examiner* a great success. In 1895 Hearst decided to go to New York and take on the master. He bought the New York *Journal* and vowed to "out-Pulitzer" Pulitzer. The inevitable resulted. To outdo each other, Pulitzer and Hearst launched crazier and crazier stunts. Not even the comic pages escaped the competitive frenzy. Pulitzer ran the *Yellow Kid,* and then Hearst hired the cartoonist away. Pulitzer hired a new one, and both papers ran the yellow character and plastered the city with yellow promotional posters. The circulation war was nicknamed *yellow journalism,* and the term came to be a derisive reference to sensational excesses in news coverage.

The yellow excesses reached a feverish peak as Hearst and Pulitzer covered the growing tensions between Spain and the United States. Fueled by hyped atrocity stories, the tension eventually exploded in war. One story, perhaps apocryphal, epitomizes the no-holds-barred competition between Pulitzer and Hearst. Although Spain had consented to all demands by the United States, Hearst sent the artist Frederic Remington to Cuba to cover the situation. Remington cabled back: "Everything is quiet. There is no trouble here. There will be no war. Wish to return." Hearst replied: "Please remain. You furnish the pictures. I'll furnish the war."

Yellow journalism had its imitators in New York and elsewhere. It is important to note, however, that not all journalism went the yellow route. *Adolph Ochs* bought the *New York Times* in 1896 and built it into a newspaper that avoided sideshows to report and comment seriously on important issues and events. The *Times*, still true to that approach, outlived the Pulitzer and Hearst newspapers in New York and today is considered among the best newspapers in the world.

The yellow tradition, however, still lives. The New York *Daily News*, founded in 1919 and almost an immediate hit, ushered in a period that some historians characterize as *jazz journalism*. It was just Hearst and Pulitzer updated in tabloid form with an emphasis on photography. Today, newspapers like the commercially successful *National Enquirer* are in the yellow tradition. So are a handful of metropolitan dailies, including Rupert Murdoch's San Antonio, Texas, *Express-News*. It is

Joseph Pulitzer

William Randolph Hearst

Journalistic Sensationalism. Rival New York newspaper publishers Joseph Pulitzer and William Randolph Hearst tried to outdo each other daily with anti-Spanish atrocity stories from Cuba, many of them trumped up. Some historians say the public hysteria fueled by Pulitzer and Hearst helped precipitate the Spanish-American War, especially after the U.S. battleship *Maine* exploded in Havana harbour. Both Pulitzer and Hearst claimed it was a Spanish attack on an American vessel, although a case can be made that the explosion was accidental.

obvious too in tabloid television programs like "Hard Copy" and "A Current Affair" and interview programs like Donahue, Oprah and Geraldo, which pander to the offbeat and the sensational.

While not as important in forming distinctive journalistic traditions as the earlier penny papers, yellow newspapers were significant in contributing to the growing feeling of nationhood in the United States, especially among the diverse immigrants arriving in massive numbers. Journalism historian Larry Lorenz put it this way: "The publishers reached out to the widest possible audience by trying to find a common denominator, and that turned out to be the human interest story. Similarities among groups were emphasized rather than differences. Readers, in their quest to be real Americans, seized on those common elements to pattern themselves after, and soon their distinctive characteristics and awareness of themselves as special groups began to fade."

JOURNALISM IN CANADA

The evolution of the press in Canada is discussed in Chapter 2. But it is interesting to note here that Canadian journalism, says Robert Fulford in the 1981 Kent Commission report, is a mix of American and British influences. He cites press historian

Wilfred Kesteron, who observes that Canadian journalists work under a libertarian press system, and that they are fueled by ideals similar to those that characterized the Partisan and Colonial periods in U.S. history. This is not surprising considering many of Canada's first journalists were displaced Americans, who immigrated to Canada in the late 1700s and early 1800s. According to Kesterton, "under the libertarian press system, the system which prevails in Canada, the twin qualities desired for the media are freedom and responsibility. That truism envisages persons of the press doing their work freely, unhampered by government controls and regulatory bodies."

This ideology of social responsibility for journalists is evident in the myriad press councils and press codes in Canada today. The concept has also been adopted by the *Canadian Journalism Foundation*. Formed in 1990, the CJF is an association of journalists, academics and other Canadian leaders. Its goals include professional development for journalists in the belief that better journalists "will result in a better informed citizenry and an improvement in the quality of the Canadian democratic process. Members of the CJC include senior CBC correspondent Knowlton Nash, Peter Desbarats of Western University and Lise Bissonnette of *Le Devoir*.

Journalism in Quebec has also been influenced by American press traditions, but has also acquired its own personality. The 1981 Kent Commission concluded that journalism in Quebec is "torn between the European and particularly French tradition of political diatribe and the American inclination towards hard news." Lysiane Gagnon, also writing for the Kent Commission's report on journalists, says that Quebec's brand of journalism tends to be more political, analytical, conceptual and personal than English Canada's.

- -

VARIABLES AFFECTING NEWS

STUDY PREVIEW The variables that determine what is reported include things beyond a journalist's control, such as how much space or time is available to tell stories. Also, a story that might receive top billing on a slow news day might not even appear on a day when an overwhelming number of major stories are breaking.

NEWS HOLE

A variable affecting what ends up being reported as news is called the *news hole*. In newspapers the news hole is the space left after the advertising department has placed all the ads it has sold in the paper. The volume of advertising determines the number of total pages, and generally, the bigger the issue, the more room for news. Newspaper editors can squeeze fewer stories into a thin Monday issue than a fat Wednesday issue.

In broadcasting, the news hole tends to be more consistent. A 30-minute television newscast may have room for only 23 minutes of news, but the format doesn't vary. When the advertising department doesn't sell all the seven minutes available for advertising, it usually is public service announcements, promotional messages and program notes—not news—that pick up the slack. Even so, the news hole can vary in broadcasting. A 10-minute newscast can accommodate more stories than a 5-minute newscast, and, as with newspapers, it is the judgment of journalists that determines which events make it.

The Price of Diversity

Listen to a few local radio stations for national news or pick up several newspapers from around your province, and you will find the same stories, often word for word from the Canadian Press. Check the editorial pages, and you will find many of the same columnists in paper after paper.

This sameness bothers media critics, who say that democracy would be better served with coverage and commentary from a greater range of sources. Also, some critics say the news services and syndicates work insidiously against good local coverage because penny-pinching media owners find stories from Timbuktu and Ulan Bator less costly than hiring local reporters. The result: Mali and Outer Mongolia are sometimes better covered than city hall.

The other side of the argument is that news services and syndicates provide a quantity and quality of coverage that hardly any local newspapers or broadcast stations could afford on their own.

How do you see this issue?

NEWS FLOW AND STAFFING

Besides the news hole, the flow of news varies from day to day. A story that might be played prominently on a slow news day can be passed over entirely in the competition for space on a heavy news day.

On one of the heaviest news days of all time, in 1989, death claimed Iran's Ayatollah Khomeini, a central figure in United States foreign policy; Chinese young people and the government were locked in a showdown in Tiananmen Square; the Polish people were voting to reject their one-party Communist political system; and a revolt was under way in the Soviet republic of Uzbekistan. That was a heavy news day, and the flow of major nation-rattling events preempted stories that otherwise would have been news.

Whether reporters are in the right place at the right time can affect coverage. A newsworthy event in Nigeria will receive short shrift if the network correspondent for Africa is occupied with a natural disaster in next-door Cameroon. A radio station's city government coverage will slip when the city hall reporter is on vacation or if the station can't afford a regular reporter at city hall. When Iraq invaded Kuwait by surprise in August 1990, it so happened that almost all the U.S. and European reporters assigned to the Persian Gulf were on vacation or elsewhere on assignment. An exception was Caryle Murphy of the *Washington Post*. Like everyone else, Murphy hadn't expected the invasion, but she had decided to make a routine trip from her Cairo bureau for a first-hand look at Kuwaiti affairs. Only by happenstance did Murphy have what she called "a front-row seat for witnessing a small nation being crushed." Competing news organizations were devoid of eyewitness staff coverage until they scrambled to fly people into the region.

PERCEPTIONS ABOUT AUDIENCE

How a news organization perceives its audience affects news coverage. The *National Enquirer* lavishes attention on unproven cancer cures that the *Toronto Star* treats briefly if at all. The *Wall Street Journal* sees its purpose as news for readers who have special interests in finance, the economy and business. NBC's Consumer News and Business Channel was established to serve an audience more interested in quick market updates, brief analysis and trendy consumer news than the kind of depth offered by the *Journal*.

The perception that a news organization has of its audience is evident in a comparison of stories on different networks' newscasts. CNN may lead newscasts with a coup d'état in another country, while Newsworld leads with a new government economic forecast, Rapid Fax on MuchMusic with the announcement of a rock group's tour, and "A Current Affair" with a six-month-old gory homicide that none of the others covered at all.

AVAILABILITY OF MATERIAL

The availability of photographs and video also is a factor in what ends up being news. Television is often faulted for overplaying visually titillating stories, such as fires, and underplaying or ignoring more significant stories that are not photogenic. Newspapers and magazines also are partial to stories with strong accompanying visuals, as shown in an especially poignant way when a Boston woman and child sought refuge on their apartment's balcony when the building caught fire. Then the balcony collapsed. The woman died on impact; the child somehow survived. The tragedy was all the more dramatic because it occurred just as firefighters were about to rescue the woman and child. Most journalists would report such an event, but in this case the coverage was far more extensive than would normally be the case because Stanley Forman of the Boston *Herald-American* photographed the woman and child plunging to the ground. On its own merits, the event probably would not have been reported beyond Boston, but with Forman's series of dramatic photographs, clicked in quick succession, the story was reported in visual media—newspapers, magazines and television—around the world.

Radio news people revel in stories when sound is available, which influences what is reported and new. A barnyard interview with a farm leader, with cows snorting in the background, is likelier to make the air than the same farm leader saying virtually the same thing in the sterile confines of a legislative committee chamber.

COMPETITION

One trigger of adrenalin for journalists is landing a scoop and, conversely, being scooped. Journalism is a competitive business, and the drive to outdo other news organizations keeps news publications and newscasts fresh with new material.

Competition has an unglamorous side. Journalists constantly monitor each other to identify events that they missed and need to catch up on to be competitive. This catch-up aspect of the news business contributes to similarities in coverage, which scholar Leon Sigal calls the *consensible nature of news*. It also is called "pack" and "herd" journalism.

In the final analysis, news is the result of journalists scanning their environment and making decisions, first on whether to cover certain events and then on how to cover them. The decisions are made against a backdrop of countless variables, many of them changing during the reporting, writing and editing processes.

NON-NEWSROOM INFLUENCES ON NEWS

STUDY PREVIEW   While journalists are key in deciding what to report and how, non-newsroom forces in news organizations sometimes play a role, too. These forces include advertiser-sensitive executives, who do not always share the truth-seeking and truth-telling agendas of journalists.

EXECUTIVE ORDERS

While reporters have significant roles in deciding what makes news, news organizations are corporate structures. The people in charge have the final word on matters big and small. It is publishers and general managers and their immediate lieutenants who are in charge. Some of these executives make self-serving decisions on coverage that gall the journalists who work for them, but such is how chains of command work.

An egregious example of front-office meddling in news judgments was alleged in a 1990 complaint to the Federal Communications Commission by radio station KCDA in Coeur d'Alene, Idaho. The station charged that the local newspaper, the Coeur d'Alene *Press*, lavished news coverage on the radio station owned by the newspaper's owner but ignored KCDA despite KCDA's extensive participation in community activities that were as newsworthy as the activities that garnered coverage for the newspaper-owned station. In one *Press* story in which mentioning KCDA was unavoidable, it was referred to only as "an obscure local radio station."

Also appalling is excessive pandering to advertiser interests. It is impossible to catalogue the extent to which journalistic autonomy is sacrificed to curry favour from advertisers, but it can occur even at generally respected news organizations. The Denver *Post*, a metro daily, once offered a shopping mall 1820 column inches of free publicity, equivalent roughly to 72 000 words, a small book, as a bonus if the mall bought 30 pages of advertising. The puffery cut into space that might have been used for substantive news.

Some news organizations obsequiously lean over backwards not to alienate advertisers, which also can undermine journalistic autonomy. NBC once invited Coca-Cola, a major advertiser, to preview a television documentary that reported the company benefited from exploited migrant agricultural workers. NBC then acceded to Coca-Cola's requests to drop certain scenes.

Such policy decisions are more common among smaller, less financially solid news organizations, whose existence can be in jeopardy if they lose advertisers. To avoid rankling advertisers, the Las Cruces, New Mexico, *Sun-News*, as an example, once had a policy against naming local businesses that were in the news in an unsavoury way. When police raided a local hotel room, the *Sun-News* offered not even a hint of which hotel was the site of the raid.

Rarely do media owners acknowledge that they manipulate news coverage to their own economic interests, which is why it is difficult to document the frequency of these abuses. Sociologists who have studied newsrooms note that publishers hire managers whose thinking coincides with their own, and these managers hire editors and reporters of the same sort. The result is that decisions made by reporters do not differ much from those the publisher would make in the same situation. With the sociology of the newsroom shaped by largely like-minded people, seldom does anyone need to order manipulation explicitly. This means most instances of slanting coverage to the wishes of advertisers or other special interests are neither recorded nor reported.

Trailing of O. J. Simpson.
News reporters sometimes operate in packs. This is because most
reporters use the same values in
deciding what their audiences want
to know. They are surrogates who
ask questions for their readers,
viewers and listeners. During the
O. J. Simpson case, reporters were
seeking information and asking
questions that the public wanted
to know.

In fairness, it must be said that media owners generally are sensitive to their truth-seeking and truth-telling journalistic responsibilities and assiduously avoid calling the shots on news coverage. Journalists who are bothered by wrong-headed news decisions have three choices: they can persuade wayward owners of the wrongness of their ways, they can comply with directives, or they can quit and go to work for a respectable journalistic organization.

ADVERTISER PRESSURE

Special interests try to exert influence on coverage, such as squelching a story or insisting on self-serving angles. Advertiser pressure can be overt. The managing editor of the Laramie, Wyoming, *Boomerang* complied with a request from the newspaper's own advertising manager not to carry a state agency's news release warning people that Bon Vivant vichyssoise, possibly tainted with lethal botulism bacteria, had been found on the shelves at a local grocery. The ad manager was fearful of losing the store's advertising. In fact, the store did yank its advertising from a Laramie radio station when it aired the story, and the station's news director reported that he was warned to back off from the story and later fired.

Generally, advertiser clout is applied quietly, as when Ralph's grocery chain cancelled a $250 000 advertising contract with the Los Angeles *Herald Examiner* after a story on supermarket overcharging and shortweighting. From a journalistic perspective, the sinister result of cancelling advertising is the possible chilling effect on future coverage.

Advertiser pressure can be even more subtle. Many airlines insist that their ads be deleted from newscasts with stories about airline crashes. This is reasonable from an airline's perspective, but it also is a policy that has the effect of encouraging stations, especially financially marginal stations, to omit crash stories, even though these stories would contribute to listeners' having a clearer sense about air safety.

To their credit, most news organizations place allegiance to their audiences ahead of pleasing advertisers, as Terry Berger, president of an advertising agency representing the Brazilian airline Varig, found out from *Condé Nast's Traveler*, a travel magazine. After an article on air pollution in Rio de Janeiro, Berger wrote the magazine: "Is your editorial policy then to see how quickly you can alienate present and potential advertisers and at the same time convince your readers to stick closer to home? I really think that if you continue with this kind of editorial information, you are doing both your readers and your advertisers a disservice. For this kind of information, people read the *New York Times*. I therefore find it necessary to remove *Condé Nast's Traveler* from Varig's media schedule." Unintimidated, the magazine's editor, Harold Evans, did not recant. Not only did Evans print the letter but he followed with this comment: "Mrs. Berger is, of course, entitled to use her judgment about where she advertises Brazil's national airline. I write not about that narrow commercial issue, but about her assertion that it is a disservice to readers and advertisers for us to print true but unattractive facts when they are relevant. This goes to the heart of the editorial policy of this magazine. . . . We rejoice in the enrichments of travel, but our aim is to give readers the fullest information, frankly and fairly, so they can make their own judgments."

PRESSURE FROM SOURCES

Journalists sometimes feel external pressure directly. At the court house, valuable sources turn cold after a story appears that they don't like. A tearful husband begs an editor not to use the name of his wife in a story that points to her as a bank embezzler. A bottle of Chivas Regal arrives at Christmas from a sports publicist who says she has appreciated excellent coverage over the past year. Most journalists will tell you that their commitment to truth overrides external assaults on their autonomy. Even so, external pressures exist.

The relationship between journalists and publicists can be troublesome. In general, the relationship works well. Publicists want news coverage for their clients and provide information and help reporters line up interviews. Some publicists, however, are more committed to advancing their clients than to advancing truth, and they work to manipulate journalists into providing coverage that unduly glorifies their clients.

Staging events is a publicity tactic to gain news coverage that a cause would not otherwise attract. Some staged events are obvious hucksterism, such as Evel Knievel's ballyhooed motorcycle leaps across vast canyons in the 1970s and local flagpole-sitting stunts by celebrity disc jockeys. Covering such events usually is part of the softer side of news and, in the spirit of fun and games and diversion, is relatively harmless.

Of more serious concern are staged events about which publicists create a mirage of significance to suck journalists and the public into giving more attention than they deserve. For example, consider:

- The false impression created when hundreds of federal workers are released from work for an hour to see an incumbent's campaign speech outside a government office building.
- The contrived "photo opportunity" at which people, props and lighting are carefully, even meticulously arranged to create an image on television.

- Stunts that bring attention to a new product and give it an undeserved boost in the marketplace.

    Staged events distort a balanced journalistic portrayal of the world. Worse, they divert attention from truly significant events.

GATEKEEPING IN NEWS

STUDY PREVIEW   The individual reporter has a lot of independence in determining what to report, but news work is a team effort. No individual acts entirely alone, and there are factors, such as gatekeeping, that affect what ends up on the printed page or over the air.

GATEKEEPERS' RESPONSIBILITIES

News dispatches and photographs are subject to changes at many points in the communication chain. At these points, called *gates*, gatekeepers delete, trim, embellish and otherwise try to improve messages.

Just as a reporter exercises judgment in deciding what to report and how to report it, judgment also is at the heart of the gatekeeping process. Hardly any message, except live reporting, reaches its audience in its original form. Along the path from its originator to the eventual audience, a message is subject to all kinds of deletions, additions and changes of emphasis. With large news organizations, this process may involve dozens of editors and other persons.

The gatekeeping process affects all news. A public relations practitioner who doesn't tell the whole story is a gatekeeper. A reporter who emphasizes one aspect of an event and neglects others is a gatekeeper. Even live, on-scene television coverage involves gatekeeping because it's a gatekeeper who decides where to point the camera, and that's a decision that affects the type of information that reaches viewers. CPAC's coverage of Parliament, for example, never shows MPs sleeping or reading a newspaper during debate, even though such happens.

Gatekeeping can be a creative force. Trimming a news story can add potency. A news producer can enhance a reporter's field report with file footage. An editor can call a public relations person for additional detail to illuminate a point in a reporter's story. A newsmagazine's editor can consolidate related stories and add context that makes an important interpretive point.

GATEKEEPERS AT WORK

Most gatekeepers are invisible to the news audience, working behind the scenes and making crucial decisions in near-anonymity on how the world will be portrayed in the evening newscast and the next morning's newspaper. Here, slightly updated, is how mass communication scholar Wilbur Schramm explained gatekeeping in 1960: "Suppose we follow a news item, let us say, from India to Indiana. The first gatekeeper is the person who sees an event happen. This person sees the event selectively, noticing some things, not others. The second gatekeeper is the reporter who talks to this 'news source.' Now, of course, we could complicate this picture by giving the reporter a number of news sources to talk to about the same event, but in any case the reporter has to decide which facts to pass along the chain,

MEDIA: PEOPLE

Susan Zirinsky

Susan Zirinsky never appears on the air, but, as a CBS field producer, she is as influential as any reporter in deciding what appears on "The CBS Evening News." Zirinsky coordinates White House coverage and decides what video footage to use to illustrate the reporter's script. During the 1984 presidential campaign, the *Washington Post* gave this account of Zirinsky at work:

"She and CBS White House correspondent Bill Plante have spent the day with the President, and after three cities in eight hours the story she has to edit and send to New York is still stacked in cassettes on the floor. Plante is writing his narration at a table, trying to find a nugget of news. She wants to include some Reagan hecklers in the piece; Plante thinks there weren't enough to be important. She appeals to New York, loses, then looks at Plante's stand-up, a shot of him talking in front of Air Force One. She tells him she's going to make it shorter. 'It's only a sentence,' he grumps. 'How much are you going to cut?'"

At the time, Zirinsky was 32. Already she had been with CBS 10 years. In college, she landed a job answering phones in the CBS Washington bureau once a week. She was typing scripts for the evening news by her senior year. After graduation she became a researcher, and at age 24, she was named an associate producer. By the time Walter Mondale was challenging Ronald Reagan for the presidency in 1984, Zirinsky had been covering the White House for almost four years.

Here is how one day went on the 1984 campaign trail:

8:30 a.m. On board a charter plane, Zirinsky issues four pages of notes to her staff of 12. They tell where every camera crew and reporter will be and when. They list the numbers of dozens of telephones that Zirinsky has had installed at airports, speech sites and other locations on this one-day, three-city Reagan campaign trip.

10:25 a.m. In Pennsylvania, as the president is speaking at the Millersville University gym, one of Zirinsky's photographers catches a protester yelling and being dragged off by two Reagan supporters.

1:00 p.m. From a third-floor window of the white-columned Media, Pennsylvania, courthouse, photographers tape powerful panoramas of 13 000 people jamming a dead-end street to hear the president.

1:30 p.m. Zirinsky is on a bus for the president's third campaign stop. Plante calls from a helicopter, en route to the same speech, to say that the president took a few minutes to chat with reporters while catching his own helicopter at Media. Nothing worth reporting was said, Plante reports.

6:15 p.m. After the president's third stop, in Parkersburg, Pennsylvania, Zirinsky is slaving over her computerized editing equipment set up on a teacher's desk at a local school. Zirinsky finishes splicing crowd and speech shots into Plante's stand-up. It is dispatched to New York, a whole 15 minutes before Dan Rather begins the evening newscast.

8:00 p.m. Zirinsky's charter flight lands back in Washington. Her day is done.

Covering Politics. Most journalists have a keen interest in covering government and political process because those are the vehicles through which the people in a democracy create public policy. Diane Sawyer at the 1992 Democratic National Convention interviewed party leaders and delegates as the party's platform took shape. That platform proved to be the basis for the Clinton presidency.

what to write, what shape and colour and importance to give to the event. The reporter gives his message to an editor, who must decide how to edit the story, whether to cut or add or change. Then the message goes to a news service where someone must decide which of many hundreds of items will be picked up and telegraphed to other towns, and how important the story is, and therefore how much space it deserves.

"At a further link in the chain, this story will come to a news service and here again an editor must decide what is worth passing on to the newspapers and broadcasting stations. The chain leads us on to a regional and perhaps a state news service bureau, where the same decisions must be made; always there is more news than can be sent on—which items, and how much of the items, shall be retained and retransmitted? And finally when the item comes to a local newspaper, an editor must go through the same process, deciding which items to print in the paper.

"Out of news stories gathered by tens of thousands of reporters around the world, only a few hundred will pass the gatekeepers along the chains and reach a local newspaper editor, who will be able to pass only a few dozen of those on to the newspaper reader."

GATEKEEPING: THE HOMOLKA AND BERNARDO TRIALS

The trials of *Paul Bernardo* and *Karla Homolka*, provide an interesting case study of gatekeeping. The St. Catharines, Ontario, couple were convicted in the abduction and deaths of Kristen French of St. Catharines and Leslie Mahaffey of nearby Burlington. During the course of a regular shift, most reporters go about their duties as gatekeeper without much thought; it becomes second nature. However, reporters on this beat were made keenly aware of their role as gatekeepers and the power they held.

In 1993, at Karla Homolka's trial, Judge Francis Kovacs issued the following orders about how information relating to the trial was to be reported:

- Only accredited Canadian news media could attend the trial.
- The public was to be banned from the courtroom, with certain exceptions.
- No foreign media reporters were to be allowed in the courtroom.
- There would be a ban on publication of the circumstances of the murders, but certain procedural matters could be printed/broadcast.

The reason Kovacs gave for the ban was simple; it was to help ensure that Paul Bernardo received a fair trial. The ban proved to be problematic because much of the banned information was broadcast on American television and posted on the Internet in various newsgroups. But the role of Canadian journalists as gatekeepers was clearly defined; the gate had been locked. Journalists were only to report news that had been officially released by the court. Most journalists felt the ban was wrong as it interfered with the autonomy of their work and went against all the ideals Canadian journalism was based on, but most reporters complied with the ruling.

While the ban became the topic of discussion surrounding Homolka's trial, it's interesting to note that for many journalists, having to deal with the lifting of the ban at Paul Bernardo's trial in 1995 proved to be a much more difficult task. Kirk Makin of the *Globe and Mail* described the Bernardo beat as, "a hyperactive little community, consumed by deadlines and a sense that we were involved in something big. Those of us who were together for the entire trial shared the camaraderie of veterans, if only because the things we heard and saw were often too searing to convey to friends and family. Particularly in the beginning, the mind was unwilling, the tongue unable."

At the start of the Bernardo trial, the publication ban on evidence given at the earlier Homolka trial was lifted and many journalists were pleased to at last be able to file reports. Ben Chin, reporter for CITY-TV in Toronto, expressed relief: "For two or three years now we've been carrying around these secrets, things we were prohibited from reporting. Now, all of a sudden we can, it's kind of liberating."

While reporting the details of Homolka's trial might have been liberating, other factors made reporting difficult for the gatekeeper during the Bernardo trial. These factors included:

- The volume of evidence released, not only about Bernardo, but all the information and analysis surrounding Homolka's trial;
- The nature of the evidence itself which was graphically violent and sexual. How did one report such horrible acts?

Anne Marie Owens held a unique position as gatekeeper. A journalist for the St. Catharines *Standard*, she was the reporter assigned to the story when Kristen French was abducted in 1992 until the conviction of Paul Bernardo in 1995. Her experience on the Bernardo beat sheds some interesting light on the role of the gatekeeper. Most studies of the news-gathering process tend to state that news beats are highly routine. But these two trials were anything but routine. Homolka's trial lasted less than two days. Owens describes it as orchestrated and neatly packaged. You were given the information and told what to report.

Bernardo's trial was different. In contrast to Homolka's trial, there was an abundance of information. Like Makin, Owens found the facts difficult to write about. Not only did she find the story repulsive, but she was also a reporter in a community that was trying to understand how something so horrible could happen in their hometown. The rapes and murders had shattered what Gans might refer to as the "small town pastoralism" of St. Catharines. Owens was also writing stories that might be read by the victims' families and friends. Owens remembers "listening to stuff that is sometimes unfathomable. The information that came out was so unlike anything else that the *Standard* normally covers. I had anticipated that there would be explicit information and details that would become, as gruesome as they were, relevant. There was so much awful information. Our job wasn't to give people all of it, it was to allow people to understand what had happened and give them enough details so they knew what happened. That was tough."

Broadcasters also found it difficult to do their job. While readers can avoid the details in a story by not reading them, in broadcasting, once the words are spoken, they are heard by the audience. Al Van Alstine, news director for CKTB, a local St. Catharines radio station, remembers agonizing over newscasts. Paul Hunter of CBC News said he had difficulty listening to and reporting the details of the murders knowing that the French and Mahaffey families were sitting not far from him in the courtroom. Even after editing the stories with graphic evidence, announcers would often preface a broadcast news story by saying that the content might be offensive to some.

Some people complained about the extensive coverage the media gave the trial, while others praised the media for their work. Most journalists would no doubt be sympathetic to members of their audience who took exception to the content of their stories; the details were horrific. But the journalists were only doing their job under unique and very trying circumstances.

GLOBAL GATEKEEPING: THE NEWS AGENCIES

STUDY PREVIEW   Because gathering news is expensive, especially when it comes from far away, news organizations set up agencies, usually called wire services, news services, or networks to reduce the cost and then share the resulting stories. Today, global news services, led by the Associated Press, have more influence than most people realize on what is reported and how it is told.

COMPETITION FOR FAR-AWAY NEWS

Sam Gilbert took great pride in his coffee house. At seven stories, it was the tallest building in the United States. It dominated the Boston waterfront. Gilbert's was a popular place, partly because of an extensive collection of the latest European newspapers that he maintained in a reading room. In 1811, with a second war imminent with Britain, Gilbert announced that his patrons no longer would have to wait for ships to dock to have the latest news. Forthwith, he said, an employee would row out to ships waiting to enter the harbour and rush back with packets of the latest news. Newspapers up and down the seaboard picked up Gilbert's idea, and publishers scrambled to outdo each other by buying the fastest sloops.

In time, complex courier systems caught ships arriving at Halifax, Nova Scotia, and rushed news by pony and sloop to Boston and New York. Competition escalated, especially after Samuel Morse invented the telegraph in 1844 and coastal cities began to be linked by wire.

ASSOCIATED PRESS

The competition was spirited, especially in New York, where 10 newspapers raced to beat each other with foreign dispatches. The competition escalated costs, and in

MEDIA ABROAD

Reuter's Pigeon Service

Much of Europe had been linked by telegraph by the late 1840s, but a 100-mile gap remained between the financial centres of Brussels in Belgium and Aachen in Prussia. Young *Paul Julius Reuter* established a carrier pigeon service, with the birds carrying dispatches tied to their legs, and he immediately attracted banking customers. Reuter then moved to London to pick up the latest American news from the new trans-Atlantic cable for his pigeon delivery. In 1858 he offered his service to newspapers via telegraph.

In 1984, after years of being owned by newspapers in Britain, Australia and New Zealand, Reuters became a publicly traded company. Newly aggressive, the company beefed up its financial market reporting and expanded its domestic U.S. service. Today, Reuters serves 6500 media organizations worldwide, including 290 in the United States. Including clients in the business and financial community, Reuters has 27 000 subscribers worldwide. The service is offered in 11 languages.

Besides Reuters, AP and UPI, two other news services have extensive global networks:

■ **Agence France-Presse.** Paris-based AFP was founded by *Charles Havas* in 1835. Using carrier pigeons, Havas supplied Paris newspapers by noon with news that had happened that same morning in London and Brussels. It was from Havas that young Paul Julius Reuter learned the carrier pigeon business before setting off on his own.

Paul Julius Reuter

Today, AFP has 2000 people in 150 bureaus worldwide, including 850 full-time journalists. Text, photo, audio and video services are transmitted in Arabic, English, French, German, Spanish and Portuguese to 500 newspaper, 350 radio and 200 television clients, and to 99 national news agencies that pass AFP stories on to more media outlets. AFP has more than 50 U.S. media clients.

■ **TASS.** This Moscow-based news agency was founded in 1918, just after the Bolshevik Revolution. Today TASS supplies reports in Russian, English, French, German, Spanish and Arabic to 5500 media and nonmedia subscribers.

Until the Communist party was disbanded in 1991, TASS's editorial direction was from the party's central committee. The fall of Soviet communism left TASS in disarray about its mission. It continues, however, as the global news service of choice in some of the former Soviet bloc.

1846, one of New York's scrappiest news merchants, *David Hale* of the *Journal of Commerce*, brought five of his competitors together to discuss combining their efforts in order to reduce expenses. The concept was simple. Competing newspapers would rely on a common organization, the Harbor News Association, and share both the material and the expenses. The name evolved into the *Associated Press*.

Today the Associated Press is the world's largest news-gathering organization, with bureaus in 71 countries. In the United States, the AP has 142 bureaus in state capitals and major cities. Like its predecessor organization, it remains a nonprofit cooperative. Member newspapers each own a share based on circulation and numerous other factors. Each newspaper is obligated to furnish its local stories to the AP for distribution to other member newspapers. The AP also has its own staff, 1100 journalists in the United States and 480 abroad, to generate stories for all members. Periodically the expense of operating the AP is tallied, and members are billed for their share. The budget is about $300 million. Policies are set by member newspapers, which meet regularly.

The AP sells its news to magazines and even government agencies, and it operates profit-making news script, audio and video services for radio and television newsrooms. Only newspapers, however, are full members with a controlling voice in the organization's policies.

These numbers give a sense of the AP's size:

- 3000 employees nationwide, including journalists, management and support personnel.
- 1700 United States newspapers, including 1460 daily newspaper members.
- 6000 television, cable and station outlets.
- 1000 radio subscribers to AP Network News, which is the largest single radio network in the United States.
- 8500 foreign subscribers in 112 countries.

UNITED PRESS INTERNATIONAL

As the AP evolved, it limited membership to one newspaper per city. The policy upset newspaper-chain owner *E. W. Scripps*, who was denied AP membership for the new papers he was founding in the 1880s because older papers already had exclusive AP franchises. In 1907 Scripps founded the *United Press* for newspapers that the AP shut out. The heart of Scripps's new service was his own newspapers, but the service also was a profit-seeking enterprise available to any and all newspapers willing to subscribe.

William Randolph Hearst followed in 1909 with the *International News Service*. Both UP and INS tried to match the comprehensive Washington and foreign service of the Associated Press, but the AP proved impossible to derail. Even when the AP suffered a major setback, losing a 1945 U.S. Supreme Court decision that forced it to abandon exclusivity, the result spurred AP growth. Non-AP newspapers joined the co-op by the dozen, which hurt United Press and Hearst's INS.

In 1958 UP and INS merged to form the *United Press International*, but the new company, in reality a subsidiary of the Scripps-Howard newspaper chain, failed to meet profit expectations and eventually went on the selling block. Nobody wanted it. The British news service *Reuters*, anxious for a toehold in the United States, surveyed UPI's assets and decided against buying. In the 1980s UPI went through a series of owners. There were attempts at corporate reorganization, technological economies and sales blitzes, but several owners later the service was anything but secure.

CANADIAN PRESS

The *Canadian Press* (CP) supplies news to both French and English Canadian journalists. Founded in 1917, the Press is a cooperative venture owned and funded by daily newspapers in Canada. As with the Associated Press, Canadian papers share their local news with other members within the cooperative. The head office is in Toronto, but CP has other bureaus in Fredericton, Halifax, Victoria, Calgary, Winnipeg, Quebec City and Ottawa.

Prior to the arrival of CP, newspapers received their information from the Associated Press via the Canadian Pacific Railway. To complement the AP service, the CPR would pay freelancers along their routes to gather information to be distributed across Canada. In 1907 CPR told the three Winnipeg newspapers that their AP reports would be telegraphed to them from Minnesota. Not only would their service be cut, but the cost was to be doubled. Looking for a cheaper way to fill the void of Canadian news, the three newspapers formed their own news agency, the *Western Associated Press* (WAP). The new service provided news stories for several western papers. WAP would also carry news from the United Press, Hearst News Service and Publishers Press. It grew to the point where it became a strong competitor for AP and the CPR in Canada. A series of legal battles ensued. They ended with CPR getting out of the news distribution business and a series of Canadian newspapers picking up the AP contract until CP was officially launched in 1917.

While most of the news delivered by CP is about Canada, it will also often send reporters around the world to cover foreign events that are of interest to Canadians. If CP doesn't send one of its own reporters to cover an international event, it will use a freelance reporter based in that part of the world. These freelancers are called stringers. Other foreign news stories carried by CP come from Associated Press, Agence France-Press and Reuters.

Some facts about CP:

- It has 460 employees.
- Eighty-eight newspapers are members of CP
- CP's picture service provides almost a thousand photos a week.
- Newspapers can receive about 300 columns of news per day and print more than 100.
- CP has a French-language news service, called la Presse Canadienne (PC) in Montreal, as well as a French radio service, Nouvelle Télé-Radio (NTR).
- Like the Associated Press, Canadian Press also makes its news services available to businesses, governments and other organizations for a fee.

Twenty-six million dollars of CP's budget come from members of the CP newspaper collective. This will change shortly. Due to less advertising revenue and higher newsprint costs, members of CP are asking that their fees be reduced. The process of cuts to CP's operating budget began shortly after the Southam chain threatened to pull out of Canadian Press and to expand their own news-gathering services. Southam papers account for 18 of CP's member newspapers, while papers owned by Conrad Black, including Sterling and Hollinger newspapers, account for over half of CP's newspapers. When budget cuts to CP were announced, Southam's pullout was called off.

BROADCAST NEWS

Broadcast News (BN) is a news service for Canadian broadcasters. It's a collective between CP and Canada's broadcasters, which was created in 1954. Before then, broadcasters bought news stories from newspapers and CP and rewrote them for broadcast. BN operates 24 hours a day, seven days a week and provides news in both official languages to over 600 subscribers. Member stations are encouraged to exchange stories through BN. To provide a Canadian perspective on newsworthy events, BN has reporters in Ottawa, all provincial legislatures and in Washington.

The following are the services provided by BN:

- BN Data Service provides hourly news summaries and features such as weather, provincial news updates, entertainment, sports, health and lifestyle. BN's basic data service can provide more than 700 news stories per day to its members.
- BN Audio Service provides both hourly newscasts and actualities (sometimes called "voicers"), which can be used in a newscast.
- BN's Cablestream Service is a news service used by 150 cable companies across Canada. It's a text-only service that gives cable TV subscribers news, sports and business information 24 hours a day, seven days a week.

SYNDICATE INFLUENCE ON NEWS

STUDY PREVIEW   News organizations buy ready-to-run features, including political columns, from organizations called *syndicates*. Because syndicates sell the same features to many organizations, their influence is substantial.

NEWSPAPER SYNDICATES

Today, syndicates offer a wide range of material, usually on an exclusive basis. In major cities with competing newspapers, some features go to the highest bidder. Generally, rates are based on circulation. A small daily might spend $150 a week for 30 to 50 syndicated features. A metropolitan newspaper might spend $500 a week for a single comic strip.

Here are the major features distributed by syndicates, some of which are important as news and commentary, others of which are pure diversion:

- **Political Columns.** Commentator *David Lawrence* introduced the syndicated political column in 1916, providing modest-budget local newspapers with a low-cost tie to Washington. *Walter Lippmann*, the most influential columnist in U.S. history, appeared in hundreds of newspapers as a syndicated feature from 1929 into the 1960s.
- **Political Cartoons.** *Bill Mauldin*'s powerful World War II cartoons received a nationwide audience by syndication. Look at political cartoons on your local newspaper's editorial page, and you will see a note that identifies the cartoonist's home newspaper and, unless the cartoonist is local, the name of the syndicate that distributed it.
- **Comics.** Early syndicates offered stand-alone cartoons. In 1907 "Mutt and Jeff" became the first daily strip. Comics were packed on a single page in the 1920s and became a major circulation builder. In 1984 *Charles Schultz*'s "Peanuts" established a landmark as the first strip to appear in 2000 newspapers.
- **Lovelorn Columns.** Writing as *Dorothy Dix*, Elizabeth Meriwether Gilmer became "Mother Confessor" to millions in 1916 with the first column to the lovelorn. It was predecessor to today's columns by sisters *Abigail Van Buren* and *Ann Landers*. In the 1920s Gilmer earned an unheard-of $90 000 a year from syndication, more than any single newspaper could have paid a columnist.
- **How-to Columns.** Among available columns are "Shelby Lyman on Chess," and June Roth's "Nutrition Hotline."
- **Reviews.** Book, movie, television and video reviews are provided by syndicates. They range from high-brow criticism to the low-brow "Joe Bob Goes to the Drive-In."

Lincoln Weeps. Bill Mauldin's editorial cartoon captured the sorrow of the nation when U.S. President John F. Kennedy was shot fatally in 1963. The cartoon needed no caption. Americans everywhere recognized the figure of Lincoln from the District of Columbia memorial, and everyone understood Mauldin's portrayal.

- **Games.**   Syndicates offer dozens of crosswords, games and puzzles. Horoscopes and astrology columns are other staples.
- **Literature.**   Some syndicates buy serialization rights to memoirs and books, giving newspapers that sign up for them a truncated prepublication series. Leading magazines supply stories to newspapers through syndicates.

Syndicates also offer picture, graphics and art services. Many syndicates offer all the editorial copy that's needed for topical advertising supplements, such as spring car-care tabloids and September back-to-school issues.

JOURNALISM TRENDS

STUDY PREVIEW   News has taken two divergent paths in content in recent years. Some news organizations have moved into sophisticated, interpretative and investigative reporting. Others have emphasized superficial, tantalizing news.

EXPLORATORY REPORTING

Norman Cousins acquired his reputation as a thinker when he edited the magazine *Saturday Review.* A premier journal under Cousins, the magazine tackled issues in depth and with intelligence. A few years later, Cousins said he couldn't find much of that kind of journalism in magazines any more: "The best magazine articles in the U.S. today are appearing not in magazines but in newspapers." Cousins was taking note of a profound late 20th-century change in the concept of news. Newspapers and to a lesser extent television were tackling difficult issues that earlier were almost the exclusive provinces of magazines. Cousins especially admired the

Investigative Journalism. Dogged pursuit of meticulous factual detail became a new wrinkle in 20th-century journalism after *Washington Post* reporters Carl Bernstein and Bob Woodward unearthed the Watergate scandal. For months they pursued tips that a break-in at the Democratic Party national headquarters in the Watergate hotel, office, and apartment complex in Washington, D.C., had been authorized high in the Republican White House and that the White House then had tried to cover it up. In the end, for the first time in American history, a president resigned.

Los Angeles Times, which runs thoroughly researched, thoughtful pieces. It is not unusual for the *Los Angeles Times* to commit weeks, even months, of reporters' time to develop major stories, nor is that unusual at other major newspapers and some smaller ones.

Although newspapers have never been devoid of in-depth coverage, the thrust through most of their history has been to chronicle events: meetings, speeches, deaths, catastrophes. The emphasis began changing noticeably in the 1960s as it dawned on journalists that chronicling easily identifiable events was insufficient to capture larger, more significant issues and trends.

The failure of event-based reporting became clear when northern cities were burning in race riots in the late 1960s. Journalists had missed one of the 20th century's most significant changes: the northward migration of southern blacks. Had journalists covered the migration and provided information on the festering social divisions that resulted, there might have been a chance to develop public policies before frustration over racial injustices blew up with heavy losses of life and property and great disruption.

The superficiality of mere chronicling was underscored in early coverage of the Vietnam War. By focusing on events, journalists missed asking significant questions about the flawed policies until it was too late.

Newspapers expanded significantly beyond a myopic focus on events in the 1970s for three reasons:

- Recognition that old ways of reporting news were not enough.
- Larger reporting staffs that permitted time-consuming enterprise reporting.
- Better-educated reporters and editors, many with graduate degrees.

Newspapers, profitable as never before, were able to hire larger staffs that permitted them to try more labour-intensive, exploratory kinds of journalism. Instead of merely responding to events, newspapers, particularly big ones, began digging for stories. Much of this investigative journalism was modeled on the *Washington Post*'s doggedness in covering Watergate, the White House-authorized break-in at the Democratic national headquarters during the 1972 presidential campaign. Twenty years earlier, the Watergate break-in scandal probably would not have gone beyond three paragraphs from the police beat. In 1972, however, the persistence of *Post* reporters Carl Bernstein and Bob Woodward posed so many questions about morality in the White House that eventually Nixon resigned and 25 aides went to jail.

As late as 1960, many daily newspapers were still hiring reporters without college degrees. By 1970 that had changed, and many newspaper reporters were acquiring advanced degrees and developing specialties. Major newspapers hired reporters with law degrees for special work and encouraged promising reporters to go back to college for graduate work in science, business, medicine and the environment. The result was a new emphasis on proactive reporting in which journalists did not wait for events to happen but went out looking, even digging, for things worth telling.

SOFT NEWS

The success of the *National Enquirer*, whose circulation began to skyrocket in the 1960s, was not unnoticed, and when Time, Inc. launched *People* magazine and the *New York Times* launched *Us* magazine, gossipy celebrity news gained a kind of respectability. In this period, the newspaper industry began sophisticated research to identify what readers wanted, then fine-tuned the content mix that would improve market penetration. As a result, many dailies added "People" columns. The news services began receiving requests for more off-beat, gee-whiz items of the sensational sort. Newspapers have always run such material, but more is being printed today to appeal to a broader audience. Many newspapers today also carry more consumer-oriented stories, life-style tips, and entertainment news. This is called *soft news.*

Traditionalists decry the space that soft news takes in many newspapers today, but soft news generally has not displaced hard news. Rather, newspapers fit additional hard news, as well as soft news, into larger newspapers. The *news hole*, the space left after advertisements are put in a newspaper, increased from 19 pages on average in 1970 to 24 pages today.

CHAPTER WRAP-UP

Journalism is an art, not a science. Judgments, rather than formulas, determine which events and issues are reported and how—and no two journalists approach any story exactly the same way. This leaves the whole process of gathering and telling news subject to second-guessing and criticism. Journalists ask themselves all the time if there are ways to do a better job. All journalists can do is try to find truth and to relate it accurately. Even then, the complexity of modern news-gathering—which involves many people, each with an opportunity to change or even kill a story—includes dozens of points at which inaccuracy and imprecision can creep into a story that started out well.

The hazards of the news-gathering process are most obvious with foreign coverage. Even if the reporter is able to gather information and put it into a meaningful context, the story passes through many gatekeepers, all of whom can modify it, before it reaches an American newsroom. Then copy editors, headline writers, photo editors, caption writers and others can take even more cracks at a story.

It is no wonder that the coverage that ends up in print and on the air does not please everyone. At the same time, the news media receive some unfair criticism. The most frequent is the charge that the media slant coverage. The fact, according to respected surveys, is that the political orientation of journalists largely coincides with that of the rest of the population. Other studies have found that the values that journalists bring to their work are mainstream cultural values, including ethnocentrism and faith in democracy and capitalism.

The consolidation of news-gathering, through services like the Associated Press, has created great economies in covering far-away events and issues. Broadcast News and the Canadian Press offer a Canadian perspective. These services permit local newspapers and broadcast stations to offer more thorough coverage than they could with their own resources. The flip side is that far-away coverage is less expensive than hiring local reporters, which raises serious questions about the appropriate balance between hometown and far-away coverage. The same questions can be raised about syndicates, which provide high-quality political commentary, cartoons, comics and other materials inexpensively to local newspapers and stations.

QUESTIONS FOR REVIEW

1. What contemporary news practices are rooted in the colonial, partisan, penny, and yellow periods of history?

2. What personal values do journalists bring to their work? Does this affect what is reported and how?

3. What variables beyond journalists' control affect news?

4. What external pressures, from outside the media, affect news reporting?

5. What responsibilities do journalists have as gatekeepers?

6. What is the relationship between global news services and the newspapers you read and the newscasts you hear?

7. What is the relationship between syndicates and the newspapers you read?

8. Is there a contradiction between the two contemporary journalistic trends of exploratory reporting and soft news?

QUESTIONS FOR CRITICAL THINKING

1. The 19-year-old son of the premier of a troubled Central American country in which the CIA has deep involvement died, perhaps of a drug overdose, aboard a Northwest Airlines plane en route from Tokyo to Singapore. On the plane was a young female country singer, his frequent companion in recent weeks. The plane was a Boeing 747 manufactured in Washington state. Northwest's corporate headquarters is in Minnesota. The death occurred at 4 a.m. Eastern time.

Consider the six elements of news—proximity, prominence, timeliness, consequence, currency and drama, and discuss how this event might be reported on morning television newscasts in St. John's, Minneapolis, Nashville, Seattle and the District of Columbia. How about in Managua? Singapore? Tokyo? Rome? Istanbul? Johannesburg? What if the victim were an ordinary college student? What if the death occurred a week ago?

2. Explain news judgment.

3. How do news hole and news flow affect what is reported in the news media?

4. *Time* and *Maclean's* carry cover stories on the same subject one week. Does this indicate that executives of the magazine have conspired, or is it more likely to be caused by what Leon Sigal calls the *consensible nature of news*?

5. How does the nature of news provide ammunition to conservatives to criticize the news media as leftist promoters of change?

6. Discuss whether the news media reflect mainstream values. Do you see evidence in your news media of an underlying belief that democracy, capitalism, rural small-town life, individualism and moderation are virtues?

7. Consider Herbert Gans's view that the media cover disorder from the perspective of identifying ways to restore order. Then consider the role of the media in reporting on the Bernardo/Homolka trials.

8. If a college president calls a news conference and makes a major announcement, who are the gatekeepers who determine how the announcement is covered in the campus newspaper?

9. The major global news services are the Canadian Press, the Agence France-Presse, the Associated Press, Reuters, TASS and United Press International. Discuss their similarities and differences.

10. How important is it for Canadians to have services like Broadcast News and Canadian Press?

11. Consider the advantages and disadvantages of your local daily newspaper running both the Ann Landers and the Dear Abby advice columns.

12. Compare how U.S. journalists covered the O.J. Simpson trial with how Canadian journalists reported the Bernardo trial. What were the similarities in the coverage? The differences?

▌**F**OR **FURTHER LEARNING**

L. Brent Bozell III and Brent H. Baker, eds. *And That's the Way It Isn't: A Reference Guide to Media Bias* (Media Research Center, 1990). Bozell and Baker compile a great amount of evidence, much of it circumstantial, to demonstrate a leftist tilt in the U.S. mass media.

Canada. *Canadian News Services* (Ottawa: Supply & Services, 1981). Volume 6 of the Kent Commission on newspapers.

Canada. *The Journalists* (Ottawa: Supply and Services, 1981). Volume 2 of the Kent Commission on newspapers.

Peter Desbarats. *Guide to the Canadian News Media* (Harcourt Brace, 1990).

Daniel J. Czitrom. *Media and the American Mind: From Morse to McLuhan* (University of North Carolina Press, 1982). Czitrom explores the effect of technological innovations, particularly the telegraph, movies and radio, and popular and scholarly responses to them.

Hazel Dicken-Garcia. *Journalistic Standards in the Nineteenth Century* (University of Wisconsin Press, 1989). Dicken-Garcia traces the idea that the press should be a purveyor of information, not only a forum for partisanship, back to the time before the penny press period.

Edwin and Michael Emery. *The Press and America*, 4th ed. (Prentice Hall, 1984). The Emerys offer an encyclopedic chronology of American mass media back to its roots in authoritarian England.

Mark Fishman. *Manufacturing the News* (University of Texas Press, 1980). Fishman argues that the conventions of gathering news shape what ends up being reported as much as events themselves.

Thomas L. Friedman. *From Beirut to Jerusalem* (Farrar, Straus & Giroux, 1989). Friedman, of the *New York Times*, reveals a lot about being a foreign correspondent in this insightful look at anarchy in Beirut, Arab-Israeli tensions and Arab politics.

Herbert J. Gans. *Deciding What's News: A Study of CBS Evening News, NBC Nightly News, Newsweek and Time* (Pantheon, 1979). A sociologist examines how the values journalists bring to their work affect the news that is reported.

Jane T. Harrigan. *Read All About It! A Day in the Life of a Metropolitan Newspaper* (Globe Pequot Press, 1987). Harrigan, a journalist, tracks hundreds of newspaper people from 6 a.m. until midnight as they produce an issue of the Boston *Globe*. Along the way, she explains how journalists decide which events to report.

Norman E. Isaacs. *Untended Gates: The Mismanaged Press* (Columbia University Press, 1986). Isaacs, who has edited several major American dailies, argues that the lapses of media ethics can be blamed on top-level managers who are reluctant to involve themselves in newsroom decisions.

Brooke Kroeger. *Nellie Bly: Daredevil, Reporter, Feminist* (Random House, 1994). Kroeger, a former news reporter, unearthed court documents and lost letters for this meticulous, detailed account of an innovative reporting pioneer.

Molly Moore. *A Woman at War: Storming Kuwait With the U.S. Marines* (Scribner's, 1993). Moore, a *Washington Post* reporter, explains the difficulties of getting breaking stories back to the newsroom when military personnel control your movement and access. Moore is especially good at recounting the psychological impact of pending combat on soldiers.

Michael Parenti. *Inventing Reality: The Politics of the Mass Media* (St. Martin's, 1988).

Michael Schudson. *Discovering the News: A Social History of American Newspapers* (Basic Books, 1978). Schudson chronicles the development of journalism as a profession in the United States, focusing on changing concepts of news values and objectivity along the way.

Pamela J. Shoemaker with Elizabeth Kay Mayfield. *Building a Theory of News Content: A Synthesis of Current Approaches* (*Journalism Monographs*, No. 103, June 1987).

Shoemaker and Mayfield attempt to bring coherence to the leading theories on the factors that contribute to events being reported.

David H. Weaver and G. Cleveland Wilhoit. *The American Journalist: A Portrait of U.S. News People and Their Work*, 2nd ed. (Indiana University Press, 1991). This comprehensive profile updates the authors' 1986 work and an earlier 1971 study, which also bears reading: John W. C. Johnstone, Edward J. Slawski and William W. Bowman. *The News People: A Sociological Portrait of American Journalists and Their Work* (University of Illinois Press, 1976).

FOR **KEEPING** **UP** TO **DATE**

Among publications that keep current on journalistic issues are *Columbia Journalism Review*, *Quill*, *American Journalism Review*, *Editor & Publisher*, *Media* and *News Inc.*

Bridging the gap between scholarly and professional work is *Newspaper Research Journal*.

PUBLIC RELATIONS
Winning Hearts and Minds

Public relations is a persuasive communication tool that uses the mass media

Public relations grew out of public disfavour with big business

Public relations is an important institutional management tool

Public relations includes promotion, publicity, lobbying, fundraising, crisis management

Public relations usually involves a candid, proactive relationship with the mass media

Public relations organizations are working to improve the image of their craft

M E D I A   I N   T H E O R Y

Public Relations as "Sleaze?"

Public relations operates in the realm of what Canadian *Joyce Nelson* calls the "legitimacy gap," in her book *The Sultans of Sleaze: Public Relations and the Media.* The term legitimacy gap was coined by business professor Prakesh Sethi to describe the difference between a corporate image and the corporate reality. Nelson applies Jungian psychology to the term in her analysis of public relations. She argues that a corporation has two sides: a persona and a shadow. The persona is its corporate image, the positive image that is promoted via advertising; the shadow is its dark side, which is not usually seen in the news media and certainly not in advertising. According to Nelson, the shadow may include "the ways in which their [the corporation's] activities infringe upon our health and safety, our environment, to our oppression or that of others, despite what all their persona-related activity would like us to believe." When something happens that threatens the persona and reveals the shadow of a corporation, public relations professionals are called to fix the problem.

Nelson provides an interesting example. Within two weeks during the summer of 1981, Ontario Hydro was involved in two environmental accidents. First it dumped heavy water containing 3500 curies of radiation into the Ottawa River. The event received front page coverage in the *Globe* and was reported on television news. A week later, almost 4000 gallons of radioactive water was accidentally spilled at Ontario Hydro's Bruce Nuclear Power Plant. More than twice as much tritium—about 8000 curies—was released in the accident. These incidents created a problem for Ontario Hydro. The nuclear power industry's persona is centred around concern for public safety and the environment. But Nelson argues that these spills raised questions about the safety of nuclear power, revealing Hydro's shadow.

The second incident received less coverage in both the *Globe and Mail* and the *Toronto Star*. One of the reasons for this may have been "information overload;" perhaps the news media were simply tired of writing about problems at nuclear power plants. According to Nelson, another reason the second accident received less negative coverage had to do with the well-crafted press release that ended up as a news story in the *Toronto Star*. Consider the lead of the news story: "Armed with mops, pails and pumps, an Ontario Hydro crew has recovered 3400 gallons of radioactive heavy water at the Bruce Nuclear Power plant." This passage succeeds in diverting attention from the accident by focusing instead on the clean-up. Any suspicions the reader may have about the corporation's shadow are discarded. The story goes on to outline the cost of the clean-up in detail, which underlines Hydro's commitment to protecting the environment, whatever the cost and thus reinforces its corporate image, or persona. The story makes no mention of damage to the surrounding area.

Nelson sees public relations as the art of controlling information. In theoretical terms, this can be viewed as agenda-setting. Nelson argues that there is a serious problem when public relations professionals can shape, either entirely or in part, the content of a newspaper or newscast. A well-written and well-publicized press release, like the one written about the spill of heavy water, not only starts the process of communication but effectively ends it as well by determining the discourse surrounding it.

IMPORTANCE OF PUBLIC RELATIONS

STUDY PREVIEW   Public relations is a persuasive communication tool that people can use to motivate other people and institutions to help them achieve their goals.

A YOUNG GIRL'S STORY

In tearful and dramatic testimony, a 14-year-old Kuwaiti girl told a congressional committee that she had witnessed horrible atrocities when Iraqi troops invaded her homeland. She described soldiers pulling babies out of hospital incubators and leaving them on the floor to die. This was October 1990, while U.S. President George Bush was engaged both in massive military build-up to retake Kuwait from the Iraqis and in a massive campaign at home to convince Congress and the American people that military intervention was justified.

The horrible Iraqi deeds described by the Kuwaiti girl helped President Bush win the battle at home. Over the next few days, he cited her testimony in at least 10 speeches. On one occasion he even took some literary licence to whip up public feeling against the Iraqis by saying they "scattered babies like firewood."

Within a few days, Congress voted narrowly to let President Bush proceed with the war preparations. Of course, much more than the girl's testimony shaped public feelings, but for many people her account was riveted indelibly in their minds. Also, the testimony, as well as the U.S. military intervention, marked a huge success for the giant Hill and Knowlton public relations company.

After the Iraqi blitzkrieg into Kuwait in August 1990, well-heeled Kuwaiti leaders who had fled their country founded a group called Citizens for a Free Kuwait to generate U.S. support for their cause. They hired Hill and Knowlton, which has 290 employees in Washington alone, to send lobbyists to Congress to make their client's case. The company arranged for Kuwaiti sympathizers to give television, radio, newspaper and magazine interviews. Fact sheets and updates were widely distributed. Hill and Knowlton even arranged for Citizens for a Free Kuwait to make a $50 000 (U.S.) gift to a private foundation operated by one member of Congress.

Hill and Knowlton was engaged in classic public relations activities: advising a client on how to present the best possible case to groups it wants to win over to its view and then helping the client accomplish its purposes. For Hill and Knowlton's services, the exiled Kuwaiti government paid $11.9 million. It was a bargain, to whatever extent the expenditure contributed to the multination military and diplomatic mobilization against Iraq and the eventual expulsion of Iraqis from Kuwaiti soil. The Kuwaitis got the most bang for their buck, however, from the testimony of 14-year-old Nayirah al-Sabah.

Early in October, two months after the Iraqi invasion, officials from the Kuwaiti embassy in Washington escorted Nayirah to the Hill and Knowlton office to tell her story. The potential for the girl's story was clear right away to Lauri Fitz-Pegado, a senior H&K vice president. The agency contacted House member Tom Lantos, co-chair of the congressional Human Rights Caucus, and set up a hearing for Nayirah to testify. The news media were advised to be there for dynamite revelations. Then Fitz-Pegado began coaching Nayirah for the appearance.

The hearing lived up to Hill and Knowlton's advance billing. Nayirah choked back tears as she explained that she had been working as a volunteer at the hospital under an assumed name, and then she told about the dreadful infanticides. Among other atrocities she described was how teen-age friends had been tortured with electricity. CNN carried the testimony live, evening newscasts led with it, newspapers bannered it, and magazines featured it. Amnesty International, which tracks political terrorism worldwide, reported the baby massacre based on Nayirah's testimony, and the Red Crescent cited it before the United Nations.

Later, it turned out that Hill and Knowlton may have been duped. Although many Iraqi atrocities occurred in Kuwait, investigators were never able, even after the war, to corroborate Nayirah's story of the baby massacre. Furthermore, journalists raised questions about a cozy connection between H&K and Congressman Tom Lantos, who arranged the hearing at which Nayirah testified. Questions were raised whether Citizens for a Free Kuwait was a legitimate grassroots organization or a front manufactured for Kuwaiti interests by Hill and Knowlton. Additional doubts surfaced when it was learned that Nayirah was actually the daughter of the Kuwaiti ambassador, which had not been announced at the hearings. To that issue, Hill and Knowlton said it had needed to protect her and her family members from Iraqi death squads.

Some observers minimized the fuss, which came three months after Nayirah's mesmerizing testimony, as part of the rough-and-tumble reality of big-league

Tearful and Compelling. Fourteen-year-old Nayirah al-Sabah told Congress that she had witnessed Iraqi troops committing atrocities in her Kuwaiti homeland. Her testimony, it was learned later, was arranged by the Hill and Knowlton public relations agency, and her claims were wildly exaggerated in an attempt to arouse U.S. public sentiment against the Iraqi invaders so they would intervene militarily. Critics have raised serious questions about the appropriateness of Hill and Knowlton's role in trying to influence U.S. public policy on behalf of Kuwaiti clients.

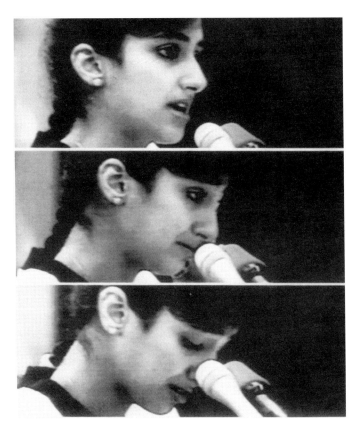

adversarial American politics. Anyone involved in the process, including public relations agencies, is going to get bloodied from time to time. Through it all, H&K defended its performance on behalf of Citizens for a Free Kuwait by saying it never had any reason to doubt Nayirah's veracity. No one doubted that Hill and Knowlton had succeeded at a crucial point in winning support for the United States to go to war against Iraq.

DEFINING PUBLIC RELATIONS

It's unfortunate, but the term *public relations* sometimes is used loosely. Some people think it means backslapping, glad-handing and smiling prettily to make people feel good. It's not uncommon for a secretary or receptionist to list "public relations" on a résumé. The fact, however, is that public relations goes far beyond good interpersonal skills. A useful definition is that public relations is a management tool for leaders in business, government and other institutions to establish beneficial *relationships* with other institutions and groups. Four steps are necessary for public relations to accomplish its goals:

IDENTIFY EXISTING RELATIONSHIPS.   In modern society, institutions have many relationships. A college, for example, has relationships with its students, its faculty, its staff, its alumni, its benefactors, the neighbourhood, the community, the legislature, other colleges, accreditors of its programs, perhaps unions. The list could go on and on. Each of these constituencies is called a *public*—hence the term *public relations.*

EVALUATE THE RELATIONSHIPS.   Through research, the public relations practitioner studies these relationships to determine how well they are working. This evaluation is an ongoing process. A college may have excellent relations with the legislature one year and win major appropriations, but after a scandal related to the president's budget the next year, legislators may be downright unfriendly.

DESIGN POLICIES TO IMPROVE THE RELATIONSHIPS. The job of public relations people is to recommend policies to top management to make these relationships work better, not only for the organization but also for the partners in each relationship. *Paul Garrett*, a pioneer in corporate relations, found that General Motors was not seen in friendly terms during the Great Depression, which put the giant auto-maker at risk with many publics, including its own employees. GM, he advised, needed new policies to seem neighbourly—rather than as a far-removed, impersonal, monolithic industrial giant.

IMPLEMENT THE POLICIES.   Garrett used the term *enlightened self-interest* for his series of policies intended to downsize GM in the eyes of many of the company's publics. Garrett set up municipal programs in towns with GM plants, and grants for schools and scholarships for employees' children. General Motors benefited from a revised image and, in the spirit of enlightened self-interest, so did GM employees, their children and their communities.

Public relations is not a mass medium itself, but PR uses the media as tools to accomplish its goals. To announce GM's initiatives to change its image in the 1930s, Paul Garrett issued news releases that he hoped newspapers, magazines and radio stations would pick up. The number of people in most of the publics with which public relations practitioners need to communicate is so large that it can be reached only through the mass media. The influence of public relations on the news media is extensive. Half of the news in many newspapers originates with formal statements or news releases from organizations that want something in the paper. It is the same with radio and television.

PUBLIC RELATIONS IN A DEMOCRACY

Misconceptions about public relations include the idea that it is a one-way street for institutions and individuals to communicate *to* the public. Actually, the good practice of public relations seeks two-way communication between and among all the people and institutions concerned with an issue.

A task force established by the Public Relations Society of America to explore the stature and role of the profession concluded that public relations has the potential to improve the functioning of democracy by encouraging the exchange of information and ideas on public issues. The task force made these points:

- Public relations is a means for the public to have its desires and interests felt by the institutions in our society. It interprets and speaks for the public to organizations that otherwise might be unresponsive, and it speaks for those organizations to the public.
- Public relations is a means to achieve mutual adjustments between institutions and groups, establishing smoother relationships that benefit the public.

Crisis Management. Something went wrong at a Union Carbide chemical factory at Bhopal, India, and more than 2000 people died. It was the worst industrial accident in history. Union Carbide fumbled at first in dealing with media inquiries. Company guards denied access to a reporter who wanted to visit a Union Carbide plant in West Virginia that manufactured the same chemical as the Bhopal plant. A few days later, however, the company invited reporters inside the gates en masse. The turnaround represented a realization that shutting out the news media was engendering public suspicions about Union Carbide's culpability in the Bhopal disaster. In contrast, openness can inspire public confidence.

- Public relations is a safety valve for freedom. By providing means of working out accommodations, it makes arbitrary action or coercion less likely.
- Public relations is an essential element in the communication system that enables individuals to be informed on many aspects of subjects that affect their lives.
- Public relations people can help activate the social conscience of the organizations for which they work.

ORIGINS OF PUBLIC RELATIONS

STUDY PREVIEW   Many big companies found themselves in disfavour in the late 1800s for ignoring the public good to make profits. Feeling misunderstood, some moguls of industry turned to Ivy Lee, the father of public relations, for counsel on gaining public support.

MOGULS IN TROUBLE

Nobody would be tempted to think of *William Henry Vanderbilt* as very good at public relations. In 1882, it was Vanderbilt, president of the New York Central Railroad, who said, "The public be damned," when asked about the effect of changing train schedules. Vanderbilt's utterance so infuriated people that it became a banner in the populist crusade against robber barons and tycoons in the late 1800s. Under populist pressure, state governments set up agencies to regulate railroads. Then the national government established the Interstate Commerce Commission to control freight and passenger rates. Government began insisting on safety standards. Labour unions formed in the industries with the worst working conditions, safety records and pay. Journalists added pressure with muckraking exposés on excesses in the railroad, coal and oil trusts; on meat-packing industry frauds; and on patent medicines.

The leaders of industry were slow to recognize the effect of populist objections on their practices. They were comfortable with *social Darwinism*, an adaptation of *Charles Darwin*'s survival-of-the-fittest theory. In fact, they thought themselves forward-thinking in applying Darwin's theory to business and social issues. It was only a few years earlier, in 1859, that Darwin had laid out his biological theory in *On the Origin of Species by Means of Natural Selection*. To cushion the harshness of social Darwinism, many tycoons espoused a paternalism toward those whose "fitness" had not brought them fortune and power. No matter how carefully put, the paternalism seemed arrogant to the "less fit."

George Baer, a railroad president, epitomized both social Darwinism and paternalism in commenting on a labour strike: "The rights and interests of the laboring man will be protected and cared for not by labor agitators but by the Christian men to whom God in His infinite wisdom has given the control of the property interests of the country." Baer was quoted widely, further fueling sentiment against big business. Baer may have been sincere, but his position was read as a cover for excessive business practices by barons who assumed superiority to everyone else.

Meanwhile, social Darwinism came under attack as circuitous reasoning: economic success accomplished by abusive practices could be used to justify further abusive practices, which would lead to further success. Social Darwinism was a dog-eat-dog outlook that hardly jibed with democratic ideals, especially not as described in the preamble to the U.S. Constitution, which sought to "promote the general welfare, and secure the blessings of liberty" for everyone—not for only the chosen "fittest." Into these tensions at the turn of the century came public relations pioneer Ivy Lee.

THE IDEAS OF IVY LEE

Coal mine operators, like the railroad magnates, were held in the public's contempt at the turn of the century. Obsessed with profits, caring little about public sentiment or even the well-being of their employees, the mine operators were vulnerable in the new populist wave. Mine workers organized, and 150 000 in Pennsylvania went out on strike in 1902, shutting down the anthracite industry and disrupting coal-dependent industries, including the railroads. The mine operators snubbed reporters, which probably contributed to a pro-union slant in many news stories and worsened the operators' public image. Not until six months into the strike, when President Theodore Roosevelt threatened to take over the mines with Army troops, did the operators settle.

Shaken finally by Roosevelt's threat and recognizing Roosevelt's responsiveness to public opinion, the mine operators began reconsidering how they went about their business. In 1906, with another strike looming, one operator heard about *Ivy*

Lee, a young publicist in New York who had new ideas about winning public support. He was hired. In a turnabout in press relations, Lee issued a news release that announced, "The anthracite coal operators, realizing the general public interest in conditions in the mining regions, have arranged to supply the press with all possible information." Then followed a series of releases with information attributed to the mine operators by name—the same people who earlier had preferred anonymity and refused all interview requests. There were no more secret strike strategy meetings. When operators planned a meeting, reporters covering the impending strike were informed. Although reporters were not admitted to the meetings, summaries of the proceedings were given to them immediately afterward. This relative openness eased long-standing hostility toward the operators, and a strike was averted.

Lee's success with the mine operators began a career that rewrote the rules on how corporations deal with their various publics. Among his accomplishments were:

CONVERTING INDUSTRY TOWARD OPENNESS.   Railroads had notoriously secretive policies not only about their business practices but even about accidents. When the Pennsylvania Railroad sought Ivy Lee's counsel, he advised against suppressing news—especially on things that inevitably would leak out anyway. When a train jumped the rails near Gap, Pennsylvania, Lee arranged for a special car to take reporters to the scene and even take pictures. The Pennsylvania line was applauded in the press for the openness, and coverage of the railroad, which had been negative for years, began changing. A "bad press" continued plaguing other railroads that persisted in their secretive tradition.

TURNING NEGATIVE NEWS INTO POSITIVE NEWS.   When the U.S. Senate proposed investigating International Harvester for monopolistic practices, Lee advised the giant farm implement manufacturer against reflexive obstructionism and silence. A statement went out announcing that the company, confident in its business practices, not only welcomed but also would facilitate an investigation. Then began a campaign that pointed out International Harvester's beneficence toward its employees. The campaign also emphasized other upbeat information about the company.

PUTTING CORPORATE EXECUTIVES ON DISPLAY.   When workers at a Colorado mine went on strike, company guards fired machine guns and killed several men. More battling followed, during which two women and 11 children were killed. It was called the *Ludlow Massacre*, and John D. Rockefeller Jr., the chief mine owner, was pilloried for what had happened. Rockefeller was an easy target. Like his father, widely despised for the earlier Standard Oil monopolistic practices, John Jr., tried to keep himself out of the spotlight, but suddenly mobs were protesting at his mansion in New York and calling out "shoot him down like a dog." Rockefeller asked Ivy Lee what he should do. Lee began whipping up articles about Rockefeller's human side, his family and his generosity. Then, on Lee's advice, Rockefeller announced he would visit Colorado to see conditions himself. He spent two weeks talking with miners at work and in their homes and meeting their families. It was a news story that reporters could not resist, and it unveiled Rockefeller as a human being, not a far-removed, callous captain of industry. One myth-shattering episode occurred one evening when Rockefeller, after a brief

Ludlow Massacre. Colorado militiamen opened fire during a 1914 mine labor dispute and killed women and children. Overnight, John D. Rockefeller became the object of public hatred. It was a Rockefeller company that owned the mine, and even in New York, where Rockefeller lived, there were rallies asking for his head. Public relations pioneer, Ivy Lee, advised Rockefeller to tour the Ludlow area as soon as tempers cooled to show his sincere concern and to begin work on a labour contract to meet the concerns of miners. Rockefeller ended up a popular character in the Colorado mining camps.

Ivy Lee

address to miners and their wives, suggested that the floor be cleared for a dance. Before it was all over, John D. Rockefeller Jr. had danced with almost every miner's wife, and the news stories about the evening did a great deal to mitigate antagonism and distrust toward Rockefeller. Back in New York, with Lee's help, Rockefeller put together a proposal for a grievance procedure, which he asked the Colorado miners to approve. It was ratified overwhelmingly.

AVOIDING PUFFERY AND FLUFF.   Ivy Lee came on the scene at a time when many organizations were making extravagant claims about themselves and their products. Circus promoter *P. T. Barnum* made this kind of hyping a fine art in the late 1800s, and he had many imitators. It was an age of puffed-up advertising claims and fluffy rhetoric. Lee noted, however, that people soon saw through hyperbolic claims and lost faith in those who made them. In launching his public relations agency in 1906, he vowed to be accurate in everything he said and to provide whatever verification anyone requested. This became part of the creed of good practice in public relations, and it remains so today.

PUBLIC RELATIONS ON A NEW SCALE

The potential of public relations to rally support for a cause was demonstrated on a gigantic scale in World War I and again in World War II. In 1917 President Woodrow Wilson, concerned about widespread antiwar sentiment, asked *George Creel* to head a new government agency whose job was to make the war popular. The Creel Committee cranked out news releases, magazine pieces, posters, even movies. A list of 75 000 local speakers was put together to talk nationwide at school programs, church groups and civic organizations about making the world safe for democracy. More than 15 000 committee articles were printed. Never before had public relations been attempted on such a scale—and it worked. World War I became a popular cause even to the point of inspiring people to buy Liberty Bonds, putting up their own money to finance the war outside the usual taxation apparatus.

When World War II began, an agency akin to the Creel Committee was formed. Veteran journalist *Elmer Davis* was put in charge. The new *Office of War Information* was public relations on a bigger scale than ever before.

The Creel and Davis committees employed hundreds of people. Davis had 250 employees handling news releases alone. These staff members, mostly young, carried new lessons about public relations into the private sector after the war. These were the people who shaped corporate public relations as we know it today.

STRUCTURE OF PUBLIC RELATIONS

STUDY PREVIEW   In developing sound policies, corporations and other institutions depend on public relations experts who are sensitive to the implications of policy on the public consciousness. This makes public relations a vital management function. Besides a role in policymaking, public relations people play key roles in carrying out institutional policy.

POLICY ROLE OF PUBLIC RELATIONS

When U.S. giant AT&T needed somebody to take over public relations in 1927, the president of the company went to magazine editor *Arthur Page* and offered him a vice presidency. Before accepting, Page laid out several conditions. One was that he have a voice in AT&T policy. Page was hardly on an ego trip. He had seen too many corporations that regarded their public relations arm merely as an executor of policy. Page considered PR itself as a *management function*. To be effective as vice president for public relations, Page knew that he must contribute to the making of high-level corporate decisions as well as executing them.

Today, experts on public relations agree with Arthur Page's concept: When institutions are making policy, they need to consider the effects on their many publics. That can be done best when the person in charge of public relations, ideally at the vice presidential level, is intimately involved in decision-making. The public relations executive advises the rest of the institution's leaders on public perceptions and the effects that policy options might have on perceptions. Also, the public relations vice president is in a better position to implement the institution's policy for having been a part of developing it.

HOW PUBLIC RELATIONS IS ORGANIZED

No two institutions are organized in precisely the same way. At General Motors, 200 people work in public relations. In smaller organizations, PR may be one of several hats worn by a single person. Except in the smallest operations, the public relations department usually has three functional areas of responsibility:

EXTERNAL RELATIONS.   This involves communication with groups and people outside the organization, including customers, dealers, suppliers and community leaders. The external-relations unit usually is responsible for encouraging employees to participate in civic activities. Other responsibilities include arranging promotional activities like exhibits, trade shows, conferences and tours.

Public relations people also lobby government agencies and legislators on behalf of their organization, keep the organization abreast of government regulations and legislation, and coordinate relations with political candidates. This may include fund-raising for candidates and coordinating political action committees.

In hospitals and nonprofit organizations, a public relations function may include recruiting and scheduling volunteer workers.

War Popular.   Contrary to myth, World War I did not begin as a popular cause with Americans. In fact, there were antidraft riots in many cities. This prompted President Woodrow Wilson to ask journalist George Creel to launch a major campaign to persuade Americans that the war was important to make the world safe for democracy. Within months, Americans were financing much of the war voluntarily by buying government bonds. This poster was only one aspect of Creel's work, which demonstrated that public relations principles could be applied on a massive scale.

George Creel

INTERNAL RELATIONS.   This involves developing optimal relations with employees, managers, unions, shareholders and other internal groups. In-house newsletters, magazines and brochures are important media for communicating with organizations' internal audiences.

MEDIA RELATIONS.   Communication with large groups of people outside an organization is practicable only through the mass media. An organization's coordinator of media relations responds to news media queries, arranges news conferences and issues news releases. These coordinators coach executives for news interviews and sometimes serve as their organization's spokesperson.

PUBLIC RELATIONS AGENCIES

Even though many organizations have their own public relations staff, they may go to public relations agencies for help on specific projects or problems. Hundreds of companies specialize in public relations counsel and related services. It is a big business. Income at global PR agencies like Burson-Marsteller runs about $200 million a year.

The biggest agencies offer a full range of services on a global scale. Hill and Knowlton has offices in Cleveland, its original home; Dallas; Frankfurt; Geneva; London; Los Angeles; New York, now its headquarters; Paris; Rome; Seattle; and Washington, D.C. The agency will take on projects anywhere in the world, either on its own or by working with local agencies.

Besides full-service agencies, there are specialized public relations companies, which focus on a narrow range of services. For example, clipping services cut out and provide newspaper and magazine articles and radio and television items of interest to clients. Among specialized agencies are those that focus exclusively on

Perrier Is Back. In 1990, when traces of cancer-causing benzene were found in Perrier, the bottled French mineral water, Perrier's reputation was in jeopardy. So were sales of $100 million a year in the United States alone. The company acted promptly to meet this challenge. First, release all available information about the contamination. Second, explain there was no significant health risk from the minute amounts of benzene. Third, point out that the company voluntarily recalled 160 million bottles from distribution channels worldwide because the contents did not meet their standards. Fourth, relaunch the product. Fifth, put Perrier President Ronald V. Davis in touch with the public vouching for Perrier's purity and quality controls. Photographs of Davis quaffing Perrier were soon in the news media everywhere. This was all followed, three weeks after the recall, by an advertising campaign, "Perrier Is Back." Sales rebounded.

MEDIA DATABANK

Major Public Relations Agencies

These are the largest public relations agencies in the U.S. Because some agencies are part of larger companies that don't break out data on their subordinate units, some data here are estimates.

Company	Income Worldwide	Employees Worldwide	Company	Income Worldwide	Employees Worldwide
Burson-Marsteller	$204 million	2100	Fleishman-Hillard	$59 million	600
Shandick	166 million	1900	Ketchum	45 million	400
Hill and Knowlton	149 million	1600	Rowland	44 million	500
Omnicon	66 million	1000	Ogilvy Adams & Rinehart	36 million	300
Edelman	60 million	700	Manning, Selvage & Lee	31 million	300

political campaigns. Others coach corporate executives for news interviews. Others coordinate trade shows.

Some agencies bill clients only for services rendered. Others charge clients just to be on call. Hill and Knowlton, for example, has a minimum $5000-a-month retainer fee. Agency expenses for specific projects are billed in addition. Staff time usually is at an hourly rate that covers the agency's overhead and allows a profit margin. Other expenses are usually billed with a 15 to 17 percent markup.

PUBLIC RELATIONS SERVICES

STUDY PREVIEW Public relations deals with publicity and promotion, but it also involves less visible activities. These include lobbying, fund-raising and crisis management. Public relations is distinct from advertising.

ACTIVITIES BEYOND PUBLICITY

Full-service public relations agencies provide a wide range of services built on two of the cornerstones of the business: *publicity* and *promotion*. These agencies are ready to conduct media campaigns to rally support for a cause, create an image or turn a problem into an asset. Publicity and promotion, however, are only the most visible services offered by public relations agencies. Others include:

LOBBYING. Every province has public relations practitioners whose specialty is representing their clients to legislative bodies and government agencies. In one sense, lobbyists are expediters. They know local traditions and customs, and they know who is in a position to affect policy. Lobbyists advise their clients, which include trade associations, corporations, public interest groups and regulated utilities and industries, on how to achieve their goals by working with legislators and government regulators. Many lobbyists call themselves "government relations specialists."

POLITICAL COMMUNICATION. Every provincial capital has political consultants whose work mostly is advising candidates for public office. Services include campaign management, survey research, publicity, media relations and image consulting. Political consultants also work on elections, referendums, recalls and other public policy issues.

IMAGE CONSULTING.   Image consulting has been a growing specialized branch of public relations since the first energy crisis in the 1970s. Oil companies, realizing that their side of the story was not getting across, turned to image consultants to groom corporate spokespersons, often chief executives, to meet reporters one on one and go on talk shows. The groomers did a brisk business, and it paid off in countering the stories and rumours that were blaming the oil companies for skyrocketing fuel prices.

Jacqueline Thompson, author of the *Directory of Personal Image Consultants*, listed 53 entries in 1981 and has been adding up to 157 new entries a year since then. About these consultants, said Thompson: "They will lower the pitch of your voice, remove your accent, correct your 'body language,' modify your unacceptable behavior, eliminate your negative self-perception, select your wardrobe, restyle your hair, and teach you how to speak off the cuff or read a speech without putting your audience to sleep."

FINANCIAL PUBLIC RELATIONS.   Financial public relations dates to the 1920s and 1930s. It is the job of people in financial PR to know not only the principles of public relations but also the complex regulations governing the promotion of securities in corporate mergers, acquisitions, new issues and stock splits.

FUND-RAISING.   Some public relations people specialize in fund-raising and membership drives. Many university and community colleges, for example, have their own staffs to perform these functions. Others look to fund-raising firms to manage capital drives. Such an agency employs a variety of techniques, from mass mailings to phonathon soliciting, and charges a percentage of the amount raised. This is a growing field, given the current economic climate, which has led both the federal and provincial governments to cut back on grants and funding.

CONTINGENCY PLANNING.   Many organizations rely on public relations people to design programs to address problems that can be expected to occur. Airlines, for example, need detailed plans for handling inevitable plane crashes—situations requiring quick, appropriate responses under tremendous pressure. When a crisis occurs, an organization can turn to public relations people for advice on dealing with it. Some agencies specialize in *crisis management*, which involves picking up the pieces either when a contingency plan fails or when there was no plan to deal with a crisis.

POLLING.   Public-opinion sampling is essential in many public relations projects. Full-service agencies can either conduct surveys themselves or contract with companies that specialize in surveying.

EVENTS COORDINATION.   Many public relations people are involved in coordinating a broad range of events, including product announcements, news conferences and convention planning. Some in-house public relations departments and agencies have their own artistic and audio-visual production talent to produce brochures, tapes and other promotional materials. Other agencies contract for those services.

PUBLIC RELATIONS AND ADVERTISING

Both public relations and advertising involve persuasion, but most of the similarities end there. Public relations has responsibility in shaping an organization's policy. It is a management activity. Advertising is not. The work of advertising is much narrower. It focuses on selling a service or product after all the management decisions have been made. Public relations "sells" points of view and images, which are intangibles and therefore hard to measure. In advertising, success is measurable with tangibles, like sales, that can be calculated from the bottom line.

When an organization decides it needs a persuasive campaign, there is a choice between public relations and advertising. One advantage of advertising is that the organization controls the message. By buying space or time in the mass media, an organization has the final say on what it says in its advertising messages.

In public relations, in contrast, an organization tries to influence the media to tell its story its way, but the message that goes out is actually up to the media. A news reporter, for example, may lean heavily on a public relations person for information about an organization, but the reporter may also gather information from other sources, and, in the end, it is the reporter who writes the story. The result, usually, is that a news story carries more credibility than advertisements with mass audiences. The disadvantage to an organization is the risk that comes with surrendering control over the message that goes to the public.

For many persuasive campaigns, organizations use both public relations and advertising. Increasingly, public relations and advertising people find themselves

Taking on the Media. After ABC television reported that tobacco companies spiked cigarettes to make them more addictive, R.J. Reynolds responded with a multiprong campaign to tell its side. The tobacco company sued ABC. The company also ran advertorials in the *Wall Street Journal* and elsewhere featuring the chairman of the company. Adversarial responses to the media are not mainstream public relations, but they are becoming more frequent. General Motors used adversarial public relations against NBC after the network rigged a GM truck to explode in order to support a claim that they were prone to fires in collisions. GM filed a suit and went public with evidence that NBC's video was staged. After extracting an apology from a humiliated NBC, GM dropped its suit.

working together. This is especially true in corporations that have adopted *total marketing plans*, which attempt to coordinate advertising as a marketing tool with promotion and publicity of the sort that pubic relations experts can provide. Several major advertising agencies, aware of their clients' shift to total marketing, have acquired or established public relations subsidiaries to provide a wider range of services under their roof.

It's this overlap that has prompted some advertising agencies to move more into public relations. The WWP Group of London, a global advertising agency, has acquired both Hill and Knowlton, the third-largest public relations company in the United States, and the Ogilvy PR Group, the ninth largest. The Young & Rubicam advertising agency has three public relations subsidiaries: Burson-Marsteller, the largest; Cohn & Wolf, the 13th; and Creswell, Munsell, Fultz & Zirbel, the 50th. These are giant enterprises, which reflect the conglomeration and globalization of both advertising and public relations.

Public relations and advertising also overlap in *institutional advertising*, which involves producing ads not to sell goods or services but to promote an institution's image or position on a public issue.

MEDIA RELATIONS

STUDY PREVIEW Public relations people generally favour candour in working with the news media. Even so, some organizations opt to stonewall journalistic inquiries. An emerging school of thought in public relations is to challenge negative stories aggressively and publicly.

OPEN MEDIA RELATIONS

The common wisdom among public relations people today is to be open and candid with the mass media. It is a principle that dates to Ivy Lee, and case studies abound to confirm its effectiveness. A classic case study on this point is the Tylenol crisis.

Johnson & Johnson had spent many years and millions of dollars to inspire public confidence in its product Tylenol, and by 1982 the product was the leader in a crowded field of headache remedies with 36 percent of the market. Then disaster struck. Seven people in Chicago died after taking Tylenol capsules laced with cyanide. James Burke, president of Johnson & Johnson, and Lawrence Foster, vice president for public relations, moved quickly. Within hours, Johnson & Johnson:

- Halted the manufacture and distribution of Tylenol.
- Removed Tylenol products from retailers' shelves.
- Launched a massive advertising campaign requesting people to exchange Tylenol capsules for a safe replacement.
- Summoned 50 public relations employees from Johnson & Johnson and its subsidiary companies to staff a press centre to answer media and consumer questions forthrightly.
- Ordered an internal company investigation of the Tylenol manufacturing and distribution process.
- Promised full cooperation with government investigators.
- Ordered the development of tamper-proof packaging for the reintroduction of Tylenol products after the contamination problem was resolved.

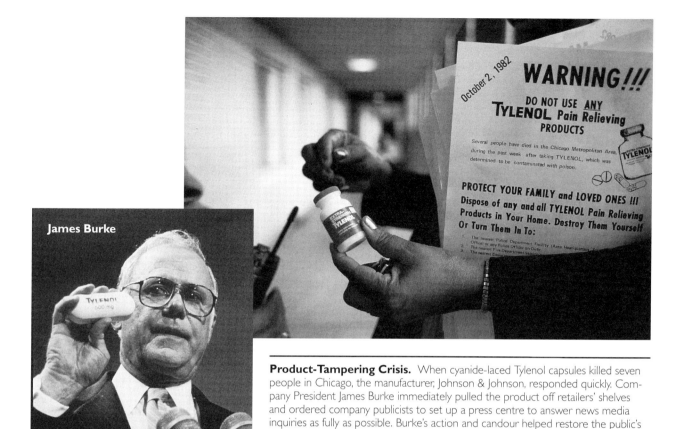

James Burke

Product-Tampering Crisis. When cyanide-laced Tylenol capsules killed seven people in Chicago, the manufacturer, Johnson & Johnson, responded quickly. Company President James Burke immediately pulled the product off retailers' shelves and ordered company publicists to set up a press centre to answer news media inquiries as fully as possible. Burke's action and candour helped restore the public's shaken confidence in Tylenol, and the product resumed its significant market share after the crisis ended. It turned out that it had been a disturbed person outside Johnson & Johnson's production and distribution system who had contaminated the capsules rather than a manufacturing lapse.

Investigators determined within days that an urban terrorist had poisoned the capsules. Although the news media exonerated Johnson & Johnson of negligence, the company nonetheless had a tremendous problem: how to restore public confidence in Tylenol. Many former Tylenol users were reluctant to take a chance, and the Tylenol share of the analgesic market dropped to 6 percent.

To address the problem, Johnson & Johnson called in the Burson-Marsteller public relations agency. Burson-Marsteller recommended a media campaign to capitalize on the high marks the news media had given the company for openness during the crisis. Mailgrams went out inviting journalists to a 30-city video teleconference to hear James Burke announce the reintroduction. Six hundred reporters turned out, and Johnson & Johnson officials took their questions live.

To stir even wider attention, 7500 *media kits* had been sent to newsrooms the day before the teleconference. The kits included a news release and a bevy of supporting materials: photographs, charts and background information.

The resulting news coverage was extensive. On average, newspapers carried 32 column inches of copy on the announcement. Network television and radio as well as local stations also afforded heavy coverage. Meanwhile, Johnson & Johnson executives, who had attended a workshop on how to make favourable television appearances, made themselves available as guests on the network morning shows and talk shows such as "Donahue" and "Nightline." At the same time, Johnson & Johnson distributed 80 million free coupons to encourage people to use Tylenol again.

The massive media-based public relations campaign worked. Within a year, Tylenol had regained 80 percent of its former market share, and today, in an increasingly crowded analgesic field, Tylenol is again the market leader with annual sales of $670 million, compared with $520 million before the cyanide crisis.

PROACTIVE MEDIA RELATIONS

Although public relations campaigns cannot control what the media say, public relations people can help shape how news media report issues by taking the initiative. In the Tylenol crisis, for example, Johnson & Johnson reacted quickly and decisively and took control of disseminating information, which, coupled with full disclosure, headed off false rumours that could have caused further damage.

PROACTIVE CRISIS RESPONSES.   A principle in crisis management is to seize leadership on the story. This involves anticipating what journalists will want to know and providing it to them before they even have time to formulate their questions. Ivy Lee did this time and again, and Johnson & Johnson did it in 1982.

For successful crisis management, public relations people need strong ongoing relationships with an organization's top officials. Otherwise, when a crisis strikes, they likely will have difficulty rounding up the kind of breaking information they need to deal effectively with the news media. During the 1991 Persian Gulf war, Pentagon spokesperson Pete Williams received high marks as a public relations person for shaping news coverage of the conflict. Williams did this by tapping his close working relationships with Defence Secretary Dick Cheney and the Joint Chiefs of Staff for information favourable to the war effort. At regular news briefings, sometimes several a day, Williams provided so much grist for the journalistic mill that reporters were overwhelmed putting it together for stories, which reduced the time available for them to go after stories on their own. The war was reported largely as the Pentagon wanted.

ONGOING MEDIA RELATIONSHIPS.   Good media relations cannot be forged in the fire of a crisis. Organizations that survive a crisis generally have a history of solid media relations. Their public relations staff people know reporters, editors and news directors on a first-name basis. They avoid hyping news releases on routine matters, and they work hard at earning the trust of journalists.

Many public relations people, in fact, are seasoned journalists themselves, and they understand how journalists go about their work. It is their journalistic background that made them attractive candidates for their PR jobs.

SOUND OPERATING PRINCIPLES.   An underlying strength that helped see Johnson & Johnson through the Tylenol crisis was the company's credo. The credo was a written vow that Johnson & Johnson's first responsibility was to "those who use our products and services." The credo, which had been promoted in-house for years, said: "Every time a business hires, builds, sells or buys, it is acting *for the people* as well as *for itself*, and it must be prepared to accept full responsibility."

With such a sound operating principle, Johnson & Johnson's crisis response was, in some respects, almost reflexive. Going silent, for example, would have run counter to the principles that Johnson & Johnson people had accepted as part of their corporate culture for years.

AMBIVALENCE IN MEDIA RELATIONS

Despite the advantages of open media relations, there are companies that choose not to embrace that approach. The business magazine *Fortune* has listed these major corporations as notorious for not even returning phone calls when journalists call:

- Amerada Hess, the huge crude oil and natural gas company.
- Winn-Dixie, the southern supermarket chain.
- Texas Instruments, the semiconductor company, which felt stung by 1983 media coverage of a $145 million loss.

Some corporations take a middle ground, currying media coverage selectively. Giant IBM, which receives 30 000 media queries a year, frets that news coverage would underscore its sheer size. IBM turns away questions on many issues, including the company's long-term planning. The corporation's PR chief, Seth McCormick, spurns Ivy Lee's maxim that corporate executives should be "on display." In an interview, McCormick told *Fortune:* "We control what is said about the company through the sparsity of heads for the outside world to talk to. We like it that way."

Although IBM ignores the common wisdom about media relations, the corporation shows up frequently in rankings of the most respected companies in the nation. An imponderable question is whether IBM's reputation is due to its posture on media relations or in spite of it.

Procter & Gamble is another major company that generally is tight-lipped about how it conducts its business, with the notable exception of product promotions. Another notable exception was Procter & Gamble's full-scale public relations campaign in the 1980s to squelch persistent rumours that its corporate symbol—the moon and stars—had roots in Satanism.

ADVERSARIAL PUBLIC RELATIONS

Public relations took on aggressive, even feisty tactics when Mobil Oil decided in the 1970s not to take media criticism lightly any more. *Herb Schmertz*, vice president for Mobil's public affairs, charted a new course by:

- Filing formal complaints with news organizations when coverage was unfair in the company's view.
- Taking Mobil's case directly to the general public with paid advertising, *advertorials* as they are called, a splicing of the words "advertising" and "editorial," that explained the company's views.
- Sending corporate representatives on media tours to spread Mobil's side to as many constituencies as possible.

Schmertz's energetic counterattacks were a departure from conventional wisdom in pubic relations, which was to let criticism go unanswered or, at most, to complain privately to executives of news organizations about negative coverage as

Joseph Hazelwood

Lawrence Rawl

Messing Up. The Exxon public-relations operations bungled badly when a tanker went aground off Alaska in 1989, causing a gigantic environmental disaster. Exxon Chairman Lawrence Rawl remained silent for a week. Exxon was slow to mobilize its cleanup crews and then blamed Coast Guard and state authorities for delays. Also, Exxon tried to handle media inquiries with a one-person press centre, which was hardly sufficient. Things worsened. Amid media finger-pointing at the captain of the ship, Joseph Hazelwood, Exxon publicly abandoned him. Public sympathy shifted to the captain when it turned out that the media had given him a worse rap than he was due.

unwarranted. The conventional wisdom was that a public response would only bring more attention to the negative coverage.

In abandoning passivity, Mobil was adapting what sports fans call the Red Auerbach technique. Auerbach, the legendary coach of the Boston Celtics, was known for criticizing referees. He realized they would never change a call, but he believed that refs would be less inclined to make questionable calls against the Celtics if they knew that Auerbach would jump all over them. Mobil President Rawleigh Warner Jr. explained the new Mobil policy this way: "People know that if they take a swipe at us, we will fight back."

Schmertz employed the full range of PR tools in 1974 when ABC aired a television documentary that raised critical questions about the U.S. oil industry. Mobil objected first to ABC and then fired off a formal complaint to the National News Council, a volunteer media watchdog group. Mobil claimed 32 inaccuracies and instances of unfairness and requested that the council investigate. Mobil also issued an unusually lengthy news release, quoting from the documentary and offering point-by-point rebuttals.

Six Mobil executives were given a crash course on giving good interviews and sent out to meet the news media. In two years, the executives and other Mobil representatives appeared on 365 television and 211 radio shows and talked with 80 newspaper reporters. Schmertz encouraged them to take the offensive. To counter the ABC impression that the oil industry still engaged in the bad practices of its past, Schmertz told executives to stress that such information was outdated. "Put the shoe on the other foot," he said, advising the Mobil executives to say the impression left by the ABC documentary was "comparable to Mobil's producing a documentary about today's television industry and pointing to a 1941 FCC decree requiring RCA to rid itself of one of its networks as evidence of a current conspiracy."

Advertorials were part of Mobil's initiatives. Under Schmertz, as much as $6 million a year went into newspaper and magazine ads, explaining the company's position. Mobil also began producing its own television programs on energy issues and providing them free to stations. The programs had a journalistic tone, and many stations ran them as if they were actual documentaries rather than part of Mobil's media campaign.

The jury is still out on whether Schmertz's aggressive sparring is good policy. Most organizations continue to follow the traditional thinking that taking on the media only generates more attention about the original bad news. On the other hand, Schmertz's approach has been tried by some major corporations. Bechtel, Illinois Power and Kaiser Aluminum all have called for independent investigations of stories that reflected badly on them.

Another adversarial approach, although not recommended by most public relations people, is for an offended organization to sever relations with the source of unfavourable news—an information boycott. In 1954, in a spectacular pout, General Motors cut off contact with *Wall Street Journal* reporters and withdrew advertising from the newspaper. This approach carries great risks:

- By going silent, an organization loses avenues for conveying its message to mass audiences.
- An organization that yanks advertising to punish detractors is perceived negatively for coercively wielding its economic might.
- An organization that quits advertising in an effective advertising medium will lose sales.

Mobil Advertorial. Many public relations practitioners seek to avoid confrontation, but Herb Schmertz of Mobil bought space in newspapers and magazines beginning in the 1970s to lay out his company's positions on controversial issues and even to be confrontational. Schmertz tackled the news media when he felt Mobil had not received a fair shake in coverage. These position statements are called "advertorials" because they are in space purchased as advertising and their content is like an editorial.

Herb Schmertz

A boycott differs from Schmertz's adversarial approach in an important respect. Schmertz responds to negative news by contributing to the exchange of information and ideas, which is positive in a democratic society. An information boycott, on the other hand, restricts the flow of information. Today, GM's policy has returned to the conventional wisdom of not arguing with anyone who buys paper by the ton and ink by the barrel.

PROFESSIONALIZATION

 STUDY PREVIEW Public relations has a tarnished image that stems from shortsighted promotion and whitewashing techniques of the late 1800s. While some dubious practices continue, PR leaders are working to improve standards.

A TARNISHED HERITAGE

Unsavoury elements in the heritage of public relations remain a heavy burden. P. T. Barnum, whose name became synonymous with hype, attracted crowds to his stunts and shows in the latter 1800s with extravagant promises. Sad to say, some promoters still use Barnum's tactics. The claims for snake oils and elixirs from Barnum's era live on in commercials for pain relievers and cold remedies. The early response of tycoons to muckraking attacks, before Ivy Lee came along, was *white-washing*—covering up the abuses but not correcting them. It is no wonder that the term "PR" sometimes is used derisively. To say something is "all PR" means it lacks substance. Of people whose apparent positive qualities are a mere façade, it may be said that they have "good PR."

Although journalists rely heavily on public relations people for information, many journalists look with suspicion on PR practitioners. Not uncommon among seasoned journalists are utterances like: "I've never met a PR person I couldn't distrust." Such cynicism flows partly from the journalists' self-image as unfettered truth seekers whose only obligation is serving their audiences' needs. PR people, on the other hand, are seen as obligated to their employers, whose interests do not always dovetail with the public good. Behind their backs, PR people are called "flaks," a takeoff on the World War II slang for antiaircraft bursts intended to stop enemy bombers. PR *flakkers*, as journalists use the term, interfere with journalistic truth seeking by putting forth slanted, self-serving information, which is not necessarily the whole story.

The journalism-PR tension is exacerbated by a common newsroom view that PR people try to get free news hole space for their messages rather than buy airtime and column inches. This view may seem strange considering that 50 to 90 percent of all news stories either originate with or contain information supplied by PR people. It is also strange considering that many PR people are former news reporters and editors. No matter how uncomfortable PR people and journalists are as bedfellows, they are bedfellows nonetheless.

Some public relations people have tried to leapfrog the negative baggage attached to the term "PR" by abandoning it. *Public information, public affairs, corporate communication* and plain old *communication* have been used by public relations firms as synonyms for PR.

STANDARDS AND CERTIFICATION

Founded in 1948, the *Canadian Public Relations Society* (CPRS), with 1500 members, has a different approach: improving the quality of public relations work, whatever the label. The association adopted the following code of professional standards. Although CPRS is a Canadian association, its codes clearly reflect lessons learned in both the U.S. and Canada.

CANADIAN PUBLIC RELATIONS SOCIETY CODE OF PROFESSIONAL STANDARDS

Members of the Canadian Public Relations Society, Inc. are pledged to maintain the spirit and ideals of the following stated principles of conduct and to consider these essentials to the practice of public relations.

- A member shall practice public relations according to the highest professional standards.
- A member shall deal fairly and honestly with the communications media and the public.
- A member shall practice the highest standards of honesty, accuracy, integrity and truth, and shall not knowingly disseminate false or misleading information.
- A member shall deal fairly with past or present employers/clients, with fellow practitioners, and with members of other professions.

- A member shall be prepared to disclose the name of their employer or client for whom public communications are made and refrain from associating themselves with anyone that would not respect such policy.
- A member shall protect the confidences of present, former and prospective employers/clients.
- A member shall not represent conflicting or competing interests without the express consent of those concerned, given after a full disclosure of the facts.
- A member shall not guarantee specified results beyond the member's capacity to achieve.
- Members shall personally accept no fees, commissions, gifts or any other considerations for professional services from anyone except employers or clients for whom the services were specifically performed.

(Reprinted by permission of the CPRS.)

In a further professionalization step, CPRS established a certification process. Those who meet the criteria and pass exams are allowed to place *APR*, which stands for *accredited public relations professional*, after their names. The criteria are:

- Being recommended by an already accredited CPRS member.
- Five years of full-time professional experience.
- Passing an eight-hour written examination on public relations principles, techniques, history and ethics.
- Passing an oral exam conducted by three professionals.

The process is rigorous. Typically, a third of those who attempt the examination fail it the first time. Once earned, certification needs to be renewed through continuing education, and the right to use "APR" can be taken away if a member violates the CPRS code. About 1300 CPRS members hold APR certification.

CHAPTER WRAP-UP

When Ivy Lee hung up a shingle in New York for a new publicity agency in 1906, he wanted to distance himself from the huckstering that marked most publicity at the time. To do that, Lee issued a declaration of principles for the new agency and sent it out to editors. Today, Lee's declaration remains a classic statement on the practice of public relations. It promised that the agency would deal only in legitimate news about its clients, and no fluff. It invited journalists to pursue more information about the agency's clients. It also vowed to be honest and accurate.

Here's Lee's declaration: "This is not a secret press bureau. All our work is done in the open. We aim to supply news. This is not an advertising agency; if you think any of our matter ought properly to go to your business office, do not use it. Our matter is accurate. Further details on any subject treated will be supplied promptly, and any editor will be assisted most cheerfully in verifying directly any statement of fact. Upon inquiry, full information will be given to any editor concerning those on whose behalf an article is sent out. In brief, our plan is, frankly and openly, on behalf of the business concerns and public institutions, to supply to the press and the public of the United States prompt and accurate information concerning subjects which is of value and interest to the public to know about."

The declaration hangs in many public relations shops today.

QUESTIONS FOR REVIEW

1. What is public relations? How is public relations connected to the mass media?

2. Why did big business become interested in the techniques and principles of public relations beginning in the late 1800s?

3. How is public relations a management tool?

4. What is the range of activities in which public relations people are involved?

5. What kind of relationship do most people strive to have with the mass media?

6. Why does public relations have a bad image? What are public relations professionals doing about it?

7. What is the legitimacy gap?

QUESTIONS FOR CRITICAL THINKING

1. When Ivy Lee accepted the Pennsylvania Railroad as a client in 1906, he saw the job as "interpreting the Pennsylvania Railroad to the public and interpreting the public to the Pennsylvania Railroad." Compare Lee's point with Arthur Page's view of public relations as a management function.

2. A U.S. federal grand jury indicted the Chrysler Corporation in 1987 for disconnecting odometers from 60 000 new vehicles, giving them to company executives to drive, sometimes hundreds of miles, then reconnecting the odometers and selling the cars as new. Chrysler Chairman Lee Iacocca called a news conference, admitted the practice "went beyond dumb and reached all the way to stupid," promised it would not happen again, and offered to compensate people who bought the "new" cars. Would Ivy Lee endorse how Iacocca dealt with the situation?

3. How would a corporate leader of the 1880s have handled the Chrysler odometer tampering?

4. How are public relations practitioners trying to overcome the complaints from journalists that they are flakkers interfering with an unfettered pursuit of truth?

5. What was the contribution of the Committee on Public Information, usually called the Creel Committee, to public relations after World War I?

6. How do public relations agencies turn profits?

7. When does an institution with its own in-house public relations operation need to hire a PR agency?

8. Explain the concept of enlightened self-interest.

9. How did the confluence of the following three phenomena at the turn of the century contribute to the emergence of modern public relations?

The related concepts of social Darwinism, a social theory; laissez-faire, a government philosophy; and paternalism, a practice of business.

Muckraking, which attacked prevalent abuses of the public interest.

Advertising, which had grown since the 1830s as a way to reach great numbers of people.

10. Showman P. T. Barnum epitomized 19th-century press agentry with extravagant claims, like promoting the midget Tom Thumb as a Civil War general. To attract crowds to a tour by an unknown European soprano, Jenny Lind, Barnum labeled her "the Swedish Nightingale." Would such promotional methods work today? Keep in mind that Barnum, explaining his methods, once said, "There's a sucker born every minute."

11. How can the Sapir-Whorf hypothesis be tied into the process of public relations?

FOR FURTHER LEARNING

Scott M. Cutlip, Allen H. Center and Glen M. Broom. *Effective Public Relations,* 6th cd. (Prentice Hall, 1985). This widely used introductory textbook touches all bases.

Ray Eldon Hiebert. *Courtier to the Crowd: The Story of Ivy Lee and the Development of Public Relations* (Iowa State University Press, 1966). Professor Hiebert's flattering biography focuses on the enduring public relations principles articulated, if not always practised, by Ivy Lee.

George S. McGovern and Leonard F. Guttridge. *The Great Coalfield War* (Houghton Mifflin, 1972). This account of the Ludlow Massacre includes the success of the Ivy Lee–inspired campaign to rescue the Rockefeller reputation but is less than enthusiastic about Lee's corporate-oriented perspective and sometimes shoddy fact gathering.

Kevin McManus. "Video Coaches." *Forbes* 129 (June 7, 1982). McManus provides additional background on the emerging field of image consulting.

Lael M. Moynihan. "Horrendous PR Crises: What They Did When the Unthinkable Happened." *Media History Digest* 8 (Spring–Summer 1988):1, 19–25. Moynihan, a consumer relations specialist, details eight major cases of crisis management through proven public relations principles.

Joyce Nelson. *The Sultans of Sleaze* (Between the Lines, 1989). Nelson offers a critical look at the profession.

Herbert Schmertz and William Novak. *Good-bye to the Low Profile: The Art of Creative Confrontation* (Little, Brown, 1986). Combative Herb Schmertz passes on the lessons he learned as Mobil Oil's innovative public relations chief, including how-tos for advertorials and preparation of executives for interviews with journalists.

Perry Dean Young. *God's Bullies: Power Politics and Religious Tyranny* (Henry Holt, 1982). Young provides a quick look at contemporary image consulting.

FOR KEEPING UP TO DATE

The trade journal *O'Dwyer's PR Services* tracks the industry on a monthly basis.

Other sources of ongoing information are *Public Relations Journal, Public Relations Quarterly* and *Public Relations Review* and *Marketing* Magazine.

ADVERTISING Selling Goods and Services

Advertising uses psychology to tap audience interests

Advertising contributes to prosperity, finances most of the mass media and facilitates intelligent consumer decision making

Most advertising messages are carried through the mass media

Advertising agencies create and place ads for advertisers

Advertisements are carefully placed in media to reach appropriate audiences for products and services

Tactics include brand names, lowest common denominators, positioning, redundancy

A globalization of the advertising industry has created opportunities and problems

Advertising messages have shifted from "buyer beware" to "seller beware"

Advertising people need to solve problems created by ad clutter and creative excesses

M E D I A   I N   T H E O R Y

Research and Psychology

Content analysis and semiotic analysis are two ways to look at ads.

ANALYZING ADS

If research means to "look again," the question becomes *how* can we look at ads? As artifacts of com-munication, advertisements can be considered texts to be read and analyzed. Two ways in which communication scholars do this is through content analysis and semiotic analysis.

As a research tool, content analysis has its roots in the social sciences. It's an empirical method that measures denotation (or first-order signifieds) in an ad. In other words, it counts what is physically present in an advertisement and nothing more. It is an objective, structured and scientific way of looking at ads. A simple content analysis might involve counting the number of women in ads for household products and comparing them to the number of men in the same type of ad. If the research indicated that more women than men were being used to sell these products, the researcher might claim that this is an example of sexism in advertising, as women are represented in terms of traditional stereotypes. Content analysis is often used by MediaWatch, which is a national, volunteer organization that keeps an eye on sexism in the media. Through content analysis, MediaWatch studies have been able to uncover the following examples of sexism in Canadian media:

- In radio ads, 68 percent of women appear in the role of consumer; women are rarely seen in the role of expert or celebrity.
- In TV commercials, male voice-overs outnumber female voice-overs by a ratio of 2 to 1.

Unlike content analysis, semiotic analysis has its roots in the humanities. As we've seen before, it's a method used to look at connotation (or second-order signifieds) in ads. Instead of following the structured, scientific format of content analysis, semiotics analyzes an ad in terms of the interplay of signs, signifiers and signifieds. In this way, the researcher can uncover the ideology or mythology in an ad or a series of ads.

Griselda Pollock, in "What's Wrong with Images of Women?" offers a unique and simple semiotic method for reading sexism in an ad. The myths behind the signs for both men and women need to be addressed because it's hard to talk about good or bad images of women (or men, for that matter) without comparing how the opposite gender is represented in advertising images. Pollock therefore argues that a semiotic analysis of gender images needs to treat men and women as separate signs; each with specific signifiers and signifieds. She argues that the idea of images of women "needs to be challenged and replaced by the notion of woman as a signifier in an ideological discourse in which one can identify the meanings that are constructed in relation to other signifiers ... A useful device for initiating this kind of work is the use of male/female reversals."

Her classic example of female/male reversals is the juxtaposition of a 19th-century French nude photo of a woman holding a tray of apples up to her breasts, bearing the caption *Achetez les pommes*, with a nude man, holding a tray of bananas near his crotch. While the example is a humorous one, it does uncover certain mythologies about how images of men and women are constructed. The first image is a redundant one; women are often compared to fruit in Western culture. The second image is entropic because it is unexpected. Pollock's point is this: if the ad creates a strange connotation when a man is put in place of a woman, you have uncovered what communication theorists call the dominant ideology and what Barthes would call myth. The role reversal may also be done by substituting "he" for "she" in advertising copy.

Both semiotic analysis and content analysis have strengths and weaknesses. In "Social Communication in Advertising," Leiss, Klein and Jhally explain that while content analysis is an objective method of looking at ads and works best on a large scale using many ads, it doesn't really explain how audiences interpret and decode the images within the text itself. They say that semiotic analysis works well if you are reading a single ad.

MOTIVATIONAL RESEARCH

Whatever naïveté North Americans had about opinion-shaping was dispelled by the mid-20th century. Sinister possibilities were realized in the work of Joseph Goebbels, the Nazi minister of propaganda and public enlightenment. In the Pacific, the Japanese aimed the infamous Tokyo Rose radio broadcasts at GIs to lower their morale. Then, during the Korean War, a macabre fascination developed with the so-called brainwashing techniques used on American prisoners of war. In this same period, the work of Austrian psychiatrist Sigmund Freud, which emphasized hidden motivations and repressed sexual impulses, was being popularized in countless books and articles.

No wonder, considering this intellectual context, advertising people in the 1950s looked to the social sciences to find new ways to woo customers. Among the advertising pioneers of this period was Ernest Dichter, who accepted Freud's claim that people act on motivations that they are not even aware of. Depth interviewing, Dichter felt, could reveal these motivations, which could then be exploited in advertising messages.

Dichter used his interviewing, called motivational

research, for automotive clients. Rightly or wrongly, Dichter determined that the American male was loyal to his wife but fantasized about a mistress. Men, he noted, usually were the decision makers in purchasing a car. Then, in what seemed a quantum leap, Dichter equated sedans, which were what most people drove, with wives. Sedans were familiar, reliable. Convertibles, impractical for many people and also beyond their reach financially, were equated with mistresses—romantic, daring, glamorous. With these conclusions in hand, Dichter devised advertisements for a new kind of sedan without a centre door pillar. The hardtop, as it was called, gave a convertible effect when the windows were down. The advertising clearly reflected Dichter's thinking: "You'll find something new to love every time you drive it." Although they were not as solid as sedans and tended to leak air and water, hardtops were popular among automobile buyers for the next 25 years.

Dichter's motivational research led to numerous campaigns that exploited sexual images. For Ronson lighters, the flame, in phallic form, was reproduced in extraordinary proportions. A campaign for Ajax cleanser, hardly a glamour product, had a white knight charging through the street, ignoring law and regulation with a great phallic lance. Whether consumers were motivated by sexual imagery is hard to establish. Even so, many campaigns flowing from motivational research worked.

SUBLIMINAL ADVERTISING

The idea that advertising can be persuasive at subconscious levels was taken a step further by market researcher Jim Vicary, who coined the term subliminal advertising. Vicary claimed in 1957 that he had studied the effect of inserting messages like "Drink Coca-Cola" and "Eat popcorn" into movies. The messages, although flashed too fast to be recognized by the human eye, still registered in the brain and, said Vicary, prompted moviegoers to rush to the snack bar. In experiments at a New Jersey movie house, he said, Coke sales increased 18 percent and popcorn almost 60 percent. Vicary's report stirred great interest, and also alarm, but researchers who tried to replicate his study found no evidence to support his claim.

Despite Vicary's dubious claims, psychologists have identified a phenomenon they call subception, in which certain behaviour sometimes seems to be triggered by messages perceived subliminally. Whether the effect works outside laboratory experiments and whether the effect is strong enough to prod a consumer to go to buy something is uncertain. Nevertheless, there remains a widespread belief among the general population that subliminal advertising works, and fortunes are being made by people who peddle various devices and systems with extravagant claims that they can control human behaviour. Among these are the "hidden" messages in stores' sound systems that say shoplifting is not nice.

This idea that advertising is loaded with hidden messages has been taken to extremes by Wilson Bryan Key, who spins out books alleging that plugs are hidden in all kinds of places for devil worship, homosexuality and a variety of libertine activities. He has accused the Nabisco people of baking the word "sex" into Ritz crackers. At Howard Johnson restaurants, he has charged, placemat pictures of plates heaped with clams portray orgies and bestiality. Though widely read, Key offers no evidence beyond his own observations and interpretations. In advertising circles, his views are dismissed as amusing but wacky. The view of Nabisco and Howard Johnson is less charitable.

In 1990 Wilson Bryan Key's views suffered a serious setback. He was a primary witness in a highly publicized Nevada trial on whether the Judas Priest heavy metal album "Stained Glass" had triggered the suicide of an 18-year-old youth and the attempted suicide of his 20-year-old friend. The families said that the pair had obsessed about a Judas Priest album that dealt with suicide and that one song was subliminally embedded with the words "Do it" over and over. The families' attorneys hired Key as an expert witness to help make their point. From Key's perspective, the case did not go well. Millions of television viewers who followed the trial strained to make out the supposed words "Do it," but even when isolated from the rest of the music, they were almost impossible to make out. It turned out the sounds were neither lyrics nor even vocal but rather instrumental effects. Members of Judas Priest testified that they had not equated the sound to any words at all and had inserted it for artistic effect, hardly to encourage suicide. The jury sided with Judas Priest, and Key left town with his wobbly ideas on subliminal messages having taken a serious blow under a jury's scrutiny.

David Ogilvy, founder of the Ogilvy & Mather agency, once made fun of claims like Key's, pointing out the absurdity of "millions of suggestible consumers getting up from their armchairs and rushing like zombies through the traffic on their way to buy the product at the nearest store." The danger of "Vote Bolshevik" being flashed during the "NBC Nightly News" is remote, and whether it would have any effect is dubious.

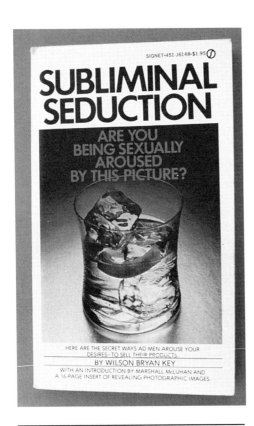

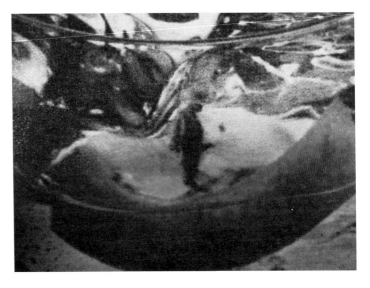

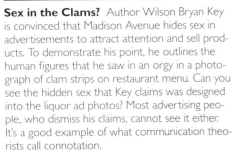

Sex in the Clams? Author Wilson Bryan Key is convinced that Madison Avenue hides sex in advertisements to attract attention and sell products. To demonstrate his point, he outlines the human figures that he saw in an orgy in a photograph of clam strips on restaurant menu. Can you see the hidden sex that Key claims was designed into the liquor ad photos? Most advertising people, who dismiss his claims, cannot see it either. It's a good example of what communication theorists call connotation.

IMPORTANCE OF ADVERTISING

STUDY PREVIEW   Advertising is key in a consumer economy. Without it, people would have a hard time even knowing what products and services are available. Advertising, in fact, is essential to a prosperous society. Advertising also is the financial basis of contemporary mass media.

ADVERTISING AND CONSUMER ECONOMIES

Advertising is a major component of modern economies. When the GNP is up, so is advertising spending. When the GNP falters, as it did in the early 1990s, many manufacturers, distributors and retailers pull back their advertising expenditures. The essential role of advertising in a modern consumer economy is obvious if you think about how people decide what to buy. If a shoe manufacturer were unable to tout the virtues of its footwear by advertising in the mass media, people would have a hard time learning about the product, let alone knowing that it is what they want.

ADVERTISING AND PROSPERITY

Advertising's phenomenal continuing growth has been a product of a plentiful society. In a poor society with a shortage of goods, people line up for necessities like food and clothing. Advertising has no role and serves no purpose when survival is the question. With prosperity, however, people have not only discretionary income but also a choice of ways to spend it. Advertising is the vehicle that provides information and rationales to help them decide how to enjoy their prosperity.

Besides being a product of economic prosperity, advertising contributes to prosperity. By dangling desirable commodities and services before mass audiences, advertising can inspire people to greater productivity, so that they can have more income to buy the things that are advertised.

Advertising also can introduce efficiency into the economy by allowing comparison shopping without in-person inspections of all the alternatives. Efficiencies also can result when advertising alerts consumers to superior and less costly products and services, which displace outdated, outmoded and inefficient offerings.

Said Howard Morgens when he was president of Procter & Gamble: "Advertising is the most effective and efficient way to sell to the consumer. If we should ever find better methods of selling our type of products to the consumer, we'll leave advertising and turn to these other methods." Veteran advertising executive David Ogilvy made the point this way: "Advertising is still the cheapest form of selling. It would cost you $25,000 to have salesmen call on a thousand homes. A television commercial can do it for $4.69." McGraw-Hill, which publishes trade magazines, has offered research that a salesperson's typical call costs $178, a letter $6.63, and a phone call $6.35. For 17 cents, says McGraw-Hill, an advertiser can reach a prospect through advertising. Although an advertisement does not close a sale, it introduces the product and makes the salesperson's job easier and quicker.

ADVERTISING AND DEMOCRACY

Advertising took off as a modern phenomenon in the United States more than elsewhere, which has given rise to a theory that advertising and democracy are connected. This theory notes that Americans, early in their history as a democracy, were required by their political system to hold individual opinions. They looked for information so that they could evaluate their leaders and vote on public policy.

Place-Based Media. Advertisers are dabbling with alternatives to the traditional media for delivering their messages. Newspapers stand to lose grocery advertising to in-store coupon dispensers like this Actmedia device, located right on the shelf near the advertised product. Advertisers using Actmedia pay to have the devices stocked with up to 1500 coupons a month.

This emphasis on individuality and reason paved the way for advertising: Just as people looked to the mass media for information on political matters, they also came to look to the media for information on buying decisions.

In authoritarian countries, on the other hand, people tend to look to strong personal leaders, not reason, for ideas to embrace. This, according to the theory, diminishes the demand for information in these nondemocracies, including the kind of information provided by advertising.

Advertising has another important role in democratic societies in generating most of the operating revenue for newspapers, magazines, television and radio. Without advertising, many of the media on which people rely for information and for the exchange of ideas on public issues would not exist as we know them.

ORIGINS OF ADVERTISING

STUDY PREVIEW   Advertising is the product of great forces that have shaped modern society, beginning with Gutenberg's movable type that made mass-produced messages possible. Without the mass media, there would be no vehicle to carry advertisements to mass audiences. Advertising also is a product of the democratic experience; of the Industrial Revolution and its spin-offs, including vast transportation networks and mass markets; and of continuing economic growth.

STEPCHILD OF TECHNOLOGY

Advertising is not a mass medium, but it relies on media to carry its messages. *Johannes Gutenberg*'s movable type, which permitted mass production of the printed word, made mass-produced advertising possible. First came flyers, then advertisements in newspapers and magazines. In the 1800s, when technology created high-speed presses that could produce enough copies for larger audiences, advertising used them to expand markets. With the introduction of radio, advertisers learned how to use electronic communication. Then came television.

Flyers were the first form of printed advertising. The British printer *William Caxton* issued the first printed advertisement in 1468 to promote one of his books. Early newspapers listed cargo arriving from Europe and invited readers to come, look and buy.

INDUSTRIAL REVOLUTION SPIN-OFFS

Steam-powered presses made large press runs possible. Factories drew great numbers of people to jobs within geographically small areas to which newspapers could be distributed quickly. The jobs also drew immigrants who were eager to learn—from newspapers as well as other sources—about their adopted country. Industrialization also created unprecedented wealth, giving even labourers a share of the new prosperity. A consumer economy was emerging, although it was primitive by today's standards.

A key to the success of the early penny press was that, at a penny a copy, its newspapers were affordable for almost everyone. Of course, production expenses exceeded a penny a copy. Just as the commercial media do today, the penny express looked to advertisers to pick up the slack. As Ben Day wrote in his first issue of the New York *Sun*: "The object of this paper is to lay before the public, at a price within the means of everyone, all the news of the day, and at the same time afford an advantageous medium for advertising." Day and imitator penny press publishers sought larger and larger circulations, knowing that merchants would see the value in buying space to reach so much buying power.

National advertising took root in the 1840s as railroads, another creation of the Industrial Revolution, spawned new networks for mass distribution of manufactured goods. National brands developed, and their producers looked to magazines, also delivered by rail, to promote sales. By 1869 the rail network linked the Atlantic and Pacific coasts.

PIONEER AGENCIES

By 1869 most merchants recognized the value of advertising, but they grumbled about the time it took away from their other work. In that grumbling, a young Philadelphia man sensed opportunity. *Wayland Ayer*, age 20, speculated that merchants, and even national manufacturers, would welcome a service company to help them create advertisements and place them in publications. Ayer feared, however, that his idea might not be taken seriously by potential clients because of his youth and inexperience. So when Wayland Ayer opened a shop, he borrowed his father's name for the shingle. The father was never part of the business, but the agency's name, *N. W. Ayer & Son*, gave young Ayer access to potential clients, and the first advertising agency was born.

The Ayer agency had forerunners in space brokers who, beginning in 1842 with *Volney Palmer*, bought large blocks of newspaper space at a discount, broke up the space, and resold it to advertisers at a markup, usually 25 percent. Space brokers, however, did not create advertisements. The Ayer agency not only created ads but also offered the array of services that agencies still offer clients today:

- Counsel on selling products and services.
- Design services, that is, actually creating advertisements and campaigns.
- Expertise on placing advertisements in advantageous media.

ADVERTISING AGENCIES

STUDY PREVIEW   Central in modern advertising are the agencies that create and place ads on behalf of their clients. These agencies are generally funded by the media in which they place ads. In effect, this makes agency services free to advertisers.

AGENCY STRUCTURE

Full-service advertising agencies conduct market research for their clients, design and produce advertisements, and choose the media in which the advertisement will run. The 500 leading agencies employ 120 000 people worldwide. The responsibilities of people who work at advertising agencies fall into these broad categories:

CREATIVE POSITIONS. This category includes copywriters, graphics experts and layout people. These creative people generally report to creative directors, art directors and copy supervisors.

CLIENT LIAISON. Most of these people are *account executives*, who work with clients. Account executives are responsible for understanding clients' needs, communicating those needs to the creative staff, and going back to clients with the creative staff's ideas.

MEDIA BUYING. Agency employees called *media buyers* determine the most effective media in which to place ads and then place them.

MARKET RESEARCH. Agency research staffs generate information on target consumer groups, data that can guide the creative and media staffs.

Many agencies also employ technicians and producers who turn ideas into camera-ready proofs, colourplates, videotape, and film and audio cartridges, although a lot of production work is contracted to specialty companies. Besides full-service agencies, there are creative boutiques, which specialize in preparing messages; media buying houses, which recommend strategy on placing ads; and other narrowly focused agencies.

AGENCY–MEDIA RELATIONS

Because agencies are so influential in deciding where advertisements are placed, the mass media give them a 15 percent discount. A newspaper that lists $100 per column inch as its standard rate charges agencies only $85. The agencies, however, bill their clients the full $100 and keep the 15 percent difference. This discount, actually a *commission system*, is available only to agencies. Besides the 15 percent commission, agencies receive an additional 2 percent discount from media units by paying cash for space and time. Because these media discounts are offered only to ad agencies, advertisers themselves would not receive them if they did their advertising work in-house.

The commission system causes a problem for agencies because their income is dependent on the frequency with which advertisements are placed. The fluctuations can be great, which makes it difficult for the agencies to meet their regular payroll. To even out their income, some agencies have shifted to a *fee system*.

Arrangements vary, but it is common for the client to be billed for the agency's professional time and research plus an agreed-on percentage. The fee system reduces gigantic fluctuations in agency income when clients change their media spending because revenue is derived from fees for services, not a percentage of space and time purchases. Another advantage of the fee system is that clients who pay fees for services are not suspicious that their agencies are being self-serving when they recommend bigger and bigger campaigns.

MEDIA ROLE IN CREATING ADVERTISING

Agencies are the most visible part of the advertising industry, but more advertising people work outside agencies than for agencies. The media themselves have advertising staffs that work with agency media buyers on placing advertisements. These staffs, comprised of *ad reps*, also design and produce material for smaller advertisers. Broadcast networks, magazines and radio and television stations also have their own sales staffs.

An extension of media advertising staffs are *brokers* who solicit national advertising and pass it on to their newspaper and station clients at a fee. Many broker agencies are specialized.

ADVERTISER ROLE IN ADVERTISING

Most companies, although they hire agencies for advertising services, have their own advertising expertise among the in-house people who develop marketing strategies. These companies look to ad agencies to develop the advertising campaigns that will help them meet their marketing goals. For some companies, the *advertising director* or *advertising manager* is the liaison between the company's marketing strategists and the ad agency's tacticians. Large companies with many products have in-house *brand managers* for this liaison.

Although it is not the usual pattern, some companies have in-house advertising departments and rely hardly at all on agencies.

PLACING ADVERTISEMENTS

STUDY PREVIEW   The placement of advertisements is a sophisticated business. Not only do different media have inherent advantages and disadvantages in reaching potential customers, but so do individual publications and broadcast outlets.

MEDIA ADVERTISING PLANS

Agencies create *media plans* to insure that advertisements reach the right target audience. Developing a media plan is no small task. Consider the number of media outlets available: daily newspapers, weeklies, general-interest magazines, radio stations and television stations. Other possibilities include direct mail, billboards, blimps, skywriting and even printing the company's name on pencils.

Media buyers have formulas for deciding which media are best for reaching potential customers. The most common formula is called *CPM*, short for *cost per thousand.* If airtime for a radio advertisement costs 7.2 cents per thousand listeners, and if space for a magazine advertisement costs 7.3 cents per thousand readers, and if both can be expected to reach equally appropriate target audiences, and if all other things are equal, radio—with the lower CPM—will be the medium of choice.

Media buyers have numerous sources of data to help them decide where advertisements can be placed for the best results. The *Audit Bureau of Circulations*, created by the newspaper industry in 1914, provides reliable information based on independent audits of the circulation of most newspapers. Survey organizations like *Nielsen* and the *Bureau of Broadcast Measurement* (BBM) conduct surveys on television and radio audiences. *Standard Rate and Data Service* publishes volumes of information on media audiences, circulations and advertising rates.

Placing advertisements involves more than just calculating CPM. Even if the numbers favour the *National Enquirer* over the *New Yorker*, advertisements for $80-an-ounce perfumes and world cruises would be wasted in the *Enquirer*, just as ads for high-grade barley seed would be pointless on an urban radio station, no matter how much less expensive on a CPM basis than a strong farm station in the Midwest.

MEDIA FOR ADVERTISING

Here are the pluses and minuses of major media as advertising vehicles:

NEWSPAPERS.   The hot relationship that media theorist Marshall McLuhan described between newspapers and their readers attracts advertisers. Newspaper readers are predisposed to consider information in advertisements seriously. Studies show that people, when ready to buy, look more to newspapers than to other media. Because newspapers are tangible, readers can refer back to advertisements just by picking up the paper a second time, which is not possible with ephemeral media like television and radio. Coupons are possible in newspapers. Newspaper readers tend to be older, better educated and higher earning than television and radio audiences. Space for newspaper ads usually can be reserved as late as 48 hours ahead, and 11th-hour changes are possible.

However, newspapers are becoming less valuable for reaching young adults with advertising messages. To the consternation of newspaper publishers, there has been an alarming drop among these people in recent years, and it appears that, unlike their parents, young adults are not picking up the newspaper habit as they mature.

Another drawback to newspapers as an advertising medium is that, being printed on cheap paper, the ads do not look as good as in slick magazines. Also, most people recycle their newspapers within a day or so, which means that, unlike magazines, there is not much opportunity for readers to happen upon an ad a second or third time.

MAGAZINES.   As another print medium, magazines have many of the advantages of newspapers, plus longer *shelf life*, an advertising term for the amount of time that an advertisement remains available to readers. Magazines remain in the home for weeks, sometimes months, which offers greater exposure to advertisements. People share magazines, which give them high *pass-along circulation*. Magazines are more prestigious, with slick paper and splashier graphics. With precise colour separations and enameled papers, magazine advertisements can be beautiful in ways that newspaper advertisements cannot. Magazines, specializing as they do, offer more narrowly defined audiences than newspapers.

On the downside, magazines require reservations for advertising space up to three months in advance. Opportunities for last-minute changes are limited, often impossible.

RADIO.   Radio stations with narrow formats offer easily identified target audiences. Time can be bought on short notice, with changes possible almost until airtime. Comparatively inexpensive, radio lends itself to repeated play of advertisements to drive home a message introduced in more expensive media like television. Radio lends itself to jingles that can contribute to a lasting image.

However, radio offers no opportunity for a visual display, although the images listeners create in their minds from audio suggestions can be more potent than those set out visually on television. Radio is a mobile medium that people carry with them. The extensive availability of radio is offset, however, by the fact that people tune in and out. Another negative is that many listeners are inattentive. Also, there is no shelf life.

TELEVISION.   As a moving and visual medium, television can offer unmatched impact, and the rapid growth of both network and local television advertising, far outpacing other media, indicates its effectiveness in reaching a diverse mass audience.

Drawbacks include the fact that production costs can be high. So are rates. The expense of television time has forced advertisers to go to shorter and shorter advertisements. A result is *ad clutter*, a phenomenon in which advertisements compete against each other and reduce the impact of all of them. Placing advertisements on television is a problem because demand outstrips the supply of slots, especially during prime hours. Slots for some hours are locked up months, even whole seasons, in advance. Because of the audience's diversity and size, targeting potential customers with any precision is difficult with television—with the exception of emerging narrowly focused cable services.

SATURATION ADVERTISING

An emerging twist on advertisement placement is *saturation advertising*, which Chris Whittle has pioneered through some of his alternative media publications, including the Larger Agenda books and his video services. With this approach, an advertiser selects a media vehicle that seems right for its products or services and then buys all the ad space that is available. Besides saturating a targeted audience, this approach blocks out the competition.

Asked how he would spend General Motors's $13 billion advertising budget through the 1990s, Whittle, applying the saturation idea, said he would advise GM to:

- Become sole sponsor of the summer and winter Olympics ($2.6 billion).
- Buy all the ad space for one week in every newspaper and magazine and on every television and radio station, as well as every billboard and milk carton, to advertise GM cars ($2 billion).
- Hire 8000 bright university graduates to take the 8 million people who bought Fords the previous year to a $100 lunch to explain the virtue of GM cars ($2 billion).

- Send the 8000 bright university grads back to their lunch partners three years later with a new GM car to drive for a week ($2 billion).
- Build showrooms in the 300 largest indoor malls and allow shoppers to inspect new cars without being hassled by salespeople and to book a test drive ($1 billion).
- Buy every commercial slot on Cable News Network for a whole year.
- Buy every commercial slot on ABC, CBS and NBC during the 25th anniversary of Earth Day in 1995 and sponsor environmental television programs ($200 million).
- Engage filmmaker Steven Spielberg to create an adventure trilogy to be shown at special screenings for the 10 million people who bought a Japanese car the previous year ($200 million).

PITCHING MESSAGES

STUDY PREVIEW When the age of mass production and mass markets arrived, common wisdom in advertising favored aiming at the largest possible audience of potential customers. These are called lowest common denominator approaches, and such advertisements tend to be heavy-handed, so that no one can possibly miss the point. Narrower pitches, going for segments of the mass audience, permit more deftness, subtlety and imagination.

IMPORTANCE OF BRANDS

A challenge for advertising people is the modern-day reality that mass-produced products aimed at large markets are essentially alike: Toothpaste is toothpaste is toothpaste. When a product is virtually identical to the competition, how can one toothpaste-maker move more tubes?

BRAND NAMES. By trial and error, tactics were devised in the late 1800s to set similar products apart. One tactic, promoting a product as a *brand name*, aims to make a product a household word. When it is successful, a brand name becomes almost the generic identifier, like *Coke* for cola and *Kleenex* for facial tissue.

Techniques of successful brand name advertising came together in the 1890s for an English product, Pears' soap. A key element in the campaign was *multimedia saturation*. Advertisements for Pears' were everywhere, in newspapers and magazines and on posters, vacant walls, fences, buses and street posts. Redundancy hammered home the brand name. "Good morning. Have you used Pears' today?" became a good-natured greeting among Britons that was still being repeated 50 years later. Each repetition reinforced the brand name.

BRAND IMAGE. *David Ogilvy*, who headed the Ogilvy & Mather agency, developed the *brand image* in the 1950s. Ogilvy's advice: "Give your product a first-class ticket through life."

Ogilvy created shirt advertisements with the distinguished Baron Wrangell, who really was a European nobleman, wearing a black eye patch—and a Hathaway shirt. The classy image was reinforced with the accoutrements around Wrangell: exquisite models of sailing ships, antique weapons, silver dinnerware. To some, seeing Wrangell's setting, the patch suggested all kinds of exotica. Perhaps he had lost an eye in a romantic duel or a sporting accident.

Explaining the importance of image, Ogilvy once said: "Take whisky. Why do

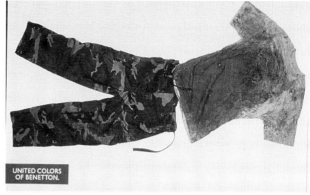

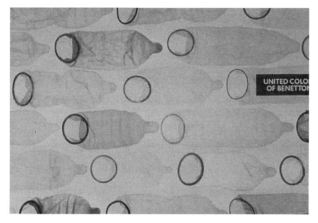

Benetton with Message. For years Benetton, the global casual clothing retailer, has run controversial ads drawing attention to social issues more than the company's products. A 1994 campaign in 25 countries featured a bloody military uniform from Bosnia, recovered from the family of a young man who died in combat. It was a haunting photo. Oliviero Toscani, Benetton's creative director who shoots the company's ads, says the goal is to position Benetton as a socially conscious marketer. The attention-getting 1991 "flying condoms" ad, said Toscani, was aimed to combat the disease AIDS. Even so, in the United States, *Self, Mademoiselle* and *Cosmopolitan* rejected it for fear of offending readers. There were objections also with a follow-up campaign that Benetton claimed celebrated love, but which some cautious publications thought trod too closely on taboos. Some Benetton ads are quite *entropic* and are excellent texts to decode using semiotic techniques.

Oliviero Toscani

First-Class Ticket. In one of his most noted campaigns, advertising genius David Ogilvy featured the distinguished chair of the company that bottled Schweppes mixers in classy locations. Said Ogilvy: "It pays to give products an image of quality—a first-class ticket." Ogilvy realized how advertising creates impressions. "Nobody wants to be seen using shoddy products," he said.

The man from Schweppes is here

Meet Commander Edward Whitehead, Schweppesman Extraordinary from London, England, where the house of Schweppes has been a great institution since 1794.

Commander Whitehead has come to these United States to make sure that every drop of Schweppes Quinine Water bottled here has the original flavor which has long made Schweppes

the only mixer for an authentic Gin and Tonic.

He imports the original Schweppes elixir, and the secret of Schweppes unique carbonation is locked in his brief case. "Schwesppervescence," says the Commander, "lasts the whole drink through."

It took Schweppes almost a hundred years to bring the flavor of their Quinine Water to its

present bittersweet perfection. But it will take you only thirty seconds to mix it with ice and gin in a highball glass. Then, gentle reader, you will bless the day you read these words.

P.S. If your favorite store or bar doesn't yet have Schweppes, drop a card to us and we'll make the proper arrangements. Address Schweppes, 30 East 60th Street, New York City.

some people choose Jack Daniel's, while others choose Grand Dad or Taylor? Have they tried all three and compared the taste? Don't make me laugh. The reality is that these three brands have different images which appeal to different kinds of people. It isn't the whisky they choose, it's the image. The brand image is 90 percent of what the distiller has to sell. Give people a taste of Old Crow, and tell them it's Old Crow. Then give them another taste of Old Crow, but tell them it's Jack Daniel's. Ask them which they prefer. They'll think the two drinks are quite different. They are tasting images."

LOWEST COMMON DENOMINATOR

Early brand-name campaigns were geared to the largest possible audience, sometimes called an *LCD*, or *lowest common denominator*, approach. The term "LCD" is adapted from mathematics. To reach an audience that includes members with IQs of 100, the pitch cannot exceed their level of understanding, even if some people in the audience have IQs of 150. The opportunity for deft touches and even cleverness is limited by the fact they might be lost on some potential customers.

Lowest common denominator advertising is best epitomized in contemporary advertising by *USP*, short for *unique selling proposition*, a term coined by *Rosser Reeves* of the giant Ted Bates agency in the 1960s. Reeves's prescription was simple: Create a benefit of the product, even if from thin air, and then tout the benefit authoritatively and repeatedly as if the competition doesn't have it. One early USP campaign flaunted that Schlitz beer bottles were "washed with live steam." The claim sounded good—who would want to drink from dirty bottles? However, the fact was that every brewery used steam to clean reusable bottles before filling them again. Furthermore, what is "live steam"? Although the implication of a competitive edge was hollow, it was done dramatically and pounded home with emphasis, and it sold beer. Just as hollow as a competitive advantage was the USP claim for Colgate toothpaste: "Cleans Your Breath While It Cleans Your Teeth."

Perhaps to compensate for a lack of substance, many USP ads are heavy-handed. Most people have heard about fast-fast-fast relief from headache remedies or that heartburn relief is spelled R-O-L-A-I-D-S. USP can be unappealing, as acknowledged even by the chairman of Warner-Lambert, which makes Rolaids, who once laughed that his company owed the American people an apology for insulting their intelligence over and over with Bates's USP slogans. Warner-Lambert was also laughing all the way to the bank over the USP-spurred success of Rolaids, Efferdent, Listermint and Bubblicious.

A unique selling proposition, however, need be neither hollow nor insulting. *Leo Burnett*, founder of the agency bearing his name, refined the USP concept by insisting that the unique point be real. For Maytag, Burnett took the company's slight advantage in reliability and dramatized it with the lonely Maytag repairman.

Market Segments

Rather than pitching to the lowest common denominator, advertising executive *Jack Trout* developed the idea of *positioning*. Trout worked to establish product identities that appealed not to the whole audience but to a specific audience. The cowboy image for Marlboro cigarettes, for example, established a macho attraction beginning in 1958. Later, something similar was done with Virginia Slims, aimed at women.

Positioning helps distinguish products from all the LCD clamour and noise. Advocates of positioning note that there are more and more advertisements and that they are becoming noisier and noisier. Ad clutter, as it is called, drowns out individual advertisements. With positioning, the appeal is focused and caters to audience segments, and it need not be done in such broad strokes.

Campaigns based on positioning have included:

- Johnson & Johnson's baby oil and baby shampoo, which were positioned as an adult product by advertisements featuring athletes.
- Alka-Seltzer, once a hangover and headache remedy, which was positioned as an upmarket product for stress relief among health-conscious, success-driven people.

Redundancy Techniques

You'll remember from Chapter 1 that a redundant message is one that's easy to decode. Advertising people learned the importance of *redundancy* early on. To be effective, an advertising message must be repeated, perhaps thousands of times.

Redundancy, however, is expensive. To increase effectiveness at less cost, advertisers use several techniques:

- **Barrages.** Scheduling advertisements in intensive bursts called *flights* or *waves.*
- **Bunching.** Promoting a product in a limited period, like running advertisements for school supplies in late August and September.
- **Trailing.** Running condensed versions of advertisements after the original has been introduced, as AT&T did with its hostility advertisements on workplace tensions beginning in 1987. Powerful 60-second advertisements introduced the campaign, followed in a few weeks by 15-second versions. Automakers introduce new models with multipage magazine spreads, following with single-page placements.
- **Multimedia Trailing.** Using less expensive media to reinforce expensive advertisements. Relatively cheap drive-time radio in major markets is a favourite follow-through to expensive television advertisements created for major events like the Super Bowl.

CONGLOMERATION AND GLOBALIZATION

STUDY PREVIEW A tremendous consolidation in the advertising business occurred in the 1980s. Agencies bought agencies, and some of the resulting super agencies continued their acquisitions abroad. Today, these global agencies are beset with problems that came with the early 1990s worldwide recession.

ACQUISITION BINGE

In the late 1970s under U.S. President Carter, the American government backed off on antitrust actions and other regulatory controls, paving the way for a great number of mergers and consolidations in American business. Advertising was no exception, and many agencies swallowed up others. The Reagan and Bush administrations continued the hands-off-business approach into the 1980s and 1990s, and dominant big businesses, including major advertising agencies, became even more so.

The demassification of the mass media was also a factor. Several big agencies, whose favoured choice for most clients had been network television for 40 years, realized that the network audience was fragmenting, and they had to find a new way to do business. These agencies lacked in-house expertise at direct-mail advertising and other emerging advertising media, so they began buying smaller, specialized ad shops, successful regional agencies, and public relations companies to fill in the gaps.

While U.S. agencies were consolidating, there was also an international consolidation occurring that wiped out the traditional dominance of U.S. advertising agencies abroad. Not only did some foreign agencies like Dentsu of Japan become giant multinational organizations, but an upstart London agency, Saatchi & Saatchi, went on an acquisition binge that absorbed several U.S. agencies. The result is fewer but bigger agencies.

This globalization of the advertising business had detractors who were concerned that the new super agencies, all based in leading Western societies, would further diminish indigenous values in less developed countries under the steamroller they called "cultural imperialism." Many ad people saw the situation differently, arguing that people buy only what they want and that it would be the choice of

Third World people whether to respond to advertising that originates with multinational advertising agencies. Also, noted advertising guru David Ogilvy, successful advertising always is adapted to local conditions: "The advertising campaigns for these brands will emanate from the headquarters of multinational agencies but will be adapted to respect differences in local culture." If local appeals and themes are necessary to sell a product, those are the ones that will be employed.

Some of the leading ad agencies in Canada are part of conglomerates:

- The largest agency in Canada, BBDO of Canada, is a subsidiary of Omnicom of New York. Omnicom's annual income is close to $1.8 billion.
- Ogilvy and Mather is part of the WWP Group, a worldwide conglomerate that has its headquarters in London, England. Ogilvy and Mather's yearly income is $2.8 billion, making it the largest ad agency in the world.
- Young and Rubicam's head office is in New York. Worldwide, they earn about $1 billion a year.

AGENCY CONSOLIDATION PROBLEMS

The agency consolidation of the 1980s was driven mostly by two factors. First, agencies that were turning huge profits had money to spend on acquisitions, and other profitable agencies were attractive acquisition targets. Second, banks and other lending institutions were willing to finance highly leveraged acquisitions. The pace of acquisitions came to a halt in the worldwide recession that developed in 1990, and some of the new super agencies began to unravel.

With the recession, many manufacturers, retailers and other advertisers cut back on spending. Agency revenue plummeted. As a result, the source of money for super agencies to repay loans disappeared. Some agencies shut down subsidiary

MEDIA DATABANK

Top 10 Advertising Agencies in Canada

Here are the largest Canadian advertising agencies ranked by their gross revenue. Many of these are international companies.

Agency	Major Clients	Gross Revenue
BBDO Canada	Apple, Kraft, Molson	$54.7 million
Cossette Communication/Marketing	Bell Canada, Saturn Saab Isuzu, Provigo	48.7 million
MacLaren McCann Canada	Black and Decker, Royal Bank, Coca-Cola	40.0 million
Young and Rubicam Group of Companies Limited	Colgate, Ford, Xerox	31.7 million
Leo Burnett	Cadbury, Fruit of the Loom, VISA	26.1 million
Ogilvy and Mather (Canada)	Eaton's, *Financial Post*, Scott's Hospitality	26.0 million
FCB Canada	Air Canada, Royal Canadian Mint	24.9 million
BCP Canada	Canada Post, TVA, Canadian Airlines International	24.7 million
Vickers and Benson	BBS, Bank of Montreal, M & M Meat Shops	16.8 million
Palmer Jarvis Communications	Clearly Canadian Beverages, Manitoba Telephones, Nabob	16.0 million

(Source: *Marketing* Magazine's 1996 Agency Ranking, June 24, 1996)

agencies or consolidated them. There were massive layoffs, and businesses were scaled back. Some agencies bought time to get their finances back in order under the auspices of bankruptcy courts. Even still, the prospects for some of these troubled agencies remain unsure.

ADVERTISING REGULATION

STUDY PREVIEW The "buyer beware" underpinning of much of 19th-century advertising has given way to "seller beware." Today, advertising is regulated on many fronts, by the media that carry advertisements, by the advertising industry itself and by governmental agencies.

GATEKEEPING REGULATION BY MEDIA

A dramatic reversal in thinking about advertising has occurred in the 20th century. The earlier *caveat emptor* mindset, "buyer beware," tolerated extravagant claims. Anybody who believed that the same elixir could cure dandruff, halitosis and cancer deserved to be conned, or so went the thinking. Over the years, due partly to the growing consumer movement, the thinking changed to *caveat venditor*, "seller beware," placing the onus on the advertiser to avoid misleading claims and to demonstrate the truth of claims.

In advertising's early days, newspapers and magazines skirted the ethics question posed by false advertisements by saying their pages were open to all advertisers. Under growing pressure, publications sometimes criticized dubious advertisements editorially, but most did not ban them. *Edward Bok*, who made *Ladies' Home Journal* a runaway success in the 1890s, crusaded against dishonest advertising. In one exposé on Lydia E. Pinkham's remedies for "female maladies," Bok reported that Lydia, to whom women readers were invited in advertisements to write for advice, had been dead for 22 years. Yet the advertisements continued.

In 1929, NBC adopted a code of ethics to preclude false or exaggerated claims. Other networks followed. At the peak of the networks' concern about broadcast standards, it was estimated that half the commercials for products were turned away for violating network codes. Codes for broadcast advertising have come and gone over the years, all voluntary with stations that chose to subscribe.

The print media also have seen a variety of industry-wide codes, all voluntary. Most publications spurn misleading advertisements. Many university and community college newspapers refuse advertisements from term-paper services. Some metropolitan papers turn away advertisements for pornographic movies.

A case can be made that the media do not go far enough in exercising their prerogative to ban dubious advertisements. Critics argue that on nettling questions, such as the morality of printing ads for carcinogenic tobacco products, with major revenue at stake, many newspapers and magazines sidestep a moral judgment, run the advertisements and reap the revenue. The critics note, for example, that most commercial broadcasters ran cigarette advertisements until the federal government intervened. The media, so goes the argument, are too devoted to profits to do all the regulating they should.

INDUSTRY SELF-REGULATION

The advertising industry itself has numerous organizations that try, through ethics codes and moral suasion, to eradicate falsity and deception. Besides the explicit purposes of these self-policing mechanisms, their existence can be cited by advertising people to argue that their industry is able to deal with misdeeds itself with a minimum of government regulation.

THE CANADIAN ADVERTISING FOUNDATION   The Canadian Advertising Foundation (CAF) is a national industry association committed to assuring the integrity and viability of advertising through industry self-regulation. Its members include advertisers, media organizations, and suppliers to the advertising sector.

CAF administers the *Canadian Code of Advertising Standards*, first published in 1963, as the principal instrument of advertising self-regulation. Through its national and regional Advertising Standards Councils, consumer complaints about advertising are accepted, reviewed, and adjudicated. CAF also administers other advertising self-regulatory codes; provides broadcast advertising commercial clearance services for food and non-alcoholic beverage, cosmetic, and child-directed advertising, and broadcast and print clearances for tobacco advertising; provides consultative services to the advertising industry; and administers the industry's *Trade Dispute Procedure*.

THE CODE

The *Canadian Code of Advertising Standards* has been approved and is supported by all participating organizations, and is designed to help set and maintain standards of honesty, truth, accuracy, fairness and taste in advertising. ...

No advertising shall be prepared or knowingly exhibited by the participating organizations which contravenes this Code of Standards.

The clauses should be adhered to both in letter and in spirit. Advertisers and advertising agencies must be prepared to substantiate their claims promptly to the Council upon request.

1. Accuracy, Clarity

    (a) Advertisements must not contain inaccurate or deceptive claims, statements, illustrations, or representations, either direct or implied, with regard to price, availability or performance of a product or service. In assessing the truthfulness and accuracy of a message, the concern is not with the intent of the sender or precise legality of the presentation. Rather, the focus is on the message as received or perceived, that is, the general impression conveyed by the advertisement.

    (b) Advertisements must not omit relevant information in a manner which is deceptive.

    (c) All pertinent details of an advertised offer must be clearly stated.

    (d) Disclaimers or asterisked information must not contradict more prominent aspects of the message and should be located and presented in such a manner as to be clearly visible.

2. Disguised Advertising Techniques

No advertisement shall be presented in a format or style which conceals its commercial intent.

3. Price Claims

    (a) No advertisement shall include deceptive price claims or discounts, unrealistic price comparisons or exaggerated claims as to worth or value. "Regular Price," "Suggested Retail Price," "Manufacturer's List Price," and "Fair Market Value" are deceptive terms when used by an advertiser to indicate a savings, unless they represent prices at which a reasonable number of the item was actually sold within the preceding six months in the market place where the advertisement appears.

    (b) Where price discounts are offered, qualifying statements such as "up to," "XX off," etc., must be in easily readable type, in close proximity to the prices quoted, and, where practical, legitimate regular prices must be included.

    (c) Prices quoted in advertisements in Canadian media, other than in Canadian funds, must be so identified.

4. Bait and Switch

Advertisements must not misrepresent the consumer's opportunity to purchase the goods and services at the terms presented. If supply of the sale item is limited, or the seller can fulfil only limited demand, this must be clearly stated in the advertisement.

5. Guarantees

No advertisement shall offer a guarantee or warranty, unless the guarantee or warranty is fully explained as to conditions and limits and the name of the guarantor or warrantor is provided, or it is indicated where such information may be obtained.

6. Comparative Advertising

Advertisements must not discredit, disparage or attack unfairly other products, services, advertisements, or companies or exaggerate the nature or importance of competitive differences.

7. Testimonials

Testimonials, endorsations, or representations of opinion or preference must reflect the genuine, reasonably current opinion of the individual(s), group or organization making such representations, and must be based upon adequate information about or experience with the product or service being advertised, and must not otherwise be deceptive.

8. Professional or Scientific Claims

Advertisements must not distort the true meaning of statements made by professionals or scientific authorities. Advertising claims must not imply they have a scientific basis which they do not truly possess. Any scientific, professional or authoritative claims or statements must be applicable to the Canadian context, unless otherwise clearly stated.

9. Imitation

No advertiser shall imitate the copy, slogans, or illustrations of another advertiser in such a manner as to mislead the consumer.

10. Safety

Advertisements must not display a disregard for public safety or depict situations which might encourage unsafe or dangerous practices, particularly when portraying products in normal use.

11. Exploitation of Persons with Disabilities

Advertisements must not hold out false hope in the form of a cure or relief, either on a temporary or permanent basis, for persons who have disabilities.

12. Superstition and Fears

Advertisements must not exploit superstitions or play upon fears to mislead the consumer.

13. Advertising to Children

Advertising which is directed to children must not exploit their credulity, lack of experience, or their sense of loyalty, and must not present information or illustrations which might result in their physical, emotional or moral harm.

Child-directed advertising in the broadcast media is separately regulated by the Broadcast Code for Advertising to Children, also administered by the Canadian Advertising Foundation. Advertising to children in Quebec is prohibited by the Quebec Consumer Protection Act.

14. Advertising to Minors

Products prohibited from sale to minors must not be advertised in such a way as to appeal particularly to persons under legal age and people featured in advertisements for such products must be, and clearly be seen to be, adults under the law.

15. Taste, Public Decency

It is recognized that standards of taste are subjective and vary widely from person to person and community to community, and are, indeed, subject to constant change. Advertising must not present demeaning or derogatory portrayals of individuals or groups; must not exploit violence, sexuality, children, the customs, convictions or characteristics of religious or ethno-cultural groups, persons with disabilities or any other person, group or institution in a manner which is offensive to generally prevailing standards.

One of the codes published by the CAF deals with sexism in advertising. The following is from the CAF's *Gender Portrayal Guidelines*, published in 1994:

1. Authority

Advertising should strive to provide an equal representation of women and men in roles of authority both for the characters within the actual advertising scenario and when representing the advertiser through announcers, voice-overs, experts and on-camera authorities.

Comment:

While advertisers have made noticeable progress in providing equal representation of men and women in roles of authority, some disparity still exists. In particular, individual advertisers should give equal consideration to women in the area of voice-overs.

2. Decision-Making

Women and men should be portrayed equally as single decision-makers for all purchases including big-ticket items. Where joint decision-making is reflected, men and women should be portrayed as equal participants in the decision-making process whether in the workplace or at home.

Comment:

Both women and men are active decision-makers for all categories of personal and household purchases as well as in the workforce. Advertising should reflect this reality.

3. Sexuality

Advertising should avoid the inappropriate use or exploitation of sexuality of both women and men.

Comment:

Exploiting is interpreted as a presentation in which sexuality is on display merely for the gratification of others.

When sexuality is relevant to the product being advertised or is part of the creative scenario, it should be treated with sensitivity and respect for the individual(s).

Advertising should specifically avoid the following:

(i) Sexualization

There is nothing wrong with positive, relevant sexuality in advertising which portrays a person in control of and celebrating her/his sexuality. However, people must not be portrayed as primarily sexual or defined by their sexuality. Clothes, behaviours, positions and poses, camera angles, camera as voyeur, language, audio track, and/or product placement can all contribute, implicitly or explicitly, to sexualization.

(ii) Sexualization of Children

Boys and girls under 16 must not be portrayed as displaying adult sexual characteristics. Similarly, adult women must not be portrayed as girls or with child-like characteristics while maintaining adult sexual characteristics.

(iii) Gender Role Stereotype

Social and sexual interactions must portray women and men as equals and must not reinforce stereotypes, such as, male dominant/female submissive.

(iv) Irrelevant Associations

a) Using or displaying a woman's sexuality in order to sell a product that has no relation to sexuality is by definition sexually exploitative.

b) Advertising must avoid the exploitation of nudity and the irrelevant segmentation of body parts.

(v) Sexual Harassment
Advertising must not portray sexual harassment as acceptable or normal behaviour in either covert or overt ways, and should avoid representing women as prey or objects of uncontrolled desire.

(vi) Objectification and Commodization
People must not be sexually portrayed as objects, toys, animals or with animal-like characteristics. Nor should products be attributed with negative gender stereotypical characteristics.

4. Violence
Neither sex should be portrayed as exerting domination over the other by means of overt or implied threats, or actual force.

Comment:
   Men and women should be portrayed equally as in control of their person and their surroundings. Images and texts which imply domination, aggression or violence, or enjoyment of the same, should not be used.

5. Diversity
Advertising should portray both women and men in the full spectrum of diversity and as equally competent in a wide range of activities both inside and outside the home.

Comment:
   Today in Canadian society there is no single contemporary family structure. Men and women take part in a broad variety of responsibilities, occupations, lifestyles and activities. This diversity should be portrayed in advertising.
   Further, women and men of various ages, appearances and backgrounds should be considered when creating advertising.

6. Language
Advertising should avoid language that misrepresents, offends or excludes women or men.

Comment:
   The equality of the sexes should be reflected through the use of gender neutral language, e.g. fire fighter instead of fireman and synthetic instead of man-made. Language should also reflect the equal dignity of both genders e.g. men and women rather than men and girls; and must not include pejorative or inappropriate terms.

(Codes reprinted by permission of CAF)

Consumers may complain to the CAF if they think an advertisement doesn't comply with current codes. In 1995, 764 complaints were handled by the CAF, down from 908 in 1994. Most of these ads fell under the "Taste and Public Decency" clause. Of the 764 complaints, 170 were upheld, citing violations of the Code of Advertising Standards; 13 complaints about gender portrayal were also upheld.
   Other industry codes administered by the CAF include:

- Broadcast Code for Advertising to Children.
- Agriculture and Agri-food Canada's Guide to Food Labelling and Advertising.
- Advertising Code of Standards for Cosmetics, Toiletries and Fragrances.
- The Tobacco Industry Voluntary Packaging and Advertising Code.

Miracle Cures. Potions and gizmos for curing just about whatever ails you led to government regulation of advertising.

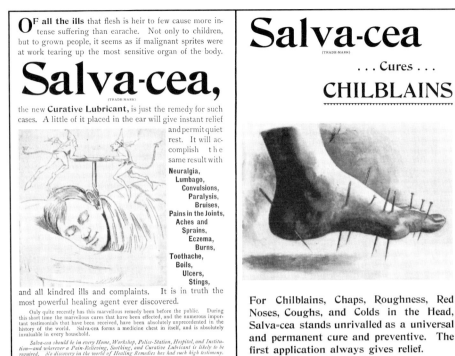

UNRESOLVED PROBLEMS AND ISSUES

STUDY PREVIEW   People are exposed to such a blur of ads that advertisers worry that their messages are being lost in the clutter. Some advertising people see more creativity as the answer so people will want to see and read ads, but there is evidence that creativity can work against an ad's effectiveness.

ADVERTISING CLUTTER

Leo Bogart of the Newspaper Advertising Bureau noted that the number of advertising messages doubled through the 1960s and 1970s, and except for the recession at the start of the 1990s, the trend continues. This proliferation of advertising creates a problem—too many ads. CBS squeezed so many ads into its coverage of the 1992 winter Olympics that some viewers felt the network regarded the games as a sideshow. Even in regular programming, the frequency of ads has led advertisers to fret that their individual ads are being lost in the clutter. The problem has been exacerbated by the shortening of ads from 60 seconds in the early days of television to today's widely used 15-second format.

At one time, the National Association of Broadcasters in the U.S. had a code limiting the quantity of commercials. The Federal Communications Commission let station owners know that it supported the NAB code, but in 1981, as part of the Reagan administration's deregulation, the FCC backed away from any limitation. In 1983 a federal court threw out the NAB limitation as a monopolistic practice.

Ad clutter is less an issue in the print media. Many people buy magazines and newspapers to look at ads as part of the comparative shopping process. Even so, some advertisers, concerned that their ads are overlooked in massive editions, such as a seven-pound metro Sunday newspaper or a 700-page bridal magazine, are looking for alternative means to reach potential customers in a less cluttered environment.

The clutter that marks much of commercial television and radio today may be alleviated as the media fragment further. Not only will demassification create more specialized outlets, such as narrowly focused cable television services, but there will be new media. Videodiscs, for example, can be delivered by mail, and videotext can be called up on home computer screens. The result will be advertising aimed at narrower audiences.

EXCESSES IN CREATIVITY

Advertisers are reviewing whether creativity is as effective an approach as hard sell. *Harry McMahan* studied Clio Awards for creativity in advertising and discovered that 36 agencies that produced 81 winners of the prestigious awards for advertisements had either lost the winning account or gone out of business.

Predicts advertising commentator E. B. Weiss: "Extravagant license for creative people will be curtailed." The future may hold more heavy-handed pitches, perhaps with over-the-counter regimens not only promising fast-fast-fast relief but also spelling it out in all caps and boldface with exclamation marks: **F-A-S-T! F-A-S-T! F-A-S-T!!!**

Favourite Print Advertisements. Video Storyboard Tests Inc. interviews more than 22 000 people for its annual list of the most memorable advertisements. Guess was among several print media winners announced in 1993.

AN OVERRATED MARKETING TOOL?

Long-held assumptions about the effectiveness of advertising itself are being questioned. *Gerald Tellis*, a researcher, put together a sophisticated statistical model that found that people are relatively unmoved by television advertisements in making brand choices, especially on mundane everyday products like toilet paper and laundry detergents.

Tellis's conclusions began with consumer purchasing studies. Not surprisingly, considering its self-interest, the advertising industry has challenged Tellis's studies. Meanwhile, Tellis and other scholars have continued the studies.

The jury is still out on whether Tellis is correct in his doubts about television advertising, on whether the style of advertising makes a difference, or on whether it is just ads for generic products, such as toilet paper and detergent, that are virtually identical and that fail to influence consumers when they are in the store picking products off the shelves.

CHAPTER WRAP-UP

The role of advertising in mass media cannot be overstated. Without advertising, most media would go out of business. In fact, in the 1960s, when advertisers switched to television from the giant general-interest magazines, those magazines went under. Today, the rapid expansion of cable networks is possible only because advertisers are buying time on the new networks to reach potential customers. In one sense, advertisers subsidize readers, viewers and listeners who pay only a fraction of the cost of producing publications and broadcasts. The bulk of the cost is paid by advertisers, who are willing to do so to make their pitches to potential customers who, coincidentally, are media consumers.

Besides underwriting the mass media, advertising is vital for a prosperous, growing consumer economy. It triggers demand for goods and services, and it enables people to make wise choices by providing information on competing products. The result is efficiency in the marketplace, which frees more capital for expansion. This all speaks to an intimate interrelationship involving advertising in a democratic and capitalistic society.

Today, as democracy and capitalism are reintroduced in Central and Eastern Europe, advertising can be expected to have an essential role in fostering new consumer economies. Advertising agencies will be called on for their expertise to develop campaigns for goods and services. This process will provide a greater revenue base for the mass media in these countries, which will result in better journalistic and entertainment content.

QUESTIONS FOR REVIEW

1. Why is advertising essential in a capitalistic society?
2. Trace the development of advertising since the time of Johannes Gutenberg.
3. What is the role of advertising agencies?
4. Why do some advertisements appear in some media and not other media?
5. What are the major tactics used in advertising? Who devised each one?
6. How do advertising people use psychology and research to shape their messages?

7. What are the advantages and the problems of the globalization of the advertising industry?
8. Does advertising still follow the "buyer beware" dictum?
9. What are some problems and unanswered issues in advertising?
10. What are the basic differences between content and semiotic analysis?
11. What are some of the codes of the Canadian Advertising Foundation?

QUESTIONS FOR CRITICAL THINKING

1. How does the development of modern advertising relate to Johannes Gutenberg's technological innovation? To the Industrial Revolution? To long-distance mass transportation? To mass marketing?
2. Why does advertising flourish more in democratic than in autocratic societies? In a capitalistic more than in a controlled economy? In a prosperous society?
3. What were the contributions to advertising of Volney Palmer, Wayland Ayer, Rosser Reeves, Jack Trout, Ernest Dichter, Wilson Bryan Key and David Ogilvy?
4. What are the responsibilities of advertising account executives, copywriters, media buyers, researchers, brand managers, ad reps, brokers?
5. What are the advantages of the commission system for advertising agency revenue? Of the fee system? The disadvantages of both?
6. Describe these advertising tactics: brand-name

promotion, unique selling proposition, lowest common denominator approach, positioning and redundancy.
7. Ad clutter is an emerging problem. How is it a problem? What can be done about it?
8. Develop a content analysis of a single issue of a magazine. In terms of the first-order signifieds, look at signs that are easily quantifiable, like gender or race.
9. Using the same magazine as you used in question 8, develop a semiotic analysis of one or two of the ads. How do the signs work to create connotation? What meanings lie in the ad's connotations that were missed in the content analysis?
10. Try using Pollock's model of gender reversal in advertising. Describe how the signified changes when you change the signifier; i.e., replace a man with a woman or vice versa.

FOR FURTHER LEARNING

Mary Billard. "Heavy Metal Goes on Trial." *Rolling Stone* (July 12–26, 1990):582–583 double issue, 83–88, 132. Billard examines the events leading to a shotgun suicide of a Nevada youth whose family claimed that subliminal messages in a Judas Priest song led him to do it.

Stephen Fox. *The Mirror Makers: A History of American Advertising and Its Creators* (Morrow, 1984).

Wilson Bryan Key. *Subliminal Seduction: Ad Media's Manipulation of a Not So Innocent America* (New American Library, 1972). Sex appeal has a special dimension for Key, who argues that an advertisement for Gilbey's gin

has the letters s-e-x carefully carved in ice cubes in an expensive *Time* magazine advertisement. Key offers no corroborating evidence in this and later books, *Media Sexploitation* (New American Library, 1976), *The Clam-Plate Orgy: And Other Subliminal Techniques for Manipulating Your Behavior* (New America, 1980) and *The Age of Manipulation* (Holt, 1989).

Otto Kleppner, Thomas Russell and Glenn Verrill. *Advertising Procedure*, 8th ed. (Prentice Hall, 1990).

William Liess, Stephen Klein and Sut Jhally. *Social Communication in Advertising* (Nelson Canada, 1990). The authors provide a broadly based, theoretical overview of advertising in North America.

Bob Levenson. *Bill Bernbach's Book: A History of the Advertising That Changed the History of Advertising* (Random House, 1987). Levenson focuses on the "creative revolution" typified in the Bernbach agency's "Think Small" Volkswagen advertisements of the 1950s and early 1960s.

Nancy Millman. *Emperors of Adland: Inside the Advertising Revolution* (Warner Books, 1988). This fast-paced book by a Chicago newspaper columnist traces the mergers of advertising agencies in the 1980s and questions whether mega-agencies are good for advertising.

David Ogilvy. *Confessions of an Advertising Man* (Atheneum, 1963). The man who created a leading agency explains his philosophy in this autobiography. In *Ogilvy on Advertising* (Vintage, 1985), Ogilvy offers lively advice about effective advertising.

Griselda Pollock. "What's Wrong with Images of Women?" in *Screen Education* 24 (Autumn, 1977).

Anthony Pratkanis and Elliot Aronson. *Age of Propaganda: The Everyday Use and Abuse of Persuasion* (W. H. Freeman, 1992). Pratkanis and Aronson, both scholars, provide a particularly good, lively status report on "subliminal sorcery."

Michael Schudson. *Advertising: The Uneasy Persuasion: Its Dubious Impact on American Society* (Basic Books, 1984). Schudson, a media theorist, challenges the effectiveness of advertising while exploring the ideological impact of advertisements.

FOR KEEPING UP TO DATE

Weekly trade journals are *Advertising Age* and *AdWeek*. Scholarly publications include *Journal of Marketing Research* and *Journal of Advertising*. The *New York Times* regularly reports on the industry.

Marketing Magazine is an excellent trade journal that looks at marketing advertising and public relations from a Canadian perspective.

MASS MEDIA
Effects on Individuals

Most media scholars today believe the effects of the mass media generally are cumulative over time

Individuals choose some mass media over others for the satisfactions they anticipate

Individuals have substantial control over mass media effects on them

Mass media have a significant role helping children learn society's expectations of them

Scholars differ on whether media-depicted violence triggers aggressive behaviour

The mass media set the agenda for what people are interested in and talk about

The mass media can work against citizen involvement in political processes

M E D I A   I N   T H E O R Y

Agressive Reaction

Has your stomach ever tightened at a scary moment during a movie? Your skin tingled? These are the responses that the moviemaker, an expert at effective storytelling, had intended. They work, however, only if the moviemaker has succeeded at sweeping you into the story line. This process of getting "into" the story requires suspending disbelief. It is not unique to movies. In all fiction, no matter what the medium, the storyteller needs to move the audience from knowing the story is fictitious, which is disbelief, to going along with it and being affected, which is the suspending of disbelief. In a movie, you have suspended disbelief if you grab the arm of the person next to you to survive a frightening turn of events on the screen, or if you scream, or gasp, or cry.

There is no question that the media affect people, but there is considerable debate about whether these effects are momentary or long term and whether these effects can prompt people into antisocial behaviour. Some outspoken media critics charge that media-depicted male violence against women leads to rape on the streets and at home. There is wide concern that children are especially susceptible to violence on television and the movies and imitate media violence in their own lives. What are your own experiences with the effects of media depictions of antisocial behaviour?

- Have you ever been inspired to an antisocial act because you saw it on the screen?
- Do you know anyone who has?
- Do you worry that children might be affected by media depictions of violence in ways that you never were?
- Does concern for your own safety increase after seeing violence depicted on the media?

These are the kinds of questions addressed in this chapter.

EFFECTS STUDIES

STUDY PREVIEW   Early mass communication scholars assumed that the mass media were so powerful that ideas and even ballot-box instructions could be inserted as if by hypodermic needle into the body politic. Doubts arose in the 1940s about whether the media were really that powerful, and scholars began shaping their research questions on assumptions that media effects were more modest. Recent studies are asking about long-term, cumulative media effects.

MEDIA EFFECTS: THE CASE OF *WAR OF THE WORLDS*

The boy genius Orson Welles was on a roll. By 1938, at age 23, Welles's dramatic flair had landed him a network radio show, "Mercury Theater on the Air," at prime time on CBS on Sunday nights. The program featured adaptations of well-known literature. For their October 30 program, Welles and his colleagues decided on a scary 1898 British novel. Their enthusiasm faded five days before airtime when writer Howard Koch concluded that the novel did not lend itself to radio. Koch said that he in effect was required to create a one-hour original play and five days was not enough time, but neither was there time to switch to another play. The Thursday rehearsal was flat. Koch, frantic, scrambled to rewrite the script, but the Saturday rehearsal was disappointing too. Little did Welles expect that Koch's loose adaptation of H. G. Wells's *War of the Worlds* would become one of broadcasting's most memorable programs.

Orson Welles opened with the voice of a wizened chronicler from some future time, intoning eerily: "We know now that in the early years of the 20th century this world was being watched closely by intelligences greater than man's. ..." Welles's unsettling monologue was followed by an innocuous weather forecast, then hotel dance music. To casual listeners, the monologue seemed a mistake dropped inadvertently into typical radio music. Then the music was interrupted by a news bulletin. An astronomer reported several explosions on Mars, propelling something at enormous velocity toward Earth. The bulletin over, listeners were transported back to the hotel orchestra. After applause, the orchestra started up again, only to be interrupted: Seismologists had picked up an earthquake-like shock in New Jersey. Then it was one bulletin after another. A

Orson Welles. Young Orson Welles scared the living daylights out of several million radio listeners with the 1938 radio drama "War of the Worlds." Most of the fright was short-lived, though. All but the most naive listeners quickly realized that Martians really had not devastated the New Jersey militia as they marched toward the Hudson River to destroy Manhattan.

huge cylinder had crashed into a New Jersey farm. On the scene, a reported asked what happened.

> FARMER: A hissing sound. Like this: sssssssss . . . kinda like a fourt' of July rocket.
> REPORTER: Then what?
> FARMER: Turned my head out the window and would have swore I was to sleep and dreamin'.
> REPORTER: Yes?
> FARMER: I seen a kinda greenish streak and then zingo! Somethin' smacked the ground. Knocked me clear out of my chair!

The story line accelerated. Giant Martians moved across the countryside spewing fatal gas. One at a time, reporters at remote sites vanished off the air. The Secretary of the Interior came on: "Citizens of the nation: I shall not try to conceal the gravity of the situation. . . . Placing our faith in God we must continue the performance of our duties, each and every one of us, so that we may confront this destructive adversary with a nation united, courageous, and consecrated to the preservation of human supremacy on this earth."

Meanwhile, the Martians decimated the Army and were wading across the Hudson River. Amid sirens and other sounds of emergency, a reporter on a Manhattan rooftop described the monsters advancing through the streets. He passed on bulletins that Martian cylinders were coming down in St. Louis, Chicago, near Buffalo, all over the country. From his vantage, he described the Martians felling people by the thousands and moving in on him, the gas crossing Sixth Avenue, then Fifth Avenue, then 100 yards away, then 50 feet. Then silence. A lonely ham radio voice somehow became patched into the network: 2X2L calling CQ . . . 2X2L calling CQ . . . 2X2L calling CQ, New York . . . Isn't there anyone on the air? . . . Isn't there anyone? . . . Anyone? . . ." Silence.

To the surprise of Orson Welles and his crew, the drama triggered widespread mayhem. Neighbours gathered in streets all over the country, wet towels to their faces to slow the gas. In Newark, New Jersey, people, many undressed, fled their apartments. Said a New York woman, "I never hugged my radio so closely. . . . I held a crucifix in my hand and prayed while looking out my open window to get a faint whiff of gas so that I would know when to close my window and hermetically seal my room with waterproof cement or anything else I could get a hold of. My plan was to stay in the room and hope that I would not suffocate before the gas blew away." A Midwest man told of his grandparents, uncles, aunts and children, on their knees, "God knows but we prayed. . . . My mother went out and looked for Mars. Dad was hard to convince or skeptical or sumpin', but he even got to believing it. Brother Joe, as usual, got more excited than he could show. Brother George wasn't home. Aunt Gracie, a good Catholic, began to pray with Uncle Henry. Lily got sick to her stomach. I prayed harder and more earnestly than ever before. Just as soon as we were convinced that this thing was real, how petty all things on earth seemed; how soon we put our trust in God."

In one Pacific Northwest village, a power outage reinforced the panic. Switchboards throughout the country were swamped by people trying to call relatives, fueling the hysteria. The telephone volume in northern New Jersey was up 39 percent. Most CBS stations reported a six-fold increase in calls. Many people jumped into their cars to drive to safety but did not know where to go and so just drove around, which put hysterical strangers in touch with each other.

Researchers estimate that one out of six people who heard the program, more than one million in all, suspended disbelief and braced for the worst.

The effects were especially amazing considering that:

- An announcer identified the program as fiction at four points.
- Almost 10 times as many people were tuned to a popular comedy show on another network.
- The program ran only one hour, an impossibly short time for the sequence that began with the blastoffs on Mars, included a major military battle in New Jersey, and ended with New York's destruction.

Unwittingly, Orson Welles and his Mercury Theater crew had created an evening of infamy and raised questions about media effects to new intensity. In this chapter, you will learn what scholars have found out about the effects of the mass media on individuals.

POWERFUL EFFECTS THEORY

The first generation of mass communication scholars thought the mass media had a profound, direct effect on people. Their idea, called *effects theory*, drew heavily on social commentator *Walter Lippmann*'s influential 1922 book, *Public Opinion*. Lipp-

Opinion Leaders

Imagine the value of being able to identify opinion leaders if you were running a political campaign, handling an advertising account, or managing a public relations campaign. Since the introduction of the two-step flow model in mass communication theory, researchers have tried to identify who these influential people are. In 1971 scholars Everett Rogers and Floyd Shoemaker pulled together the research on the question and concluded that opinion leaders generally are distinguished from their followers because they:

■ Pay attention to the mass media more avidly and thoroughly.
■ Are especially accessible to their followers.
■ Hold higher social status.
■ Are more involved in community affairs, which gives them access to people in positions of responsibility and power who can effect changes.

■ Are more cosmopolitan, which can take the form of being knowledgeable, widely travelled and experienced.
■ Tend to be more innovative in crises or other situations necessitating change.

Identifying opinion leaders is elusive, as epitomized by the comment of one waitress. The waitress said she decided how to vote because she overheard a customer "who looked like he knew what he was talking about." She didn't even know the man.

Name as many opinion leaders as you can in your neighbourhoods, schools, churches and other organizations in your community. How about provincial, national and even world opinion leaders? Be sure you have supporting rationales.

mann argued that we see the world not as it really is but as "pictures in our heads." The "pictures" of things we have not experienced personally, he said, are shaped by the mass media. The powerful impact that Lippmann ascribed to the media was a precursor of the effects theory that evolved among scholars over the next few years.

Yale psychologist *Harold Lasswell*, who studied World War II propaganda, embodied the effects theory in his famous model of mass communication: *Who, Says what, In which channel, To whom, With what effect*. At their extreme, effects theory devotees assumed that the media could inject information, ideas and even propaganda hypodermically into the public. The theory was explained in terms of a hypodermic needle model or bullet model. Early effects scholars would agree that newspaper coverage and endorsements of political candidates decided elections.

The early scholars did not see that the hypodermic metaphor was hopelessly simplistic. They assumed wrongly that individuals are passive and absorb uncritically and unconditionally whatever the media spew forth. The fact is that individuals read, hear and see the same things differently. Even if they did not, people are exposed to many, many media—hardly a single, monolithic voice. Also, there is a scepticism among media consumers that is manifested at its extreme in the saying, "You can't believe a thing you read in the paper." People are not mindless, uncritical blotters.

MINIMALIST EFFECTS THEORY

Scholarly enthusiasm for the hypodermic needle model dwindled after two massive studies of voter behaviour. The studies, led by sociologist *Paul Lazarsfeld* were the first rigorous tests of media effects on an election. Lazarsfeld's researchers went back to 600 people several times to discover how they developed their campaign opinions. Rather than citing particular newspapers, magazines or radio stations, as had been expected, these people generally mentioned friends and acquaintances. The media had hardly any direct effect. Clearly, the hypodermic needle model was off base, and the effects theory needed rethinking. From that rethinking emerged the *minimalist effects theory*, which included:

TWO-STEP FLOW MODEL.   Minimalist scholars devised the two-step flow model to show that voters are motivated less by the mass media than by people they know personally and respect. These people, called *opinion leaders*, include many clergy, teachers and neighbourhood merchants, although it is impossible to list categorically all those who comprise opinion leaders. Not all clergy, for example, are influential, and opinion leaders are not necessarily in an authority role. The minimalist scholars' point is that personal contact is more important than media contact. The two-step flow model, which replaced the hypodermic needle model, showed that whatever effect the media have with the majority of the population is through opinion leaders. Later, as mass communication research became more sophisticated, the two-step model was expanded into a *multistep flow model* to capture the complex web of social relationships that affects individuals.

STATUS CONFERRAL.   Minimalist scholars acknowledge that the media create prominence for issues and people by giving them coverage. Conversely, neglect relegates issues and personalities to obscurity. Related to this *status conferral* phenomenon is *agenda setting*. Professors *Maxwell McCombs* and *Don Shaw*, describing the agenda-setting phenomenon in 1972, said the media do not tell people *what to think* but tell them *what to think about*. This is a profound distinction. In covering a political campaign, explain McCombs and Shaw, the media choose which issues or topics to emphasize, thereby setting the campaign's agenda. "This ability to affect cognitive change among individuals," say McCombs and Shaw, "is one of the most important aspects of the power of mass communication."

NARCOTICIZING DYSFUNCTION.   Some minimalists claim that the media rarely energize people into action, such as getting them to go out to vote for a candidate. Rather, they say, the media lull people into passivity. This effect, called *narcoticizing dysfunction*, is supported by studies that find that many people are so overwhelmed by the volume of news and information available to them that they tend to withdraw from involvement in public issues. Narcoticizing dysfunction occurs also when people pick up a great deal of information from the media on a particular subject—poverty, for example—and believe that they are doing something about a problem when they are really only smugly well-informed. Intellectual involvement becomes a substitute for active involvement.

CUMULATIVE EFFECTS THEORY

In recent years some mass communication scholars have parted from the minimalists and resurrected the powerful effects theory, although with a twist that avoids the simplistic hypodermic needle model. German scholar *Elisabeth Noelle-Neumann*, a leader of this school, conceded that the media do not have powerful immediate effects but argues that effects over time are profound. Her *cumulative effects theory* notes that nobody can escape either the media, which are ubiquitous, or the media's messages, which are driven home with redundancy. To support her point, Noelle-Neumann cites multimedia advertising campaigns that hammer away with the same message over and over. There's no missing the point. Even in news reports there is a redundancy, with the media all focusing on the same events.

Noelle-Neumann's cumulative effects theory has troubling implications. She says that the media, despite surface appearances, work against diverse, robust public consideration of issues. Noelle-Neumann bases her observation on human psychology, which she says encourages people who feel they hold majority viewpoints to speak out confidently. Those views gain credibility in their claim to be dominant when they are carried by the media, whether they are really dominant or not. Meanwhile, says Noelle-Neumann, people who perceive that they are in a minority are inclined to speak out less, perhaps not at all. The result is that dominant views can snowball through the media and become consensus views without being sufficiently challenged.

To demonstrate her intriguing theory, Noelle-Neumann has devised the ominously labeled *spiral of silence model*, in which minority views are intimidated into silence and obscurity. Noelle-Neumann's model raises doubts about the libertarian concept that the media provide a marketplace in which conflicting ideas fight it out fairly, each receiving a full hearing.

USES AND GRATIFICATIONS STUDIES

STUDY PREVIEW   Beginning in the 1940s, many mass communication scholars shifted from studying the media to studying media audiences. These scholars assumed that individuals use the media to gratify needs. Their work, known as uses and gratifications studies, focused on how individuals use mass media—and why.

CHALLENGES TO AUDIENCE PASSIVITY

As disillusionment with the powerful effects theory set in after the Lazarsfeld studies of the 1940s, scholars reevaluated many of their assumptions, including the idea that people are merely passive consumers of the mass media. From the reevaluation came research questions about why individuals tap into the mass media. This research, called *uses and gratifications studies*, explored how individuals choose certain media outlets. One vein of research said people seek certain media to gratify certain needs.

These scholars worked with social science theories about people being motivated to do certain things by human needs and wants, such as seeking water, food and shelter as necessities and wanting to be socially accepted and loved. These scholars identified dozens of reasons that people use the media, among them surveillance, socialization and diversion.

SURVEILLANCE FUNCTION

With their acute sense of smell and sound, deer scan their environment constantly for approaching danger. In modern human society, surveillance is provided for individuals by the mass media, which scan local and global environments for information that helps individuals make decisions to live better, even survive.

News coverage is the most evident form through which the mass media serve this *surveillance function*. From a weather report, people decide whether to wear a raincoat; from the Bay Street averages, whether to invest; from the news, whether the president will have their support. Although most people don't obsess about being on top of all that's happening in the world, there is a touch of the "news junkie" in everybody. All people need reliable information on their immediate environment. Is snow expected? Is the bridge fixed? Are vegetable prices coming down? Most of us are curious about developments in politics, economics, science and other fields. The news media provide a surveillance function for their audiences, surveying the world for information that people want and need to know.

It is not only news that provides surveillance. From drama and literature, people learn about great human issues that give them a better feel for the human condition. Popular music and entertainment, conveyed by the mass media, give people a feel for the emotional reactions of other human beings, many very far away, and for things going on in their world.

SOCIALIZATION FUNCTION

Except for recluses, people are always seeking information that helps them fit in with other people. This *socialization function*, a lifelong process, is greatly assisted by the mass media. Without paying attention to the media, for example, it is hard to participate in conversations about how the Expos did last night, or Atom Egoyan's latest movie. Jay Leno's monologues give late-night television watchers a common experience with their friends and associates the next day, as do the latest movie and the evening news.

Using the media can be a social activity, bringing people together. Gathering around the radio on Sunday night for the Mercury Theater in the 1930s was a family activity. Going to the movies or watching "Hockey Night in Canada" with friends is a group activity.

The media also contribute to togetherness by creating commonality. Friends who subscribe to *Maclean's* have a shared experience in reading the weekly cover story, even though they do it separately. The magazine helps individuals maintain social relationships by giving them something in common. In this sense, the media are important in creating community, even nationhood and perhaps, with global communication, a fellowship of humankind.

Less positive as a social function of the mass media is *parasocial interaction*. When a television anchor looks directly into the camera, as if talking with individual viewers, it is not a true social relationship that is being created. The communication is one-way without audience feedback. However, because many people enjoy the sense of interaction, no matter how false it is, many local stations encourage on-camera members of the news team to chat among themselves, which furthers the impression of an ongoing conversation with an extended peer group that includes the individual viewer.

This same false sense of reciprocal dialogue exists also among individuals and their favourite political columnists, lovelorn and other advice writers, and humourists. Some people have the illusion that the friends David Letterman interviews on his program are their friends, and so are Pamela Wallin and Larry King's. It is also illusory parasocial interaction when someone has the television set on for companionship.

DIVERSION FUNCTION

Through the mass media, people can escape everyday drudgery, immersing themselves in a soap opera, a murder mystery or pop music. The result can be stimulation, relaxation or emotional release.

STIMULATION.   Everybody is bored occasionally. When our senses—sight, hearing, smell, taste and touch—are without sufficient external stimuli, a sensory vacuum results. Following the physicist's law that a vacuum must be filled, we seek new stimuli to correct our sensory deprivation. In modern society the mass media are almost always handy as boredom-offsetting stimulants. It's not only in boring situations that the mass media can be a stimulant. To accelerate the pace of an already lively party, for example, someone can put on quicker music and turn up the volume.

RELAXATION.   When someone's sensory abilities are overloaded, the media can be relaxing. Slower, softer music sometimes can help. Relaxation, in fact, can come through any change of pace. In some situations, a high-tension movie or book can be as effective as a lullaby.

RELEASE.   People can use the mass media to blow off steam. Somehow a Friday night horror movie dissipates the frustration pent up all week. So can a good cry over a tear-jerking book.

Using the mass media as a stimulant, relaxant or release is quick, healthy escapism. Escapism, however, can go further, as when soap-opera fans so enmesh themselves in the programs that they perceive themselves as characters in the story line. Carried too far, escapism becomes withdrawal. When people build on media portrayals to the point that their existence revolves on living out the lives of, say, Elvis Presley or Marilyn Monroe, the withdrawal from reality has become a serious psychological disorder.

CONSISTENCY THEORY

Gratifications scholars learned that people generally are conservative in choosing media, looking for media that reinforce their personal views. Faced with messages consistent with their own views and ones that are radically different, people pay attention to the one they're comfortable with and have slight recall of contrary views. These phenomena—selective exposure, selective perception, selective retention and selective recall—came to be called *consistency theory*.

Consistency theory does a lot to explain media habits. People read, watch and listen to media with messages that don't jar them. The theory raised serious questions about how well the media can meet the democratic ideal that the media be a forum for the robust exchange of divergent ideas. The media can't fulfill their role as a forum if people hear only what they want to hear.

INDIVIDUAL SELECTIVITY

STUDY PREVIEW   Individuals choose to expose themselves to media whose perspective and approach reinforce their personal interests and values. These choices, called selective exposure, are consciously made. Similar selectivity phenomena are at work subconsciously in how individuals perceive and retain media content.

SELECTIVE EXPOSURE

People make deliberate decisions in choosing media. For example, outdoors enthusiasts choose *Field & Stream* at the newsrack. Academics subscribe to *Saturday*

Night. Young rock fans watch MuchMusic, while country fans will tune in to Country Music Television. People expose themselves to media whose content relates to their interests. In this sense, individuals exercise control over the media's effects on them. Nobody forces these selections on anybody.

This process of choosing media, called *selective exposure*, continues once an individual is involved in a publication or a broadcast. A hunter who seldom fishes will gravitate to the hunting articles in *Field & Stream*, perhaps even skipping the fishing pieces entirely. On MuchMusic, a hard-rock aficionado will be attentive to wild music and tune in during "The Power Hour," but will take a break when the video jock announces that a mellow piece will follow the commercial.

SELECTIVE PERCEPTION

The selectivity that occurs in actually reading, watching and listening is less conscious than in selective exposure. No matter how clear a message is, people see and hear egocentrically. This phenomenon, known as *selective* or *autistic perception*, was demonstrated in the 1950s by researcher Roy Carter, who found that physicians concerned about socialized medicine at the time would hear "social aspects of medicine" as "socialized medicine." Rural folks on the Prairies, anxious for news about farming, thought they heard the words "farm news" on the radio when the announcer said "foreign news."

Scholars Eugene Webb and Jerry Salancik explain it this way: "Exposure to information is hedonistic." People pick up what they want to pick up. Webb and Salancik state that nonsmokers who read an article about smoking focus subconsciously on passages that link smoking with cancer, being secure and content, even joyful, in the information that reinforces the wisdom of their decision not to smoke. In contrast, smokers are more attentive to passages that hedge the smoking–cancer link. In using the mass media for information, people tend to perceive what they want. As social commentator Walter Lippmann put it, "For the most part we do not first see and then define, we define first and then see." Sometimes the human mind distorts facts to square with predispositions and preconceptions.

SELECTIVE RETENTION AND RECALL

Experts say that the brain records forever everything to which it is exposed. The problem is recall. While people remember many things that were extremely pleasurable or that coincided with their beliefs, they have a harder time calling up the memory's file on other things.

"Selective forgetting" happens to mothers when they tend to deemphasize or even forget the illnesses or disturbances of pregnancy and the pain of birth. This phenomenon works the opposite way when individuals encounter things that reinforce their beliefs.

Nostalgia also can affect recall. For example, many mothers grossly predate when undesirable behaviour like thumb sucking was abandoned. Mothers tend also to suggest precocity about the age at which Suzy or José first walked or cut the first tooth. In the same way, people often use rose-coloured lenses, not 20/20 vision, in recalling information and ideas from the media.

In summary, individuals have a large degree of control over how the mass media affect them. Not only do individuals make conscious choices in exposing

themselves to particular media, but also their beliefs and values subconsciously shape how their minds pick up and store information and ideas. The phenomena of selective exposure, selective perception and selective retention and recall are overlooked by people who portray the mass media as omnipotent and individuals as helpless and manipulated pawns.

The 1938 "War of the Worlds" scare demonstrates this point. The immediate response was to heap blame on the media, particularly *Orson Welles* and CBS, but panic-stricken listeners bore responsibility too. A Princeton University team led by psychologist *Hadley Cantril*, which studied the panic, noted that radio listeners brought to their radio sets predispositions and preconceptions that contributed to what happened. Among their subconscious baggage:

- A preconception, almost a reverence, about radio, especially CBS, as a reliable medium for major, breaking news.
- A predisposition to expect bad news, created by a decade of disastrous global economic developments and another war imminent in Europe.
- Selective perception, which caused them to miss announcements that the program was a dramatization. While many listeners tuned in late and missed the initial announcement, others listened straight through the announcements without registering them.
- An awe about scientific discoveries, technological progress and new weapons, which contributed to gullibility.
- Memories from World War I about the horror of gas warfare.
- An inability to test the radio story with their own common sense. How, for example, could the Army mobilize for a battle against the Martians within 20 minutes of the invasion?

SOCIALIZATION

STUDY PREVIEW   The mass media have a large role in initiating children into society. This socialization process is essential to perpetuating cultural values, but some people worry that it can be negative if the media report and portray undesirable behaviour and attitudes, such as violence and racism.

MEDIA'S INITIATING ROLE

Nobody is born knowing how to fit into society. This is learned through a process that begins at home. Children imitate their parents and brothers and sisters. From listening and observing, children learn values. Some behaviour is applauded, some is scolded. Gradually this culturization and socialization process expands to include friends, neighbours, school and at some point the mass media.

In earlier times, the role of the mass media came late because books, magazines and newspapers required reading skills that were learned in school. The media were only a modest part of early childhood socialization. Today, however, television is omnipresent from the cradle. A young person turning 18 will have spent more time watching television than in any other activity except sleep. Television, which requires no special skills to use, has displaced much of the socializing influence that once came from parents. "Sesame Street" imparts more information on the value of nutrition than Mum's admonition to eat spinach.

By definition, socialization is *prosocial*. Children learn that motherhood, baseball and apple pie are valued, that buddies frown on tattling, that honesty is virtuous, and that hard work is rewarded. The stability of a society is assured through the transmission of such values to the next generation.

ROLE MODELS

The extent of media influence on individuals may never be sorted out with any precision, in part because every individual is a distinct person and because media exposure varies from person to person. Even so, some media influence is undeniable. Consider the effect of entertainment idols as they come across through the media. Many individuals, especially young people casting about for an identity all their own, groom themselves in conformity with the latest heartthrob. Consider the Mickey Mantle butch haircuts in the 1950s, Elvis Presley ducktails in the 1960s, Beatle mopheads in the 1970s, and punk spiking in the 1980s. Remember all the Madonna look-alikes in high schools a few years ago? This imitation, called *role modeling*, even includes emulating speech mannerisms of whoever is hip at the moment— "Know what I mean?" "Grody to the max." "Isn't that special." "Not!"

No matter how quirky, fashion fads are not terribly consequential, but serious questions can be raised about whether role modeling extends to behaviour. Many people who produce media messages recognize a responsibility for role modeling. Whenever Batman and Robin leaped into their Batmobile in the campy 1960s television series, the camera always managed to show them fastening their seat belts. Many newspapers have a policy to mention in accident stories whether seat belts were in use. In the 1980s, as concern about AIDS mounted, moviemakers went out of their way to show condoms as a precaution in social situations. For example, in the movie *Broadcast News*, the producer character slips a condom into her purse before leaving the house on the night of the awards dinner.

If role modeling can work for good purposes, such as promoting safety consciousness and disease prevention, it would seem that it could also have a negative

Role Models. The Simpson family, a Fox television network and CanWest-Global success in the early 1990s, may seem mere fun to most viewers, but media characters, even in cartoon, are role models for many people. It is no wonder that many parents and educators were concerned about Bart Simpson's irreverent attitudes toward authority figures.

effect. Such was the argument against the 1988 movie *Colors*, which was built around Los Angeles gang violence. Said Curtis Sliwa, leader of the Guardian Angels, which opposed the movie, "It doesn't take much creative analysis to know that this could foment a problem. . . . It's almost like a how-to movie. It starts with a drive-by shooting." When the movie opened, two teenagers at one movie house were shot, one fatally, and police made 13 arrests at another theatre. Experts were divided, as might be expected, on whether or not the violence was inspired by depictions on the screen.

STEREOTYPING

Close your eyes. Think "professor." What image forms in your mind? Before 1973 most people would have envisioned a harmless, absent-minded eccentric. Today, the image is more likely to be the brilliant, sometimes brutal Professor Kingsfield portrayed by John Houseman in the 1973 movie and subsequent television series "The Paper Chase." Both the absent-minded pre-1973 professor and the steel-trap post-1973 Kingsfield are images known as stereotypes. Both flow from the mass media. While neither is an accurate generalization about professors, both have long-term impact.

Stereotyping is a kind of shorthand that can facilitate communication. Putting a cowboy in a black hat allows a movie director to sidestep complex character explanation and move quickly into a story line, because moviegoers hold a generalization about cowboys in black hats. They are the bad guys—a stereotype. Newspaper editors pack lots of information into headlines by drawing on stereotypes held by the readers. Consider the extra meanings implicit in headlines that refer to the "Castro regime," or a "Southern belle," or a "college jock." Stereotypes paint broad strokes that help create impact in media messages, but they are also a problem. A generalization, no matter how useful, is inaccurate. Not all Scots are cheap, nor are all Bay Street brokers crooked, nor are all college jocks dumb—not even a majority.

By using stereotypes, the mass media perpetuate them. With benign stereotypes, there is no problem, but the media can perpetuate social injustice with stereotypes. In the late 1970s, the U.S. Civil Rights Commission found that blacks on network television were portrayed disproportionately in immature, demeaning or comic roles. By using a stereotype, television was not only perpetuating false generalizations but also being racist. Worse, network thoughtlessness was robbing black people of strong role models.

Feminists have leveled objections that women are both underrepresented and misrepresented in the media. One study by sociologist Eve Simson found that most female television parts were decorative, played by pretty California women in their 20s. Worse were the occupations represented by women, said Simson. Most frequent were prostitutes, at 16 percent. Traditional female occupations—secretaries, nurses, flight attendants and receptionists—represented 17 percent. Career women tended to be man-haters or domestic failures. Said Simson, "With nearly every family, regardless of socioeconomic class, having at least one TV set and the average set being turned on 6.3 hours per day, TV has emerged as an important source for promulgating attitudes, values and customs. For some viewers, it is the only major contact with outside 'reality,' including how to relate to women. Thus, not only is TV's sexism insulting, but it is also detrimental to the status of women."

Media critics like Simson call for the media to become activists to revise demeaning stereotypes. While often right-minded, such calls can interfere with accurate portrayals. In the 1970s, Italian-American activists, for example, lobbied successfully against Mafia characters being identified as Italian.

SOCIALIZATION VIA EAVESDROPPING

The mass media, especially television, have eroded the boundaries that people once respected between the generations, genders and other social institutions. Once adults whispered when they wanted to discuss certain subjects, like sex, when children were around. Today, children eavesdrop on all kinds of adult topics by seeing them depicted on television. Though meant as a joke, these lines ring true today to many squirming parents:

> **Father to Friend:** My son and I had that father-and-son talk about the birds and the bees yesterday.
> **Friend:** Did you learn anything?

Joshua Meyrowitz, a communication scholar, brought the new socialization effects of intergenerational eavesdropping to wide attention with his 1985 book, *No Sense of Place*. In effect, the old socially recognized institution of childhood, which long had been protected from "big-people issues" like money, divorce and sex, was disappearing. From television sitcoms, kids today learn that adults fight and goof up and sometimes are just plain silly. These are things kids may always have been aware of in a vague sense, but now they have front row seats.

Television also cracked other protected societal institutions, such as the "man's world." Through television, many women entered the man's world of the locker room, the fishing trip, and the workplace beyond the home. Older mass media, including books, had dealt with a diversity of topics and allowed people in on the "secrets" of other groups, but the ubiquity of television and the ease of access to it accelerated the breakdown of traditional institutional barriers.

MEDIA-DEPICTED VIOLENCE

STUDY PREVIEW Some individuals mimic aggressive behaviour they see in the media, but such incidents are exceptions. Some experts argue, in fact, that media-depicted violence actually reduces real-life aggressive behaviour.

TELEVISION VIOLENCE AND CANADIAN CHILDREN

- The average Canadian child spends about the same amount of time watching television as he or she does in school.
- By the time a Canadian child reaches 12 years of age, she or he has seen 12 000 violent deaths on television.
- According to the University of Laval, children's programs contain 68 percent more violence than those for adults.

LEARNING ABOUT VIOLENCE

The mass media help bring young people into society's mainstream by demonstrating dominant behaviours and norms. This prosocial process, called *observational learning*, turns dark, however, when children learn deviate behaviours from the media. In Manteca, California, two teenagers, one only 13, lay in wait for a friend's father in his own house and attacked him. They beat him with a fireplace poker, kicked him and stabbed him, and choked him to death with a dog chain. Then they poured salt in his wounds. Why the final act of violence, the salt in the wounds? The 13-year-old explained that he had seen it on television. While there is no question that people can learn about violent behaviour from the media, a major issue of our time is whether the mass media are the cause of aberrant behaviour.

Individuals on trial for criminal acts occasionally plead that "the media made me do it." That was the defence in a 1974 California case in which two young girls playing on a beach were raped with a beer bottle by four teenagers. The rapists told police they had picked up the idea from a television movie they had seen four days earlier. In the movie, a young woman was raped with a broom handle, and in court, the youths' attorneys blamed the movie. The judge, as is typical in such cases, threw out media-projected violence as an unacceptable scapegoating defence and held the young perpetrators responsible.

Although the courts have never accepted transfer of responsibility as a legal defence, it is clear that violent behaviour can be imitated from the media. Some experts, however, say that the negative effect of media-depicted violence is too often overstated and that media violence actually has a positive side.

MEDIA VIOLENCE AS POSITIVE

People who downplay the effect of media portrayals of blood, guts and violence often refer to a *cathartic effect*. This theory, which dates to ancient Greece and the philosopher *Aristotle*, suggests that watching violence allows individuals vicariously to release pent-up everyday frustration that might otherwise explode dangerously. By seeing violence, so goes the theory, people let off steam. Most advocates of the cathartic effect claim that individuals who see violent activity are stimulated to fantasy violence, which drains off latent tendencies toward real-life violence.

In more recent times, scholar *Seymour Feshbach* has conducted studies that lend support to the cathartic effect theory. In one study, Feshbach lined up 625 junior high school boys at seven California boarding schools and showed half of them a steady diet of violent television programs for six weeks. The other half were shown nonviolent fare. Every day during the study, teachers and supervisors reported on each boy's behaviour in and out of class. Feshbach found no difference in aggressive behaviour between the two groups. Further, there was a decline in aggression among boys watching violence who were determined by personality tests to be more inclined toward aggressive behaviour.

Opponents of the cathartic effect theory, who include both respected researchers as well as reflexive media bashers, were quick to point out flaws in Feshbach's research methods. Nonetheless, his conclusions carried considerable weight because of the study's unprecedented massiveness—625 individuals. Also, the study was conducted in a real-life environment rather than in a laboratory, and there was a consistency in the findings.

PRODDING SOCIALLY POSITIVE ACTION

Besides the cathartic effects theory, an argument for portraying violence is that it prompts people to socially positive action. This happened after NBC aired "The Burning Bed," a television movie about an abused woman who could not take any more and set fire to her sleeping husband. The night the movie was shown, battered-spouse centres were overwhelmed with calls from women who had been putting off doing anything to extricate themselves from relationships with abusive mates.

On the negative side, one man set his estranged wife afire and explained that he was inspired by "The Burning Bed." Another man who beat his wife senseless gave the same explanation.

MEDIA VIOLENCE AS NEGATIVE

The preponderance of evidence is that media-depicted violence has the potential to cue real-life violence, and most catharsis theorists concede that this is a possibility. The *aggressive stimulation theory*, however, is often overstated to the point that it comes across smacking of the now generally discredited bullet, or hypodermic needle, theory of mass communication. The fact is that few people act out media violence in their own lives.

An exaggerated reading of the aggressive stimulation theory became impressed in the public mind, indelibly it seems, after a 1963 *Look* magazine article by Stanford University researcher *Albert Bandura*. In his research, Bandura had found that there was an increase in aggressive responses by children shown films of people aggressively punching and beating on large inflated clowns called Bobos. After the film, the children's toys were taken away except for a Bobo doll, which, Bandura reported, was given a beating—just like on the film. The inference was that the children modeled their behaviour on the film violence. Bandura also conducted other experiments that all pointed in the same direction.

Wow, Pow, Zap. The notion that media-depicted violence triggers real-life violence gained currency in the 1960s after researcher Albert Bandura wrote a *Look* magazine article about his Bobo doll research. Kids in a laboratory began really whacking Bobos after seeing people doing the same thing in a film. There is a continuing debate, however, about whether people were accurate in inferring that media violence directly causes real violence. Bandura himself has been dismayed at some of the simplistic conclusions that have been drawn from the *Look* article.

The *Bobo doll studies* gained wide attention, but, as with most research on the contentious media-triggered violence issue, other scholars eventually became critical of Bandura's research methodologies. One criticism is that he mistook child playfulness with the Bobo dolls for aggressiveness. Even so, everyone who has been stirred to excitement by a violent movie knows from personal experience that there is an effect, and the early publicity on the Bobo studies seemed to verify that growing societal violence was caused by the media.

Such cause-and-effect connections frequently are inferred from individual incidents that are widely played in the news media. Here is a sampler:

■ After watching the movie *Warlock* 10 times, 14-year-old Sandy Charles of Saskatchewan killed an eight-year-old boy by stabbing him with a knife and then beating him with a beer bottle and a rock. After killing him, he cut strips of skin from his victim and boiled them down. The movie claimed that if you drank boiled-down fat from a virgin, it would give you the power to fly. Charles wanted to fly.

■ Fifteen year-old Ronald Zamora of Miami, a fan of the television police shows "Kojak" and "Police Woman," murdered an 83-year-old female neighbour, and then said he was the victim of "involuntary subliminal television intoxication."

■ Before going to the electric chair, serial killer Ted Bundy reported that media depictions inspired him to stalk women and kill them.

■ Twenty-nine people shot themselves playing Russian roulette in separate incidents across the U.S. after watching the movie "The Deer Hunter," which keeps cutting to a high-tension Russian roulette Saigon gambling scene.

Inferences from such anecdotal cases have contributed to the common notion that media-depicted violence leads directly to aggressive and violent behaviour. This widely held notion was also supported by casual readings of numerous serious studies, among them:

■ Researcher Monroe Lefkowitz identified third graders who watched a lot of violent television, and then, 10 years later, found that these individuals were rated by their peers as "aggressive."

■ Psychologist Leonard Berkowitz showed violent film scenes to children and college students and then moved them to a lab where they were given push buttons and told that they could administer electric shocks to an individual who, depending on the experiment, either had insulted them or resembled a violent character in the film, or who, they were told, had made a mistake on an exam and needed a reminder. Those who had seen the violence on film pushed their shock buttons more and longer than other subjects who had not seen the film.

■ A mental health institute reported that serious fights in high schools were more common among students who watched violent television programs.

RECENT CANADIAN RESEARCH

A media researcher from the University of Winnipeg, Wendy Josephson, challenges some of the most common criticisms about the links between violence on television and increased levels of aggression in children. For example, while some may argue that there is no conclusive proof that watching violence on television will cause violent behaviour in children, Josephson says to simply look at recent research studies; the vast majority of reports, including studies by the CRTC, the House of Commons Standing Committee on Communications and Culture and the Royal Commission on Violence in the Communications Industry claim there is a link between television viewing and violence. She claims that although earlier studies from the 1950s and 1960s might have been methodologically flawed, recent studies have improved research designs and, as a result, provide more reliable data.

Some of the other assumptions Josephson challenges include:

The effect is too small to make a difference.
While television is only one agent of socialization that will influence how aggressive a child is, it is probably just as important as other variables like social class and gender, while being easier to control.

There is no clear definition of violence.

Different researchers may have used various definitions of what violent behaviour is, but they have a common theme—one person deliberately hurting another. When Canadians talk about violence, we refer to a set of shared experiences and examples.

Violence on television only reflects the violent society we live in.

This is absolutely untrue, says Josephson. Television crime is about 10 times more violent than crime in real life. Saturday morning cartoons are particularly violent. The average cartoon has about 20 to 25 violent acts per hour; in prime time, there are about five violent acts per hour.

Violence is on TV because that's what people want to watch.

Some research indicates that while violence may be a selling feature of both children's and adults' programs, there are other conventions of television, such as fast-paced editing, which make programs popular among children. Josephson says that it's the producers of television who use violence to their own advantage. The storylines of many children's shows are similar—simple conflict that can be communicated visually, fast-paced action, the building of suspense and action that is easy to break up by commercials. In short, producers use violence as a hook to keep kids tuned in to their program.

"Theodore the Tugboat." Canadian programs like "Theodore the Tugboat" don't resort to the violence of other popular children's shows like "Sailor Moon." Psychologists, such as Josephson, argue that children's programming doesn't need violence or rapid editing to be effective.

Josephson also asks Canadian television producers to try to avoid this kind of hook. She urges producers of children's shows to reduce the amount of violence and to contextualize the violence that is still included. Violence should not be used simply as comic relief or as an easy way to solve problems. The consequences of these acts need to be addressed, especially in programming for older children and teens. As for networks and television stations, she suggests they be careful when scheduling programs early in the day or late in the afternoon as this is prime time for many Canadian children, especially for "latch-key" kids who get home before their parents.

CATALYTIC THEORY

Simplistic readings of both cathartic and aggressive stimulation effects research can yield extreme conclusions. A careful reading, however, points more to the media having a role in real-life violence but not necessarily triggering it and doing so only infrequently—and only if several non-media factors are also present. For example, evidence suggests that television and movie violence, even in cartoons, is arousing and can excite some children to violence, especially hyperactive and easily excitable children. These children, like unstable adults, become wrapped up psychologically with the portrayals and are stirred to the point of acting out. However, this happens only when a combination of other influences is also present. Among these other influences are:

- Whether violence portrayed in the media is rewarded. In 1984 researcher David Phillips found that the murder rate increases after publicized prizefights, in which the victor is rewarded, and decreases after publicized murder trials and executions, in which, of course, violence is punished.
- Whether media exposure is heavy. A lesson from Monroe Lefkowitz's research and dozens of other studies is that aggressive behavioural tendencies are strongest among people who see a lot of media-depicted violence. This suggests a cumulative media effect rather than a single hypodermic injection leading to violence.
- Whether a violent person fits other profiles. Studies have found correlations between aggressive behaviour and many variables besides violence viewing. These include income, education, intelligence and parental child-rearing practices. This is not to say that any of these third variables cause violent behaviour. The suggestion, rather, is that violence is far too complex to be explained by a single factor.

Most researchers note too that screen-triggered violence is increased if the aggression:

- Is realistic and exciting, like a chase or suspense sequence that sends adrenalin levels surging.
- Succeeds in righting a wrong, like helping an abused or ridiculed character get even.
- Includes situations or characters similar to those in the viewer's own experience.

All these things would prompt a scientist to call media violence a *catalyst*. Just as the presence of a certain element will allow other elements to react explosively but itself not be part of the explosion, the presence of media violence can be a factor in real-life violence but not a cause by itself. This *catalytic theory* was articulated by scholars *Wilbur Schramm*, *Jack Lyle* and *Edwin Parker*, who investigated the effects of television on children and came up with this statement in their 1961 book, *Television in the Lives of Our Children*, which has become a classic on the effects of media-depicted violence on individuals: "For *some* children under *some* conditions, *some* television is harmful. For other children under the same conditions, or for the same children under *other* conditions, it may be beneficial. For *most* children, under *most* conditions, *most* television is probably neither particularly harmful nor particularly beneficial."

SOCIETALLY DEBILITATING EFFECTS

Media-depicted violence scares far more people than it inspires to violence, and this, according to *George Gerbner*, a leading researcher on screen violence, leads some people to believe the world is more dangerous than it really is. Gerbner calculates that 1 in 10 television characters is involved in violence in any given week. In real life, the chances are only about 1 in 100 per *year*. People who watch a lot of television, Gerbner found, see their own chances of being involved in violence nearer the distorted television level than their local crime statistics or even their own experience would suggest. It seems that television violence leads people to think they are in far greater real-life jeopardy than they really are.

The implications of Gerbner's findings go to the heart of a free and democratic society. With exaggerated fears about their safety, Gerbner says, people will demand greater police protection. They are also likelier, he says, to submit to established authority and even to accept police violence as a tradeoff for their own security.

TOLERANCE OF VIOLENCE

An especially serious concern about media-depicted violence is that it has a numbing, callousing effect on people. This *desensitizing theory*, which is widely held, says not only that individuals are becoming hardened by media violence but also that society's tolerance for such antisocial behaviour is increasing.

Media critics say the media are responsible for this desensitization, but many media people, particularly movie and television directors, respond that it is the desensitization that has forced them to make the violence in their shows even more graphic. They explain that they have run out of alternatives to get the point across when the story line requires that the audience be repulsed. Some movie critics, of course, find this explanation a little too convenient for gore-inclined moviemakers and television directors, but even directors not inclined to gratuitous violence feel their options for stirring the audience have become scarcer. The critics respond that this is a chicken-or-egg question and that the media are in no position to use the desensitization theory to excuse increasing violence in their products if they themselves contributed to the desensitization. And so the argument goes on about who is to blame.

Desensitization is apparent in news also. The absolute ban on showing the bodies of crime and accident victims in newspapers and on television newscasts, almost universal a few years ago, is becoming a thing of the past. No longer do newsroom practices forbid showing body bags or even bodies. During the

Desensitization. Critics of media violence said slasher movies like *Halloween 5* were desensitizing people, especially teenagers, to the horrors of violence. That concern now has been transferred to video games. In one Mortal Kombat sequence, a crowd shouts encouragement for Kano to rip the heart out of Scorpion, his downed protagonist. Kano waves the dismembered heart to the crowd, which roars approvingly. Although scholars disagree about whether media violence begets real-life violence, most do agree that media violence leaves people more accepting of violence around them in their everyday lives.

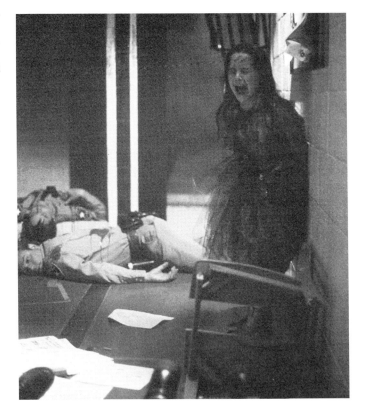

1991 Persian Gulf war, U.S. television had no reluctance about airing videos of allied troops picking up the bodies of hundreds of strafed Iraqi soldiers and hurling them, like sacks of flour, onto flatbed trucks for hauling to deep trenches, where the cameras recorded the heaped bodies being unceremoniously bulldozed over with sand.

In summary, we know far less about media violence than we need to. Various theories explain some phenomena, but the theories themselves do not dovetail. The desensitizing theory, for example, explains audience acceptance of more violence, but it hardly explains research findings that people who watch a lot of television actually have heightened anxiety about their personal safety. People fretting about their own safety hardly are desensitized.

THE V-CHIP

One Canadian who was concerned about the effects of television violence on his children is *Tim Collings*, who teaches engineering at Simon Fraser University. His solution: the *violence-chip*, or *V-chip*, for short. Once installed inside the television, the chip will allow parents to predetermine what level of violence is acceptable. Shows are rated according to their level of violence: 0 for family fare, 5 for graphic sex and violence. This rating is embedded into the signal in much the same way as closed-captioning. Parents and caregivers simply take their remote control and enter the violence level that is appropriate, depending on the time of day and who's watching. If the level of violence exceeds the pre-set level, the TV will block out the show. Both Canadian and American television sets will eventually have to come with the V-chip preinstalled. Until that time, it will be provided by the cable companies for a nominal fee.

The V-chip does have its critics. For example, artists and producers want to know who will decide what rating a show receives. Some producers feel that the V-chip promotes a kind of unspoken censorship because the content of their shows will now have a label (rating) attached to them. Others worry that the V-chip ratings may cause them to lose advertising revenue. Will a high violence rating affect other ratings and revenues? Will advertisers not sponsor programs that have been rated 4 or 5 or will some groups in society boycott products that do sponsor violent shows?

The V-chip is only part of the solution. Education is another key to minimizing the effects of television and violence. The Alliance for Children and Television for Health Canada produces a kit to help parents educate their children about watching television. Their suggestions include asking children these questions while watching a program with them:

- Do you like this program?
- Why do you like/don't you like this program?
- How do you think the program is going to end?
- How does this make you feel?
- Could this ending happen in real life?
- How could you solve that problem?

By inviting children to ask questions about the programs they watch, parents increase the likelihood that they will grow up with a higher degree of media literacy. These kits can be purchased for about $60 from the Alliance.

Violence and Supervision.
Many cable companies make literature available to parents. Brochures, like this one from the Canadian Cable Television Association, help educate both children and parents about television violence and its effects.

MEDIA AGENDA-SETTING FOR INDIVIDUALS

STUDY PREVIEW Media coverage helps define the things people think about and worry about. This is called agenda-setting. It occurs as the media create awareness of issues through their coverage, which lends importance to those issues. The media don't set agendas unilaterally, but they look to their audiences in deciding their priorities for coverage.

MEDIA SELECTION OF ISSUES

When the New York police wanted more subway patrols, their union public relations person asked officers to call him with every subway crime. He passed the accounts, all of them, on to newspapers and television and radio stations. He could not have been more pleased with his media blitz. News coverage of subway crime, he later boasted, increased several thousand percent, although there had been no appreciable change in the crime rate itself. Suddenly, for no reason other than dramatically stepped-up coverage, people were alarmed. Their personal agendas of what to think about—and worry about—had changed. The sudden new concern, which made it easier for the union to argue for more subway patrols, was an example of media *agenda-setting* at work. The police's PR person lured news media decision makers into putting subway crime higher on their lists of issues to be covered, and individuals moved it up on their lists of personal concerns.

The agenda-setting phenomenon has been recognized for a long time. Sociologist *Robert Park*, writing in the 1920s, articulated the theory in rejecting the once-popular notion that the media tell people what to think. As Park saw it, the media create awareness of issues more than they create knowledge or attitudes. Today, agenda-setting theorists put it this way: The media do not tell people *what to think* but *what to think about.* Agenda-setting occurs at several levels:

CREATING AWARENESS.   Only if individuals are aware of an issue can they be concerned about it. Concern about parents who kill their children becomes a major issue with media coverage of spectacular cases. In 1994 Susan Smith, a South Carolina woman, attracted wide attention with her horrific report that her sons, ages three and one, had been kidnapped. The story darkened later when the woman confessed to driving the family car into the lake and drowning the boys herself. Over several days of intense media attention, the nation learned not only the morbid details of what happened but also became better informed about a wide range of parental, family and legal issues that the coverage brought to the fore.

ESTABLISHING PRIORITIES.   People trust the news media to sort through the events of the day and make order of them. Lead-off stories on a newscast or on page one are expected to be the most significant. Not only does how a story is played affect people's agendas, but so do the time and space afforded it. Lavish graphics can propel an item higher.

PERPETUATING ISSUES.   Continuing coverage lends importance to an issue. A single story on a bribed senator might soon be forgotten, but day-after-day follow-ups can fuel ethics reforms. Conversely, if gatekeepers are diverted to other stories, a hot issue can cool overnight—out of sight, out of mind.

INTRAMEDIA AGENDA-SETTING

Agenda-setting also is a phenomenon that affects media people, who constantly monitor one another. Reporters and editors many times are concerned more with how their peers are handling a story than with what their audience wants. Sometimes the media harp on one topic, making it seem more important than it really is, until it becomes tedious.

The media's agenda-setting role extends beyond news. Over time, life-styles and values portrayed in the media can influence not just what people think about but what they do. Hugh Hefner's *Playboy* magazine of the 1950s helped to usher in the sexual revolution. Advertising has created a redefinition of American values by whetting an appetite for possessions and glamorizing immediate gratification.

Even so, individuals exercise a high degree of control in their personal agendas. For decades, William Randolph Hearst campaigned with front-page editorials in all his newspapers against using animals in research, but animal rights did not become a pressing public issue. Even with the extensive media coverage of the Constitutional debate polls found that many Canadians were still apathetic about the state of the nation. For the most part, these were people who chose to tune out the coverage. The fact is that journalists and other creators of media messages cannot automatically impose their agendas on individuals. If people are not interested, an issue won't become part of their agendas. The individual values at work in the processes of selective exposure, perception and retention can thwart media leadership in agenda-setting.

Also, media agendas are not decided in a vacuum. Dependent as they are on having mass audiences, the media take cues for their coverage from their audiences. Penny press editors in the 1830s looked over the shoulders of newspaper readers on the street to see what stories attracted them and then shaped their coverage accordingly. Today, news organizations tap the public pulse through scientific sampling to deliver what people want. The mass media both exert leadership in agenda-setting and mirror the agendas of their audiences.

MEDIA-INDUCED ANXIETY AND APATHY

STUDY PREVIEW The pervasiveness of the mass media is not necessarily a good thing, according to some theorists who say a plethora of information and access to ideas and entertainment can induce information anxiety. Another theory is that the news media even encourage passivity by leaving an impression that their reporting is so complete that there's nothing left to know or do.

INFORMATION ANXIETY

The *New York Times* had a landmark day on November 13, 1987. It published its largest edition ever—5.45 kg, 1612 pages and 12 million words. How could anyone, even on a quiet Sunday, manage all that information? One of the problems in contemporary life is the sheer quantity of information technology allows us as a society to gather and disseminate. Even a relatively slender weekday edition of the *New York Times* contains more information than the average person in the 17th century was likely to come across in a lifetime, according to Richard Saul Wurman in his book *Information Anxiety*.

While educated people traditionally have thirsted for information, the quantity has become such that many people feel overwhelmed by what is called *information pollution*. We are awash in it and drowning, and the mass media are a factor in this. Consider college students at a major metropolitan campus:

- They pass newspaper vending machines and racks with a dozen different papers—dailies, weeklies, freebies—en route to class.
- On the radio, they have access to 40 stations.
- In their mailbox, they find a solicitation for discount subscriptions to 240 magazines.
- They turn on their television during a study break and need to choose among 50 channels.
- At lunch, they notice advertisements everywhere—on the placemat, on the milk carton, on table standups, on the butter pat, on the walls, on the radio coming over the public-address system, on the pen used to write a cheque.
- At the library, they have almost instant on-line access through computer systems to more information than any human being could possibly deal with.

Compounding the quantity of information available is the accelerating rate at which it is available. Trend analyst John Naisbitt has made the point with this example: When President Lincoln was shot in 1865, people in London learned about it five days later. When President Reagan was shot in 1981, journalist Henry Fairlie, in his office one block away, heard about the assassination attempt from his London editor who had seen it on television and phoned Fairlie to get him to go to the scene. Databases to which almost every college student today has access are updated day by day, hour by hour, even second by second.

It is no wonder that conscientious people who want good and current data to form their judgments and opinions, even to go about their jobs, feel overwhelmed. Wurman, who has written exclusively on this frustration, describes *information anxiety* as the result of "the ever-widening gap between what we understand and what we think we should understand."

The solution is knowing how to locate relevant information and tune out the rest, but even this is increasingly difficult. Naisbitt reported in *Megatrends* that scientists planning an experiment are spending more time figuring out whether someone somewhere already has done the experiment than conducting the experiment itself.

On some matters, many people do not even try to sort through all the information that they have available. Their solution to information anxiety is to give up. Other people have a false sense of being on top of things, especially public issues, because so much information is available.

MEDIA-INDUCED PASSIVITY

One effect of the mass media is embodied in the stereotypical couch potato, whose greatest physical and mental exercise is heading to the refrigerator during commercials. Studies indicate that the typical North American spends four to six hours a day with the mass media, mostly with television. The experience is primarily passive, and it has been blamed, along with greater mobility and access to more leisure activities, for major changes in how people live their lives.

- **Churches and Lodges.** The role of church auxiliaries and lodges, once central in community social life with weekly activities, has diminished.
- **Neighbourhood Taverns.** Taverns at busy neighbourhood corners and rural crossroads once were the centre of political discussion in many areas, but this is less true today.
- **Participatory Sports.** Despite the fitness and wellness craze, more people than ever are overweight and out of shape, which can be partly attributed to physical passivity induced by television and media-based homebound activities.

While these phenomena may be explained in part by people's increased use of the mass media and the attendant passivity, it would be a mistake not to recognize that social forces besides the media have contributed to them.

WELL-INFORMED FUTILITY

The news media take pride in purveying information to help people be active and involved in public matters, but, ironically, the media contribute insidiously to passivity by lulling people into accepting news reports as the last word on a subject. To attract and impress audiences, reporters use techniques to enhance their credibility, coming across as more authoritative than they really are and making their stories seem comprehensive and complete. Consider the well-groomed, clear-spoken television reporter on Parliament Hill whose 40-second report seems to address all inherent questions. The slickness in presentation works against the journalistic ideal of promoting intelligent citizen involvement in the political and social process by seeming to be so complete that nothing more can be said. The result is called the *syndrome of well-informed futility*. Readers, listeners and viewers feel satisfied that they're fully informed, which becomes an end in itself rather than actual involvement. This phenomenon works against democracy, which is predicated on citizen involvement, not apathy.

As agenda-setters, the mass media may also be working against the democratic ideal. The greater the role of the media in choosing the society's issues and fashions and even setting the values, the less the role of the people at a grassroots level.

CHAPTER WRAP-UP

The mass media influence us, but scholars are divided about how much. There is agreement that the media help initiate children into society by portraying social and cultural values. This is a serious responsibility because portrayals of aberrant behaviour, like violence, have effects, although we are not sure about their extent. This is not to say that individuals are unwitting pawns of the mass media. People choose what they read and what they tune in to, and they generally filter the information and images to conform with their preconceived notions and personal values.

In other respects too, the mass media are a stabilizing influence. The media try to fit into the lives of their audiences. An example is children's television programs on weekend mornings when kids are home from school but still on an early-rising schedule. The media not only react to audience life-styles but also contribute to the patterns by which people live their lives, like going to bed after the late news. In short, the media have effects on individuals and on society, but it is a two-way street. Society is a shaper of media content, but individuals make the ultimate decisions about subscribing, listening and watching. The influence issue is a complex one that merits further research and thought.

QUESTIONS FOR REVIEW

1. Why have most media scholars abandoned the powerful and minimalist effect theories for the cumulative theory?

2. What is the uses and gratifications approach to mass media studies?

3. Do individuals have any control over mass media effects on them?

4. What role do the mass media have in socializing children?

5. How do scholars differ on whether media-depicted violence triggers aggressive behaviour?

6. What is meant when someone says: "The mass media don't tell people what to think as much as tell them what to think about"?

7. Does being informed by mass media necessarily improve citizen involvement in political processes?

QUESTIONS FOR CRITICAL THINKING

1. Although generally discredited by scholars now, the powerful effects theory once had many adherents. How do you explain the lingering popularity of this thinking among many people?

2. Name at least three opinion leaders who influence you on issues that you do not follow closely in the media. On what issues are you yourself an opinion leader?

3. Give specific examples of each of the seven primary mass media contributing to the lifelong socialization process. For starters, consider a current nonfiction best-selling book.

4. Explain how selective exposure, selective perception and selective retention would work in the imaginary case of a devout Muslim who was studying English literature at Harvard University at the time Salman Rushdie's book *The Satanic Verses* was published. You may want to check newsmagazines in February and March 1989 for background.

5. Discuss the human needs that the mass media help satisfy in terms of the news and entertainment media.

6. Among the functions that the mass media serve for individuals are diversion and escape. Is this healthy?

7. Explain the prosocial potential of the mass media in culturization and socialization. What about the media as an antisocial force in observational learning?

8. Cite at least three contemporary role models who you can argue are positive. Explain how they might also be viewed as negative. Cite three role models who you can argue are negative.

9. What stereotype comes to your mind with the term "Uncle Remus"? Is your image of Uncle Remus one that would be held universally? Why or why not?

10. How can serious scholars of mass communication hold such diverse ideas as the cathartic, aggressive stimulation and catalytic theories? Which camp is right?

11. Compare American programming to Canadian programming. Which is more violent? Why?

FOR FURTHER LEARNING

George Comstock. *Television in America* (Sage, 1980). Professor Comstock's Chapter 5, "Growing Up," offers a quick review of research on television and violence, the effects of television commercials, and socialization.

Diana Coulter. "A Kid's Eye View of TV." *Toronto Star* (May 31, 1996).

Tanya Davis. "The Ratings Game," *Maclean's* (June 17, 1996).

Cham Eyal, Jim Winter and Maxwell McCombs. "The Agenda-Setting Role in Mass Communication." In Michael Emery and Ted Curtis Smythe, *Reading in Mass Communication: Concepts and Issues in the Mass Media*, 6th ed. (Wm. C. Brown, 1986), 169–174. The authors, all scholars, trace the development of agenda-setting theory and identify the status of research.

Leo W. Jeffres. *Mass Media: Processes and Effects* (Waveland, 1986). Professor Jeffres discusses the variety of perspectives that attempt to understand the mysterious process of mass communication and then focuses on effects of the media on individuals and on society.

Wendy L. Josephson, Ph D. *Television Violence: A Review of the Effects on Children of Different Ages* (Department of Canadian Heritage, 1995). A good review of the literature which focuses on the effects of television violence on six age groups: infants, toddlers, preschoolers, elementary-school children and teenagers. It can be ordered by calling 1-800-896-267-1291.

Robert M. Liebert, Joyce N. Spafkin and Emily S. Davidson. *The Early Window: Effects of Television on Children and Youth*, 2nd ed. (Pergamon, 1985). This compendium covers the broad range of studies on television and children with special emphasis on research into media-depicted violence.

Joshua Meyrowitz. *No Sense of Place: The Impact of Electronic Media on Social Behaviour* (Oxford, 1985). Professor Meyrowitz says television allows everybody, adult and child alike, to eavesdrop into other generations, which has eroded if not undone intergenerational distinctions that once were essential components of the social structure.

John Naisbitt. *Megatrends: Ten New Directions Transforming Our Lives* (Warner, 1982). Naisbitt identifies trends in society, particularly the shift from the industrial age to the information age.

Williard D. Rowland, Jr. *The Politics of TV Violence: Policy Uses of Communication Research* (Sage, 1983). Rowland argues that the mass media have used a heavy hand behind the scenes to dilute research findings that screen violence begets real-life violence. Rowland, a scholar, goes back to the Payne studies in the late 1920s.

Richard Saul Wurman. *Information Anxiety* (Doubleday, 1989). Wurman discusses information overload as a modern problem for individuals and suggests ways to deal with it.

FOR KEEPING UP TO DATE

Among numerous scholarly journals that publish research on media effects are the *Journal of Communication*, *Journalism Quarterly*, *Journal of Broadcasting & Electronic Media* and *Mass Communication Review*.

Also valuable is *Mass Communication Review Yearbook* published annually by Sage of Beverly Hills, Calif.

There are several brochures and pamphlets about television violence that can be obtained from both government and industry sources: The Media Awareness Network in Ottawa; 1-800-896-3342. National Clearinghouse on Family Violence; 1-800-267-1291.

"The Prime Time Parent Kit" may be ordered from the Alliance for Children and Television for Health Canada at 416-515-0466.

MASS MEDIA
and Society

The mass media seek to reach large audiences rather than to extend cultural sensitivity

The mass media contribute to stability in the society by providing common rituals

People communicate with generations into the future and with far-away people through the mass media

Scholar Marshall McLuhan foresaw television easing the alienation of human beings from their true nature

Societies that dominate economically and politically export their values elsewhere for better or worse

MEDIA IN THEORY

Mass Media and Fundamental Change

The detribalization theory says the written word changed tribal communities by deemphasizing interpersonal communication. Written communication engaged the mind, not the senses, and, according to the theory, a lonely, cerebral-based culture resulted. Now, as sense-intensive television displaces written communication, retribalization is creating a global village.

HUMAN ALIENATION

An intriguing, contrarian assessment of the media's effects on human society was laid out by Canadian theorist *Marshall McLuhan* in the 1960s. McLuhan argued that the print media had alienated human beings from their natural state. In pre-mass media times, McLuhan said, people acquired their awareness about their world through their own observation and experience and through their fellow human beings, whom they saw face to face and with whom they communicated orally. As McLuhan saw it, this was a pristine communal existence—rich in that it involved all the senses, sight, sound, smell, taste and touch. This communal, tribal state was eroded by the written word, which involved the insular, meditative act of reading. The printing press, he said, compounded this alienation from humankind's tribal roots. The written word, by engaging the mind, not the senses, begat *detribalization*, and the printing press accelerated it.

According to McLuhan, the printed word even changed human thought processes. In their tribal state, he said, human beings responded spontaneously to everything that was happening around them. The written word, in contrast, required people to concentrate on an author's relatively narrow, contrived set of data that led from Point A to Point B to Point C. Following the linear serial order of the written word was a lonely, cerebral activity, unlike participatory tribal communication, which had an undirected, helter-skelter spontaneity.

TELEVISION AND THE GLOBAL VILLAGE

McLuhan saw television bringing back tribalization. While books, magazines and newspapers engaged the mind, television engaged the senses. In fact, the television screen could be so loaded with data that it could approximate the high level of sensual stimuli that people found in their environments back in the tribal period of human history. Retribalization, he said, was at hand because of the new, intensely sensual communication that television could facilitate. Because television could far exceed the reach of any previous interpersonal communication, McLuhan called the new tribal village a *global village*.

With retribalization, McLuhan said, people will abandon the print media's linear intrusions on human nature. Was McLuhan right? His disciples claim that certain earmarks of written communication—complex story lines, logical progression and causality—are less important to today's young people, who grew up with sense-intensive television. They point to the music videos of the 1980s, which excited the senses but made no linear sense. Many teachers say children are having a harder time finding significance in the totality of a lesson. Instead, children fasten on to details.

As fascinating as McLuhan was, he left himself vulnerable to critics who point out that, in a true nonlinear spirit, he was selective with evidence and never put his ideas to rigorous scholarly examination. McLuhan died in 1980. Today the jury remains divided, agreeing only that he was a provocative thinker.

MASS MEDIA ROLE IN CULTURE

STUDY PREVIEW The mass media are inextricably linked with culture because it is through the media that creative people have their strongest sway. While the media have the potential to disseminate the best creative work of the human mind and soul, some critics say the media are obsessive about trendy, often silly subjects. These critics find serious fault with the media's concern for *pop culture*, claiming it squeezes out things of significance.

MEDIA'S TRANSMISSION OF VALUES

Robert and Linda Lichter met while working on a massive study of major media decision makers. Later they married and formed the Center for Media and Public Affairs in Washington, which today is a research organization on the mass media and social change. One of the most troubling findings of the Lichters and co-researcher Stanley Rothman is that the major media are out of touch with the people. This conclusion comes out of massive studies of the people who run the entertainment media.

Media Elite. Researchers Linda and Robert Lichter and Stanley Roth-man say that the people who create most of television's entertainment programming have a liberal outlook that influences their shows. According to the Lichter-Rothman studies, this "media elite" is overwhelmingly urban, secular and antagonistic to business and other powerful institutions in society. As a group, these people have far more education and higher incomes than the general population. Because they move in relatively small social circles of like-minded and similarly situated people largely from Los Angeles and New York, these media leaders are insulated from what most Americans are thinking.

The Lichter-Rothman studies say that television executives and key creative people are overwhelmingly liberal on the great social issues of our time. More significantly, the studies have found that the programming these people produce reflects their political and social outlook. For example:

- Television scripts favour feminist positions in 71 percent of the shows, far more than public-opinion surveys find among the general population.
- Three percent of television murders are committed by blacks, compared to half in real life.
- Two out of three people are portrayed in positive occupations on television, but only one out of three businesspeople is depicted in a positive role.

These examples, according to the Lichters and Rothman, indicate a bias toward feminism and minority people and against businesspeople. The Lichter-Rothman work documents a dramatic turnaround in television entertainment fare. Two generations ago, leading programs, ranging from sitcoms like "Leave It to Beaver" and dramatic programs like "Wagon Train" extolled traditional values. In the 1970s came programs like "Mork and Mindy" and "All in the Family" that questioned some values. Today, network schedules make plenty of room for programs like "L.A. Law" and "Murphy Brown" that examine nontraditional views and exhibit a dramatically different social orientation than, say, "Leave It to Beaver."

It is hazardous, of course, to paint too broad a picture of contemporary television, where a sitcom like "The Cosby Show" is much in the 1950s mode, but the Lichters and Rothman, by analyzing 620 shows over a 30-year period, argue persuasively that there has been a dramatic shift. They characterize the shift this way: "Television's America may once have looked like Los Angeles' Orange County writ large—Waspish, businesslike, religious, patriotic and middle class. Today it better resembles San Francisco's Marin County—trendy, self-expressive, culturally diverse and cosmopolitan."

The Lichter-Rothman studies indicate that this liberal, urban and secular "media elite," which creates television entertainment programming, is moving farther and farther away from traditional values. This might be just an interesting phenomenon, except that, to critics, this media elite is subverting American culture by glamorizing alternative life-styles and values. The Lichters and Rothman add fuel to this concern by noting that television's creative people not only deal with vexed issues but, both subtly and overtly, slant the issues to their point of view.

This raises all kinds of serious questions about the mass media's effects on society. Can the media change bedrock social values? If values can be changed, are they really bedrock? While there is no doubt that the media affect society, how much do they do so? And how do these effects work? In this chapter you will learn what many leading researchers and scholars have concluded in their studies and reflections so far. You also will learn that much remains a mystery.

ELITIST VERSUS POPULIST VALUES

The mass media can enrich society by disseminating the best of human creativity, including great literature, music and art. The media also carry a lot of lesser things that reflect the culture and, for better or worse, contribute to it. Over time, a continuum has been devised that covers this vast range of artistic material that requires sophisticated and cultivated tastes to appreciate. This is called *high art*. At the other extreme is *low art*, which requires little sophistication to enjoy.

One strain of traditional media criticism has been that the media underplay great works and concentrate on low art. This *elitist view* argues that the mass media do society a disservice by pandering to low tastes. To describe low art, elitists sometimes use the German word *kitsch*, which translates roughly as garish or trashy. The word captures their disdain. In contrast, the *populist view* is that there is nothing unbecoming in the mass media's catering to mass tastes in a democratic, capitalist society.

In a widely cited 1960 essay, "Masscult and Midcult," social commentator *Dwight Macdonald* made a virulent case that all popular art is kitsch. The mass media, which depend on finding large audiences for their economic base, can hardly ever come out at the higher reaches of Macdonald's spectrum.

This kind of elitist analysis was given a larger framework in 1976 when sociologist *Herbert Gans* categorized cultural work along socioeconomic and intellectual lines. Gans said that classical music, as an example, appealed by and large to people of academic and professional accomplishments and higher incomes. These were *high-culture* audiences, which enjoyed complexities and subtleties in their art and entertainment. Next came *middle-culture* audiences, which were less abstract in their interests and liked prime-time television. *Low-culture* audiences were factory

Identifying Kitsch

Although *quality* is an elusive term, students of the mass media need to come to grips with it to assess media performance. Are the media realizing their potential to enrich the culture? Are the media being responsible when they pander to the lowest common denominator in cultural sensitivity to attract the largest possible audiences?

Where do you fit on a scale of cultural appreciation? Where do you expect to fit in another year? Two years? Ten years?

To address these questions, the high-brow, middle-brow and low-brow breakdown is useful. For example: A gourmet works at developing a sophisticated taste for food. Such taste has not been acquired yet by a child who wolfs down two catsup-oozing hamburgers and cannot conceive of a better meal.

On a high-brow/low-brow scale of quality, where do these fit?

■ The Winnipeg Symphony Orchestra's recorded performance of Gershwin's *Strike Up The Band Overture.*

■ An album of singer Anne Murray's most romantic music.

■ A video of a Tom Cochrane concert.

Some media content is hard to fit into pigeonholes easily. Keep this difficulty in mind when you classify:

■ Robert Wise's 1961 movie of the Broadway musical *West Side Story.*

■ *Romeo and Juliet,* performed for video at the annual Stratford, Ontario, Shakespeare festival.

■ *Atlantic* magazine.

■ The *National Enquirer.*

■ The "MacNeil-Lehrer Report" on the Public Broadcasting System.

■ The "Oprah Winfrey" syndicated television talk show program.

■ The "Wheel of Fortune" television game show.

■ The Fox television series "The Simpsons."

and service workers whose interests were more basic; whose educational accomplishments, incomes and social status were lower; and whose media tastes leaned toward kung fu movies, comic books and supermarket tabloids.

Gans was applying his contemporary observations to flesh out the distinctions that had been taking form in art criticism for centuries—the distinctions between high art and low art.

HIGH-BROW. The high art favoured by elitists generally can be identified by its technical and thematic complexity and originality. High art often is highly individualistic because the creator, whether a novelist or a television producer, has explored issues in fresh ways and often with new and different methods. Even when a collaborative effort, a piece of high art is distinctive. High art requires a sophisticated audience to appreciate it fully. Often it has enduring value, surviving time's test as to its significance and worth.

The sophistication that permits an opera aficionado to appreciate the intricacies of a composer's score, the poetry of the lyricist and the excellence of the performance sometimes is called *high-brow.* The label has grim origins in the idea that a person must have great intelligence to have refined tastes, and a high "brow" is necessary to accommodate such a big brain. Generally the term is used by people who disdain those who have not developed the sophistication to enjoy, for example, the abstractions of a Fellini film, a Matisse sculpture or a Picasso painting. High-

Assessing Newspapers. The level of intellectual interest that is necessary to enjoy and appreciate high-end news coverage, like that in the *New York Times*, is much more sophisticated than that to enjoy low-end tabloids. The audiences of such diverse publications correlate with educational background, professional accomplishment, income and social status.

brows generally are people who, as Gans noted, are interested in issues by which society is defining itself and look in literature and drama for stories on conflicts inherent in the human condition and between the individual and society.

MIDDLE-BROW. Middle-brow tastes recognize some artistic merit but without a high level of sophistication. There is more interest in action than abstractions, in Captain Kirk aboard the starship *Enterprise* than in the childhood struggles of Ingmar Bergman that shaped his films. In socioeconomic terms, middle-brow appeals to people who take comfort in media portrayals that support their status quo orientation and values.

LOW-BROW. Someone once made this often-repeated distinction: High-brows talk about ideas, middle-brows talk about things, and low-brows talk about people. Judging from the circulation success of the *National Enquirer* and other supermarket tabloids, there must be a lot of low-brows in contemporary North America. Hardly any sophistication is needed to recognize the machismo of Rambo, the villainy of Simon Legree, the heroism of Superman, or the sexiness of Madonna.

THE CASE AGAINST POP ART

Pop art is of the moment, including things like mood rings, hula-hoops and grunge garb—and trendy media fare. Even elitists may have fun with pop, but they traditionally have drawn the line at anyone who mistakes it as having serious artistic merit. Pop art is low art that has immense although generally short-lived popularity.

Elitists see pop art as contrived and artificial. In their view, the people who create *popular art* are masters at identifying what will succeed in the marketplace and then providing it. Pop art, according to this view, succeeds by conning people into liking it. When Nehru jackets were the fashion rage in the late 1960s, it was not because they were superior in comfort or utility or aesthetics, but because promoters sensed profits could be made in touting them via the mass media as new and cashing in on easily manipulated mass tastes. It was the same with Cabbage Patch dolls, pet rocks, showy petticoats and countless other faddy products.

The mass media, according to the critics, are obsessed with pop art. Partly this is because the media are the carriers of the promotional campaigns that create popular followings but also because competition within the media creates pressure to be first, to be ahead, to be on top of things. The result, say elitists, is that junk takes precedence over quality.

Much is to be said for this criticism of pop art. The promotion of the screwball 1960s sitcom "Beverly Hillbillies," for example, created an eager audience that otherwise might have been reading Steinbeck's critically respected *Grapes of Wrath*. An elitist might chortle, even laugh at the unbelievable antics and travails of the Beverly Hillbillies, who had their own charm and attractions, but an elitist would be concerned all the while that low art was displacing high art in the marketplace and that the society was the poorer for it.

POP ART REVISIONISM

Pop art has always had a few champions among intellectuals, although their voices were usually drowned out in the din of elitist pooh-poohing. In 1965, however, essayist *Susan Sontag* wrote an influential piece, "One Culture and the New Sensibility," which prompted many elitists to take a fresh look at pop art.

POP ART AS EVOCATIVE.   Sontag made the case that pop art could raise serious issues, just as could high art. She wrote: "The feeling given off by a Rauschenberg painting might be like that of a song by the Supremes." Sontag soon was being called the high priestess of *pop intellectualism*. More significantly, the Supremes were being taken more seriously, as were a great number of Sontag's avant-garde and obscure pop artist friends.

POPULARIZATION OF HIGH ART.   Sontag's argument noted that the mass appeal of pop artists meant that they could convey high art to the masses. A pop pianist like Liberace might omit the trills and other intricacies in performing a sonata, but he nonetheless gave a mass audience an access to Mozart that otherwise would never occur. Sontag saw a valuable service being performed by artists who both understood high art and could "translate" it for unsophisticated audiences, a process known as *popularization*.

As Sontag saw it, the mass media were at the fulcrum in a process that brings diverse kinds of cultural products and audiences together in exciting, enriching ways. The result of popularization, Sontag said, was an elevation of the cultural sensitivity of the whole society.

POP ART AS A SOCIETAL UNIFIER.   In effect, Sontag encouraged people not to look at art on the traditional divisive, class-conscious, elitist-populist continuum. Artistic value, she said, could be found almost anywhere. The word "camp" gained circulation among 1960s elitists who were influenced by Sontag. These high-brows began finding a perversely sophisticated appeal in pop art as diverse as Andy Warhol's banal soup cans and the outrageous "Batman." The mass media, through which most people experienced Warhol and all people experienced "Batman," became recognized more broadly than ever as a societal unifier.

The Sontag-inspired revisionist look at pop art coincides with the view of many mass media historians that the media have helped bind the society rather than divide it. Radio united Canada effectively in the 1940s. Later, so did network television. In short, the mass media are purveyors of cultural production that contributes to social cohesion, whether it be high art or low art.

HIGH ART AS POPULAR.   While kitsch may be prominent in media programming, it hardly elbows out all substantive content. In 1991, for example, Ken Burns's public television documentary, *The Civil War*, outdrew low art prime-time network programs five nights in a row. It was a glaring example that high art can appeal to people across almost the whole range of socioeconomic levels and is not necessarily driven out by low art. Burns's documentary was hardly a lone example. Another, also from 1991, was Franco Zeffirelli's movie *Hamlet*, starring pop movie star Mel Gibson, which was marketed to a mass audience and yet could hardly be dismissed by elitists as kitsch.

SOCIAL STABILITY

STUDY PREVIEW   The mass media create rituals around which people structure their lives. This is one of many ways that the media contribute to social stability. The media foster socialization through adulthood, contributing to social cohesion by affirming believes and values and helping reconcile inconsistent values and discrepancies between private behaviour and public morality.

MEDIA-INDUCED RITUAL

Northwest Airlines pilots, flying their Stratocruisers over the Dakotas in the 1950s, could tell when the late-night news ended on WCCO, the powerful Minneapolis radio station. They could see lights at ranches and towns all across the Dakotas going off as people, having heard the news, went to bed. The 10 o'clock WCCO news had become embedded as a ritual. Today, for people on the East and West Coasts, where most television stations run their late news at 11 p.m., the commonest time to go to bed is 11:30, after the news. Like other rituals that mark a society, media-induced rituals contribute order and structure to the lives of individuals.

The effect of media-induced rituals extends even further. Collectively, the lifestyles of individuals have broad social effect. Consider just these two effects of evening newspapers, an 1878 media innovation:

EVENING NEWS.   E.W. Scripps changed people's habits with his evening newspapers, first in Cleveland and 1878, then elsewhere. Soon, p.m. papers outnumbered a.m. papers. The new habit, however, was not so much for *evening newspapers* as for *evening news*, as newspaper publishers discovered a hundred years later when television siphoned readers away with evening newscasts. The evening ritual persists, even though the medium is changing as p.m. newspapers go out of business or retreat to mornings.

COMPETITIVE SHOPPING.   In the era before refrigeration and packaged foods, household shopping was a daily necessity. When evening newspapers appeared, housewives, who were the primary shoppers of the period, adjusted their routines to read the paper the evening before their morning trips to the market. The new ritual allowed time for more methodical bargain hunting, which sharpened retail competition.

Besides shaping routines, ritual contributes to the mass media's influence as a shaper of culture. At 8:15 a.m. every Sunday, half the television sets in Japan are tuned to "Serial Novel," a tear-jerking series that began in the 1950s. Because so many people watch, it is a common experience that is one element in the identification of contemporary Japanese society. In North American society, a ritual that marked the society for years was "Dallas," Friday, 9 p.m. Eastern time, 8 p.m. Central time. A Canadian ritual is watching "Hockey Night in Canada" on Saturday nights.

THE MEDIA AND THE STATUS QUO

In their quest for profits through large audiences, the mass media need to tap into their audience's common knowledge and widely felt feelings. Writers for network sitcoms avoid obscure, arcane language. Heroes and villains reflect current morals. Catering this way to a mass audience, the media reinforce existing cultural beliefs and values. People take comfort in learning through the media that they fit into their community and society, which furthers social cohesion. This is socialization continued beyond the formative years. It also is socialization in reverse, with the media taking cues from the society and playing them back.

The media's role in social cohesion has a negative side. Critics say that the media pander to the lowest common denominator by dealing only with things that fit the status quo easily. The result, the critics note, is a thwarting of artistic exploration beyond the mainstream. Critics are especially disparaging of predictable, wooden characters in movies and television and of predictability in the subjects chosen for the news.

Demanding a Better Life. Muscovites rioted against their government in 1993 when it became clear that the first wave, post-Communist reformers could not deliver the Western-style prosperity that the Russian people had learned about through the mass media. They were acting out a process called "diffusion of innovation." Through media coverage of Western consumer economies, the people knew there was a better way, and they wanted their leaders to adopt the innovations that would make them prosperous also.

A related negative aspect of the media's role as a contributor to social cohesion is that dominant values too often go unchallenged, which means that some wrong values and practices persist. Dudley Clendinen, a newspaper editor who grew up in the U.S. South, faults journalists for, in effect, defending racism by not covering it: "The news columns of Southern papers weren't very curious or deep or original in the late 1940s and 1950s. They followed sports and politics actively enough, but the whole rational thrust of Southern culture from the time of John C. Calhoun on had been self-defensive and maintaining. It had to be, to justify the unjustifiable in a society dedicated first to slavery and then to segregation and subservience. Tradition was everything, and the news pages were simply not in the habit of examining the traditions of the South."

THE MEDIA AND COGNITIVE DISSONANCE

The media are not always complacent. Beginning in the late 1950s, after the period to which Clendinen was referring, media attention turned to racial segregation. News coverage, literary comment, and dramatic and comedy portrayals began to point up flaws in the status quo. Consider the effect, through the mass media, of these individuals on racism:

- **John Howard Griffin.** In 1959 Griffin, a white journalist, dyed his skin black for a six-week odyssey through the South. His book, *Black Like Me*, was an inside look at being black in America. It had special credibility for the white majority because Griffin was white.
- **George Wallace.** The mass audience saw the issue of segregation personified in news coverage of Governor George Wallace physically blocking black students

Cognitive Dissonance. Many white Americans from racist backgrounds found themselves challenging their own values when the U.S. federal government adopted proactive civil rights policies in the 1950s and 1960s. This dissonance escalated as these people followed news coverage of the long-overdue demands of blacks for fair treatment, as in this 1963 march. Some white racists resolved the discrepancy by abandoning racism. Many others simply retreated from discussion on the issue.

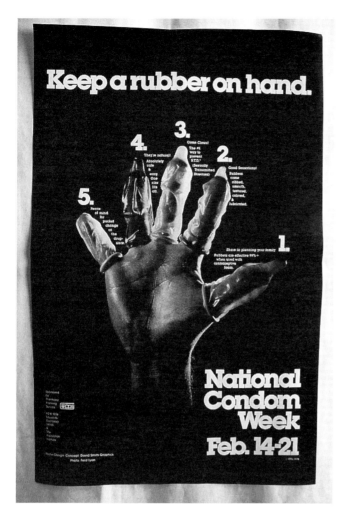

Influencing Mores. Safe sex campaigns, prompted by the AIDS crisis, have used the mass media to discourage promiscuity, unprotected intercourse and high-risk sexual practices. The messages work. One indicator is that the average age that young people become sexually active is going up. Another indicator is rising condom sales. Long-term government campaigns about the dangers of smoking have also been effective, as measured by dropping cigarette sales. The campaigns of organizations, such as Mothers Against Drunk Driving, commonly known as MADD, have seriously influenced views of excessive drinking as unfashionable.

from attending the University of Alabama. The indelible impression was that segregation could be defended only by a clenched fist and not by reason.

- **Martin Luther King Jr.** News photographers captured the courage and conviction of Martin Luther King Jr. and other civil rights activists, black and white, taking great risks through civil disobedience to object to racist public policies.
- **Archie Bunker.** Archie Bunker, a television sitcom character, made a laughing-stock of bigots.

To some people, the media coverage and portrayals seemed to exacerbate racial tensions. In the longer run, however, media attention contributed to a new consensus through a phenomenon that psychologists call *cognitive dissonance*. Imagine white racists as they saw George Wallace giving way to U.S. federal troops under orders from the White House. The situation pitted against each other two values held by individual racists—segregation as a value and an ordered society as symbolized by the presidency. Suddenly aware that their personal values were in terrible disharmony, or *dissonance*, many of these racists avoided the issue. Instead of continuing to express racism among family and friends, many tended to be silent. They may have been as racist as ever, but they were quiet, or watched their words carefully. Gradually their untenable view is fading into social unacceptability. This is not to say that racism does not persist. It does, and continues to manifest itself in American life although, in many ways, in forms much muted since the media focused on the experiment of John Howard Griffin, the clenched fist of George Wallace, and the crusade of Martin Luther King Jr.

When the media go beyond pap and the predictable, they are examining the cutting edge issues by which the society defines its values. Newsmagazines, newspapers and television, utilizing new printing, photography and video technology in the late 1960s, put war graphically into American living rooms, pointing up all kinds of discrepancies between Pentagon claims and the Vietnam reality. Even the glamorized, heroic view of war, which had persisted through history, was countered by media depictions of the blood and death. Unable to resolve the discrepancies, some people withdrew into silence. Others reassessed their views and then, with changed positions or more confident in their original positions, they engaged in a dialogue from which a consensus emerged. And the United States, the mightiest power in history, began a militarily humiliating withdrawal. It was democracy at work, slowly and painfully, but at work.

AGENDA-SETTING AND STATUS CONFERRAL

Media attention lends a legitimacy to events, individuals and issues that does not extend to things that go uncovered. This conferring of status occurs through the media's role as agenda-setters. It puts everybody on the same wavelength, or at least a similar one, which contributes to social cohesion by focusing our collective attention on issues we can address together. Otherwise, each of us could be going in separate directions, which would make collective action difficult if not impossible.

Nannygate. Friends and associates didn't take much notice when insurance executive Zoe Baird hired illegal aliens for household work—after all, "everybody did it." But when Baird was under scrutiny as President Clinton's appointee for attorney general in 1993, the revelations about her skirting the law in hiring domestic help became a classic collision between private actions and public morality. President Clinton withdrew the nomination. Mass media coverage of morality issues reminds society to keep re-evaluating its values.

MEDIA AND MORALITY

A small-town wag once noted that people read the local newspaper not to find out what is going on, which everybody already knows, but to find out who got caught. The observation was profound. The mass media, by reporting deviant behaviour, help enforce society's moral order. When someone is arrested for burglary and sentenced, it reaffirms for everybody that human beings have property rights.

Beyond police blotter news, the mass media are agents for reconciling discrepancies between *private actions* and *public morality*. Individually, people tolerate minor infractions of public morality, like taking pencils home from work. Some people even let life-threatening behaviour go unreported, like child abuse. When the deviant behaviour is publicly exposed, however, toleration ceases and social processes come into action that reconcile the deviance with public morality. The reconciling process maintains public norms and values. Consider Douglas Ginsburg. In the 1970s, Ginsburg, a young law professor, smoked marijuana at a few parties. It was a misdemeanour, but Ginsburg's friends tolerated it, and not a word was said publicly. In 1988, however, when President Reagan nominated Ginsburg to the U.S. Supreme Court, reporter Nina Totenberg of National Public Radio reported Ginsburg's transgressions. Exposed, he withdrew his name. There was no choice. His private action, publicly exposed, could not be tolerated, and his withdrawal maintained public norms and values, without which a society cannot exist.

This same phenomenon occurred in the 1980s when homelessness became a public issue. For years, homeless people in every major city had slept in doorways and alleys and, during winter, at steam vents. The homeless were seen but invisible. When social policies and economic factors in the 1980s sent the numbers skyrocketing, homelessness became a media issue that could not be ignored, and the society had to do something. Under the glare of media attention, people brought their private behaviour, which had been to overlook the problem, into conformity with the tenet of public morality that says we are all our brothers' keepers. Reform policies to relieve homelessness began moving through political channels.

CULTURAL TRANSMISSION

STUDY PREVIEW   The mass media transmit cultural values through history. Past generations talk to us through mass media, mostly books, just as we, often not realizing it, talk to future generations. The media also diffuse values and ideas contemporaneously.

HISTORICAL TRANSMISSION

Human beings have a compulsion to leave the wisdom they have accumulated for future generations. There is a compulsion, too, to learn from the past. In olden times, people gathered around campfires and in temples to hear storytellers. It was a ritual through which people learned the values that governed their community.

Five thousand years ago, the oral tradition was augmented when Middle Eastern traders devised an alphabet to keep track of inventories, transactions and rates of exchange. When paper was invented, clay tablets gave way to scrolls and eventually books, which became the primary vehicle for storytelling. Religious values were passed on in holy books. Military chronicles laid out the lessons of war. Literature provided lessons by exploring the nooks and crannies of the human condition.

Books remain the primary repository of our culture. For several centuries, it has been between hard covers, in black ink on paper, that the experiences, lessons and wisdom of our forebears have been recorded for posterity. Other mass media today share in the preservation and transmission of culture over time. Consider these archives:

- Museum of Broadcasting in New York, with 1200 hours of television documentaries; great performances, productions, debuts and series; and a sample of top-rated shows.
- Library for Communication and Graphic Arts at Ohio State University, whose collection includes editorial cartoons.
- Vanderbilt Television News Archive in Nashville, Tennessee, with 7000 hours of network nightly news programs and special coverage such as political conventions and space shots.
- CBC archives, with hundreds of hours of radio and TV news programs.

CONTEMPORARY TRANSMISSION

The mass media also transmit values among contemporary communities and societies, sometimes causing changes that otherwise would not occur. Anthropologists have documented that mass communication can change society. When Edmund Carpenter introduced movies in an isolated New Guinea village, the men adjusted their clothing toward the Western style and even remodeled their houses. This phenomenon, which scholars call *diffusion of innovations*, occurs when ideas move through the mass media. Consider the following:

- **Music, Fashion and Pop Culture.** In modern-day pop culture, the cues come through the media, mostly from New York, Hollywood and Nashville.
- **Third World Innovation.** The United Nations creates instructional films and radio programs to promote agricultural reform in less developed parts of the world. Overpopulated areas have been targets of birth control campaigns.
- **Democracy in China.** As China opened itself to Western tourists, commerce and mass media in the 1980s, the people glimpsed Western democracy government and prosperity, which precipitated pressure on the Communist government to westernize and resulted in the 1989 Tiananmen Square confrontation. A similar phenomenon was a factor in the *glasnost* relaxations in the Soviet Union in the late 1980s.
- **Demise of Main Street.** Small-town businesses are boarding up as rural people see advertisements from regional shopping malls, which are farther away but offer greater variety and lower prices than Main Street Canada.

Scholars note that the mass media can be given too much credit for the diffusion of innovations. Diffusion almost always needs reinforcement through interpersonal communication. Also, the diffusion hardly ever is a one-shot hypodermic injection but a process that requires redundancy in messages over an extended period. The 1989 outburst for democracy in China did not happen because one Chinese person read Thomas Paine one afternoon, nor do rural people suddenly abandon their local Main Street for a Wal-Mart 40 miles away. The diffusion of innovations typically involves three initial steps in which the mass media can be pivotal:

- **Awareness.** Individuals and groups learn about alternatives, new options and possibilities.

- **Interest.** Once aware, people need to have their interest further whetted.
- **Evaluation.** By considering the experience of other people, as relayed by the mass media, individuals evaluate whether they wish to adopt an innovation.

The adoption process has two additional steps in which the media play a small role: the trial stage, in which an innovation is given a try, and the final stage, in which the innovation is either adopted or rejected.

CULTURAL INTRUSION

STUDY PREVIEW   Some experts claim that the export of American and Western popular culture is latter-day imperialism, motivated by profit and without concern for its effect on other societies. This theory of cultural dominance claims too that Third World countries are pawns of the Western-based global entertainment media and news services. Other experts disagree, saying the charges of cultural imperialism are overblown and hysterical.

LATTER-DAY IMPERIALISM

Some scholars claim that international communication has a dark side, which they call *cultural imperialism*. Their view is that the media are like the 19th-century European colonial powers, exporting Western values, often uninvited, to other cultures. At stake, these critics say, is the cultural sovereignty of non-Western nations. These critics note that the international communication media have their headquarters in the United States and also in the former European colonial powers. The communication flow, they claim, is one way, from the powerful nations to the weak ones. The result, as they see it, is that Western values are imposed in an impossible-to-resist way. A Third World television station, for example, can buy a recycled American television program for far less than it costs to produce an indigenous program. The same holds true for Canadian broadcasters.

Scholar *Herbert Schiller*, who wrote *Mass Communications and American Empire*, argued that the one-way communication flow is especially insidious because the Western productions, especially movies and television, are so slick that they easily outdraw locally produced programs. As a result, says Schiller, the Western-controlled international mass media preempt native culture, a situation he sees as robbery, just like the earlier colonial tapping of natural resources to enrich the home countries.

The presence of American popular culture in Canada is easy to spot. American movies, television, pop music, books and magazines are everywhere, and so is their residue—life-styles, fashions, fads. Even in Japan, which might seem resistant to cultural invasions because of its economic might, American cultural influence is omnipresent. Magazine House, a Tokyo publishing company, has brought out one successful magazine after another, blatantly imitating Western pop culture even in titling its magazines. Among them: *Popeye*, for high school boys; *Olive*, for junior high school girls; *Tarzan* on fitness and life-style; *Brutus*, for college men; *Gulliver*, a travel magazine; and *Croissant*, for middle-aged women. Throughout the world, in Japan and elsewhere, the American soap opera "Dallas" plays and replays.

American cultural hegemony has been partly blamed on the global dominance of American advertising agencies. Said British commentator Philip Kleinman: "All over the world, ad men look to Madison Avenue as Moslems look to Mecca."

Television Everywhere. The influence of Western society has permeated cultures around the world, which critics say results in a superimposition of Western values and styles that erode worthy but fragile cultural values elsewhere. Here, cultural intrusion shows itself with latter-day Bedouins outside Raqqa, Syria, and in a rural home in Hungary.

DEFENDING WESTERN HEGEMONY

Being leaders of pop culture abroad, says advertising executive David Ogilvy, does not necessarily mean that American values are being imposed abroad. Most Ogilvy & Mather employees abroad, he notes, are not American. When agencies use American campaigns, they modify them to fit the local culture. In addition, local subsidiaries of multinational agencies create many of their campaigns. Some of the outcry against American agencies abroad, according to Ogilvy, has little to do with any cultural invasion but is a cry for profits. Locally owned agencies, he says, "have a habit of wrapping themselves in their national flag and appealing to their governments for protection against foreign invaders. They accuse us of imposing an alien culture, particularly in countries that have little culture of their own."

Some people could accuse Ogilvy of insensitivity, but he also defines another way of viewing transcultural mass communication. The goal of advertising, Ogilvy reminds critics, is to sell goods—regardless of where advertisements originate. Just because a campaign was invented elsewhere does not make it an insult to anyone's self-respect.

In some ways, cultural imperialism is in the eyes of the beholder. Some Latin American countries, for example, scream "cultural imperialism" at the United States but don't object when Mexico exports soap operas to the rest of Latin America, as do Brazil and Argentina. Although they are exercising a form of cultural imperialism, nobody puts the label on them. Media observer Larry Lorenz, who has studied this phenomenon, explains it this way: "What is occurring is simply

Cultural Intrusion. When Tokyo children grow up loving American pop culture characters like Minnie and Mickey Mouse, is native Japanese culture being lost? Scenes like this, at Disneyland in Tokyo, lead some scholars to question whether American cultural icons and values are displacing others around the globe. This type of cultural imperialism worries many Canadian communication scholars, given Canada's proximity to the U.S.

Americanizing the World

British traders introduced opium in China in the 1600s. The habit spread, and soon the British had a profitable trade importing opium to Chinese ports and exporting silver to pay for it. Resentful at British profits from the death and misery they had introduced, the Chinese government acted in 1839 against any further opium importation. In response, the British bombarded Canton, and the Opium War ensued.

Today, a similar struggle, dubbed the Second Opium war is under way. Yielding to American trade pressure, Japan, South Korea and Taiwan lifted bans on foreign tobacco in 1987, and the Marlboro man instantly became a familiar poster figure. Propelled by huge advertising budgets and American-style promotion, United States tobacco sales increased 24-fold almost overnight in Taiwan, to 5.1 billion cigarettes a year.

Is this cultural imperialism at its worst? Massachusetts Congressman Chet Atkins called it "the ultimate ugly Americanism." Noting that the U.S. government had mounted an extensive domestic campaign against smoking, Atkins said, "We are sending a message through our trade negotiators that Asian lungs are more expendable than American lungs." In Taiwan, a leading antismoking activist, David Yen, said, "We want American friendship, machinery and food—but not your drugs."

Meanwhile, the Marlboro man, taller in the saddle than ever, rides on. Smoking in Japan, South Korea and Taiwan continues to grow to record levels.

Samurai Cowboy. For better or worse, American culture has permeated cultures almost everywhere on the globe. In Tokyo, a number of country and western bars have found legions of customers eager to don a Stetson, light a Marlboro, twang a guitar and sing Willie Nelson music. American beer is big too. Critics fret that American cultural icons and values are squeezing out indigenous cultural production and values. "Cultural imperialism," they call it. Canadian culture, it seems, is not alone in falling under the influence of American pop culture.

---

internationalism brought on by the ever more sophisticated media of mass communication."

The cultural imperialism theory has other doubters among scholars. The doubters note that the theory is a simplistic application of the now-discredited hypodermic needle model of mass communication. Media messages do not have immediate direct effects. In challenging the idea of cultural imperialism as a world-changing, sinister force, scholar Michael Tracey notes that the U.S. soap opera "Dallas" is available in many different countries but is not as popular as home-produced soaps, and is almost completely ignored in many countries even though, because it can be bought cheap, it is run and re-run. In 1982, Tracey noted, "Dallas" was 69th in the Brazilian television ratings and 109th in the Mexican—hardly a world-beater.

Also overstated are charges that news from Europe and the United States dominates coverage in other parts of the world. One study found that 60 to 75 percent of the foreign news in the Third World is about other Third World countries, mostly those nearby. While the giant Western news services, AP, Agence France-Presse, Reuters, UPI and to a lesser degree TASS, are the main purveyors of foreign news, the coverage that reaches Third World audiences is extremely parochial.

TRANSNATIONAL CULTURAL ENRICHMENT

Some scholars see transnational cultural flow in more benign terms than Herbert Schiller and his fellow cultural imperialism theorists. George Steiner has noted that European and American culture have been enriched, not corrupted, by the continuing presence of Greek mythology over 2000 years. In a homely way, sociologist Michael Tracey makes a similar point:

"I was born in a working-class neighbourhood called Oldham in the north of England. Before the First World War, Oldham produced most of the world's spun cotton. It is a place of mills and chimneys, and I was born and raised in one of the areas of housing—called St. Mary's—built to serve those mills. I recently heard a record by a local group of folk singers called the Oldham Tinkers, and one track was about Charlie Chaplin. This song was apparently very popular with local children in the years immediately after the First World War. Was that evidence of the cultural influences of Hollywood, a primeval moment of the imperialism of one culture, the subjugation of another? It seems almost boorish to think of it that way. Was the little man not a deep well of pleasure through laughter, a pleasure that was simply universal in appeal? Was it not Chaplin's real genius to strike some common chord, uniting the whole of humanity? Is that not, in fact, the real genius of American popular culture, to bind together, better than anything, common humanity?"

Despite the controversy alleging cultural imperialism and the arguments to debunk it, the issue is not settled. Many Third World countries, speaking through the United Nations, have demanded subsidies from Western nations to finance local cultural enterprises. They also have demanded a policy voice in the major Western-operated global news services.

CHAPTER WRAP-UP

The mass media have caused fundamental changes in human communication. When Gutenberg introduced movable type in the 15th century, people began shifting from largely intuitive interpersonal communication to reading, which, says Canadian communication theorist Marshall McLuchan, required a different kind of concentration. The result, according to McLuhan, was less spontaneous communication, an alienation among individuals and a fragmented society. With electronic, visual media like television, which engage numerous senses and require less cerebral participation than reading, McLuhan saw a return to communication more consistent with human nature. He called it *retribalization*. Not everyone accepts McLuhan's vision, but there is agreement that the mass media profoundly affect society.

The mass media do not operate in a vacuum. The people who decide media content are products of the society, and the necessity to turn a profit requires that the media be in touch with the society's values or lose audience. In one sense, this reality of capitalism works against the media venturing too far from mainstream values. Critics say the media pander too much to popular tastes and ignore culturally significant works that could enrich society. An alternate view, more charitable to the media, is that great works trickle down to mass audiences through media popularization.

The media contribute both to social stability and to change. A lot of media content gives comfort to audiences by reinforcing existing social values. At the same time, media attention to nonmainstream ideas, in both news and fiction forms, requires people to reassess their values and, over time, contributes to social change.

QUESTIONS FOR REVIEW

1. Why are mass media more interested in reaching large audiences than in contributing to cultural sensitivity?

2. How do the mass media contribute to stability in the society?

3. What are historical and cultural transmission?

4. How did scholar Marshall McLuhan foresee that television would ease the human alienation that he said was created by the mass-produced written word?

5. Are their disadvantages when dominant societies export their values elsewhere?

QUESTIONS FOR CRITICAL THINKING

1. Why do the mass media find little room for great works that could elevate the cultural sensitivity of the society?

2. Explain essayist Susan Sontag's point that the mass media bring culturally significant works to mass audiences through the popularization process.

3. Give examples of how people shape their everyday lives around rituals created by the mass media. Also, give examples of how the mass media respond to social rituals in deciding what to present and how and when to do it.

4. Why would a radical social reformer object to most mass media content?

5. How has cognitive dissonance created through the mass media worked against racial separatism in American society since the 1950s?

6. How do the mass media help determine the issues that society sees as important?

7. How do the media contribute to social order and cohesion by reporting private acts that deviate from public morality? You might want to consider the 1992 presidential campaign of Bill Clinton, or any of the televangelism scandals.

8. Give examples of the mass media allowing cultural values to be communicated through history to future societies. Also, give examples of contemporary cultural transmission.

9. Explain scholar Marshall McLuhan's theory that the mass-produced written word has contributed to an alienation of human beings from their true nature. How did McLuhan think television could reverse this alienation?

10. Is *imperialism*, a word with strong negative implications, the best term to describe the transmission of cultural ideas and values from America to Canada?

FOR FURTHER LEARNING

Howard Hampton. "Out of Our Heads." *Gannett Center Journal* 1:133-147. Hampton, an arts critic, reviews current thinking on the media and pop culture. This entire issue of the *Gannett Center Journal* is devoted to articles on the arts and the media.

S. Robert Lichter, Linda S. Lichter and Stanley Rothman. *Watching America: What Television Tells Us About Our Lives* (Prentice Hall, 1991).

Marshall McLuhan. *The Gutenberg Galaxy: The Making of Typographic Man* (University of Toronto Press, 1967). Most of the array of McLuhan's speculations about media effects can be found in this book and in his earlier *Understanding Media: The Extensions of Man* (McGraw-Hill, 1964).

Herbert Schiller. *Mass Communications and American Empire* (Kelley, 1969). Schiller sees "imperial network" of American forces, including the media, building a cultural dominance in less developed parts of the world.

Susan Sontag. "One Culture and New Sensibility." *Against Interpretation* (Farrar Straus & Giroux, 1966). Sontag sees pop art as a vehicle for bringing cultural sensitivity to mass audiences.

Michael Tracey. "The Poisoned Chalice: International Television and the Idea of Dominance." *Daedalus* 114 (Fall 1985):4, 17-56. Tracey sees cultural imperialism as an overstated theory that is unsupported by evidence and hardly sinister.

FOR KEEPING UP TO DATE

Recommended are *The Canadian Journal of Communication, Critical Studies in Mass Communication, Journal of Popular Culture, Journal of American Culture* and *Journal of International Popular Culture*, all scholarly publications.

MASS MEDIA
in a Political Environment

National media systems conform to the political systems within which they operate

Modern authoritarian media systems use censorship, licensing, bribery and repression to control the mass media

Communist media systems differ from authoritarian systems in their premises about the nature of truth

Libertarian media systems are optimistic about the capabilities of human reason

Modern North American media practices emphasize social responsibility more than libertarian freedom

MEDIA IN THEORY

Distinguishing Media Systems

Scholars Fred Siebert, Theodore Peterson and Wilbur Schramm created models for looking at national media systems in a pioneering work, Four Theories of the Press. Their book, published in 1956, helped many later scholars make sense of the roles that mass media play in vastly different political systems.

Siebert, Peterson and Schramm identified authoritarian, communist and libertarian models, and also a

latter-day adaptation of libertarianism that they called social responsibility. There is quibbling about whether social responsibility should be a separate model, but the point really is how these models offer a systematic picture of the mass media in different nations.

Review the characteristics of media in different systems in the following table, and then see where a national media system that you or your classmates know about fits in. A good starting point would be England in the latter years of Henry VIII's reign. How about Canada? Classmates who have lived abroad or studied foreign political systems can help with other countries.

Remember, a model is never perfect, and no national media system fits into a Siebert, Peterson and Schramm pigeonhole exactly. Some developed, relatively stable countries, like the United States, are better fits than countries in the developing world that are still working out their political systems. A special challenge is where to plug in Mexico: The country has privately owned media, but criticism of government, while allowed, can bring indirect sanctions from the government. Where would Canada's mixed system fit?

	Authoritarian	**Communist**	**Libertarian**	**Social Responsibility**
Who Owns the Mass Media?	Privately owned.	State owned.	Privately owned.	Privately owned.
Is Criticism of Government Allowed?	No.	Yes, but ideology is off-limits.	Yes, even encouraged.	Yes, as long as it is responsible.
Who Decides What the Media Will Say?	The media.	The state.	The media.	Experts.
Who Decides What the Media Will Not Say?	The state.	The state.	The media.	Experts.
Who Enforces Decisions on Media Content?	The state.	The state.	Nobody.	Ideally the media, perhaps the state.

POLITICAL-MEDIA SYSTEMS

STUDY PREVIEW   Authoritarian governments, including modern-day dictatorships, regard the mass media as subservient: The government is beyond challenge. In libertarian systems, the media decide their content independent of government control. Frequently they challenge government policy. Communist systems conceive of government and media as partners in the common task of moving the society to a perfected state.

AUTHORITARIAN

Through the history of the mass media, dating to Johannes Gutenberg, authoritarian political systems have been the most common. At that time it generally was the monarchy that had great power over the expression of ideas. England was an authoritarian state that permitted neither open inquiry nor free expression. In this century, Nazi Germany, Franco's Spain and Third World dictatorships have continued the authoritarian tradition. An assumption in authoritarian systems is that the government is infallible, which means its policies are beyond question. The media role in the society is subservience to government.

LIBERTARIAN

Later, when democracies developed, first in the United States and Canada and then in France and elsewhere in western Europe, the role of the mass media was substantially different. These were libertarian countries whose political systems encouraged free expression. In democratic countries, the mass media have great liberty as unbridled forums for the expression and exchange of ideas. Leading libertarian systems today include the United States, Japan, England, Canada and the

Authoritarian Execution.
Authoritarian governments prevent mass media criticism of their policies using numerous methods, including execution. In authoritarian England, the Crown made public spectacles of executions, as in the case of John of Barneveld in 1619, above, which had a chilling effect on other people who might have challenged the Crown.

other Western democracies. Libertarianism has great faith in the wisdom of the people, who utilize the mass media to arrive at decisions on public policy. Governments, which are elected to carry out the will of the people, are under the independent scrutiny of the mass media.

COMMUNIST

Political philosopher Karl Marx inspired the youngest political and media system, which came into existence after the 1917 Bolshevik revolution in Russia. Communist mass media are regarded as government's partners in moving the society toward a perfect state. This political-media system suffered a major setback after 1990 with the overthrow of communism in the Soviet Union and in most of the countries in central Europe. It still remains the system in China and in several smaller countries, including Albania and Cuba.

AUTHORITARIAN SYSTEMS

STUDY PREVIEW   England in the 1500s and 1600s was the prototypical authoritarian state. The government asserted control over the press when it became apparent that the mass-produced written word could be used to encourage dissent and even revolution among the people. To control the mass media, authoritarian governments use censorship, licensing, repression and bribery. Defenders of authoritarian systems argue that their regimes are infallible. Others argue that bridled media are necessary for political and social stability.

ENGLAND UNDER HENRY VIII

When Johannes Gutenberg invented movable type in the 1400s, making mass production of the written word possible, authorities were enthusiastic. Early printers produced Bibles and religious tracts, which were consistent with the values of the intertwined institutions of state and church. It did not occur to anybody that the new invention might be used for heretical or traitorous purposes. Later, occasional tracts appeared that challenged the authorities, but their threat was easily dismissed because, even in the early 1500s, printing still was mostly in Latin, which could be read only by the ruling elite. Most common people were unable to read even their native language, let alone Latin. The printed word seemed an unlikely vehicle for the foment of popular revolution.

Within two generations, however, the comfortable relationship between the authorities and the fast-growing printing industry changed, and the authorities clamped down. What happened in England was typical. In 1529, after Dutch tracts that challenged royal authority began showing up in England, *King Henry VIII* outlawed imported publications. He also decreed that every English printer must be licensed. Printers caught producing anything objectionable to the crown lost their licences, in effect being put out of business. Remaining in the government's good graces brought favours. A licence meant a guaranteed local monopoly and a lock on government and church printing jobs.

Henry VIII's clampdown, a turnabout in official attitudes toward the press, was triggered by major social and political changes that were occurring in England:

- Literacy was increasing. More common people were learning to read. It became apparent that wider literacy increased the possible effect of seditious and heretical ideas on the general population.
- A mercantile class was emerging. Merchants and tradespeople were accumulating modest wealth, which permitted discretionary time in their lives and the lives of

MEDIA: PEOPLE

John Twyn

John Twyn died a particularly gruesome death. In 1663 Twyn, a printer, published a book that held that the monarch should be accountable to the people. While hardly a radical concept today, the idea was heretical in 17th-century England, where kings considered themselves divinely appointed. Twyn, who had not even written the book but merely printed it, was arrested and convicted of seditious libel. His sentence: "You shall be hanged by the neck, and being alive, shall be cut down and your privy members shall be cut off, your entrails shall be taken from your body, and you living, the same to be burnt before your eyes."

The political climate in England and the other modern Western democracies has changed dramatically since John Twyn's time. But mass communicators are still profoundly affected by the political systems within which they operate. The Committee to Protect Jour-

nalists, which tracks repression against the press, reports that dozens of reporters are jailed every year. In 1989 there were 65 journalists in 16 countries in prison or held hostage. A 66th was confined by the state to a psychiatric ward.

Even in a democracy with a constitution guaranteeing free expression and a free press, journalists are sentenced to jail from time to time, usually for refusing to identify their confidential sources when asked to do so by a judge. There are even stories of reporters' lives being threatened. *Washington Post* reporters Carl Bernstein and Bob Woodward said they learned their lives were in danger as they dug into 1972 Nixon re-election campaign scandals. In that same period, columnist Jack Anderson reported that a government plot had been hatched in the Justice Department to assassinate him for his Watergate reporting.

their families. This mercantile class, not needing to work from dawn to dusk to survive, had sufficient time to contemplate matters of state, religion and things in general. These were people who read, and a sense was developing among them that their interests as a group did not always coincide with the Crown's.

- Parliament was developing as an expression of popular will. Mercantilists found Parliament could be a powerful forum for challenging the Crown's policies, and they began using it to those ends.
- Printers were becoming bolder. The growing volume of material produced by the young printing industry included more political books and tracts, some disturbing to the Crown. The Crown perceived the threat as being all the worse because printed words were more frequently in English, not Latin, which dramatically increased their potential to stir up the masses.

Frederick Siebert, a scholar on the authoritarian English press, describes the main function of the mass media in an authoritarian system this way: "to support and advance the policies of government as determined by the political machinery then in operation." Siebert's phrase "then in operation" points out how fickle an authoritarian system can be. In 1530, when England under Henry VIII was still a Catholic state, a man was executed for selling a book by a Protestant author. Only 50 years later, after the government had rejected Catholicism, a printer was executed for printing a Catholic pamphlet. In an authoritarian system, the media are subservient to government and adjust their coverage to coincide with changes in government policy.

METHODS OF AUTHORITARIAN CONTROL

Censorship usually comes to mind as an authoritarian method to control the mass media, but censorship is labour intensive and inefficient. Other methods include licensing, bribery and repression.

CENSORSHIP.   Authoritarian regimes have found numerous ways, both blatant and subtle, to control the mass media. Censorship is one. The most thorough censoring requires that manuscripts be read by governmental agents before being printed or aired. To work, prepublication censorship requires a governmental agent in every newsroom and everywhere else that mass media messages are produced. This is hardly practicable, although governments sometimes establish elaborate censorship bureaucracies during wartime to protect sensitive military information and to ban information that runs counter to their propaganda. Even democracies have required reporters to run battlefield stories past censors.

LICENSING.   Authoritarian governments generally favour less obtrusive methods of control than censorship. Henry VIII introduced a licensing system that limited the printing trade to people who held royal patents. The mechanism for bestowing these licences rested with the Stationers Company, a trade association. Royal patents were available only to association members, and membership was tightly controlled. To stay in the Crown's favour, the Stationers Company expelled members who produced forbidden materials, in effect putting them out of business.

Four hundred years later, Nazi Germany used a more complex system. Under the guise of improving the quality of news, entertainment and culture, *Joseph*

Irrepressible. Author Salman Rushdie was the target of a death contract issued by Iran's religious-political leader, Ayatollah Ruhollah Khomeini, who found blasphemy in Rushdie's book *Satanic Verses*. Rushdie was forced into hiding, but the Ayatollah's attempt to suppress the book backfired. Instead, it whetted public interest in the book, which became a best-seller, and fueled readership for follow-up Rushdie books.

Goebbels, the minister of propaganda and public enlightenment, established guilds to which "cultural workers" had to belong. There were "chambers," as these guilds were called, for advertising, film, literature, music, the press, radio and theatre. The chambers could deny membership to cultural workers whose work did not qualify. As Nazi anti-Semitism became frenzied, however, the chambers shifted their membership criteria to exclude Jews. Membership in the press chamber, for example, was limited to third-generation so-called Aryans.

The Spanish dictator *Francisco Franco*, who came to power in 1936, employed rigid licensing. News organizations could hire only people listed on an official register of journalists. To be on the list required graduation from one of Franco's three-year journalism schools, which wove political indoctrination into the curriculum. The success of the schools, from Franco's perspective, was further assured because admission was limited to students who were sympathetic to the generalissimo.

BRIBERY.   Germany's "Iron Chancellor," Otto von Bismarck, maintained an immense fund for bribing editors, which kept much of the German press of the 1860s on his side. The practice is institutionalized in much of the impoverished Third World today, where journalists, earning barely subsistence salaries, accept gratuities on the side for putting certain stories in the paper and on the air.

Bribery also can occur when a government controls supplies that are necessary for the media to function. Franco cut newsprint deliveries to a Spanish newspaper in the early 1960s after several promonarchist articles appeared. In Mexico, a country with no newsprint manufacturing plants, PIPSA, a quasigovernment agency, allocates imported newsprint. The goal, purportedly, is to assure an even stream of paper to newspapers and magazines. In practice, however, a correlation exists between articles unfavourable to the regime and either interruptions in paper delivery or the delivery of inferior paper. The publisher of a slick magazine gets the

Authoritarianism in the Video Age

Thwarting alien ideas, always the goal of authoritarian regimes, is becoming more and more difficult, thanks to technology. Even in Henry VIII's time, when there were relatively few presses, it was impossible to track down all the sources of printed dissent. In the 20th century, ditto machines, photocopiers and fax machines compounded the frustration.

Then, in the 1980s, came low-cost videotape cameras, which anybody could operate, and videocassette recorders, which allowed people to watch forbidden things privately. Journalist Richard Zoglin, writing in *Time* magazine, said, "No matter how firm a clamp is placed on a nation's media, it can be thwarted by a determined opposition armed with video cameras." Videotape was both subverting authoritarian governments and spurring profound cultural changes:

- Strongly anti-Soviet videos, such as *Rambo,* were being bootlegged behind the Iron Curtain, where their entertainment value kept them in high demand.
- Amazon Indians were toting camcorders to meetings with Brazilian officials to, as one leader put it, "catch their lies and make them hold true to their promises."
- Palestinians were taping brutally wounded hospital patients as evidence of Israeli excesses in suppressing the revolutionary Intifada movement.
- Muslim theocracies were finding it impossible to intercept underground copies of video porn like *Debbie Does Dallas* and *Nude Jell-O Wrestling.*
- The government's pretence of democracy was exposed in Mexico, Panama and other countries by people with camcorders who recorded election fraud on videotapes that were inexpensively duplicated and put into wide circulation.

Camcorders in the Amazon. Video technology gives oppressed people a low-cost weapon to document promises by governments they don't trust. In the Amazon, the Kayapo tribe videotaped negotiations with Brazilian officials about a proposed dam.

- Distrust between Pakistanis and Indians was being undermined as Hindi music videos made their way north across the border to eager viewers and as Pakistani soap operas made their way south.

message quickly when PIPSA will supply only very rough pulp. This is subtle bribery: Publications that play ball with the regime receive a payoff in supplies essential for doing business.

REPRESSION.   Authoritarian rulers are at their most obvious when they arrest journalists who challenge their authority. Execution is the ultimate sanction. While such extreme action usually comes only after, not before, an article critical of the regime appears, it still has a chilling effect on other journalists. To learn that a fellow journalist was dragged away in the middle of the night for writing a critical article is mighty intimidating to other journalists considering similar pieces.

EFFECTIVENESS OF CONTROLS

Authoritarian controls have short-term effectiveness, but the truth is impossible to suppress for very long. In Franco's Spain, which was allied with Germany in World War II, the news media were mum for years about Nazi atrocities against Jews. Despite the media blackout, the Spanish people were aware of the Holocaust. People do not receive all their information from the mass media, and if they tend to doubt the accuracy or thoroughness of an authoritarian medium, they pay special attention to alternative sources of information, such as talking to travelers, reading contraband publications and listening secretly to transborder newscasts.

Not even prepublication censorship can stop truth. If censors purge parts of a foreign correspondent's story, editors indicate in notes inserted in the truncated story that it was subject to censorship. When reporters are denied access to censor-controlled satellite uplinks, telephones and other ways to transmit their stories, they hitch a ride elsewhere to file their stories, albeit later. Even when an authoritarian government expels journalists, stories get out. During the apartheid violence in South Africa in the late 1980s, the government monitored foreign publications and

Divine Right. King James I, who fancied himself a scholar, wrote a treatise in 1598 that claimed monarchies were legitimate because of a pipeline to God. His theory, called the divine right of kings, is a classic defence of authoritarian political and media systems.

newscasts for stories it did not like and then ousted the foreign correspondents who produced them. The result was that news gathering in South Africa was more difficult, but it hardly stopped the reporting of government abuses. Journalists instead relied on travelers to get information out of South Africa about what was happening.

In some authoritarian countries, the mass media are so compliant with the regime that the government seldom needs to crack down. In Mexico, for example, President Miguel de la Madrid Hurtado suggested in 1983 that publishers pay reporters more so that they would be less susceptible to bribes for writing favourable stories. Respectfully but forcefully, the publishers said that they would not. In 1989, de la Madrid's successor, President Carlos Salinas de Gortar, proposed that PIPSA be done away with, but the publishers objected strenuously, and PIPSA remained. In another example of media commitment to authoritarianism, the operator of the private Mexican television network has proclaimed himself "a soldier of the PRI." The PRI has long been Mexico's controlling political party, and the network executive was saying that he would do nothing to disrupt the status quo. With that sort of attitude expressed at the top, the troops in the newsroom are not even threatened by external censorship. In short, in some countries, control of the media by government is a joint operation of the media and the government. Media owners willingly, even eagerly acquiesce.

NATURE OF TRUTH

Authoritarian media systems make sense to anyone who accepts the premise that the government, whether embodied in a king or a dictator, is right in all that it says and does. Such a premise is anathema to most North Americans, but a mere 400 years ago it was mainstream Western thought. King James VII of Scotland, who later became *King James I* of England, made an eloquent argument for the *divine right of kings* in 1598. He claimed that legitimate kings were anointed by the Almighty and thereby were better able to express righteousness and truth than anyone else. By definition, therefore, anybody who differed with the king was embracing falsity and probably heresy.

The authoritarian line of reasoning justifies suppression on numerous grounds:

- Truth is a monopoly of the regime. Commoners can come to know it only through the ruler, who, in King James's thinking, has an exclusive pipeline to the Almighty. Advocates of authoritarianism have little confidence in individuals.
- Challenges to the government are based on falsity. It could not be otherwise, considering the premise that government is infallible.
- Without strong government, the stability necessary for society to function may be disrupted. Because challenges to government tend to undermine stability and because the challenges are presumed to be false to begin with, they must be suppressed.

To the authoritarian mind, journalists who support the government are purveying truth and should be rewarded. The unfaithful, who criticize, are spreading falsity and should be banished. It all makes sense if King James was right with his divine right theory. It was no wonder that sedition was a high crime.

An inherent contradiction in authoritarianism is the premise that the ruler is uniquely equipped to know truth. Experience over the centuries makes it clear that monarchs and dictators come in many stripes. Regimes have been known to change in midstream, as in Henry VIII's change of heart on Roman Catholicism. A fair question to put to authoritarian advocates is whether Henry was right when he was a Catholic, or later when he was an Anglican.

COMMUNIST SYSTEMS

STUDY PREVIEW   Many people equate authoritarian media systems with communist ones, but there are fundamental differences. The concepts of truth and how human beings can come to know truth, for example, are widely divergent.

MARXIST UNDERPINNINGS

The German philosopher *Karl Marx*, who wrote in the mid-1800s, had the idea that humankind was evolving toward a perfect state. As Marx saw it, people eventually would be living in such perfect social harmony that they would not even need government to maintain social order. The process, he said, might take a long time, centuries perhaps, but the evolution was inevitable.

In the interim before "perfection," Marx called for governments to recognize the inevitability of history and adopt policies to hasten the evolution toward the perfect state. The mass media, he said, should be government's partners in facilitating these undeniable historical processes.

In 1917, after Bolshevik revolutionaries replaced the authoritarian Russian czars, Marxists established a different kind of government, and it became the prototypical communist state until the collapse of the Soviet Union in 1991. Although the Soviet Union's successor states have moved away from the communist model, the media system of the former Soviet Union remains the best way to understand how the media are designed to work in China and other remaining communist states such as Cuba.

MARXIST NOTION OF TRUTH

The Bolshevik-created Soviet government had many earmarks of brutal authoritarianism, but its philosophical underpinnings were different. The Marxist notion of truth, for example, was radically different.

The pre-communist Russian czars, like Henry VIII and most other monarchs, had claimed an inherited superiority in developing a perfect understanding. Coming to know truth was a matter of tapping into revelation, a kind of communion with God. Only by heeding their divinely anointed ruler could common people approach such perfect understanding.

The Marxists, in contrast, said that coming to know truth was simply to recognize the inevitability of history: Historical process was truth, and truth was historical process. In short, people need not look beyond ideology for truth. Marxism's implications for the mass media were profound.

Marxist *Vladimir Lenin*, who founded the Soviet state as well as the Communist party newspaper *Pravda*, called for the media to be "collective propagandists, agitators and organizers." The 1925 Soviet constitution was clear: The fundamental purpose of the press was "to strengthen Communist social order."

***Pravda* in Translation.** Minnesota businessman Charles Cox began publishing an English translation of the leading Soviet daily, *Pravda,* something the Russians do not do. In 1985, Cox was faithful in text, layout and graphics to the original. Early subscribers were primarily government agencies (both U.S. and foreign) and colleges and universities. The paper was distributed to 21 nations around the world. But at $630 a year there were not enough subscribers to keep Cox's enterprise going.

Communist Mastermind. Vladimir Lenin, who created the Soviet Union out of the 1917 Bolshevik revolution, conceived of the mass media as government's partner in moving society toward perfection. Under this concept, leaders of the government and the Communist Party held key posts in the media. After the collapse of the Soviet Union in the early 1990s, the people who ran the country's newspapers and magazines and broadcast media found it difficult to switch to the new reality of democracy in a Western vein.

MEDIA UNIFIED WITH GOVERNMENT

Authoritarian and communist media are structured differently. Most authoritarian systems are rooted in capitalism. The mass media are owned by people whose business is to make money, and the profit motive is a major factor in deciding what goes to print and what is put on the air. In general, authoritarian governments interfere only on issues directly affecting the government's ability to stay in power and maintain social order. Most of the time, the media in authoritarian states operate independent of government.

In communist countries, the economic structure is socialist. Unconcerned about profit, communist media people choose to provide coverage that furthers the government's ideological goals. In fact, media decision makers usually are government officials chosen because they are in tune with Marx's central idea on the inevitability of historical processes. When the Soviet Union was in full flower as a communist state, for example, the editors of the leading publications were all high officials in the Communist Party. One media scholar called it akin to having the vice president of the United States editing the *Washington Post.*

In practice, communist governments and media often fall short of their ideological mandate and appear authoritarian. Still, Marxist roots show through. A Polish journalist who defected to the United States when Poland was still a communist state gave this account of a gang rape he covered: "The story did not appear in its original form. The details of the incident were heavily toned down, as they would have marred the image of happy and idealistic youngsters building socialism." In an authoritarian system, in contrast, ideology would not be a factor in deciding how to report such a story.

Also unlike authoritarian systems, communist media criticize government. Throughout the history of the Soviet Union, the media were loaded with stories on official bungling and inefficiency, although usually at a low level, such as a factory commissar who was looking the other way at warehouse thievery. Typical was "Bring the Parasites to Account," a *Pravda* story on chronic production shortages blamed on bad managers. Soviet newspapers and magazines invited readers to be whistle-blowers. The accusations were investigated, and the resulting stories were intended to discourage practices that were retarding the arrival of a perfect state.

Off-limits in the communist media, however, is criticism of Marxist ideology, which is accorded the sacred respect that ultimate truth deserves.

LIBERTARIAN SYSTEMS

STUDY PREVIEW   Libertarian thinkers have faith in the ability of human beings to come to know great truths by applying reason. Libertarians feel that a robust, open exchange of ideas will eliminate flawed notions and reinforce good ones. This process, however, may take time because people individually and collectively make short-term mistakes.

OPTIMISM ABOUT THE HUMAN MIND

Physicists love telling young science pupils the story of an English lad, Isaac Newton, who, sitting in an orchard one late-summer day, was struck on the head by a falling apple. Voilà! At that moment the law of gravity was instantly clear to Isaac Newton. It is a good story, though not a true one. Deriving the law of gravitation was a much more sophisticated matter for Newton, the leading 17th-century physicist, but the orchard story lives on. It is a story also told to pupils in their first world history class to illustrate a period in intellectual history called the *Enlightenment*. In this version, young Newton not only discovered gravity at the very instant that he was bumped on the head, but he also realized that he could come to know great truths like the law of gravity by using his own mind. He did not need to rely on a priest or a monarch or anyone else claiming a special relationship with God. He could do it on his own. This revelation, say the history teachers, was a profound challenge to authoritarian premises and ushered in the era of rationalist thinking that marks the modern age. Individually and together, people were capable of learning the great truths, called the *natural law*, unassisted by governing authorities. The insight of the Enlightenment was that human beings are rational beings. It marked the beginning of quantum progress in the sciences. The insight also contributed to the development of *libertarianism*, which held the intellectual roots of modern democracy.

MARKETPLACE OF IDEAS

An English writer, *John Milton*, was the pioneer libertarian. In his 1644 pamphlet *Areopagitica*, Milton made a case for free expression based on the idea that individual human beings were capable of discovering truth if given the opportunity. Milton called for a *marketplace of ideas* in which people could choose from the range of human ideas and values, just as shoppers pinch a lot of fruits and vegetables at the produce market until they find the best. Milton's marketplace of ideas was not a place but a concept. It existed whenever people exchanged ideas, whether in conversation or letters or the printed word.

Milton was eloquent in his call for free expression. He saw no reason to fear any ideas, no matter how subversive, because human beings inevitably would choose the best ideas and values. "Let [Truth] and Falsehood grapple: whoever knew Truth put to the worse in a free and open encounter?" he wrote. Milton reasoned that people would gain confidence in their own ideas and values if they tested them continually against alternative views. It was an argument against censorship. People need to have the fullest possible selection in the marketplace if they are going to go home with the best product, whether vegetables or ideas. Also, bad ideas should be present in the marketplace because, no matter how obnoxious, they might contain a grain of truth worth considering.

Milton acknowledged that people sometimes err in sorting out alternatives, but these mistakes are corrected as people continually reassess their values against competing values in the marketplace. Milton saw this truth seeking as a never-

MEDIA ABROAD

Journalism Colombia-Style

Journalistic War Zone. Reporting the news takes special courage in Colombia, where drug lords take terrorist initiatives when they are unhappy with coverage. In September 1989, the newspaper *El Espectador* in Bogota was bombed. One person died and 70 were injured. Damage totaled $2.5 million, including the loss of 1200 tons of newsprint.

Journalists in some countries do their work in fear of authoritarian governments. In Colombia the dangers are from the cocaine cartels, which object to being covered in the news media. From 1985 to 1989, at least 33 Colombian journalists were killed. Dozens more have fled the country after receiving death threats.

The leading newspaper, *El Espectador,* has been a particular target. Gunmen on motorcycles shot the editor and the newspaper's lawyer on a street in 1986. In 1989 two other *El Espectador* employees were similarly cut down on the street. More than 70 people were injured when a bomb planted in a pickup truck blew up at the newspaper's plant.

Here is a look at the working news media in Colombia:

- Security guards hold machine guns on visitors at the entrance to the Caricol radio station in Bogota.
- Five metre concrete walls topped by razor-wire lines surround *El Colombiano's* newspaper plant in Medellin.
- A photographer for Colombian Television tucks a .38-calibre revolver in his battery-pack belt.
- Armed guards and bullet-proof cars protect television reporters as they make their rounds.

ending, lifelong human pursuit, which meant that people would shed flawed ideas and values for better ones over time. Milton called this a *self-righting process.*

LIBERTARIANS AND RELIGION

Early libertarian headiness over the potential of the human mind created conflicts with religious authorities. The traditional clerics were authoritarian, with an essentially negative view of human nature. According to some theologians, people were incapable of fulfilling their human nature on their own. Libertarians, on the other hand, were intoxicated with the belief that human beings could fulfill their nature and come to know ultimate truths by applying reason alone. Implicit in libertarianism, it seemed, was that traditional religion was an extraneous vestige of less-enlightened times.

The conflict has not been entirely resolved, but many modern libertarians note that the natural law, which they claim can be learned through human analytical processes, coincides with the ultimate truths to which churches in an authoritarian period sought to bring the faithful. The reconciliation equates the libertarians' notion of natural law with the religious notion of God's will. The American thinker *Carl Becker* addressed the conflict in 1945 when he updated John Milton with this summation of libertarianism: "If men were free to inquire about all things, to form opinions on the basis of knowledge and evidence, and to utter their opinions freely, the competition of knowledge and opinion in the marketplace of rational discourse would ultimately banish ignorance and superstition and enable men to shape their conduct and their institutions in conformity with the fundamental and *invariable laws of nature* and the *will of God.*"

FREEDOM AND RESPONSIBILITY

STUDY PREVIEW   An uneasiness developed in the 20th century over the validity of the libertarian assumptions necessary for the marketplace of ideas to work. In 1947 a private panel, the Hutchins Commission, gave voice to this uneasiness in identifying abuses of press freedom and recommending a change in emphasis from a *free* to a *responsible* press. This new emphasis came to be called the *social responsibility* concept, and it gradually was adopted by the media as a modification of traditional libertarian thinking.

FLAWED LIBERTARIAN ASSUMPTIONS

The novelist and muckraker *Upton Sinclair* raised questions about the integrity of newspapers in his novel *The Brass Check*, published in 1919. Sinclair offered a look inside an imaginary newsroom in which powerful interests could bribe their way into print. He outlined how newspapers could abuse their freedom. The doubts that Sinclair planted about the news media grew. Many people were bothered about one-sidedness in newspapers, especially as consolidations reduced the number of competing newspapers. Orson Welles's 1941 movie *Citizen Kane*, based on newspaper publisher William Randolph Hearst, undermined public confidence in the people who ran newspapers. So did the quirkiness of other prominent publishers, such as *Robert McCormick*, who turned the *Chicago Tribune* into a campaign vehicle for simplified spellings like "thru" for "through," "frate" for "freight" and "buro" for "bureau." McCormick was always quick to defend his eccentricities, as well as the *Tribune's* blatantly right-wing news coverage, in the name of a free press. Ameri-

Marketplace of Ideas. John Milton gave the world the marketplace of ideas concept in his 1644 pamphlet *Areopagitica,* which paved the way for libertarianism. Milton said that everyone should be free to express ideas, no matter how traitorous, blasphemous, deleterious or just plain silly, for the consideration of other people. It was a strong argument against restrictions on free expression.

cans, imbued with libertarian idealism, were hesitant to challenge McCormick and other media barons but there were growing doubts by the late 1940s about whether modern society provided a proper environment for the marketplace of ideas. These doubts concerned basic libertarian assumptions:

PEOPLE ARE CAPABLE OF DISTINGUISHING TRUTH. In their enthusiasm about human nature, libertarians assumed that people are involved in a life-long quest for knowledge, truth and wisdom. There was evidence aplenty, however, that many people could not care less about the great questions of human existence. People might be capable of sorting truth from falsity in the marketplace of ideas, but many do not work at it.

MEDIA ARE DIVERSE. Libertarians imagined a world of so many diverse publications that there would be room for every outlook. In the 20th century, however, some people saw a reduction in media diversity. Cities with several newspapers lost papers one by one to the point that in the 1940s few cities had more than two newspapers. Only three broadcast networks dominated radio coverage of national and international affairs.

MEDIA INDEPENDENCE. Libertarianism assumes that truth-seeking individuals exchange ideas in an unstructured, free-wheeling marketplace. As governments picked up public relations skills, however, the media have experienced varying degrees of manipulation, which has detracted from their role as the vehicles of the marketplace. Also, the reliance of media on advertising means that media whose coverage is not attractive to advertisers are squeezed out of existence.

EASY ACCESS TO MEDIA. The libertarian notion of all citizens engaging in great dialogues through the media seemed naïve to some people. Few newspapers published more than a half a dozen reader letters a day, and the reduction in the number of cities with multiple newspapers had further devalued newspapers as a vehicle for citizen exchange.

Impetus to Social Responsibility.
The blue-ribbon Hutchins Commission called in 1947 for the media to be more socially responsible, but not until the 1950s did news people begin a serious self-assessment of their practices. One trigger of the self-assessment was the damage that resulted from news coverage of false charges by Wisconsin Senator Joseph McCarthy that communists had infiltrated federal agencies. The reporting that McCarthy made the allegations was literally accurate, but it failed to raise essential questions about McCarthy's credibility. When the news media realized they had been duped by McCarthy, and that the American people had been duped through them, there developed an emphasis on reporting to put events "in a context that makes them meaningful," as the Hutchins Commission had recommended in 1947.

Electronic Town Hall. Ross Perot took his bid for the presidency directly to the people with live televised speeches and appearances on talk shows. This bypassed the usual processes that the news media use in boiling down, summarizing and packaging the news. Bypassing media gate-keepers allowed Perot to maintain more control over his messages. Other candidates also are using new technology to communicate directly with voters.

HUTCHINS COMMISSION

Doubts about some libertarian assumptions took firm shape in 1947 when magazine tycoon *Henry Luce* gave a grant of $200 000 to an old college friend, *Robert Maynard Hutchins*, to study the American press. Hutchins, chancellor of the University of Chicago, assembled a group of scholars. Like the Davey and Kent Commissions in Canada, the *Hutchins Commission*, as it was called, issued a bombshell report that expressed concern that the news media were becoming too powerful. The commission cited the growth of newspaper chains. To Luce's dismay, the commission also seemed concerned about the power of magazine groups like his own

Murphy Brown and Baby. When television character Murphy Brown found herself pregnant and unwed,
then Vice-President Dan Quayle made a political issue
out of it. It was a bad example, he said. Quayle was
assuming that Brown somehow was undermining family
values among the millions of people who watched the
program regularly. Whether Quayle was overly concerned is open to debate: Some experts say the media
mirror social values, including those that are in flux;
other experts say that the media are in the vanguard of
ushering in change and setting the direction for evolving
values; others say the media both follow and lead.
Whatever the case, mother and baby are doing fine.

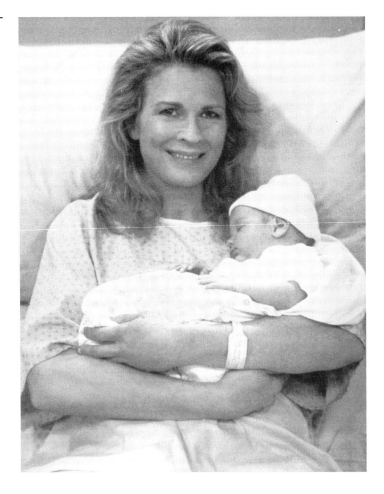

Time, Life and *Fortune.* The commission said the news media needed to be more
responsible and specifically called on the press to provide:

- A truthful, comprehensive and intelligent account of the day's events in a con-
  text that makes them meaningful.
- A forum for exchange of comment and criticism, including contrary ideas.
- A representative picture of society's constituent groups, including blacks and
  other minorities.
- Coverage that challenges society's goals and values and helps clarify them.

Luce was livid. He had established the commission hoping to blunt criticism
that his own magazines were one-sided and too powerful. It backfired. The commission raised serious questions about news media practices that Luce and other
media barons had defended in the name of freedom of the press. *Robert McCormick*,
publisher of the *Chicago Tribune*, mounted a tirade and commissioned a book to rip
the commission's report apart. Newspaper trade associations went on record that
the republic was best served when nobody was looking over journalists' shoulders.
Freedom of the press, they argued, was at stake when government or anybody else,
including a private group of eggheads under Robert Hutchins's direction, tried to

prescribe what the press should do. The same argument was made by Canadian newspapers after the two Royal Commissions looked into newspapers.

RESPONSIBILITY VERSUS PROFITABILITY

The mass media's concern for social responsibility is sometimes at odds with the imperative placed on media managers to turn profits, which is reasonable in a capitalistic system. However, profitability can be damaged by socially responsible journalism. For example:

- Newspapers can keep costs down with fewer pages and more ads than news.
- A major grocery chain threatens to discontinue advertising if a television station proceeds with a story about unsanitary practices in the grocery store's delicatessens.
- Most advertisers buy space and time in media geared for upscale audiences with buying power. This may exclude the poor and some minority groups.
- A reporter proposes a significant investigative project that is journalistically promising, but the time and expense, and possible legal costs, would undercut the station's profitability.

The fact is that the mass media today, particularly the news media, are pursuing divergent policies. Doing what is right journalistically does not always coincide with doing what will enhance profits, and doing what is profitable can work against good journalism.

In short, good journalism and good profits are not always easy partners. Financially strong newspapers are in better positions to resist forces that can work against good journalism, but there are some news organizations that have built their financial strength by bowing to powerful influences and diluting their journalistic aggressiveness.

EXCEPTIONS TO SOCIAL RESPONSIBILITY

Despite the evidence that the news media operate in a more socially responsible framework today than before, there are exceptions. Some media companies, particularly absentee chain owners of many smaller papers, begrudge newsroom expenditures and do not even run editorials regularly. Some newspapers find it cheaper to print news-service stories from remote parts of the globe than to send a reporter to the courthouse every day.

There have been many exceptions to social responsibility in Canada, including:

- K.C. Irving's newspaper monopoly. In the 1960s, Irving owned all five of New Brunswick's English dailies. He was chastized in 1970 by the Davey Committee for not carrying reports about the New Brunswick Water Authority's new antipollution regulations for pulp mills in his newspapers. In addition to owning the five newspapers, Irving also owned one of the largest pulp mills in New Brunswick.
- The Kitchener Market controversy in the 1970s. This involved a debate about whether the old Kitchener market should be replaced with a new building in the downtown area. Media owners and managers did not represent the opinions of those opposed to the new market, while giving extensive coverage to those who supported the initiative. A letter to the editor in favour of the new market was planted in the *Kitchener-Waterloo Record*.

Campaigning with a Sax.
Political candidates have learned to take their campaigns live directly to the people via radio and television. Bill Clinton did it with entertainment program appearances during the 1992 elections, including the "Arsenio Hall Show" where he played the saxophone. This form of campaigning through electronic media bypasses journalists who once were an intermediary between candidates and voters.

- The reluctance of two small-town newspapers to report news about water pollution. In Tilsonburg and Ingersoll, Ontario, local papers gave little coverage to reports on a contaminated well.

CHAPTER WRAP-UP

A nation's political and media systems mirror each other. Democracies have libertarian media systems in which government functions under the watchful eye of the independent news media. The media, in fact, are called "watchdogs" because they are expected to identify misdeeds by government and bring them to public attention.

Today, most developed Western nations are in the libertarian tradition. The development of these governing and media systems was a reaction to authoritarian systems in which the government operated dictatorially and controlled the media through a variety of means, including censorship, licensing, bribery and repression.

Authoritarian and libertarian systems spring from philosophically distinct premises. Authoritarianism, which operates today in much of the world, is doubtful about the ability of people to govern themselves. Trust is placed in a dictator, monarch or other ruler, sometimes assumed to be divinely appointed. In authoritarian systems, the media follow the leadership of the infallible governing authority. Libertarianism, on the other hand, has confidence in the ability of human beings, individually and collectively, to conduct their affairs on their own.

In the 20th century, Soviet communism emerged as a third and distinct government and media system. On a philosophical plane, communism respects neither a single leader nor the people. Instead, it trusts great historical movements to bring about, eventually, a perfect society. The government and the media are interim entities expected to facilitate and hasten the inevitable arrival of utopia. The Soviet Union, which led the way with communism, began a dramatic shift to libertarianism in the late 1980s after 60 years of frustration at making its style of communism work, but communist media systems remain in China and some tertiary communist countries.

QUESTIONS FOR **REVIEW**

1. Name the major national political and media systems in the world today.
2. How would someone defend authoritarian media systems?
3. How do communist media systems differ from authoritarian systems regarding the nature of truth?

4. How do libertarians regard human reason, and how does this figure into libertarian media systems?
5. Why have media practices shifted away from an emphasis on freedom to an emphasis on social responsibility?

QUESTIONS FOR **CRITICAL THINKING**

1. Why is it impossible for a libertarian country to have an authoritarian or communist media system? Can an authoritarian country have a libertarian or communist media system? Can a communist country have a libertarian or authoritarian system?
2. How did 16th-century England embody the thinking that still is at the heart of authoritarian media systems?
3. Describe how modern dictatorships, as well as the fascist Nazi and Mussolini regimes of the 1930s and 1940s, used the same methods of authoritarian control as Henry VIII.
4. Why are government attempts at suppressing information usually futile in the long term?
5. In the authoritarian scheme of thinking, how do

people come to know truth? In a libertarian scheme? In a communist scheme?
6. How do authoritarians view the potential of human reason? Libertarians? Communists?
7. How did Enlightenment thinking lead to libertarian media systems? Discuss this in terms of specific libertarian philosophers.
8. How did Upton Sinclair, Orson Welles and Robert Hutchins contribute to 20th-century changes in the libertarian media concept?
9. In what periods of history did the authoritarian media concept thrive? Libertarian? Communist?
10. Name as many countries as you can with a libertarian media system. Name those with an authoritarian system. Name those with a communist system.

FOR **FURTHER LEARNING**

Carl L. Becker. *Freedom and Responsibility in the American Way of Life* (Vintage, 1945). Becker, a historian, updates classic libertarianism in terms of mid-20th-century American life.

Isaiah Berlin. *Karl Marx: His Life and Environment* (Oxford University Press, 1939). This enduring biography of Marx and his ideas was written by a British scholar and diplomat.

Kevin Cash. *Who the Hell Is William Loeb?* (Amoskeog Press, 1975). A former Manchester *Union Leader* staff member writes unflatteringly about how Loeb ran New Hampshire's dominant newspaper.

Commission on Freedom of the Press. *A Free and Responsible Press* (University of Chicago, 1947). This is the Hutchins Commission report from which have sprung the social responsibility modifications of libertarian thinking about the press.

John Hannigan. "Ideology, Elites and the Canadian Mass Media." In *Communications in Canadian Society*, ed. Benjamin Singer (Addison-Wesley, 1983).

Frank Hughes. *Prejudice and the Press* (Devin-Adair, 1950). Commissioned by Robert McCormick, publisher of the *Chicago Tribune*, this is an attempt to refute the 1947 Hutchins Commission report that said the U.S.

mass media were so obsessed with freedom of the press that they overlooked an obligation to be responsible.

John C. Merrill. *An Imperative of Freedom: A Philosophy of Journalistic Autonomy* (Hastings House, 1974). Merrill, a media scholar, offers a totalitarian-anarchy continuum model of major media systems.

Fred Siebert, Theodore Peterson and Wilbur Schramm. *Four Theories of the Press* (University of Illinois Press, 1956). Siebert, Peterson and Schramm root national political and media systems in philosophical premises about the nature of knowledge, humankind and soci-

ety. *Four Theories* remains the seminal work for later treatments of the subject.

Joseph Robson Tanner. *English Constitutional Conflicts of the Seventeenth Century, 1603-1689* (Cambridge University Press, 1928). Tanner explains the intellectual foundation of James I's argument for the divine right of kings and explores how the doctrine was debated through the 1600s. Tanner's frequent citations of 17th-century documents, with their cumbersome verbiage, makes for heavy reading.

■ FOR KEEPING UP TO DATE

Index on Censorship, published in London, England, provides monthly country-by-country status reports.

Scholarly journals that carry articles on foreign media systems, international communication and media responsibility include the *Journal of Broadcasting & Electronic Media*, the *Journal of Communication* and *Journalism Quarterly.*

Professional journals that carry articles on foreign media systems and on media responsibility include *Columbia Journalism Review*, *Quill* and *American Journalism Review.*

Ongoing discussion on media responsibility also appears in the *Journal of Mass Media Ethics.*

MEDIA RESEARCH
The Quest for Useful Data

Mass media organizations are more interested in applied than theoretical research

Surveys tell the mass media about their audiences

The size of mass media audiences is measured by monitoring press runs and sales and by surveying

Mass media organizations measure the reactions of people to make informed decisions about content

Audience analysis techniques include demographic, geodemographic and psychographic breakdowns

MEDIA IN THEORY

Applied and Theoretical Research

Media-sponsored research looks for ways to build audiences, to enhance profits and to program responsibly. In contrast, mass communication scholarship asks theoretical questions that can yield new understandings, regardless of whether there is a practical application.

MEDIA-SPONSORED RESEARCH

Studies sponsored by mass media companies seek knowledge that can be put to use, or applied. This is called applied research. When broadcasters underwrite research on media violence, they want answers to help make programming decisions. Audience measures and analysis are applied research, which can be put to work to enhance profits.

Mass media research ranges from developing new technology to seeking historical lessons from previous practices. Here are some fields of applied media research:

TECHNOLOGICAL RESEARCH. Mass media companies and their suppliers finance research into technology to take economic advantage of new opportunities. Early television in the United States, for example, was spearheaded in the 1930s by RCA, which saw new opportunities for its NBC radio subsidiary. Ink manufacturers introduced nonsmudge soybean inks in the late 1980s for newspapers. Besides cutting-edge technological research, media companies also sponsor finding out ways to adapt innovations developed in other fields, such as computers and satellites, to reduce costs, improve profits and remain competitive.

PUBLIC POLICY ANALYSIS. The media have intense interests in how changes in public policy will affect their business. Analysts anticipated correctly that the television networks would go to satellites to send programs to their affiliates, but they failed to anticipate that network affiliates would use their new downlink dishes to pick up programming from non-network sources and accelerate the fragmentation of the television industry.

FINANCIAL STUDIES. Whether Merrill Lynch recommends that investors be bullish on Southam depends on how analysts interpret Southam's periodic financial reports. Even privately held media companies are subject to analysis. Competitors make decisions based on their assessment of the marketplace and all the players.

OPINION SURVEYS. When anchor Dan Rather began wearing a sweater on the "CBS Evening News," ratings improved. The network learned about the "sweater factor" from audience surveys. Survey research helps media executives make content decisions—whether to expand sports coverage, to hire a disc jockey away from the competition, or to axe a dubious sitcom. Advertisers and public relations practitioners also look to public-opinion surveys.

MASS COMMUNICATION SCHOLARSHIP

In contrast to applied research, theoretical research looks for truths regardless of practical application. Scholars consider most theoretical research on a higher level than applied research, partly because the force that drives it is the seeking of truths for their own sake rather than for any economic goal.

Profit motivated as they are, media organizations are not especially enthusiastic about funding theoretical research. There usually is no apparent or short-term economic return from theoretical scholarship. For this reason, most theoretical research occurs at major universities, whose institutional commitments include pushing back the frontiers of human knowledge, even if no economic reward is likely. Here are some of the kinds of studies and analyses that are the subject of theoretical research:

EFFECTS STUDIES. The greatest ferment in mass communication scholarship has involved questions about effects. In the 1920s, as mass communication theory took form, scholars began exploring the effects of mass communication and of the mass media themselves on society and individuals. Conversely, scholars are also interested in how ongoing changes and adjustments in society influence the mass media and their content.

PROCESS STUDIES. A continuing interest among scholars is the mystery of how the process of mass communication works. Just as human beings have developed theories to explain other great mysteries, such as thunder being caused by unhappy gods thrashing about in the heavens, mass communication scholars have developed a great many explanations to help us understand mass communication.

Examples of these theories include the diverse models that scholars have created of the mass communication process. You might recall the general, concentric circle and narrative models from Chapter 1. None of these models is as way out as the thrashing-gods explanation for thunder, but their diversity indicates that many questions still need to be asked and explored before we can ever develop the kind of understanding about mass communication that scientists now have about thunder.

GRATIFICATIONS STUDIES.   Beginning in the 1940s, studies about how and why individuals use the mass media attracted scholarly interest. These today are called uses and gratifications studies.

CONTENT ANALYSIS.   George Gerbner, a scholar of media violence, studied the 8 p.m. hour of network television for 19 years and found an average of 168 violent acts a week. Gerbner arrived at his disturbing statistic through content analysis, a research method involving the systematic counting of media content. Gerbner's tallying became a basic reference point for important further studies that correlated media-depicted violence with changes in incidents of violence in society at large.

It is also content analysis when a researcher tallies the column inches of sports in a newspaper to determine what percentage of available space goes to sports. While interesting for its own sake, such information can become a significant indicator of the changing role of sports in our culture.

MediaWatch is a national, volunteer network of feminists who monitor sexism in the media. Content analysis is one of their techniques. Through content analysis, MediaWatch studies have been able to uncover the following examples of sexism in Canadian media:

- Seventy percent of bylines in Canadian newspapers belong to men; only 305 belong to women. The *Globe and Mail* was singled out as the worst offender; 87 percent of bylines are male, 13 percent are female.
- Eighty-five percent of all interviewees on TV news are male; 15 percent are female.

HISTORICAL STUDIES.   Some scholars specialize in deriving truths about the mass media and mass communication by examining evidence from the past.

CRITICAL STUDIES.   Scholars who are engaged in critical studies question underlying institutions and their economic, philosophical and political assumptions that shape the mass media. These scholars pose provocative questions from the frameworks of diverse disciplines, questioning things that most people take for granted. The semiotic school falls under the umbrella term critical studies.

CNN Anchor Bernard Shaw

Fickle Audience.   Television executives look to survey research to find ways to reach more viewers. In 1994, CNN's ratings were down 25 percent from a year earlier. That prompted the network to scrap some soft-news programs, including "Living in the '90s," and to create new call-in sports and news programs, one with a live audience. CNN's problem is that it cannot sustain the huge audience it draws when everybody is intently interested in major news, like the O. J. Simpson case or Operation Desert Storm. The network typically draws only about 400,000 viewers. Although CNN's audience is educated, affluent and attractive to advertisers, more viewers would mean more revenue. CNN accounts for 70 percent of Turner Broadcasting System's operating earnings.

PUBLIC-OPINION SURVEYING

STUDY PREVIEW   Public-opinion polling is an important ancillary activity for the mass media. One polling technique, probability sampling, relies on statistical guidelines that can be incredibly accurate. Sad to say, less reliable survey techniques also are used, which sullies the reputation of serious sampling.

THE SURVEYING INDUSTRY

Public-opinion surveying is a business whose clients include major corporations, political candidates, and the mass media. Hundreds of companies are in the survey business, most performing advertising and product-related opinion research for private clients. During election campaigns, political candidates become major clients. There are dozens of other survey companies that do confidential research for and about the media. Their findings are important because they determine what kind of advertising will run and where, what programs will be developed and broadcast and which ones will be canceled. Some television stations even use such research to choose anchors for major newscasts.

PROBABILITY SAMPLING

Although polling has become a high-profile business, many people do not understand how questions to a few hundred individuals can tell the mood of millions. In the *probability sampling* method pioneered by George Gallup in the 1940s, four factors figure into accurate surveying:

SAMPLE SIZE.   To learn how students from a certain community college or university feel about abortion on demand, you start by asking one student. Because you can hardly generalize from one student to the whole student body of 2000, you ask a second student. If both agree, you start developing a tentative sense of how students at this college feel, but because you cannot have much confidence in such a tiny sample, you ask a third student, and a fourth and a fifth. At some point between interviewing just one and all 2000 students, you can draw a reasonable conclusion.

Statisticians have found that 384 is a magic number for many surveys. Put simply, no matter how large the population being sampled, if every member has an equal opportunity to be polled, you need ask only 384 people to be 95 percent confident that you are within 5 percentage points of a precise reading. For a lot of surveys, that is close enough. Here is a breakdown, from Philip Meyer's *Precision Journalism*, a book for journalists on surveying, on necessary sample sizes for 95 percent confidence and being within 5 percentage points:

Population Size	Sample Size
Infinity	384
500 000	384
100 000	383
50 000	381
10 000	370
5000	357
3000	341
2000	322
1000	278

Judging Surveys

A 1975 poll found that one in seven adults had been polled at least once by some survey or another.

■ Have you ever played a part in a poll or any other survey? Has anyone in your family? Any of your friends?

■ Did you see the poll results to determine whether your views coincided with the majority's?
■ Do you think that the poll extrapolated accurately from the small sample? Did you know the sample size? How it was selected? The margin of error? The confidence level?

At a community college with a total enrollment of 2000, the sample size would need to be 322 students.

SAMPLE SELECTION. Essential in probability sampling is giving every member of the population being sampled an equal chance to be interviewed. If, for example, you want to know how Kansans intend to vote, you cannot merely go to a Wichita street corner and survey the first 384 people who pass by. You would need to check a list of the state's registered voters and then divide by the magic number, 384:

$$\frac{675\,000}{384} = 1758$$

You would need to talk with every 1758th person on the list. At your school, 2000 divided by 322 would mean an interval of 6.2. Every sixth person in the student body would need to be polled.

Besides the right sample size and proper interval selection, two other significant variables affect survey accuracy: margin of error and confidence level.

MARGIN OF ERROR. For absolute precision, every person in the population must be interviewed, but such precision is hardly ever needed, and the process would be prohibitively expensive and impracticable. Pollsters, therefore, must decide what is an acceptable margin of error for every survey they conduct. This is a complex matter, but, in simple terms, you can have a fairly high level of confidence that a properly designed survey with 384 respondents can yield results within 5 percentage points, either way, of being correct. If the survey finds that two candidates for provincewide office are running 51 to 49 percent, for example, the race is too close to call with a sample of 384. If, however, the survey says that the candidates are running 56 to 44 percent, you can be reasonably confident who is ahead in the race because, even if the survey is 5 points off on the high side for the leader, the candidate at the very least has 51 percent support (56 percent minus a maximum 5 percentage points for possible error). At best, the trailing candidate has 49 percent (44 percent plus a maximum 5 percentage points for possible error).

Increasing the sample size will reduce the margin of error. Meyer gives this breakdown:

Population Size	Sample Size	Margin of Error
Infinity	384	5 percentage points
Infinity	600	4 percentage points
Infinity	1067	3 percentage points
Infinity	2401	2 percentage points
Infinity	9605	1 percentage points

Professional polling organizations that sample voters typically use sample sizes between 1500 and 3000 to increase accuracy. Also, measuring subgroups within the population being sampled requires that each subgroup, such as men and women, of Catholics and non-Catholics be presented by 384 properly selected people.

CONFIDENCE LEVEL.   With a sample of 384, pollsters can claim a relatively high 95 percent confidence level, that is, that they are within 5 percentage points of being on the mark. For many surveys, this is sufficient statistical validity. If the confidence level needs to be higher, or if the margin of error needs to be decreased, the number of people surveyed will need to be increased. In short, the level of confidence and margin of error are inversely related. A larger sample can improve confidence, just as it also can reduce the margin of error.

QUOTA SAMPLING

Besides probability sampling, pollsters survey cross-sections of the whole population. With quota sampling, a pollster checking an election campaign interviews a sample of people that includes a quota of men and women that corresponds to the number of male and female registered voters. The sample might also include an appropriate quota of Liberals, New Democrats, Conservatives, Reformers and independents; of poor, middle-income and wealthy people; of Catholics, Jews and Protestants; of the employed and unemployed; and other breakdowns significant to the pollster.

Both quota and probability sampling are valid if done correctly, but Gallup abandoned quota sampling because he could not pinpoint public opinion closer than 4 percentage points on average. With probability sampling, he regularly came within 2 percentage points.

EVALUATING SURVEYS

Sidewalk interviews cannot be expected to reflect the views of the population. The people who respond to such polls are self-selected by virtue of being at a given place at a given time. Just as unreliable are call-in polls with 800 or 900 telephone numbers. These polls test the views only of people who are aware of the poll and who have sufficiently strong opinions to want to be heard.

Journalists run the risk of being duped when special-interest groups suggest that news stories be written based on their privately conducted surveys. Some organizations selectively release self-serving conclusions.

Incompetence in designing a survey can mar results. Surveys by college research methodology classes are notorious. Results can be seriously skewed if even one student, perhaps under deadline pressure at the end of a semester, fakes data and is not caught.

Despite their current ambivalence about Clinton's health care plan, Americans feel -- by more than a two-to-one margin -- that the Clinton administration has had a positive (62%) rather than negative (28%) influence on efforts to reform the health care system. Also by a substantial margin, Democrats in Congress are seen as having a positive (52%) rather than negative (28%) influence. On the other hand, Republicans in Congress are seen as having more of a negative (51%) than positive (29%) influence.

Clinton has criticized the insurance companies and lobbyists who have strongly opposed his health care plan, and most Americans have taken his side. By more than a three-to-one margin, these groups are viewed as having a negative rather than positive influence on health reform. Doctors and hospitals are also viewed as a negative (51%) rather than positive (33%) influence.

Methodology

The current results are based on telephone interviews with a randomly selected national sample of 1,019 adults, 18 years and older, conducted June 25-28, 1994. For results based on the whole sample, one can say with 95 percent confidence that the error attributable to sampling and other random effects could be plus or minus 3 percentage points. For results based on just half the sample, the margin of error is plus or minus 5 percentage points. In addition to sampling error, question wording and practical difficulties in conducting surveys can introduce error or bias into the findings of public opinion polls.

How well do you understand the details you have heard or read so far about the debate over health care reform in this country? Would you say you understand most of those details, many of them, a few of them, or none of them at all?

Most	29%
Many	26
A few	30
None	5
No opinion	1
	100%

Do you think Congress should pass a bill to reform the health care system, or should Congress leave the health care system as it is?

Should pass a bill	69%
Leave system as is	26
No opinion	5
	100%

Would you support or oppose a health care reform package that guarantees every American private health insurance that can never be taken away?

Guaranteed Insurance - Trend

	Jan 28-30	Jun 25-28
Support	79%	77%
Oppose	16	17
No opinion	5	6
	100%	100%

Suppose Congress passes a bill which would improve the country's health care system, but would not guarantee coverage for every American. Do you think President Clinton should veto the bill and send it back to Congress, or should he sign it?

Veto if No Guaranteed Coverage? - Trend

	Jan 28-30	Jun 25-28
Veto bill		
Sign it	73%	62%
Depends (vol.)	22	26
No opinion	3	4
	2	8
	100%	100%

Which of the following do you think is the more important change that needs to take place in health care -- Making sure that Americans cannot lose their health insurance, even if they lose their job or have a medical problem, or, providing health insurance for those who cannot now afford it?

Guaranteed coverage	54%
Providing insurance	31
Both equally (vol.)	12
No opinion	3
	100%

In general, how much of the costs of health insurance should be paid by employers and how much by employees? Do you think -- Employers should pay all, employers should pay most, with employees paying some, employers and employees should share the costs equally, employees should pay most, with employers paying some, or employees should pay all?

Who Should Pay? - Trend

	Apr 16-18	Jun 25-28
Employers pay all	8%	8%
Employers pay most	46	44
Share the costs equally	35	37
Employees pay most	5	4
Employees pay all	2	3
No opinion	4	4
	100%	100%

Now I am going to read you five benefits which could be guaranteed to all Americans if Congress passes a health care reform bill this year. Which benefit among the five do you want guaranteed most: Prescription drugs; mental health and substance abuse services; care for catastrophic, long-term illnesses; dental care; nursing home care. (RANDOM ORDER) Which do you consider the second most important benefit you would want guaranteed?

Most Important Benefit
(1st & 2nd choices combined)

Catastrophic illness	69%
Nursing home care	45
Prescription drugs	39
Mental health/substance abuse	
Dental care	
None (vol.)	

The GALLUP POLL
N E W S   S E R V I C E

Volume 59, No. 9   Friday, July 1, 1994

Public Firm On Health Reform Goals

Although Unclear On Details of Clinton's Plan

By David W. Moore

PRINCETON, NJ -- Americans may not know the details of Clinton's health care reform plan, but -- according to a new Gallup poll -- they do want Congress to pass a reform bill and they are quite firm about some of the provisions they want included. Only 29% say they know most of the details of Clinton's plan, and just 39% say they have enough information to judge whether that plan is acceptable or not. But, by a margin of 69% to 26%, Americans want Congress to reform the system rather than leave it as is.

When asked about certain provisions currently being debated, the public shows a strong consensus for several items:

♦ The most important provision should be guaranteed coverage for all Americans that can never be taken away: 77% support this provision, only 17% oppose it. If Congress passes a bill without the guaranteed coverage for every American, 62% want the President to veto the bill.

♦ Guaranteed coverage is more important than universal coverage: by 54% to 31%, Americans say it is more important to provide guaranteed coverage to those who have it now than to cover those who cannot afford insurance.

♦ Controlling costs is also more important than universal coverage: by 57% to 32%, Americans say it is more important to control costs so they don't rise so fast in the future than it is to cover those who cannot afford insurance.

♦ Most Americans feel that employers should pay most (44%) or all (8%) of the costs of insurance. Another third (37%) are willing to share the costs equally, but only a few Americans feel that workers should pay most (4%) or all (3%) of the costs.

♦ Apart from routine health care, Americans most want coverage for catastrophic, long-term illnesses (69%). Nursing home care (45%) and prescription drugs (39%) are also seen as important elements in a new health care system, while mental health coverage (23%) and dental care (14%) are seen as less important among these five items.

♦ Finally, most Americans are opposed to government-financed abortions. If the government guarantees medical benefits as part of the health reform package, only one-third of Americans (34%) think abortion should be included among them, while 59% say it should not be included.

Political Impact of Health Care Reform Positive for Democrats

Americans remain split on Clinton's health care plan, with 49% opposed and 43% in favor, essentially unchanged for the past four months. Support has dropped, however, from the high point a year ago when Clinton introduced his plan, then favored by 59% of the public, and opposed by 33%.

George Gallup

The Whole Story. Reputable pollsters believe in full disclosure about how they go about doing their work. Note the detail on sample size, confidence level, margin of error and other specifics in this Gallup release to media clients.

In response to sloppy and dishonest surveying, the Associated Press insists on knowing methodology details before running poll stories. The AP tells reporters to ask:

■ **How Many Persons Were Interviewed and How Were They Selected?** Any survey of fewer than 384 persons selected randomly from the population group has a greater margin for error than usually is tolerated.

- **When Was the Poll Taken?** Opinions shift over time. During election campaigns, shifts can be quick, even overnight.
- **Who Paid for the Poll?** With privately commissioned polls, reporters should be sceptical, asking whether the results being released constitute everything learned in the survey. The timing of the release of political polls to be politically advantageous is not uncommon.
- **What Was the Sampling Error for a Poll and for Subgroups?** Margins of error exist in all surveys unless everyone in the population is surveyed. If the margin of error exceeds the margin between candidates, the results are indicative only that the race is tight.
- **How Was the Poll Conducted?** Whether a survey was conducted over the telephone or face to face in homes is important. Polls conducted on street corners or in shopping malls are not worth much statistically unless the question is what the people at a particular street corner or mall think. Mail surveys are also flawed unless surveyors follow up on people who do not answer the original questionnaires.
- **How Were Questions Worded and in What Order Were They Asked?** Drafting questions is an art. Sloppily worded questions yield sloppy conclusions. Leading questions and loaded questions can skew results. So can question sequencing.

It is at great risk that a polling company's client misrepresents survey results. Most polling companies, concerned about protecting their reputations, include a clause in their contracts with clients that gives the pollster the right to approve the release of findings. The clause usually reads: "When misinterpretation appears, we shall publicly disclose what is required to correct it, notwithstanding our obligation for client confidentiality in all other respects."

LATTER-DAY STRAW POLLS

The ABC television network dabbled, some say irresponsibly, with phone-in polling on public issues in the mid-1980s. So did Cable News Network. The vehicle was the 900 telephone number, which listeners could dial at 50 cents a call to register yea or nay on a question. MTV, the American rock music channel, did something similar that left the impression of being a legitimate public test of a recording's popularity. In Canada, TSN and MuchMusic often conduct such straw polls.

To its credit, ABC sometimes ran scientific surveys the same evening that Ted Koppel was conducting a 900 phone-in and compared the results. Sometimes the results coincided. Other times, the latter-day straw polls were nowhere near close.

Also dubious are the candid camera features, popular in weekly newspapers, in which a question is put to citizens on the street. The photos of half a dozen individuals and their comments are then published, often on the editorial page. These features are circulation builders for small publications whose financial success depends on how many local names and mug shots can be crammed into an issue, but it is only coincidental when the views expressed are representative of the population as a whole.

These roving-photographer features are at their worst when people are not given time to formulate an intelligent response. The result too often is contributions to the public babble, not public understanding. The result is irresponsible pseudojournalism. A defensible variation on the "inquiring camera" feature is used by *USA Today* for its editorial page. The newspaper maintains a cross-section panel of several hundred people nationwide. Members of the panel are asked their thoughts on a specific question and given a few days to respond. Also, panel members are chosen in part for presumed articulateness. *USA Today*'s goal is a meaningful contribution to public dialogue—not off-the-cuff chatter.

MEASURING AUDIENCE SIZE

STUDY PREVIEW   To attract advertisers, the mass media need to know the number and kinds of people they reach. This is done for the print media by audits and for the broadcast media by surveys. Although surveying is widely accepted for obtaining such data, some approaches are more reliable than others.

NEWSPAPER AND MAGAZINE AUDITS

The number of copies a newspaper or magazine puts out, called *circulation*, is fairly easy to calculate. It is simple arithmetic involving data like press runs, subscription sales and unsold copies returned from newsracks. Many publishers follow strict procedures, which are checked by independent audit organizations, such as the *Audit Bureau of Circulations*, to assure advertisers that the system is honest and circulation claims comparable.

The Audit Bureau of Circulations was formed in 1914 to remove the temptation for publishers to inflate their claims to attract advertisers and hike ad rates. Inflated claims, contagious in some cities, were working to the disadvantage of honest publishers. Today, most newspapers and magazines belong to ABC, which means that they follow the bureau's standards for reporting circulation and are subject to the bureau's audits.

Some fuzziness enters circulation data when newspapers and magazines try to count the number of people who see a single copy. The commonly used factors for this *pass-around circulation*, usually three to four readers per copy, underrate some publications and overrate others. The Audit Bureau of Circulation, however, endorses only its own firm rules for substantiating circulation claims for the print media.

BROADCAST RATINGS

Radio and television audiences are harder to measure, but advertisers have no less need for counts to help them decide where to place ads and to know what is a fair price. To keep track of broadcast audiences, a whole industry, now with about 200 companies, has developed. *ACNielsen Canada* tracks network television viewership. Since 1944, Canadian broadcast audiences have also been measured by the *Bureau of Broadcast Measurement* (BBM).

Radio ratings began in 1929 when advertisers asked American pollster *Archibald Crossley* to determine how many people were listening to network programs. Crossley checked a small sample of households and then extrapolated the data into national ratings, the same process that radio and television audience tracking companies still use, although there have been refinements.

In the 1940s, Nielsen began telling advertisers which radio programs were especially popular among men, women and children. Nielsen also divided listenership into age brackets: 18–34, 35–49, and 50 plus. These were called *demographic breakdowns.* When Nielsen moved into television monitoring in 1950, it expanded audience data into more breakdowns, including income, education, religion, occupation, neighborhood, and even which products the viewers of certain programs use frequently.

While Archibald Crossley's early ratings were sponsored by advertisers, today networks and individual stations also commission ratings to be done. The television networks pass ratings data on to advertisers immediately. Local stations usually recast the raw data for brochures that display the data in ways that put the station in the most favourable light. These brochures are distributed by station sales representatives to advertisers. While advertisers receive ratings data from the stations and networks, major advertising agencies have contracts with research companies to gather audience data to meet their specifications.

BBM and ACNielsen Canada both provide useful data for local radio and television stations. Through its Nielsen Television Index (NTI), ACNielsen also provides reports on television viewing in Canada within 10 days of a weekly survey period. NTI provides data for CTV, CBC, CanWest Global, Radio Canada, Radio-Québec, TSN, MuchMusic, YTV and Newsworld.

AUDIENCE MEASUREMENT TECHNIQUES

The primary techniques, sometimes used in combination, for measuring broadcast audiences are:

INTERVIEWS.   In his pioneer 1929 listenership polling, Archibald Crossley placed telephone calls to randomly selected households. Today, many polling companies use telephone interviews exclusively. Some companies conduct face-to-face interviews, which can elicit fuller information, although it is more expensive and time-consuming.

DIARIES.   Many ratings companies give forms to selected households to record what stations were on at particular times. Some companies distribute diaries to every member of a household. BBM's diaries go to everybody over age 12 in selected households, which provide data on age and gender preferences for certain stations and programs. Participants mail these diaries back to BBM, which tabulates the results.

BBM began using diaries to tabulate data about Canadians' viewing and listening habits in 1956. Initially, BBM issued a household diary to participants in its survey. Participants would record information about the entire household and their viewing and listening habits in this diary. In 1967, BBM started to issue personal diaries, which helped tabulate data about a specific person within that house. In 1975, the bureau began to provide separate diaries for radio and television.

Using a probability sample in each market in Canada, BBM measures television viewing on a weekly basis; while radio stations are rated for about four months each year, with an eight-week ratings period in both the spring and the fall. In larger markets, like Toronto, Montreal and Vancouver, BBM also has a summer ratings period.

BBM now asks radio listeners to answer additional questions about their favourite products, restaurants and about how much money they spend per week on food. This gives the bureau additional data that may be useful to radio stations when selling their air time. Asking questions like these may uncover opportunities for niche advertising.

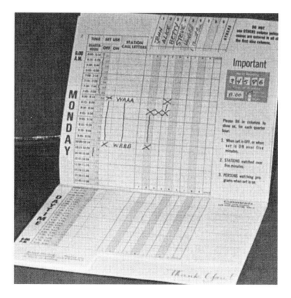

Measuring Broadcast Audiences. Many audience measurement companies ask selected households to keep diaries on their listening and viewing habits. Through statistical extrapolations, these companies claim they can discover the size of the total audience for particular programs and stations. This ACNielsen Canada diary asks participants to list who is watching, which allows broadcast executives and advertisers to learn demographic details about this audience. Under pressure for more accurate television ratings, audience measurement companies are shifting from written diaries to electronic meters. With a meter, members of participating households punch in when they start watching. With more advanced meters, punching in is not even required. The meters sense who is watching by body mass, which is programmed into the meter for every member of the household when it is installed.

METERS.   For television ratings ACNielsen Canada installs meters to record when television sets are on and to which channels they are tuned. Early devices like Nielsen's Audimeter recorded data on film cartridges, which were mailed back every two weeks to Nielsen. Today, new devices transmit data daily by telephone to Nielsen's central computer.

Though an improvement over interviews and diaries in several respects, the early meters recorded only whether a television set was turned on and to which channel it was turned—not whether anybody was watching. In many households, it came to be realized, people left the television on as background noise, which distorted the final data. To address this problem, ACNielsen Canada installed new push-button devices called *people meters* and asked people in the surveyed households to punch in personal codes to identify who was watching certain programs—mom, dad, oldsters, teenagers, little kids, or nobody at all.

Like diaries, the first people meters required participants to log their viewing dutifully. It was recognized that not everyone in every wired household could be expected to be equally conscientious about recording their "entries" and "exits." To address this problem, new *passive meters* can recognize household members automatically by body mass, which eliminates the hazard of some viewers' failing to record their watching.

CRITICISM OF RATINGS

However sophisticated the ratings services have become, they have critics. Many fans question the accuracy of ratings when their favourite television program is cancelled because the network finds the ratings inadequate. Something is wrong, they say, when the viewing preferences of a few thousand households determine network programming for the entire nation. Though it seems incredible to someone unknowledgeable about statistical probability, the sample base of major ratings services is considered sufficient to extrapolate reliably on viewership and listenership.

Ratings have problems, some inherent in differing methodologies and some attributable to human error and fudging:

DISCREPANCIES. When different ratings services come up with widely divergent findings in the same market, advertisers become suspicious. Minor discrepancies can be explained by different sampling methods, but significant discrepancies point to flawed methodology or execution.

SLANTED RESULTS. Sales reps of some local stations, eager to demonstrate to advertisers that their stations have large audiences, extract only the favourable data from survey results. It takes a sophisticated local advertiser to reconcile slanted and fudged claims. Unfortunately, this seems to be a common occurrence.

SAMPLE SELECTION. Some ratings services select their samples meticulously, giving every household in a market a statistically equal opportunity to be sampled. Some sample selections are seriously flawed: How reliable, for example, are the listenership claims of a rock 'n' roll station that puts a disc jockey's face on billboards all over town and then sends the disc jockey to a teenage dance palace to ask about listening preferences?

HYPING. Ratings-hungry stations in the U.S. have learned how to build audiences during *sweeps weeks* in February, May and November when major local television ratings are done. Consider:

- It was no coincidence in 1989 that syndicated talk-show host Geraldo Rivera took his cameras to a nudist colony during the February sweeps. It helped the local stations that buy his program to attract extra viewers in a critical sweeps period.
- Radio give-aways often coincide with ratings periods. Cars, trips and money are used to bait listeners.
- Many news departments promote sensationalistic series for the sweeps and then retreat to routine coverage when the ratings period is over. Just ahead of one 1988 Minneapolis sweeps, one station mailed out thousands of questionnaires, asking people to watch its programs and mail back the form. Accused of trickery to look good in the ratings, the station responded with a straight face that it

merely was trying a new technique to strengthen viewership. The timing, it argued, was mere coincidence.

- To boost ratings during the May 1990 sweeps, Denver television station KCNC heavily promoted a four-part series, "Blood Sport," on illegal dogfights. The series, however, turned out not to be the scandal. Unable to find any real dog-fights, reporter Wendy Bergin and photojournalists Scott Wright and Jim Stair staged a gruesome dogfight. All three ended up indicted for dogfighting for "monetary gain or entertainment," a Colorado felony punishable by four years in prison. Bergin later explained to the newspaper *Westword* that she had been pushed by a "ratings frenzy" to outdo competing stations: "Everyone was in sort of an altered state. Everybody was saying, 'We've got to beat them at 10. We've got to beat them at 10.' Nobody understood they'd moved a few degrees out of reality."

- Besides sweep weeks, there are *black weeks* when no ratings are conducted. In these periods, some stations run all kinds of odd and dull serve-the-public pro-grams that they would never consider during a sweeps period.

RESPONDENT ACCURACY.   Respondents don't always answer truthfully. People have an opportunity to tell interviewers or diaries that they watched an artsy film on Showcase instead of less classy fare. Shock radio and trash television may have more audience than the ratings show.

ZIPPING, ZAPPING AND FLUSHING.   Ratings services measure audiences for programs and for different times of day, but they do not measure whether commercials are watched. Advertisers are interested, of course, in whether

What the Audience Wants.
The mass media reduce chances for flops by testing their products on live audiences. A Hollywood company, National Research Group, charges moviemakers $200 000 for information on actors and subjects that people are interested in at the moment. NRG also test-previews movies to help determine which scenes don't go over well, and even to figure out how to end the movie. It was NRG's advice that resulted in Anne Archer's killing Glenn Close in the finale of *Fatal Attraction*. That, said NRG, was what people wanted to have happen to the rabbit-boiling Close.

the programs in which their ads are sandwiched are popular, but more important to them is whether people are watching the ads.

This vacuum in audience measurements was documented in the 1960s when somebody with a sense of humour correlated a major drop in Chicago water pressure with the Super Bowl halftime. Football fans were getting off the couch by the thousands at halftime to go to the bathroom. Advertisers were missing many people because viewers were watching the program but not the ads. This *flush factor* was also at work with all other programs. Television viewers find all kinds of things to do when the commercials come on—go to the refrigerator, let the dog in, chat with someone else watching the program. The same thing happens in radio. With a push-button car radio, drivers easily change stations whenever an ad comes up to find a station that is playing music or delivering news.

This problem has been exacerbated with the advent of hand-held television remote controls. Viewers can zip from station to station to avoid commercials, and when they record programs for later viewing they can zap out the commercials.

MEASURING AUDIENCE REACTION

STUDY PREVIEW   The television ratings business has moved beyond measuring audience size to measuring audience reaction. Today, Nielsen and Arbitron in the U.S. have systems to determine what it is about a program that stirs an audience, and also whether a particular advertisement is prompting people to buy the advertised product. Other methods to measure audience reaction include focus groups, galvanic skin checks, and prototypes.

CHECKING WHETHER ADS WORK

Today, Nielsen and Arbitron measure not only audience size and demographics for particular programs and parts of the day, but they also have devised methods to determine whether particular television advertisements are likely to prompt viewers to purchase a product.

In 1991 Nielsen launched a two-stage system, called *Comprehensive Advertising Tracking System*, which first checks the effectiveness of advertisements for competing products through pretesting. Test groups are asked their brand preferences, shown advance copies of competing television spots and then tested again on their preferences. In the second CATS stage, Nielsen tracks viewership of the competing ads when they run on the networks. With both pretest and viewership data, advertisers are better able to make informed judgments on how to place ads to counter the competition's ads and even whether to change their pitches.

Arbitron, meanwhile, has offered advertisers its *ScanAmerica* data, which tabulate both who in a household is watching a particular ad and whether the advertised product is purchased. To determine which advertised products are purchased, everyone in participating households is issued a *scanner wand* to run over the universal product code on the items they buy. If General Mills discovers that viewers who see its Wheaties ads are still buying Kellogg's Corn Flakes, General Mills knows it needs to make some changes in its advertising.

Both CATS and ScanAmerica have their detractors. CATS relies heavily on the reactions of small groups of people previewing ads, which is less precise statistically than larger samples. ScanAmerica's weakness is that it requires participants to remember to use their scanner wands. In an interview with the *Wall Street Journal*, Joel Segal, executive vice president of the McCann-Erickson agency, expressed his doubts this way: "Everytime you make a sophisticated demand of the consumer, you become less sure of the results."

FOCUS GROUPS

Television consulting companies measure audience reaction with *focus groups*. Typically an interview crew goes to a shopping centre, chooses a dozen individuals by gender and age, and offers them cookies, soft drinks and $25 each to sit down and watch a taped local newscast. A moderator then asks their reactions, sometimes with loaded and leading questions to open them up. It is a tricky research method that depends highly on the skill of the moderator. In one court case, an anchor who lost her job as a result of responses to a focus group complained that the moderator contaminated the process with prejudicial assertions and questions:

- "This is your chance to get rid of the things you don't like to see on the news."
- "Come on, unload on those sons of bitches who make $100 000 a year."
- "This is your chance to do more than just yell at the TV. You can speak up and say I really hate that guy or I really like that broad."
- "Let's spend 30 seconds destroying this anchor. Is she a mutt? Be honest about this."

Even when conducted skillfully, focus groups have the disadvantage of reflecting the opinion of the loudest respondent.

GALVANIC SKIN CHECKS

Consulting companies hired by television stations run a great variety of studies to determine audience reaction. Local stations, which originate news programs and not much else, look to these consultants for advice on news sets, story selection, and even which anchors and reporters are most popular. Besides surveys, these consultants sometimes use *galvanic skin checks*. Wires are attached to individuals in a sample group of viewers to measure pulse and skin reactions, such as perspiration. Advocates of these tests claim that they reveal how much interest a newscast evokes and whether it is positive or negative.

These tests were first used to check audience reaction to advertisements, but today some stations look to them in deciding whether to remodel a studio. A dubious use, from a journalistic perspective, is using galvanic skin checks to determine what kinds of stories to cover and whether to find new anchors and reporters. The skin checks reward short, photogenic stories like fires and accidents rather than significant stories, which tend to be longer and don't lend themselves to flashy video. The checks also favour good-looking, smooth anchors and reporters regardless of their journalistic competence. One wag was literally correct when he called this "a heart-throb approach to journalism."

PROTOTYPE RESEARCH

Before making major investments, media executives need as much information as they can obtain to determine how to enhance a project's chances for success or whether it has a chance at all. The *American Research Institute* of Los Angeles specializes in showing previews of television programs and even promotional ads to sample audiences. It is a method originated by movie studios, which invite people to advance showings and watch their reaction to decide how to advertise a new film most effectively, how to time the film's release, and even whether to re-edit the film.

When Gannett decided to establish a new newspaper, *USA Today*, it created prototypes, each designed differently, to test readers' reactions. Many new magazines are preceded with at least one trial issue to sample marketplace reaction and to show to potential advertisers.

In network television, a prototype may even make it on the air in the form of a *pilot*. One or a few episodes are tested, usually in prime time with a lot of promotion, to see if the audience goes for the program concept. Some made-for-television movies actually are test runs to determine whether a series might be spun off from the movies.

AUDIENCE ANALYSIS

STUDY PREVIEW Traditional demographic polling methods divided people by gender, age and other easily identifiable population characteristics. Today, media people use sophisticated life-style breakdowns such as geodemographics and psychographics to match the content of their publications, broadcast programs and advertising to the audiences they seek.

DEMOGRAPHICS

Early in the development of public-opinion surveying, pollsters learned that broad breakdowns had limited usefulness. Archibald Crossley's pioneering radio surveys, for example, told the number of people who were listening to network programs, which was valuable to the networks and their advertisers, but Crossley's figures did not tell how many listeners were men or women, urban or rural, old or young. Such breakdowns of overall survey data, called *demographics*, were developed in the 1930s as Crossley, George Gallup and other early pollsters refined their work.

Today, if demographic data indicate a political candidate is weak in the U.S. midwest, campaign strategists can gear the candidate's message to midwestern concerns. Through demographics, advertisers keen on reaching young women can identify magazines that will carry their ads to that audience. If advertisers seek an elderly audience, they can use demographic data to determine where to place their television ads.

While demographics remains valuable today, newer methods can break the population into categories that have even greater usefulness. These newer methods, which include geodemography, provide life-style breakdowns.

GEODEMOGRAPHICS

Computer whiz *Jonathan Robbin* provided the basis for more sophisticated breakdowns in 1974 when he began developing his *PRIZM* system for *geodemography*. From U.S. census data, Robbin grouped every zip code by ethnicity, family life cycle, housing style, mobility and social rank. Then he identified 34 factors that statistically distinguished neighbourhoods from each other. All this information was cranked through a computer programmed by Robbin to plug every zip code into 1 of 40 clusters. Here are the most frequent clusters created through PRIZM, which stands for Potential Rating Index for Zip Markets, with the labels Robbin put on them.

- **Blue-Chip Blues.** These are the wealthiest blue-collar suburbs with a median household income of $32 000 and house value of $72 600. These Blue-Chip Blues, as Robbin calls them, comprise about 6 percent of U.S. households. About 13 percent of these people are university graduates.
- **Young Suburbia.** Child-rearing outlying suburbs, 5.3 percent of U.S. population; median income, $38 600; median house value, $93 300; university grads, 24 percent.
- **Golden Ponds.** Rustic mountain, seashore or lakeside cottage communities, 5.2 percent; income, $20 100; house, $51 500; university grads, 13 percent.
- **New Beginnings.** Fringe-city areas of singles apartment complexes, garden apartments and trim bungalows, 4.3 percent; income, $24 800; house, $75 400; university grads, 19 percent.
- **New Homesteaders.** Exurban boom towns of young midscale families, 4.2 percent; income, $25 900; house, $67 200; university grads, 19 percent.
- **Share Croppers.** Primarily southern hamlets devoted to farming and light industry, 4 percent; income, $16 900; house, $33 900; university grads, 7 percent.

The potential of Robbin's PRIZM system was clear at *Time*, *Newsweek* and *McCall's*, which re-sorted subscriber lists and created new zoned editions to allow advertisers to mix and match their messages with a great variety of subaudiences of potential customers. Cadillac could choose editions aimed at these PRIZM neighbourhoods:

Adrenalin Video. Television producers know from research what kinds of videos excite viewers. During the Persian Gulf war, combat footage was repeated again and again under voice-overs that told about war developments. This led some observers to say that war coverage had become video entertainment.

Geodemographics. Many magazines can customize their advertising and editorial content to match the interests of readers through sophisticated geodemographic audience analysis. *Time* demonstrated the potential of its TargetSelect geodemographic program by printing the name of each subscriber as part of the cover art for the November 26, 1990, issue. The cover underscored the point of the lead article about the sort of TargetSelect sophistication also used by "junk mail" companies to match fliers sent through the mail with the likeliest customers for their products.

- **Blue-Blood Estates.** Wealthiest neighbourhoods; income, $70 300; house, $200 000 plus; university grads, 51 percent.

- **Money and Brains.** Posh big-city enclaves of townhouses, condos and apartments; income, $45 800; house, $159 800; university grads, 46 percent.

For its household products, Colgate-Palmolive might focus on:

- **Blue-Collar Nursery.** Middle-class, child-rearing towns; income, $30 000; house, $67 300; university grads, 10 percent.

Geodemographic breakdowns are used not only for magazine advertising but also for editorial content. At Time Warner magazines, geodemographic analysis permits issues to be edited for special audiences. *Time*, for example, has a 600 000 circulation edition for company owners, directors, board chairs, presidents, other titled officers and department heads. Among others are editions for physicians and students.

Theoretically, using PRIZM geodemographic breakdowns and other data, newsmagazines customize their agribusiness coverage for chicken farmers, offer expanded golf coverage for golf fans, and beef up articles on problems of the aged in the Gray Power and Golden Ponds PRIZM clusters. More book reviews might be added for Town and Gowns, the PRIZM cluster for university towns (income in 1974, $17 600; houses, $60 900; university grads, 28 percent).

In a 1990 stunt that demonstrated the potential for customizing magazines,

Time printed the name of each subscriber in big print as part of the cover art, using the same computerized ink-jet printing that it uses for localizing advertisements.

PSYCHOGRAPHICS

A refined life-style breakdown introduced in the late 1970s, *psychographics*, divides the population into life-style segments. One leading psychographics approach, the *Values* and *Life-Styles* program, known as VALS for short, uses an 85-page survey that was used to identify broad categories of people:

NEED-DRIVEN PEOPLE
- **Survivors.** This is a small downscale category that includes pensioners who worry about making ends meet.
- **Sustainers.** These people live from paycheque to paycheque. Although they indulge in an occasional extravagance, they have slight hope for improving their lot in life. Sustainers are a downscale category and aren't frequent advertising targets.

OUTER-DIRECTED PEOPLE
- **Belongers.** Comprising about 38 percent of the population, these people are conformists who are satisfied with mainstream values and are reluctant to change brands once they're satisfied. Belongers are not very venturesome. They tend to be churchgoers and television watchers.
- **Emulators.** Comprising 10 percent of the population, these people aspire to a better life but, not quite understanding how to do it, go for the trappings of prosperity. Emulators are status seekers, prone to suggestions on what makes the good life.
- **Achievers.** Comprising about 20 percent of the population, these are prosperous people who pride themselves on making their own decisions. They're an upscale audience to which a lot of advertising is directed. As a group, achievers aren't heavy television watchers.

INNER-DIRECTED PEOPLE
- **I-Am-Me's.** Comprising 3 percent of the population, these people work hard to set themselves apart and are susceptible to advertising pitches that offer ways to differentiate themselves, which gives them a kind of subculture conformity. SRI International, which developed the VALS technique, characterized I-Am-Me's as "a guitar-playing punk rocker who goes around in shades and sports an earring." Rebellious youth, angry and maladjusted, fit this category.
- **Experientials.** Comprising 5 percent of the population, these people are venturesome, willing to try new things in an attempt to experience life fully. They are a promising upscale audience for many advertisers.
- **Societally Conscious.** Comprising 11 percent of the population, these people are aware of social issues and tend to be politically active. The societally conscious also are upscale and inner-directed, and they tend to prefer reading to watching television.

INTEGRATED PEOPLE
- **Integrateds.** Comprising only 2 percent of the population, integrateds are both creative and prosperous—willing to try different products and ways of doing things, and they have the wherewithal to do it.

Applying psychographics is not without hazard. The categories are in flux as society and life-styles change. SRI researchers charted growth in the percentage of I-am-me's, experientials and the societally conscious in the 1980s and projected that they would be one-third of the population within a few years. Belongers were declining.

Another complication is that no person fits absolutely the mold of any one category. Even for individuals who fit one category better than another, there is no single mass medium to reach them. VALS research may show that achievers constitute the biggest market for antihistamines, but belongers also head to the medicine cabinet when they're congested.

CHAPTER WRAP-UP

The mass media are a rich field for study, partly because there are so many mysteries about how the process of mass communication works. Scholars have devised fascinating theories to explain the process, but their theories are widely divergent, and they squabble among themselves even about basic premises. Students aspiring to media careers have the special problem of trying to sort out these theories, which stem from scholarship and research on the same campuses where the work of journalism, advertising, broadcasting and public relations is taught.

Besides scholarship, often of an abstract sort, media research includes work that is distinctly practical. Publishers and broadcast executives need data on their circulations and reach in order to attract advertisers, and they are eager for research that can help them to reduce costs and tailor their product to larger or more profitable audiences. Both the media themselves and special research companies perform this kind of research.

Both theoretical research, which mostly is campus-based, and applied research, which the media eagerly fund, use many of the same tools. A unifying tool of these disparate research approaches is public-opinion sampling. It is used to track public opinion, which is essential in public relations work; to learn which television programs are the most watched, which is essential in programming and advertising decisions; and to determine the effects of media and how people use the media, which are scholarly endeavours.

QUESTIONS FOR REVIEW

1. What do surveys tell the mass media about their audiences?
2. How is the size of mass media audiences measured?
3. How is the reaction of people to the mass media measured?
4. What are techniques of audience analysis?
5. Why are mass media organizations more interested in applied than theoretical research?
6. Explain what BBM and ACNielsen Canada do.

QUESTIONS FOR CRITICAL THINKING

1. Street-corner polls are called *straw polls* because they are based on such weak methodology. Explain how quota sampling and probability sampling are improvements.

2. What is the basis for arguments that public-opinion surveys subvert democracy? What is the counterargument?

3. The Audit Bureau of Circulations and television rating services like ACNielsen Canada and BBM are essential media services to advertisers. How are these services similar? How different?

4. How can local television and radio stations manipulate their ratings?

5. Explain how applied research and theoretical research differ.

FOR FURTHER LEARNING

James Atlas. "Beyond Demographics: How Madison Avenue Knows Who You Are and What You Want." *Atlantic* 254 (October 1984):4, 49–58. Atlas explores the uses and hazards of psychographics in shaping advertising campaigns.

Charles O. Bennett. *Facts Without Opinion: First Fifty Years of the Audit Bureau of Circulations* (Audit Bureau of Circulations, 1965).

George Gallup. *The Sophisticated Poll Watcher's Guide* (Princeton Opinion Press, 1972). Gallup, a pioneer pollster, answers critics who charge that polls pervert the democratic process. Gallup argues that polling oils the wheels of democracy by helping elected leaders determine the majority will.

Shearson A. Lowery and Melvin L. DeFleur. *Milestones in Mass Communication Research: Media Effects* (Longman, 1983). Beginners will find Lowery and DeFleur's chronicle an easily followed primer on developments in mass communication research.

Philip Meyer. *Precision Journalism*, 2nd ed. (Indiana University Press, 1979). Meyer, a reporter who became a professor, explains how scholarly research methods, including survey research, can be applied in journalistic truth seeking.

Alan Prendergast. "Wendy Bergin's Exclusive Hoax." *Washington Journalism Review* 13 (October 1991):8, 30–34. Prendergast, a newspaper reporter, offers a case study on how pressure to attract viewers during a ratings period led three Denver journalists to stage an illegal dogfight to illustrate a television newscast series.

William S. Rubens. "A Personal History of TV Ratings, 1929 to 1989 and Beyond." *Feedback* 30 (Fall 1989):4, 3–15. Rubens, a former NBC vice president for research, draws on his experience for this thumbnail history of measuring broadcast audience.

Michael J. Weiss. *The Clustering of America* (Harper & Row, 1988). Weiss, a clever writer, describes Jonathan Robbin's geodemographic research and then takes the reader on a tour to view America through PRIZM eyes.

Richard Saul Wurman. *Information Anxiety* (Doubleday, 1989). Wurman, an architect, advocates new ways of organizing words and graphics to help people understand a growing deluge of information.

FOR KEEPING UP TO DATE

Public Opinion Quarterly is a scholarly publication. *American Demographics* and *Public Opinion* have a lot of general-interest content for media observers.

CHAPTER 14

ETHICS
and the Mass Media

Mass media ethics codes cannot anticipate all moral questions

Mass media people draw on numerous moral principles, not all of them consistent, to deal with ethical questions

Mass media people disagree on ethics depending on whether they favour process-based or outcome-based approaches

Some mass media people confuse ethics with obeying the law, being prudent, or adhering to accepted practices

Dubious mass media practices confound efforts to establish clear standards that would be universally accepted

MEDIA IN THEORY

Process versus Outcome

The various approaches to ethics fall into two broad categories: deontological ethics and teleological ethics. Deontologists say people need to follow good rules. Teleologists judge morality not by the rules but by the consequences of decisions.

DEONTOLOGICAL ETHICS

The Greek word "deon," which means "duty," is the heart of *deontological ethics*, which holds that people act morally when they follow good rules. Deontologists feel that people are duty bound to identify these rules.

Deontologists include people who believe that Scripture holds all the answers for right living. Their equivalent among media practitioners are those who rely entirely on codes of ethics drafted by organizations they trust. Following rules is a prescriptive form of ethics. At first consideration, ethics might seem as easy as following the rules, but not all questions are clear-cut. In complicated situations, the rules sometimes contradict each other. Some cases are dilemmas with no right option—only a choice among less-than-desirable options.

Deontological ethics becomes complicated, and also more intellectually interesting, when individuals, unsatisfied with other people's rules, try to work out their own universally applicable moral principles.

Here are some major deontological approaches:

- **Theory of divine command.** This theory holds that proper moral decisions come from obeying the commands of God, with blind trust that the consequences will be good.
- **Theory of divine right of kings.** This theory sees virtue in allegiance to a divinely anointed monarch, such as in England at the time of Henry VIII.
- **Theory of secular command.** This theory is a nonreligious variation that stresses allegiance to a dictator or other political leader from whom the people take cues when making moral decisions.
- **Libertarian theory.** This theory stresses a laissez-faire approach to ethics: Give free rein to the human ability to think through problems, and people almost always will make morally right decisions.
- **Categorical imperative theory.** This theory holds that virtue results when people identify and apply universal principles.

TELEOLOGICAL ETHICS

Unlike deontological ethics, which is concerned with the right actions, teleological ethics is concerned with the consequences of actions. The word "teleological" comes from the Greek word "teleos," which means "result" or "consequence."

Teleologists see flaws in the formal, legalistic duty to rules of deontologists, noting that great harm sometimes flows from blind allegiance to rules.

Here are some major teleological approaches:

- **Pragmatic theory.** This theory encourages people to look at human experience to determine the prob-

able consequences of an action and then decide its desirability.
- **Utilitarian theory.** This theory favours ethics actions that benefit more people than they damage—the greatest good for the greatest number.
- **Social-responsibility theory.** This theory judges actions by the good effect they have on society.

SITUATIONAL ETHICS

Firm deontologists see two primary flaws in teleological ethics:

- Imperfect foresight.
- Lack of guiding principles.

Despite these flaws, many media practitioners apply teleological approaches, sometimes labeled *situational ethics*, to arrive at moral decisions. They gather as much information as they can about a situation and then decide, not on the basis of principle but on the facts of the situation. Critics of situational ethics worry about decisions governed by situations. Much better, they argue, would be decisions flowing from principles of enduring value. With situational ethics, the same person might do one thing one day and on another day go another direction in a similar situation.

Consider a case at the *Rocky Mountain News* in Denver. Editors learned that the president of a major suburban newspaper chain had killed his parents and sister in another state when he was 18. After seven years in a mental hospital, the man completed college, moved to Colorado, lived a model life and became a successful newspaper executive. The *Rocky Mountain News* decided not to make a story of it. Said a *News* official: "The only reason for dredging up [his] past would be to titillate morbid curiosity or to shoot down, maliciously, a successful citizen."

However, when another newspaper revealed the man's past, the *Rocky Mountain News* reversed itself and published a lengthy piece of its own. Why? The newspaper that broke the story had suggested that *News* editors knew about the man's past and decided to protect him as a fellow member of the journalistic fraternity. *News* editors denied that their motivation was to protect the man. To prove it, they reversed their decision and published a story about him. The *News* explained its change of mind by saying that the situation had changed. *News* editors, concerned that their newspaper's credibility had been challenged, felt that printing a story would set that straight. Of less concern, suddenly, was that the story would titillate morbid curiosity or contribute to the destruction of a successful citizen. It was a classic case of situational ethics.

Flip-flops on moral issues, such as happened at the *Rocky Mountain News*, bother critics of situational ethics. The critics say decisions should be based on deeply rooted moral principles—not immediate, transient facts or changing peripheral contexts.

THE DIFFICULTY OF ETHICS

STUDY PREVIEW Mass media organizations have put together codes of ethics that prescribe how practitioners should go about their work. While useful in many ways, these codes neither sort through the bedeviling problems that result from conflicting prescriptions nor help much when the only open options are negative.

THE CASE OF ARTHUR ASHE

Tennis champion Arthur Ashe was glad but then leery to hear his old high school chum Doug Smith on the phone. Smith, tennis reporter for *USA Today*, wanted to see him for an interview. It was not unusual for reporters to call on Ashe. He was the first world-class American black male tennis player, and after his athletic prime he had campaigned vigorously against apartheid. But by 1992, he worried with every interview that the question of whether he had AIDS would surface.

Ashe, in fact, had AIDS. He had contracted the virus apparently in 1983 during surgery. Five years later when doctors found the infection, Ashe began therapy for the debilitating and inevitably fatal disease. He decided against going public that he had the disease, and his family and friends went along with what Ashe called "a silent and generous conspiracy to assist me in maintaining my privacy."

When Doug Smith showed up for the interview, he asked the dreaded question: "Do you have AIDS?" Although Ashe realized that some reporter some day would ask the question, it nonetheless caught him off guard. "Could be," he quipped. Then he recognized how much more revealing his words were than he intended. The secret was out.

The next afternoon, before Smith's article could appear, Ashe called a news conference to announce that he suffered from AIDS. Although he was gentle on *USA Today*, Ashe criticized the mass media for intruding into the private lives of people. In the news conference, carried live by CNN, Ashe said: "I am sorry that I have been forced to make this revelation at this time. After all, I am not running for some office of public trust, nor do I have stockholders to account to. It is only that I fall in the dubious umbrella of, quote, public figure, end of quote."

Ironically, *USA Today* had decided against going with the story, but Ashe's news conference nonetheless epitomized one of the great media ethics questions of our time: Who prevails when the mass media are at the intersection of the public's interest in knowing certain information and an individual's interest in preserving personal privacy? As with vexed ethics questions, people on both sides feel strongly and mount powerful arguments for their positions. Journalists themselves are hardly of one mind.

Private Issue? Tennis hero Arthur Ashe objected that news media inquiries about his AIDS violated his privacy.

Here are arguments supporting *USA Today*'s initiative:

- Gerry Callahan of the *Boston Herald* said the violation of Ashe's privacy was committed by whoever in his circle of friends tipped the newspaper anonymously. The newspaper, he said, merely was performing its function to check out tips.
- USA Today editor Peter Prichard told the trade journal *Editor & Publisher* that it would have been news too if someone had tipped the paper that Ashe was suffering terminal cancer. Said Prichard: "I do not see any public service in sweeping this under the rug."
- The Atlanta *Constitution* equated "public interest" in Ashe to "the deep affection people hold for him" and noted that he could not reasonably have expected to preserve his privacy much longer. "The gentle circle of conspirators that had kept his secret for three years simply had grown too large, and the evidence of his physical decline had become too marked not to be noticed," the newspaper said.

Not everyone saw it that way. *USA Today* received almost 1100 calls, with 60 people canceling their subscriptions. Among journalists, there were negative reactions too:

- Mona Charen, a syndicated columnist, wrote that the fact that Ashe was a great athlete who established a milestone for blacks was "no reason to treat his personal struggle as a peep show."
- DeWayne Wickham, whose column appears in *USA Today*, equated AIDS victims with rape victims. "Like them he too should not be twice victimized by being made to suffer from the harsh glare of the public spotlight."

As with most ethics issues, many people, including mass communicators, see both sides:

- Burl Osborne, publisher of the *Dallas Morning News*, said, "One should think about it a long time and make absolutely certain what you are doing, but I really can't fault the publication of the story in this case."

■ Gregory Favre, executive editor of the Sacramento, California, *Bee*, called it "one of those tough questions." On whether to print it, however, Favre's paper did so.

■ The Milwaukee *Journal* said it "took seriously the public's right to know about its leaders and heroes" and then added: "But the media must balance that right against the harm that can come in certain cases from the publication of damaging information." The *Journal* noted the hesitancy that some people have about disclosing AIDS as opposed to other ailments and concluded its editorial by saying: "The wise editor will, perhaps with rare exception, forgo the scoop and encourage the person to go public as a way of better controlling what is disclosed and emboldening others to reveal their own secrets about AIDS."

Much of the criticism of *USA Today's* initiative centred on "cheap scoops." Jeff Cohen, who heads the FAIR media watchdog group, said: "In recent years, mass media have been sliding down the slippery slope in pursuit of private lives of celebrities. These stories sell newspapers and pump up TV ratings, but they do little for public discourse."

Paul McMasters, executive director of the Freedom Forum, cast the incident as a no-win situation all around, as is the case with many ethics issues. Said McMasters: "The fact that Arthur Ashe is stricken with AIDS is a tragedy. The fact that he lost a measure of his privacy is a tragedy."

In this chapter, you will learn about the great principles that leading thinkers have devised over the centuries to sort through dilemmas that are part of the human condition, and how they can be applied to media issues.

PRESCRIPTIVE ETHICS CODES

The mass media abound with codes of ethics. One of the earliest was adopted in 1923, the Canons of Journalism of the American Society of Newspaper Editors. Advertising, broadcast and public relations practitioners also have codes. Many newcomers to the mass media make an erroneous assumption that the answers to all the moral choices in their work exist in the prescriptions of these codes. While the codes can be helpful, ethics is not so easy.

The difficulty of ethics becomes clear when a news reporter is confronted with a conflict between moral responsibilities to different concepts. Consider:

RESPECT FOR PRIVACY. The code of the Society of Professional Journalists prescribes that reporters will show respect for the dignity, privacy, rights and well-being of people "at all times." The SPJ prescription sounds excellent, but moral priorities such as dignity and privacy sometimes seem less important than other priorities, as many people would argue in the case of Arthur Ashe. The public interest also overrode privacy in 1988 when the Miami *Herald* staked out presidential candidate Gary Hart overnight when he had a woman friend in his Washington townhouse.

COMMITMENT TO TIMELINESS. The code of the Radio-Television News Directors Association of Canada prescribes that reporters be "accurate, comprehensive, and balanced." In practice, however, complete accuracy is jeopardized

Sold-out Edition. Perhaps the most famous news photograph of all time was Tom Howard's shot of the electric chair execution of murderer Ruth Snyder. Knowing the Sing Sing warden wouldn't agree to a photo, Howard strapped a tiny camera to his ankle and, at the right moment, lifted his trouser leg and snapped the shutter with a trip wire. The exclusive photo goosed street sales of the New York *Daily News,* which had followed the lurid trial of Snyder and her lover for killing her husband. Such stories and a focus on photo coverage, typical of the *Daily News* under founder Joseph Patterson, boosted the newspaper's circulation to more than 2 million, the largest in the nation, in the 1940s.

when reporters rush to the air with stories. It takes time to confirm details and be accurate—and that delays stories.

BEING FAIR. The code of the Canadian Public Relations Society prescribes dealing fairly with both clients and the general public. However, a persuasive message prepared on behalf of a client is not always the same message that would be prepared on behalf of the general public. Persuasive communication is not necessarily dishonest, but how information is marshaled to create the message depends on whom the PR person is serving.

CONFLICT IN DUTIES

Media ethics codes are well-intended, usually helpful guides, but they are simplistic when it comes to knotty moral questions. When media ethicians Clifford Christians, Mark Fackler and Kim Rotzoll compiled a list of five duties of mass media practitioners, some of these inherent problems became obvious.

DUTY TO SELF. Self-preservation is a basic human instinct, but is a photo-journalist shirking a duty to subscribers by avoiding a dangerous combat zone?

Self-aggrandizement can be an issue too. Many college newspaper editors are

Naming Rape Victims

The editor of the Des Moines *Register*, Geneva Overholser, faced the question of how to deal with rape in a journalistically serious way in 1990. A woman who had been assaulted and raped, Nancy Ziegenmeyer, was willing to discuss the crime in graphic detail and to describe her emotions about testifying when the assailant went on trial. Overholser decided to go ahead, and a five-part series was published.

How would you sort through these considerations in such a decision?

- Nancy Ziegenmeyer's courage could inspire other rape victims to report this largely unreported crime.
- Many people might be offended and cancel subscriptions and advertisements.
- The series could improve social awareness about rape and reduce its incidence.
- If Nancy Ziegenmeyer's name is printed, then the names of all rape victims should be published.
- Printing the name adds to the rape victim's obloquy, which can delay psychological recovery.
- Facts are facts, and they should be printed. It is not the job of the news media to keep secrets.

Can you identify other positions on this ethics question?

Overholser decided to go with the Ziegenmeyer series, including a graphic account of the assault. Critical of mainstream news media practice, Overholser argued that the media participate in the stigma of rape when they treat rape victims differently from the victims of other crimes. Also, she said, refusing to talk openly

Shielding Victims. When Patricia Bowman charged that a Kennedy scion had raped her, the media was divided on whether to name her in news coverage. It was an ethics question. Eventually Bowman went public, granting numerous interviews, including one with television network reporter Diane Sawyer. The issue has many facets. One argument is that a system of open justice requires someone making a serious charge to do so publicly. A counterargument is that publicity cruelly and needlessly increases the victim's suffering.

about rape weakens society's ability to deal with it.

On a related note, during Paul Bernardo's murder trial, the real name of one of his rape victims was not made public. Instead the woman was referred to as "Jane Doe."

invited, all expenses paid, to Hollywood movie premieres. The duty-to-self principle favours going: The trip would be fun. In addition, it is a good story opportunity, and, as a free favour, it would not cost the newspaper anything. However, what of an editor's responsibility to readers? Readers have a right to expect writers to provide honest accounts that are not coloured by favouritism. Can a reporter write straight after being wined and dined and flown across the continent by movie producers who want a gung ho story? Even if reporters rise above being affected and are true to conscience, there are the duty-to-employer and the duty-to-profession principles to consider. The newspaper and the profession itself can be tarnished by suspicions, no matter whether they are unfounded, that a reporter has been bought off.

DUTY TO AUDIENCE.   Television programs that reenact violence are popular with audiences, but are they a disservice because they frighten many viewers into inferring that the streets are more dangerous than they really are?

A journalist named Wicker tells a story about his early days on the police beat. He was covering a divorce case involving one spouse chasing the other with an ax. Nobody was hurt physically, and everyone who heard the story in the courtroom, except the divorcing couple, had a good laugh. "It was human comedy at its most ribald, and the courtroom rocked with laughter," he recalled years later. In writing his story, he captured the darkly comedic details so skillfully that his editor put the story on Page One. Wicker was proud of the piece until the next day when the woman in the case called on him. Worn out, haggard, hurt and angry, she asked, "Why did you think you had a right to make fun of me in your paper?"

The lesson stayed with him for the rest of his career. He had unthinkingly hurt a fellow human being for no better reason than evoking a chuckle, or perhaps a belly laugh, from his readers. To Wicker, the duty-to-audience principle would never again transcend his moral duty to the dignity of the subjects of his stories. Similar ethics questions are involved in whether to cite AIDS as a contributing factor to death in an obituary, whether to identify victims in rape stories, and whether to name juveniles charged with crimes.

DUTY TO EMPLOYER.   Does loyalty to an employer transcend the ideal of pursuing and telling the truth when a news reporter discovers dubious business deals involving the parent corporation? This is a growing issue as the mass media become consolidated into fewer gigantic companies owned by conglomerates. In 1989, for example, investigative reporter Peter Karl of Chicago television station WMAQ broke a story that General Electric had manufactured jet engines with untested and sometimes defective bolts. Although WMAQ is owned by NBC, which in turn is owned by General Electric, Karl's exclusive, documented and accurate story aired. However, when the story was passed on to the network itself, Marty Ryan, executive producer of the "Today" show, ordered that the references to General Electric be edited out.

DUTY TO THE PROFESSION.   At what point does an ethically motivated advertising-agency person blow the whistle on misleading claims by other advertising people?

DUTY TO SOCIETY.   Does duty to society ever transcend duty to self? To audience? To employer? To colleagues? Does ideology affect a media worker's sense of duty to society? Consider how Joseph Stalin, Adolf Hitler and Franklin Roosevelt would be covered by highly motivated communist, fascist and libertarian journalists.

Are there occasions when the duty-to-society and the duty-to-audience principles are incompatible? Nobody enjoys seeing the horrors of war, for example, but journalists may feel that their duty to society demands that they go after the most grisly photographs of combat to show how horrible war is and, thereby, in a small way, contribute to public pressure toward a cessation of hostilities and eventual peace.

MORAL PRINCIPLES

STUDY PREVIEW   Concern about doing the right thing is part of human nature, and leading thinkers have developed a great number of enduring moral principles over the centuries. The mass media, like other institutions and also like individuals, draw on these principles, but this does not always make moral decisions easy. The principles are not entirely consistent, especially in sorting through dilemmas.

THE GOLDEN MEAN

The Greek philosopher *Aristotle*, writing almost 2400 years ago, devised the *golden mean* as a basis for moral decision making. The golden mean sounds simple and straightforward: Avoid extremes and seek moderation. Modern journalistic balance and fairness are founded on this principle.

The golden mean's dictate, however, is not as simple as it sounds. As with all moral principles, application of the golden mean can present difficulties. Consider the federal law that requires over-the-air broadcasters to give "equal opportunity" to candidates for public office. If one candidate buys 30 seconds at 7 p.m. for $120, a station is obligated to allow other candidates for the same office to buy 30 seconds at the same time for the same rate. On the surface, this application of the golden mean, embodied in federal law, might seem to be reasonable, fair and morally right, but the issue is far more complex. The equality requirement, for example, gives an advantage to candidates who hold simplistic positions that can be expressed compactly. Good and able candidates whose positions require more time to explain are disadvantaged, and the society is damaged when inferior candidates win public office.

The Golden Mean. The Greek thinker Aristotle told his students almost 2400 years ago that right courses of action avoid extremes. His recommendation: moderation.

While minute-for-minute equality in broadcasting can be a flawed application of the golden mean, Aristotle's principle is valuable to media people when making moral decisions, as long as they do not abdicate their power of reason to embrace formulaic tit-for-tat measurable equality. It takes the human mind, not a formula, to determine fairness. And therein lies the complexity of the golden mean. No two human beings think exactly alike, which means that applying the golden mean involves individuals making judgment calls that are not necessarily the same. This element of judgment in moral decisions can make ethics intellectually exciting. It takes a sharp mind to sort through issues of balance and fairness.

"DO UNTO OTHERS"

The Judeo-Christian principle of "Do unto others as you would have them do unto you" appeals to most people. Not even the do-unto-others prescription, however, is without problems. Consider the photojournalist who sees virtue in serving a mass audience with a truthful account of the human condition. This might manifest itself in portrayals of great emotions, like grief. But would the photojournalist appreciate being photographed herself in a grieving moment after learning that her infant son had died in an accident? If not, her pursuit of truth through photography for a mass audience would be contrary to the "do-unto-others" dictum.

CATEGORICAL IMPERATIVES

About 200 years ago, German philosopher *Immanuel Kant* wrote that moral decisions should flow from thoroughly considered principles. As he put it, "Act on the maxim that you would want to become universal law." He called his maxim the *categorical imperative*. A categorical imperative, well thought out, is a principle that the individual who devised it would be willing to apply in all moral questions of a similar sort.

Kant's categorical imperative does not dictate specifically what actions are morally right or wrong. Moral choices, says Kant, go deeper than the context of the immediate issue. He encourages a philosophical approach to moral questions, with people using their intellect to identify principles that they, as individuals, would find acceptable if applied universally.

Kant does not encourage the kind of standardized approach to ethics represented by professional codes. His emphasis, rather, is on hard thinking. Says philosopher Patricia Smith, of the University of Kentucky, writing in the *Journal of Mass Media Ethics:* "A philosophical approach to ethics embodies a commitment to consistency, clarity, the principled evaluation of arguments, and unrelenting persistence to get to the bottom of things."

UTILITARIAN ETHICS

In the mid-1800s, British thinker *John Stuart Mill* declared that morally right decisions are those that result in "happiness for the greatest number." Mill called his idea the *principle of utility*. It sounds good to many of us because it parallels the democratic principle of majority rule, with its emphasis on the greatest good for the greatest number of people.

By and large, journalists embrace Mill's utilitarianism today, as evinced in notions like *the people's right to know*, a concept originally meant to support journalistic pursuit of information about government, putting the public's interests ahead

Universal Law. Immanuel Kant, an 18th-century German philosopher, urged people to find principles that they would be comfortable having applied in all situations. He called these principles *categorical imperatives*.

Utilitarianism. American journalists tend to like 19th-century British thinker John Stuart Mill's utilitarianism, which favours actions that result in the greatest good for the greatest number of people. This approach to ethics dovetails well with majority rule and modern democracy.

of government's interests, but which has come to be almost reflexively invoked to defend pursuing very personal information about individuals, no matter what the human cost.

PRAGMATIC ETHICS

John Dewey, an American thinker who wrote in the late 1800s and early 1900s, argued that the virtue of moral decisions had to be judged by their results. A difficulty in Dewey's *pragmatic ethics* is that people do not have perfect crystal balls to tell them for sure whether their moral actions will have good consequences.

EGALITARIAN ETHICS

In this century, philosopher *John Rawls* introduced the *veil of ignorance* as an element in ethics decisions. Choosing a right course of action, said Rawls, requires blindness to social position or other discriminating factors. An ethical decision requires that all people be given an equal hearing and the same fair consideration.

To Rawls, a brutal slaying in an upscale suburb deserves the same journalistic attention as a slaying in a poor urban neighbourhood. All other things being equal, a $20 000 bank burglary is no more newsworthy than a $20 000 embezzlement.

SOCIAL RESPONSIBILITY ETHICS

The Hutchins Commission, a learned group that studied the American mass media in the 1940s, recommended that journalists and other media people make decisions that serve the society responsibly. For all its virtues, the *social responsibility system*, like all ethics systems, has difficulties. For one thing, decision makers can only imperfectly foresee the effects of their decisions. It is not possible to predict with 100 percent confidence whether every decision will turn out to be socially responsible. Also, well-meaning people may differ honestly about how society is most responsibly served.

ETHICS AND OTHER ISSUES

STUDY PREVIEW   Right and wrong are issues in both ethics and law, but they are different issues. Obedience to law, or even to professional codes of ethics, will not always lead to moral action. There are also times when practical issues can enter moral decisions.

DIFFERENTIATING ETHICS AND LAW

Ethics and law are related but separate. Ethics is an individual matter that relates closely to conscience. Because conscience is unique to each individual, no two people have exactly the same moral framework. There are, however, issues about which there is consensus. No right-minded person condones murder, for example.

Images of Grief. After a Vietnamese husband and wife, parents of five children, were shot in a gangland slaying, photographer Eric Luse of the *San Francisco Chronicle* was assigned to the funeral. As the couple's oldest daughter came out of the services clutching her mother's photograph, Luse took this picture. Because the funeral procession was on a public street, there was no legal issue, but intrusions into private moments can also be an ethics issue. Typical of how views are divided on many ethics issues, media people saw this photo two ways. The *Chronicle* decided against running the picture on grounds that it was "very intrusive," but judges in the World Press Photo contest gave it first place. In the Picture of the Year contest, it placed third.

When there is a universal feeling, ethics becomes codified in law, but laws do not address all moral questions. It is the issues of right and wrong that do not have a consensus that make ethics difficult. Was it morally right for *USA Today* to initiate coverage of Arthur Ashe's AIDS?

The ethics decisions of an individual mass media practitioner usually are more limiting than the law. There are times, though, when a journalist may choose to break the law on the grounds of ethics. Applying John Stuart Mill's principle of "the greatest good," a radio reporter might choose to break the speed limit to reach a chemical plant where an accident is threatening to send a deadly cloud toward where her listeners live. Breaking a speed limit may seem petty, but it demonstrates that obeying the law and obeying one's conscience do not always coincide.

ACCEPTED PRACTICES

Just as there is not a reliable correlation between law and ethics, neither is there one between accepted media practices and ethics. What is acceptable at one advertising agency to make a product look good in photographs might be unacceptable at another. Even universally accepted practices should not go unexamined, for unless accepted practices are examined and reconsidered on a continuing basis, media practitioners can come to rely more on habit than on principles in their work.

PRUDENCE AND ETHICS

Prudence is the application of wisdom in a practical situation. It can be a levelling factor in moral questions. Consider the case of Irvin Lieberman, who had built his *Main Line Chronicle* and several other weeklies in the Philadelphia suburbs into aggressive, journalistically excellent newspapers. After being hit with nine libel suits, all costly to defend, Lieberman abandoned the editorial thrust of his newspapers. "I decided not to do any investigative work," he said. "It was a matter of either feeding my family or spending my whole life in court." Out of prudence, Lieberman decided to abandon his commitment to hard-hitting, effective journalism.

Courageous pursuit of morally lofty ends can, as a practical matter, be foolish. Whether Irvin Lieberman was exhibiting a moral weakness by bending to the chilling factor of libel suits, which are costly to fight, or being prudent is an issue that could be debated forever. The point, however, is that prudence cannot be ignored as a factor in moral decisions.

UNSETTLED, UNSETTLING ISSUES

STUDY PREVIEW   When mass media people discuss ethics, they talk about right and wrong behaviour, but creating policies on ethics issues is not easy. Many standard media practices press the line between right and wrong, which muddies clear-cut standards that are universally applicable and recognized. There is further muddiness because many ethics codes confuse unethical behaviour and behaviour that may appear unethical but that is not necessarily so.

PLAGIARISM

In 1988, *Chicago Tribune* editors became concerned after running a story from their Jerusalem correspondent and then discovering that some passages were incredibly similar to a story that had been printed in the *Jerusalem Post* a few days earlier.

Compare these passages:

<table>
<tr><td>The injured can be found in many homes, as well—men, women and children bearing bruises, fractures and bandaged limbs, the victims of Israeli gunfire, beatings, rubber bullets, and tear gas inhalation.

—*Chicago Tribune*</td><td>The injured can be seen in many homes: young and older men and even children with bruises and fractures, women with black and blue marks and bandaged arms—victims of beatings, rubber bullets, tear gas inhalation and sometimes gunfire.

—*Jerusalem Post*</td></tr>
</table>

The *Tribune*'s Jerusalem correspondent resigned. Some newspapers fire writers who pass off other people's work as their own. It is more common, though, to simply reassign an offending writer to a low-visibility job on the copy desk or to do nothing at all. Although many journalists talk firmly about plagiarism as unethical, the issue is not simple. The fact is that standard journalistic practices encourage a lot of "borrowing," which complicates drawing clear lines. Among factors that make journalists uncomfortable when pressed hard on plagiarism questions are:

- Institutionalized exchanging of stories.
- The role of public relations in generating news stories.
- Monitoring the competition.
- Subliminal memory and innocent recall.

SWAPPING STORIES.   Some creative work, like scholarship, requires that information and ideas be attributed to their sources. Journalists are not so strict, as shown by story swapping through the Canadian Press and Broadcast News. The Canadian Press picks up stories from its members and distributes them to other members, often without any reference to the source. Some CP publications and BN broadcasters do not even acknowledge CP as the intermediary.

Incredible as it may seem, journalistic tolerance for plagiarism allows radio stations to pirate the local newspaper for newscasts. Sometimes you can hear the announcer turning the pages. A sad joke that acknowledges this practice is that some stations buy their news at 50 cents a copy, which is cheaper than hiring reporters to cover the community. So pervasive is the journalistic tolerance for "borrowing" that few newspapers even mildly protest when their stories are pirated.

NEWS RELEASES.   In many newsrooms, the plagiarism question is clouded further by the practice of using news releases from public relations people word for word without citing the source. Even in newsrooms that rewrite releases to avoid the embarrassment of running a story that is exactly the same as the competition's, it is standard practice not to cite the source. Public relations people, who are paid for writing favourable stories on their clients, have no objections to being plagiarized, and news organizations find it an easy, inexpensive way to fill space. Despite the mutual convenience, the arrangement raises serious questions of ethics to which many in the media have not responded. The practice leaves the false impression that stories originating with news releases actually originated with the news organization. More serious is that the uncredited stories are a disservice to democracy. Marie Dunn White, in the *Journal of Mass Media Ethics*, wrote: "In order for the reader to evaluate the information he or she is receiving correctly and completely, he or she must know which information came from a press release and, therefore, may be biased."

MONITORING COMPETITION.   Competitive pressure also contributes to fuzziness on the plagiarism issue. To avoid being skunked on stories, reporters monitor each other closely to pick up tips and ideas. Generally, reporters are not particular about where they pick up information as long as they are confident that it is accurate. For background, reporters tap newsroom libraries, databases, journals, books and other sources, and, in the interest of not cluttering their stories, they do not use footnotes.

SUBLIMINAL MEMORY.   Covering breaking events has its own pressure that puts journalists at special risk. Almost every journalist who writes under the pressure of a deadline has had the experience of writing a story and later discovering that phrases that came easily at the keyboard were actually somebody else's. In their voracious pursuit of information, reporters store phrases and perhaps whole passages subliminally in their memories. This happened to a drama critic who was horrified when a reader pointed out the similarity between his review of a play and an earlier review of the same play in another newspaper. Once aware of what he had done unwittingly, the critic offered his resignation. His editors instead moved him to the copy desk.

It's this concept of *innocent recall* that concerns Canadian columnist *Don McGillivray*, who argues that plagiarism is often a simple case of unintentionally borrowing from others. Journalists are like any other group of professionals: they like to "talk shop" when in the presence of other journalists. They discuss stories they've written and articles they've read. Later, while writing a story, a journalist may subconsciously remember a certain phrase from an earlier conversation with a colleague and use it in a story. Is this plagiarism? McGillivray doesn't think so. It's simply the outcome of a psychological process.

The muddiness on the issue of journalistic plagiarism is encapsulated in the fact that the Society of Professional Journalists' ethics code makes a flat statement that plagiarism is "dishonest and unacceptable," but then sidesteps the knotty part of the issue by declining to define "plagiarism."

MISREPRESENTATION

Janet Cooke's meteoric rise at the *Washington Post* unraveled quickly the day after she received a Pulitzer Prize. Her editors had been so impressed with her story, "Jimmy's World," about a child who was addicted to heroin, that they nominated it for a Pulitzer Prize. The gripping tale began: "Jimmy is 8 years old and a third-generation heroin addict, a precocious little boy with sandy hair, velvety brown eyes and needle marks freckling the baby-smooth skin of his thin brown arms." Janet Cooke claimed that she had won the confidence of Jimmy's mother and her live-in man friend, a drug dealer, to do the story. Cooke said she had promised not to reveal their identities as a condition for her access to Jimmy.

The story, played on the front page, so shocked Washington that people demanded that Jimmy be taken away from his mother and placed in a foster home. The *Post* declined to help authorities, citing Cooke's promise of confidentiality to her sources. The mayor ordered the police to find Jimmy with or without the newspaper's help, and millions of dollars in police resources went into a door-to-door search. After 17 days, the police gave up knocking on doors for tips on Jimmy. Some doubts emerged at the *Post* about the story, but the newspaper stood behind its reporter.

Janet Cooke, 25 when she was hired by the *Post*, had extraordinary credentials. Her résumé showed a baccalaureate degree, magna cum laude, from Vassar; study at the Sorbonne in Paris; a master's degree from the University of Toledo; abilities in several languages; and two years of journalistic experience with the Toledo *Blade*. Said Ben Bradlee, editor of the *Post*, "She had it all. She was bright. She was well-spoken. She was pretty. She wrote well." She was black, which made her especially attractive to the *Post*, which was working to bring the percentage of black staff reporters nearer to the percentage of blacks in its circulation area.

"Jimmy's World" was published in September 1980. Six months later, the Pulitzer committee announced its decision and issued a biographical sheet on Janet Cooke. The Associated Press, trying to flesh out the biographical information, spotted discrepancies right away. Janet Cooke, it turned out, had attended Vassar one year but had not been graduated with the honours she claimed. The University of Toledo had no record of awarding her a master's. Suddenly, doubts that had surfaced in the days immediately after "Jimmy's World" was published took on a new intensity. The editors sat Cooke down and grilled her on the claims on which she was hired. No, she admitted, she was not multilingual. The Sorbonne claim was fuzzy. More importantly, they grilled her on whether there was really a Jimmy. The interrogation continued into the night, and finally Janet Cooke confessed all: There were no confidential sources, and there was no Jimmy. She had fabricated the story. She resigned, and the *Post*, terribly embarrassed, returned the Pulitzer.

In cases of outright fabrication, as in "Jimmy's World," it is easy to identify the lapses in ethics. When Janet Cooke emerged briefly from seclusion to explain herself, she said that she was responding to pressures in the *Post* newsroom to produce flashy, sensational copy. Most people found the explanation unsatisfying, considering the pattern of deception that went back to her falsified résumé.

There are misrepresentations, however, that are not as clearly unacceptable. Much debated are:

STAGING NEWS.   To attract favourable attention to their clients, public relations people organize *media events*. These are designed to be irresistible to journalists. Rallies and demonstrations on topical issues, for example, find their way onto front pages, magazine covers and evening newscasts because their photogenic qualities give them an edge over less visual although sometimes more significant events. The ethics question is less important for publicists, who generally are up-front about what they are doing. The ethics question is more serious for journalists, who claim that their job is to present an accurate, balanced account of a day's events but who regularly overplay staged events that are designed by publicists to be photogenic and easy to cover.

RE-CREATIONS.   A wave of *reality programs* on television that began in the late 1980s featured reenactments that were not always labeled as such. Philip Weiss, writing in *Columbia Journalism Review*, offered this litany: shadows on the wall of a woman taking a hammer to her husband, a faceless actor grabbing a tin of kerosene to blow up his son, a corpse in a wheelbarrow with a hand dangling, a detective opening the trunk of a car and reeling from the smell of a decomposing body. While mixing re-creations with strictly news footage rankles many critics, others argue that it helps people understand the situation. The same question arises with *docudramas*, which mix actual events and dramatic re-creations.

SELECTIVE EDITING.   The editing process, by its nature, requires journalists to make decisions about what is most worth emphasizing and what is least worth even including. In this sense, all editing is selective, but the term "selective editing" refers to making decisions with the goal of distorting. Selective editing can occur in drama too, when writers, editors and other media people take literary licence too far and intentionally misrepresent.

FICTIONAL METHODS.   In the late 1960s, many experiments in media portrayals of people and issues came to be called the *New Journalism*. The term was hard to define because it included so many approaches. Among the most controversial were applications of fiction-writing methods on topical issues, an approach widely accepted in book publishing but suddenly controversial when it appeared in the news media. Character development became more important than before, including presumed insights into the thinking of people being covered. The view of the writer became an essential element in much of this reporting. The defence for these approaches was that traditional, facts-only reporting could not approach complex truths that merited journalistic explorations. The profound ethics questions that these approaches posed were usually mitigated by clear statements about what the writer was attempting. Nonetheless, it was a controversial approach to the issues of the day. There was no defence when the fictional approach was complete fabrication passing itself off as reality, as in "Jimmy's World."

GIFTS, JUNKETS AND MEALS

In his 1919 book *The Brass Check*, a pioneer examination of newsroom ethics, *Upton Sinclair* told how news people took bribes to put stories in the paper. Today, media

Rigged Explosion. To illustrate a story on vehicle safety, NBC "Dateline" showed a General Motors pickup truck exploding in a collision. Not told to viewers was that the explosion had been rigged for the cameras. The misrepresentation came to light when GM filed a suit, claiming it had been wrongly damaged. For most media people, the issue was one of ethics more than law. The misrepresentation in the re-creation violated the trust that the network had cultivated for its news. After an internal investigation, changes were ordered in the "Dateline" staff, and NBC News Vice President Michael Gartner soon found himself out of a job. Also, besides apologizing to GM, which then withdrew its suit, NBC apologized to its viewers.

Courtesy Dateline NBC

ethics codes universally condemn gifts and certainly bribes, but there still are many people who curry favour with the mass media through gifts, such as a college sports information director who gives a fifth of whisky at Christmas to a sports writer as a gesture of goodwill. Favours can take many forms: media-appreciation luncheons, free trips abroad for the experience necessary to do a travel article, season passes to cover the opera, discounts at certain stores.

Despite the consistent exhortation of the ethics codes against gifts, favours, free travel and special treatment and privileges, there is nothing inherently wrong in taking them if they do not influence coverage and if the journalist's benefactor understands that. The problem with favours is more a practical one than one of ethics. Taking a favour *may or may not be bad*, but it *looks bad*. Many ethics codes do not make this important distinction.

While ethics codes are uniform against *freebies*, as gifts and favours are called, many news organizations accept free movie, drama, concert and other tickets, as well as recordings, books and other materials for review. The justification usually is that their budgets allow them to review only materials that arrive free and that their audiences would be denied reviews if the materials had to be purchased. A counterargument is that a news organization that cannot afford to do business properly should not be in business. Many news organizations, however, insist on buying tickets for their reporters to beauty pageants, sports events and other things to which there is an admission fee. A frequent exception occurs when a press box or special media facility is available. With recordings, books and free samples, some media organizations return them or pass them on to charity to avoid any appearance that they have been bought off.

When junkets are proposed, some organizations send reporters only if they can pay the fare and other expenses. An exception is made by some news organizations for trips that they could not possibly arrange on their own, such as covering a two-week naval exercise aboard a ship.

Some media organizations address the issue of impropriety by acknowledging favours. Many quiz shows say that "promotional consideration" has been provided to companies that give them travel, lodging and prizes. Just as forthright are publications that state that reviews are made possible through season passes or free samples. Acknowledging favours does not remove the questions but at least it is upfront.

VARIOUS CANADIAN CODES OF ETHICS

STUDY PREVIEW   Attitudes toward codes of ethics vary, but most Canadian media organizations have one, as do public relations and advertising associations. These codes go far beyond the question of "freebies," and at least try to address issues of social equality, controversy, offensive content, and fairness in handling complex stories.

Many media critics feel that ethics are not taken as seriously as they might be. According to writer Brian Green, one news director's perspective on ethics was as follows: "It's hard to remember you're here to drain the swamp when you're up to your ass in alligators." Peter Desbarats argues that many media critics feel that while the media may talk a good line when it comes to ethics, it's more talk than walk. Other critics feel that codes of ethics are merely public relations tools the media use to perpetuate the myth that they are holier than thou. This may or may not be true. But the fact remains that most Canadian media organizations have a code of ethics that, if nothing else, serves as a guideline to follow should an alligator creep up on them. The same applies to the public relations and advertising industries.

The study of ethics manifests itself in the world of media in the form of codes of conduct. Among the many media organizations that have codes of conduct for their members are the Canadian Association of Broadcasters, the Canadian Daily Newspaper Association and the Radio-Television News Directors Association of Canada.

THE CANADIAN ASSOCIATION OF BROADCASTERS

Self-proclaimed as the voice of Canada's private broadcasters, the *Canadian Association of Broadcasters* (CAB) was founded by 13 broadcasters in 1926 as a voluntary organization that advocated self-rule for Canada's broadcasters with little, if any, government regulation. CAB was the lobby group for Canada's radio broadcasters prior to the findings of the Aird Commission in 1928. Currently, CAB represents 151 FM radio stations, 68 television stations, one television network and 85 associate members.

In 1990 CAB formed the *Canadian Broadcast Standards Council*. This is a self-regulating council funded for and by private broadcasters in Canada. Its mandate is to promote high standards in radio and television broadcasting through self-regulation. The voluntary CBSC codes cover such areas as children's programming, news and advertising. They prohibit violence in children's programming and the use of subliminal devices in advertising and programming. They also deal with a wide range of issues, including human rights issues and sex-role stereotyping. Since 1991, the CRTC has officially recognized and supported the objectives of the CBSC.

CBSC CODE OF ETHICS—BACKGROUND.   The purpose of this Code of Ethics is to document the realization by proprietors and managers of broadcasting stations, that, as an integral part in the media of communications of this nation, their first responsibility is to the radio listeners and television viewers of Canada for the dissemination of information and news, the supply of a variety of entertainment programming to meet the various tastes of listeners, and the necessity for ethical business standards in dealing with advertisers and their agencies.

It is recognized that the most valuable asset of a broadcaster is public respect which must be earned and can be maintained only by adherence to the highest possible standards of public service and integrity.

The electronic form of publication known as private commercial broadcasting is a highly competitive business devoted to provision of service to the public in all its interests—business, political, recreational, informational, cultural and educational—for profit.

Revenues from advertising make possible non-government broadcasting and make all types of programs available to the Canadian people including news, information, education, and entertainment. Each broadcaster is responsible for the programming of the licensed station. This responsibility can only be met by bringing influence to bear upon all who have a hand in the production of programs including networks, sponsors, producers of live and recorded programs, advertising agencies and talent agencies.

Clause 1—General Programming

Recognizing the varied tastes of the public it shall be the responsibility of the broadcasting industry to so program its various stations that as far as possible, all groups of listeners and viewers shall have from these, some part of the programming devoted to their special likes and desires.

Clause 2—Human Rights

Recognizing that every person has a right to full and equal recognition and to enjoy certain fundamental rights and freedoms, broadcasters shall endeavour to ensure, to the best of their ability, that their programming contains no abusive or discriminatory material or comment which is based on matters of race, national or ethnic origin, colour, religion, age, sex, marital status or physical or mental handicap.

Clause 3—Children's Programs

Recognizing that programs designed specifically for children reach impressionable minds and influence social attitudes and aptitudes, it shall be the responsibility of member stations to provide the closest possible supervision in the selection and control of material, characterizations and plot. Nothing in the foregoing shall mean that the vigour and vitality common to children's imaginations and love of adventure should be removed. It does mean that programs should be based upon sound social concepts and presented with a superior degree of craftsmanship; that these programs should reflect the moral and ethical standards of contemporary Canadian society and encourage pro-social behaviour and attitudes. The member stations should encourage parents to select, from the richness of broadcasting fare, the best programs to be brought to the attention of their children.

Clause 4—Community Activities

It shall be the responsibility of each member station to serve to the utmost of its ability the interests of its particular community and to identify itself actively with worthwhile community activities.

Clause 5—Education

While recognizing that all programs possess, by their very nature, some educational value, member stations will do all in their power to make specific educational efforts as useful and entertaining as possible. To that end, they will continue to use their time and facilities and to cooperate with appropriate educational groups in an attempt to augment the educational and cultural influences of school, institutions of higher learning, the home and other institutions devoted to education and culture. When practical, advantage should be taken of opportunities to consult such institutions on what suitable material is available and how it may best be presented. Where practical, factual material for public enlightenment should be included by stations, networks, advertisers and their agencies.

Clause 6—News

It shall be the responsibility of member stations to ensure that news shall be represented with accuracy and without bias. The member station shall satisfy itself that the arrangements made for obtaining news ensure this results. It shall also ensure that news broadcasts are not editorial. News shall not be selected for the purpose of furthering or hindering either side of any controversial public issue, nor shall it be designed by the beliefs or opinions or desires of the station management, the editor or others engaged in its preparation or delivery. The fundamental purpose of news dissemination in a democracy is to enable people to know what is happening, and to understand events so that they may form their own conclusions.

Therefore, nothing in the foregoing shall be understood as preventing news broadcasters from analyzing and elucidating news so long as such analysis or comment is clearly labelled as such and kept distinct from regular news presentations. Member stations will, insofar as practical, endeavour to provide editorial opinion which stall be clearly labelled as such and kept entirely distinct from regular broadcasts of news or analysis and opinion.

It is recognized that the full, fair and proper presentation of news, opinion, comment and editorial is the prime and fundamental responsibility of the broadcast publisher.

Clause 7—Controversial Public Issues

Recognizing in a democracy the necessity of presenting all sides of a public issue, it shall be the responsibility of member stations to treat fairly all subjects of a controversial nature. Time shall be allotted with due regard to all the other elements of balanced program schedules, and to the degree of public interest in the questions presented. Recognizing that healthy controversy is essential to the maintenance of democratic institutions, the broadcast publisher will endeavour to encourage presentation of news and opinion on any controversy which contains an element of the public interest.

Clause 8—Advertising

Recognizing the service that commercial sponsors render to listeners and viewers in making known to them the goods and services available in their communities and realizing that the story of such goods and services goes into the intimacy of the home, it shall be the responsibility of member stations and their sales representatives to work with advertisers and agencies in improving the technique of telling the advertising story so that these shall be in good taste, simple, truthful and believable, and shall not offend what is generally accepted as the prevailing standard of good taste.

Advertising is to be made most effective not only by the use of an appropriate selling message but by earning the most favourable reaction of the public to the sponsor by providing the best possible programming. Nothing in the foregoing shall prevent the dramatization of the use, value or attractiveness of products and services. While appropriate legislation protects the public from false and exaggerated claims for drugs, proprietaries and foods, it shall be the responsibility of member stations and their sales representatives to work with the advertiser of these products and the advertising agencies to ensure that their value and use are told in words that are not offensive. Recognizing also that advertising appeals or commentaries by any advertiser that cast reflection upon the operation of a competitor or other industry or business are destructive of public confidence, it shall be the responsibility of member stations, so far as it lies within their power, to prevent such advertising appeals or commentaries being broadcast by their stations.

Broadcasters subscribing to the Code of Ethics and Clause 8 approve adherence to the complementary Canadian Code of Advertising Standards, published by the Advertising Advisory Board; the guidelines on sex-role stereotyping published by the Advertising Advisory Board; the Broadcast Code for Advertising to Children, published by the Canadian Association of Broadcasters; and to the Code of Consumer Advertising Practices for Non-Prescription Medicines, as published by the Advertising Advisory Board. The aforementioned codes and guidelines are all subject to endorsement by the Joint Board of the Canadian Association of Broadcasters from time to time.

Clause 9—Prohibition of Subliminal Devices

Broadcasters must not knowingly broadcast any advertising material or program that makes use of any subliminal technique or device "Subliminal device" means a technical device that is used to convey or attempt to convey a message to a person by means of images or sounds of very brief duration, or by any other means, without that person being aware that such a device is being used, or being aware of the substance of the message being conveyed or attempted to be conveyed.

Clause 10—Advertising on AM and FM Radio Broadcasting Stations

(a) Broadcasters recognize that they are responsible for the acceptability of advertising material which they broadcast. All commercials should be in good taste and should conform with applicable laws and regulations.

(b) Broadcasters should adhere strictly to the provisions of all industry codes or guidelines relating to advertising, such as those pertaining to children's advertising, feminine hygiene products and the advertising of alcoholic beverages.

(c) Broadcasters should ensure that the time allocated to commercial messages is not excessive at any period during the broadcast day, and particularly during high audience periods. The total quantity of commercial messages broadcast on a given station in one week should not, in any event, exceed 1750 minutes.

(d) Broadcasters should ensure in the scheduling of commercial messages that they are appropriate for the likely listening audience at the time the commercials are scheduled, and that they are both scheduled and inserted in a manner that will not detract from the effectiveness of the programming broadcast by the station.

(e) Broadcasters should ensure that advertising material within a newscast is clearly distinguishable from the news information adjacent to it. To this end, any commercial message broadcast within a newscast should not be read by the newsreader.

(f) Broadcasters should ensure that there is no influence by advertisers, or the perception of such influence, on the reporting of news or public affairs, which must be accurate, balanced and objective, with fairness and integrity being the paramount considerations governing its reporting.

Clause 11—Radio Station Contests and Promotions

(a) Broadcasters recognize that whereas station contests and promotions are legitimate and useful methods of attracting audiences, they should be conducted in such a manner that the cost of any such contest or promotion is not excessive, particularly in relation to the station's programming budget.

(b) All station contests and promotions should be conceived and conducted in good taste, and particular care should be taken to ensure that they are not likely to give rise to a public inconvenience or disturbance.

Clause 12—Television Station Contests and Promotions

(a) Broadcasters recognize that whereas station contests and promotions are legitimate and useful methods of attracting audiences, they should be conducted in such a manner that the cost of any such contest or promotion is not excessive, particularly in relation to the station's programming budget.

(b) All station contests and promotions should be conceived and conducted in good taste, and particular care should be taken to ensure that they are not likely to give rise to a public inconvenience or disturbance.

Clause 13—Advertising in Television News Programs

(a) Broadcasters should ensure that advertising material within a newscast is clearly distinguishable from the news information adjacent to it. To this end, any commercial message broadcast within a newscast should not be read by the newsreader.

(b) Broadcasters should ensure that there is no influence by advertisers, or the perception of such influence, on the reporting of news or public affairs, which must be accurate, balanced and objective, with fairness and integrity being the paramount considerations governing its reporting.

Clause 14—Treatment of Religious Programs

Broadcasters should endeavour to make available to the community adequate opportunity for presentation of religious messages and should also endeavour to assist in all ways open to them the furtherance of religious activities in the community. Recognizing the purpose of the religious broadcast to be that of promoting the spiritual harmony and understanding of humanity and that of administering broadly to the varied religious needs of the community, it shall be the responsibility of each member station to ensure that its religious broadcasts, which reach persons of all creeds and races simultaneously, shall not be used to convey attacks upon another race or religion.

Clause 15—Sex-Role Stereotyping

Recognizing that stereotyping images can and do cause negative influences, it shall be the responsibility of broadcasters to exhibit, to the best of their ability, a conscious sensitivity to the problems related to sex-role stereotyping, by refraining from exploitation and by the reflection of the intellectual and emotional equality of both sexes in programming.

Clause 16—Employees

Each member station shall endeavour to secure the highest possible type of employees and people who are qualified for and suitable to the duties for which each is hires. Every attempt shall be made to make service in the broadcasting industry an attractive and permanent career, permitting employees to contribute through their manner of living and personal attainments to the station's prestige in the community. Each employee shall receive, in addition to minimum guarantees provided by applicable legislation, fair remuneration and treatment in accordance with the standards prevailing the particular community at any time. The general intent of this section is realization that any industry is most often judged by the type of employees it attracts, the manner in which they conduct themselves and are able to live and their opinion of the industry for which they work. Recognizing this as a valuable asset, the broadcaster will do everything possible to maintain and further the best type of staff relations.

Clause 17—Adherence

(a) All future broadcasting codes which have been endorsed by the Board of Directors and ratified by the membership who subscribe to the Code, at a duly called annual meeting of the Association, shall be incorporated into the Code of Ethics.

(b) Upon adoption of this Code of Ethics by the Association, any member broadcasting station shall be granted appropriate recognition and symbol. It may then make announcement periodically of the fact it is in possession of such certification and be entitled to make appropriate oral and visual use of the Code symbol.

Clause 18—Composition of the Committee

There shall be a Code of Ethics Committee of five persons, three of whom shall be appointed by the Board of Directors and two elected by the Annual Meeting of the Association for a period not to exceed five years, and appointments may be renewed. Any vacancy in the Committee may be filled for the unexpired term by the Board of Directors. Any vacancy or absence shall not impair the powers of the remaining members of the Code of Ethics Committee to act, provided, however, that a quorum of it shall be considered as not less than three persons and such a quorum shall be present before the Code of Ethics Committee is empowered to transact business.

(Reprinted by permission of the CBSC)

Television viewers and radio listeners have filed a variety of complaints with the CBSC. In 1991 a listener objected to a remark made by an announcer at CHFX-FM in Halifax. The announcer remarked that since a local craft show closed at 4 p.m. the wives of male listeners should be home in time to make supper for them. The CBSC felt that at least two outdated myths had been perpetuated by the announcer's comments. Since the guidelines on sex-role stereotyping clearly state that women and men need to be portrayed in a wide variety of roles, the council ruled that the listener had a valid complaint.

A viewer in BC complained when CTV ran the movie *When Harry Met Sally* almost unedited in 1992. The viewer was concerned about the use of an offensive word. After investigating the issue, the CBSC discovered that CTV had warned viewers that some of the movie's content might not be acceptable to all. Therefore the CBSC concluded that the station was not at fault.

In 1992, a listener who had tuned in to a hockey game on CKNW in Vancouver complained when the play-by-play commentator referred to the lacklustre play of a defenceman as resembling that of a "drug store Indian." CKNW apologized for the comments, remarking that they were clearly in violation of the CBSC Clause 2, which prohibits the use of derogatory stereotypes based on race and ethnicity.

RADIO AND TELEVISION NEWS DIRECTORS ASSOCIATION OF CANADA

The Radio and Television News Directors Association was founded over 50 years ago. It's an international organization with affiliations in Canada. Recognizing the importance to a democracy of an informed public, the members of the RTNDA of Canada believe the broadcasting of factual, accurately reported and timely news and public affairs is vital. To this end, RTNDA members in Canada pledge to observe the following Code of Ethics, which is also administered by the CBSC:

ARTICLE ONE:
The main purpose of broadcast journalism is to inform the public in an accurate, comprehensive and balanced manner about events of importance.
ARTICLE TWO:
News and public affairs broadcasts will put events into perspective by presenting relevant background information. Factors such as race, creed, nationality or religion will be reported only when relevant. Comments and editorial opinion will be identified as such. Errors will be quickly acknowledged and publicly corrected.
ARTICLE THREE:
Broadcast journalists will not sensationalize news items, and will resist pressures, whether from inside or outside the broadcast industry, to do so. They will in no way distort the news. Broadcast journalists will not edit taped interviews to distort the meaning, intent, or actual words of the interviewee.
ARTICLE FOUR:
Broadcast journalists will always display respect for the dignity, privacy and well-being of everyone with whom they deal, and make every effort to ensure that the privacy of public persons is infringed only to the extent necessary to satisfy the public interest and accurately report the news.
ARTICLE FIVE:
Broadcast journalists will govern themselves on and off the job in such a way as to avoid conflict of interest, real or apparent.

ARTICLE SIX:

Broadcast journalists will seek to remove any impediments or bans on the use of electronic news-gathering equipment at public proceedings, believing that such access is in the public interest. They acknowledge the importance of protection of confidential information and sources.

ARTICLE SEVEN:

News directors recognize that informed analysis, comment and editorial opinion on public events and issues is both a right and a responsibility that should be delegated only to individuals whose experience and judgment qualify them for it.

ARTICLE EIGHT:

Broadcast journalists shall conduct themselves politely, keeping broadcast equipment as unobtrusive as possible. Broadcast journalists will try to prevent their presence from distorting the character or importance of events.

ARTICLE NINE:

In reporting matters that are, or may be, before the courts, broadcast journalists will ensure that their reporting does not interfere with the right of an individual to a fair trial.

ARTICLE TEN:

Reporting of criminal activities, such as hostage takings, will be done in a fashion that does not knowingly endanger lives, hamper attempts by authorities to conclude the event, offer comfort and support or provide information to the perpetrator(s). RTNDA members will not contact either the victim(s) or the perpetrator(s) of a criminal activity during the course of the event, with the purpose of conducting an interview for broadcast.

ARTICLE ELEVEN:

The RTNDA will seek to enforce this code through its members and encourage all broadcast journalists, whether RTNDA members or not, to observe its spirit. News directors will try whenever possible and within programming format constraints to publicize the existence of the Code of Ethics, and state that their news department adhere to the code. In any such announcement, it should be mentioned that copies of the code can be obtained by writing the RTNDA or the news director at the station.

(Reprinted with the permission of the RTNDA)

CANADIAN DAILY NEWSPAPER ASSOCIATION CODE OF ETHICS

The Canadian Daily Newspaper Association was founded in 1919. Its members came to include 83 Canadian dailies. In late 1996, it merged with the Newspaper Marketing Bureau to form the Canadian Newspaper Association. The CNA has not yet published its new code of ethics. Therefore a copy of the CDNA's Statement of Principles, published in 1977 and updated in 1995, follows:

PREAMBLE

This statement of principles expresses the commitment of Canada's daily newspapers to operate in the public interest. A newspaper is a vital source of information and a private business enterprise with responsibility to the community it serves.

FREEDOM OF THE PRESS

Freedom of the press is an exercise of every Canadian's right to freedom of expression guaranteed in the Charter of Rights and Freedoms. It is the right to gather and disseminate information, to discuss, to advocate, to dissent. A free press is essential to our democratic society. It enables readers to use their Charter right to receive information and make informed judgments on the issues and ideas of the time.

INDEPENDENCE

The newspaper's primary obligation is fidelity to the public good. It should pay the costs of gathering the news. Conflicts of interest, real or apparent, should be declared. The newspaper should guard its independence from government, commercial and other interests seeking to subvert content for their own purposes.

ACCURACY AND FAIRNESS

The newspaper keeps faith with readers by presenting information that is accurate, fair, comprehensive, interesting and timely. It should acknowledge its mistakes promptly and conspicuously. Sound practice clearly distinguishes among news reports, expressions of opinion, and materials produced for and by advertisers. When images have been altered or simulated, readers should be told.

COMMUNITY RESPONSIBILITY

The newspaper has responsibilities to its readers, its shareholders, its employees and its advertisers. But the operation of a newspaper is a public trust and its overriding responsibility is to the society it serves. The newspaper plays many roles: a watchdog against evil and wrongdoing, an advocate for good works and noble deeds, and an opinion leader for its community. The newspaper should strive to paint a representative picture of its diverse communities, to encourage the expression of disparate views and to be accessible and accountable to the readers it serves, whether rich or poor, weak or powerful, minority or majority. When published material attacks an individual or group, those affected should be given an opportunity to reply.

RESPECT

The newspaper should strive to treat the people it covers with courtesy and fairness. It should respect the rights of others, particularly every person's right to a fair trial. The inevitable conflict between privacy and the public good should be judged in the light of common sense and with decency.

(Reprinted by permission of the Canadian Daily Newspaper Association)

CHAPTER WRAP-UP

Mass media people need to be concerned about ethics because they can have powerful effects. But answers do not come easily. Personal information can embarrass a person inexcusably. However, it can be argued that privacy is less important, for example, with candidates for high office.

Philosophers have devised numerous systems to help individuals address moral issues. Influential is John Stuart Mill's utilitarianism, which favours choices that lead to the greatest good for the most people. Other moral principles favour more respect for individual privacy.

Moral decision making is rooted in conscience, which makes it highly individual. Attempts to bring order to moral issues in journalism and the mass media have included codes of ethics. These codes identify behaviours that are recognized as ethically troublesome, but because they are generalized statements, the codes cannot anticipate all situations. There is no substitute for human reason and common sense.

QUESTIONS FOR REVIEW

1. Why cannot ethics codes anticipate all moral questions? And does this limit the value of codes for mass media people?

2. List and explain moral principles that mass media people can use to sort through ethics questions.

3. How can mass media people come to different conclusions depending on whether they use process-based or outcome-based ethics?

4. Is ethics the same as law? As prudence? As accepted practices?

5. Discuss dubious mass media practices that are inconsistent with many moral principles.

6. Review the various Canadian ethics codes. How useful are such codes?

QUESTIONS FOR CRITICAL THINKING

1. How are traditional libertarians deontological in their approach to ethics? How is the social responsibility approach teleological?

2. As someone who reads newspapers and watches newscasts, would you favour deontological or teleological ethics? Which is easier? Which system do you think most journalists prefer?

3. Can you identify the ethics principle or system most associated with Aristotle? Immanuel Kant? John Stuart Mill? John Dewey? John Rawls? Robert Maynard Hutchins?

4. How can codes of ethics help mass media people make the right decisions? Do codes always work? Why or why not?

5. A candidate for mayor tells a news reporter that the incumbent mayor is in cahoots with organized crime. What should the reporter do before going on the air with this bombshell accusation? Why?

6. Can media people ever defend breaking the law as ethical?

7. Is there a difference between ethics and accepted practices?

FOR FURTHER LEARNING

Clifford G. Christians, Kim B. Rotzoll and Mark Fackler. *Media Ethics*, 2nd ed. (Longman, 1987). These scholars are especially good at describing Kant's categorical imperative and other philosophical systems on which media ethics can be based.

Roy Peter Clark. "The Original Sin: How Plagiarism Poisons the Press," *Washington Journalism Review* (March 1983), 43–47.

Brian Green. *Broadcast News Essentials* (Harcourt Brace, 1996). A guide to Canadian broadcast writing.

Carl Hausman. *The Decision-Making Process in Journalism* (Nelson-Hall, 1990). Hausman, a journalism professor, provides a checklist to help sort the way through ethics problems.

Walter B. Jaehnig. "Harrison Cochran—The Publisher with a Past," *Journal of Mass Media Ethics* 2 (Fall/Winter 1986–87):1, 80–88. This is a case study examination of the *Rocky Mountain News* situational ethics case. Every issue of this journal contains a media ethics problem with commentary from professional and scholarly observers.

Janet Malcolm. *The Journalist and the Murderer* (Knopf, 1990). Malcolm argues that journalists exploit their sources of information, using the relationship of author Joe McGinniss and a convicted murderer for the book *Fatal Vision*.

John C. Merrill. *The Dialectic in Journalism: Toward a Responsible Use of Press Freedom* (Louisiana State University Press, 1990). Professor Merrill, who has written several books on journalism ethics, favours philosophical frameworks for solving ethics questions rather than codes of ethics.

Nick Russell. *Morals and the Media: Ethics in Canadian Journalism* (University of British Columbia Press: 1994).

Phillip Weiss. "Bad Rap for TV Tabs," *Columbia Journalism Review* 28 (May/June 1989):1, 39–42. Weiss deals with ethics questions raised by tabloid television programs, including dramatized re-creations.

Marie Dunn White. "Plagiarism and the News Media," *Journal of Mass Media Ethics* 4 (1989):2, 265–280. White examines the hazards when journalists read their competitors for story ideas and information.

FOR KEEPING UP TO DATE

Ethicists sort through moral dilemmas involving mass communication in the scholarly *Journal of Mass Media Ethics.*

Many trade and professional journals also deal with media ethics, including *Columbia Journalism Review* and *Broadcaster.*

MASS MEDIA TOMORROW

A mass media revolution is under way because of miniaturization, digital and other technologies, and satellites

Television is evolving in a less aggressive direction than the other mass media

Newspapers are well positioned to dominate the news business in the future

Magazines may become indistinguishable from newspapers in the new media age

Radio will likely assume entirely new forms with new technologies

The new media offer advertisers new opportunities to reach narrow audiences

Many experts see everyone being connected by the information highway

Public policy will need rethinking as the media become truly global and more oriented to narrow audiences

MEDIA IN THEORY

Looking Ahead

As the forms of communication change, how will the process change? We have come full circle: to introduce the final chapter of the book, we need to review some of the ideas we examined when we began. Here's a list of questions to ask yourself when reading about the coming technological changes in Canadian communications:

- Would McLuhan classify these new media forms and their content as "hot" or "cold"?
- Are they elitist or populist?

- Who will control the new media?
- Who will control their content?
- Who will govern the new media technologies?
- Should Canadian content be protected?
- Which model best reflects the "new" communication: Laswell, Shannon and Weaver, or the Concentric Circle model?
- Which school of thought is best suited to analyze the new media, the process school or the semiotic school?
- How will old media adapt to new technology?

MASS MEDIA REVOLUTION

STUDY PREVIEW A mass media revolution is under way because of miniaturization, digital and other new technologies and satellites. An important key in new media forms is the ability to compress messages for storage and transmission.

CANADIANS AND NEW TECHNOLOGIES

Waking to music and information on the radio. Checking the latest forecast on the Weather Network. Getting some money at the bank machine on the way to work. Checking your faxes and e-mail once you get to the office. Using a cell phone on your way home to order a pizza. Calling Viewer's Choice Canada after supper to order that night's pay per view special.

Welcome to Canadians on the information highway.

If recent history has taught us anything, it's that we love to play with electronic gadgets. The following chart from a 1995 report done by Statistics Canada suggests that no matter what the form of technology, Canadians have welcomed it with open arms.

MINIATURIZATION

Until the 1950s, home radios were delicate pieces of equipment that glowed with lightbulblike tubes that amplified broadcast signals so they could be heard. Even the smallest radios, called "table models," were pieces of furniture. Then, in the 1950s, came a technological marvel: handheld battery-powered transistor radios that people could carry anywhere. While revolutionary in themselves, these transistor radios were only the beginning of an age of technological miniaturization.

The revolution began in 1947 when researchers developed the first semiconductor switch. They took pieces of glasslike silicon, really just pieces of sand, and devised a way to make them respond to a negative or positive charge. These tiny slivers of sand, called semiconductors, could function as on-off switches. The implications of semiconductors for the electronic mass media were quickly evident because they could solve problems inherent in the technology of radio at the time. For one thing, radios and their tubes were fragile. The tubes got hot and eventually burned out. Also, they consumed massive amounts of electricity. Semiconductors, on the other hand, could amplify broadcast signals without any heat, and they used hardly any electricity. Important too, semiconductors were much, much smaller than tubes. That's why transistor radios were portable, unlike the radios before them.

Miniaturization has been important not only because equipment can be smaller and more reliable but also because it can be much less expensive. The first computers in the 1940s, based on tube technology, were so big it took entire buildings

MEDIA DATABANK

Percentage of urban households[1] with selected equipment in 1994

Census metropolitan area (number of households)	Cable television	VCRs	Camcorders	Cassette or tape recorders	CD players	Home computers	Modems
Calgary (270 000)	86	82	15	81	45	31	7
Edmonton (290 000)	79	83	17	84	47	30	12
Halifax (124 000)	87	85	11	85	46	27	12
Hamilton (244 000)	87	82	14	78	48	28	4
Kitchener (133 000)	87	85	19	82	55	36	22
London (137 000)	86	83	16	85	44	29	6
Montréal (1 246 000)	69	71	11	66	38	22	7
Ottawa–Hull (352 000)	84	81	12	81	44	34	11
Québec (266 000)	68	75	10	72	44	18	3
St. Catharines–Niagara (131 000)	72	82	14	78	35	22	13
Toronto (1 365 000)	90	82	19	76	46	31	12
Vancouver (660 000)	93	81	17	83	54	36	16
Victoria (129 000)	94	79	14	87	52	36	15
Windsor (99 000)	49	80	16	77	40	25	19
Winnipeg (250 000)	85	77	12	79	40	21	14

[1]Households in census metropolitan areas.

Source: Statistics Canada, Household Surveys Division, 1994 Household Facilities and Equipment Survey.

to house them and large staffs of technicians to operate them. According to a National Academy of Science estimate, it cost $130 000 to make 125 multiplications with those computers. By 1970 the cost was a mere $4. Today it can be done for pennies.

Wilbur Schramm, in his book *The Story of Human Communication*, cited a Marquardt Corporation estimate that all the information recorded in the last 10 000 years could be stored in a cube 6 feet (1.8 m) by 6 feet by 6 feet. All 12 million books in the U.S. Library of Congress would take less than 2 cubic inches (33 cc). Miniaturization through semiconductors has brought us a long way.

DIGITAL AND OTHER TECHNOLOGIES

Telephones today are mostly point-to-point communication tools for one person to talk to another person or for the one-way transmission of data. Mass media, in contrast, allow one person to talk to hundreds if not millions of people. This distinction, however, is disappearing as telephone companies, capitalizing on semiconductor and other technologies, develop the capacity to carry messages to multiple parties. This technological revolution, making telephone systems into mass media, is based on several developments:

- **Semiconductors.** The rapid on-off switching of semiconductors allows more voices to be carried simultaneously on a single cable.

- **Optical fibre cable.** Glass fibre cable technology, often called *fibre optics*, has vastly greater capacity to carry messages than old copper cables, with better quality at less cost. In the early days of semiconductor on-off switching, people marveled that 51 calls could be carried at the same time on a copper cable. Today, with semiconductor switching combined with optical fibre cable, a single line can carry 60 000 calls simultaneously.

- **Digitization.** An outgrowth of semiconductor technology has been the digitization of data, even voices and video, for storage and transmission. A message, whether a voice on a phone line or music on a compact disc, is reduced to millions and millions of on-off signals. Miniaturization has made it possible to record a tremendous number of these on-off signals for transmission and replay. Hence, as Wilbur Schramm noted, all human knowledge could fit into about 8 cubic metres. Calgary's Shaw Cablesystems was experimenting with digital cable TV in the fall of 1996.

SATELLITES

Orbiting satellites are platforms that relay messages worldwide, including both entertainment and news. Combined with other technologies that are transforming the mass media, satellites are making the world a very small place. Not a spot on the globe is beyond the media's reach. These technologies are creating vast global commercial opportunities to supply news and entertainment without regard to national borders.

You Choose the Shot. An experiment with interactive television involved 130 households. With a remote control–type device, viewers chose which camera they wanted to see as a football game progressed: go to an end zone camera; zoom in on a tackle; zoom back on a long pass; or go to the scoreboard. Interactive media allow the consumer to send messages back to the source. The introduction of high-capacity optical fibre cable is opening the way to entirely new structures of media programming and presentation. Possibilities include on-demand music, much like a jukebox.

TELEVISION AND TELECOMPUTERS

STUDY PREVIEW   The over-air television industry is working to improve picture clarity with high-definition screens. Other media, meanwhile, are leapfrogging HDTV and going on to even better on-screen images. These include images with easily read text.

HIGH-DEFINITION TELEVISION

The over-air television industry is developing new enhanced-picture systems known variously as *HDTV*, short for high-definition television, and *ATV*, short for advanced television. Television screens in Canada and the U.S. today have 525 interlaced horizontal lines with every other line filled in at rapid intervals. This fools the eye into seeing motion, although the image is fuzzy close up and on over-size screens. The European 625-line screens are a bit sharper, and the Japanese 1 124-line HDTV screens sharper yet. But not even the Japanese system handles text well. If a whole newspaper page is transmitted, viewers can make out only the headlines. For a story to be read, the camera must zoom in on a single narrow column of type.

For HDTV, the National Television Standards Committee, which decides such things, has set 62 dots per inch as the new television transmission standard. That is wholly adequate for producing the image quality of today's 525-line screens and even HDTV screens of the future. But compared to the telecomputer standards that other media are developing, 62 dots per inch doesn't measure up at all.

TELECOMPUTERS

For on-screen images, computers use at least a 200-dot-per-inch standard, or, put another way, 40 000 dots per square inch, for fully readable text—more than 30 times what television people are planning for HDTV.

The other mass media, particularly newspapers, appear to be leapfrogging television by adapting standards developed by the computer industry to create, transmit and display readable messages. This technology involves compressing those tiny on-screen dots, called *pixels*. Television's upcoming 62-dot standard doesn't come close to the level needed for delivering text. One current computer standard for pixels, the 72 dots per inch that Apple uses for its laptop computers, is one-third sharper than the 62-dot NTSC standard. But even the laptop's 72 dots aren't sharp enough. In tests with people reading from standard books and from laptops, those using laptops moved through the material 25 percent more slowly.

As engineers discover new miniaturization techniques and ways to squeeze more capacity into computer chips, pixels will be packed more and more densely on screens. This means that superb-image, lightweight compact screens will be coming along. The term *telecomputer* is often used to distinguish this new, sharper image medium from television.

FLAT SCREENS

Technology is making flat screens possible. We see flat screens today on laptop and other small computers. These telecomputer screens contrast with the thick cathode-ray tubes of television sets, which are neither lightweight nor compact. The cost of producing television picture tubes is about as low as it will go, whereas flat screen production costs are destined to drop significantly.

Today high-density telecomputer screens cost $10 per square inch to manufacture, but with the price of computer chip technology dropping by half every 18 months,

The Eyeball as a Screen. Micro Vision is hoping to market a device that projects images directly onto the human eyeball. The VRD, short for "virtual retina display," will be small enough to mount on a pair of eyeglasses and it will give a sharper image than a 70-millimetre IMAX screen. With the VDR, people would not need television or computer screens. Micro Vision says this device eventually can be made for less than $100.

manufacturers expect high-density pixel screens to drop to $1 per square inch. This means that compact computer screens with the resolution of the best laser printers could be manufactured for $100 or less.

If the future of mass media is in personal compact reception equipment, as many futurists foresee, then the future will be with telecomputer systems because they have the flexibility people want. These screens can handle both images and text, and they are light, compact and cheap and becoming more so. The relative bulkiness and cost of television screens means they won't compete. George Gilder, a leading media technologist, is blunt: "Computers will soon blow away the broadcast television industry." Gilder says major broadcast companies that are committing themselves to television's over-air technology rather than going the telecomputer route are "in a kind of elephants' waltz into the sunset."

VIRTUAL RETINA DISPLAYS

Even before flat screens make it to market they may be obsolete. University technologists are developing a system that displays electronic images directly on the human retina. People would wear something resembling a pair of glasses that would project three-dimensional photographic-quality images with the eyeball itself as the screen. These eyeball projectors, called *virtual retina displays*, would leapfrog the competition between cathode ray tubes and flat screens.

TOMORROW'S NEWS MEDIA

STUDY PREVIEW Newspaper companies are well positioned to dominate the news business in the future and to expand into services beyond news. In the not too distant future, people will be able to call up the news they want in as much detail as they want. In effect, everyone would be able to create custom, individual news packages from massive arrays of information that will be available.

NEWSPAPERS' FUTURE

Newspapers are well into the electronic age in every way except final production and delivery. Writers do their stories on computers, and editors use advanced digital equipment to edit the copy, lay it out and make it ready for printing. The actual printing, however, is on monstrous presses whose technological heritage can be traced to Johannes Gutenberg's movable type of the 1400s. Also, just as it was 500 years ago, the product is still ink on paper—barrels and barrels of ink and reams of paper. And just as it has been for almost two centuries, the delivery of newspapers is mostly in the hands of youngsters who trot from house to house to drop the papers on doorsteps. There is a quaint irony in trusting boys and girls to deliver a million-dollar product, like an edition of a metropolitan daily, to the customers.

Do newspapers have a future? The obituary for newspapers was written prematurely twice before. Publishers once feared radio would put them out of business. It didn't happen. Later, television was a threat, and in fact television stole newspaper readers, especially in the evening, and this prompted speculation that the end for newspapers was near. That speculation is fading, however, and many futurists believe today's newspaper companies are well positioned to dominate the news business in the 21st century.

EFFICIENCY AND EFFECTIVENESS

Newspapers are a medium based on words. For the most part, visuals in newspapers and also magazines are mere enhancements to written messages. Those people who see the communication of the future as primarily video have missed the fact that video works better than words for only an extremely narrow range of messages. Media technologist George Gilder puts it this way: "Video is most effective in conveying

First Online. The *Halifax Daily News* was Canada's first on-line newspaper. Internet surfers can read local, national and international stories at the click of a button. The paper's URL is: **http://cfn.cs.dal.ca/Media/ TodaysNews/TodaysNews.html** Many other newspapers have also gone on-line in Canada.

shocks and sensations and appealing to prurient interests of large miscellaneous audiences. Images easily excel in blasting through to the glandular substances of the human community; there's nothing like a body naked or bloody or both to arrest the eye." Human communication, however, goes far beyond shock scenes and sensual appeals. People communicate mostly through words.

Television technology today, with only 525 lines on a screen, is not a good medium for written messages. Nor is television an efficient medium for relaying information. News anchors and reporters talk on air at 140 to 160 words a minute. That is not an efficient rate to communicate messages, especially considering that most people read at least 700 words a minute. Veteran network anchor Walter Cronkite once noted that the script for one edition of the CBS Evening News would take up only half the front page of the *New York Times*. Think about how many pages of a newspaper you could read in the time it takes to watch a half-hour newscast.

COMPUTER DELIVERY

The ability of computer networks to relay digitized text, images and even voice almost instantly will be the heart of tomorrow's news media. There will be no morning or afternoon newspapers. With delivery through computer networks directly to readers, news people can update their stories as events warrant and as articles are written and as visual and sound packages are produced. The product can be delivered in real time, just like television with reporters and photographers at the scene live—but with crisper telecomputer video than with television and text.

The news media of tomorrow will also have other advantages over television as we know it today, including unlimited space and time. Also, the audience will have an ability to choose individually what stories to follow instead of being forced to wait, as with today's television, for stories that interest them to come up in the newscast.

Like the *Halifax Daily News*, several Canadian newspapers are offering their news and services on-line. Many aren't making money yet, but it is a way of attracting some of the revenue they have lost over the last few years. Other on-line Canadian newspapers include the *Toronto Star*, the Toronto *Sun*, the Montreal *Gazette*, the *Ottawa Citizen* and the *Edmonton Journal*.

It's not only the major newspapers that are going on-line. Several community newspapers are also offered via the Internet. Student newspapers are also on-line, including Langara College's the *Gleanor*, the *Brunswickan* from the University of New Brunswick and the University of King's College's the *Watch*.

In 1996 Rogers Communications established the Canadian On-line Explorer (CANOE) on the World Wide Web. This multimedia news and entertainment service provides links to electronic versions of all the *Sun* newspapers, the *Financial Post*, *Maclean's* magazine and Toronto's 680 News, an all-news radio station which is also owned by Rogers.

NEWS HOLE.   People will have access to far more information than today. The "news hole" no longer will be limited by the space available in an edition or the time available in a newscast. Readers can see the headlines and then, with their screen controls, choose to go into depth with more background stories, with stories from previous days, with maps, charts and photos, and with video segments with voices and sound of news events as they happened. It will be possible to read the texts of important speeches, rather than merely read summaries, or to listen to the whole speech as it was delivered. It will be possible even to watch the actual interviews on which stories are based.

PIXELS.   Television today has a built-in disadvantage in displaying on-screen text. The current on-screen pixel density does not give the crisp resolution that is needed for people to read from their screens, except for oversized, headline-type messages. If you see words on a television screen today, they usually are bottom-of-the-screen streamers with four or five words per line at most. To show a piece of writing on screen, television producers have to zoom in so close that only a fragment of a line shows. The alternative, scrolling or panning over a written message, works for a brief message but is as distracting as would be turning the pages of a newspaper every few words.

The television industry has committed itself to relatively modest improvements in pixel density. Even with the higher resolution of HDTV, with roughly double the horizontal lines, the image will not be crisp enough to deliver text. In the meantime, newspapers plan to deliver news to telecomputer screens, which use thousands more pixels to create images. Besides text, telecomputer screens can present moving images—and do it more sharply than television. In short, telecomputer newspapers are in a good position to displace television as a medium for news.

Over-air television won't disappear as a medium all at once. It will remain satisfactory for watching movies and simple visual presentations, but because it doesn't work for texts and because telecomputer screens will do everything better, over-air television eventually will be displaced by cable-delivered media—unless sharper over-air transmission standards are adopted.

BROWSING.   Newspapers today lend themselves to browsing. People scan headlines and photos to decide what interests them. Tomorrow's on-screen newspaper also will allow browsing. With a click of a key or a mouse or button, or perhaps a voice command, readers will move to another page or even turn pages by uttering a voice command: "Next screen, please." "Sports now, please." "More photos, please." "How about those Expos?"

This browsing capacity is something that television, as it now exists, does not have. With television, if you are interested in a particular story, you have to sit through other stories until what you want comes up. This makes television a dull news medium. It also has made television a superficial medium: So viewers don't get bored waiting for the items they're interested in, television people have devised formats with short stories. Many stations and networks have a two-minute cap on stories. The result is stories that touch only on the surface of a subject.

READER CONTROL.   With telecomputer systems, people will be able to call up from newspaper databanks the news and information that interests them. Unlike over-air radio and television, people will not be compelled to watch live coverage if something else interests them more. People can create their own sequences of stories and skip ones that don't interest them. On-screen newspapers, then as now, will be a personal medium over which the reader has control. George Gilder put it this way: "Newspapers rely on the intelligence of the reader. Although the editors select and shape the matter to be delivered, readers choose, peruse, sort, queue and quaff the news and advertising copy at their own pace and volition."

Gilder offers this telling analogy: "Newspapers differ from television stations in much the way automobiles differ from trains. With the car (and the newspaper), you get in and go pretty much where you want when you want." In short, newspapers put the decision-making power in the hands of readers. Readers interact with the product, which they shape to their own needs and interests.

- -

MAGAZINES AND BOOKS

STUDY PREVIEW Magazines may become indistinguishable from newspapers in the new media age. Both magazine and book publishers already are dabbling in digitized nonpaper delivery.

MELDING MAGAZINES AND NEWSPAPERS

Like newspapers, magazines can be delivered digitally. This is happening already, with numerous magazines available on CD-ROM discs that people can play on computers and read on screen. But the future for magazines as a distinct mass medium is not clear.

As newspapers offer more and more coverage of specialized events and allow readers to browse through an incredible choice of detail and perspectives, magazines will lose their role as a specialized medium catering to special tastes and interests. For example, why would a ski enthusiast subscribe to a ski magazine if a newspaper offers unlimited access to all the information available on skiing?

Some futurists see magazines and newspapers melding into a single medium. When *Roger Fidler*, of Knight-Ridder's Information Design Laboratory, speaks of the newspaper of tomorrow, he talks about multiple layers of coverage. Readers, he says, can tap into conventional general news coverage of unfolding events by browsing through headlines to find what interests them, and, if they want more depth and detail, they can plunge into deeper levels of the subject. These deeper levels would include the kind of thorough, focused and specialized treatment we find in today's magazines. The same is true for nonnews subjects. The knitting columns in today's newspapers, to take one example, can have so many sublayers of detail and instruction and options that they could rival today's specialized magazines on knitting. If Fidler is correct, a melding of today's newspapers and magazines seems inevitable.

This melding is already beginning. In fact, if you review metropolitan daily newspapers and magazines today, you will find a lot of the content is much the same. Newspapers generally offer more background and depth in coverage than ever before, and they have a wide range of commentary on the issues of the day. Many magazines package their articles for republication by newspapers. What most separates newspapers and magazines today is presentation. Magazines are slicker and bound. Those physical distinctions will disappear when both newspapers and magazines are delivered on-screen.

ELECTRONIC BOOKS

Book publishers are dabbling with electronic delivery. Many best-sellers are read onto cassette tapes and sold to people who want to hear books, not read them, as they commute to work and go about their chores. The next step is for publishers to put books into digitized storage banks. Readers could then call them up on demand for reading on their telecomputer screens or listening via new telecomputers with voice capabilities. Publishers already sell digitized versions of books that can be read on computers. These versions could easily be installed in computer networks for readers to call up on demand.

Interim to Tomorrow. *Time* reporters are getting a taste of work in the multimedia world because editors ask them to lug hand-held video cameras to interviews. Footage is then used in CD-ROM versions of the magazine.

TOMORROW'S RADIO

STUDY PREVIEW   New transmission techniques could bring digital clarity to radio listening. This could shake up the economic structure of the radio industry.

DIGITAL RADIO

Music lovers who were in awe at the sound quality when FM stereo began playing compact discs in the 1980s are in for a big surprise. The next improvement in radio technology will use digital transmitters. Instead of taking the 0s and 1s of a CD computer code and converting them to analog signals for transmission, as stations do today, the new equipment would send the 0s and 1s themselves. Listeners with digital receivers would hear the sound as precisely and clearly as a CD on a home player.

INTERACTIVE THREAT

The digital transmission technology that excites so many radio people today may eventually lead to the radio industry's demise. Technology is finding ways to compress digital signals so more and more messages, including music and news, can be squeezed down for transmission. It is this compression that will allow people to have on-demand programming via their fibre-optic lines. Instead of waiting for your favourite song or the latest sports, you could call up what you want and it would be instantly played for you—just for you when you want it. It is the telephone and cable television companies, which now are wiring the nation and the world, that will offer these on-demand services.

Radio would still have a role for people on the go, commuting or at the beach, where they can't plug in, but that is a much smaller audience segment than radio has today. In the distant future, digital compression may reach the point that wireless over-air communication can be truly interactive, with so many messages squeezed onto the electromagnetic spectrum that on-demand services can be delivered over the air. It may still be radio stations that deliver these services, but the programming would be listener-determined, not station-determined. Radio would be like a giant jukebox. This raises fundamental questions about the structure of tomorrow's radio industry: How will advertising fit in? Will it fit in at all? Who would want to listen to happy idiot disc jockeys if they could get the music they wanted whenever they wanted it? Or the latest sports or news?

In short, the kinds of services offered by radio today will likely be subsumed in the broader media services that are being created by companies installing interactive cable links.

FINANCING THE NEW MEDIA

STUDY PREVIEW The new media present new opportunities for advertisers to reach highly defined, narrow audiences. If advertisers shift to new media, the current economic foundation of the magazine, newspaper, radio and television industries would be upended.

REACHING NARROW AUDIENCES

In the mid-1950s, when many magazines and radio stations demassified to find narrower audience segments, advertising shifted to the narrower media. The huge mass-oriented magazines lost advertising, and most went out of business. For advertisers, it was economics pure and simple: "Where can the greatest number of potential buyers of my products or services be reached for the least cost?" Advertisements for men's products shifted to media that geared themselves to male audiences. Cadillac ads went to upscale outlets, muffler ads to downscale outlets.

Now, technology has introduced a whole new ability for the mass media to reach narrower audience segments. The major television networks are losing huge segments of their audience and the major portion of their advertising to the multitude of specially focused cable channels. Newspapers have lost advertising to direct mail, which aims at audiences as narrowly defined as physicians who live in neighbourhoods with home prices averaging $800 000. Magazines also have lost advertising to direct mail.

The advertising industry will have to learn whole new ways to target sales pitches to specialized audiences. This learning may not come easily. In the 1990s, some advertising agencies turned away clients who wanted to shift from network television to direct mail. These agencies, locked into creating network television ads, hadn't developed any expertise at direct mail. To survive in an age of new, narrowly defined mass media, advertising agencies will need to adapt. Otherwise, they will shrink as new, more flexible agencies take over clients that see financial advantages in new media.

RESTRUCTURING MEDIA ECONOMICS

The current financial structure of the mass media may be turned topsy-turvy by the new media. If advertisers go to new media geared to narrower, more defined niches, media outlets that today offer massive heterogeneous audiences will lose their largest source of revenue. *Time* magazine, as an example, could not survive in its present form if advertisers shifted to newsmagazines that offered them narrower slices of the mass market that better fit their products and services. Current mass media units like *Time* would need to restructure themselves. That restructuring could mean more rounds of demassification, shifting the financial base of magazines, newspapers, television and radio from advertisers to consumers, or shutting down.

DEMASSIFY.   Just as magazines have been doing since the dawn of television, mass media could reposition themselves to seek the narrow audience segments that advertisers want to reach. In the case of *Time*, the magazine might narrow its focus to business or the arts or the biosciences. The problem for large-audience media units like *Time* is that narrowly focused publications already have staked out the demassified territory.

A variation on demassification would be splitting existing mass media outlets into numerous demassified entities. *Time*, for example, could have one edition for businesspeople, one for arts people, one for bioscientists, and many others. This already has occurred on a relatively modest scale. The newsmagazines have special editions with bulked-up coverage for certain audience segments like university and community college students, and those editions carry advertising aimed at those audience segments.

TRANSFER COSTS.   A popular mass media unit, like *Time*, could remain in largely its present form by transferring its costs from advertisers to its audience. In effect, *Time* readers would be asked to pick up a greater share of the expense of running the operation. This might mean a $10 cover price, perhaps more, to offset declining advertising revenue.

Some media observers like the idea of media consumers paying all the cost of the media directly because it purifies the media–consumer relationship. Media people then edit their messages for the audience without worrying about whether they might offend advertisers. In some media operations, say these critics, advertisers influence and taint the content.

While $10, perhaps more, for a copy of *Time* may seem like a lot, consumers already are paying the whole costs of producing the magazine, but they do it indirectly. The advertising dollars that *Time* now collects are really the dollars readers pay for the products they buy after seeing advertisements in *Time*. Those dollars end up back at the magazine anyway when advertisers pay for the space their ads occupied. The idea of consumers paying the whole cost of running the mass media directly has attractions in being so straightforward.

SHUT DOWN.   Media operations that don't reposition themselves or find alternate revenue sources when advertisers leave them will not survive. This is what happened to mass magazines in the 1960s and 1970s when their advertisers gravitated to network television. A major shakeout could occur again as more narrowly focused media outlets attract advertisers.

ADVERTISING AND DIGITAL MEDIA

Many media futurists believe today's advertising-dependent media can adapt to the digital future. One of the newspaper mockups that Knight-Ridder's Roger Fidler has put together has ads along the bottom of the screen. By touching the ad, the reader activates screen changes and gains access to more information about the product—in words, images, motion and sound. As Fidler sees it, newspaper ads can be more alive with digital delivery than the present delivery on paper, like a television picture. The reader, in control, can open up more and more screens for more information, delving deeper into information about the advertised product.

If it's an automobile advertisement, the reader could call up an index for competing brands to do a kind of comparison that's not easily done today. Or a reader could delve immediately into independent product reviews. With interactive communication, readers could easily register their interest in a product, perhaps to have a new automobile dropped off for a test drive, by clicking a key or touching a box on the screen. Automatically and instantly, the advertiser is informed about the potential customer. By touching another box, the reader could send the credit card number and address, which had been encrypted into the screens, to order a product immediately.

The new digitized media probably would not charge advertisers by the column inch, as newspapers and magazines do today. Rate structures might instead be based on electronically measured circulation, or on how well ever-changing audience demographics coincide with advertised products, or even on how long readers spend with a particular advertisement. Whatever the new structure, say futurists like Knight-Ridder's Roger Fidler, there is no reason to believe that these future newspapers and magazines will surrender any of their current advertising revenues, which today typically total more than 80 percent of their income.

If Fidler is wrong and the new digital media lose advertisers, the means are available for media consumers themselves to pay all the costs. Today's forerunners of digitized media, database services like America OnLine, CompuServe and Prodigy, charge subscription fees for people who use them. This is equivalent to the subscription price or cover price of today's magazines and newspapers, and it would not be difficult for digital media to have similar subscription fees.

INFORMATION HIGHWAY

STUDY PREVIEW   Many experts see everyone being connected by the information highway. The Internet and numerous on-line commercial networks exist today. These are forerunners of what is being called the *information superhighway* of tomorrow. The superhighway could displace today's mass media for delivering information and entertainment to mass audiences.

CYBER-CANUCKS

Some facts from a 1996 ACNielsen Canada survey of Cyber-Canucks:

- Eighteen million Canadians have access to a computer.
- One in five Canadians has some form of access to the Internet, either at home, school or at the office.
- Most Internet users are 25 to 44 years old and spend less than two hours on-line per week.
- Fifty-five percent of Internet users are male, 45 percent are female.

THE INTERNET

Like the railroads a century earlier, which bound the nation together in new ways and facilitated major economic growth, today, what is called the *information highway* is being built—an electronic network that connects libraries, corporations, government agencies and individuals.

A 1996 report from the Information Highway Advisory Council, "The Promise of the Information Highway," suggests that new technologies are at work changing the way Canadians live and work in many ways:

- Knowledge-based industries are growing faster than any other sector of the Canadian economy, especially in computer services.
- Employment in Canada's cultural sector, which makes up about 3.0 of Canada's GDP, grew by 32 percent between 1981 and 1991. As the demand increases for new forms of entertainment and information, this growth could be larger.
- Even the traditional manufacturing, resource and agricultural industries are turning to new technologies in order to compete in the global marketplace. They use technologies to find export markets and customers around the world.

These factors, combined with rapidly dropping prices for electronic equipment and the rapidly changing electronic horizon, mean that the next few years should be quite interesting, not only in terms of how Canadians will adapt to new technologies, but also in terms of how these patterns will change the way we think of the mass media.

COMMERCIAL ON-LINE SERVICES

The information highway is more than the Internet, however. Commercial enterprises, including America OnLine, CompuServe, Delphi, GEnie and Prodigy, provide packages of information and entertainment to subscribers for a fee. America OnLine, for example, offers *U.S. News and World Report*, the Associated Press and oodles of games for $8.95 a month.

MEDIA AND INFORMATION HIGHWAYS

The mass media as we know them today may be replaced by the information highway. Many companies are scrambling to position themselves on the ground floor of this developing technology. Telephone companies and cable companies are merging and entering cooperative ventures to build delivery systems to every household and business. These companies and ventures also are seeking other partners to develop packages of information and entertainment for their customers. In effect, these new ventures will be able to do what the mass media today are doing—but instead of a newspaper delivering news, it will come electronically via the information highway. The same will also be true with books, magazines, radio, television, sound recording and perhaps even movies.

Subscribers to commercial on-line services today pay for the long-distance time they use when they are plugged into the service. This may well change if the new information highway comes into general acceptance over the coming years.

At one time, the Internet tried to keep commercial interests off the network, but those restrictions are softening. The thinking is shifting toward accepting anyone who can contribute to a stronger Internet. This doesn't mean anybody and everybody is welcome. A Hollywood movie studio, for example, would be kept from transmitting feature-length movies to home viewers. The network doesn't have that kind of capacity. But futurists, noting with certainty that technology will increase the information highway's capacity exponentially over the years, believe it is destined to become an open carrier—moving from a toll road to a freeway.

In time, the information highway will not only be a vehicle for mass media companies to send their products to their consumers, but its capacity also will permit consumers to talk back. The information highway will be the backbone of the interactive mass media that will allow on-call services whenever people want them: movies on-call, news on-call, your favourite song on-call. People also will be able to place orders instantly for products they want by return message.

The information highway will make possible the national, electronic town meetings that U.S. presidential aspirant Ross Perot talked about in the 1992 presidential campaign, with the people being able to register their preferences in ongoing referendums. People will be able to review catalogues delivered by merchants via the information highway.

INFORMATION HIGHWAY IMPLICATIONS

As Canada shifts from the old resource-based economy to the new information-based economy, many policy issues are being debated regarding the Internet. "The Final Report of the Information Highway Advisory Council," published in 1995, treats the Information Highway as both a product and a process; not only should Canadian culture be reflected in the final product, but Canadians should also have a role in the process. The council was guided by three objectives: to create jobs in the new economy; to ensure that electronic services would be available at a low cost; and to preserve Canadian identity and culture. The council raised the following policy issues:

- How fast should the infrastructure be built and who will pay for it?
- Can a balance between competition and regulation be reached?
- What will be the requirements for Canadian ownership and control of these information networks?
- How can copyright be protected?
- How can Canadian culture be protected on the Information Highway?

Given the rapid rate of technological change, these kinds of issues will be the essence of any future policy discussions in Canada.

PUBLIC POLICY AND NEW MEDIA

STUDY PREVIEW Public policy will need rethinking as the media become truly global and more oriented to narrow audiences. A transition from government to conglomerate and marketplace control is already well under way.

GLOBALIZATION AND CONGLOMERATION

Nations once assumed control over the mass media within their boundaries. Dictators took absolute control. Even in democracies, governments legislated certain controls on the mass media, particularly in broadcasting. The ability of government to control media has always been vulnerable. In Henry VIII's time, Dutch news sheets were still smuggled into England despite his ban. And the U.S.-sponsored propaganda services, including Radio Free Europe, penetrated behind the Soviet Union's Iron Curtain during the Cold War. But today, with transnational communication exploding on many fronts, there is less and less governments can do.

The driving force behind transnational communication today is not so much political as economic. Transnational communication once was mostly for political reasons. Those 16th-century Dutch corantos advanced libertarian ideas that the English monarchy feared. Radio Free Europe encouraged internal revolts and new ways of thinking in Central Europe and the Soviet Union. In contrast, today it is global media conglomerates that are creating the international publishing deals and the satellite linkups that transcend national borders. Their motivations are economic— to amass huge audiences that advertisers want to reach.

With only a few exceptions, like China, governments don't feel threatened by these global media enterprises, and therefore they are less inclined to regulate them closely. By and large, the marketplace is more an influence on what these global media companies disseminate than governments are. People, not governments, are deciding whether to tune in.

CENSORSHIP ON THE INTERNET

There is an ongoing debate about censorship on the Internet. The sheer volume of information uploaded to the Internet on a daily basis—the equivalent of about 300 pages per second—makes censoring and policing the Internet difficult, if not impossible.

Some recent Canadian examples highlight the problem of censorship on the Internet:

- The University of Waterloo blocked access to several of the alt.sex newsgroups from their server in 1994, declaring them obscene.
- A convicted pedophile in Calgary was charged in 1995 with possession of pornographic images that depicted children in sexual acts. Police claim he was part of an international pornographic network specializing in kiddie porn. There was a similar child pornography case in Quebec in 1996.
- During the Bernardo murder trial, a World Wide Web page offered Canadian Internet users access to foreign newspaper and magazine articles unavailable in the Canadian media due to the publication ban. Two newsgroups, alt.fan.karla-homolka and alt.fan.paul-bernardo, also offered Internet users access to information and rumours about the crimes. This raises a provocative question: say a resident of St. Catharines, Ontario, where the killings took place, was reading a transcript about the trial posted to a newsgroup by someone in Texas, would this person be violating Canadian law?

Pornographic images, stories and games are widely available on the Internet. This material can be accessed through the World Wide Web, in newsgroups or via e-mail. The Canadian Criminal Code makes possession of these images a criminal offence, but it's not against the law in other countries. This creates an interesting situation: is a Canadian sitting at his or her computer viewing pornographic images from another country on the Internet breaking the law? While the RCMP may be able to charge people with possessing some of these images, it's impossible to track down some of the international sites that are distributing these images. Laws recognize borders, the Internet doesn't.

Jeffery Shallit teaches computer science at Waterloo and is also the treasurer of Electronic Frontier Canada, a group opposed to any form of censorship on the Internet. Shallit claims that the issue of sex on the Internet has been blown out of proportion by the traditional media. Sexual topics, he says, make up only a small portion of the thousands of Usenet discussion groups. Users have to deliberately search for sexually explicit material; they're not likely to stumble across it accidently while surfing the Internet. Shallit has developed a theory regarding new technology and sexually explicit material, known as Shallit's Laws. The first law is "every new medium of expression will be used for sex." The second law states "every new medium of expression will come under attack, usually because of Shallit's first law."

WHOLE NEW MEDIA WORLD

STUDY PREVIEW The mass media are in a technology-driven transformation that will change how we inform and entertain ourselves. Despite the changes ahead, mass communicators will still be preparing mass messages for mass audiences.

MELDING MEDIA

Gutenberg brought mass production to books, and the other primary print media, magazines and newspapers, followed. People have never had a problem recognizing the differences among books, magazines and newspapers. When sound recording and movies came along, they too were distinctive, and later so were radio and television.

Now get ready for a whole new media world in which the old, familiar distinctions will be disappearing. Technology already is influencing how media organizations deliver messages. Many of the changes so far, like satellite delivery, still rely on traditional reception equipment. People watch Viewer's Choice Canada, for example, on the same kind of television set they always did. Coming soon, however, are fundamentally new reception mechanisms.

MASS MEDIA IN THE FUTURE

While it's very difficult to predict what forms of technology will be available in the future, several recent developments seem to indicate that Canadian consumers should be ready for some changes in home and business technology:

- *Cable Modems.* In 1995 Rogers Communications launched the Wave in Newmarket, Ontario. This allows users to connect their computers to the Internet using a co-axial cable, the same kind used to bring cable television into our homes. This connection is faster than conventional telephone company modems; data is transfered about 10 times faster this way. Rogers and other cable companies, such as Shaw and Western Co-Axial, are marketing the service not only to individuals but to schools and other instititutions.
- *DirecPC.* By renting or buying a small dish, Internet users can connect using satellites. This service transfers data faster than cable modems and can transfer data about 15 times faster than a modem connected to a regular phone line.
- *ISDN.* The Integrated Services Digital Network is offered by Bell Canada to both residential and business customers. It uses a direct digital connection, not a modem, to transfer data at about four times the speed of an analogue modem.

Some say that whatever dazzling changes are ahead for the mass media, the essentials will remain the same as today: *mass communicators* preparing *mass messages* for delivery via the process of *mass communication* to *mass audiences.* Others argue

Interactive Media

Hooked on the mass media, we allow them to shape how we put our daily lives together. If the CBC airs "Hockey Night in Canada" at 7:30 p.m., millions of people make it a point to be there to see it. We choose one car over another because it's equipped with a tape player. We choose a route to work that goes past a newsstand to pick up the morning paper. We haul the radio outside to listen while we wash our cars.

Some cracks in this slavery to the mass media have already been introduced through technology. Home VCRs, for example, permit the automatic taping of television programs for later replay. And video rentals free us from the showing times at the local cinema.

New technology will ease even more of our slavery to media schedules and also give us new options to improve our lives. Consider:

- How do you decide today what brand of sneakers you want to buy? How could your personal interactive media, like the Internet, change how you make your decision?
- To read a best-selling book today, most people go to a bookstore or library, join a book club or borrow the book from a friend. Could there be a more convenient way for you to acquire the book when interactive media are available?
- When you want the latest news in the evening now, you tune to a newscast on television or radio. Then you wait for what you're interested in. How would this change with interactive media?
- Futurists have been talking about the "cashless society" for years. Could interactive media make the cashless society possible?

that the process will be more democratic, allowing anyone with access to a computer and a modem an opportunity to communicate his or her message.

CHAPTER WRAP-UP

The mass media as we know them today are about to meld in a technological convergence in which the technological differences among the media will disappear. This convergence is fueled by accelerated miniaturization of equipment and the ability to compress data into tiny digital bits for storage and transmission. And all the media, whether they traditionally have relied on print, electronic or photographic technology, are involved in the convergence. *USA Today*'s Kevin Mania, writing in *Quill* magazine, put it this way: "All the devices people use for communicating and all the kinds of communication have started crashing together into one massive mega-media industry. The result is that telephone lines will soon carry TV shows. Cable TV will carry telephone calls. Desktop computers will be used to watch and edit movies. Cellular phone-computers the size of a notepad will dial into interactive magazines that combine text, sound and video to tell stories."

These changes represent a media revolution because they will affect the fundamental relationship between the media and their audiences. Two-way communication will be possible for the first time, with people being able to extract what they want from the media when they want it. This interactive relationship, as it is called, will enable people to check on a Blue Jays score, a fire raging down the road or an obscure bill in the provincial legislature by hitting a few buttons on a remote control, rather than waiting for the morning newspaper or scanning through TV and radio channels hoping to catch a report. Movies, market data and the latest Margaret Atwood novel will be on tap too.

There may be fewer media, but there will be more messages than ever. This means that messages will be going to narrower and narrower segments of the mass audience. This will be a nightmare for advertising people, who will have thousands more channels to choose from in deciding where to place their clients' ads. Advertisers themselves, however, will welcome the ability to zero in on their likeliest potential customers and thereby save dollars they waste today in sending messages to large audiences that include people with scant interest in the product.

At the heart of the melded media are the fibre-optic lines that telephone and cable companies are laying to transmit massive amounts of data. A single strand can carry 50 copies of a medium-sized novel in a second—hundreds of times faster than the existing copper cable television lines and thousands of times faster than copper telephone lines. Fibre-optic lines, which have many strands, are the backbone of the coming information highways.

Public policy will need rethinking as the media converge. The old regulatory distinctions between print and broadcast media will need to be reassessed. There also are global implications because of the virtual impossibility of stopping media signals, particularly those relayed by satellite, at national borders. With the new media, authoritarian governments will find their traditional controls of media content won't work any more.

Whatever changes are ahead, however, the heart of mass communication remains with people preparing messages for mass audiences. The work of mass communicators is in gathering, digesting and packaging information, whether it be news, entertainment or persuasion. Newspapers as we know them may disappear, and so may television and books and the other traditional media. But the demand for creating media messages of all kinds will grow as technology enables the mass media to cater to more specific audience segments. For mass communicators, the future is in the content, not the hardware.

QUESTIONS FOR REVIEW

1. What technologies are fueling the mass media revolution?

2. Why are other mass media set to leapfrog television technologically?

3. Why are newspapers well positioned to dominate the news business in the future?

4. Why are magazines probably going to be subsumed by newspapers in the new media age?

5. What are the prospects for radio in the near and distant future?

6. What new opportunities do the new media present advertisers?

7. What will the information highway do?

8. Why is media technology forcing a rethinking of public policy in Canada?

9. How will new media forms affect the fundamental structure of media people preparing media messages for dissemination through the mass communication process to mass audiences?

⬛Q⬛UESTIONS FOR CRITICAL THINKING

1. Will it be possible to condense all human knowledge smaller than the approximately 8 cubic metres cited by media scholar Wilbur Schramm in his book *The Story of Human Communication*?

2. Why is the television industry hesitant about moving to the pixel-dense screens the computer industry and other media are developing?

3. Why would media scholar George Gilder disagree with the notion that pictures are more important than words—and even the old adage that a picture is worth a thousand words?

4. How can books make the shift from being a print medium to being an electronic medium? Should they?

5. How are digital radio, national radio and interactive radio all risks for people now in the radio business?

6. How will the economics of the mass media be reshaped as technology makes it possible to narrow even more closely to specific audiences?

7. What improvements for the Internet information highway are coming in the years ahead?

8. One traditional justification for government regulation of the broadcast media is being wiped out by emerging marketplace realities. How so?

9. What makes books, magazines, newspapers, sound recordings, movies, radio and television different from one another? What will become of these distinctions in coming years?

10. How can the RCMP keep track of pornography on the Internet? Should they bother?

⬛F⬛OR FURTHER LEARNING

Robert Brehl. "Brave New World," *Toronto Star* (March 30, 1996).

Canada, The Information Highway Advisory Council. *The Challenge of the Information Highway* (1995). Available at www.info.ic.gc.ca/info-highway/ih.html

Jim Carroll, Rick Broadhead. *The 1997 Canadian Internet Handbook* (Prentice Hall Canada, 1996).

"Crime in Cyberspace," *Maclean's* (May 22, 1995) pp. 50–58.

Joshua Eddings. *How the Internet Works* (Ziff-Davis Press, 1994). An excellent primer.

Roger Fidler. *Mediamorphosis* (forthcoming). Fidler, a technologist for Knight-Ridder newspapers, makes a case that it is newspapers that are positioned to dominate the mass media of the future.

Martha FitzSimons, editor. *Media, Democracy and the Information Highway* (Freedom Forum Media Studies Center, 1993). This conference report on national information policy is an excellent starting point on the major issues involving rapidly changing technology.

George Gilder. *Life after Television: The Coming Transformation of Media and American Life* (Norton, 1992). Gilder is excellent at explaining the contrasting technology of television and the telecomputer. Gilder writes regularly for the *Forbes* magazine supplement *ASAP.*

John R. Levine and Carol Naroudi. *The Internet for Dummies* (IDG Books, 1996). This how-to for beginning Internet users is loaded with information on the information highway.

Robert Lucky. *Silicon Dreams* (St. Martin's, 1989). Lucky argues that words are more important in mass communication than images. This is fortunate, he notes, because more words can be stored digitally than photographs.

Jack Lyle and Douglas B. McLeod. *Communication, Media and Change* (Mayfield, 1993).

Kevin Maney. "Will the Techno Tsunami Wash Us Out?" *Quill* 82 (March 1994):2, 16–18. Maney, a newspaper reporter, discusses career implications of media convergence on the careers of media people. This issue of *Quill* has additional articles on the subject.

John V. Pavlik and Everette E. Dennis, editors. *Demystifying Media Technology* (Mayfield, 1993).

Wilbur Schramm. *The Story of Human Communication* (Harper & Row, 1988). In this work, which capped his distinguished career of scholarship, Schramm covers the whole sweep of communication history, with peeks at where it is headed.

APPENDIX 1

INTERNET RESOURCES Websites

Visit our Website at: www.phcanada.com

ASSOCIATIONS/SOCIETIES

Canadian Association of Broadcasters
www.cab-acr.ca

Canadian Cable Television Association
www.ccta.ca

Canadian Daily Newspaper Association
fox.nstn.ca/~bcantley/cdna.html

Friends of Canadian Broadcasting
friendscb.org

Canadian Public Relations Society
www.cprs.ca

Public Relations Society of America
www.prsa.org/

Radio Television News Directors Association
www.rtnda.org

BOOKS

Prentice Hall Canada
www.phcanada.com

FILM

Columbia Tri-Star
www.sony.com

Disney
www.disney.com

Independent Film Channel
www.ifctv.com

MCA/Universal
www.mca.com.

MGM
www.mgmua.com

Miramax Films
www.miramax.com

National Film Board of Canada
www.nfb.org

Paramount
www.paramount.com

Twentieth Century Fox
www.fox.com

GOVERNMENT

CRTC
www.crtc.gc.ca

MEDIA RESEARCH

ACNielsen Canada
www.acnielsen.ca

NEWSPAPERS/MAGAZINES

Associated Press
www.trib.com/NEWS/APwire.html

Canadian Living
www.canadian-living.com

Canadian Press
www.canpress.ca

Financial Post
www.canoe.ca/fp/home.html

Globe and Mail
www.theglobeandmail.com

Halifax Daily News
www.atcon.com/media/daily/News.html

Hollinger
www.suntimes.com/hollinger/link.html

Maclean's
www.canoe.ca/Maclean's/home.html

New York Times
www.nytimes.com

Saturday Night
www.enews.com/magazines/sn

Southam
www.southam.ca

Sun Newspapers
www.canoe.ca/PlanetSun/home.html

Time
www.timeinc.com/time/magazine/magazine

Toronto Star
www.t-o.com

USA Today
www.usatoday.com

Canadian Newspapers on the Internet
www.synapse.net/~radio/print.htm#canada

RADIO

Airwaves Journal
www.airwaves.com

CBC
radioworks.cbc.ca

Radio and Records
www.rronline.com

Canadian Radio Stations on the Internet
wmbr.mit.edu/stations/ca.html

TELEVISION

A&E
www.aetv.com

ABC
www.abc.com

Alliance Television
www.alliance.ca/TV/tvlinks

Baton Broadcasting
baton.com

BCTV
tv.bc.sympatico.ca

Bravo!
www.citytv.com

CBC
www.cbc.ca

CBS
www.cbs.com

CNN
www.cnn.com

CPAC
www.screen.com/CPAC

Discovery
www.discovery.com

Fox
www.foxnetwork.com

Learning Channel
www.discovery.com

MuchMusic
www.muchmusic.com

NBC
www.nbc.com

PBS
www.pbs.org

Rogers
www.rogers.com

Showcase Television
www.screen.com/Showcase

SRC
www.src-mtl.com

TSN
www.tsn.ca

Viewer's Choice
www.ppv.com

APPENDIX 2

BROADCASTING ACT (part)

38–39 ELIZABETH II

CHAPTER 11

An Act respecting broadcasting and to amend certain Acts in relation thereto and in relation to radiocommunication

[Assented to 1st February, 1991]

Her Majesty, by and with the advice and consent of the Senate and House of Commons of Canada, enacts as follows:

SHORT TITLE

1. This Act may be cited as the *Broadcasting Act.*

∗ ∗ ∗

PART I

…

GENERAL

Broadcasting Policy for Canada

Declaration   **3.** (1) It is hereby declared as the broadcasting policy for Canada that

(*a*) the Canadian broadcasting system shall be effectively owned and controlled by Canadians;

(*b*) the Canadian broadcasting system, operating primarily in the English and French languages and comprising public, private and community elements, makes use of radio frequencies that are public property and provides, through its programming, a public service essential to the maintenance and enhancement of national identity and cultural sovereignty;

(*c*) English and French language broadcasting, while sharing common aspects, operate under different conditions and may have different requirements;

(*d*) the Canadian broadcasting system should

   (i) serve to safeguard, enrich and strengthen the cultural, political, social and economic fabric of Canada,

(ii) encourage the development of Canadian expression by providing a wide range of programming that reflects Canadian attitudes, opinions, ideas, values and artistic creativity, by displaying Canadian talent in entertainment programming and by offering information and analysis concerning Canada and other countries from a Canadian point of view,

(iii) through its programming and the employment opportunities arising out of its operations, serve the needs and interests, and reflect the circumstances and aspirations, of Canadian men, women and children, including equal rights, the linguistic duality and multicultural and multiracial nature of Canadian society and the special place of aboriginal peoples within that society, and

(iv) be readily adaptable to scientific and technological change;

(*e*) each element of the Canadian broadcasting system shall contribute in an appropriate manner to the creation and presentation of Canadian programming;

(*f*) each broadcasting undertaking shall make maximum use, and in no case less than predominant use, of Canadian creative and other resources in the creation and presentation of programming, unless the nature of the service provided by the undertaking, such as specialized content or format or the use of languages other than French and English, renders that use impracticable, in which case the undertaking shall make the greatest practicable use of those resources;

(*g*) the programming originated by broadcasting undertakings should be of high standard;

(*h*) all persons who are licensed to carry on broadcasting undertakings have a responsibility for the programs they broadcast;

(*i*) the programming provided by the Canadian broadcasting system should

(i) be varied and comprehensive, providing a balance of information, enlightenment and entertainment for men, women and children of all ages, interests and tastes,

(ii) be drawn from local, regional, national and international sources,

(iii) include educational and community programs,

(iv) provide a reasonable opportunity for the public to be exposed to the expression of differing views on matters of public concern, and

(v) include a significant contribution from the Canadian independent production sector;

(*j*) educational programming, particularly where provided through the facilities of an independent educational authority, is an integral part of the Canadian broadcasting system;

(*k*) a range of broadcasting services in English and in French shall be extended to all Canadians as resources become available;

(*l*) the Canadian Broadcasting Corporation, as the national public broadcaster, should provide radio and television services incorporating a wide range of programming that informs, enlightens and entertains;

(*m*) the programming provided by the Corporation should

   (i) be predominantly and distinctively Canadian,

   (ii) reflect Canada and its regions to national and regional audiences, while serving the special needs of those regions,

   (iii) actively contribute to the flow and exchange of cultural expression,

   (iv) be in English and in French, reflecting the different needs and circumstances of each official language community, including the particular needs and circumstances of English and French linguistic minorities,

   (v) strive to be of equivalent quality in English and in French,

   (vi) contribute to shared national consciousness and identity,

   (vii) be made available throughout Canada by the most appropriate and efficient means and as resources become available for the purpose, and

   (viii) reflect the multicultural and multiracial nature of Canada;

(*n*) where any conflict arises between the objectives of the Corporation set out in paragraphs (*l*) and (*m*) and the interests of any other broadcasting undertaking of the Canadian broadcasting system, it shall be resolved in the public interest, and where the public interest would be equally served by resolving the conflict in favour of either, it shall be resolved in favour of the objectives set out in paragraphs (*l*) and (*m*);

(*o*) programming that reflects the aboriginal cultures of Canada should be provided within the Canadian broadcasting system as resources become available for the purpose;

(*p*) programming accessible by disabled persons should be provided within the Canadian broadcasting system as resources become available for the purpose;

(*q*) without limiting any obligation of a broadcasting undertaking to provide the programming contemplated by paragraph (*i*), alternative television programming services in English and in French should be provided where necessary to ensure that the full range of programming contemplated by that paragraph is made available through the Canadian broadcasting system;

(*r*) the programming provided by alternative television programming services should

   (i) be innovative and be complementary to the programming provided for mass audiences,

   (ii) cater to tastes and interests not adequately provided for by the programming provided for mass audiences, and include programming devoted to culture and the arts,

   (iii) reflect Canada's regions and multicultural nature,

   (iv) as far as possible, be acquired rather than produced by those services, and

   (v) be made available throughout Canada by the most cost-efficient means;

(*s*) private networks and programming undertakings should, to an extent consistent with the financial and other resources available to them,

(i) contribute significantly to the creation and presentation of Canadian programming, and

(ii) be responsive to the evolving demands of the public; and

(*t*) distribution undertakings

(i) should give priority to the carriage of Canadian programming services and, in particular, to the carriage of local Canadian stations,

(ii) should provide efficient delivery of programming at affordable rates, using the most effective technologies available at reasonable cost,

(iii) should, where programming services are supplied to them by broadcasting undertakings pursuant to contractual arrangements, provide reasonable terms for the carriage, packaging and retailing of those programming services, and

(iv) may, where the Commission considers it appropriate, originate programming, including local programming, on such terms as are conducive to the achievement of the objectives of the broadcasting policy set out in this subsection, and in particular provide access for underserved linguistic and cultural minority communities.

Further declaration

(2) It is further declared that the Canadian broadcasting system constitutes a single system and that the objectives of the broadcasting policy set out in subsection (1) can best be achieved by providing for the regulation and supervision of the Canadian broadcasting system by a single independent public authority.

NAME INDEX

SUBJECT INDEX

prototype research,
355–6
Audiences
consistency theory, 277
crossover, 19
flawed libertarian
assumption, 334
function of media for,
275–7
high-culture, 302
information anxiety,
294–5
low-culture, 302
passivity, 274, 295
and role models, 280–1
selective media
exposure, 277–8
selective perception,
278
selective retention and
recall, 278–9
uses and gratification
studies, 275
well-informed futility,
295–6
See also Mass audiences;
Surveys
Audimeter, 351
Audion tube, 111
Audit Bureau of
Circulations, 250
Audits, circulation, 349
Australia, 49
Australian, 49
Authoritarian political
media systems
bribery, 325–6
capitalism, 330
censorship, 324
circumvention of
controls, 327–8
compliance, 328
contraband
publications, 327
divine right of kings,
328
England under Henry
VIII, 322–4
expulsion of
journalists, 327
Franco's Spain, 321,
325
function of media in,
324
inherent contradiction,
326–7
licensing, 323, 324–5
methods of control,
324–7

Nazi Germany, 321,
324–5
repression, 326–7
royal patents, 323, 324
Third World
dictatorships, 321
truth, 328–9
Autistic perception, 278

B
Bachman Turner
Overdrive, 79, 86
Band, The, 87
Bank of America, 144
Bank of Montreal, 258
Bare Naked Ladies, 87
Batman, 141, 147
Baton Broadcasting
System, 169
BBC, 116
BBDO Canada, 257, 258
BBS, 258
BCP Canada, 258
BCTV television, 169
*Beatles: An Analysis of the
Communist Use of
Music, The*, 101
Beau-Marks, 87
Beautiful music format,
118, 121
Bechtel, Illinois Power,
235
Bell Canada, 258
Bell Laboratories, 82
Bells, The, 79, 86
Belongers, 359
Benetton, 253
Berliner Gramophone
Company, 81
Bernardo trial, 202–3,
406
Bertelsmann, 98
"Bestiality Dial-a-Porn",
124
Better Homes & Gardens,
63
Between Friends, 150
"Beverley Hillbillies",
305
"Beverly Hills, 90210",
166
"Big Yellow Taxi", 80
Billboard, 66, 92
Billy Jack, 78
Binary numbers, 84
Birth of a Nation, The,
140, 147
Black and Decker, 258

"Black Like Me", 308
Black music, 80, 956
Black Robe, 148
Black weeks, 353
Blackboard Jungle, 137
Block bookings, 134, 146
"Blood Sport", 353
Blood, Sweat and Tears,
86
Blow-up, 145
Blue Jays baseball, 169
Blue-Blood Estates, 358
Blue-Chip Blues, 357
Blue-Collar Nursery,
358
BN Audio Service, 208
BN Data Service, 208
Board of Broadcast
Governors (BBG),
117, 161
*Bob and Carol and Ted and
Alice*, 137
Body Fashions, 66
Bolshevik Revolution,
205, 329
Bon Vivant vichyssoise,
198
Bonnie and Clyde, 137
Books, 7–8
as cultural repository,
312
electronic, 399
impact of television on,
155
and movable type, 34
revenue, 12–3
Bootleg recordings, 97
"Born to Be Wild", 78
"Born in the U.S.A.",
103
Boston Celtics, 235
Boston College, 124
Boston Herald, 49, 365
Boston *Herald-American*,
196
"Boy in the Bubble", 80
Boycott, information,
235–6
Brass Check, The, 333,
378
Brave One, The, 133
Bravo!, 149, 176
Brazil, 315
Broadcast News, 203–4,
375
*Broadcast New*s, 280
Broadcast ratings
audience measurement
for commercials,

353–4
criticisms of, 352–4
demographic
breakdowns,
349–50
diaries, 350
discrepancies, 352
hyping of, 352–3
interviews, 350
measurement
techniques, 350–2
meters, 351
radio, 349
respondent accuracy,
353
sample selection, 352
slanted results, 352
television, 350, 351
Broadcaster, 66, 67
Broadcasting Acts
(Canada), 161–2
Brown lung disease issue,
67
Brunswickan, 397
Brutus, 313
Bubblicious, 255
Buckshot philosophy, 89
Budweiser, 147
Bull Durham, 147
Bullet model. *See* Effects
theory
Bulletin, 69
Bureau of Broadcast
Measurement
(BBM), 155, 173,
250, 349, 350
"Burning Bed, The", 284
Burson-Marsteller, 226,
227, 231
Business Channel, 196
Business Week, 69
*Busy Man's Magazin*e, 62
Buyouts. *See*
Conglomeration

C
Cable companies, 400,
404
Cable Modems, 407
Cable News Network.
See CNN
Cable television
advertising, 17
in Canada, 173
competition with
networks, 166
demassification, 72
documentary films, 130

emergence of, 158–9,
163, 170
and networks, 177
pay-per-view, 176–7,
178
video channel, 89, 94
See also Subscriber
television;
Television industry
Cablecaster, 67
Cablestream Service, 208
Cadbury, 258
Calgary Herald, 40
Callin shows, 123–4
"Camel News Caravan",
167
"Canada AM", 169
Canada Cup, 117
Canada Post, 258
*Canada's Cultural
Industries*, 99, 162
Canadian Advertising
Foundation (CAF),
259, 262, 263
Canadian Airlines
International, 258
Canadian Association of
Broadcasters
(CAB), 110, 161,
380
Canadian Association of
Recording Arts and
Sciences (CARAS),
87
Canadian Association of
Retired Persons, 66
Canadian Biograph
Company, 149
Canadian Broadcast
Standards Council,
380, 385
Canadian Broadcasting
Act, 117
Canadian Broadcasting
Corporation. *See*
CBC
Canadian Code of
Advertising
Standards, 259–261
Canadian Copyright Act,
92–3, 97
Canadian Daily News-
paper Association
(CDNA), 380, 386
Canadian Film Develop-
ment Corporation,
144, 150

on-screen newspapers, 398–99
Telefilm, 144, 150
Telephone companies, 392, 400, 404
Telephones, 392
Television
advanced, 394
advent of, 37
as advertising medium, 251
advertising revenue, 50
broadcast ratings, 350, 351
Canadian content, 161
Canadian viewers, 156
colour, 160
competition for radio audience, 118
content trap, 137
editing and taping, 164
entertainment programming, 164–5
evesdropping, 282–3
high-definition, 394
impact of, 155–7
interactive, 173
interview programs, 193
in Japan, 175
live broadcasts, 164
onscreen text, 398
ownership statistics, 6
pay, 138
"pilots", 174
point-of-purchase commercials, 17
political values, 157, 301
popularity of, 154–5
retribalization theory of, 300
sitcoms, 165, 282
"tabloid journalism", 166, 193
technological development, 157, 160, 173, 176, 177
violence, 283–8, 289
See also News; Telecomputers; Television industry
Television in America, 157
Television industry
advertising revenue, 177
American dual national system, 162-3

audience tracking, 173
bias against businesspeople, 301
Canadian broadcasting system, 160–2
competition for viewers, 170–3
entertainment production, 174–5
feminist bias, 301
freelance producers, 174
independent stations, 171
independent video production houses, 176
independently produced entertainment programs, 174
local stations, 162–3
motion pictures, 175
network affiliates, 163–4
news production, 174
off-network programs, 175
pro-minorities bias, 301
production of advertisement, 175–6
program standards, 165–6
sexism in, 171
social agenda, 301
sweeps week, 352–3
syndicators, 175
traditional networks in Canada, 169
traditional networks in U.S., 170
traditional values, 302
Television in the Lives of Our Children, 289
Terminator, 2, 141
Texas Instruments, 233
"Theme from S.W.A.T.", 79
"Theodore the Tugboat", 287
"These Eyes", 86
Third World countries, 317
Thirty-two Short Films about Glenn Gould, 150
"This Hour Has Seven

Days", 168
Thomas hearings, 133
Thomson, 39, 40, 41, 42
3M, 82
Tiananmen Square, 195, 312
Time Inc., 176
Time magazine, 11, 12, 56, 62, 336, 357, 358, 359
Canadian edition, 62
foreign editions, 69
Time Warner, 69, 90, 91, 99, 142, 356
Time-Life, 99
Tip sheets, 92
Titanic, 119
TMN, 13, 150, 173
Tobacco, 316
"Today" show, 369
Tokyo Broadcasting System, 175
Toledo *Blade*, 377
Top, 40 format, 118, 119
Toronto News, 47
Toronto Star, 41, 47–8, 216, 397
Toronto *Telegram*, 37
Torstar Corporation, 48
Toshiba, 68
Town and Gowns, 358
Trade journals, 66–7
"Traders", 169
Tragically Hip, The, 79, 87
Transducer, 84
Tri-Star Pictures, 99, 146
Trick effects, 60
Trooper, 87
TSN, 163, 173, 176, 348
Turner Broadcasting System, 343
Turner Network Television (TNT), 159
TV Bureau of Canada, 155
TV Guide, 49, 64
TV Ontario, 13
TVA, 258
Twentieth-Century-Fox Film Corporation, 136, 147, 170
"20/20", 130
"Twin Peaks", 26
Two-step flow model, 274
Tylenol, 230–2

U
U.S. Civil Rights Commission, 282
U.S. Justice Department, 134
U.S. Supreme Court, 134, 206
Ugly Ducklings, 78
"Undun", 86
UNI, 98
United Nations, 317
United Press, 206, 207
United Press International, 206, 317
United-Paramount Theaters, 170
Unitel, 17
Universal Pictures, 98, 141
University of Alabama, 309
University of King's College, 397
University of New Brunswick, 397
University of Waterloo, 406
Unmodulated wave, 113
Upper Canada Gazette, 37
Us, 62
USA for Africa project, 79–80
USA entertainment network, 177
USA Today, 38, 45–6, 349, 356, 364, 365, 366
Use and gratification studies, 275
Utilitarianism, ethics, 371–2
Uzbekistan, 195

V
V for Victory, 149
V-chip, 291
Values and Life-Styles (VALS) program, 359–60
Vancouver *Province*, 40, 41
Vancouver *Sun*, 40, 41
Vanderbilt Television News Archive, 312
Vanity Fair, 67

Varig, 199
Vassar, 377
Viacom, 146
Vibration-sensitive recording, 81–2
Vickers and Benson, 258
Victor Talking Machine Co., 85
Victoria *Gazette*, 37
Video, home, 138, 166
Video News and Reviews, 70
Video Storyboard Tests Inc., 265
Videodiscs, 265
Videotext, 265
Vietnam War, 80, 210, 310
Viewer's Cable, 173, 178
Viewer's Choice, 173
Village Voice, 53–4
Vinyl records, 83
Violence
aggressive stimulation theory of, 284–6
catalytic theory, 288–9
cathartic effect of, 283–4
desensitization theory of, 289
fear of, 289
learned behaviour, 283
recent research, 286–8
and socially positive action, 284
tolerance of, 289, 291
Virginia Slims, 255
Virtual retina displays, 395
VISA, 258
Vision, 176
Visuals, 57. *See also* Photographs
Vitascope projector, 132
Voilà Québec, 70

W
"W5", 168
"Wagon Train", 301
Waking Up the Neighbours, 78
Walkman, 90
Wall Street Journal, 13, 44, 66, 229, 235
Want ads, 51
"War of the Worlds", 270–2, 279
Warlock, 285
Warner, 85, 89, 91

PHOTO CREDITS

CHAPTER ONE p. 3 CBC Television; p. 5, AP/Wide World Photos; p. 8, J. Barr/Gamma Liaison; p. 9, David Dempster; p. 9 (inset), AP/Wide World Photos; p. 17, Courtesy of Video Cart, Inc.; p. 18, Sport Scope; p. 22 (inset left), Courtesy of AT&T Archives; p. 22 (inset right), News and Publications Service, Stanford University; p. 24, Reprinted from *The Columbia Journalism Review*, May/June 1994 ©

CHAPTER TWO p. 33 (all three), North Wind Picture Archives; p. 45, Reprinted by permission of *The Wall Street Journal*, © 1994, Dow Jones & Company, Inc. All rights reserved worldwide; p. 45 (inset), *The Wall Street Journal*; p. 46, *USA Today*; p. 47, *Toronto Star*; p. 49, AP/World Wide Photos; p. 52 MetroValley Newspaper Group; pp. 58-59 (top), © 1911 Charles D. Walcott, National Geographic Society; p. 58 (bottom left), George Strock, *Life Magazine* © 1944 Time, Inc.; p. 58 (bottom right), Joe Scherschel, *Life Magazine* © 1958 Time, Inc.; p. 59 (bottom left), Margaret Bourke-White, *Life Magazine* © 1936 Time, Inc.; p. 59 (bottom right), UPI/Bettmann; p. 61, AP/Wide World Photos; p. 63 *Maclean's Magazine*; p. 68, *Reader's Digest*; p. 70, Copyright © 1992 Watterson. Reprinted with permission of Universal Press Syndicate. All rights reserved

CHAPTER THREE p. 81, UPI/Bettmann; p. 82, Bettmann; p. 86, AP/Wide World Photos; p. 88, Craig Robertson/Toronto Sun; p. 91, AP/Wide World Photos; p. 93, Rex Miller; p. 95, Bettmann; p. 98, Peter Charlesworth/JB Pictures; p. 101, Mark Seliger/Outline; p. 102, Jacques M. Chenet/Gamma Liaison

CHAPTER FOUR p. 109, CBC Television; p. 111, UPI/Corbis-Bettman; p. 112, KUOM, The University of Minnesota; p. 113 (all), AP/Wide World Photos; p. 119 (both), Bettmann; p. 120, Chip Hires/Gamma Liaison; p. 121, ABC Radio, Chicago; p. 122, AP/Wide World Photos; p. 123, Jeff Slocomb/Outline

CHAPTER FIVE p. 129 (left), Frank Trapper/Sygma; p. 129 (right) Gamma Liaison; p. 129 (bottom), The Kobal Collection; p. 130 (left), Culver Pictures; p. 130 (right), AP/Wide World Photos; p. 131, The Kobal Collection; p. 132, The Kobal Collection; p. 134, AP/Wide World Photos; p. 136, Van Bucher; p. 139 (top), Bettmann; p. 139 (bottom), J. R. Eyerman, *Life Magazine* © 1958 Time, Inc.; p. 141, Bettmann; p. 143, Stephen P. Allen/Gamma Liaison.

CHAPTER SIX p. 158, AP/Wide World Photos; p. 163, Patrick Pagnano/CBS; p. 165, UPI/Bettmann; p. 166, The Kobal Collection; p. 167, Edinger/Gamma Liaison; p. 168, CBC Television; p. 171, Mike Maple/Woodfin Camp & Associates; p. 172 (top), Paula Lerner/Woodfin Camp & Associates; p. 172 (bottom), Library of Congress; p. 176, AP/Wide World Photos; p. 178, NASA

CHAPTER SEVEN p. 185, AP/Wide World Photos; p. 186, John Chiasson/Gamma Liaison; p. 188, Bettmann, hand colouring by North Wind Picture Archives; p. 189 (left), Bettmann; p. 189 (right), North Wind Picture Archives; p. 191, Culver Pictures; p. 192, UPI/Bettmann; p. 193 (top), Culver Pictures; p. 193 (left), Bettmann; p. 193 (bottom), Culver Pictures; p. 198, David Butow/Black Star; p. 201, Susan Zirinsky; p. 202, Charles/Gamma Liaison; p. 205, Culver Pictures; p. 209, © 1963 Mauldin/*Chicago Sun Times*; p. 210 (left), Superstock; p. 210 (right), UPI/Bettmann

CHAPTER EIGHT p. 218 (all), Naum Kazhdan/NYT Pictures; p. 220, A. Tannenbaum/Sygma; p. 223, Colorado Historical Society; p. 223 (inset), AP/Wide World Photos; p. 225 (left), The Granger Collection; p. 225 (right), AP/Wide World Photos; p. 226, Anthony Barboza; p. 229, David Grossman; p. 231, Kevin Horan; p. 231 (inset), Sygma; p. 234 (top), Sygma; p. 234 (middle left, middle right, bottom), AP/Wide World Photos; p. 236 (left), Herb Schmertz; p. 236 (right), Van Bucher

CHAPTER NINE p. 244 (all), Wilson Bryan Key; p. 246, Actmedia; p. 253 (all), United Colors of Benetton; p. 254 (both), Ogilvy & Mather; p. 257, Greg Girard/Contact Press Images; p. 264, North Wind Picture Archives; p. 265, Guess, Inc.

CHAPTER TEN p. 271, Culver Pictures; p. 279, David Dempster; p. 281, AP/Wide World Photos; p. 285, Dr. Albert Bandura; p. 287, Cochran Entertainment Inc.; p. 290 (top), A. Markfield/Gamma Liaison; p. 290 (bottom), Chenet/Gamma Liaison

CHAPTER ELEVEN p. 301 (left), Center for Media and Public Affairs; p. 301 (right), Fredrich Cantor; p. 304 (left), Copyright © 1994 by The New York Times Company. Reprinted by permission. *The New York Times*; p. 304 (right), *The National Enquirer*, photo by David Grossman; p. 307,

Nickelsberg/Gamma Liaison; p. 308, AP/Wide World Photos; p. 309, John Nordell/JB Pictures; p. 310, AP/Wide World Photos; p. 314 (top), Y. Gellie/P. Maitre/Matrix; p. 314 (bottom), MTV Europe; p. 315, Gamma Liaison; p. 316, Catherine Karnow/Woodfin Camp & Associates

CHAPTER TWELVE p. 322, North Wind Picture Archives; p. 325, AP/Wide World Photos; p. 326, Stephen Ferry/JB Pictures; p. 327, Stock Montage; p. 330 (left), AP/Wide World Photos; p. 330 (right), Bettmann; p. 332, Timothy Ross/JB Pictures; p. 334, Culver Pictures; p. 335 (top), Carl Mydans, *Life Magazine* © Time Warner, Inc.; p. 335 (bottom), AP/Wide World Photos; p. 336, AP/Wide World Photos; p. 338, AP/Wide World Photos

CHAPTER THIRTEEN p. 343, Roger Hutchins/

Woodfin Camp & Associates; p. 347, Gallup Poll News Service; p. 347 (inset), AP/Wide World Photos; p. 351 (both), Nielsen Media Research; p. 353, The Kobal Collection; p. 357, CNN; p. 358, Copyright © 1990 The Time Inc. Magazine Company. Reprinted with permission

CHAPTER FOURTEEN p. 365, AP/Wide World Photos; p. 367, N.Y. Daily News Photo; p. 368, Susan Greenwood/Gamma Liaison; p. 370, Bettmann; p. 372 (both), North Wind Picture Archives; p. 373, Eric Luse, *San Francisco Chronicle*; p. 378, Charles Steiner/JB Pictures

CHAPTER FIFTEEN p. 393, Ira Wyman/Sygma; p. 395, Kevin R. Morris; p. 396 *The Daily News*, Halifax; p. 400, David Grossman.